"Clark Morrison and Scott Birkey, two of California's most respe
attorneys, have made a major contribution to the field, and to th
or practice it. *Natural Resource Regulation in California* offers a clear, authoritative
and eminently readable source of information on federal and state wildlife, wetlands
and conservation law. This publication doesn't limit itself to relevant federal and
California statutes, but also addresses critically important, related topics such as
conservation easements, mitigation banking, cultural resources, and the public
trust doctrine. *Natural Resource Regulation in California* is must reading for anyone
interested in learning about the field of natural resources law, and deserves to be on
every environmental practitioner's bookshelf."

—RICHARD M. FRANK, *Professor of Environmental Practice,*
Director, California Environmental Law & Policy Center, School of Law,
University of California, Davis

"California's commitment to being a leader in natural resource conservation has
resulted in an impressive and expansive set of laws and regulations. When this is
combined with the body of federal statutory and regulatory law, the outcome is
complex. Clark Morrison and Scott B. Birkey have written a comprehensive and
understandable guide that allows the reader to understand the connections, content,
and practical application of endangered species and wetlands law and regulation.
This guide will be useful to both the novice and the seasoned practitioner."

—KIM DELFINO, *Defenders of Wildlife*

"California has a wide range of rare and vulnerable natural resources that are protected
under one of the most powerful and complex regulatory schemes in the United
States. Morrison and Birkey's comprehensive overview of natural resource regulation
in California explains the relevant state and federal laws, regulations, and policies
and provides a practical guide to compliance that will be useful to experienced
practitioners as well as those new to this area of the law."

—CHRIS BEALE, *Resources Law Group, LLP*

Publisher's Note

Before you rely on the information in this book, be sure you are aware that some changes in the statutes, regulations, or case law may have gone into effect since the date of publication. The book, moreover, provides general information about the law. Readers should consult their own attorneys before relying on the representations found herein.

NATURAL RESOURCE

REGULATION

IN CALIFORNIA

A PRACTICAL GUIDE TO AGENCY

PERMITTING AND PROCEDURES

FIRST EDITION

Clark Morrison and Scott B. Birkey

NATURAL RESOURCE REGULATION IN CALIFORNIA

A PRACTICAL GUIDE TO AGENCY PERMITTING AND PROCEDURES

First Edition

Solano Press Books

Post Office Box 773

Point Arena, California 95468

tel: 800 931-9373

fax: 707 884-4109

email: spbooks@solano.com

interior design: Catherine Courtenaye

figure design: Rachel Grunig

index: Louisa Emmons

print edition: ISBN 978-1-938166-31-0

Kindle e-book: ISBN 978-1-938166-32-7

Natural Resource Regulation in California is printed on stock comprised of 10 percent post-consumer fiber with soy-based ink formulated for minimally low VOC emissions.

Cover photo: Marsh Creek Reservoir, Scott Hein. Hein is a photographer and a member of the Board of Directors of Save Mount Diablo, which has helped to preserve tens of thousands of acres around Mount Diablo, often through mitigation provided by land use projects.

Notice: This book is designed to assist you in understanding environmental law and policy. It is necessarily general in nature and does not discuss all exceptions and variations to general rules. Also, it may not reflect the latest changes in the law. It is not intended as legal advice and should not be relied on to address legal problems. You should always consult an attorney for advice regarding your specific factual situation.

AT A GLANCE

CONTENTS

PART I: THREATENED, ENDANGERED, AND OTHER PROTECTED SPECIES

PART II: WETLANDS AND OTHER AQUATIC RESOURCES

PART III: OTHER RESOURCES AND PROCESSES

PREFACE

THIS BOOK IS INTENDED FOR ANYONE SEEKING AN UNDERSTANDING of the complexities of state and federal wetlands and endangered species permitting in California. Although written primarily from a legal perspective, this book is not just for lawyers. It should be useful also to students, teachers, planners, biologists, resource managers, local government officials, consultants, and members of the public. We hope it serves as a practical guide offering both a broad perspective for our readers and detailed information on the agencies, laws, regulations, and policies that govern the permitting process.

Part I of this book covers the full panoply of state and federal species-related laws that govern development in California. In addition to the federal Endangered Species Act (Chapter 1) and the California Endangered Species Act (Chapter 2), Part I covers avian protections (e.g., the Migratory Bird Treaty Act, the Bald and Golden Eagle Protection Act, and California Fish and Game Code protections for avian species) (Chapter 3); statutory protections for plant species (including the California Native Plant Protection Act and the California Desert Native Plants Act) (Chapter 4), and fish species (e.g., Magnuson-Stevens) (Chapter 5); and various other categories of protected wildlife including California's fully protected and other special-status species (Chapter 6).

Part II covers wetlands and other waters of the United States and the State of California, which are governed by Section 404 of the federal Clean Water Act (Chapter 7) and California's Porter-Cologne Water Quality Control Act (Chapter 8), respectively. Part II also covers California's regulatory structure for rivers, streams, and lakes under Section 1600 of the California Fish and Game Code (Chapter 9) which, in many cases, governs resources that are also covered by the Clean Water Act or Porter-Cologne.

Part III addresses a number of subjects that do not fit neatly within the species- and wetlands-related themes of Parts I and II. In particular, Chapter 10 describes the means by which mitigation is accomplished in California through conservation-related transactional structures such as conservation easements, permittee-responsible projects, mitigation, and conservation banks. Chapter 11 explains the structure and use of regional conservation plans including habitat conservation plans, natural community conservation plans, and regional conservation investment strategies. Finally, Part III covers certain other discrete categories of natural resources that are often implicated during species- or wetlands-related permitting. These include discussions of cultural resource protections under the National Historic Preservation Act and California's AB 52 (Chapter 12); bay and coastal resource protections administered by the Bay Conservation and Development Commission, and the California Coastal Commission (Chapter 13); and the role of the public trust doctrine in shaping environmental policy in the State of California (Chapter 14).

Because the authors had to stop somewhere, certain specialized subjects were excluded from coverage in this book. For example, this book does not cover California water law. Nor does it cover laws or regulations relating to specific industry sectors such as energy, mining, forestry, or agriculture. Moreover, although this book covers the discharge of dredged or fill material into state and federal waters, it does not otherwise include broader discussions of surface or groundwater pollution or storm water regulation except where needed for context. Finally, although from time to time this book touches on requirements of the California Environmental Quality Act and National Environmental Policy Act—and these statutes are of paramount importance in resource agency permitting in California—this book is not a treatise on either statute.

The reader should not rely on this guide as an authoritative source of legal advice. First, although intended to provide a broad overview for the practitioner, this book does not cite to every case, regulation, guidance document, or other source of authority relevant to the subjects covered. This is particularly true with respect to federal law, where we have concentrated on Ninth Circuit and U.S. Supreme Court opinions as examples of how different subjects are treated. Moreover, where we do discuss cases or other sources of authority, we cite to them only for specific illustrative purposes; in many instances the information we provide here may be incomplete or lacking in context.

Second, the regulatory environment in California, and nationwide, is changing at a break-neck pace. It is certain that aspects of this book will be outdated on the date of its publication. While we intend to update the book from time to time, it will be the reader's responsibility to track changes in the law in the meantime.

As this is our first edition, we encourage our readers to let us know of any errors requiring correction (of which we expect many); disagreements they may have with our expressed positions or occasional biases arising out of our experience as counsel to private and public permittees (of which we expect more than a few); or additional subjects that might be helpful to include in future editions (all of which we will gladly consider).

ACKNOWLEDGMENTS

We were supported in this endeavor by a number of our colleagues. Our contributors included Christian Cebrian (Bay Conservation and Development Commission), Tim Paone (Coastal Commission), Linda Klein (cultural resources), Stephanie Straka (plant protections), Jimmy Purvis (fish and avian protections), Ashley Weinstein-Carnes (conservation planning), and Julia Stein, who now serves as Supervising Attorney at UCLA's Frank G. Wells Environmental Law Clinic and Project Director of the Emmett Institute on Climate Change and the Environment (waters of the State). Each of these contributors devoted considerable personal time to this project, and we are grateful for their sacrifices. Christian and Tim deserve special mention as the primary authors of Chapter 13 (Bay and Coastal Resources), and Linda as the primary author of Chapter 12 (Cultural Resources). We are greatly appreciative of the administrative and technical support provided by our able assistants, Susan Berger Law and Sandy E'Bell, law librarian Justine Morgan, and word processor Howard Moore. We are in debt to our partners, particularly our chair Mario Camara and team leaders Michael Zischke and Annie Mudge, for encouraging this project and supporting generously the participation of all of these contributors.

We thank also the professionals who provided extraordinarily helpful comments on various chapters of this book. Our peer reviewers included Chris Beale at Resources Law Group (California Endangered Species Act); Travis Hemmen at Westervelt Ecological Services (conservation transactions); Jim Monroe, U.S. Fish and Wildlife Service Office of the Solicitor (ret.) (federal Endangered Species Act); Brian Plant at Remy, Moose & Manley (waters of the United States); Lisa Westwood at ECORP Consulting (cultural resources); David Zippin at ICF International (conservation planning); and Steve Foreman at LSA (fully protected species). Also, many of our friends in the consulting community were generous in providing the photos of flora and fauna contained in this book.

Thanks to Ling-Yen Jones and Natalie Macris, who brought us into the Solano Press fold, and our editor/designer Catherine Courtenaye, who guided us through countless revisions and painstaking discussions about Bluebook citations, the presentation of "bulleted" lists, and how to deal with the ubiquitous acronyms of environmental law.

We wish to acknowledge the many hard-working and dedicated public servants we have worked with over the last 30 years. Our friends at the agencies have incredibly difficult jobs and deserve far more credit and thanks than they may receive from those of us in the regulated community.

It goes without saying that the greatest contributors to this book were our ever-patient spouses, Rebecca Galler and Rachel Birkey, and Clark's daughters, Islay and Margo. To our families, this book is as much your accomplishment as it is ours. Thank you so much for your enthusiasm and support. We dedicate this book to you, and to our parents who raised us in the outdoors and showed us how to appreciate all things natural and wild.

ABOUT THE AUTHORS

Clark Morrison and Scott Birkey practice land use and natural resource law in San Francisco with the law firm Cox, Castle & Nicholson. Together, they have over 50 years of combined experience. Their practice focuses on the permitting of complex private and public projects under Section 404 of the Clean Water Act, Porter-Cologne, the state and federal Endangered Species Acts, and the other state and federal laws covered in this treatise. Their experience includes environmental permitting and defense, environmental review under CEQA and NEPA, habitat conservation planning, mitigation and conservation banking, conservation easements and other transactional structures, and legislative and regulatory advocacy.

Clark and Scott are alumni of and have taught at U.C. Berkeley School of Law, which is home to one of the finest environmental law programs in the United States. During his time at Berkeley Law, Scott served as Editor-in-Chief of *Ecology Law Quarterly*. Scott and Clark speak and write regularly on natural resource matters. In addition to their traditional law practices, Scott and Clark devote much of their time assisting The Nature Conservancy in its efforts to conserve natural resources throughout the western United States.

The authors' interest in natural resource law is both personal and professional.

Clark spent his childhood in Anchorage, Alaska, as the son of a land man for the Standard Oil Company of California. Clark's father spent much of his time on the North Slope negotiating land deals with the State of Alaska, the federal government and the Alaska Native Corporations, bringing home caribou sausage for the family to eat and drafts of oil leases that served as drawing paper for the kids. Clark learned to fish and camp in the Chugach Mountains and the Kenai Peninsula, and he remains an avid outdoorsman today.

Scott is a third-generation natural resource legacy. His father was a surveyor for NOAA, spending his time on ships mapping out coastlines. His grandfather worked for the U.S. Bureau of Reclamation (Department of the Interior) and then the Soil Conservation Service (USDA) helping ranchers and farmers in Wyoming and Montana to establish irrigation systems. Scott was born and raised in Wyoming where he learned to love the outdoors, and most summers Scott can be located only with a good GPS as he wanders throughout the Sierra Nevada.

INTRODUCTION

The Resource Agencies

Any given project may be subject to the permitting requirements of more than a half dozen resource agencies, each of which possesses or exercises different priorities, substantive requirements, jurisdictional scopes and even lexicons. This chapter introduces the primary state and federal agencies involved in permitting natural resource impacts in California.

CDFW or the "Department" =
California Department of Fish
and Wildlife

STATE AGENCIES

The primary state agencies with permitting authority in California include the California Department of Fish and Wildlife, the California Fish and Game Commission, the State Water Resources Control Board, and the Regional Water Quality Control Boards. The California Office of Historic Preservation, which has an ancillary role in many permit processes, is not discussed here, but is described in context in Chapter 12. Also described in other chapters are the California Coastal Commission and the Bay Conservation and Development Commission.

California Department of Fish and Wildlife

The California Department of Fish and Wildlife (CDFW or the Department) has its origins in the California Fish and Game Commission, dating back to 1870. The administrative functions of that commission were eventually assumed by the Division of Fish and Game, housed within the Department of Natural Resources, in 1927. In 1951, the Division was elevated by statute to a department level (then known as the Department of Fish and Game). The following year, the Department was restructured to establish five regional offices, a pre-cursor to the seven-region structure that exists today.

The Department later became a part of California's Natural Resources Agency, which also includes the Department of Water Resources, the Department of Parks and Recreation, the Department of Forestry and Fire Protection, the California Conservation Corps, the Department of Conservation, and the Office of Exposition Park Management. Now named the Department of Fish and Wildlife (rather than Fish and Game), CDFW is responsible for the implementation of California's fish and wildlife laws, including hunting and fishing regulations. The Department also plays a non-regulatory role, working with other state and federal agencies to manage California's fish and wildlife resources.

CDFW is separated into seven geographical regions, each of which has a regional headquarters. They are: The Northern Region (Region 1), headquartered in Redding; the North Central Region (Region 2), headquartered in Rancho Cordova; the Bay Delta Region (Region 3), headquartered in Napa; the Central Region (Region 4), headquartered in Fresno; the South Coast Region (Region 5), headquartered in San Diego; the Inland Deserts Region (Region 6), headquartered in Ontario; and the Marine Region (Region 7), headquartered in Monterey.

The Department consists of several non-geographic divisions and offices, including divisions for administration, ecosystem conservation, law enforcement, wildlife and fisheries, and data and technology, and offices for communications, equal opportunity, legislative affairs, spill prevention and response, and the general counsel. The Department has a law enforcement division, which is divided into four districts: the North Coast District, Northern District, Central District, and Southern District. Most relevant to this book, the Department's "Habitat Conservation Planning" branch is responsible for administering the Department's permitting programs. Those programs include approving incidental take permits pursuant to the California Endangered Species Act (CESA), providing trustees and responsible agency reviews under the California Environmental Quality Act (CEQA), administering the Lake and Streambed Alteration Program, and overseeing conservation banking efforts.

The Department is the state's principal agency for the regulation of impacts to fish and wildlife resources. Most notably, the Department is authorized under CESA to issue incidental take permits for listed and candidate species, as well as the Natural Community Conservation Planning Act (NCCPA), which provides for broad-based conservation plans that provide incidental take authority for both CESA-protected species and "fully protected species." The Department also issues Lake and Streambed Alteration Agreements pursuant to Fish and Game Code 1602, which agreements impose measures for the protection of fish and wildlife resources in connection with certain actions that may substantially affect the channel or bank of a river, stream, or lake.

Through its banking program, the Department coordinates with other state agencies and promulgates policy and guidance for the establishment and operation of conservation and mitigation banks. The Department also administers a regional planning and permitting program known as "Regional Conservation Investment Strategies." Finally, the Department reviews and comments upon environmental documents and impacts arising from project activities that may affect fish or wildlife resources.

The Department's role is not limited to the review and consideration of permits. CDFW is a trustee agency in California, which carries with it a broad, non-regulatory mission in the protection of California's fish and wildlife resources. This mission exists both under the public trust doctrine, but also the Department's broad conservation mandate under CESA and other statutes, including Sections 1801 and 1802 of the Fish and Game Code, which explicitly identify the Department's public trust mission. The scope of the Department's duties are expansive, and a quick review of the Department's web-site will provide abundant information on its important, non-regulatory obligations.

California Fish and Game Commission

The California Fish and Game Commission (Commission) was the first state wildlife conservation agency in the country, having been established in 1870 as the "Board of Fish Commissioners" to provide for the restoration and preservation of fish in California waters. The Board of Fish Commissioners was renamed in 1909 as the Fish and Game Commission, and the administrative functions of the original commission were assumed by the Division of Fish and Game (i.e., the predecessor to CDFW). In 1945, through constitutional amendment, the Commission received responsibility for promulgating regulations to manage sport fishing and hunting, and later assumed responsibility for the listing of species under CESA. The Commission's current responsibilities, including those under CESA, are set forth below.

CESA = California Endangered Species Act

CEQA = California Environmental Quality Act

NCCPA = Natural Community Conservation Planning Act

Commission = California Fish and Game Commission

SWRCB = State Water
Resources Control Board, or
"State Water Board"

The Commission consists of five members who serve in six-year staggered terms. Commissioners are appointed by the governor subject to confirmation by the California State Senate. The Commission meets twelve times a year and annually elects one member as the president and another as the vice president. The president of the Commission chairs all public meetings and signs correspondence that results from Commission action. The president also serves as a member of the Wildlife Conservation Board, discussed in greater detail below.

The Commission has three committees: the Wildlife Resources Committee, the Tribal Committee, and the Marine Resources Committee. Each committee is chaired or co-chaired by no more than two commissioners. Commissioners are assigned to their respective committees annually, typically by majority vote of the Commission at the same time the president is elected. Committee meetings are less formal than Commission meetings and are generally designed to allow for additional discussion and presentations on regulatory proposals under consideration. However, committees cannot take formal action independent of the full Commission, so the committees serve to make recommendations to the Commission. In addition to these three committees, the Commission sometimes forms ad hoc committees to address particular short-term issues under consideration by the Commission.

Per the Fish and Game Code, the Commission has been delegated a number of responsibilities by the Legislature. As discussed above, the Commission formulates the general policies for conduct by CDFW. It also has the authority to regulate game seasons, methods of take for game animals and sport fishing, control of non-native species, establishment and regulation of protected lands and waters such as marine protected areas and ecological reserves, listing and delisting of threatened and endangered species under CESA, and acceptance of mitigation lands on behalf of the state. The Commission assumes a quasi-judicial role as the agency that considers appeals to revocation or suspension of licenses and permits issued pursuant to the Fish and Game Code. The Commission is also responsible for prescribing the terms and conditions for issuance, revocation, or suspension of certain licenses and permits issued by CDFW.

State Water Resources Control Board and Regional Water Quality Control Boards

California's State Water Resources Control Board (SWRCB or the "State Water Board") administers the state's system for issuing, managing, or monitoring California's water rights systems. The State Water Board also serves as a sister agency to the California Department of Water Resources in the implementation of the Sustainable Groundwater Management Act.

In addition to its authority over water rights, the State Water Board holds authority to set statewide policy with respect to water quality. The State Water Board's responsibilities include, for example, the identification of "beneficial uses" of water to be protected in California. The State Water Board also allocates funds, coordinates the regulatory efforts of the nine Regional Water Quality Control Boards (RWQCBs or the "Regional Water Boards"), and reviews petitions challenging decisions made by the Regional Water Boards.

On the federal side, the Clean Water Act delegates authority to the State of California, acting through the State Water Board and the Regional Water Boards (collectively, Water Boards), to develop and administer the state's "National Pollutant Discharge Elimination System" (NPDES). The NPDES program regulates point source discharges—discharges from a specific source, like a pipe or ditch—to waters of the United States. Also as a part of the NPDES program, the Water Boards regulate storm water pollution through general construction permits and permits to local agencies for storm water treatment facilities.

Most importantly for the purposes of this book, the Water Boards administer the state's permitting system under the Porter-Cologne Water Quality Control Act, California's principal water quality statute. In the federal wetland permitting context, the Water Boards have authority under Section 401 of the Clean Water Act to review and "certify" permits proposed for issuance by the U.S. Army Corps of Engineers. Where federal waters are not present, the Water Boards regulate the discharge of dredged or fill material under Porter-Cologne through the issuance of waste discharge requirements (WDRs).

Except for projects that cross regional boundaries, the Regional Water Boards have principal responsibility for issuing certifications and WDRs for projects within their geographic jurisdiction in accordance with Porter-Cologne and Section 401. However, in certain instances—for example, the issuance of general WDRs applicable to a class of project throughout the state—the State Water Board is the entity that initially issues a permit or certification. Similarly, enforcement decisions are generally made first by the Regional Water Boards, which are appealable to the State Water Board, but at times the State Water Board may initiate its own enforcement proceedings.

The State Water Board is comprised of five appointed members selected on the basis of qualifications in the fields of water supply, water quality, and water rights. Each board member must fill one of five different specialty positions: civil engineer, professional engineer, water quality expert, attorney member/water rights expert, and public member. The agency has a significant staff, including divisions covering Water Quality, Water Rights, Legislative Affairs, and Enforcement, all of which are overseen by an Executive Director appointed by the board itself.

There are nine RWQCBs across the state,[1] the geographic boundaries of which are organized around the hydrological boundaries of the major water basins in California. Accordingly, more than one Regional Water Board may have jurisdiction within a single county. For example, both the San Francisco and Central Coast Regional Water Boards

DWR = California Department of Water Resources

SGMA = Sustainable Groundwater Management Act

RWQCB = Regional Water Quality Control Board, or "Regional Water Board"

NPDES = National Pollutant Discharge Elimination System

WDR = waste discharge requirement

1   These include the following regions: North Coast (Region 1), San Francisco (Region 2), Central Coast (Region 3), Los Angeles (Region 4), Central Valley (Region 5), Lahontan (Region 6), Colorado River (Region 7), Santa Ana (Region 8), and San Diego (Region 9).

USFWS or the "Service" = U.S.
Fish and Wildlife Service

NMFS or NOAA Fisheries =
National Oceanic and
Atmospheric Administration's
National Marine Fisheries
Service

USACE or the "Corps" = U.S.
Army Corps of Engineers

EPA = Environmental Protection
Agency

exercise jurisdiction in San Mateo and Santa Clara counties, and the Central Coast, Los Angeles, Central Valley, and Lahontan Regional Water Boards all exercise jurisdiction within some portion of Kern County. Each of the nine Regional Water Boards is comprised of seven board members appointed by the governor on the basis of demonstrated interest or proven ability in the field of water quality, including water pollution control, water resource management, water use, or water protection, and each Regional Water Board is managed by an executive officer appointed by the board of that region.

FEDERAL AGENCIES

The primary agencies involved in regulating natural resources at the federal level are the U.S. Fish and Wildlife Service (USFWS or "the Service"), the National Oceanic and Atmospheric Administration's National Marine Fisheries Service (NMFS or NOAA Fisheries), the U.S. Army Corps of Engineers (USACE or "the Corps"), and the U.S. Environmental Protection Agency (EPA). The roles and responsibilities of these four agencies are described below. Other federal agencies may play a role in project permitting, depending on the location or impacts of a proposed project, and they are described where appropriate in other parts of this book.

U.S. Fish and Wildlife Service

The Service[2] is an agency within the U.S. Department of the Interior, and it is responsible for conserving, protecting, and enhancing fish and wildlife and their habitats for the continuing benefit of the American people through federal programs relating to migratory birds, endangered species, interjurisdictional fish and marine mammals, and inland sport fisheries.[3] Most notably for the purposes of this book, it administers the federal Endangered Species Act.

The Service's internal manuals identify three basic objectives for the agency: (1) to assist in the development and application of an environmental stewardship ethic for our society, based on ecological principles, scientific knowledge of fish and wildlife, and a sense of moral responsibility; (2) to guide the conservation, development, and management of the nation's fish and wildlife resources; and (3) to administer a national program to provide the public opportunities to understand, appreciate, and wisely use fish and wildlife resources. These objectives are stated to support the Service's mission of conserving, protecting, and enhancing fish and wildlife and their habitats for the continuing benefit of the American people.[4]

Among its many functions, the Service acquires, protects, and manages unique ecosystems necessary to sustain fish and wildlife such as migratory birds, resident species, and endangered species; and promulgates and enforces regulations for the protection of migratory birds, marine mammals, fish and other non-endangered wildlife from illegal

2 NMFS is commonly referred to also as the "Service" and, collectively with USFWS, as the "Services." For the purposes of this book, and to avoid confusion, we often use the term "Service" exclusively to refer to USFWS.

3 FWM# 327 (March 6, 1998), available at https://www.fws.gov/policy/022fw1.html.

4 *Id.*

taking, transportation, or sale within the United States or from foreign countries.[5] In this book we are primarily concerned with the Service's role in administering the provisions of the ESA.

The State of California is located within the Service's Pacific Southwest Region (Region 8). Region 8 also includes the state of Nevada and the Klamath Basin within the state of Oregon. The Region's headquarters are located in Sacramento, California, and managed by a regional director, deputy regional director, and assistant regional directors for the various programs administered by the Service. In California, the Service is administered through its Sacramento headquarters and various field offices, including Klamath Falls, Yreka, Arcata, Sacramento (which includes Coast-Bay, Sacramento Valley, San Joaquin Valley, and Sierra-Cascades divisions), Reno, Southern Nevada, Ventura and Carlsbad.[6]

The field offices carry out a variety of functions but, when it comes to permitting, they are charged with the implementation of Section 7 (consultation with federal agencies) and Section 10 (habitat conservation plans) of the ESA.

As noted above, the Service has regulatory authority over projects subject to the federal Endangered Species Act,[7] including Section 9 enforcement of unauthorized take of special-status species, Section 7 consultation, and Section 10 incidental take permits and habitat conservation plans. The Service administers the Endangered Species Act as it applies to terrestrial species and non-anadromous fish species. The Service also has regulatory authority over projects subject to the Migratory Bird Treaty Act[8] and the Bald and Golden Eagle Protection Act.[9]

National Marine Fisheries Service

NMFS is a division of the National Oceanic and Atmospheric Administration, which is in the Department of Commerce. NMFS is responsible for the stewardship of the nation's ocean resources and their habitat. The agency derives its authority from numerous statutes, including the federal Endangered Species Act, the Magnuson-Stevens Fishery Conservation and Management Act, and the Marine Mammal Protection Act. Along the West Coast, the agency manages fishery resources for salmon and steelhead, over 90 species of groundfish, coastal pelagic fish such as anchovy and sardine, and highly migratory species such as billfish, sharks and tuna.[10]

The State of California is located entirely with NMFS' West Coast Region. The California Coastal Office includes three offices, which are located in Arcata, Santa Rosa,

---

5   *Id.*

6   USFWS, About the Pacific Southwest Regional Office, available at https://www.fws.gov/cno/about_us.html.

7   16 U.S.C. § 1531 *et seq.*

8   *Id.* §§ 703–712.

9   *Id.* § 668.

10 NOAA Fisheries, What We Do, available at http://www.westcoast.fisheries.noaa.gov/whatwedo/overview/what_we_do_overview.html.

and Long Beach. The California Central Valley Office includes one office in Sacramento. Both regions are managed by assistant regional administrators, who administer a variety of different regulatory sub-branches.

Like the Service, NMFS has regulatory authority over projects subject to the ESA,[11] and has parallel responsibilities including Section 9 enforcement, Section 7 consultations, and Section 10 incidental take permits in accordance with approved habitat conservation plans. While the Service administers the ESA relative to terrestrial species and pelagic fish, NMFS administers the ESA as it applies to marine mammals (which are also governed by the Marine Mammal Protection Act[12] administered by NMFS), ocean species, and anadromous fish species. As an agency within the Department of Commerce, the agency also has regulatory authority under the Magnuson-Stevens Fishery Conservation and Management Act.[13]

U.S. Army Corps of Engineers

The Corps has long held a role in the protection of America's navigable waterways, primarily for the purposes of military defense and commerce, the regulatory principles of which are now found primarily in the Rivers and Harbors Act of 1899. But the Corps' role has evolved over the years into the area of environmental regulation, and the agency is responsible under Section 404 of the Clean Water Act for protecting the integrity of the nation's wetlands and other waters.

It may seem odd that the Corps maintains primary authority under the Clean Water Act (under the watchful eye of EPA), but in a sense this is an outgrowth of its original role in the protection of navigability. In fact, when the modern version of the Clean Water Act came to the forefront in 1972, it was thought that the Corps' jurisdiction was limited to navigable waters. Over the subsequent 45 years, however, various rulemakings and litigation have pushed the boundaries of the Corps' authority to the extent that—at least under the Clean Water Act—it issues permits for waters that are not at all navigable-in-fact. But the debate continues today and, as of the date of publication, the Trump Administration had promulgated draft regulations that would pare back the scope of Corps (and EPA) jurisdiction more closely to its original "navigable" boundaries.

The State of California is located with the Corps' South Pacific Division (SPD), which is headquartered in San Francisco. Within the SPD, California is divided into three Corps Districts: Sacramento District, with District headquarters in Sacramento; Los Angeles District, with District headquarters in Los Angeles; and San Francisco District, with District headquarters in San Francisco.

Although the Corps' regulatory program is overseen by the Assistant Secretary of the Army for Civil Works housed in the Pentagon, it is implemented primarily by a

---

11   16 U.S.C. § 1531 *et seq.*

12   *Id.* § 1361 *et seq.*

13   *Id.* § 1801 *et seq.*

civilian staff with military officers posted in the Corps' regional divisions, which are led by a commander (typically a General) and a deputy commander, and in each of the districts by a district engineer. The main face of the Corps, however, is the civilian regulatory chief in each of the districts, who reports to the district engineer.

As noted above, the Corps has two primary sources of regulatory jurisdiction. First, the Corps regulates the discharge of fill or dredged material into waters of the United States pursuant to Section 404 of the Clean Water Act.[14] This role is carried out in coordination with EPA, which promulgates standards for the issuance of permits under Section 404 (including the so-called "404(b)(1) Guidelines"), reviews certain types of Jurisdictional Determinations, has the power to elevate and veto Corps permits, and has initial responsibilities for formal enforcement proceedings. Second, the Corps regulates the obstruction or alteration of navigable waters of the United States pursuant to Section 10 of the Rivers and Harbors Act of 1899.[15] The Corps carries out this role without any oversight by EPA (except to the extent that permitting under the RHA also involves permitting under Section 404).

U.S. Environmental Protection Agency

While EPA is the nation's primary watchdog over water and air quality issues, particularly to the extent those issues implicate issues of public health, the agency shares a role with the Corps in the federal wetlands program. Although the Corps is the primary permit-issuing agency, EPA plays an oversight role in that permit process and in jurisdictional questions, and often plays a primary role in enforcement actions.

The State of California is located in EPA's Region 9 (Pacific Southwest). Region 9 is headquartered in San Francisco, with field offices located in Los Angeles and San Diego. The region is led by a Regional Administrator who is in charge of several divisions arranged around topical areas. Issues arising under the Clean Water Act are handled by wetland personnel housed within the region's Water Division.

As noted above, EPA has authority to participate in various aspects of the Section 404 permitting process, including review of certain types of Jurisdictional Determinations, elevating Corps permit decisions involving "Aquatic Resources of National Importance," vetoing Corps permits in certain circumstances, enforcing violations of the Clean Water Act, and prescribing standards for the issuance of permits under Section 404. These authorities have placed EPA in the role of watchdog over the Corps, a role which often creates some tension between the two agencies.

---

14 33 U.S.C. § 1344.

15 *Id.* § 403.

PART I

THREATENED, ENDANGERED, AND OTHER PROTECTED SPECIES

in this chapter . . .

CHAPTER 1

The Federal Endangered Species Act

This chapter provides an overview of the federal Endangered Species Act, which offers protection to threatened and endangered species listed pursuant to this Act. The chapter covers both the substantive protections and the permitting program administered by the U.S. Fish and Wildlife Service and the National Marine Fisheries Service.

HISTORY OF THE ESA

The Endangered Species Act of 1973[1] (ESA) is the cornerstone of the nation's statutory structure for the protection of at-risk species. A good synopsis of the Act's legislative history and underpinnings can be found in the U.S. Supreme Court's landmark decision *Tennessee Valley Authority v. Hill,*[2] which was the first Supreme Court case to consider the meaning and scope of the ESA. The following summarizes the Supreme Court's more detailed exegesis of the Act.

The first major congressional concern for the preservation of endangered species had come with passage of the Endangered Species Act of 1966.[3] In that legislation, Congress gave the Secretary of the Interior power to identify "the names of the species of native fish and wildlife found to be threatened with extinction,"[4] as well as authorization to purchase land for the conservation, protection, restoration, and propagation of "selected species" of "native fish and wildlife" threatened with extinction.[5]

Declaring the preservation of endangered species a national policy, the 1966 Act directed all federal agencies both to protect these species and "insofar as is practicable and consistent with the[ir] primary purposes,"[6] to "preserve the habitats of such threatened species on lands under their jurisdiction."[7] The 1966 statute did not include a broad prohibition on the taking of endangered species, however, except on federal lands,[8] and even in those federal areas the Secretary was authorized to allow the hunting and fishing of endangered species.[9]

In 1969, Congress enacted the Endangered Species Conservation Act,[10] which continued the provisions of the 1966 Act while at the same time broadened federal involvement in the preservation of endangered species. Under the 1969 legislation, the Secretary of the Interior was empowered to list species "threatened with worldwide extinction."[11] In addition, the importation of any such species into the United States was prohibited.[12] An indirect approach to the taking of endangered species was also adopted in the Conservation Act by way of a ban on the transportation and sale of wildlife taken in violation of any federal, state, or foreign law.[13]

---

1   16 U.S.C. § 1531 *et seq.*

2   437 U.S. 153 (1978).

3   80 Stat. 926, repealed, 87 Stat. 903.

4   *Id.* § 1(c), 80 Stat. 926

5   *Id.* §§ 2(a)–(c), 80 Stat. 926–27.

6   *Id.* § 1(b), 80 Stat. 926.

7   *Id.*

8   *Id.* § 4(c), 80 Stat. 928.

9   *Id.* § 4(d)(1), 80 Stat. 928.

10   83 Stat. 275, repealed, 87 Stat. 903.

11   *Id.* § 3(a), 83 Stat. 275.

12   *Id.* § 2, 83 Stat. 275.

13   *Id.* §§ 7(a)–(b), 83 Stat. 279.

Despite the fact that the 1966 and 1969 legislation represented "the most comprehensive of its type to be enacted by any nation"[14] up to that time, Congress was soon persuaded that a more expansive approach was needed if the newly declared national policy of preserving endangered species was to be realized.

In shaping legislation to further deal with the problem of species extinction, Congress started from the finding that "[t]he two major causes of extinction are hunting and destruction of natural habitat."[15] Of these twin threats, Congress was informed that the greater threat was destruction of natural habitats.[16] Witnesses recommended, among other things, that Congress require all land-managing agencies "to avoid damaging critical habitat for endangered species and to take positive steps to improve such habitat."[17]

As it was finally passed, the Endangered Species Act of 1973 represented the most comprehensive legislation for the preservation of endangered species enacted by any nation. Its stated purposes were "to provide a means whereby the ecosystems upon which endangered species and threatened species depend may be conserved," and "to provide a program for the conservation of such . . . species."[18] Virtually all dealings with endangered species, including taking, possession, transportation, and sale, were prohibited,[19] except in narrow circumstances.[20] The Secretary of the Interior was also given extensive power to develop regulations and programs for the preservation of endangered and threatened species.[21] Citizen involvement was encouraged by the Act, with provisions allowing interested persons to petition the Secretary to list a species as endangered or threatened,[22] and bring civil suits in U.S. district courts to compel compliance with the Act.[23]

The Supreme Court's conclusions in *TVA v. Hill* after considering the Act's legislative history and text are unequivocal:

> The plain intent of Congress in enacting this statute was to halt and
> reverse the trend toward species extinction, whatever the cost. This is
> reflected not only in the stated policies of the Act, but in literally every

---

14 *TVA*, 437 U.S. at 176 fn.22 (quoting Hearings on Endangered Species before the Subcommittee of the House Committee on Merchant Marine and Fisheries, 93d Cong., 1st Sess., 202 (1973) (statement of Assistant Secretary of the Interior) (hereinafter cited as 1973 House Hearings)).

15 S. Rep. No. 93-307, p. 2 (1973).

16 See 1973 House Hearings 236 (statement of Associate Deputy Chief for National Forest System, Dept. of Agriculture); *id.* at 241 (statement of Director of Mich. Dept. of Natural Resources); *id.* at 306 (statement of Stephen R. Seater, Defenders of Wildlife); Lachenmeier, The Endangered Species Act of 1973: Preservation or Pandemonium?, 5 Environ. Law 29, 31 (1974).

17 1973 House Hearings 241 (statement of Director of Mich. Dept. of Natural Resources).

18 16 U.S.C. § 1531(b).

19 *Id.* § 1538.

20 *Id.* § 1539(b).

21 *Id.* § 1533(d).

22 *Id.* § 1533(c)(2).

23 *Id.* § 1540(c) & (g).

USFWS = U.S. Fish and Wildlife
Service

section of the statute. All persons, including federal agencies, are specifically instructed not to "take" endangered species, meaning that no one is "to harass, harm, pursue, hunt, shoot, wound, kill, trap, capture, or collect" such life forms.[24]

This view is largely reflected in all the case law that follows from *TVA v. Hill*, and in many ways fuels the fire for those seeking to overturn or weaken the ESA. As described below, there have been many attempts since then to legislatively chip away at the ESA, and arguments have been made attacking the Act's constitutional legitimacy. Most of these efforts have been unsuccessful and thus far the Act remains intact.

CONSTITUTIONALITY OF THE ESA

The ESA is no stranger to controversy. Although the statute was enacted with broad-based support across the political spectrum, as the federal government began implementing the statute, that support began to show signs of strain. The difficulties showcased in *TVA v. Hill* regarding the endangered snail darter and construction of the Tellico Dam began a national debate over the Act that continues to this day.

Judicial attacks against the ESA generally have been framed as Commerce Clause issues, typically directed at species that are present within only one state and therefore do not cross state lines. Recent U.S. Supreme Court cases that do not involve the ESA but do concern the Commerce Clause have trended toward the view that Congress' powers under the Commerce Clause are more restricted, particularly in those instances where only a tenuous relationship exists between the regulated activity and interstate commerce.[25] This case law has given some opponents a legal foothold in arguments against the constitutionality of the ESA.

One of the most important decisions on this issue is the Tenth Circuit Court of Appeal's decision *People for the Ethical Treatment of Property Owners v. U.S. Fish & Wildlife Service*.[26] In this case, the USFWS promulgated a regulation that prohibited the take of the Utah prairie dog, a threatened species that is present only within the state of Utah and on non-federal land. An organization calling itself People for the Ethical Treatment of Property Owners, or "PETPO," challenged the regulation on the grounds that neither the Commerce Clause[27] nor the Necessary and Proper Clause of the U.S. Constitution authorizes Congress to regulate take of the Utah prairie dog on non-federal land.[28] The District Court for the District of Utah agreed with PETPO,

---

24 16 U.S.C. §§ 1532(14), 1538(a)(1)(B).

25 See, e.g., *United States v. Lopez*, 514 U.S. 549 (1995).

26 852 F.3d 990 (10th Cir. 2017).

27 The Commerce Clause gives Congress the authority "[t]o regulate Commerce with foreign Nations, and among the several States, and with the Indian Tribes." U.S. Const. art. I, § 8, cl. 3.

28 Importantly, PETPO conceded that Congress has the power under the Property Clause of the U.S. Constitution to regulate take of the Utah prairie dog on federal land. *People for the Ethical Treatment of Property Owners*, 852 F.3d at 999 fn. 4.

and granted summary judgment in their favor on the ground that these constitutional provisions do not authorize Congress to regulate take of the Utah prairie dog on non-federal land.

Utah prairie dog. Photo: Bernd Thaller

The Tenth Circuit reversed the District Court on this issue. The court began its analysis by identifying the three categories of activity that the Commerce Clause authorizes Congress to regulate: (1) use of the channels of interstate commerce; (2) instrumentalities of interstate commerce, or persons or things in interstate commerce; and (3) activities that substantially affect interstate commerce.[29] Focusing on the third category, the court explained that, based on U.S. Supreme Court precedent, "the Commerce Clause authorizes regulation of noncommercial, purely intrastate activity that is an essential part of a broader regulatory scheme that, as a whole, substantially affects interstate commerce (i.e., has a substantial relation to interstate commerce)."[30] Using that framework for analysis, the court concluded that "Congress had a rational basis to believe that regulation of the take of the Utah prairie dog on non-federal land is an essential part of the ESA's broader regulatory scheme which, in the aggregate, substantially affects interstate commerce."[31] As such, the court held that the regulation on non-federal land of take of a purely intrastate species, like the Utah prairie dog, under the ESA is a constitutional exercise of congressional authority under the Commerce Clause.[32]

The holding in *PETPO* is generally consistent with other decisions evaluating Commerce Clause challenges to the ESA.[33]

AGENCIES THAT ADMINISTER THE ESA

Two federal agencies administer the ESA: (1) the U.S. Fish and Wildlife Service; and (2) the National Marine Fisheries Service. For purposes of this chapter, both of these agencies will be referred to collectively as the "Service," unless otherwise noted.

---

29 *People for the Ethical Treatment of Property Owners*, 852 F.3d at 1000 (quoting *United States v. Lopez*, 514 U.S. 549, 558–59 (1995)).

30 *Id.* at 1002.

31 *Id.*

32 *Id.* at 1008. Because the court reached its decision based on the Commerce Clause analysis, it did not consider the constitutionality of the regulation under the Necessary and Proper Clause.

33 See *Alabama-Tombigbee Rivers Coalition v. Kempthorne*, 477 F.3d 1250 (11th Cir. 2007) (rejecting Commerce Clause challenge to final rule listing the Alabama sturgeon as endangered under the theory that "Congress has exceeded the power granted to it under the Commerce Clause by authorizing protection of the Alabama Sturgeon"); see also *Markle Interests, L.L.C. v. U.S. Fish & Wildlife Service*, 827 F.3d 452, 475–77 (5th Cir. 2016) (aggregating all ESA critical-habitat designations and upholding Service's designation of private, purely intrastate land for purely intrastate frog species under the Commerce Clause); *GDF Realty Invs., Ltd. v. Norton*, 326 F.3d 622, 640 (5th Cir. 2003) (concluding that regulation of purely intrastate cave species takes "is an essential part of" ESA's larger regulatory scheme); *Gibbs v. Babbitt*, 214 F.3d 483, 487 (4th Cir. 2000) ("This regulation [prohibiting take of red wolves] is also sustainable as 'an essential part of a larger regulation of economic activity, in which the regulatory scheme could be undercut unless the intrastate activity were regulated.'" (quoting *Lopez* 514 U.S. at 561)).

USFWS or the "Service" = U.S. Fish and Wildlife Service

NMFS = National Marine Fisheries Service

U.S. Fish and Wildlife Service

The U.S. Fish and Wildlife Service (USFWS) is an agency within the Department of the Interior. The USFWS has primary responsibility for terrestrial and freshwater organisms under the ESA. For more information regarding the USFWS and its administrative structure within the state of California, see Introduction: The Resource Agencies.

National Marine Fisheries Service

The National Marine Fisheries Service (NMFS) is an agency within the National Oceanic Atmospheric Administration, which itself is an agency within the U.S. Department of Commerce. NMFS's primary responsibilities are mainly marine wildlife such as whales and anadromous fish (i.e., fish species such as salmon that spend portions of their life cycle both in the ocean and within freshwater streams). For more information regarding NMFS and its administrative structure within the state of California, see Introduction: The Resource Agencies.

THE LISTING PROCESS

The foundation of the ESA's regulatory power is the Service's authority to identify species as either endangered or threatened and to place them on the endangered or threatened species list subject to the Act's protection.

Listing a Species

The ESA establishes by statute two categories of species subject to protection—endangered species and threatened species.[34] The term "endangered species" means "any species which is in danger of extinction throughout all or a significant portion of its range."[35] The term "threatened species" means "any species which is likely to become an endangered species within the foreseeable future throughout all or a significant portion of its range."[36] Although the term "foreseeable future" is not defined in the statute, regulations proposed by the Service in July 2018 (the "Proposed Regulations") would specify that the term "foreseeable future" extends only so far into the future as the Service "can reasonably determine that the conditions potentially posing a danger of extinction in the future are *probable*."[37]

The Secretaries of the Interior and Commerce are obligated to publish and maintain a list of all species determined to be endangered or threatened.[38] The Secretaries have

---

34 16 U.S.C. § 1531(b) (establishing as purposes of the Act "to provide a means whereby the ecosystems upon which endangered species and threatened species depend may be conserved, [and] to provide a program for the conservation of such endangered species and threatened species").

35 *Id.* § 1532(6).

36 *Id.* § 1532(20).

37 83 Fed. Reg. 35,193 *et seq.*

38 16 U.S.C. § 1533(c)(1).

PROPOSED REVISIONS TO
ENDANGERED SPECIES ACT REGULATIONS

On July 19, 2018, the Trump Administration issued proposed revisions to three sets of Endangered Species Act regulations administered by the Service. These proposed revisions would make several changes, as summarized below:

> **Rescission of Protection for Threatened Species under ESA Section 4(d) (83 Fed. Reg. 35,174).** The ESA prohibits the take of species listed as "endangered." The take prohibition does not apply to "threatened" species unless the Service adopts a rule extending that protection to threatened species. The Service relies on a "blanket" 4(d) rule automatically extending protections to threatened species. The proposed rule would rescind the blanket 4(d) rule and permit the Service to extend protection on a species-by-species basis (e.g., similar to the special 4(d) rules for California coastal gnatcatcher and California tiger salamander).

> **Restrictions on Listing of Species and Designation of Critical Habitat (83 Fed. Reg. 35,193).** The ESA prescribes certain standards for the listing of threatened and endangered species. The proposed rule would allow introduction of economic data into some listing decisions (for informational purposes) despite statutory requirements that listings are supposed to be made based upon the best available scientific information. The proposed rule would also narrow the "forward look" employed by the Service to determine whether a species is threatened with future endangerment. This change would, among other things, limit the agency's need to consider the impacts of climate change in some listing decisions.

> The ESA requires the Service to designate "critical habitat" for a listed species at the time of listing "to the maximum extent prudent." A critical habitat designation increases the level of protection afforded a listed species from a jeopardy standard to a recovery standard. The proposed rule would clarify the circumstances under which the Service can decline to designate critical habitat. More significantly, it would limit the Service's ability to designate as critical habitat areas that are not currently occupied by a listed species.

> **Other Section 7 Reforms (83 Fed. Reg. 35,178).** The proposed rule would change a number of definitions and procedural steps associated with Section 7 consultations, including "adverse modification of critical habitat," "Effects of the Action," "Environmental Baseline," and "Programmatic Consultations."

As of the publication date of this book, these proposed rules have not yet been finalized.

NOAA = National Oceanic and
Atmospheric Administration

delegated this authority to the U.S. Fish and Wildlife Service and the NOAA National Marine Fisheries Service.[39]

On its own initiative and through notice-and-comment rule-making,[40] the Service may list a species as endangered or threatened based on any one or a combination of the following factors:

> the present or threatened destruction, modification, or curtailment of its habitat or range

> overutilization for commercial, recreational, scientific, or educational purposes

> disease or predation

> the inadequacy of existing regulatory mechanisms

> other natural or manmade factors affecting its continued existence[41]

The Act provides that the Service must make these determinations based solely on the best scientific and commercial data available after conducting a review of the status of the species and after taking into account those efforts, if any, being made by any state or foreign nation, or any political subdivision of a state or foreign nation, to protect such species, whether by predator control, protection of habitat and food supply, or other conservation practices, within any area under its jurisdiction, or on the high seas.[42]

The regulations add to these statutory requirements by requiring that the Service must make its listing decisions "*solely* on the basis of the best available scientific and commercial information regarding a species' status, without reference to possible economic or other impacts of such determination."[43] This concept may be somewhat eroded, however, by the Proposed Regulations discussed above. Under the Proposed Regulations,[44] the clause prohibiting reference to economic and other impacts would be deleted. Although the ESA itself prohibits the Service from considering economic impacts, in its proposal the Service explains that economic information "may be informative to the public" and thus made a part of the record.

Interested persons have the ability to petition the Service to add species to the list or to remove species from the endangered or threatened species list.[45] The primary purpose of the Act's petition process is to empower the public, in effect, to direct the attention of the Service to (1) species that may be imperiled and may warrant listing, but whose status the Service has not yet determined, (2) changes in the nature or magnitude of a listed species' threats or other circumstances that may warrant reclassification of

---

39   50 C.F.R. § 402.01(b).

40   *Northwest Ecosystem Alliance v. U.S. Fish & Wildlife Serv.,* 475 F.3d 1136, 1137 (9th Cir. 2007).

41   16 U.S.C. § 1533(a)(1)(A)–(E); 50 C.F.R. § 424.11(c).

42   16 U.S.C. § 1533(b)(1)(A). The Service is also required to give consideration to species which have been designated as requiring protection from unrestricted commerce by any foreign nation, or pursuant to any international agreement; or identified as in danger of extinction, or likely to become so within the foreseeable future, by any state agency or by any agency of a foreign nation that is responsible for the conservation of fish or wildlife or plants. *Id.* § 1533(b)(1)(B).

43   50 C.F.R. § 424.11(b) (emphasis in original).

44   83 Fed. Reg. 35,193 *et seq.*

45   50 C.F.R. § 424.14. See also, e.g., *Northwest Ecosystem Alliance,* 475 F.3d at 1137–38.

that species' status (i.e., "down-listing" the species from an endangered species to a threatened species, or "up-listing" from a threatened species to an endangered species) or delisting of the species (i.e., removing the species from the endangered list or the threatened list), or (3) information that would support making revisions to critical habitat designations.[46]

Petitioners must provide notice to the state agency responsible for the management and conservation of fish, plant, or wildlife resources in each state where the species that is the subject of the petition occurs. This notification must be made at least 30 days prior to submission of the petition.[47] In California, this notification must be provided to the California Department of Fish and Wildlife.

The petition must clearly identify itself as such, be dated, and include the following information:

> the name, signature, address, telephone number, if any, and the association, institution, or business affiliation, if any, of the petitioner

> the scientific name and any common name of a species of fish or wildlife or plants that is the subject of the petition. Only one species may be the subject of a petition, which may include, by hierarchical extension based on taxonomy and the Act, any subspecies or variety, or (for vertebrates) any potential distinct population segments of that species.

> a clear indication of the administrative action the petitioner seeks (e.g., listing of a species)

> a detailed narrative justifying the recommended administrative action that contains an analysis of the information presented

> literature citations that are specific enough for the Service to readily locate the information cited in the petition, including page numbers or chapters as applicable

> electronic or hard copies of supporting materials, to the extent permitted by U.S. copyright law, or appropriate excerpts or quotations from those materials (e.g., publications, maps, reports, letters from authorities) cited in the petition

> information to establish whether the subject entity is a "species" as defined in the Act

> information on the current and historical geographic range of the species, including the states or countries intersected, in whole or part, by that range

> copies of the notification letters or electronic communication which petitioners provided to the state agency or agencies responsible for the management and conservation of fish, plant, or wildlife resources in each state where the species that is the subject of the petition currently occurs[48]

---

46   Endangered and Threatened Wildlife and Plants; Revisions to the Regulations for Petitions, 81 Fed. Reg. 66,462, 66,462 (Sept. 27, 2016).

47   50 C.F.R. § 424.14(b).

48   *Id.* § 424.14(c).

In addition to the information described above, the Service's determination as to whether the petition provides substantial scientific or commercial information indicating that the petitioned action may be warranted will depend in part on the degree to which the petition includes the following types of information:

> information on current population status and trends and estimates of current population sizes and distributions, both in captivity and the wild, if available

> identification of the factors under Section 4(a)(1) of the Act that may affect the species and where these factors are acting upon the species

> whether and to what extent any or all of the factors alone or in combination identified in Section 4(a)(1) of the Act may cause the species to be an endangered species or threatened species (i.e., the species is currently in danger of extinction or is likely to become so within the foreseeable future), and, if so, how high in magnitude and how imminent the threats to the species and its habitat are

> information on adequacy of regulatory protections and effectiveness of conservation activities by states as well as other parties, that have been initiated or that are ongoing, that may protect the species or its habitat

> a complete, balanced representation of the relevant facts, including information that may contradict claims in the petition[49]

If a request does not meet the requirements related to the contents of a petition, the Service will generally reject the request without making a finding, and will, within a reasonable timeframe, notify the sender and provide an explanation of the rejection. However, the Service retains discretion to process a petition where it determines there has been substantial compliance with the relevant requirements.[50] To the maximum extent practicable and within 90 days after receiving such a petition, the Service must make a finding as to whether the petition presents substantial scientific or commercial information indicating that the petitioned action may be warranted.[51] If the petition is found to present such information, the Service must "promptly" commence a

---

49 50 C.F.R. § 424.14(d).

50 *Id.* § 424.14(f)(1).

51 *Id.* § 424.14(h)(1). "Substantial scientific or commercial information" refers to credible scientific or commercial information in support of the petition's claims such that a reasonable person conducting an impartial scientific review would conclude that the action proposed in the petition may be warranted. Conclusions drawn in the petition without the support of credible scientific or commercial information will not be considered "substantial information." *Id.* § 424.14(h)(1)(i). The "substantial scientific or commercial information" standard must be applied in light of any prior reviews or findings the Service has made on the listing status of the species that is the subject of the petition. Where the Service has already conducted a finding on, or review of, the listing status of that species (whether in response to a petition or on the Service's own initiative), the Service will evaluate any petition received thereafter seeking to list, delist, or reclassify that species to determine whether a reasonable person conducting an impartial scientific review would conclude that the action proposed in the petition may be warranted despite the previous review or finding. Where the prior review resulted in a final agency action, a petitioned action generally would not be considered to present substantial scientific and commercial information indicating that the action may be warranted unless the petition provides new information not previously considered. *Id.* § 424.14(h)(1)(iii).

review of that species.[52] While the species is being considered for listing, it is referred to as a "candidate species."[53]

Within 12 months after receiving a petition that is found to present substantial information indicating that the petitioned action may be warranted, the Service must make one of the following findings:

> the petitioned action is not warranted, in which case the Service must promptly publish such finding in the Federal Register

> the petitioned action is warranted, in which case the Service must promptly publish in the Federal Register a general notice and the complete text of a proposed regulation to implement such action

> the petitioned action is warranted, but that (1) the immediate proposal and timely promulgation of a final regulation implementing the petitioned action is precluded by pending proposals to determine whether any species is an endangered species or a threatened species, and (2) expeditious progress is being made to add qualified species to either of the lists and to remove from the lists species for which the protections of the ESA are no longer necessary. If these two requirements are satisfied, then the Service must promptly publish such finding in the Federal Register, together with a description and evaluation of the reasons and date on which the finding is based[54]

The ESA provides that "any negative finding" relative to whether a petition presents substantial scientific or commercial information, and "any finding" relative to whether the petitioned action is or is not warranted, is subject to judicial review.[55]

If the Service determines the petitioned action is warranted, then it must provide a notice of a proposed rule to carry out the action of listing the species. The notice must include a summary of factors affecting the species or its designated critical habitat.[56] In addition to publishing notice of the proposal in the Federal Register, the Service must give actual notice of the proposed regulation to the state agency in each state and county in which the species is believed to occur and invite the comment of each such agency and jurisdiction.[57] In addition to other noticing requirements, the Service must also give notice of the proposed regulation to any federal agencies, local authorities, or private individuals or organizations known to be affected by the rule.[58] Finally, the Service must

---

52 16 U.S.C. § 1533(b)(3)(A); 50 C.F.R. § 424.14(h)(2). The Act also specifies that the Service must "promptly" publish each finding as to whether the petition presents such substantial scientific or commercial information in the Federal Register. *Id.*

53 50 C.F.R. § 424.02 (defining "candidate" as "any species being considered by the Secretary for listing as an endangered or threatened species, but not yet the subject of a proposed rule").

54 *Id.* § 1533(b)(3)(B)(i)–(iii); 50 C.F.R. § 424.14(h)(2).

55 50 C.F.R. § 1533(b)(3)(C)(ii).

56 50 C.F.R. § 424.16(b).

57 *Id.* § 424.16(c)(1)(ii).

58 *Id.* § 424.16(c)(1)(iii); see *id.* § 424.16(c)(iv) & (v) for other noticing requirements.

publish a summary of the proposed regulation in a newspaper of general circulation in each area of the United States in which the species is believed to occur.[59]

The regulations require that the Service allow at least 60 days for public comment following publication in the Federal Register of the proposed rule. This period may be extended or reopened upon a finding by the Service that there is good cause to do so.[60] The Service must promptly hold at least one public hearing if any person so requests within 45 days of publication of the proposed rule.[61]

Within one year of the publication of the rule, the Service must publish in the Federal Register either (1) a final rule to implement the Service's determination; (2) a notice withdrawing the proposed rule upon a finding that available evidence does not justify the action proposed by the rule; or (3) a notice extending the one-year period by an additional period of not more than six months because there is substantial disagreement among scientists knowledgeable about the species regarding the sufficiency or accuracy of the available data relevant to the determination.[62]

Publication of a final rule to list a species must provide a summary of factors affecting the species.[63] A final rule takes effect not less than 30 days after it is published in the Federal Register, except as otherwise provided for good cause, and not less than 90 days after publication in the Federal Register of the proposed rule and actual notification of any affected state agencies and counties.[64] If a state agency submits comments disagreeing in whole or in part with a proposed rule, and the Service issues a final rule that is in conflict with such comments, or if the Service fails to adopt a regulation for which a state agency has made a petition for listing, then the Secretary must provide such agency with a written justification for the failure to adopt a rule consistent with the agency's comments or petition.[65]

The lists of endangered and threatened wildlife and plant species are maintained in the Service's regulations in the Code of Federal Regulations.[66] At least once every five years the Service must conduct a review of each listed species to determine whether it should be delisted or reclassified. A notice announcing those species under active review must be published in the Federal Register. The Service may also review the status of any species at any time based upon a petition or upon other data available to the Service.[67]

---

59   50 C.F.R. § 424.16(c)(1)(vi).

60   *Id.* § 424.16(c)(2).

61   *Id.* § 424.16(c)(3).

62   *Id.* § 424.17(a)(1).

63   *Id.* § 424.18(a).

64   *Id.* § 424.18(b).

65   *Id.* § 424.18(c).

66   *Id.* § 17.11 (endangered and threatened wildlife list); *id.* § 17.12 (endangered and threatened plants list).

67   *Id.* § 424.21.

Delisting a Species

Listed species may also be considered for delisting, i.e., removal from the lists of endangered or threatened species.[68] The factors considered in delisting a species are the same as those used in listing an endangered or threatened species, essentially requiring that the factors requiring the listing of the species in the first instance no longer justify the continued listing of the species. As discussed above, these factors include (1) the present or threatened destruction, modification, or curtailment of a species, habitat, or range; (2) overutilization for commercial, recreational, scientific, or educational purposes; (3) disease or predation; (4) the inadequacy of existing regulatory mechanisms; or (5) other natural or manmade factors affecting its continued existence.[69] If adopted, the Proposed Regulations would specifically state that the standard for a decision to delist a species "is the same as the standard not to list it in the first instance."[70]

Bald eagle. Photo: Becky Matsubara. Licensed under CC 2.0.

The removal must be supported by the best scientific and commercial data available to the Service after conducting a review of the status of the species. A species may be delisted only if such data substantiate that it is neither endangered nor threatened for one or more of the following reasons:

(1) *Extinction.* Unless all individuals of the listed species had been previously identified and located and were later found to be extirpated from their previous range, a sufficient period of time[71] must be allowed before delisting to indicate clearly that the species is extinct.

(2) *Recovery.* The principal goal of the Service is to return listed species to a point at which protection under the Act is no longer required. A species may be delisted on the basis of recovery only if the best scientific and commercial data available indicate that it is no longer endangered or threatened.

(3) *Original data for classification in error.* Subsequent investigations may show that the best scientific or commercial data available when the species was listed, or the interpretation of such data, were in error.

When considering a delisting or other revision to the lists, the Service must consult as appropriate with affected states, interested persons and organizations, other affected federal agencies, and, in cooperation with the Secretary of State, with the country or countries in which the species concerned are normally found or whose citizens harvest such species from the high seas. Data reviewed by the Service may include, but are not limited to scientific or commercial publications, administrative reports, maps or other graphic materials, information received from experts on the subject, and comments from interested parties. After this consultation and based on these determination requirements above, the Service may change the listed status of the species.[72]

---

68 *Id.* § 424.10.

69 *Id.* § 424.11(d) (referring to the listing factors set forth in § 424.11(c)).

70 83 Fed. Reg. 35,193 *et seq.*

71 Neither the statute nor the regulations provide a mechanism for determining whether a sufficient amount of time has elapsed. In the authors' experience, this time period may be longer than 50 years.

72 50 C.F.R. § 424.10.

DPS = distinct population
segment

Generally, the processes described above regarding the listing of species apply to the delisting of species, and practitioners should consult those same provisions in the Code of Federal Regulations related to listing or revisions to the status of listed species.

Distinct Population Segments

An issue that often arises regarding the definition of species is the meaning of the term "distinct population segment". The Act defines "species" as including "any subspecies of fish or wildlife or plants, and any distinct population segment of any species of vertebrate fish or wildlife which interbreeds when mature."[73] Thus, under the ESA, the Service can designate a particular population of a species as a distinct population segment and then consider that distinct population segment a species for listing purposes.[74]

The ESA does not define the term "distinct population segment" (commonly referred to as "DPS"). DPS questions are highly fact-specific, and as a general rule, the courts will defer to the Service's DPS determinations. For example, in *In re Polar Bear Endangered Species Act Listing*,[75] the Court of Appeals for the District of Columbia Circuit considered an argument raised by plaintiffs challenging the Service's decision to list the polar bear as a threatened, rather than an endangered, species. The plaintiffs argued that the Service should have divided the species into distinct population segments for the purposes of its listing decision. Citing the Service's analysis in the administrative record, the court explained the Service's determination as to "small genetic differences" among polar bears and other findings supported the Service's conclusions that "physiology, demographics, behavior, and life history strategies of the species" were not sufficient to distinguish population segments under the DPS Policy.[76]

The U.S. Fish and Wildlife Service issued policy guidance on the meaning and application of the term "distinct population segment" in its *Policy Regarding the Recognition of Distinct Vertebrate Population Segments Under the Endangered Species Act* ("DPS Policy").[77] The ability to designate and list distinct population segments allows the Service to provide different levels of protection to different populations of the same species. Accordingly, the Service does not have to list an entire species as endangered when only one of its populations faces extinction.[78]

73 16 U.S.C. § 1532(16).

74 *National Ass'n of Home Builders v. Norton*, 340 F.3d 835, 842 (9th Cir. 2003).

75 709 F.3d 1 (D.C. Cir. 2013).

76 *Id.* at 12.

77 Policy Regarding the Recognition of Distinct Vertebrate Population Segments, 61 Fed. Reg. 4722 (Feb. 7, 1996). The Policy was subject to an as-applied challenge in *Northwest Ecosystem Alliance v. U.S. Fish & Wildlife Service*, 475 F.3d 1136 (9th Cir. 2007). The Ninth Circuit Court of Appeals held that the DPS Policy is entitled to deference under the U.S. Supreme Court's *Chevron* standard, which is a deferential standard that applies "when it appears that Congress delegated authority to the agency generally to make rules carrying the force of law, and that the agency interpretation claiming deference was promulgated in the exercise of that authority." *Id.* at 1141 (citing *Chevron U.S.A., Inc. v. Natural Res. Def. Council, Inc.*, 467 U.S. 837 (1984), and quoting *United States v. Mead Corp.*, 533 U.S. 218 (2001)); see also *Trout Unlimited v. Lohn*, 559 F.3d 946, 954 (9th Cir. 2009). The court then went on to uphold the DPS Policy as a reasonable construction of the term "distinct population segment" in the ESA. *Id.* at 1143–45.

78 *National Ass'n of Home Builders*, 340 F.3d at 842 (citing 61 Fed. Reg. at 4725).

The DPS Policy establishes three criteria for a Distinct Population Segment,[79] which the agency must assess sequentially:

(1) discreteness of the population segment in relation to the remainder of the species to which it belongs

(2) the significance of the population segment to the species to which it belongs

(3) the population segment's conservation status in relation to the Act's standards for listing (i.e., is the population segment, when treated as if it were a species, endangered or threatened?)[80]

The first criterion in the sequence, "discreteness," requires that the population segment be either "markedly separated from other populations of the same taxon as a consequence of physical, physiological, ecological, or behavioral factors" or "delimited by international governmental boundaries within which differences in control of exploitation, management of habitat, conservation status, or regulatory mechanisms exist that are significant."[81]

The purpose of the discreteness standard is to ensure that a distinct population segment is "adequately defined and described," allowing for the effective administration of the ESA.[82] This standard distinguishes a population from other members of its species but does not require "absolute separation."[83] A population is discrete if it is "markedly separated from other populations of the same taxon as a consequence of physical, physiological, ecological, or behavioral factors," or if it is "delimited by international governmental boundaries within which differences in control of exploitation, management of habitat, conservation status, or regulatory mechanisms exist that are significant" in light of the ESA.[84]

If a population is discrete, the Service then considers the "biological and ecological significance" of the population to the taxon to which it belongs. The purpose of the significance element is "to carry out the expressed congressional intent that this authority [to list distinct population segments] be exercised sparingly as well as to concentrate conservation efforts undertaken under the [ESA] on avoiding important losses of genetic diversity."[85] The Service determines the significance of a discrete population by considering the following non-exclusive factors:

(1) persistence of the discrete population segment in an ecological setting unusual or unique for the taxon

79   In *Northwest Ecosystem Alliance v. U.S. Fish & Wildlife Serv.*, 475 F.3d 1136 (9th Cir. 2007), the Ninth Circuit identifies the first two criteria as two "factors" for the Service's consideration and based on those two factors of discreteness and significant, a population qualifies as a distinct population segment. According to the court, "[i]f a population is deemed to be a [distinct population segment], the inquiry then proceeds to whether it is endangered or threatened." *Id.* at 1138.

80   61 Fed. Reg. at 4725

81   *Id.*

82   *National Ass'n of Home Builders*, 340 F.3d at 842 (9th Cir. 2003) (citing 61 Fed. Reg. at 4724).

83   *Id.*

84   *Id.* (citing 61 Fed. Reg. at 4725).

85   *National Ass'n of Home Builders*, 340 F.3d at 844 (citing 61 Fed. Reg. at 4724).

(2) evidence that loss of the discrete population segment would result in a significant gap in the range of a taxon

(3) evidence that the discrete population segment represents the only surviving natural occurrence of a taxon that may be more abundant elsewhere as an introduced population outside its historic range

(4) evidence that the discrete population segment differs markedly from other populations of the species in its genetic characteristics[86]

The first, second, and fourth factors have been the subject of further substantive interpretation by the courts.

First Factor: Ecological Setting. In *Northwest Ecosystem Alliance v. U.S. Fish & Wildlife Service*,[87] the Ninth Circuit Court of Appeals considered a challenge to the Service's determination that certain populations of the Washington gray squirrel were not distinct population segments. With respect to the first factor, the plaintiffs contested the Service's finding that certain geographic regions in Washington did not constitute unusual or unique ecological settings for this taxon. The court upheld the Service's conclusion that the differences in habitat between these geographic regions and other regions in the state were "not so great" as to constitute a "unique or unusual ecological setting" for the western gray squirrel.[88]

Second Factor: Significant Gap in the Range. In *National Association of Home Builders v. Norton*,[89] the Ninth Circuit Court of Appeals considered the Service's decision to list the Arizona pygmy-owl population as a distinct population segment for purposes of the ESA. As to the second factor, the court evaluated whether the Service arbitrarily determined that the loss of the discrete Arizona pygmy-owl population would cause a gap in the range of its taxon and that such a gap would be significant. The court explained that the DPS Policy does not define what constitutes a "gap" for purposes of the second significance factor, but because the meaning of "gap" is ambiguous, the Service was entitled to deference in interpreting its own regulations, unless that interpretation is plainly erroneous. Plaintiffs argued that this particular owl population was at the periphery of its range, and so therefore its loss could not constitute a "gap," because by analogy, a gap by definition constitutes a gap in the "middle of a fence, not at its end." The court rejected this argument, noting that even the loss of a peripheral population, however small, would create an empty geographic space in the range of a taxon.[90] The court then evaluated the Service's bases for finding that the gap was significant: (1) decrease in the genetic variability of the taxon; (2) reduction in the current range of the taxon; (3) reduction in the historic range of the taxon; and (4) extirpation of the western pygmy-owls from the United States. After evaluating the Service's rationales for

---

86   *Id.* (citing 61 Fed. Reg. at 4725).

87   475 F.3d 1136 (9th Cir. 2007).

88   *Id.* at 1145–46.

89   340 F.3d 835 (9th Cir. 2003).

90   *Id.* at 845–46.

making these determinations, the court concluded that the Service did not articulate a reasoned basis for finding that the gap created by the loss of the discrete Arizona pygmy-owl population would be significant to the taxon as a whole.[91]

In *Northwest Ecosystem Alliance v. U.S. Fish & Wildlife Service*,[92] the Ninth Circuit evaluated the Service's determination that the hypothetical loss of the Washington population of gray squirrels would not be of biological and ecological significance to the taxon as a whole. The court took into account the Service's consideration of evidence regarding the squirrel's behavior, morphology, and home range size, and upheld its determination that any gap caused by the loss of the Washington population would not be significant because the population lacks biologically distinctive traits. Notably, the court rejected an argument by plaintiffs that a serious reduction in the squirrel's geographic range suffices to satisfy the "significant gap" factor, finding instead that the "significance" inquiry under the DPS Policy is not limited to geographic factors.[93]

Fourth Factor: Marked Genetic Differences. The Ninth Circuit Court of Appeals in *National Association of Home Builders v. Norton*[94] evaluated the Service's argument that since the eastern and western pygmy-owls had potentially different genetic characteristics, the extirpation of the Arizona pygmy-owls would result in the loss of genetic distinctness associated with the Arizona pygmy-owls from the western United States. The court found that the Service did not present evidence of marked genetic differences between pygmy-owls in Arizona and northwestern Mexico. The court also found that only a "potential" genetic difference existed between the western and eastern pygmy-owl populations, which is contrary to the requirement that an "actual" genetic difference exists, and those actual genetic differences be appreciable. The court therefore concluded that the Service did not articulate a rational basis for its finding that the discrete Arizona pygmy-owl population is significant to its taxon under the fourth significance factor.[95]

The Ninth Circuit also evaluated this factor in *Northwest Ecosystem Alliance v. U.S. Fish & Wildlife Service*.[96] In this case, the court evaluated whether the Service properly determined whether the Washington gray squirrel population's genetic characteristics differed "markedly" from the remainder of the subspecies' range.[97] The Service based its decision on a peer-reviewed study of genetic differences among gray squirrel populations in Washington, Oregon, and California. The court evaluated the Service's analysis of these data and determined that it "must defer to the agency's interpretation of complex scientific data."[98]

---

91 *Id.* at 849–50.

92 475 F.3d 1136 (9th Cir. 2007).

93 *Id.* at 1148 (noting that on its face the DPS Policy considers ecological, historical, and genetic factors in addition to geography).

94 340 F.3d 835 (9th Cir. 2003).

95 *Id.* at 851–52.

96 475 F.3d 1136 (9th Cir. 2007).

97 *Id.* at 1149–50.

98 475 F.3d 1136, 1150 (9th Cir. 2007).

ESU = evolutionarily significant unit

If a population is deemed to be a distinct population segment, the inquiry then proceeds to whether it is endangered or threatened.[99]

Evolutionarily Significant Units

Because of their natural history, NMFS regulates certain populations of anadromous fish species, namely salmon and steelhead, based on concepts derived from the "distinct population segment" approach to applying ESA mandates. These populations are referred to as "evolutionarily significant units."

The Ninth Circuit Court of Appeals has provided a good narrative for how the regulations governing ESUs have developed. The discussion below is taken from the court's decision in *Trout Unlimited v. Lohn*,[100] one of the most important cases on the issue of ESUs. As the court explains, NMFS has adopted regulations applying the ESA's mandates to salmon and steelhead populations on the Pacific coast that have been modified over the years in response to scientific evidence and to legal challenges. In 1991, NMFS issued a policy statement defining a distinct population segment, and hence a "species" under the ESA, as an "evolutionarily significant unit" (ESU) for purposes of regulating salmon and steelhead populations ("ESU Policy").[101]

Based on the ESU Policy, an ESU "must satisfy two criteria . . . (1) It must be substantially reproductively isolated from other conspecific population units; and (2) It must represent an important component in the evolutionary legacy of the species."[102] The first criterion—reproductive isolation—is based upon "movements of tagged fish, recolonization rates of other populations, measurements of genetic differences between populations, and evaluations of the efficacy of natural barriers." The second criterion— the population's contribution to the evolutionary legacy of the species—is based upon "the ecological/genetic diversity of the species as a whole. In other words, if the population became extinct, would this event represent a significant loss to the ecological/ genetic diversity of the species?"[103]

Five years later, NMFS and the U.S. Fish and Wildlife Service adopted the DPS Policy discussed above. As described above, the DPS Policy slightly modified the three factors to be considered in a listing decision for a distinct population segment. The DPS Policy describes these factors as (1) the "[d]iscreteness of the population segment in relation to the remainder of the species to which it belongs," (2) "[t]he significance of the population segment to the species to which it belongs," and (3) "[t]he population segment's conservation status in relation to the [ESA's] standards for listing (i.e., is the

Salmon in the Lower American River. Photo: Dan Cox/USFWS. Licensed under CC 2.0.

99 *Northwest Ecosystem Alliance*, 475 F.3d at 1138; *Trout Unlimited v. Lohn*, 559 F.3d 946, 949 (9th Cir. 2009).

100 559 F.3d 946 (9th Cir. 2009).

101 Policy on Applying the Definition of Species, 56 Fed. Reg. 58,612, 58,618 (Nov. 20, 1991) (the "ESU Policy").

102 *Id.*

103 *Id.*

population segment, when treated as if it were a species, endangered or threatened?).”[104] NMFS applies the joint policy to steelhead populations but the original 1991 policy to Pacific salmon populations.[105]

In 1993, NMFS concluded that hatchery fish could be part of the same ESU as natural fish. The agency issued an Interim Hatchery Policy which reasoned that “[g]enetic resources important to the species’ evolutionary legacy may reside in hatchery fish as well as in natural fish.”[106] Hatchery fish otherwise meeting the two criteria for a natural population’s ESU would nevertheless be excluded from that ESU, and not included in the listed species, if information indicated that: (1) the hatchery population in question is of a different genetic lineage than the listed natural populations, (2) artificial propagation has produced appreciable changes in the hatchery population in characteristics that are believed to have a genetic basis, or (3) there is substantial uncertainty about the relationship between existing hatchery fish and the natural population.[107]

Although hatchery fish could be part of the same ESU as natural fish, NMFS decided that, absent exceptional circumstances, only natural fish could be listed as endangered or threatened.[108] NMFS determined that only those hatchery fish “considered to be essential for recovery [of the natural population]” could be listed alongside the natural fish.[109] According to the Interim Hatchery Policy, hatchery fish might be considered “essential to recovery” if “the natural population faces a high, short-term risk of extinction, or if the hatchery population is believed to contain a substantial proportion of the genetic diversity remaining in the species.”[110]

The Interim Hatchery Policy lasted only until 2001, when Alsea Valley Alliance, an environmental organization, successfully challenged NMFS’s decision to distinguish between natural and hatchery fish for listing purposes, after finding both to be within the same ESU. Applying the Interim Hatchery Policy, NMFS had included nine hatchery populations of Oregon coast coho salmon within the same ESU as natural coho salmon but had listed only the natural portion of the ESU as threatened.[111] Alsea Valley challenged that distinction in the U.S. District Court for the District of Oregon, arguing that “the ESA does not allow the Secretary to make listing distinctions below that of species, subspecies or a distinct population segment of a species.”[112]

---

104 Policy Regarding the Recognition of Distinct Vertebrate Population Segments, 61 Fed. Reg. 4722, 4725 (Feb. 7, 1996).

105 *Id.* at 4722.

106 Interim Policy on Artificial Propagation of Pacific Salmon, 58 Fed. Reg. 17,573, 17,574 (Apr. 5, 1993).

107 *Id.* at 17,575.

108 See *id.* (“In general, [hatchery] fish will not be included as part of the listed species.”).

109 *Id.*

110 *Id.*

111 See 50 C.F.R. § 227.4 (1999); 63 Fed. Reg. 42,587, 42,589 (Aug. 10, 1998).

112 *Alsea Valley Alliance v. Evans (Alsea I)*, 161 F. Supp. 2d 1154, 1161 (D. Or. 2001).

The district court agreed with Alsea Valley, concluding that "NMFS may consider listing only an entire species, subspecies or distinct population segment."[113] Because NMFS had placed the hatchery coho and the natural coho in the same ESU, the district court reasoned, NMFS was required to list both hatchery and natural coho as endangered, or neither hatchery nor natural coho as endangered. Accordingly, the district court struck down the Oregon coast coho listing as arbitrary and capricious.

Rather than appeal the district court's decision, NMFS revised its Interim Hatchery Policy to eliminate the distinction between natural and hatchery fish in listing determinations. After 162 days of public comment, NMFS issued a Final Hatchery Listing Policy on June 28, 2005.[114]

The 2005 Hatchery Listing Policy reaffirms that hatchery fish may be part of the same ESU as natural fish but alters NMFS's listing practices in several ways. To comply with *Alsea I*, the Hatchery Listing Policy provides that hatchery fish that are part of the same ESU as natural fish "will be included in any listing of the ESU."[115] In addition, the Hatchery Listing Policy requires NMFS to consider the status of the ESU as a whole rather than the status of only the natural fish within the ESU when determining whether an ESU should be listed as endangered or threatened.[116] However, under the policy, a listing determination still places primary importance on the viability of natural, self-sustaining populations, providing that "[h]atchery fish will be included in assessing an ESU's status in the context of their contributions to conserving natural self-sustaining populations."[117] The Hatchery Listing Policy also requires status determinations to be based upon abundance, productivity, genetic diversity, and spatial distribution of the ESU.[118] Noting that hatchery fish can be both helpful and harmful to natural fish, the policy also allows NMFS to use its discretionary authority via Section 4(d) regulations to provide for the take of certain hatchery fish, even if the ESU to which they belong is listed as threatened.[119]

Around this time, NMFS issued Section 4(d) regulations with respect to the taking of ESUs deemed threatened. Under these regulations, naturally spawned and hatchery salmon with intact adipose fins may not be taken.[120] On the other hand, hatchery fish with clipped adipose fins may be taken.[121]

In *Trout Unlimited v. Lohn*,[122] plaintiffs challenged NMFS's decision in accordance with the 2005 Hatchery Listing Policy to downlist a population of Upper Columbia River

113 *Id.*

114 See Policy on the Consideration of Hatchery-Origin Fish, 70 Fed. Reg. 37,204 (June 28, 2005).

115 *Id.* at 37,215.

116 *Id.*

117 *Id.*

118 *Id.*

119 *Id.* at 37,215–16.

120 See Endangered and Threatened Species: Final Listing Determinations for 16 ESUs of West Coast Salmon, 70 Fed. Reg. 37,160, 37,194–95 (June 28, 2005).

121 *Id.*

122 559 F.3d 946 (9th Cir. 2009).

steelhead from endangered to threatened. The Upper Columbia River steelhead is an inland steelhead ESU in the Columbia River Basin upstream from the Yakima River in Washington to the U.S.-Canada border. Environmental conservation organizations challenged NMFS's rejection of their petitions to separate natural fish and hatchery fish into different ESUs, and the downlisting of the Upper Columbia River steelhead ESU from "endangered" to "threatened." As part of its second claim, the organizations argued that the 2005 Hatchery Listing Policy impermissibly required NMFS to consider the status of the entire ESU rather than just the natural components of the ESU when making listing determinations, and that NMFS's decisions were arbitrary and capricious and failed to employ "the best scientific and commercial data available" in violation of the ESA.

A number of trade associations intervened, challenging NMFS's listing policies on opposite grounds. Relying on *Alsea I*, the trade associations' core claim was that the ESA does not allow NMFS to make any distinctions between hatchery fish and natural fish once NMFS has included them in the same ESU. The trade associations' basic contention was that once NMFS defines an ESU, it may not further distinguish between members of that ESU when making its listing determinations.

The Ninth Circuit Court of Appeals held that NMFS's decision not to split natural and hatchery fish into separate ESUs was not arbitrary and capricious based on its view that it was required to defer to NMFS resolution of certain scientific questions related to this issue. As to the claim that the decision to downlist the Upper Columbia River steelhead violated the ESA because the listing determination was based on the status of the entire ESU rather than the status of only the natural fish within the ESU. According to plaintiffs, basing listing determinations on the status of the entire ESU was arbitrary and capricious because the ESU's central purpose is to preserve natural populations rather than artificial ones. The court responded to this issue by first pointing out that the ESA's primary goal is to preserve the ability of natural populations to survive in the wild. "The statute mentions artificial propagation merely as a means 'to bring any endangered species or threatened species to the point at which the measures provided pursuant to [the ESA] are no longer necessary.'"[123] The court then held that the Hatchery Listing Policy was consistent with the ESA and with its statutory goal of preserving natural populations. The court explained that the Policy calls for a status review of the entire "species." Finally, the court held that NMFS's decision to downlist the species was based on the best scientific evidence available, in light of the extensive scientific data used by NMFS to approach its decision.[124]

The court then considered arguments by the trade association that NMFS impermissibly distinguished between hatchery and naturally spawned salmon. "Once an ESU is defined to include both hatchery and naturally spawned fish, the [trade association] contends that any further differentiation within the ESU is error .... Thus, the [trade association] maintains that considering hatchery and naturally spawned fish separately

123 *Id.* at 957 (quoting 16 U.S.C. § 1523(3)).
124 *Id.* at 957–59.

during the listing process violated the ESA . . . ."[125] The court rejected these arguments, first, because it found nothing in the ESA that required NMFS to treat hatchery and naturally spawned fish equally, and second, because the ESA's legislative history does not address how such biological distinctions should affect the process by which NMFS makes its listing determination. "If NMFS were attempting to list something less than an ESU, the [trade association's] arguments might have some merit. However, no party in this case claims that NMFS has listed anything but an entire ESU."[126]

"Throughout All or a Significant Portion of Its Range" Determinations

Another important consideration in the listing process is whether the species should be considered endangered or threatened in light of its status "throughout all or a significant portion of its range."[127] The ESA and its implementing regulations do not define what constitutes a "significant portion of [a species'] range" for the purpose of the listing determination.

One court has noted that, "[s]tanding alone, the phrase 'in danger of extinction throughout . . . a significant portion of its range' is puzzling," and that "the phrase 'extinc[t] throughout . . . a significant portion of its range' is something of an oxymoron."[128] "The statute is therefore inherently ambiguous, as it appears to use language in a manner in some tension with ordinary usage."

In *Defenders of Wildlife v. Norton*, the Ninth Circuit Court of Appeals struggled with this language in the context of the Service's decision not to list the flat-tailed horned lizard as a threatened species. In making this determination, the Service interpreted this language to mean that a species is eligible for protection under the ESA if it "faces threats in enough key portions of its range that the *entire species* is in danger of extinction, or will be within the foreseeable future."[129] The court noted that this interpretation assumes that a species is in danger of extinction in a "significant portion of its range" only if it is in danger of extinction everywhere."[130] The court determined this interpretation was unacceptable because it had the effect of rendering the phrase superfluous in light of the fact that the statute already defines "endangered species" as those species that are "in danger of extinction throughout all . . . of [their] range."[131]

The court then evaluated the plaintiff's interpretation of this phrase, which relied on a more quantitative approach, arguing that the projected loss of 82 percent of the lizard's habitat constitutes "a substantial portion of its range." The court concluded that

---

125 *Id.* at 959.

126 *Id.* at 960.

127 "The term 'endangered species' means any species which is in danger of extinction throughout all or a significant portion of its range." 16 U.S.C. § 1532(6). "The term 'threatened species' means any species which is likely to become an endangered species within the foreseeable future throughout all or a significant portion of its range." *Id.* § 1532(20).

128 *Defenders of Wildlife v. Norton*, 258 F.3d 1136, 1140–41 (9th Cir. 2001).

129 *Id.* at 1141 (emphasis in original).

130 *Id.*

131 *Id.* at 1141–42.

this approach was problematic because it does not make sense to assume that the loss of a predetermined percentage of habitat or range would necessarily qualify a species for listing, and because Congress could have—but did not—included in the ESA a bright line percentage appropriate for determining when listing was necessary.[132]

Instead of adopting either of the parties' interpretations, the court drew from the legislative history of the ESA and concluded "that a species can be extinct 'throughout . . . a significant portion of its range' if there are major geographical areas in which it is no longer viable but once was."[133] "Those areas need not coincide with national or state political boundaries, although they can." The court concluded that the Service did not apply this standard or even expressly consider the "extinction throughout . . . a significant portion of its range" issue at all, and that if the Service had done so, it "might have determined that the lizard is indeed in danger of "extinction throughout . . . a significant portion of its range."[134] As such, the court concluded that the Service's decision to not list the lizard was arbitrary and capricious.

In July 2014, the Service issued its Final Policy on Interpretation of the Phrase "Significant Portion of Its Range" in the ESA's Definition of "Endangered Species" and "Threatened Species."[135] This Policy was in response to the Ninth Circuit's ruling in *Defenders of Wildlife v. Norton*,[136] "which indicates that "with respect to the statutory language 'throughout all or a significant portion of its range,' [the Service] should give words on either side of the 'or' operational meaning."[137] According to the Policy:

> A portion of the range of a species is "significant" if the species is not currently endangered or threatened throughout all of its range, but the portion's contribution to the viability of the species is so important that, without the members in that portion, the species would be in danger of extinction, or likely to become so in the foreseeable future, throughout all of its range.[138]

The Policy adopts the following approach to implementing the phrase "significant portion of its range."

> First, if a species is found to be endangered or threatened throughout only a significant portion of its range, the entire species is listed as endangered or threatened, respectively, and the Act's protections apply to all individuals of the species wherever found.

132 *Id.* at 1143–44.

133 *Id.* at 1145.

134 *Id.* at 1145–46.

135 79 Fed. Reg. 37,578 (July 1, 2014).

136 258 F.3d 1136 (9th Cir. 2001).

137 79 Fed. Reg. 37,578, 37,579–80 (July 1, 2014).

138 *Id.* at 37,578.

Second, a portion of the range of a species is "significant" if the species is not currently endangered or threatened throughout its range, but the portion's contribution to the viability of the species is so important that, without the members in that portion, the species would be in danger of extinction, or likely to become so in the foreseeable future, throughout all of its range.

Third, the range of a species is considered to be the general geographical area within which that species can be found at the time the Service makes any particular status determination. This range includes those areas used throughout all or part of the species' life cycle, even if they are not used regularly (e.g., seasonal habitats). Lost historical range is relevant to the analysis of the status of the species, but it cannot constitute a significant portion of a species' range.

Fourth, if a species is endangered or threatened throughout a significant portion of its range, and the population in that significant portion is a valid distinct population segment, the Service will list the distinct population segment rather than the entire taxonomic species or subspecies.

Initially, the courts upheld the Service's 2014 Policy interpreting "significant portion of its range."[139] However, in *Center for Biological Diversity v. Jewell*,[140] the District Court for the District of Arizona found that "the Service's goal in creating the [2014 Policy] was to give as little substantive effect as possible to the ["significant portion of its range"] language of the ESA in order to avoid providing range-wide protection to a species based on threats in a portion of the species' range." As such, this court found that the 2014 Policy frustrates the purposes of the ESA and therefore was arbitrary and capricious in violation of the Administrative Procedure Act. The District Court for the Northern District of California agreed with this reasoning in *Desert Survivors v. U.S. Dep't of the Interior*.[141] Given this judicial history, the legal status of the 2014 Policy remains uncertain.

SECTION 4(d) PROTECTIONS FOR THREATENED SPECIES

The Service has broad authority to issue regulations for the conservation of threatened species. As described above, the ESA prohibits take of endangered species pursuant to Section 9 by mandating that endangered species may not be "take[n]," meaning that no one may "harass, harm, pursue, hunt, shoot, wound, kill, trap, capture or collect" them.

---

139 See *Humane Soc'y v. Zinke*, 865 F.3d 585, 605 (D.C. Cir. 2017); *Defenders of Wildlife v. Jewell*, 176 F. Supp. 3d 975, 1007–10 (D. Mont. 2016).

140 248 F. Supp. 3d 946, 958 (D. Ariz. 2017).

141 Case No. 16-cv-01165-JCS (May 15, 2018).

A threatened species, on the other hand, is subject to the Service's discretionary protection.[142] This protection is governed and established by Section 4(d) of the ESA.

Section 4(d) specifies that "[w]henever any species is listed as a threatened species . . . the [Service] shall issue such regulations as [the Service] deems necessary and advisable to provide for the conservation of such species."[143] "Conservation" measures "may include regulated taking" in "the extraordinary case where population pressures within a given ecosystem cannot be otherwise relieved."[144] To determine which regulations are "necessary and advisable," the Service has informally explained that it uses "the best available information to determine which regulations are needed to conserve threatened species."[145] According to the Service, this information may come in the form of published scientific papers, input from species' experts, or other written materials. Public involvement during the rulemaking process can help the Service identify those activities and programs that may affect the species as well as potential changes to the prohibitions.

Using its Section 4(d) authority under the ESA, the U.S. Fish and Wildlife Service (but not the National Marine Fisheries Service) extended the prohibition of take to all threatened species by regulation in 1978, often referred to as the Blanket 4(d) Rule.[146] Thus, the take of threatened species is prohibited by regulation. However, this Blanket 4(d) Rule for threatened species can be modified by a species-specific "4(d) Special Rule." These "4(d) Special Rules" take the place of the normal protection of the ESA[147] and typically target the protections offered by the 1978 Blanket 4(d) Rule. In the absence of a 4(d) Special Rule, threatened species nonetheless get all of the protections that endangered species automatically get through Section 9.

The Blanket 4(d) Rule was challenged by industry groups in the Court of Appeals for the District of Columbia Circuit in *Sweet Home Chapter of Communities for a Great Oregon v. Babbitt*.[148] Plaintiffs argued that Section 4(d) of the ESA requires the Service to extend the prohibitions to threatened species on a species-by-species basis, and that the ESA requires the Service to explain in each instance why it is "necessary and advisable" to apply the prohibitions to a threatened species. Plaintiffs also argued that the text of the ESA established that Congress intended regulations extending the Section 9 prohibitions to threatened species to apply only to individual species. They also pointed to

---

142 *Trout Unlimited*, 559 F.3d at 950 (citing 16 U.S.C. § 1533(d)).

143 16 U.S.C. § 1533(d).

144 *Id.*

145 See U.S. Fish and Wildlife Service, Endangered Species Act Special Rules, Questions and Answers (available at https://www.fws.gov/mountain-prairie/factsheets/ESA%20SpecialRules%20Factsheet_020714.pdf).

146 50 C.F.R. § 17.31(a). The District of Columbia Court of Appeals described this regulation as serving to, "at one fell swoop, bring[ ] all threatened fish and wildlife species into the protective net" of the Section 9 prohibitions. *Sweet Home Chapter of Communities for a Great Oregon v. Babbitt*, 1 F.3d 1 (D.C. Cir. 1993) ("In short, the [Service] has, with this regulation, established a regime in which the prohibitions established for endangered species are extended automatically to all threatened species by a blanket rule and then withdrawn as appropriate, by special rule for particular species and by permit in particular situations.").

147 50 C.F.R. § 17.31(c).

148 1 F.3d 1 (D.C. Cir. 1993).

legislative history demonstrating this intent. The court rejected all of these arguments and held that the Blanket 4(d) Rule does not violate the ESA.[149]

The Service primarily uses 4(d) Rules for two purposes. First, the Service uses these rules to incentivize proactive conservation efforts, by streamlining ESA compliance for actions that have long-term benefits but might result in "take" in the short term. Second, the Service uses 4(d) Rules to target the take prohibitions to streamline ESA compliance for actions that result in low levels of take but do not contribute to the threats facing a species' continued existence. This streamlining can reduce ESA conflicts allowing some "de minimis" activities to continue to occur, while focusing the Service's attention on the threats that make a difference to the species' recovery.[150]

Regulations proposed by the Service in July 2018 (the "Proposed Regulations")[151] would amend Sections 17.31 and 17.71 of the Service's regulations to eliminate the Blanket 4(d) Rule for species that are listed as threatened after the effective date of the Proposed Regulations. Instead, at the time of listing a species as threatened, the species would have protection against take only if the Service promulgates a species-specific 4(d) rule.

CRITICAL HABITAT

In enacting the ESA, Congress viewed habitat loss as a significant factor contributing to species endangerment. Habitat destruction and degradation have been contributing factors causing the decline of a majority of species listed as threatened or endangered. The present or threatened destruction, modification, or curtailment of a species' habitat or range is included in the Act as one of the factors on which to base a determination of threatened or endangered species status. One of the tools provided by the Act to conserve species is the designation of critical habitat.[152]

The purpose of critical habitat is to identify the areas that are essential to the species' recovery. Once critical habitat is designated, it can contribute to the conservation of listed species is several ways. For the practitioner, one of the most important legal protections created by the designation of critical habitat is the regulatory protection established by Section 7(a)(2) of the Act. Section 7(a)(2) requires that federal agencies ensure, in consultation with the Service, that their actions are not likely to destroy or adversely modify critical habitat. The designation of critical habitat ensures that the federal government considers the effects of its actions (including the issuance of permits to private applicants, for example) on habitat important to species' conservation and avoids or modifies those actions that are likely to destroy or adversely modify

149 *Id*. See also *Center for Biological Diversity v. Salazar*, 695 F.3d 893 (9th Cir. 2012) (concerning the Rule 4(d) Regulations applicable to polar bears in the context of whether an Incidental Take Statement was required for a Biological Opinion).

150 See U.S. Fish and Wildlife Service, Endangered Species Act Special Rules, Questions and Answers (available at https://www.fws.gov/mountain-prairie/factsheets/ESA%20SpecialRules%20Factsheet_020714.pdf).

151 83 Fed. Reg. 35,174.

152 Listing Endangered and Threatened Species and Designating Critical Habitat; Implementing Changes to the Regulations for Designating Critical Habitat, Final Rule, 81 Fed. Reg. 7414, 7414 (Feb. 11, 2016).

critical habitat.[153] Therefore, the designation of critical habitat can result in significant regulatory controls.

Authority and Bases for Designation

Concurrent with its determination that a species is endangered or threatened, the Service must to the "maximum extent prudent and determinable . . . designate any habitat of such species which is then considered to be critical habitat."[154] The Service's regulations further specify that the Service may "designate critical habitat, delete . . . critical habitat, . . . [or] revise the boundary of an area designated as critical habitat."[155]

The Act provides the specific bases for designating or revising critical habitat:

> The [Service] shall designate critical habitat, and make revisions thereto, . . . on the basis of the best scientific data available and after taking into consideration the economic impact, the impact on national security, and any other relevant impact, of specifying any particular area as critical habitat. The [Service] may exclude any area from critical habitat, unless he determines, based on the best scientific and commercial data available, that the failure to designate such area as critical habitat will result in the extinction of the species concerned.[156]

The Service's regulations elaborate on the application of the phrase "maximum extent prudent and determinable" in designating critical habitat. According to the regulations, the Service will, "to the maximum extent prudent and determinable," propose and finalize critical habitat designations concurrent with issuing proposed and final listing rules, respectively. If designation of critical habitat is not prudent or if critical habitat is not determinable, the Service will state the reasons for not designating critical habitat in the publication of proposed and final rules listing a species. The Service will make a final designation of critical habitat on the basis of the best scientific data available, after taking into consideration the probable economic, national security, and other relevant impacts of making such a designation in accordance with the Service's regulations, as further described below.

Under the Service's regulations, a designation of critical habitat is not "prudent" when any of the following situations exist: (1) the species is threatened by taking or other human activity, and identification of critical habitat can be expected to increase the degree of such threat to the species; or (2) such designation of critical habitat would not be beneficial to the species.

The Proposed Regulations would delete the clause stating that designation is not prudent if it is not beneficial, and would replace that clause with four new analytical prongs, the most important of which would allow the Service to avoid designating critical habitat

---

153 *Id.* at 7414–15.

154 16 U.S.C. § 1533(a)(3)(A)(i).

155 50 C.F.R. § 424.10.

156 16 U.S.C. § 1533(b)(2).

where present or threatened impacts to a species' habitat is not a threat to the species *or* the habitat threat stems solely from causes that cannot be addressed in the context of Section 7 consultations (e.g., impacts associated with global climate change).[157] The Service could also determine that designation is not prudent if: no areas meet the definition of critical habitat; the species occurs primarily outside the United States (and thus designation would provide negligible conservation value); or the Service otherwise determines that designation of critical habitat would not be prudent.[158]

Designation of critical habitat is not "determinable" when one or both of the following situations exist: Data sufficient to perform required analyses are lacking; or the biological needs of the species are not sufficiently well known to identify any area that meets the definition of "critical habitat."

Where designation of critical habitat is prudent and determinable, the Service will identify specific areas within the geographical area occupied by the species at the time of listing *and* any specific areas outside the geographical area occupied by the species to be considered for designation as critical habitat. The Service will identify, at a scale determined by the Service to be appropriate, specific areas within the geographical area occupied by the species for consideration as critical habitat. The Service will:[159]

(1) Identify the geographical area occupied by the species at the time of listing.

(2) Identify physical and biological features essential to the conservation of the species at an appropriate level of specificity using the best available scientific data. This analysis will vary between species and may include consideration of the appropriate quality, quantity, and spatial and temporal arrangements of such features in the context of the life history, status, and conservation needs of the species.

(3) Determine the specific areas within the geographical area occupied by the species that contain the physical or biological features[160] essential to the conservation of the species.

(4) Determine which of these features may require special management considerations or protection.[161]

Under the Service's current regulations, the Service will identify, at a scale determined by the Service to be appropriate, specific areas outside the geographical area

---

157 83 Fed. Reg. 35,193 *et seq.*

158 *Id.*

159 50 C.F.R. § 424.12(b)(1)(i)–(iv).

160 "Physical or biological features" is a term defined in the Section 7 regulations to mean:
> The features that support the life-history needs of the species, including but not limited to, water characteristics, soil type, geological features, sites, prey, vegetation, symbiotic species, or other features. A feature may be a single habitat characteristic, or a more complex combination of habitat characteristics. Features may include habitat characteristics that support ephemeral or dynamic habitat conditions. Features may also be expressed in terms relating to principles of conservation biology, such as patch size, distribution distances, and connectivity.

> *Id.* § 424.02.

161 "Special management considerations or protection" is a term defined in the Section 7 regulations to mean "methods or procedures useful in protecting the physical or biological features essential to the conservation of listed species." 50 C.F.R. § 424.02.

occupied by the species that are essential for its conservation, considering the life history, status, and conservation needs of the species based on the best available scientific data.[162] Although the Service under President Obama had amended its regulations to eliminate earlier restrictions on when unoccupied areas could be designated, the Service under President Trump has proposed (in the Proposed Regulations) to limit designations of unoccupied areas to only those situations when limiting the designation to occupied areas would (1) be inadequate to ensure the conservation of the species; or (2) result in less efficient conservation for the species.[163] Moreover, any designation of unoccupied areas must be based upon a determination that there is a reasonable likelihood "that the area will contribute to the conservation of the species."

The Service's regulations require that each critical habitat area will be shown on a map, with more detailed information discussed in the preamble of the rulemaking documents published in the Federal Register and made available from the lead field office of the Service responsible for such designation. Textual information may be included for purposes of clarifying or refining the location and boundaries of each area or to explain the exclusion of sites (e.g., paved roads, buildings) within the mapped area. Each area will be referenced to the state(s), county(ies), or other local government units within which all or part of the critical habitat is located. Unless otherwise indicated within the critical habitat descriptions, the names of the state(s) and county(ies) are provided for informational purposes only and do not constitute the boundaries of the area. Ephemeral reference points (e.g., trees, sand bars) may not be used in any textual description used to clarify or refine the boundaries of critical habitat.

The regulations also provide that when several habitats, each satisfying the requirements for designation as critical habitat, are located in proximity to one another, the Service may designate an inclusive area as critical habitat.[164] The Service may designate critical habitat for those species listed as threatened or endangered but for which no critical habitat has been previously designated. For species listed prior to November 10, 1978, the designation of critical habitat is at the discretion of the Service.

The Service's authority to designate critical habitat is restricted. The Act prohibits the Service from designating critical habitat on "any lands or other geographical areas owned or controlled by the Department of Defense, or designated for its use, that are subject to an Integrated Natural Resources Management Plan [INRMP] prepared under Section 670a of [Title 16 of the U.S.C.], if the [Service] determines in writing that such plan provides a benefit to the species for which critical habitat is proposed for designation."[165] In determining whether such a benefit is provided, the Service must consider:

> the extent of the area and features present

> the type and frequency of use of the area by the species

INRMP = Integrated Natural Resources Management Plan

---

162 *Id.* § 424.12(b)(2).

163 83 Fed. Reg. 35,193 *et seq.*

164 50 C.F.R. § 424.12(c).

165 16 U.S.C. § 1533(a)(3)(B)(i); 50 C.F.R. § 424.12(g) & (h).

> the relevant elements of the INRMP in terms of management objectives, activities covered, and best management practices, and the certainty that the relevant elements will be implemented

> the degree to which the relevant elements of the INRMP will protect the habitat from the types of effects that would be addressed through a destruction-or-adverse-modification analysis[166]

Process for Designation

The ESA establishes a process for requests to designate, remove, or revise critical habitat. Any interested person may submit a written petition making any of these requests.[167] The Service's regulations enumerate the requirements for a petition. A petition must clearly identify itself as such, be dated, and contain the following information:[168]

(1) the name, signature, address, telephone number, if any, and the association, institution, or business affiliation, if any, of the petitioner

(2) the scientific name and any common name of a species of fish or wildlife or plants that is the subject of the petition; only one species may be the subject of a petition, which may include, by hierarchical extension based on taxonomy and the Act, any subspecies or variety, or (for vertebrates) any potential distinct population segments of that species

(3) a clear indication of the administrative action the petitioner seeks (e.g., revision of critical habitat)

(4) a detailed narrative justifying the recommended administrative action that contains an analysis of the information presented

(5) literature citations that are specific enough for the Service to readily locate the information cited in the petition, including page numbers or chapters as applicable

(6) electronic or hard copies of supporting materials, to the extent permitted by U.S. copyright law, or appropriate excerpts or quotations from those materials (e.g., publications, maps, reports, letters from authorities) cited in the petition

(7) copies of the notification letters or electronic communication which petitioners provided to the state agency or agencies responsible for the management and conservation of fish, plant, or wildlife resources in each state where the species that is the subject of the petition currently occurs

For a petition to revise critical habitat, petitioners must provide notice to the state responsible for the management and conservation of fish, plant, or wildlife resources in each state where the species that is the subject of the petition occurs. This notification must be made at least 30 days prior to submission of the petition.[169] "To the maximum

---

166 50 C.F.R. § 424.12(h)(1)–(4).

167 *Id.* § 424.14(a).

168 *Id.* § 424.14(c). Item (8) from the list in this section of the Code of Federal Regulations has been omitted because it addresses petitions to list, delist, or reclassify species.

169 *Id.* § 424.14(b).

extent practicable," within 90 days after receiving a petition of an interested person to revise a critical habitat designation, the Service must make a finding as to whether the petition presents substantial scientific information indicating that the revision may be warranted.[170] According to the Service's regulations, the Service's determinations as to whether the petition provides substantial scientific information indicating that the petitioned action may be warranted will depend in part on the degree to which the petition includes the following types of information:[171]

(1) a description and map(s) of areas that the current designation does not include that should be included, or includes areas that should no longer be included, and a description of the benefits of designating or not designating these specific areas as critical habitat; petitioners should include sufficient supporting information to substantiate the requested changes, which may include GIS data or boundary layers that relate to the request, if appropriate

(2) a description of physical or biological features[172] essential for the conservation of the species and whether they may require special management considerations or protection[173]

(3) for any areas petitioned to be added to critical habitat within the geographical area occupied by the species at time it was listed, information indicating that the specific areas contain one or more of the physical or biological features (including characteristics that support ephemeral or dynamic habitat conditions) that are essential to the conservation of the species and may require special management considerations or protection. The petitioner should also indicate which specific areas contain which feature.

(4) for any areas petitioned for removal from currently designated critical habitat within the geographical area occupied by the species at the time it was listed, information indicating that the specific areas do not contain the physical or biological features (including characteristics that support ephemeral or dynamic habitat conditions) that are essential to the conservation of the species, or that these features do not require special management considerations or protection

(5) for areas petitioned to be added to or removed from critical habitat that were outside the geographical area occupied by the species at the time it was listed,

---

170 16 U.S.C. § 1533(b)(3)(D)(i). The Service must promptly publish such finding in the Federal Register. *Id.*

171 50 C.F.R. § 424.14(e)(1)–(6).

172 "Physical or biological features" is a term defined in the Section 7 regulations to mean:
    The features that support the life-history needs of the species, including but not limited to, water characteristics, soil type, geological features, sites, prey, vegetation, symbiotic species, or other features. A feature may be a single habitat characteristic, or a more complex combination of habitat characteristics. Features may include habitat characteristics that support ephemeral or dynamic habitat conditions. Features may also be expressed in terms relating to principles of conservation biology, such as patch size, distribution distances, and connectivity.
    Id. § 424.02.

173 "Special management considerations or protection" is a term defined in the Section 7 regulations to mean "methods or procedures useful in protecting the physical or biological features essential to the conservation of listed species." *Id.*

> information indicating why the petitioned areas are or are not essential for the conservation of the species
>
> (6) a complete, balanced representation of the relevant facts, including information that may contradict claims in the petition

If a request does not meet the requirements for petitions, the Service will generally reject the request without making a finding, and will, within a reasonable timeframe, notify the sender and provide an explanation of the rejection. However, the Service retains discretion to process a petition where the Service determines there has been substantial compliance with the relevant requirements.[174] If a request does meet the requirements for petitions, the Service will acknowledge receipt of the petition by posting information on the Service's website.[175] If the petitioner provides supplemental information before the initial finding is made and states that it is part of the petition, the new information, along with the previously submitted information, is treated as a new petition that supersedes the original petition, and the statutory timeframes will begin when such supplemental information is received.[176]

To the maximum extent practicable, within 90 days of receiving a petition to revise a critical habitat designation, the Service will make a finding as to whether the petition presents substantial scientific information indicating that the revision may be warranted. The Service will publish such finding in the Federal Register.[177] In this context, "substantial scientific information" refers to credible scientific information in support of the petition's claims such that a reasonable person conducting an impartial scientific review would conclude that the revision proposed in the petition may be warranted. Conclusions drawn in the petition without the support of credible scientific information will not be considered "substantial information."[178] The Service will consider the information received, and it may also consider other information readily available at the time the determination is made in reaching its initial finding on the petition. The Service is not required to consider any supporting materials cited by the petitioner if the cited documents are not provided in accordance with the Service's regulations.[179]

If the Service finds that the petition presents substantial information that the requested revision may be warranted, the Service will determine, within 12 months after receiving the petition, how to proceed with the requested revision, and will promptly publish notice of that intention in the Federal Register.[180] The Department's determination of whether to implement or not such a revision is subject to notice in the Federal

---

174 *Id.* § 424.14(f)(1).

175 *Id.* § 424.14(f)(2).

176 *Id.* § 424.14(g).

177 *Id.* § 424.14(i)(1).

178 *Id.* § 424.14(i)(1)(i).

179 *Id.* § 424.14(i)(1)(ii).

180 16 U.S.C. § 1533(b)(3)(D)(ii); 50 C.F.R. § 424.14(i)(2).

Register, and that notice period is subject to extensions under certain circumstances.[181] A petitioner may withdraw the petition at any time during the petition process by submitting such request in writing. If a petition is withdrawn, the Service may, at its discretion, discontinue action on the petition finding, even if the Service has already made a 90-day finding that there is substantial information indicating that the requested action may be warranted.[182]

The rulemaking process for designating or revising critical habitat is described in the Service's regulations. A notice of a proposed rule to carry out this action must contain a detailed description of the proposed action and a summary of the data on which the proposal is based, showing the relationship of such data to the rule proposed. The summary will, to the maximum extent practicable, include a brief description and evaluation of those activities (whether public or private) that, in the opinion of the Service, if undertaken, may adversely modify such habitat or may be affected by such designation. The detailed description of the action must include a map of the critical habitat area and may also include proposed text that clarifies or modifies the map. The notice must also include a summary of factors affecting the species and/or its designated critical habitat.[183]

With respect to the process to designate or revise critical habitat, the Service must:[184]

> publish notice of the proposal in the Federal Register

> give actual notice of the proposed regulation to the state agency in each state in which the species is believed to occur and to each county or equivalent jurisdiction therein in which the species is believed to occur, and invite the comment of each such agency and jurisdiction

> give notice of the proposed regulation to any federal agencies, local authorities, or private individuals or organizations known to be affected by the rule

> insofar as practical, and in cooperation with the Secretary of State, give notice of the proposed regulation to list, delist, or reclassify a species to each foreign nation in which the species is believed to occur or whose citizens harvest the species on the high seas, and invite the comment of such nation

> give notice of the proposed regulation to such professional scientific organizations as the Service deems appropriate

> publish a summary of the proposed regulation in a newspaper of general circulation in each area of the United States in which the species is believed to occur

At least 60 days must be allowed for public comment following publication in the Federal Register of a rule proposing the listing, delisting, or reclassification of a species, or the designation or revision of critical habitat. The Service may extend or reopen the period for public comment on a proposed rule upon a finding that there is good cause to

181 16 U.S.C. § 1533(b)(6).

182 50 C.F.R. § 424.14(k).

183 *Id.* § 424.16(b).

184 *Id.* § 424.16(c)(1).

do so. A notice of any such extension or reopening must be published in the Federal Register and must specify the basis for so doing.[185]

The Service must promptly hold at least one public hearing if any person so requests within 45 days of publication of a proposed regulation to designate or revise critical habitat. Notice of the location and time of any such hearing must be published in the Federal Register not less than 15 days before the hearing is held.[186]

Determinations Related to Critical Habitat Designations

Within one year of the publication of a rule proposing to designate or revise critical habitat, the Service must publish one of the following in the Federal Register:[187]

> a final rule to implement such determination or revision

> a finding that such revision should not be made

> a notice withdrawing the proposed rule upon a finding that available evidence does not justify the action proposed by the rule[188]

> a notice extending such one-year period by an additional period of not more than six months because there is substantial disagreement among scientists knowledgeable about the species concerned regarding the sufficiency or accuracy of the available data relevant to the determination or revision concerned

A final rule designating critical habitat of an endangered or a threatened species must to the extent permissible be published concurrently with the final rule listing such species, unless the Service determines that (1) it is essential to the conservation of such species that it be listed promptly; or (2) critical habitat of such species is not then determinable. In which case, the Service, with respect to the proposed regulation to designate such habitat, may extend the one-year period by not more than one additional year. Not later than the close of such additional year the Service must publish a final regulation, based on such data as may be available at that time, designating, to the maximum extent prudent, such habitat.[189]

The final rule must contain a detailed description of the action being finalized, a summary of the comments and recommendations received in response to the proposal, summaries of the data on which the rule is based and the relationship of such data to the final rule, and a description of any conservation measures available under the rule. The rule must also provide a summary of factors affecting the species relevant to the critical habitat designation.[190] The rule must also include a detailed description of the action

185 50 C.F.R. § 424.16(c)(2).

186 *Id.* § 424.16(c)(3).

187 *Id.* § 424.17(a)(1)(i)–(iv).

188 If a proposed rule is withdrawn, the notice of withdrawal must set forth the basis upon which the proposed rule has been found not to be supported by available evidence. The Service shall not again propose a rule withdrawn under such provision except on the basis of sufficient new information that warrants a re-proposal. *Id.* § 424.17(a)(3).

189 *Id.* § 424.17(b).

190 *Id.* § 424.18(a).

including a map of the critical habitat area and may also include rule text that clarifies or modifies the map. The map itself, as modified by any rule text, constitutes the official boundary of the designation.[191]

A final rule must take effect (1) not less than 30 days after it is published in the Federal Register, except as otherwise provided for good cause found and published with the rule; and (2) not less than 90 days after publication in the Federal Register of the proposed rule, and actual notification of any affected state agencies and counties or equivalent jurisdictions.[192]

Exclusions from Critical Habitat

At the time of publication of a proposed rule to designate critical habitat, the Service will make available for public comment the draft economic analysis of the designation. The draft economic analysis will be summarized in the Federal Register notice of the proposed designation of critical habitat.[193] Prior to finalizing the designation of critical habitat, the Service will consider the probable economic, national security, and other relevant impacts of the designation upon proposed or ongoing activities. The Service considers impacts at a scale that the Service determines to be appropriate and will compare the impacts with and without the designation. Impacts may be qualitatively or quantitatively described.[194]

The Service has discretion to exclude any particular area from the critical habitat upon a determination that the benefits of such exclusion outweigh the benefits of specifying the particular area as part of the critical habitat. In identifying those benefits, in addition to the mandatory consideration of impacts conducted pursuant to the Service's regulations, the Service assigns the weight given to any benefits relevant to the designation of critical habitat. The Service, however, will not exclude any particular area if, based on the best scientific and commercial data available, the Service determines that the failure to designate that area as critical habitat will result in the extinction of the species concerned.[195]

Important Case Law Regarding the Designation and Application of Critical Habitat

The issue of critical habitat designations has generated a significant amount of case law. For example, in *Arizona Cattle Growers' Association v. Salazar*,[196] an industry association challenged the Service's designation of critical habitat for the Mexican spotted owl. The association argued that the Service unlawfully designated areas containing no owls as "occupied" habitat and that the Service calculated the economic impacts of

191 *Id.* § 424.18(a)(1).
192 *Id.* § 424.18(b).
193 *Id.* § 424.19(a).
194 *Id.* § 424.19(b).
195 *Id.* § 424.19(c).
196 606 F.3d 1160 (9th Cir. 2010).

the designation by applying an impermissible "baseline" approach. As to the first issue, the court held that the Service has "authority to designate as 'occupied' areas that the owl uses with sufficient regularity that it is likely to be present during any reasonable span of time."[197]

As to the second issue, the court explained that the Service applied a "baseline" approach to the economic analysis, and under this approach, any economic impacts of protecting the owl that would occur regardless of the critical habitat designation—in particular, the burdens imposed by listing the owl—are treated as part of the regulatory "baseline" and are not factored into the economic analysis of the effects of the critical habitat designation. Plaintiffs argued that this was error and that the Service was required to apply a "co-extensive" approach in which the agency ignores the protection of a species that results from the listing decision in considering whether to designate an area as critical habitat. Any economic burden that designating an area would cause must be counted in the economic analysis, even if the same burden is already imposed by listing the species and, therefore, would exist even if the area were not designated.[198] To evaluate this issue, the court noted that the co-extensive approach relied on an interpretation of the phrase "destruction or adverse modification" that was subsequently struck down by the Ninth Circuit in *Gifford Pinchot Task Force v. U.S. Fish & Wildlife Service*, discussed in more detail below. As a result of that decision, the court concluded that the Service may use the baseline approach in analyzing critical habitat designations.[199]

One of the most important decisions regarding the application of the critical habitat in the Section 7 context is *Gifford Pinchot Task Force v. U.S. Fish & Wildlife Service*.[200] In *Gifford Pinchot*, several environmental organizations challenged six Biological Opinions issued by the Service in connection with timber harvests in certain forests of the Northwest that authorized the incidental take of the threatened northern spotted owl. Among other things, the plaintiffs challenged the Biological Opinions on the critical habitat requirements of a Section 7 consultation. In particular, plaintiffs argued that the Service's interpretation of "adverse modification" is unlawful in the context of a Section 7 consultation, which requires that in every Biological Opinion the consulting agency must ensure that the proposed action "is not likely to jeopardize the continued existence of" an endangered or threatened

---

197 *Id.* at 1165. Notably, the court also found that it is "possible for the [Service] to go too far. Most obvious is that the agency may not determine that areas unused by owls are occupied merely because those areas are suitable for future occupancy. Such a position would ignore the ESA's distinction between occupied and unoccupied areas." *Id.* at 1167. The court further explained: "[D]etermining whether an area is occupied or merely will be occupied in the future may be complicated in the context of migratory or mobile species. The fact that a member of the species is not present in an area at a given instant does not mean the area is suitable only for future occupancy if the species regularly uses the area." *Id.*

198 *Id.* at 1172. The plaintiffs relied on the Tenth Circuit Court of Appeals' decision in *New Mexico Cattle Growers Association v. U.S. Fish & Wildlife Service*, 248 F.3d 1277 (10th Cir. 2001), for this argument.

199 *Id.* at 1173.

200 378 F.3d 1059 (9th Cir. 2004).

species and that the federal action will not result in the "destruction or adverse modification" of the designated "critical habitat" of the listed species.

The plaintiffs' argument focused on the definition of "destruction or adverse modification" as "[a] direct or indirect alteration that appreciably diminishes the value of critical habitat for both the survival and recovery of a listed species. Such alterations include, but are not limited to, alterations adversely modifying any of those physical or biological features that were the basis for determining the habitat to be critical."[201] The plaintiffs argued that this definition "sets the bar too high because the adverse modification threshold is not triggered by a proposed action until there is an appreciable diminishment of the value of critical habitat for both survival and recovery."

The Ninth Circuit Court of Appeals agreed with the plaintiffs. The court considered the language in the definition, particularly the language "that appreciably diminish[] the value of critical habitat for *both* the survival *and* recovery of a listed species."[202] The court explained:

> This regulatory definition explicitly requires appreciable diminishment of the critical habitat necessary for survival before the "destruction or adverse modification" standard could ever be met. Because it is logical and inevitable that a species requires more critical habitat for recovery than is necessary for the species survival, the regulation's singular focus becomes "survival." Given this literal understanding of the regulation's express definition of "adverse modification," we consider whether that definition is a permissible interpretation of the ESA.[203]

The court concluded that the definition of "adverse modification" "reads the 'recovery' goal out of the adverse modification inquiry; a proposed action 'adversely modifies' critical habitat if, and only if, the value of the critical habitat for survival is appreciably diminished." In light of this,

> The [Service] could authorize the complete elimination of critical habitat necessary only for recovery, and so long as the smaller amount of critical habitat necessary for survival is not appreciably diminished, then no "destruction or adverse modification," as defined by the regulation, has taken place. This cannot be right. If the [Service] follows its own regulation, then it is obligated to be indifferent to, if not to ignore, the recovery goal of critical habitat.[204]

The court explained that this "offends" the ESA because the ESA was enacted to both "forestall the extinction of species" and "allow a species to recover to the point where it may be delisted." The court also noted that the ESA defines "critical habitat" as

201 *Id.* at 1069 (quoting 50 C.F.R. § 402.02).

202 *Id.* (quoting with emphasis added 50 C.F.R. § 402.02).

203 *Id.*

204 *Id.* at 1069–70.

including specific areas that are "essential to the conservation of the species." According to the court, this demonstrates that Congress intended that "conservation and survival be two different (though complementary) goals of the ESA." The definition of "adverse modification" is inconsistent with this view because it would essentially find that adverse modification to critical habitat can only occur "when there is so much critical habitat lost that a species' very survival is threatened." To define "destruction or adverse modification" of critical habitat to occur only when there is appreciable diminishment of the value of critical habitat for both survival and conservation fails to provide protection of habitat when necessary only for species' recovery. According to the court, this is contrary to Congress's intent in the ESA. Thus, the court held that the regulatory definition of "adverse modification" was unlawful.[205]

As a result of the *Gifford Pinchot* decision, the Service adopted a final rule[206] in 2016 that amended the definition of "destruction or adverse modification" to read:

> [a] direct or indirect alteration that appreciably diminishes the value of critical habitat for the conservation of a listed species. Such alterations may include, but are not limited to, those that alter the physical or biological features essential to the conservation of a species or that preclude or significantly delay development of such features.[207]

The Proposed Regulations would amend this definition by deleting the second sentence and adding the phrase "as a whole" to the end of the first sentence.[208] That is, in making a "destruction or adverse modification" finding, the Service would evaluate the question in the context of the entire area of the critical habitat designation, and not simply destruction or adverse modification occurring within only the action area or the areas immediately around it.

Another important decision regarding the designation of critical habitat is the U.S. Supreme Court's decision in *Weyerhaeuser Co. v. U.S. Fish & Wildlife Service*.[209] This case concerns the dusky gopher frog, which was listed as endangered in 2001. The Service proposed designating as part of the frog's critical habitat property in Louisiana, which the Service referred to as "Unit 1." The frog had once lived in Unit

---

205 *Id.* at 1077. The court cites the Fifth Circuit Court of Appeals' decision in *Sierra Club v. U.S. Fish & Wildlife Service*, 245 F.3d 434 (5th Cir. 2001), which reached the same conclusion regarding the "critical habitat" language and the same regulatory definition of "destruction or adverse modification." The court quotes the following from that decision:
> "Conservation" is a much broader concept than mere survival. The ESA's definition of "conservation" speaks to the recovery of a threatened or endangered species. Indeed, in a different section of the ESA, the statute distinguishes between "conservation" and "survival." Requiring consultation only where an action affects the value of critical habitat to both the recovery and survival of a species imposes a higher threshold than the statutory language permits.
> *Id.* at 1070 (quoting *Sierra Club*, 245 F.3d at 441–42).

206 Interagency Cooperation – Endangered Species Act of 1973, as Amended; Definition of Destruction or Adverse Modification of Critical Habitat, 81 Fed. Reg. 7214 (Feb. 11, 2016).

207 50 C.F.R. § 402.02.

208 83 Fed. Reg. 35,178 *et seq.*

209 Case No. 17-71, _____ U.S. _____ (Nov. 27, 2018).

1, but the land had long been used as a commercial timber plantation, and no frogs had been spotted there for decades. Moreover, Unit 1 no longer contained habitat suitable for the frog, and instead would have required some degree of modification in order to support a sustainable population of the frog. Nonetheless, the Service designated the property as unoccupied critical habitat because its rare, high-quality breeding ponds and distance from existing frog populations made it essential for the species' conservation.

The owner of Unit 1 challenged the Service's designation of the property as critical habitat, arguing among other things that the property's closed-canopy timber plantation could not be critical habitat for the frog because the frog lives in open-canopy forests. In a unanimous decision,[210] the Supreme Court held that an area is eligible for designation as critical habitat only if it is actually habitat for the species. According to the Court, the ESA states that when the Service lists a species as endangered it must also "designate any habitat of such species which is then considered to be critical habitat."[211] The ESA does not authorize the Service to designate the area as critical habitat unless it is also habitat for the species. Because the court of appeals had no occasion to interpret the term "habitat" or to assess the Service's administrative findings regarding Unit 1, the Supreme Court remanded the case back to the Fifth Circuit Court of Appeals.

RECOVERY PLANS

In certain circumstances, the ESA requires the Service to prepare a "recovery plan" for species listed as either endangered or threatened. More specifically, the Service must "develop and implement [recovery plans] for the conservation and survival of endangered species and threatened species . . . , unless [the Service] finds that such a plan will not promote the conservation of the species."[212] In developing and implementing these plans, the Service must, to the maximum extent practicable, "give priority to those endangered species or threatened species . . . that are most likely to benefit from such plans, particularly those species that are, or may be, in conflict with construction or other development projects or other forms of economic activity."

The contents of a recovery plans include:

(1) a description of such site-specific management actions as may be necessary to achieve the plan's goal for the conservation and survival of the species

(2) objective, measurable criteria which, when met, would result in a determination . . . that the species be removed from the list

(3) estimates of the time required and the cost to carry out those measures needed to achieve the plan's goal and to achieve intermediate steps toward that goal[213]

210 The opinion was 8-0. Justice Kavanaugh took no part in the consideration or decision of the case.
211 Id. (quoting 16 U.S.C. § 1533(a)(3)(A)(i)).
212 16 U.S.C. § 1533(f)(1).
213 Id. § 1533(f)(1)(B)(i)–(iii).

The Act requires the Service to provide public notice and an opportunity for public review and comment on draft plans before they receive final approval, and the Service is required to consider all information presented during the public comment period before it approves the plan.[214]

Both the U.S. Fish and Wildlife Service and NMFS (NOAA Fisheries) have prepared several recovery plans for listed species in California. Examples of recovery plans in California include:

> NOAA Fisheries, Southern Oregon/Northern California Coast Coho Salmon Recovery Plan (2014)[215]

> NOAA Fisheries, California Coastal Chinook Salmon, Northern California Steelhead, and Central California Coast Steelhead (2016)[216]

> U.S. Fish and Wildlife Service, Recovery Plan for the Central California Distinct Population of the California Tiger Salamander (2017)[217]

> U.S. Fish and Wildlife Service, Recovery Plan for Vernal Pool Ecosystems of California and Southern Oregon (2005)[218]

> U.S. Fish and Wildlife Service, Recovery Plan for Upland Species of the San Joaquin Valley, California (1998)[219]

> U.S. Fish and Wildlife Service, Recovery Plan for the Santa Ana Sucker (2017)[220]

Although the ESA requires the Department to "implement" recovery plans, they are intended to serve only as guidance and planning documents. Most recovery plans include disclaimer language stating that: "Recovery plans are guidance and planning documents only; identification of an action to be implemented by any public or private party does not create a legal obligation beyond existing legal requirements."[221]

Courts have confirmed the Service's view that recovery plans are meant to serve only as guidance and planning documents. For example, in *Cascadia Wildlands v. Thrailkill*, plaintiffs argued that a Biological Opinion prepared for a fire recovery project was inconsistent with a recovery plan for the northern spotted owl. The District Court for the

---

214 *Id.* § 1533(f)(4) & (f)(5).

215 Available at http://www.westcoast.fisheries.noaa.gov/protected_species/salmon_steelhead/recovery_planning_and_implementation/southern_oregon_northern_california_coast/SONCC_recovery_plan.html.

216 Available at http://www.westcoast.fisheries.noaa.gov/protected_species/salmon_steelhead/recovery_planning_and_implementation/north_central_california_coast/coastal_multispecies_recovery_plan.html.

217 Available at https://www.fws.gov/sacramento/outreach/2017/06-14/docs/Signed_Central_CTS_Recovery_Plan.pdf.

218 Available at https://www.fws.gov/sacramento/es/Recovery-Planning/Vernal-Pool/Documents/Vernal%20Pool%20Recovery%20Plan%20Executive%20Summary.pdf.

219 Available at http://www.fwspubs.org/doi/suppl/10.3996/052015-JFWM-045/suppl_file/052015-jfwm-045.s2.pdf?code=ufws-site.

220 Available at https://ecos.fws.gov/docs/recovery_plan/20170228_Final%20SAS%20RP%20Signed.pdf.

221 See, e.g., U.S. Fish and Wildlife Service, Recovery Plan for the Santa Ana Sucker (2017) at iii.

District of Oregon rejected this argument on the basis that "recovery plans do not have the force of law," and as such, "[t]hey are not binding on federal agencies."[222]

TAKE PROHIBITION AND EXCEPTIONS FOR INCIDENTAL TAKE

Definition of Take

Section 9 of the ESA makes it illegal for any private or public entity to "take" an endangered species. In particular, the Act specifies that it is "unlawful for any person . . . to . . . take any [endangered species of fish or wildlife] within the United States or the territorial sea of the United States."[223] The term "take" means "to harass, harm, pursue, hunt, shoot, wound, kill, trap, capture, or collect, or to attempt to engage in any such conduct."[224] The Act does not further define the terms it uses to define "take," but the Service's regulations define the terms "harass" and "harm":

> Harass in the definition of "take" in the Act means an intentional or negligent act or omission which creates the likelihood of injury to wildlife by annoying it to such an extent as to significantly disrupt normal behavioral patterns which include, but are not limited to, breeding, feeding, or sheltering . . . .

> [¶]

> Harm in the definition of "take" in the Act means an act which actually kills or injures wildlife. Such act may include significant habitat modification or degradation where it actually kills or injures wildlife by significantly impairing essential behavioral patterns, including breeding, feeding or sheltering.[225]

Standards That Apply to Take

The definition of take is articulated in Section 9 of the ESA. The Ninth Circuit Court of Appeal has addressed the issue of whether the standard for "taking" species is different under Section 9 as compared to Section 7. In *Arizona Cattle Growers' Association v. U.S.*

---

222 49 F. Supp. 3d 774, 786–87 (D. Or. 2014). See also *Friends of Blackwater v. Salazar*, 691 F.3d 428, 432–34 (D.C. Cir. 2012); *Fund for Animals v. Rice*, 85 F.3d 535, 547 (11th Cir. 1996) ("By providing general guidance as to what is required in a recovery plan, the ESA 'breathes discretion at every pore.'"); *California Native Plant Soc'y v. U.S. Environmental Protection Agency*, No. 06-03604, 2007 WL 2021796, at *21 (N.D. Cal. July 10, 2007); *Conservation Northwest v. Kempthorne*, No. 04-1331, 2007 WL 1847143, n.2 (W.D. Wash. June 25, 2007); *Biodiversity Legal Foundation v. Norton*, 285 F. Supp. 2d 1, 14 (D.D.C. 2003) ("[T]he Court is generally persuaded by the Eleventh Circuit's reasoning in [*Rice*], and agrees that the . . . Recovery Plan was merely a guideline, which FWS had discretion to follow."); *National Wildlife Fed'n v. National Park Service*, 669 F. Supp. 384, 388 (D. Wyo. 1987) ("Plaintiffs would urge upon this Court that the language § 1533(f) obligates the Secretary to develop and implement a recovery plan, and that, once developed, all concerned agencies must adhere to it. The language does not so say."). But see *Southwest Center for Biological Div. v. Bartel*, 470 F. Supp. 2d 1118, 1136–37 (S.D. Cal. 2006) (finding that the Service must consider the standards and other information in a recovery plan to evaluate the effect of an incidental take permit on species discussed in the plan and whether mitigation is adequate).

223 16 U.S.C. § 1538(a)(1)(B).

224 *Id.* § 1532(19).

225 50 C.F.R. § 17.3.

Fish & Wildlife Service,[226] the court considered an argument raised by the Service that the word "taking" as using in Section 7 should be interpreted more broadly than in the context of Section 9, relying upon the different purposes, i.e., protective (Section 7) as opposed to punitive (Section 9), served by each section. The Service argued that a taking as construed in Section 7 should encompass those situations in which harm to a listed species was "possible" or "likely" in the future due to the proposed action, and thus, the Section 7 incidental take definition should be interpreted more broadly than the definition of take under Section 9.[227]

The court rejected this argument in light of the Act's structure and its legislative history. According to the court, the Act's structure and legislative history show Congress's intent to enact one standard for "taking" within both Section 7(b)(4), governing the preparation of Incidental Take Statements, and Section 9, imposing civil and criminal penalties for violation of the ESA. Based on legislative reports from the 1982 amendments to the ESA that enacted Section 7(b)(4), the court concluded the need for a Section 7 safe harbor provision only emerges when there is an actual or prospective taking under Section 9. A broader interpretation of Section 7 would allow the Service to "engage in widespread land regulation even where no Section 9 liability could be imposed," which "would turn the purpose behind the 1982 Amendment on its head."[228]

Take Due to Habitat Modification

Because "harm" may include "significant habitat modification or degradation," a "take" prohibited by Section 9 can occur when an action resulting in habitat modification significantly impairs the breeding, feeding, or sheltering of a protected species. The U.S. Supreme Court upheld this interpretation of the Service's regulations in the landmark decision *Babbitt v. Sweet Home Chapter of Communities for a Great Oregon.*[229] The Court reasoned that the ordinary understanding of the word "harm" "naturally encompasses habitat modification that results in actual injury or death to members of an endangered or threatened species."[230] Moreover, the "broad purpose of the ESA" supported the Service's decision "to extend protection against activities that cause the precise harms Congress enacted the statute to avoid."[231] Finally, the Court explained that Congress understood the Section 10 incidental take permit and habitat conservation plan process as regulating "indirect as well as deliberate takings," supporting the Service's view "that activities not intended to harm an endangered species, such as habitat modification, may constitute unlawful takings under the ESA unless the Secretary permits them."[232]

226 273 F.3d 1229 (9th Cir. 2001).

227 *Id.* at 1237.

228 *Id.* at 1239.

229 515 U.S. 687 (1995).

230 *Id.* at 697.

231 *Id.* at 698.

232 *Id.* at 701.

In *Defenders of Wildlife v. Bernal*,[233] the Ninth Circuit further elaborated on the question of when habitat modification will constitute a harm:

> Harming a species may be indirect, in that the harm may be caused by habitat modification, but habitat modification does not constitute harm unless it "actually kills or injures wildlife." The Department of Interior's definition of harm was upheld against a facial challenge to its validity in [*Babbitt*]. In upholding the definition of "harm" as encompassing habitat modification, the Supreme Court emphasized that "every term in the regulation's definition of "harm" is subservient to the phrase "an act which actually kills or injures wildlife."[234]

However, mere habitat degradation is not always sufficient to constitute harm under the ESA. In *National Wildlife Federation v. Burlington Northern Railroad*,[235] the Ninth Circuit held as much, and further explained that to regulate habitat degradation that merely retards recovery of a depleted species, "[plaintiff] would have to show significant impairment of the species' breeding or feeding habits and prove that the habitat degradation prevents, or possibly retards, recovery of the species."[236]

The court's view in *National Wildlife Federation* is consistent with the Service's regulations, which adopts a definition of "harm" specifying that habitat modification or degradation "actually kills or injures wildlife."[237] The Federal Register notice for these regulations further elaborate:

> [T]he word "actually" before the words "kills or injures" . . . makes it clear that habitat modification or degradation, standing alone, is not a taking pursuant to section 9. To be subject to section 9, the modification or degradation must be significant, must significantly impair essential behavioral patterns, and must result in actual injury to a protected wildlife species.[238]

Exceptions to Prohibited Take

Section 10(a) of the ESA contains exceptions to the Section 9 "take" prohibitions. Section 10(a)(1)(A) authorizes the Service to issue permits for scientific purposes or to enhance the propagation or survival of listed species. Section 10(a)(1)(A) permits are also required:

> > when a reasonable and prudent alternative calls for scientific research that will result in take of the species

---

233 204 F.3d 920 (9th Cir. 1999).

234 *Id.* at 924–25 (citation omitted); see also *Marbled Murrelet v. Babbitt*, 83 F.3d 1060 (9th Cir. 1996) (discussing generally the propriety of projecting harm through habitat modification so long as the habitat modification will cause actual killing or injury of protected species).

235 23 F.3d 1508 (9th Cir. 1994).

236 *Id.* at 1513.

237 50 C.F.R. § 17.3.

238 46 Fed. Reg. 54,748 (1981) (emphasis in original).

GUIDANCE ON INCIDENTAL TAKE PERMIT TRIGGERS

On April 26, 2018, the Trump Administration issued its "Guidance on Trigger for an Incidental Take Permit Under Section 10(a)(1)(B) of the Endangered Species Act Where Occupied Habitat or Potentially Occupied Habitat Is Being Modified." The memorandum states that a Section 10(a)(1)(B) incidental take permit is only needed in situations where a non-federal project is likely to result in "take" of a listed species of fish or wildlife. The memorandum further explains that habitat modification in and of itself does not necessarily constitute take.

Relying on the landmark U.S. Supreme Court decision *Babbitt v. Sweet Home Chapter of Communities for a Great Oregon*, 515 U.S. 687 (1995), the memorandum concludes that the law clearly requires that in order to find that habitat modification constitutes a taking of listed species under the definition of "harm," all aspects of the harm definition must be triggered.

Accordingly, the memorandum identifies three questions that can serve as a flow-chart before a determination is made that an action involving habitat modification is likely to result to take:

> Is the modification of habitat significant?

> If so, does that modification also significantly impair an essential behavior pattern of a listed species?

> Is the significant modification of the habitat, with a significant impairment of an essential behavior pattern, likely to result in the actual killing or injury of wildlife?

All three components of the definition are necessary to meet the regulatory definition of "harm" as a form of take through habitat modification under Section 9 of the ESA, with the "actual killing or injury of wildlife" as the most significant component of the definition.

> when the agency, applicant or contractor plans to carry out additional research not required by an Incidental Take Statement that would involve direct take (if this is part of the action evaluated pursuant to Section 7 consultation and direct take is contemplated, a permit is not needed)

> for species surveys associated with Biological Assessments that result in take, including harassment[239]

The permitted activity for Section 10(a)(1)(A) permits must not operate to the disadvantage of the species and must be consistent with the purposes and policy set forth in Section 2 of the Act. Intra-Service Section 7 consultation must be conducted prior to issuance of a Section 10(a)(1)(A) permit.[240]

Section 10(a)(1)(B) of the Act allows non-federal parties planning activities that have no federal nexus, but which could result in the incidental taking of listed animals, to

239 Section 7 Handbook at p. 2-4.
240 *Id.*

apply for an incidental take permit. The application must include a habitat conservation plan (HCP) setting forth the proposed actions, determining the effects of those actions on affected fish and wildlife species and their habitats (often including proposed or candidate species), and defining measures to minimize and mitigate adverse effects. For additional details regarding Section 10(a)(1)(B) incidental take permits and HCPs, see Chapter 13 (Conservation Planning).

HCP = Habitat Conservation Plan

The Service's *Consultation Handbook: Procedures for Conducting Consultation and Conference Activities Under Section 7 of the Endangered Species Act* (March 1998) ("Section 7 Handbook") acknowledges the practical realities associated with the HCP process, which can be onerous and time consuming. As described in the Handbook, in some HCP planning areas, parties may strive to find a federal nexus to avoid the HCP process altogether. The Handbook encourages the Service to advise these parties of the differences between incidental take capabilities under Sections 7 and 10. Although the issuance of an incidental take permit under Section 10 must not jeopardize the continued existence of a listed species, Section 10 expressly authorizes the Service to minimize and mitigate, to the maximum extent practical, the adverse impacts to the species (supplying some benefit to the species such as land acquisition of habitat restoration or enhancement to offset unavoidable effects of the action). Mitigation may or may not reduce the actual number of individuals the Service anticipates will be taken as a result of project implementation. For incidental take considerations under Section 7, minimization of the level of take on the individuals affected is required. Also, the Incidental Take Statement in a Section 7 Biological Opinion does not provide assurances against future obligations or requirements to minimize or mitigate harm resulting from the authorized take, unlike the assurances provided by the regulations governing the issuance and administration of Section 10(a)(1)(B) permits. The action agency is responsible for reinitiating consultation should their actions result in exceeding the level of incidental take.[241]

CONFERENCE PROCESS

In some instances, an action agency may be considering permits for a development project that would be located on property where species that are proposed for listing as either endangered or threatened are present or likely to be present. For those projects, a project proponent may seek confirmation that its project will not require further regulation under the ESA should that species ultimately be listed. The ESA contemplates this scenario in Section 7(a)(4).

Section 7(a)(4) of the Act provides that each federal agency must "confer with the [Service] on any agency action which is likely to jeopardize the continued existence of any species proposed to be listed [as endangered or threatened] or result in the destruction or adverse modification of critical habitat proposed to be designated for such species."

---

241 *Id.* at pp. 2-4 to 2-5.

According to the Section 7 Handbook, Section 7(a)(4) was added to the Act to provide a mechanism for identifying and resolving potential conflicts between a proposed action and proposed species or proposed critical habitat at an early planning stage. While consultations are required when the proposed action may affect listed species, a conference is required only when the proposed action is likely to jeopardize the continued existence of a proposed species or destroy or adversely modify proposed critical habitat. However, federal action agencies may request a conference on any proposed action that may affect proposed species or proposed critical habitat. The Service also can request a conference after reviewing available information suggesting a proposed action is likely to jeopardize proposed species or destroy or adversely modify proposed critical habitat.[242]

The term "conference" is further defined in the Service's regulations as "a process which involves informal discussions between a federal agency and the Service under Section 7(a)(4) of the Act regarding the impact of an action on proposed species or proposed critical habitat and recommendations to minimize or avoid the adverse effects."[243]

The Service's regulations provide further details on the conference process. Under the regulations, each federal agency shall confer with the Service on any action which is likely to jeopardize the continued existence of any proposed species or result in the destruction or adverse modification of proposed critical habitat. The conference is designed to assist the federal agency and any applicant in identifying and resolving potential conflicts at an early stage in the planning process.[244]

The federal agency shall initiate the conference with the Service. The Service may request a conference if, after a review of available information, it determines that a conference is required for a particular action.[245]

A conference between a federal agency and the Service shall consist of informal discussions concerning an action that is likely to jeopardize the continued existence of the proposed species or result in the destruction or adverse modification of the proposed critical habitat at issue. Applicants may be involved in these informal discussions to the greatest extent practicable. During the conference, the Service will make advisory recommendations, if any, on ways to minimize or avoid adverse effects. If the proposed species is subsequently listed or the proposed critical habitat is designated prior to completion of the action, the federal agency must review the action to determine whether formal consultation is required.[246]

As described in the Section 7 Handbook, conferences may involve informal discussions among the Service, the action agency, and the applicant (if any). During the conference, the Service may assist the action agency in determining effects and may advise

---

242 Section 7 Handbook at p. 6-1.

243 50 C.F.R. § 402.02.

244 *Id.* § 402.10(a).

245 *Id.* § 402.10(b).

246 *Id.* § 402.10(c).

the action agency on ways to avoid or minimize adverse effects to proposed species (or candidate species if present, and voluntarily considered by the action agency and/or the applicant) or proposed critical habitat. Although not required by the Act, the Service encourages the formation of partnerships to conserve candidate species since these species by definition may warrant future protection under the Act.[247]

If requested by the federal agency and deemed appropriate by the Service, the conference may be conducted in accordance with the procedures for formal consultation. An opinion issued at the conclusion of the conference may be adopted as the Biological Opinion when the species is listed or critical habitat is designated, but only if no significant new information is developed (including that developed during the rulemaking process on the proposed listing or critical habitat designation) and no significant changes to the federal action are made that would alter the content of the opinion. An Incidental Take Statement provided with a Conference Opinion (described in more detail below) does not become effective unless the Service adopts the opinion should the proposed listing becomes final.[248]

The conclusions reached during a conference and any recommendations must be documented by the Service and provided to the federal agency and to any applicant. The style and magnitude of this document will vary with the complexity of the conference. If formal consultation also is required for a particular action, then the Service will provide the results of the conference with the Biological Opinion.[249]

The Section 7 Handbook describes in more detail the conference report issued by the Service after informal conference. Following informal conference with the action agency, the Service issues a conference report containing recommendations for reducing adverse effects. These recommendations are advisory because the action agency is not prohibited from jeopardizing the continued existence of a proposed species or destroying or adversely modifying proposed critical habitat until the species is listed or critical habitat is designated. However, as soon as a listing becomes effective, the prohibition against jeopardy or adverse modification applies regardless of the action's stage of completion. Therefore, action agencies should utilize the conference report's recommendations to avoid likely future conflicts.[250]

The Section 7 Handbook provides additional details on the conference process, particularly relative to an aspect of the process it refers to as "formal conference." According to the Handbook, action agencies may request formal conference on a proposed action. Although the regulations permit the Service to decide whether formal conference is appropriate, generally formal conferences should be provided if requested.

Formal conferences follow the same procedures as formal consultation. The opinion issued at the end of a formal conference is called a Conference Opinion. It follows

---

247 Section 7 Handbook at p. 6-1.

248 50 C.F.R. § 402.10(d).

249 *Id.* § 402.10(e).

250 Section 7 Handbook at pp. 6-1 to 6-2.

the contents and format of a Biological Opinion. However, the Incidental Take Statement provided with a Conference Opinion does not take effect until the Services adopt the Conference Opinion as a Biological Opinion on the proposed action—after the species is listed.

With respect to the timeframes for formal conferences, the Section 7 regulations provide no specific schedule for conferences. According to the Section 7 Handbook, however, by policy, formal conferences will follow the same timeframes as formal consultations. The timing of a formal conference can be affected by a final listing action. If a proposed species is listed during the conference, and the proposed action still may affect the species, the formal conference ends and formal consultation begins. The subsequent formal consultation timeframes begin with the request from the action agency for initiation of formal consultation.

With respect to the format of a Conference Opinion, the Section 7 Handbook addresses two types of conferences: stand-alone conference and conference included in a formal consultation. A stand-alone Conference Opinion addresses only proposed species or proposed critical habitat and has the same format and contents as a final Biological Opinion. Once the proposed listing or critical habitat proposal is made final, the action agency writes the Service requesting that the Conference Opinion be confirmed as a Biological Opinion.[251]

In those circumstances where the conference is included in a formal consultation, the Section 7 Handbook explains that, when both listed and proposed species or designated and proposed critical habitats are affected by a proposed action, the Service advises the action agency of the presence of the proposed species or proposed critical habitat and determines whether the agency wants them considered during the formal consultation. If the agency does not, the Service may include a notice of the need to confer in the consultation if there is a likely jeopardy to proposed species or adverse modification to proposed critical habitat. However, if proposed species or proposed critical habitat are considered in a formal consultation, the analyses for these species/critical habitats are included in the same sections as the listed species.

Requests for Service confirmation of a Conference Opinion must be in writing. The Service must respond within 45 calendar days, and, within that period, may adopt the Conference Opinion as the Biological Opinion issued through formal consultation if no significant changes have occurred in the proposed action or the information used in the conference. When the Conference Opinion is adopted in this manner, it satisfies an action agency's Section 7 consultation requirements. If the Service denies the confirmation request, it advises the action agency to initiate formal consultation unless the "may affect" situation has been eliminated.[252]

The Section 7 Handbook includes the following illustration describing the conference process (see Figure 1-1.).

251 Section 7 Handbook at p. 6-5.

252 *Id.* at p. 6-6.

FIGURE 1-1. CONFERENCE PROCESSES
Source: Section 7 Handbook at p. 6-3, Fig. 6-1.

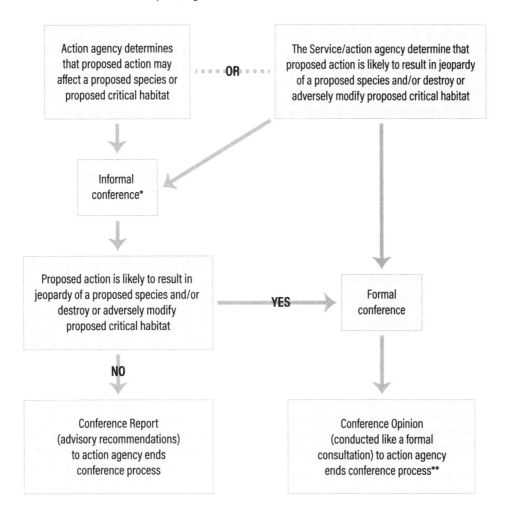

* Informal discussions can occur at any time.
**The incidental take statement does not become effective unless the Service adopts the opinion as final once the species is listed and/or critical habitat is designated.

SECTION 7 CONSULTATIONS

One of the most important elements of the federal ESA is the Section 7 consultation process. In fact, the Ninth Circuit Court of Appeals has referred to this process as the "heart of the ESA."[253] The Act requires each federal agency to:

> insure that any action authorized, funded, or carried out by such agency . . . is not likely to jeopardize the continued existence of any endangered species or threatened species or result in the destruction or adverse modification of habitat of such species which is determined . . . to be critical.[254]

---

253 *Western Watersheds Project v. Kraayenbrink*, 632 F.3d 472, 495 (9th Cir. 2010).

254 16 U.S.C. § 1536(a)(2); 50 C.F.R. § 402.01.

The Section 7 process can be complex. The Service issued its *Consultation Handbook: Procedures for Conducting Consultation and Conference Activities Under Section 7 of the Endangered Species Act* in March 1998 to "provide[ ] internal guidance and establish[ ] national policy for conducting consultation and conferences" pursuant to Section 7.[255] Practitioners should be aware of the Section 7 Handbook, as it contains helpful guidance and explanations of the Section 7 process. The summaries and descriptions below incorporate references to the Handbook where relevant.

Section 7 Triggers

Section 7 is triggered when a federal agency proposes to "authorize[ ], fund[ ], or carr[y] out" any action.[256] This language is fairly broad[257] and typical examples of agency actions triggering this requirement are the issuance of Clean Water Act Section 404 permits by the U.S. Army Corps of Engineers and the issuance of right-of-way grants by the U.S. Bureau of Land Management. Indeed, the Service's own issuance of an Endangered Species Act Section 10 incidental take permit and approval of a Habitat Conservation Plan constitutes an agency action that triggers Section 7 requirements. In those instances where the Service itself is issuing a permit, the Service must conduct what is referred to as "intra-Service Section 7 consultation."

Section 7(a)(2) makes no legal distinction between the trigger for its requirement that agencies consult with the Service and the requirement that agencies shape their actions so as not to jeopardize endangered species. Instead, the statute provides that agencies "shall, in consultation with and with the assistance of the [Service], insure that any action authorized, funded, or carried out by such agency . . . is not likely to jeopardize the continued existence of any endangered species or threatened species or result in the destruction or adverse modification of [critical] habitat of such species . . . ." An agency's obligation to consult is thus in aid of its obligation to shape its own actions so as not to jeopardize listed species, not independent of it. Both the consultation obligation and the obligation to "insure" against jeopardizing listed species are triggered by "any action authorized, funded, or carried out by such agency," and both apply if such an "action" is under consideration. As such, a consulting agency cannot take the position that it must consult under Section 7 but that it is not permitted to take into account the impacts of an action on listed species.[258]

---

255 U.S. Fish and Wildlife Service & National Marine Fisheries Service, Endangered Species Act Consultation Handbook: Procedures for Conducting Section 7 Consultations and Conferences at Foreword (March 1998).

256 16 U.S.C. § 1536(a)(2).

257 See *Pacific Rivers Council v. Thomas*, 30 F.3d 1050, 1054–55 (9th Cir. 1994) ("In short, there is little doubt that Congress intended to enact a broad definition of agency action in the ESA . . . ."); see also *Conner v. Burford*, 848 F.2d 1441 (9th Cir. 1988); *Lane County Audubon Soc'y v. Jamison*, 958 F.2d 290 (9th Cir. 1992); *Natural Resources Defense Council v. Houston*, 146 F.3d 1118, 1125 (9th Cir. 1998).

258 *Defenders of Wildlife v. U.S. Environmental Protection Agency*, 420 F.3d 946, 961 (9th Cir. 2005).

The Section 7 requirements "apply to all actions in which there is discretionary Federal involvement or control."[259] As such, an important consideration in determining whether Section 7 applies is whether there is "discretionary Federal involvement or control."[260]

For example, in *Natural Resources Defense Council v. Houston*,[261] the Ninth Circuit Court of Appeals considered whether the renewal of water service contracts pursuant to the Reclamation Act of 1939 is properly subject to Section 7 consultation. Certain water districts argued that the Bureau of Reclamation had no discretion to alter the terms of the renewal contracts, particularly the quantity of water delivered, and thus, the contract renewals did not trigger Section 7 consultation. The court noted that although the ESA does not apply "where there is no agency discretion to act,"[262] there was "some discretion available to the Bureau during the negotiation process."[263] Among other things, the court found persuasive the fact that the Bureau had discretion to alter key terms in the contract and may be able to reduce the amount of water available for sale if necessary to comply with the ESA.[264]

In *Defenders of Wildlife v. U.S. Environmental Protection Agency*,[265] the Service determined in a Biological Opinion that EPA had no choice but to disregard the impacts to listed species related to the transfer of permitting authority under the Clean Water Act from EPA to the State of Arizona. The State of Arizona and others argued that the Clean Water Act specifies that EPA "shall approve" state applications for the transfer of permitting authority if those applications meet certain enumerated factors. They argued that this therefore precluded EPA "discretion" to act on behalf of listed species, and that Section 7 did not apply because the Service's regulations state that Section 7 applies "to all actions in which there is discretionary Federal involvement or control."

The court rejected this argument primarily on the basis that prior "discretionary . . . involvement or control" cases hold Section 7(a)(2) inapplicable if the agency in question had "no ongoing regulatory authority" and thus was not an entity responsible for decision-making with respect to the particular action in question.[266] The court also

---

259 50 C.F.R. § 402.03; see *National Wildlife Fed'n v. National Marine Fisheries Service*, 481 F.3d 1224, 1233 (9th Cir. 2007).

260 50 C.F.R. § 402.03.

261 146 F.3d 1118 (9th Cir. 1998).

262 *Id.* at 1125–26 (citing *Sierra Club v. Babbitt*, 65 F.3d 1502, 1509 (9th Cir. 1995)).

263 *Id.* at 1126.

264 *Id.*

265 420 F.3d 946 (9th Cir. 2005).

266 *Id.* at 968 (citing *Wash. Toxics Coalition v. EPA*, 413 F.3d 1024, 1033 (9th Cir. 2005)). The court provided the following as examples of cases in which it has relied on the "discretionary . . . involvement" regulation to find Section 7(a)(2) inapplicable where the agency lacked any decisionmaking authority over the action of the kind challenged: *Ground Zero Ctr. for Non-Violent Action v. U.S. Dep't of the Navy*, 383 F.3d 1082, 1092 (9th Cir.2004) (holding that the action at issue fell outside the agency's authority because the risk of harm to listed species arose from the President's decision regarding the Navy's nuclear submarine force, not the Navy's obedience to that order); *Marbled Murrelet v. Babbitt*, 83 F.3d 1068, 1074 (9th Cir.1996) (holding Section 7(a)(2) inapplicable where a different agency made the ultimate decisions, while the respondent agency "merely provided advice," without authorizing, funding or carrying out anything).

noted other cases in which it had found Section 7(a)(2) inapplicable where the challenged action was legally foreordained by an earlier decision, such as where the agency lacked the ability to amend an already-issued permit "to address the needs of endangered or threatened species."[267] The court explained that by contrast, it has held that Section 7(a)(2) does apply where the agency in question had continuing decisionmaking authority over the challenged action.[268] In light of this case law, the court held that the ESA "confers authority and responsibility on agencies to protect listed species when the agency engages in an affirmative action that is both within its decisionmaking authority and unconstrained by earlier agency commitments."[269]

In *National Wildlife Federation v. National Marine Fisheries Service*,[270] the Ninth Circuit evaluated similar arguments in the context of a Section 7 consultation involving the effects of proposed operations of Federal Columbia River Power System dams and related facilities on listed fish in the lower Columbia and Snake Rivers. NMFS issued a Biological Opinion finding that these operations would not jeopardize the thirteen listed salmonid species present in these rivers. NMFS used a hypothetical "reference operation" to exclude from the proposed action's impacts the effects of related operations NMFS deemed were "nondiscretionary." This approach resulted in NMFS excluding dams that were already in existence, as well as other elements of the System's operations such as irrigation, flood control, and power generation.

Citing *Defenders of Wildlife v. U.S. Environmental Protection Agency*, the court rejected this approach, explaining that although the action agencies "may not *now* be said to 'authorize, fund, or carry out' the basic existence of the [operations'] dams,"[271] Section 7(a)(2) applies where the agency in question has "continuing decisionmaking authority over the challenged action."[272] The court also was not persuaded by NMFS's argument that competing mandates for flood control, irrigation and power production created obligations that fell outside of the agency's discretion. "NMFS may not avoid

267 *Id.* (citing *Envtl. Prot. Info. Ctr. v. Simpson Timber Co.*, 255 F.3d 1073, 1082 (9th Cir. 2001) (cited in *Wash. Toxics*, 413 F.3d at 1032) (applying § 402.16, which has similar language to § 402.03); *Sierra Club v. Babbitt*, 65 F.3d 1502, 1509 (9th Cir. 1995) (cited in *Wash. Toxics*, 413 F.3d at 1032) (holding that Section 7(a)(2) did not apply because the agency had no "[]ability to influence" a project based on a right-of-way granted prior to the Endangered Species Act's enactment)).

268 *Id.* at 968–69 (citing *Wash. Toxics*, 413 F.3d at 1032 (holding that Section 7(a)(2) applies to EPA's registration of pesticides because of its "ongoing discretion to register pesticides, alter pesticide registrations, and cancel pesticide registrations"); *Turtle Island Restoration Network v. Nat'l Marine Fisheries Serv.*, 340 F.3d 969 (9th Cir. 2003) (holding that Section 7(a)(2) applies to the granting of permits—a quintessential "authorizing" action— for future fishing); *Sierra Club*, 65 F.3d at 1508 (citing *O'Neill v. United States*, 50 F.3d 677, 680–81 (9th Cir. 1995), and noting that Section 7 applies to already-approved projects "if the project's implementation depended on an additional agency action"); *Envtl. Prot. Info. Ctr.*, 255 F.3d at 1082; *Natural Res. Def. Council v. Houston*, 146 F.3d 1118, 1125–26 (9th Cir. 1998) (holding that Section 7(a)(2) applies to "renewal of water contracts" because the agency had power to set the terms of—that is, to "authorize"—the renewed contracts, and was not bound to reaffirm merely the previously-negotiated terms); *Pac. Rivers Council v. Thomas*, 30 F.3d 1050, 1053 (9th Cir. 1994) (holding that Section 7(a)(2) did apply when there was "ongoing agency action" in that the agency retained power to authorize and carry out land use decisions)).

269 *Id.* at 967.

270 481 F.3d 1224 (9th Cir. 2007).

271 *Id.* at 1234 (emphasis added).

272 *Id.*

determining the limits of the action agencies' discretion by using a reference operation to sweep so-called 'nondiscretionary' operations into the environmental baseline, thereby excluding them from the requisite ESA jeopardy analysis."[273]

Other characteristics of the agency action also are relevant to determining whether the Section 7 consultation process is triggered. In *Lane County Audubon Society v. Jamison*,[274] the Bureau of Land Management prepared a document in response to the listing of the northern spotted owl as a threatened species intended to provide management guidelines as a strategy for the conservation of the owl. BLM did not consult with the Service on the theory that the strategy was not an "action" under Section 7 because it was a voluntarily created "policy statement." The court held that "without a doubt," the strategy was an agency action because it "sets forth criteria for harvesting owl habitat," and in light of the court's broad interpretation of the term "agency action," should have been subject to Section 7 consultation.[275]

In *Pacific Rivers Council v. Thomas*,[276] the Ninth Circuit considered whether certain Land and Resource Management Plans prepared by the U.S. Forest Service constituted an agency action that required consultation with the NMFS as to possible effects on the Snake River chinook salmon. The Forest Service argued that because these Plans were adopted before the salmon were listed as a threatened species, the Plans were not agency actions requiring Section 7 consultation. The Ninth Circuit rejected this argument and found that the Plans were important programmatic documents that set out guidelines for resource management in the forests involved in that case. As such, the court held that the Plans constituted "continuing agency action requiring consultation" under Section 7.[277] The court explained: "[B]ecause the [Plans] have an ongoing and long-lasting effect even after adoption, we hold that the [Plans] represent ongoing agency action."[278] Thus, the Forest Service should have consulted with NMFS as required under the ESA.

Obligation of Action Agency to "Insure" Against Jeopardy

The text of Section 7 is unequivocal, and the U.S. Supreme Court's decisions in *Tennessee Valley Authority v. Environmental Protection Agency* established that this text in particular "admits of no exception."[279] The Ninth Circuit Court of Appeals has considered the basic question of what the language "shall . . . insure that any action authorized, funded or carried out by such agency" requires each agency to do. In *Defenders of Wildlife v. U.S. Environmental Protection Agency*,[280] the court evaluated this question against the directives established in the *Tennessee Valley Authority* decision. The court explained that the

273 *Id.* at 1235.
274 958 F.2d 290 (9th Cir. 1992).
275 *Id.* at 293–94.
276 30 F.3d 1050 (9th Cir. 1994).
277 *Id.* at 1051.
278 *Id.* at 1053.
279 437 U.S. 153, 180 (1978).
280 420 F.3d 946 (9th Cir. 2005).

ordinary meaning of "insure" requires agencies to take action. "Unless an agency has the authority to take measures necessary to prevent harm to endangered species, it is impossible for that agency to 'make certain' that its actions are not likely to jeopardize those species."[281] Again, turning to *Tennessee Valley Authority*, the court explained, "[*Tennessee Valley Authority's*] analysis of the legislative history of the [ESA] confirms that the authority conferred on agencies to protect listed species goes beyond that conferred by agencies' own governing statutes." Thus, the court held that "the obligation of each agency to 'insure' that its covered actions are not likely to jeopardize listed species is an obligation in addition to those created by the agencies' own governing statute."[282]

Scope of the Agency Action

The scope of the agency action is often an issue when the action is a long-term planning or development project, or when the overall project is comprised of both federal and non-federal action elements. As the Ninth Circuit has explained, "[T]he scope of the agency action is crucial because the ESA requires the Biological Opinion to analyze the effect of the entire agency action."[283] Generally, the courts interpret the term "agency action" broadly.[284]

In *Conner v. Burford*,[285] the U.S. Forest Service initiated consultation with the Service as to the sale of oil and gas leases in certain National Forests in Montana pursuant to the Mineral Leasing Act of 1920. The Service issued Biological Opinions assessing the environmental effects of the lease sales. The Service divided the oil and gas activities into stages and addressed the effects of only the leasing stage on the basis that there was insufficient information available to issue a Biological Opinion beyond the

281 *Id.* at 963–67. Practitioners should note, however, that amendments in 1978 to the ESA, largely in response to the Tellico Dam litigation, created the Endangered Species Committee, often referred to as the "God Squad." This committee is composed of seven Cabinet-level members: the administrator of the Environmental Protection Agency, the administrator of the National Oceanic and Atmospheric Administration, the chairman of the Council of Economic Advisers, a representative from the state affected, the Secretary of the Agriculture, the Secretary of the Army, and the Secretary of the Interior. This committee has the authority to allow for the extinction of a species by exempting a federal agency from Section 7 requirements. To exempt a species, five of the seven members must vote in favor of the exemption. The following conditions must be met for a species to be considered for exemption: (1) there are no reasonable and prudent alternatives to the agency action; (2) the benefits of the action clearly outweigh the benefits of alternative courses of action consistent with conserving the species or its critical habitat, and such action is in the public interest; (3) the action is of regional or national importance; and (4) neither the federal agency concerned nor the exemption applicant made any irreversible or irretrievable commitment of resources prohibited by Section 7(d). 16 U.S.C. §§ 1536(e)–(p).

282 The court noted, however, that other Circuit Courts of Appeals have considered the question of whether Section 7(a)(2) provides additional authority to agencies, beyond that conferred by their governing statutes, to protect listed species from the impact of affirmative federal actions. The reasoning of those circuits reflect a circuit split on these question, with two circuits reading Section 7(a)(2) consistent with the Ninth Circuit's view and two concluding that Section 7 does not itself authorize agencies to protect listed species even when it is their own action that is jeopardizing them. The D.C. Circuit and the Fifth Circuit views on this issue are contrary to the Ninth Circuit, Eighth Circuit, and First Circuit's views. Compare *Defenders of Wildlife v. Administrator, EPA*, 882 F.2d 1294, 1299 (8th Cir. 1989), and *Conservation Law Found. v. Andrus*, 623 F.2d 712, 715 (1st Cir. 1979) with *Am. Forest & Paper Ass'n v. EPA*, 137 F.3d 291, 294, 298–99 (5th Cir. 1998), and *Platte River Whooping Crane Critical Habitat Maint. Trust v. FERC*, 962 F.2d 27, 34 (D.C. Cir. 1992).

283 *Conner v. Burford*, 848 F.2d 1441 (9th Cir. 1988).

284 *TVA*, 437 U.S. at 173 & n.18; *Conner*, 848 F.2d at 1453.

285 848 F.2d 1441 (9th Cir. 1988).

initial lease phase. As such, the Biological Opinion did not assess the potential impact that post-leasing oil and gas activities might have on protected species. Instead, the Service relied on "incremental-step consultation," contemplating that additional biological evaluations would be prepared prior to all subsequent activities and that the lessees' development proposals would be modified to protect species.[286]

The Ninth Circuit rejected this approach and held that Section 7 of the ESA required the Service in this case to consider all phases of the agency action, which includes post-leasing activities, in its Biological Opinion. Because the Service did not do this, it failed to prepare the Biological Opinion based on the best data available. Even though the precise location and extent of future oil and gas activities were unknown at the time, extensive information about the behavior and habitat of the species in the areas covered by the leases was available. "[I]ncomplete information about post-leasing activities does not excuse the failure to comply with the statutory requirement of a comprehensive Biological Opinion using the best information available."[287] Thus, the court held that the Service violated the ESA by failing to use the best information available to prepare a comprehensive Biological Opinion considering all stages of the agency action, and thus failing to adequately assess whether the agency action was likely to jeopardize the continued existence of any threatened or endangered species.[288]

Pursuant to the Service's regulations, the scope of the geographic area to be analyzed during the Section 7 process must be defined. That scope is referred to as the "action area," which must include "all areas to be affected directly or indirectly by the Federal Action and not merely the immediate area involved in the action."[289] Courts generally acknowledge that the determination of the action area requires application of scientific methodology and, thus, is within the agency's discretion. But the Service's administrative record must contain sufficient information justifying the scope of that analysis.

For example, in *Native Ecosystems Council v. Dombeck*,[290] the U.S. Forest Service prepared a Biological Assessment as part of the Section 7 process to analyze the effects that a proposed timber sale may have on certain listed species and their habitat, most notably the grizzly bear. The Biological Assessment identified an action area that covered what the Forest Service determined was the "largest geographic area within which effects would be considered." This area extended several miles in one direction but only 1.5 miles in another direction, just stopping short of a nearby sheep grazing allotment. Plaintiffs argued that the action area should have included this grazing allotment because of the potential harm to grizzly harms resulting from the removal or killing of bears due to conflicts with the livestock. The court acknowledged that the determination of the scope of an analysis area

286 *Id.* at 1451–53.

287 *Id.* at 1454.

288 *Id.*

289 50 C.F.R. § 402.02.

290 304 F.3d 886 (9th Cir. 2002).

requires application of scientific methodology and, as such, is within the agency's discretion. The court explained, however, that nothing in the record allowed it to conclude that the agency complied with its own regulations when choosing its analysis area. According to the court, "The [Biological Assessment] contains no discussion of scientific methodology, relevant facts, or rational connections linking the project's potential impacts with the Management Subunit's boundaries." Thus, the court held that the Forest Service's Biological Assessment was inadequate because it did not provide support for its choice of analysis area.[291]

Best Available Scientific and Commercial Data

The ESA requires the action agency to provide the best scientific and commercial data available concerning the impact of the proposed project on listed species or designated critical habitat.[292] The Section 7 regulations provide additional requirements. Under the regulations, the action agency must provide the Service with the best scientific and commercial data available or which can be obtained during the consultation for an adequate review of the effects that an action may have upon listed species or critical habitat. This information may include the results of studies or surveys conducted by the action agency or the "designated non-federal representative," which is defined as the person designated by the action agency as its representative to conduct informal consultation and/or to prepare any Biological Assessment.[293] The action agency must provide any applicant with the opportunity to submit information for consideration during the consultation.[294]

Case law in the Ninth Circuit Court of Appeals has established that the ESA does not require perfection from the Service. For example, in *Alaska Oil and Gas Association v. Jewell*,[295] the Service evaluated critical habitat designation for the polar bear, and in so doing, focused on the "primary constituent elements" essential to protecting the polar bear. The Ninth Circuit determined that the district court held the Service to a standard of specificity that the ESA does not require. The court concluded that the ESA "requires use of the best available technology, not perfection."[296]

Similarly, in *San Luis & Mendota Water Authority v. Jewell*,[297] the Ninth Circuit considered a Biological Opinion prepared by the Service that concluded that the Central Valley Project and the State Water Project jeopardize the continued existence of the threatened delta smelt and its habitat in the confluence of the San Francisco Bay and the Sacramento-San Joaquin Delta. The District Court concluded that the Service failed to

291 *Id.* at 902–03.

292 16 U.S.C. § 1536(a)(2) ("In fulfilling the requirements of this paragraph each agency shall use the best scientific and commercial data available.").

293 50 C.F.R. § 402.02.

294 *Id.* § 402.14(d).

295 815 F.3d 544 (9th Cir. 2016).

296 *Id.* at 555 (quoting *Bldg. Indus. Ass'n of Superior Cal. v. Norton*, 247 F.3d 1241, 1247 (D.C. Cir. 2001)) (noting that, while the agency "may not base its listings on speculation or surmise" where there is no superior data, "occasional imperfections do not violate [the ESA].").

297 747 F.3d 581 (9th Cir. 2014).

consider the best science available in reaching this determination. The Ninth Circuit began analysis of this issue by first noting that, although the Service must employ "the best scientific and commercial data available," it is "not required to support its finding that a significant risk exists with anything approaching scientific certainty."[298] After evaluating the numerous scientific modeling and data sources, the court ultimately deferred to the agency's decision consistent with well-established case law indicating such deferral is proper, and concluded that the Service's determinations in the Biological Opinion was not arbitrary and capricious.[299]

The Section 7 Handbook provides additional guidance on the "best available scientific and commercial data." According to the Handbook, if relevant data are known to be available to the agency or will be available as the result of ongoing or imminent studies, the Service should request those data and any other analyses required by the Section 7 regulations or suggest that consultation be postponed until those data or analyses are available.[300]

The Handbook further specifies that where significant data gaps exist there are two options: (1) if the action agency concurs, extend the due date of the Biological Opinion until sufficient information is developed for a more complete analysis; or (2) develop the Biological Opinion with the available information giving the benefit of the doubt to the species. If the action agency or the applicant insists consultation be completed without the data or analyses requested, the Biological Opinion or informal consultation letter should document that certain analyses or data were not provided and why that information would have been helpful in improving the data base for the consultation. In formal consultation, this statement usually appears in the "effects of the action" section. The Service is then expected to provide the benefit of the doubt to the species concerned with respect to such gaps in the information base.[301]

Section 7 Process

As interpreted by the Ninth Circuit Court of Appeals, the ESA prescribes a three-step process to ensure compliance with its substantive provisions under Section 7 by federal agencies. Each of the first two steps serves as a screening function to determine if the successive steps are required.

Early Consultation

The first step is that an agency proposing to take an action must inquire of the Service whether any threatened or endangered species "may be present" in the area of the proposed action.[302] The Service's regulations refer to this initial step as "early consultation."

298 *Id.* at 592–93 (citing 16 U.S.C. § 1536(a)(2); *Indus. Union Dep't v. Am. Petroleum Inst.*, 448 U.S. 607, 656 (1980) (plurality opinion)).

299 *Id.* at 610.

300 Section 7 Handbook at p. 1-6.

301 *Id.* (citing H.R. Conf. Rep. No. 697, 96th Cong., 2nd Sess. 12 (1979)).

302 16 U.S.C. § 1536(c)(1).

Early consultation is designed to reduce the likelihood of conflicts between listed species or critical habitat and proposed actions and occurs prior to the filing of an application for a federal permit or license. Although early consultation is conducted between the Service and the federal agency, the prospective applicant should be involved throughout the consultation process.[303]

If a prospective applicant has reason to believe that the prospective action may affect listed species or critical habitat, it may request the federal agency to enter into early consultation with the Service. The prospective applicant must certify in writing to the federal agency that (1) it has a definitive proposal outlining the action and its effects and (2) it intends to implement its proposal, if authorized.[304]

If the federal agency receives the prospective applicant's certification, then the federal agency must initiate early consultation with the Service.[305] This request must be in writing and contain the information required for a request to initiate formal consultation and, if the action is a major construction activity, the Biological Assessment.[306]

The procedures and responsibilities for early consultation are the same as outlined in the regulations regarding formal consultation, except that all references to the "applicant" must be treated as the "prospective applicant" and all references to the "Biological Opinion" or the "Opinion" must be treated as the "preliminary Biological Opinion."[307]

The contents and conclusions of a preliminary Biological Opinion are the same as for a Biological Opinion issued after formal consultation except that the Incidental Take Statement provided with a preliminary Biological Opinion does not constitute authority to take listed species.[308]

A preliminary Biological Opinion may be confirmed as a Biological Opinion issued after formal consultation if the Service reviews the proposed action and finds that there have been no significant changes in the action as planned or in the information used during the early consultation. A written request for confirmation of the preliminary Biological Opinion should be submitted after the prospective applicant applies to the federal agency for a permit or license but prior to the issuance of such permit or license. Within 45 days of receipt of the federal agency's request, the Service must either: (1) confirm that the preliminary Biological Opinion stands as a final Biological Opinion; or (2) if the findings noted above cannot be made, request that the federal agency initiate formal consultation.[309]

---

303 50 C.F.R. § 402.11(a).

304 *Id.* § 402.11(b).

305 In the authors' experience, these provisions are rarely invoked by applicants. However, for those projects that qualify, early consultation may be an effective means to resolve issues early on in the process.

306 50 C.F.R. § 402.11(c).

307 *Id.* § 402.11(d).

308 *Id.* § 402.11(e).

309 *Id.* § 402.11(f).

The bar for determining whether evaluation of an agency action must move beyond to the next step in the process is fairly low. For example, in *Thomas v. Peterson*,[310] the Ninth Circuit Court of Appeals noted with no equivocation: "Once an agency is aware that an endangered species may be present in the area of its proposed action, the ESA requires it to prepare a Biological Assessment to determine whether the proposed action is likely to affect the species and therefore requires formal consultation with the [Service]."[311] Presumably, this directive applies to both endangered and threatened species, given that the court also noted previously in this decision that Section 7(c)(1) requires an agency proposing to take an action must inquire of the Service "whether any threatened or endangered species 'may be present' in the area of the proposed action."[312]

In *Western Watersheds Project v. Kraayenbrink*,[313] the Bureau of Land Management issued 18 amendments to its grazing regulations and determined that the amendments would not affect listed species or their habitat based on the view that the amendments were "purely administrative." The court took into consideration "resounding evidence" that the amendments "may affect" listed species and their habitat. This evidence consisted primarily of expert declarations that indicated the amendments were not purely administrative. For example, the evidence indicated that the amendments would alter ownership rights to water on public lands; increase the barriers to public involvement in grazing management; and substantially delay enforcement on "failing allotments" in ways that would have a substantive effect on special status species. As such, the court concluded that the Bureau's no effect finding and resulting decision not to consult were arbitrary and capricious under the ESA.[314]

The Section 7 Handbook includes an illustration depicting typical steps during the early consultation process (see Figure 1-2.).

Informal Consultation and the Biological Assessment

Most consultations are conducted informally with the action agency or a designated non-federal representative. As summarized in the Section 7 Handbook, informal consultations:

> clarify whether and what listed, proposed, and candidate species or designated or proposed critical habitats may be in the action area

> determine what effect the action may have on these species or critical habitats

> explore ways to modify the action to reduce or remove adverse effects to the species or critical habitats

---

310 753 F.2d 754 (9th Cir. 1985).

311 *Id.* at 763 (internal quotation marks omitted).

312 *Id.*; see also *Western Watersheds Project v. Kraayenbrink*, 632 F.3d 472, 496 (9th Cir. 2010) ("The minimum threshold for an agency action to trigger consultation with [the Service] is low . . . .").

313 632 F.3d 472 (9th Cir. 2010).

314 *Id.* at 498.

FIGURE 1-2. EARLY CONSULTATION PROCESS

Source: Section 7 Handbook at p. 7-2, Fig. 7-1.

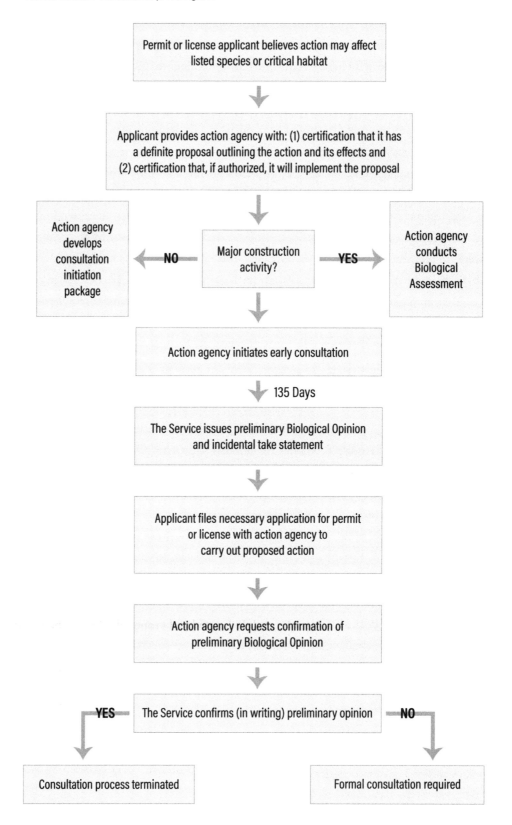

> determine the need to enter into formal consultation for listed species or designated critical habitats, or conference for the proposed species or proposed critical habitats

> explore the design or modification of an action to benefit the species[315]

If endangered or threatened species "may be present" in the area of the proposed action, then the action agency must determine whether the action "may affect listed species or habitat." This determination usually takes place during informal consultation.

Informal consultation is an optional process that includes all discussions, correspondence, etc., between the Service and the federal agency or the designated non-federal representative, designed to assist the federal agency in determining whether formal consultation or a conference is required. If during informal consultation it is determined by the federal agency, with the written concurrence of the Service, that the action is not likely to adversely affect listed species or critical habitat, the consultation process is terminated, and no further action is necessary.[316] During informal consultation, the Service may suggest modifications to the action that the federal agency and any applicant could implement to avoid the likelihood of adverse effects to listed species or critical habitat.[317]

To determine whether an "action may affect listed species or critical habitat," the action agency may be required to prepare a Biological Assessment that "evaluate[s] the potential effects of the action on listed and proposed species and . . . critical habitat and determine[s] whether any such species or habitat are likely to be adversely affected by the action."[318]

The Service's regulations define a "Biological Assessment" as "the information prepared by or under the direction of the [f]ederal agency concerning listed and proposed species and designated and proposed critical habitat that may be present in the action area and the evaluation of potential effects of the action on such species and habitat."[319] This Biological Assessment may be part of an Environmental Impact Statement or Environmental Assessment prepared pursuant to the National Environmental Policy Act (NEPA).[320]

The purpose of the Biological Assessment is to evaluate the potential effects of the action on listed and proposed species and designated and proposed critical habitat and determine whether any such species or habitat are likely to be adversely affected by the action. The Biological Assessment is also used in determining whether formal consultation or a conference (i.e., when a species is proposed for listing) is necessary.[321]

NEPA = National Environmental Policy Act

The proposed revisions to the Section 7 regulations include changes to the deadlines for informal consultation. As explained in the proposed rule, informal consultation is an optional process that includes all discussions, correspondence, etc., between the Service and the action agency to assist the action agency in determining whether formal consultation is required. Currently, there is no deadline for the Service to complete an informal consultation, unlike formal consultations, which by regulation should be completed within 90 days unless extended under the terms at Section 402.14(e) of Title 50 of the Code of Federal Regulations. The proposed revisions to the Section 7 regulations would add a 60-day deadline, subject to extension by mutual consent, for informal consultations. (83 Fed. Reg. 35.170 (July 25, 2018).)

---

315 Section 7 Handbook at p. 3-1.

316 50 C.F.R. § 402.13(a).

317 *Id.* § 402.13(b).

318 *Id.* § 402.12.

319 *Id.* § 402.02.

320 *Thomas v. Peterson*, 753 F.2d 754, 763 (9th Cir. 1985).

321 50 C.F.R. § 402.12(a).

For federal actions that are considered "major construction activities," the Service's regulations provide that "any person . . . may prepare a Biological Assessment under the supervision of the federal agency and in cooperation with the Service consistent with the procedures and requirements" of the Service's regulations.[322] The Biological Assessment must be completed before any contract for construction is entered into and before construction is begun.[323]

The federal agency or the designated non-federal representative must convey to the Service either (1) a written request for a list of any listed or proposed species or designated or proposed critical habitat that may be present in the action area; or (2) a written notification of the species and critical habitat that are being included in the Biological Assessment.[324]

Within 30 days of receipt of the notification of, or the request for, a species list, the Service must either concur with or revise the list or, in those cases where no list has been provided, advise the federal agency or the designated non-federal representative in writing whether, based on the best scientific and commercial data available, any listed or proposed species or designated or proposed critical habitat may be present in the action area. In addition to listed and proposed species, the Service will provide a list of candidate species that may be present in the action area. Candidate species refers to any species being considered by the Service for listing as endangered or threatened species but not yet the subject of a proposed rule. Although candidate species have no legal status and are accorded no protection under the Act, their inclusion will alert the federal agency of potential proposals or listings.[325]

If the Service advises that no listed species or critical habitat may be present, the federal agency need not prepare a Biological Assessment and further consultation is not required. If only proposed species or proposed critical habitat may be present in the action area, then the federal agency must confer with the Service if required under the regulations regarding conferences on proposed species or proposed critical habitat, but preparation of a Biological Assessment is not required unless the proposed listing and/ or designation becomes final.[326]

If a listed species or critical habitat may be present in the action area, the Service will provide a species list or concur with the species list provided. The Service also will provide available information (or references thereto) regarding these species and critical habitat and may recommend discretionary studies or surveys that may provide a better information base for the preparation of an assessment. Any recommendation for studies

---

322 *Id.* § 402.12(b)(1).

323 *Id.* § 402.12(b)(2).

324 *Id.* § 402.12(c).

325 *Id.* § 402.12(d).

326 *Id.* § 402.12(d)(1).

or surveys must not be construed as the Service's opinion that the federal agency has failed to satisfy the information standard of Section 7(a)(2) of the Act.[327]

If the federal agency or the designated non-federal representative does not begin preparation of the Biological Assessment within 90 days of receipt of (or concurrence with) the species list, the federal agency or the designated non-federal representative must verify (formally or informally) with the Service the current accuracy of the species list at the time the preparation of the assessment is begun.[328]

The contents of a Biological Assessment are at the discretion of the federal agency and will depend on the nature of the federal action. The following may be considered for inclusion:[329]

> the results of an on-site inspection of the area affected by the action to determine if listed or proposed species are present or occur seasonally

> the views of recognized experts on the species at issue

> a review of the literature and other information

> an analysis of the effects of the action on the species and habitat, including consideration of cumulative effects, and the results of any related studies

> an analysis of alternate actions considered by the federal agency for the proposed action

If a proposed action requiring the preparation of a Biological Assessment is identical, or very similar, to a previous action for which a Biological Assessment was prepared, the federal agency may fulfill the Biological Assessment requirement for the proposed action by incorporating by reference the earlier Biological Assessment, plus any supporting data from other documents that are pertinent to the consultation, into a written certification that:[330]

> the proposed action involves similar impacts to the same species in the same geographic area

> no new species have been listed or proposed or no new critical habitat designated or proposed for the action area

> the Biological Assessment has been supplemented with any relevant changes in information

The federal agency or the designated non-federal representative shall complete the Biological Assessment within 180 days after its initiation (receipt of or concurrence with the species list) unless a different period of time is agreed to by the Service and the federal agency. If a permit or license applicant is involved, the 180-day period may not be extended unless the agency provides the applicant, before the close of the 180-day

---

327 *Id.* § 402.12(d)(2).

328 *Id.* § 402.12(d).

329 *Id.* § 402.12(f).

330 *Id.* § 402.12(g).

period, with a written statement setting forth the estimated length of the proposed extension and the reasons why such an extension is necessary.[331]

The federal agency must submit the completed Biological Assessment to the Service for review. The Service will respond in writing within 30 days as to whether or not it concurs with the findings of the Biological Assessment. At the option of the federal agency, formal consultation may be initiated concurrently with the submission of the assessment.[332]

The federal agency must use the Biological Assessment in determining whether formal consultation or a conference is required. If the Biological Assessment indicates that there are no listed species or critical habitat present that are likely to be adversely affected by the action and the Service concurs, then formal consultation is not required. If the Biological Assessment indicates that the action is not likely to jeopardize the continued existence of proposed species or result in the destruction or adverse modification of proposed critical habitat, and the Service concurs, then a conference is not required.[333] If the Biological Assessment indicates that the proposed action is "likely to adversely affect" listed species or critical habitat present in the action area, then formal consultation is required. As such, the results of the Biological Assessment are used in (1) determining whether to request the federal agency to initiate formal consultation or a conference, (2) formulating a Biological Opinion, or (3) formulating a preliminary Biological Opinion.[334]

Below is a flowchart showing the informal consultation process (see Figure 1-3.).

Concurrence/Nonconcurrence Letters

Following review of the Biological Assessment or other pertinent information, another informal effort may be appropriate to try to eliminate any residual adverse effects of the proposed action. If that effort results in elimination of potential impacts, the Service will concur in writing that the action, as revised and newly described, is not likely to adversely affect listed species or designated critical habitat. Since concurrence depends upon implementation of the modifications, the concurrence letter must clearly state any modifications agreed to during informal consultation. If agreement cannot be reached, the Service will advise the action agency to initiate formal consultation.[335]

Although not required, an action agency may request written concurrence from the Service that the proposed action will have no effect on listed species or critical habitat. This concurrence is useful for the administrative record. When the Biological Assessment or other information indicates that the action has no likelihood of adverse

331 50 C.F.R. § 402.14(i).

332 *Id.* § 402(j).

333 *Id.* § 402.12(k)(1).

334 *Id.* § 402.12(k)(2).

335 Section 7 Handbook at p. 3-12.

FIGURE 1-3. INFORMAL CONSULTATION PROCESS
Source: Section 7 Handbook at p. 3-3, Fig. 3-1.

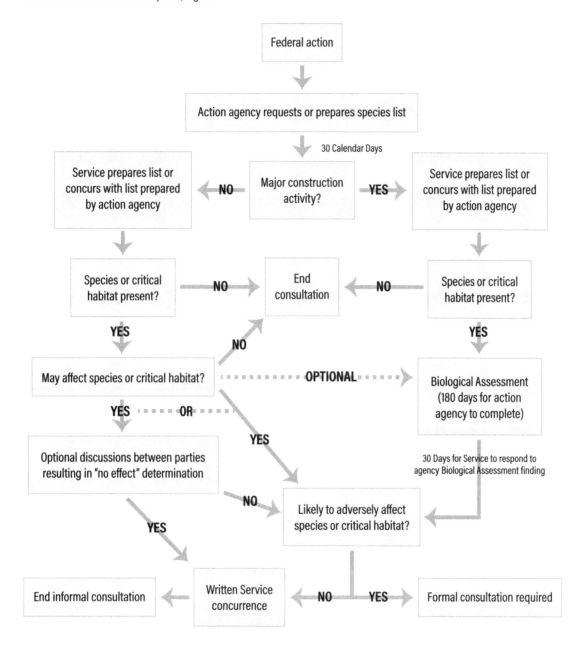

effect (including evaluation of effects that may be beneficial, insignificant, or discountable), the Service provides a letter of concurrence, which completes informal consultation. The analysis, based on review of all potential effects, direct and indirect, is
documented in the concurrence letter. If the nature of the effects cannot be determined,
benefit of the doubt is given to the species. The Section 7 Handbook advises the Service
not to concur in these instances.[336]

336 *Id.*

After evaluating the potential for effect, the Service makes one of the following determinations:

> **No effect.** The appropriate conclusion when the action agency determines its proposed action will not affect listed species or critical habitat.

> **Is not likely to adversely affect.** The appropriate conclusion when effects on listed species are expected to be discountable, or insignificant, or completely beneficial. "Beneficial effects" are contemporaneous positive effects without any adverse effects to the species. "Insignificant effects" relate to the size of the impact and should never reach the scale where take occurs. "Discountable effects" are those extremely unlikely to occur. Based on best judgment, a person would not: (1) be able to meaningfully measure, detect, or evaluate insignificant effects; or (2) expect discountable effects to occur.

> **Nonconcurrence.** If the Service does not agree with the action agency's determination of effects or if there is not enough information to adequately determine the nature of the effects, a letter of non-concurrence is provided to the action agency.

> **Is likely to adversely affect.** The appropriate conclusion if any adverse effect to listed species may occur as a direct or indirect result of the proposed action or its interrelated or interdependent actions, and the effect is not: discountable, insignificant, or beneficial. (See definitions above.) In the event the overall effect of the proposed action is beneficial to the listed species, but also is likely to cause some adverse effects, then the proposed action "is likely to adversely affect" the listed species. An "is likely to adversely affect" determination requires formal Section 7 consultation.[337]

A fourth finding is possible for proposed species or proposed critical habitat:

> **Is likely to jeopardize proposed species/adversely modify proposed critical habitat.** The appropriate conclusion when the action agency or the Service identifies situations in which the proposed action is likely to jeopardize the continued existence of the proposed species or adversely modify the proposed critical habitat. If this conclusion is reached, conference is required.[338]

Formal Consultation and the Biological Opinion

The Service's regulations require that each federal agency must review its actions at the earliest possible time to determine whether any action may affect listed species or critical habitat. If such a determination is made, formal consultation is required.[339] The Service may request a federal agency to enter into consultation if it identifies any action of that agency that may affect listed species or critical habitat and for which there has been no consultation. When such a request is made, the Service must forward to the federal agency a written explanation of the basis for the request.[340]

337 *Id.*
338 *Id.* at pp. 3-12 to 3-13.
339 50 C.F.R. § 402.14(a).
340 *Id.*

Formal consultation is not required if the federal agency determines, with the written concurrence of the Service, that the proposed action is not likely to adversely affect any listed species or critical habitat.[341] This is often referred to colloquially as a "concurrence determination." Formal consultation also is not required if a preliminary Biological Opinion, issued after "early consultation," is confirmed as the final Biological Opinion.[342]

According to the Section 7 Handbook, formal consultation becomes necessary when: (1) the action agency requests consultation after determining the proposed action may affect listed species or critical habitat (however, if the Service concurs in writing that the proposed action is not likely to adversely affect any listed species or critical habitat, i.e., the effects are completely beneficial, insignificant, or discountable, then formal consultation is not required); or (2) the Service, through informal consultation, does not concur with the action agency's finding that the proposed action is not likely to adversely affect the listed species or critical habitat.[343]

The Section 7 Handbook summarizes the determinations that are made during the formal consultation process:

> Formal consultations determine whether a proposed agency action(s) is likely to jeopardize the continued existence of a listed species (jeopardy) or destroy or adversely modify critical habitat (adverse modification). . . . They also determine the amount or extent of anticipated incidental take in an incidental take statement. Formal consultations perform several other functions: they (1) identify the nature and extent of the effects of [f]ederal (agency) actions on listed species and critical habitat; (2) identify reasonable and prudent alternatives, if any, when an action is likely to result in jeopardy or adverse modification; (3) provide an exception for specified levels of "incidental take" otherwise prohibited under section 9 of the Act; (4) provide mandatory reasonable and prudent measures to minimize the impacts of incidental take to listed species; (5) identify ways the action agencies can help conserve listed species or critical habitat when they undertake an action; and (6) provide an administrative record of effects on species that can help establish the species' environmental baseline in future biological opinions.[344]

The Section 7 Handbook also provides the following overview for when formal consultation is required and for the overall goals of formal consultation:

> If an action agency determines a proposed action "may affect" listed species or designated critical habitat, formal consultation is required . . . . No formal consultation is required if the action agency finds, with the Services written concurrence that the proposed action "may affect, but is not likely to

---

341 *Id.* § 402.14(b)(1).

342 *Id.* § 402.14(b)(2).

343 Section 7 Handbook at p. 2-6.

344 *Id.* at p. 4-1.

adversely affect" listed species or critical habitat . . . . This finding can be made only if ALL of the reasonably expected effects of the proposed action will be beneficial, insignificant, or discountable. The action agency must request concurrence, in writing, from the Service for this finding. When action agencies request formal consultation on actions not likely to adversely affect listed species or designated critical habitat, the Service should explain that informal consultation/concurrence letters are adequate to complete Section 7 compliance, but that they will enter into formal consultation if the action agency desires.

Although the formal consultation process must result in a biological opinion reaching either a jeopardy or no jeopardy to listed species (or adverse or no adverse modification of critical habitat) finding, the process is flexible and can be adapted at any point to respond to project modifications agreed to by the action agency or the applicant. Moreover, in locations where numerous actions impact a species, changes in the baseline due to successive effects can be addressed on a continuing basis using biological opinions. Such a series of biological opinions can be used like building blocks to first establish a concern, then warn of potential impacts, and finally result in a jeopardy call. Successive biological opinions can be used to monitor trends in the species' baseline, making predictions of the impacts of future actions more reliable. Extrapolation of a diminishing baseline can help show where future jeopardy thresholds may be reached.[345]

To initiate formal consultation, the federal agency must submit a written request to the Service that includes the following:

> a description of the action to be considered
> a description of the specific area that may be affected by the action
> a description of any listed species or critical habitat that may be affected by the action
> a description of the manner in which the action may affect any listed species or critical habitat and an analysis of any cumulative effects
> relevant reports, including any Environmental Impact Statement, Environmental Assessment, or Biological Assessment prepared
> any other relevant available information on the action, the affected listed species, or critical habitat[346]

Formal consultation must not be initiated by the federal agency until any required Biological Assessment has been completed and submitted to the Service. For a "major construction activity," the action agency is required to submit a Biological Assessment if

---

345 *Id.* at pp. 4-1 to 4-2.
346 50 C.F.R. § 402.14(c)(1)–(6).

PROPOSED REVISIONS TO SECTION 7 REGULATIONS— INITIATING FORMAL CONSULTATION

The proposed revisions to the Section 7 regulations include clarifications regarding the information needed in order to start the Section 7 consultation process. This would be a proposed revision to Section 402.14(c) of Title 50 of the Code of Federal Regulations. As explained in the proposed rule, this change would clarify what is necessary to initiate formal consultation.

In particular, the proposed revisions would describe the information from the action agency necessary to initiate consultation. This set of information is commonly called the "initiation package." Consistent with Section 402.06 (coordination with other environmental reviews), the Service is proposing in Section 402.14(c) to allow other documents to serve as initiation packages, such as: a document prepared for the sole purpose of providing the Service with information relevant to an agency's consultation, a document that has been prepared under NEPA or other authority that contains the necessary information to initiate consultation, or other such documents (e.g., grant application, California Environmental Quality Act Environmental Impact Report, etc.) that meet the requirements for initiating consultation.

When such documents consider two or more alternative actions, the request for consultation must describe the specific alternative or action proposed for consultation and the specific locations in the document where the relevant information is found. The Service evaluates only the action agency's proposed alternative during the consultation process. If the action agency either adopts another alternative as its final agency action, or substantively modifies the proposed alternative, reinitiation of consultation may be required.

The proposed regulations describe categories of information that should be in an initiation package to initiate formal consultation. Information must be provided in a sufficient level of detail consistent with the nature and scope of the proposed action. Consistent with the Service's existing practice, the requirement to include sufficient detail ensures the Service has enough information to understand the action as proposed and conduct an informed analysis of the effects of the action, including with regard to those measures intended to avoid, minimize, or offset effects. Such information should include a description of the proposed action, including any measures intended to avoid, minimize, or offset the effects of the proposed action, a description of the area affected (the action area), information about species or critical habitat in the action area, a description of potential effects of the proposed action on individuals of any listed species or critical habitat, a description of the cumulative effects, a summary of information from the applicant, if any, and any other relevant information. (83 Fed. Reg. 35,178 (July 25, 2018).)

listed species or designated critical habitat may be present in the action area.[347] Any request for formal consultation may encompass, subject to the approval of the Service, a number of similar individual actions within a given geographical area or a segment of a comprehensive plan. This does not relieve the federal agency of the requirements for considering the effects of the action as a whole.[348]

The federal agency requesting formal consultation shall provide the Service with the best scientific and commercial data available or which can be obtained during the consultation for an adequate review of the effects that an action may have upon listed species or critical habitat. This information may include the results of studies or surveys conducted by the federal agency or the designated non-federal representative. The federal agency must provide any applicant with the opportunity to submit information for consideration during the consultation.[349]

An action agency's package initiating consultation must be reviewed "promptly" by the Service to determine if: (1) all of the information required by the regulations has been provided; and (2) whether the information includes the best scientific and commercial data available. The "other relevant information" requirement gives the Service an opportunity to determine what project-specific information is needed to develop the Biological Opinion. The action agency is obligated to submit the best data available or "which can be obtained during the consultation . . . ."[350] Although not required by the Section 7 regulations, a topographic map showing the affected area is a useful addition to the initiation package.[351]

Formal consultation is "initiated" on the date the request is received, if the action agency provides all the relevant data required by the Section 7 regulations. If all required data are not initially submitted, then formal consultation is initiated on the date on which all required information has been received. Within 30 working days of receipt of an initiation package, the Service should provide written acknowledgment of the consultation request, advise the action agency of any data deficiencies, and request either the missing data or a written statement that the data are not available.[352]

Formal consultation concludes within 90 days after its initiation unless extended as provided below.[353] If an applicant is not involved, the Service and the federal agency may mutually agree to extend the consultation for a specific time period. If an applicant is involved, the Service and the federal agency may mutually agree to extend the consultation provided that the Service submits to the applicant, before the close of the 90 days, a written statement setting forth:

> the reasons why a longer period is required

---

347 Section 7 Handbook at p. 4-4.

348 50 C.F.R. § 402.14(c).

349 *Id.* § 402.14(d).

350 Section 7 Handbook at p. 4-5 (citing 50 C.F.R. § 402.14(d)).

351 *Id.*

352 *Id.* at pp. 4-5 to 4-6.

353 50 C.F.R. § 402.14(e).

> the information that is required to complete the consultation

> the estimated date on which the consultation will be completed[354]

A consultation involving an applicant cannot be extended for more than 60 days without the consent of the applicant. Within 45 days after concluding formal consultation, the Service shall deliver a Biological Opinion to the federal agency and any applicant.[355]

When the Service determines that additional data would provide a better information base from which to formulate a Biological Opinion, the Service may request an extension of formal consultation and request that the federal agency obtain additional data to determine how or to what extent the action may affect listed species or critical habitat. If formal consultation is extended by mutual agreement, the federal agency shall obtain, to the extent practicable, that data which can be developed within the scope of the extension. The responsibility for conducting and funding any studies belongs to the federal agency and the applicant, not the Service. The Service's request for additional data is not to be construed as the Service's opinion that the federal agency has failed to satisfy the information standard of Section 7(a)(2) of the Act. If no extension of formal consultation is agreed to, the Service will issue a Biological Opinion using the best scientific and commercial data available.[356]

Service responsibilities during formal consultation are as follows:

(1) Review all relevant information provided by the federal agency or otherwise available. Such review may include an on-site inspection of the action area with representatives of the federal agency and the applicant.

(2) Evaluate the current status of the listed species or critical habitat.

(3) Evaluate the effects of the action and cumulative effects on the listed species or critical habitat.

(4) Formulate its Biological Opinion as to whether the action, taken together with cumulative effects, is likely to jeopardize the continued existence of listed species or result in the destruction or adverse modification of critical habitat.

(5) Discuss with the federal agency and any applicant the Service's review and evaluation of items (1) through (3) above, the basis for any finding in the Biological Opinion, and the availability of reasonable and prudent alternatives (if a jeopardy opinion is to be issued) that the agency and the applicant can take to avoid violation of Section 7(a)(2). The Service will utilize the expertise of the federal agency and any applicant in identifying these alternatives. If requested, the Service must make available to the federal agency the draft Biological Opinion for the purpose of analyzing the reasonable and prudent alternatives. The 45-day period in which the Biological Opinion must be delivered will not be suspended unless the federal agency secures the written

354 *Id.* § 402.14(e)(1)–(3).

355 *Id.* § 402.14(e).

356 *Id.* § 402.14(f).

consent of the applicant to an extension to a specific date. The applicant may request a copy of the draft opinion from the federal agency. All comments on the draft Biological Opinion must be submitted to the Service through the federal agency, although the applicant may send a copy of its comments directly to the Service. The Service will not issue its Biological Opinion prior to the 45-day or extended deadline while the draft is under review by the federal agency. However, if the federal agency submits comments to the Service regarding the draft Biological Opinion within 10 days of the deadline for issuing the opinion, the Service is entitled to an automatic 10-day extension on the deadline.

(6) Formulate discretionary conservation recommendations, if any, which will assist the federal agency in reducing or eliminating the impacts that its proposed action may have on listed species or critical habitat.

(7) Formulate a statement concerning incidental take, if such take is reasonably certain to occur.

(8) In formulating its Biological Opinion, any reasonable and prudent alternatives, and any reasonable and prudent measures, the Service will use the best scientific and commercial data available and will give appropriate consideration to any beneficial actions taken by the federal agency or applicant, including any actions taken prior to the initiation of consultation.

If an action agency determines that an endangered or threatened species "is likely to be affected," then the agency must engage in formal consultation with the Service.[357] The term "formal consultation" is defined by the Service's regulations and is intended to specifically refer to the "process between the Service and the [f]ederal agency that commences with the [f]ederal agency's written request for consultation under Section 7(a)(2) of the Act and concludes with the Service's issuance of the Biological Opinion under Section 7(n)(3) of the Act."[358]

As alluded to in the definition of "formal consultation," the formal consultation process results in a written statement, referred to as a Biological Opinion, explaining how the proposed action will affect the species or its habitat. The Service's regulations define a "Biological Opinion" as "the document that states the opinion of the Service as to whether or not the [f]ederal action is likely to jeopardize the continued existence of listed species or result in the destruction or adverse modification of critical habitat."[359]

If the Service concludes that the proposed action will "jeopardize the continued existence of any [listed] species or threatened species or result in the destruction or adverse modification of [critical habitat],"[360] then the Biological Opinion must outline any "reasonable and prudent alternatives" that the Service believes will avoid that

357 50 C.F.R. § 402.14.

358 *Id.* § 402.02.

359 *Id.*

360 16 U.S.C. § 1536(a)(2).

PROPOSED REVISIONS TO SECTION 7 REGULATIONS— PROGRAMMATIC CONSULTATIONS

The proposed changes to the Section 7 regulations include the definition of "programmatic consultation." As explained in the proposed rule, the Service is proposing the addition of this term to codify an optional consultation technique that is being used with increasing frequency and to promote the use of programmatic consultations as effective tools that can improve both process efficiency and conservation in consultations. The proposed rule would allow the use of programmatic consultations to evaluate the effects of multiple actions anticipated within a particular geographic area; or to evaluate action agency programs that guide implementation of the agency's future actions by establishing standards, guidelines, or governing criteria to which future actions will adhere. The concept is that, by consulting on the program, plan, policy, regulation, series, or suites of activities as a whole, the Service can reduce the number of single, project-by-project consultations, streamline the consultation process, and increase predictability and consistency for action agencies.

As described in the proposed rule, two types of programmatic consultations are contemplated:

> **Programmatic consultations that address multiple similar, frequently occurring, or routine actions expected to be implemented in particular geographic areas.** These are generally categories of actions for which there is a good understanding of the likely effects on resources listed under the ESA, although the categories encompass future site-specific actions of which the precise details are not yet known. They do not rely on, or specifically incorporate by reference, consultations on a higher level of federal action or plan.

> **Programmatic consultations that address a proposed program, plan, policy, or regulation providing a framework for future actions.** These programmatic consultations cover programs, plans, governing policies, or regulations where the action agency is generally not able to provide detailed specificity about the number, location, timing, frequency, precise methods and intensity of the activities expected to be implemented, or to determine the site-specific adverse effects the activities will have on listed species or critical habitat. In these cases, the Service conducts a more generalized review of effects and provides the appropriate Section 7(a)(2) determination in a letter of concurrence or Biological Opinion for the programmatic consultation. In the future, when the site-specific information is known, and it is determined the project "may affect" a listed species or critical habitat, typically a subsequent consultation is completed. That subsequent consultation may be referred to as a "step-down" or "tiered consultation." The subsequent consultation commonly incorporates by reference portions of the previous consultation on the program, plan, policy, or regulations. (83 Fed. Reg. 35,178 (July 25, 2018).)

consequence.[361] As a practical matter, the determination as to whether reasonable and prudent alternatives exists occurs during the Service's review of the Biological Opinion.

If the Biological Opinion concludes that the agency action will not result in jeopardy or adverse habitat modification, or if it offers reasonable and prudent alternatives to avoid that consequence, the Service must provide the agency with a written statement, known as an Incidental Take Statement, specifying the "impact of such incidental taking on the species," any "reasonable and prudent measures that the [Service] considers necessary or appropriate to minimize such impact," and setting forth "the terms and conditions . . . that must be complied with by the [f]ederal agency . . . to implement [those measures]."[362]

The Service must also specify whether any "incidental taking" of protected species will occur, specifically "any taking otherwise prohibited, if such taking is incidental to, and not the purpose of, the carrying out of an otherwise lawful activity."[363] Its determination that an incidental taking will result leads to the publication of the Incidental Take Statement, identifying areas where members of the particular species are at risk.

Formal consultation is terminated with the issuance of the Biological Opinion. If during any stage of consultation, a federal agency determines that its proposed action is not likely to occur, the consultation may be terminated by written notice to the Service. If during any stage of consultation, a federal agency determines, with the concurrence of the Service, that its proposed action is not likely to adversely affect any listed species or critical habitat, the consultation is terminated.[364]

Below is a flowchart showing the formal consultation process (see Figure 1.4.).

Applicant's Role in the Consultation Process

The Section 7 Handbook identifies the applicant's role in the consultation process. If the federal agency identifies an applicant, the Service and the action agency meet their obligations to that party through the following:

> the action agency provides the applicant an opportunity to submit information for consideration during the consultation
> the applicant must be informed by the action agency of the estimated length of any extension of the 180-day timeframe for preparing a Biological Assessment, along with a written statement of the reasons for the extension
> the timeframes for concluding formal consultation cannot be extended beyond 60 days without the applicant's concurrence
> the applicant is entitled to review draft Biological Opinions obtained through the action agency, and to provide comments through the action agency (see further discussion below)

361 *Id.* § 1536(b)(3)(A).
362 *Id.* § 1536(b)(4).
363 *Id.*; 50 C.F.R. § 17.3.
364 50 C.F.R. § 402.14(*l*)(1)–(3).

FIGURE 1-4. FORMAL CONSULTATION PROCESS
Source: Section 7 Handbook at p. 4-3, Fig. 4-1.

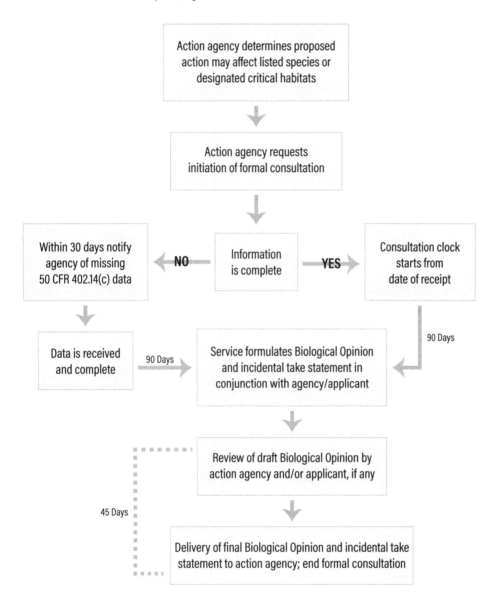

> the Service will discuss the basis of their biological determination with the applicant and seek the applicant's expertise in identifying reasonable and prudent alternatives to the action if likely jeopardy or adverse modification of critical habitat is determined

> the Service provides the applicant with a copy of the final Biological Opinion

The Regulations specify that the Service must not work directly with or take comments directly from the applicant without knowledge or consent of the action agency.[365]

The Section 7 regulations specifically state that the applicant has the ability to participate in the formal consultation process. For example, the regulations state that the action agency must provide the applicant with the opportunity to submit information

365 Section 7 Handbook at p. 2-13.

for consideration during the consultation.[366] In addition, the Service is required to discuss with the action agency and the applicant the Service's review and evaluation and the basis for any finding in the Biological Opinion.[367] The Service is also required to discuss with the action agency and the applicant the availability of reasonable and prudent alternatives (if a jeopardy opinion is to be issued), and to utilize the expertise of the action agency and the applicant in identifying these alternatives.[368]

Perhaps most importantly, the Section 7 regulations allow the applicant to review the draft Biological Opinion. The regulations state:

> The applicant may request a copy of the draft opinion from the [action agency]. All comments on the draft biological opinion must be submitted to the Service through the [action agency], although the applicant may send a copy of its comments directly to the Service. The Service will not issue its biological opinion prior to the 45-day or extended deadline while the draft is under review by the [action agency]. However, if the [action agency] submits comments to the Service regarding the draft biological opinion within 10 days of the deadline for issuing the opinion, the Service is entitled to an automatic 10-day extension on the deadline.[369]

The Section 7 Handbook provides more guidance on the Service's authority to release draft documents for review. According to the Handbook, providing action agencies or applicants an opportunity to discuss a developing Biological Opinion, preliminary opinion, or conference may result in productive discussions that may reduce or eliminate adverse effects. If an action agency asks to review a draft opinion or a draft conference report or opinion, the Service should provide a draft. The Section 7 regulations do not specify how an action agency should ask for this review. Generally, a telephone (or presumably electronic mail) request from the equivalent of a field supervisor or higher official, documented in the administrative record, is sufficient.[370]

Applicants can request draft opinion/conference documents through the action agency. When an action agency then requests this document for the applicant, the Service must inform the action agency that, once released to an applicant, the document may no longer be considered an interagency memorandum exempt from the disclosure requirements of the Freedom of Information Act.[371]

If an action agency or an applicant has comments on a draft opinion or conference document, the action agency must provide those comments to the Service in writing for the record. An applicant may copy the Service with the comments it provides to the

---

366 50 C.F.R. § 402.14(d).

367 *Id.* § 402.14(g)(5).

368 *Id.*

369 *Id.*

370 Section 7 Handbook at p. 1-12.

371 *Id.* (citing 5 U.S.C. § 552(b)(5)).

action agency. The Service will consider an applicant's comments or concerns when they are officially transmitted by the action agency.[372]

Timing Requirements

The Section 7 consultation process has statutory timing requirements.[373] As described above, formal consultation must be concluded within a 90-day period beginning on the date on which the consultation was initiated, or within such other period of time as is mutually agreed upon by the Service and the action agency.[374]

In the case of an agency action involving a permit or license applicant, the Service and the action agency may not mutually agree to conclude consultation within a period exceeding 90 days unless, before the close of the 90th day:

> in the event the consultation period proposed to be agreed to will end before the 150th day after the date on which consultation was initiated, and the Service submits to the applicant a written statement setting forth the reasons why a longer period is required, the information that is required to complete the consultation, and the estimated date on which consultation will be completed; or

> in the event the consultation period proposed to be agreed to will end 150 or more days after the date on which consultation was initiated, and the Service obtains the consent of the applicant to such period[375]

These statutory and regulatory timing requirements for the Section 7 process can be a key factor in evaluating approaches to obtaining incidental take authorization for a project that may impact listed species or their habitat. In contrast to the Section 7 process outlined above, the process for obtaining a Section 10 incidental take permit does not include any similar statutory or regulatory timing requirements. For that reason, obtaining incidental take authorization through the Section 7 process can be quicker and more certain than the Section 10 process. However, because the Section 7 process can only be invoked when a federal agency action is involved (i.e., when the project has a nexus with a federal agency action), such as a Clean Water Act Section 404 permit issued by the U.S. Army Corps of Engineers, the Section 7 incidental take authorization and the timing requirements associated with that process only apply to those projects requiring federal permits, funding, or other federal actions.

Irreversible and Irretrievable Commitment of Resources

An issue that often comes up in the context of Section 7 consultation is the question of whether and to what extent development can go forward during the consultation process.

---

372 *Id.* (citing 50 C.F.R. § 402.14(g)(5)).

373 Practitioners should be aware that the remedy for non-compliance with these timelines exists in the Administrative Procedure Act, not the Endangered Species Act. Under the Administrative Procedure Act, courts must "compel agency action unlawfully withheld or unreasonably delayed" (5 U.S.C. § 555(b)).

374 16 U.S.C. § 1536(b)(1)(A).

375 *Id.* § 1536(b)(1)(B).

PROPOSED REVISIONS TO SECTION 7 REGULATIONS—EXPEDITED CONSULTATIONS

The proposed revisions to the Section 7 regulations include the addition of a new provision titled "Expedited Consultations." This new provision would provide an opportunity for more streamlined consultation, particularly for actions that have minimal adverse effects or predictable effects based on previous consultation experience. As explained in the proposed rule, this consultation process is proposed to provide an efficient means to complete formal consultation on projects ranging from those that have a minimal impact, to those projects with a potentially broad range of effects that are known and predictable, but that are unlikely to cause jeopardy or destruction or adverse modification. The proposed rule cites as an example a habitat-restoration project that results in high conservation value for the species but may have a small amount of incidental take through construction or monitoring. This kind of project would likely lend itself to this type of consultation.

The proposed rule would require two important elements. The first element is the mutual agreement between the Service and the action agency that this form of consultation is appropriate for the proposed action. The second element is the development of a sufficient initiation package (as described in Section 402.14(c) of the regulations) that provides all the information needed to allow the Service to prepare a streamlined consultation response within mutually agreed-upon expedited timeframes. (83 Fed. Reg. 35,178 (July 25, 2018).)

The ESA specifically addresses this issue in Section 7(d). This section specifies that after initiation of formal consultation, the Service and the permit or license applicant may not make "any" irreversible or irretrievable commitment of resources with respect to the agency action which has the effect of foreclosing the formulation or implementation of any reasonable and prudent alternative measures which would avoid jeopardizing the continued existence of listed species or resulting in the destruction or adverse modification of critical habitat.[376] As further stated in the Service's regulations, "This prohibition is in force during the consultation process and continues until the requirements of Section 7(a)(2) are satisfied. This provision does not apply to the conference requirement for proposed species or proposed critical habitat under Section 7(a)(4) of the Act."[377]

The Section 7 Handbook provides some guidance on these statutory provisions. According to the Handbook, Section 7(d) was added to the Act in 1978 as part of the package that created the take exemption process. Congress intended this provision to avoid future Tellico Dam scenarios by forbidding certain irreversible and irretrievable

---

376 16 U.S.C. § 1536(d); 50 C.F.R. § 402.01(a).

377 50 C.F.R. § 402.09.

resource commitments during consultation, thus keeping open all opportunities to develop reasonable and prudent alternatives.[378]

According to the Section 7 Handbook, not all irreversible and irretrievable commitments of resources are prohibited. The formulation or implementation of any reasonable and prudent alternatives must be foreclosed by the resource commitment to violate Section 7(d). Thus, resource commitments may occur as long as the action agency retains sufficient discretion and flexibility to modify its action to allow formulation and implementation of an appropriate reasonable and prudent alternative. Destroying potential alternative habitat within the project area, for example, could violate Section 7(d). This Section 7(d) restriction remains in effect from the determination of "may effect" until the action agency advises the Service which reasonable and prudent alternative will be implemented if the Biological Opinion finds jeopardy or adverse modification. The Section 7 Handbook states that the failure to observe this provision can disqualify the agency or applicant from seeking a take exemption under Section 7.[379]

The action agency may choose not to implement the Service's reasonable and prudent alternative; instead, the action agency can choose to develop an alternative based on what they perceive as the best available scientific and commercial data. It is the responsibility of the action agency, not the Service, to determine the validity of the action agency's alternative. If the agency's alternative is challenged in court, the standard for review will be whether the decision was arbitrary and capricious under the Administrative Procedure Act. The validity of the action agency's decision will determine whether Section 7(a)(2) has been satisfied and whether Section 7(d) is applicable. If it is determined that the action agency's decision is not valid, that agency would be taking the risk of noncompliance with the Act.[380]

The Service does not provide an opinion on the question of resource commitments. Under the exemption process, that question is ultimately referred to the Endangered Species Committee for resolution. However, the Service will notify federal agencies of the Section 7(d) prohibition when formal consultation is initiated. Similarly, under Section 7(c), Biological Assessments must be completed for "major construction activities" before any contracts are entered into or construction is begun.[381]

The Ninth Circuit Court of Appeals has clarified that the prohibition against "irreversible and irretrievable" commitments of resource is not triggered unless and until consultation has been initiated.[382] This is so in those cases involving the reinitiation of consultation, as well.[383] If consultation has been initiated, however, much of the case law on this issue is fairly categorical. For example, in *Lane County Audubon Society v. Jamison*,[384]

---

378 Section 7 Handbook at p. 2-7.

379 *Id.*

380 *Id.* (citing 51 Fed. Reg. 19,940 (June 3, 1986)).

381 *Id.* at pp. 2-7 to 2-8.

382 *Pacific Rivers Council v. Thomas*, 30 F.3d 1050, 1057 (9th Cir. 1994).

383 *Id.* at 1056–57.

384 958 F.2d 290 (9th Cir. 1992).

the Ninth Circuit Court of Appeals held that the Bureau of Land Management could not go forward with any new sales of timber until consultation on a forest management plan and its effect on a threatened species was completed. That court further held that timber sales constituted a per se irreversible and irretrievable commitment of resources under Section 7(d) and thus could not go forward during the consultation period.[385]

Reinitiation of Consultation

Section 7 provides for the reinitiation of the Section 7 consultation process in the event certain changes occur or new information is obtained after the initial process has been completed. According to the Service's regulations:

> Reinitiation of formal consultation is required and shall be requested by the federal agency or by the Service, where discretionary federal involvement or control over the action has been retained or is authorized by law and:

> (1) if the amount of extent of taking specified in the Incidental Take Statement is exceeded

> (2) if new information reveals effects of the action that may affect listed species or critical habitat in a manner or to an extent not previously considered

> (3) if the identified action is subsequently modified in a manner that causes an effect to the listed species or critical habitat that was not considered in the Biological Opinion; or

> (4) if a new species is listed or critical habitat designated that may be affected by the identified action[386]

Caution should be exercised when seeking to "amend" a Biological Opinion in light of "updates" to a Biological Opinion or new information. The Ninth Circuit Court of Appeals has expressed significant reservations about so-called "amendments" to a Biological Opinion, treating them instead as reinitiation triggers. For example, in *Gifford Pinchot Task Force v. U.S. Fish & Wildlife Service*,[387] the Service sought to amend several Biological Opinions to include certain "baseline updates" for a National Forest. The court explained: "As a general rule, such 'updates' are prohibited because they would render the consultation process 'meaningless' and would allow the [Service] to issue 'unsupported Biological Opinions knowing that it could search for evidentiary support if the opinion was later challenged.' As we have recognized, the discovery of new facts does not justify an 'amendment' to the [Biological Opinion], but mandates reinitiating formal consultations."[388]

---

385 *Id.* at 295.

386 50 C.F.R. § 402.16.

387 378 F.3d 1059 (9th Cir. 2004).

388 *Id.* at 1077 (citing *Ariz. Cattle Growers' Ass'n v. U.S. Fish & Wildlife Serv.*, 273 F.3d 1229, 1245 (9th Cir. 2001)).

PROPOSED REVISIONS TO SECTION 7 REGULATIONS— REINITIATION OF CONSULTATION

The proposed revisions to the Section 7 consultations pertaining to reinitiation of consultation comprise two separate changes.

First, the Service proposes to remove the term "formal" from the title and text of this section to acknowledge that the requirement to reinitiate consultation applies to all Section 7(a)(2) consultations.

Second, the Service proposes to amend this section to address issues arising under the Ninth Circuit's decision in *Cottonwood Environmental Law Center v. U.S. Forest Service,* 789 F.3d 1075 (9th Cir. 2015), *cert. denied,* 137 S. Ct. 293 (2016). As explained in the proposed rule, the court in the *Cottonwood* decision held that the Forest Service was required to reinitiate consultation on certain forest management plans due to the designation of Canada lynx critical habitat. The court held that, even if an approved land management plan is considered to be a completed action, the Forest Service nonetheless was obligated to reinitiate consultation since it retained "discretionary [f]ederal involvement or control" over the plan. *Cottonwood,* 789 F.3d at 1084–85.

The Service proposes to clarify that the duty to reinitiate does not apply to an existing programmatic land management plan prepared pursuant to the Federal Land Policy Management Act, 43 U.S.C. § 1701 *et seq.,* or the National Forest Management Act, 16 U.S.C. § 1600 *et seq.* when a new species is listed or new critical habitat is designated.

The proposed rule explains that the Service is reaffirming that only affirmative discretionary actions are subject to reinitiation, and the mere existence of a programmatic land management plan is not affirmative discretionary action. See generally *Southern Utah Wilderness Alliance v. Norton,* 542 U.S. 55 (2004). See also *National Ass'n of Homebuilders v. Defenders of Wildlife,* 551 U.S. 644 (2007).

The proposed rule also explains that this new regulation restates its position that, while a completed programmatic land management plan does not require reinitiation upon the listing of new species or critical habitat, any on-the-ground subsequent actions taken pursuant to the plan must be subject to a separate Section 7 consultation if those actions may affect the newly listed species or critical habitat. (83 Fed. Reg. 35,178 (July 25, 2018).)

The Section 7 Handbook essentially reiterates the Section 7 regulations pertaining to reinitiation of consultation. According to the Handbook, the Section 7 regulations outline four general conditions for reinitiating formal consultation: (1) the amount or extent of incidental take is exceeded; (2) new information reveals effects of the action that may affect listed species or critical habitat in a manner or to an extent not previously considered; (3) the action is modified in a manner causing effects to listed species or critical habitat not previously considered; (4) a new species is listed or critical habitat designated that may be affected by the action.[389]

As described in the Handbook, when the action agency determines that one or more of the four conditions requiring reinitiation of formal consultation has occurred, consultation must be reinitiated. Similarly, if the Service recognizes that any of these conditions have occurred, written advice is provided to the action agency of the need to reinitiate consultation. Documentation of a reinitiated consultation must be in writing, and must contain sufficient information to record the nature of the change in the action's effects and the rationale for amending analyses of anticipated incidental take or the reasonable and prudent alternatives or measures.[390]

Reinitiations involving major changes in effects analyses or changes in the Service's Biological Opinion are addressed fully in a new consultation. A reinitiation based on a new species listing or critical habitat designation is treated as a new consultation, although data in the original opinion may be referenced when the action has not changed.[391]

BIOLOGICAL OPINIONS

Contents of a Biological Opinion

The Act sets forth the required contents of a Biological Opinion:

> [T]he [Service] shall provide to the [action agency] and the applicant, if any, a written statement setting forth the [Service's] opinion, and a summary of the information on which the opinion is based, detailing how the agency action affects the species or its critical habitat. If jeopardy or adverse modification is found, the [Service] shall suggest those reasonable and prudent alternatives which [the Service] believes would not [jeopardize the continued existence of any endangered species or threatened species or result in the destruction or adverse modification of habitat of such species] and can be taken by the [action agency] or applicant in implementing the agency action.[392]

The Service's regulations also set forth certain requirements for a Biological Opinion. As described in the Section 7 regulations, a Biological Opinion must include:

---

389 Section 7 Handbook at p. 4-63.

390 *Id.* at pp. 4-64 to 4-65.

391 *Id.* at p. 4-65.

392 16 U.S.C. § 1536(b)(3)(A).

> a summary of the information on which the opinion is based

> a detailed discussion of the effects of the action on listed species or critical habitat

> the Service's opinion on whether the action is likely to jeopardize the continued existence of a listed species or result in the destruction or adverse modification of critical habitat (a "jeopardy" Biological Opinion); or, the action is not likely to jeopardize the continued existence of a listed species or result in the destruction or adverse modification of critical habitat (a "no jeopardy" Biological Opinion). A "jeopardy" Biological Opinion shall include reasonable and prudent alternatives, if any. If the Service is unable to develop such alternatives, it will indicate that to the best of its knowledge there are no reasonable and prudent alternatives.[393]

In those cases where the Service concludes that an action (or the implementation of any reasonable and prudent alternatives) and the resultant incidental take of listed species will not violate Section 7(a)(2) of the Act, the Service must provide an Incidental Take Statement with the Biological Opinion.

The Service may also provide with the Biological Opinion a statement containing discretionary conservation recommendations. Conservation recommendations are advisory and are not intended to carry any binding legal force.[394]

Incidental Take Statements

Perhaps the most important element of a Biological Opinion is the Incidental Take Statement. The Service must specify in a Biological Opinion whether any "incidental taking" of protected species will occur, specifically "any taking otherwise prohibited, if such taking is incidental to, and not the purpose of, the carrying out of an otherwise lawful activity." The Service's determination that an incidental taking will result leads to the publication of the "Incidental Take Statement," which identifies areas where members of the particular species are at risk.

The Act requires that an Incidental Take Statement:

(i) specifies the impact of such incidental taking on the species

(ii) specifies those reasonable and prudent measures that the [Service] considers necessary or appropriate to minimize such impact

(iii) in the case of marine mammals, specifies those measures that are necessary to comply with [provisions in the U.S. Code regarding the conservation and protection of marine mammals]

(iv) sets forth the terms and conditions (including, but not limited to, reporting requirements) that must be complied with by the federal agency or applicant (if any), or both, to implement the measures specified under clauses (ii) and (iii)[395]

---

393 50 C.F.R. § 402.14(h).

394 *Id.* § 402.14(j).

395 16 U.S.C. § 1536(b)(4)(C).

The Incidental Take Statement functions as a safe harbor provision immunizing persons from Section 9 liability and penalties for takings committed during activities that are otherwise lawful and in compliance with its terms and conditions.[396] If the terms and conditions of the Incidental Take Statement are disregarded and a taking does occur, the action agency or the applicant may be subject to potentially severe civil and criminal penalties under Section 9.[397] The Ninth Circuit has characterized the Incidental Take Statement as "an advisory opinion,"[398] which is consistent with the U.S. Supreme Court's view that the action agency is "technically free to disregard the Biological Opinion and proceed with its proposed action," but that "it does so at its own peril."[399]

In general, Incidental Take Statements set forth a "trigger" that, when reached, results in an unacceptable level of incidental take, invalidating the safe harbor provision, and requiring the parties to reinitiate consultation. Ideally, this "trigger" should be a specific number.[400] For some species or in certain circumstances, it may be difficult to specify the amount or extent of authorized take with any degree of exactness. In *Arizona Cattle Growers' Association v. U.S. Fish & Wildlife Service*,[401] the Ninth Circuit Court of Appeal held that an exact numerical limit is not required. Incidental Take Statements can use a combination of numbers and estimates, so long as the Service establishes that no such numerical value could be practically obtained.[402] In those circumstances, the use of ecological conditions as a surrogate for defining the amount or extent of incidental take is reasonable so long as those conditions are linked to the take of the protected species.[403] The Ninth Circuit has explained that a "causal link" in this context does not mean that the Service must demonstrate a specific number, "only that it must establish a link between the activity and the taking of species before setting forth specific conditions."[404]

One issue that has emerged is when the Service must include an Incidental Take Statement in a Biological Opinion. The Ninth Circuit Court of Appeals in *Arizona Cattle Growers' Association v. U.S. Fish & Wildlife Service* confirmed that the ESA does not dictate that the Service must issue an Incidental Take Statement irrespective of whether any

396 *Id.* § 1536(o) (providing that any such incidental taking "shall not be considered to be a prohibited taking of the species concerned").

397 *Arizona Cattle Growers' Ass'n v. U.S. Fish & Wildlife Service*, 273 F.3d 1229, 1239 (9th Cir. 2001).

398 *Id.*

399 *Bennett v. Spear*, 520 U.S. 154, 170 (1997).

400 *Arizona Cattle Growers' Ass'n*, 273 F.3d at 1249 (citing as examples *Mausolf v. Babbitt*, 125 F.3d 661 (8th Cir. 1997) (snowmobiling activity may take no more than 2 wolves); *Fund for Animals v. Rice*, 85 F.3d 535 (11th Cir. 1996) (municipal landfill may take 52 snakes during construction and an additional 2 snakes per year thereafter); *Mt. Graham Red Squirrel v. Madigan*, 954 F.2d 1441 (9th Cir. 1992) (telescope construction may take 6 red squirrels per year); *Ctr. for Marine Conservation v. Brown*, 917 F. Supp. 1128 (S.D. Tex. 1996) (shrimping operation may take 4 hawksbill turtles, 4 leatherback turtles, 10 Kemp's ridley turtles, 10 green turtles, or 370 loggerhead turtles)).

401 273 F.3d 1229 (9th Cir. 2001).

402 *Id.* at 1250.

403 *Id.* (citing Section 7 Handbook at pp. 4-47 to 4-48).

404 *Id.*

incidental takings will occur.[405] In other words, an Incidental Take Statement is not required if no incidental takings are foreseen.[406] Accordingly, an Incidental Take Statement is required only if a taking will occur. Among other things, the court found persuasive the legislative history behind provisions in the Act explaining that "if the sole purpose of the Incidental Take Statement is to provide shelter from Section 9 penalties, . . . it would be nonsensical to require the issuance of [an] Incidental Take Statement when no takings cognizable under Section 9 are to occur."[407] The court therefore held that "absent rare circumstances such as those involving migratory species, it is arbitrary and capricious to issue an Incidental Take Statement when the Fish and Wildlife Service has no rational basis to conclude that a take will occur incident to the otherwise lawful activity."[408] Put another way, "[I]t would be unreasonable for the Fish and Wildlife Service to impose conditions [pursuant to an Incidental Take Statement] on otherwise lawful land use if a take were not reasonably certain to occur as a result of that activity."[409]

The *Arizona Cattle Growers' Association* decision is important because it effectively requires that a listed species must actually be present on the property in order to justify the Service's imposition of conditions on the lawful use of that land through the Section 7 process.[410] This principle applies even if the concern is prospective, not current, harm to the species. According to the court, "the regulations mandate a separate procedure for reinitiating consultation if different evidence is later developed."[411] Another important principle established by this decision is that the action agency and the applicant are not required "to prove that [a listed species] does not exist on the [property subject to the federal action], . . . both because it would require [the action agency or the applicant] to meet the burden statutorily imposed on the agency, and because it would be requiring [them] to prove a negative."[412] As such, "merely speculative evidence that habitat modification . . . may impact" a listed species is not sufficient to justify the Service's imposition of an Incidental Take Statement and the terms and conditions that attach to it.[413] Without evidence that a take would occur as a result of the action, issuing an Incidental Take Statement imposing conditions on the otherwise lawful use of land is arbitrary and capricious.[414] However, if the Service can articulate a causal connection between the activity and the "actual killing or injury" of a protected species, then the issuance of the Incidental Take Statement will not be considered arbitrary and capricious.[415]

---

405 *Id.* at 1241.

406 *Id.* (citing *National Wildlife Fed'n v. National Park Serv.*, 669 F. Supp. 384, 389–90 (D. Wyo. 1987)).

407 *Id.* (citing H.R. Rep. No. 97-567, at 26 (1982)).

408 *Id.* at 1242.

409 *Id.* at 1243.

410 *Id.* at 1244 ("Where the agency purports to impose conditions on the lawful use of that land without showing that the species exists on it, it acts beyond its authority in violation of [the Administrative Procedure Act].").

411 *Id.*

412 *Id.*

413 *Id.*

414 *Id.* at 1246.

415 *Id.* at 1248–49.

The Section 7 Handbook includes additional guidance regarding the purpose and required contents of an Incidental Take Statement. According to the Handbook, as a matter of policy, the Service requires that an Incidental Take Statement be included in all formal consultations, except those only involving plants, thus assuring the action agency that this element of formal consultation has been considered.

As to the meaning of "incidental take," the Handbook explains that properly interpreting an Incidental Take Statement requires familiarity with Section 9 of the Act, which identifies acts that are prohibited when dealing with any endangered and some threatened species of fish and wildlife. When the consultation involves listed plants, the agency is advised that the Act does not prohibit incidental take of these species. However, as described in the Handbook, the Service may offer cautions regarding the deliberate removal or disturbance of plants. The Ninth Circuit has held that the ESA does not require Biological Opinions to contain Incidental Take Statements for listed plant species.[416]

As discussed above, the term "take" is defined to mean "to harass, harm, pursue, hunt, shoot, wound, kill, trap, capture, or collect, or to attempt to engage in any such conduct." Most of these terms are applied as commonly understood. However, the terms "harass" and "harm" have been further defined by the Service's regulations, as follows:

> Harass means an intentional or negligent act or omission which creates the likelihood of injury to wildlife by annoying it to such an extent as to significantly disrupt normal behavior patterns which include, but are not limited to, breeding, feeding, or sheltering.

> Harm means an act which actually kills or injures wildlife. Such acts may include significant habitat modification or degradation when it actually kills or injures wildlife by significantly impairing essential behavioral patterns including breeding, feeding or sheltering.[417]

A 1981 USFWS Solicitor's opinion (Appendix D, #SO-1) expands on these concepts, concluding that an act that harasses wildlife must demonstrate the likelihood of injury to the species and some degree of fault, whether intentional or negligent. Thus, a private landowner who wishes to develop land that serves as habitat for listed wildlife is not harassing that wildlife if reasonable measures are taken to avoid their injury. However, if the modification of such habitat would likely result in death or injury, the species nevertheless would be "harmed."

---

416 *Center for Biological Diversity v. Bureau of Land Management*, 833 F.3d 1136, 1145 (9th Cir. 2016); see also *Cal. Native Plant Soc'y v. Norton*, No. 01CV1742 DMS, 2004 WL 1118537, at *8 (S.D. Cal. Feb. 10, 2004) ("In the absence of a prohibition on the 'take' of plant species, Defendants are correct that 'such take cannot occur, and no incidental take statement is needed.'"). Cf. *N. Cal. River Watch v. Wilcox*, 547 F. Supp. 2d 1071, 1075 (N.D. Cal. 2008), *aff'd*, 633 F.3d 766 (9th Cir. 2010) ("[S]ection 10—allowing a private party to apply for an incidental take permit—applies only to fish and wildlife; there is no section 10 incidental take permit provision for endangered plants.").

417 50 C.F.R. § 17.3. NMFS has not defined the terms "harass" or "harm."

On June 29, 1995, the Supreme Court upheld the Service's definition of harm to include adverse modification of habitat in *Babbitt v. Sweet Home Chapter of Communities for a Great Oregon*. Identifying habitat modifications that harm individuals of a species involves understanding the species' life history. For example, the Florida scrub jay is highly territorial and relies for its existence on food cached within its territory. A project that destroys occupied habitat and thus the food supply for that family group increases the likelihood of their starvation. Similarly, a number of birds are highly site-tenacious, returning year after year to the same nesting site. Removal of nesting habitat on that site is likely to result in loss of the pair's reproductive capability and may result in loss of the pair for lack of available feeding or nesting habitat. Opening up or fragmenting the habitat may similarly affect the species by introducing increased predation or parasitism.

The Section 7 Handbook further explains that Incidental Take Statements exempt action agencies and their permittees from the Act's Section 9 prohibitions if they comply with the reasonable and prudent measures and the implementing terms and conditions of Incidental Take Statements. In order to be considered in an Incidental Take Statement, any taking associated with an agency's action must meet the following three criteria. The taking must:

> not be likely to jeopardize the continued existence of listed species or destroy or adversely modify designated critical habitat

> result from an otherwise lawful activity

> be incidental to the purpose of the action

An agency action can meet the first criterion if (1) reasonable and prudent alternatives identified in a jeopardy or adverse modification Biological Opinion eliminate the likelihood of jeopardy to the species or adverse modification of designated critical habitat or (2) the Service makes a finding of no jeopardy or no adverse modification. When the taking associated with the proposed action violates any one of these criteria, the Service provides documentation supporting that determination and a statement that such taking is prohibited by Section 9.

In issuing an Incidental Take Statement, the Service provides a statement of anticipated incidental take with reasonable and prudent measures, as appropriate, to minimize such take. This statement provides an exemption from the taking prohibitions of Section 9 only when the agency and/or applicant demonstrate clear compliance with the implementing terms and conditions. These terms and conditions implement reasonable and prudent measures designed to minimize the impact of incidental take on the species as described in the Incidental Take Statement and are binding on the action agency.

In preparing an Incidental Take Statement, the Service is responsible for documenting the amount or extent of take anticipated; writing reasonable and prudent measures with implementing terms and conditions that are clear, precise, and enforceable; and including reporting requirements that assure timely compliance with the terms and conditions described.

NEPA = National Environmental
Policy Act

According to the Section 7 Handbook, the Incidental Take Statement provides non-discretionary measures that are necessary and appropriate to minimize the impact of incidental take. In a Biological Opinion where there are a number of reasonable and prudent alternatives provided to eliminate jeopardy to a species, there may be varying levels of incidental take associated with the alternatives. In that case, the Biological Opinion may contain different Incidental Take Statements, each with reasonable and prudent measures and terms and conditions, for each reasonable and prudent alternative.[418]

Description of the Proposed Action and Scope of the Action Area

The Section 7 Handbook provides helpful guidance on what should be included in the project description in the Biological Opinion. According to the Handbook, the Biological Opinion should provide descriptions of the proposed action and the action area (area including all direct and indirect effects). The description of the proposed action does not have to be comprehensive if details can be referenced from NEPA documents or other descriptions provided. However, some small actions may not have complete or formal descriptions of the proposed action, or the project's components may be scattered throughout a biological evaluation (or similar document), draft NEPA documents, draft plans for different portions of the action, miscellaneous policy and guidance documents, letters, telephone records, meeting notes, and other documents. In such cases, a comprehensive project description in the Biological Opinion is vital to determining the scope of the proposed action. The Service provides the draft project description to the action agency for review to eliminate any inaccuracies regarding the scope of the action. This section should summarize enough information for the reader to understand and evaluate the action under consideration in the Biological Opinion.[419]

An important component of the description of the proposed action is the definition of the "action area." Subsequent analyses of the environmental baseline, effects of the action, and levels of incidental take are based upon the action area as determined by the Service. If the Service determines that the action area differs from that described by the action agency or applicant, the Service should discuss its rationale for the change with the action agency or applicant. Occasionally, an action agency or an applicant disagrees with the Service's delineation of the action area. This generally occurs when impacts to the species/habitat result from indirect or interrelated/interdependent effects. Reaching agreement on the description of the action area is desirable, but ultimately the Service is responsible for this biological determination.[420]

Determining the action area relates only to the action proposed by the action agency. Even if the applicant has an alternative not requiring federal permits or funding, this does not enter into the Service's analysis. Such alternatives can be discussed in the reasonable and prudent alternatives or conservation recommendations if the alternative

418 Section 7 Handbook at p. 4-53.

419 *Id.* at p. 4-15.

420 *Id.* at p. 4-53.

THE ENBRIDGE DECISION

An important case concerning the scope of the Service's take authorization under Section 7 is *Sierra Club v. United States Army Corps of Engineers*, 803 F.3d 31 (D.C. Cir. 2015), sometimes referred to as the "Enbridge decision." The Enbridge decision presented an interesting challenge for California projects resulting in take of both aquatic and terrestrial species, including species (e.g., California red-legged frog, California tiger salamander) that depend on both aquatic and terrestrial environments. Because Enbridge purports to limit the scope of a Section 7 Incidental Take Statement to take occurring within the limits of Corps jurisdiction, an applicant would be required to supplement the Section 7 take statement with an *additional* incidental take permit under Section 10 of the ESA in accordance with a habitat conservation plan. It did not take long for the Corps and the Service to recognize the inefficiencies associated with such a result.

In 2017, accordingly, the Corps and the Service exchanged letters identifying a workaround to the Enbridge problem. Under this agreement in principle, the Corps would initiate formal consultation by providing a Biological Assessment that "evaluates the larger project as a whole and is inclusive of all anticipated effects of the larger project (including those resulting from interrelated or inter-dependent activities) to listed species and critical habitat, along with consideration of cumulative effects." In its Incidental Take Statement, the Service would provide coverage for all of those impacts, distinguishing between those falling within the Corps' jurisdiction and those that "must be implemented directly by the applicant if the take exemption is to apply."

Recognizing the potential Enbridge problem, the Service indicated that it "will exercise its enforcement discretion and not [S]ection 11(e) enforcement action against the applicant in these situations . . . ," but recognized that the applicant may still face some exposure to a citizen suit brought under Section 11(g) of the ESA.

The Corps and the Service have in fact been following this process in California. Should the Trump Administration succeed in limiting significantly the definition of waters of the United States, then this process may ultimately be put to the test through judicial challenge. The authors believe this process to be defensible, but the question has yet to be decided.

California tiger salamander. Photo: USFW. Licensed under CC 2.0.

California red-legged frog. Photo: John Kunna. Licensed under CC 2.0.

is within the agency's jurisdiction. The action area should be determined based on consideration of all direct and indirect effects of the proposed agency action. For example, if the proposed action is a wetland fill (requiring a federal permit) to accommodate access to a proposed development (the actual area of impact to the species), then the development is included in the action area. Whether or not the applicant can build a road that does not impact the wetland, the analysis of effects of the action still encompasses the proposed development.[421]

Describing the proposed action also includes any conservation measures proposed as part of the action. When used in the context of the Act, "conservation measures" represent actions pledged in the project description that the action agency or the applicant will implement to further the recovery of the species under review. Such measures may be tasks recommended in the species' recovery plan, should be closely related to the action, and should be achievable within the authority of the action agency or applicant. For example, degraded habitat acquired by the applicant adjacent to the area to be developed may be improved as a conservation measure prior to project completion so that individuals depending on the habitat to be destroyed by development can be relocated or allowed to relocate on the improved site.[422]

In this example, the activity carries out a recognized conservation need for the species. The beneficial effects of the conservation measure are taken into consideration for both jeopardy and incidental take analyses. However, the Section 7 Handbook reminds the reader that the objective of the incidental take analysis under Section 7 is minimization, not mitigation. If the conservation measure only protects off-site habitat and does not minimize impacts to affected individuals in the action area, the beneficial effects of the conservation measure are irrelevant to the incidental take analysis. Since conservation measures are part of the proposed action, their implementation is required under the terms of the consultation. However, conservation recommendations (which may be provided at the end of the consultation package) are discretionary suggestions made by the Service for consideration by the action agency or applicant.[423]

On the following pages are illustrations from the Section 7 Handbook that provide useful guidance in determining the scope of an action area (see Figures 1-5, 1-6, 1-7, 1-8).

Environmental Baseline

For purposes of Section 7, the environmental baseline is defined under current regulations as the past and present impacts of all federal, state, or private actions and other human activities in an action area, the anticipated impacts of all proposed federal projects in an action area that have already undergone formal or early Section 7 consultation, and the impact of state or private actions that are contemporaneous with the consultation in process.[424]

421 *Id.* at p. 4-18.
422 *Id.* at p. 4-19.
423 *Id.*
424 50 C.F.R. § 402.02.

The Section 7 Handbook provides additional guidance on what constitutes the environmental baseline for purposes of a Biological Opinion. According to the Handbook, the environmental baseline section of the Biological Opinion includes an analysis of the effects of past and ongoing human and natural factors leading to the current status of the species, its habitat (including designated critical habitat), and ecosystem, within the action area. The environmental baseline is a "snapshot" of a species' health at a specified point in time. It does not include the effects of the action under review in the consultation.[425]

As to the status of the species within the action area, unless the species' range is wholly contained within the action area, this analysis is a subset of the species' range-wide status. The purpose is to analyze the effects on the species and/or critical habitat at the action level. For example, the following issues are considered:

> the percent or amount of the species range or designated critical habitat in the action area

> whether the effect is quantitative, qualitative, or both

> the distribution of the affected and unaffected habitat

> if critical habitat will be impacted, the effect on the constituent elements

As to the factors affecting the species environment within the action area, this analysis describes factors affecting the environment of the species or critical habitat in the action area. The baseline includes state, tribal, local, and private actions already affecting the species or that will occur contemporaneously with the consultation in progress. Unrelated federal actions affecting the same species or critical habitat that have completed formal or informal consultation are also part of the environmental baseline, as are federal and other actions within the action area that may benefit listed species or critical habitat.[426]

An agency action can be removed from the environmental baseline analysis under any of the following conditions:

> an action agency notifies the Services in writing that a previously proposed action will not be implemented

> a Biological Opinion for the proposed action (not an ongoing action) is no longer valid because reinitiation of consultation is required and the action agency has been so informed in writing by the Service, or has requested that the Service reinitiate consultation

> alternatives have been implemented that remove all adverse effects[427]

An important case involving environmental baselines in the context of a Section 7 Biological Opinion is *National Wildlife Federation v. National Marine Fisheries Service*.[428] In this case, NMFS issued a Biological Opinion addressing the effects of proposed operations of the Federal Columbia River Power System dams and related facilities on listed fish in the lower Columbia and Snake Rivers. NMFS found that these operations would not jeopardize the 13 salmonid species listed as threatened or endangered in the area,

---

425 Section 7 Handbook at p. 4-22.

426 *Id.*

427 *Id.* at p. 4-23.

428 524 F.3d 917 (9th Cir. 2008).

FIGURE 1-5. EXAMPLE OF AN ACTION AREA WITHIN THE SPECIES RANGE
Source: Section 7 Handbook at p. 4-16, Fig. 4-3.

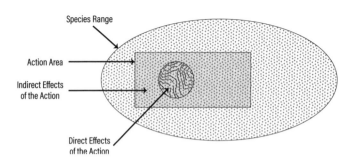

FIGURE 1-6. EXAMPLE OF AN ACTION AREA THAT ENCOMPASSES THE SPECIES RANGE
Source: Section 7 Handbook at p. 4-16, Fig. 4-4.

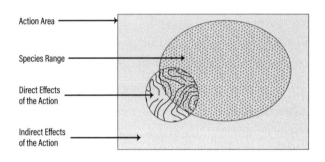

FIGURE 1-7. DETERMINING THE ACTION AREA
Source: Section 7 Handbook at p. 4-18, Fig. 4-6.

A dam on the Platte River in Colorado (project site) also may affect the water regime for whooping crane critical habitat (action area) 150 miles downstream in Nebraska.

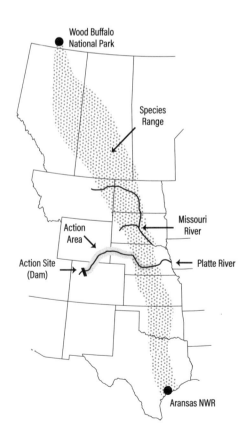

FIGURE 1-8. EXAMPLE OF AN ACTION AREA
INVOLVING AN EFFECT NOT AT THE PROJECT SITE

Source: Section 7 Handbook at p. 4-17, Fig. 4-5.

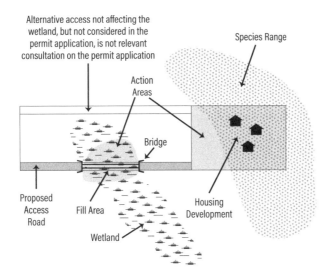

nor would the operations adversely modify their critical habitat. In so doing, NMFS included in the environmental baseline for the proposed action the existing operations, various supposedly nondiscretionary dam operations, and all past and present impacts from discretionary operations. NMFS also adopted a "reference operation" approach, purportedly in order to account for the existence of the system's dams. The reference operation consisted of the dams and a hypothetical regime for operating them, which, according to NMFS, was the most beneficial to listed fishes of any possible operating regime. NMFS also found, though, that certain aspects of FCRPS operations—such as operations relating to irrigation, flood control, and power generation—were nondiscretionary, given the dams' existence, and that those aspects should not be considered part of the action under ESA review.[429]

The Ninth Circuit Court of Appeals held that the Biological Opinion impermissibly failed to incorporate degraded baseline conditions into its jeopardy analysis. According to the court, the Biological Opinion initially evaluated the effects of the proposed action as compared to the reference operation, rather than focusing its analysis on whether the action effects, when added to the underlying baseline conditions, would tip the species into jeopardy. The court explained that "even where baseline conditions already jeopardize a species, an agency may not take action that deepens the jeopardy by causing additional harm."[430] The court noted that this approach is consistent with its prior decisions concerning baseline analyses for Section 7: "[t]he proper baseline analysis is not the

429 *Id.* at 925–26.

430 *Id.* at 930.

PROPOSED REVISIONS TO SECTION 7 REGULATIONS—DEFINITION OF EFFECTS

The reader should note that, under the Proposed Regulations, these various categories of effects (i.e., direct, indirect, cumulative and those of interrelated and interdependent actions) would be eliminated and replaced with a single definition of effects that includes "all effects on the listed species or critical habitat that are caused by the proposed action, including the effects of other activities that are caused by the proposed action." This new definition essentially captures how the Service already, as described below, employs a "but for" causation test in evaluating effects under the Section 7 Handbook (particularly with respect to interrelated and interdependent actions). That is, effects include any that are "caused by" the proposed action, and an effect is not caused by the action unless "the effect . . . or activity . . . would not occur but for the proposed action and it is reasonably certain to occur." (83 Fed. Reg. 35,178 (July 25, 2018).)

proportional share of responsibility the federal agency bears for the decline in the species, but what jeopardy might result from the agency's proposed actions in the present and future human and natural contexts."[431]

Effects of the Action

The Section 7 Handbook provides guidance on the "effects of the action" section in a Biological Opinion. As the Handbook explains, this section includes an analysis of the direct, indirect, and cumulative effects of the proposed action on the species and/or critical habitat and its interrelated and interdependent activities. See discussion below regarding the scope of the effects analysis and how these effects are defined and analyzed.

Scope of Analysis and Factors to Be Considered

The case law indicates that a negative impact on listed species is the likely direct or indirect effect of an agency's action only if the agency has some control over that result. Otherwise, the requisite nexus is absent. For example, in *National Wildlife Federation v. Coleman*, the Fifth Circuit Court of Appeals held in one of the earliest and most important cases on the issue of indirect effects under Section 7 that the Department of Transportation was responsible for development encouraged by interstate highway construction, because the Department did "control this development to the extent that [it] control[s] the placement of the highway and interchanges."[432]

A similar standard was endorsed by the U.S. Supreme Court in *Department of Transportation v. Public Citizen*[433] in the context of the National Environmental Policy

---

431 *Id.* (citing *Pac. Coast Fed'n of Fishermen's Ass'ns v. U.S. Bureau of Reclamation*, 426 F.3d 1082, 1093 (9th Cir. 2005)).

432 529 F.2d 359, 374 (5th Cir. 1976).

433 541 U.S. 752 (2004).

Act. *Public Citizen* concerned the application of NEPA regulations to the U.S. Department of Transportation's regulations governing safety rules for Mexican trucks traveling on American roads. The NEPA regulations share with the ESA regulations a similar definition of "indirect effects."[434] The question in *Public Citizen* was whether the Department of Transportation was required under NEPA to develop an Environmental Impact Statement with regard to the pollution caused by the entry of Mexican trucks onto U.S. highways under the North American Free Trade Agreement. The Court held "that where an agency has no ability to prevent a certain effect due to its limited statutory authority over the relevant actions, the agency cannot be considered a legally relevant 'cause' of the effect."[435]

The U.S. Supreme Court relied on the reasoning in *Public Citizen* to articulate the principle that "an agency cannot be considered the legal 'cause' of an action that it has no statutory discretion not to take."[436] In *National Association of Homebuilders v. Defenders of Wildlife*,[437] the Court considered the State of Arizona's application to run the Clean Water Act pollution permitting program in Arizona, and in connection with the decision whether to transfer this permitting authority from EPA to the state, the Service's decision to issue a Biological Opinion premised on the proposition that EPA lacked the authority to take into account the impact of that decision on endangered species and their habitat. The Court explained that: "[Section 7's] no-jeopardy duty covers only discretionary agency actions and does not attach to actions (like the NPDES permitting transfer authorization) that an agency is required by statute to undertake once certain specified triggering events have occurred." The Court held that deference was due to the Service's reasonable interpretation of Section 7 as applying only to "actions in which there is discretionary Federal involvement or control," and that since the transfer of NPDES permitting authority is not discretionary, but rather is mandated once a state has met the criteria set forth in the Clean Water Act, it follows that a transfer of NPDES permitting authority does not trigger Section 7's consultation and no-jeopardy requirements.

The Section 7 Handbook describes eight factors that should be considered in the analysis of a proposed action's effects on species and their habitat. These factors include:

> **Proximity of the action:** to the species, management units, or designated critical habitat units.

> **Distribution:** geographic areas where the disturbance occurs (e.g., may be several small or one large area).

> **Timing:** relationship to sensitive periods of a species' lifecycle.

---

434 Compare 40 C.F.R. § 1508.8(b) ("Indirect effects . . . are caused by the action and are later in time or farther removed in distance, but are still reasonably foreseeable.") with 50 C.F.R. § 402.02 ("Indirect effects are those that are caused by the proposed action and are later in time, but still are reasonably certain to occur.").

435 *Pub. Citizen*, 541 U.S. at 770; see also *id.* at 767 (analogizing "cause" inquiry for purpose of defining "indirect effects" to proximate cause inquiry in tort law).

436 *National Ass'n of Homebuilders v. Defenders of Wildlife*, 551 U.S. 644, 667 (2007).

437 551 U.S. 644 (2007).

> **Nature of the effect**: effects of the action on elements of a species' lifecycle, population size or variability, or distribution; or on the primary constituent elements of the critical habitat, including direct and indirect effects.

> **Duration:** The effects of a proposed action on listed species or critical habitat depend largely on the duration of its effects. Three potential categories of effects are: (1) a short-term event whose effects are relaxed almost immediately (pulse effect), (2) a sustained, long-term, or chronic event whose effects are not relaxed (press effect), or (3) a permanent event that sets a new threshold for some feature of a species' environment (threshold effect). For many species, a proposed action producing a single, short-term effect is less likely to jeopardize the continued existence of a species than a long-term chronic event or the permanent alteration of a species' habitat.

> **Disturbance frequency:** the mean number of events per unit of time affects a species differently depending on its recovery rate. If the disturbance frequency is less than the species' recovery rate, the species might persist in the face of the disturbance. If the disturbance frequency equals the species' recovery rate, the species becomes more sensitive to the effects of other disturbances. If the disturbance frequency is greater than a species' recovery rate, the species will be unable to recover between disturbances. Disturbance frequency is an important consideration when evaluating the accumulating effects of proposed actions on listed species and/or designated critical habitat, particularly when it is combined with information on a species' recovery rate.

> **Disturbance intensity:** the effect of the disturbance on a population or species as a function of the population or species' state after the disturbance. For example, a disturbance reducing the size of a population or critical habitat unit by 40 percent is more intense than a disturbance reducing population or unit size by 10 percent.

> **Disturbance severity:** the effect of a disturbance on a population or species as a function of recovery rate. The longer the recovery rate, the more severe the disturbance. For example, a disturbance from which a species or habitat takes 10 years to recover is more severe than a disturbance requiring 2 years for recovery. A severe disturbance makes a population or species more susceptible to the effects of multiple actions.

Analysis of Direct Effects

The Section 7 Handbook defines "direct effects" as the direct or immediate effects of the project on the species or its habitat, e.g., driving an off-road vehicle through the nesting habitat of the piping plover may destroy its ground nest; building a housing unit may destroy the habitat of an endangered mouse. Direct effects result from the agency action including the effects of interrelated actions and interdependent actions (see below for more details). Future federal actions that are not a direct effect of the action under consideration (and not included in the environmental baseline or treated as indirect effects) are not considered in a Biological Opinion, as those actions would themselves be subject to the Section 7 consultation process.

Analysis of Indirect Effects

The Section 7 Handbook defines "indirect effects" as being caused by or result from the proposed action, are later in time, and are reasonably certain to occur, e.g., predators may follow off-road vehicle tracks into piping plover nesting habitat and destroy nests; the people moving into the housing unit bring cats that prey on the listed mice located in the adjacent habitat. Indirect effects may occur outside of the area directly affected by the action.

Indirect effects may include other federal actions that have not undergone Section 7 consultation but will result from the action under consideration. In order to treat these actions as indirect effects in the Biological Opinion, they must be reasonably certain to occur, as evidenced by appropriations, work plans, permits issued, or budgeting; they follow a pattern of activity undertaken by the agency in the action area; or they are a logical extension of the proposed action.

Non-federal activities with indirect effects can also be predicted, particularly for ongoing projects that have a past pattern of use that is anticipated to continue. The Section 7 Handbook provides an example of such a situation. A very complex example of indirect effects arose in determining effects of renewing water service contracts from a large reclamation project (Friant Unit of the Central Valley Project) in the San Joaquin Valley of California. Upon checking with other federal and state agencies, the Service determined that the distribution of water for agricultural use on the higher east side of the Valley provided a hydrologic head maintaining the groundwater table on the west side of the Valley at a level making it economical to pump. As a result, occupied habitats for several species on the west side of the Valley were being destroyed because the pumped water could be used to convert this land to agriculture. The California Department of Water Resources provided trend data indicating a continuing conversion of habitat of 10,000 to 30,000 acres per year. These data were used to assess future non-federal effects of the project.

Several court cases provide examples of indirect effects of a proposed action. In *National Wildlife Federation v. Coleman*,[438] the court ruled that indirect effects of private development resulting from proposed construction of highway interchanges had to be considered as impacts of a proposed federal highway project, even though the private development had not been planned at the time the highway project was proposed. In another case, *Riverside Irrigation District v. Andrews*,[439] the court ruled that the U.S. Army Corps of Engineers must consider the effects of consumptive water uses made

438 529 F.2d 359 (5th Cir.), *cert. denied,* 429 U.S. 979 (1976).

439 758 F.2d 508 (10th Cir. 1985).

possible by a proposed dam on critical habitat for whooping cranes 150 miles away, in addition to the local impacts of placing fill for the dam.

Analysis of Cumulative Effects

The Section 7 Handbook provides guidance on the analysis of cumulative effects. According to the Handbook, the Section 7 regulations require the action agency to provide an analysis of cumulative effects, along with other information, when requesting initiation of formal consultation. Additionally, the Service is required to consider cumulative effects in formulating their Biological Opinions.

The Handbook sets forth the following paragraph it advises the Service to use to introduce the cumulative effects section in a Biological Opinion:

> Cumulative effects include the effects of future State, tribal, local or private actions that are reasonably certain to occur in the action area considered in this biological opinion. Future Federal actions that are unrelated to the proposed action are not considered in this section because they require separate consultation pursuant to section 7 of the Act.

According to the Handbook, the concept of cumulative effects is frequently misunderstood as it relates to determining likely jeopardy or adverse modification. Cumulative effects include effects of future state, tribal, local, and private actions, not involving a federal action, that are reasonably certain to occur within the action area under consideration. Future federal actions requiring separate consultation (unrelated to the proposed action) are not considered in the cumulative effects section.

As the Handbook explains, the "reasonably certain to occur" clause is a key factor in assessing and applying cumulative effects in Biological Opinions. First, cumulative effects involve only future non-federal actions: past and present impacts of non-federal actions are part of the environmental baseline. Indicators of actions "reasonably certain to occur" may include but are not limited to: approval of the action by state, tribal or local agencies or governments (e.g., permits, grants); indications by state, tribal or local agencies or governments that granting authority for the action is imminent; project sponsors' assurance the action will proceed; obligation of venture capital; or initiation of contracts.

The more state, tribal or local administrative discretion remaining to be exercised before a proposed non-federal action can proceed, the less there is a reasonable certainty the project will be authorized. Speculative non-federal actions that may never be implemented are not factored into the "cumulative effects" analysis. At the same time, "reasonably certain to occur" does not require a guarantee the action will occur. The action agency and the Service should consider the economic, administrative, and legal hurdles remaining before the action proceeds.

The Handbook provides the following example to help illustrate these points.

Formal consultation was conducted with the Federal Highway Administration (FHWA) on construction of a new highway in Latimer County, Oklahoma. The endangered American burying beetle is known to use forest and forest/edge habitats within the immediate area of the highway, and activities disturbing the soil surface of the beetle's habitat can impact reproduction. Intensive surface mining for coal and natural gas development were occurring in Latimer County and within the action area. Both of these activities would "benefit" from the new highway but were independent of the highway construction. Coal mining, regulated by the Office of Surface Mining, was not considered a cumulative effect because it requires section 7 consultation. Future natural gas development is a cumulative effect as it is regulated by the State. The frequent occurrence of new drilling sites in the area indicated this activity was "reasonably certain to occur" in the future. Further, several landowners in the action area had recently signed contracts to sell their mineral rights to gas companies.

The cumulative effects analysis is the last step or factor considered in formulating the Biological Opinion. Sometimes, cumulative effects can be the deciding factor in determining the likelihood of jeopardy or adverse modification. However, this is frequently the least documented part of Biological Opinions, due to the lack of definitive information on future state, tribal, local, or private actions that are unrelated to the action undergoing consultation.

Gathering information on cumulative effects often requires more effort than merely gathering information on a proposed action. One of the first places to seek cumulative effects information is in documents provided by the action agency such as NEPA analyses for the action. The Service can review the broader NEPA discussion of cumulative effects and apply the Act's narrower cumulative effects definition.

When addressing a Section 7 action within a larger Section 10(a)(1)(B) planning area, non-federal proposals for development in the Habitat Conservation Plan (HCP) are considered cumulative effects for that planning area until the Section 7 consultation for the Section 10(a)(1)(B) permit is completed, at which time the effects of those projects become part of the environmental baseline for future consultations.

Analysis of Interrelated and Interdependent Actions

The Section 7 Handbook provides guidance on analyzing "interrelated and interdependent actions." According to the Handbook, effects of the action under consultation are analyzed together with the effects of other activities that are interrelated to, or interdependent with, that action.

An interrelated activity is an activity that is part of the proposed action and depends on the proposed action for its justification. An interdependent activity is an activity that has no independent utility apart from the action under consultation.[440]

As a practical matter, the analysis of whether other activities are interrelated to, or interdependent with, the proposed action under consultation should be conducted by applying a "but for" test. The biologist should ask whether another activity in question would occur "but for" the proposed action under consultation. If the answer is "no," that the activity in question would not occur but for the proposed action, then the activity is interrelated or interdependent and should be analyzed with the effects of the action. If the answer is "yes," that the activity in question would occur regardless of the proposed action under consultation, then the activity is not interdependent or interrelated and would not be analyzed with the effects of the action under consultation.

The Handbook points out that interrelated or interdependent activities are measured against the proposed action. That is, the relevant inquiry is whether the activity in question should be analyzed with the effects of the action under consultation because it is interrelated to, or interdependent with, the proposed action. The Handbook cautions against reversing this analysis by analyzing the relationship of the proposed action against the other activity. For example, as cited below, if the proposed action is the addition of a second turbine to an existing dam, the question is whether the dam (the other activity) is interrelated to or interdependent with the proposed action (the addition of the turbine), not the reverse.

The Handbook provides examples to help the reader "better understand how the interdependent or interrelated analysis should work."

> **First example:** The Corps of Engineers requests consultation for construction of a dam which requires a section 404 permit. The dam will provide water to private irrigation canals that will come on line once the dam is completed. The private irrigation canals are interrelated to the proposed dam and must be considered in a biological opinion for the larger water development project since they would not be in existence "but for" the presence of the proposed dam under consultation. Similarly, a power turbine to be constructed concurrently with the dam cannot function and has no independent utility "but for" the dam and is, therefore, interrelated with the project. Thus, the effects of this turbine on fish passage and water quality are to be considered in the biological opinion on the proposed dam.

440 Section 7 Handbook at p. 4-27. The Handbook specifically identifies language in the Section 7 regulations that it characterizes as confusing. According to the Handbook,
> [T]he regulations refer to the action under consultation as the "larger action." In fact, the use of the term "larger" has proven to be confusing when applied in the case of a modification to an existing project. Instead of keeping the inquiry on whether other activities are interrelated to or interdependent with the modification, it has unintentionally and inappropriately shifted the focus to an inquiry on whether the modification itself is interrelated to or interdependent with the "larger" action or project.

Id. (citing 50 C.F.R. § 402.02).

Ten years after construction of the dam, a federal permit is needed to add a second turbine to the dam to increase power generation. The addition of the turbine, as the proposed action under consultation, is now the "larger action" against which the "but for" test for interrelated or interdependent effects would be applied. The pre-existing dam has independent utility without the new turbine and therefore is not interrelated to, or interdependent with, the proposed action. Ongoing effects of the existing dam are already included in the Environmental Baseline and would not be considered an effect of the proposed action under consultation. Activities which would be interdependent and interrelated to the proposed turbine could include construction of new power lines or conversion of natural habitat if the additional power capacity allowed for the development of a manufacturing facility that was dependent upon the new power grid.

Later, a new federal safety law requires the dam operator to construct a fuse plug on an existing spillway which improves response to emergency flood conditions. Construction of the fuse plug is now the proposed "larger action." Again, the existing dam is not interdependent or interrelated to the proposed fuse plug because it does not depend upon the proposed action for its existence. That is, the test is not whether the fuse plug in some way assists or facilitates in the continued operation of the pre-existing project, but instead whether the water project could not exist "but for" the fuse plug. Because the answer is that the project would exist independent of the fuse plug, the operation of that project is not interrelated or interdependent. Accordingly, the biologist would not consider the effects of the dam to be effects of the "larger" action under consultation (the proposed construction of the fuse plug). However, if the fuse plug would allow a greater flow of water through the spillway, thereby requiring the operator to increase the depth of the spillway channel and armor it with concrete, such activities would be interrelated to the proposed action.

Second example: Another example would be a proposed agency action to enlarge the water supply storage capacity of an existing flood control reservoir. An existing water supply system into which the stored water will be released does not depend on the proposed action, and hence is not interrelated.

When one or more Federal actions are determined by the Services to be interdependent or interrelated to the proposed action, or are indirect effects of the proposed action, they are combined in the consultation and a lead agency is determined for the overall consultation.

The "but for" analysis used for interdependent or interrelated actions has been upheld by the Ninth Circuit Court of Appeals. In *Sierra Club v. Bureau of Land Management*,[441] plaintiffs challenged a decision by the U.S. Bureau of Land Management to grant a right-of-way over federal land for a wind energy project developed on private land by a renewable energy company. Plaintiffs argued that the BLM was required to consider the effects of the wind project as an activity interrelated to and/or interdependent with the road project, thereby requiring consultation under the ESA. The court found that the private wind project was not part of the federal road project and was not dependent on it. Because the renewable energy company was prepared to use a private access road to complete the wind project if the federal road project did not materialize, the federal road project was not the "but for" cause of the private wind project. The court noted further that both projects were independent and had utility separate and apart from each other: "the wind project was viable with or without the right-of-way over federal land, and the road project served the independent purposes of dust control, reducing erosion, and controlling unauthorized vehicle access to a national trail." The court concluded: "In sum, these projects fail the 'but for' causation test, and neither is an integral part of the other, neither depends on the other for its justification, and each has utility independent from the other."[442]

Analysis of Beneficial Effects

Beneficial effects are defined in the Section 7 Handbook as those effects of an action that are wholly positive, without any adverse effects, on a listed species or designated critical habitat.[443] Determination that an action will have beneficial effects is a "may affect" situation. However, since there are no adverse effects, formal consultation is not required. Biological Opinions may discuss beneficial effects if the applicant requests it, or if a Biological Assessment considers numerous species, some with adverse effects, and one or more with beneficial effects.

The Handbook provides the following example. The National Park Service proposes to modify an existing rock climbing management plan that allows climbing in historic peregrine falcon nesting areas. The new plan restricts climbing activities to areas outside of a zone 1/4 mile-wide on either side of active peregrine falcon aeries during the breeding season. This protects the birds from human disturbance and eliminates take that could occur if an adult was flushed from an aerie with eggs or young needing incubation or brooding to survive. Therefore, the effects are wholly beneficial.[444]

---

441 786 F.3d 1219 (9th Cir. 2015).

442 *Id.* at 1225.

443 Section 7 Handbook at p. 4-25.

444 *Id.*

Jeopardy Analysis

The Section 7 Handbook provides helpful guidance in understanding the Service's approach to the jeopardy analysis in a Biological Opinion.

In determining whether an action is likely to jeopardize the continued existence of a species, the action is viewed against the aggregate effects of everything that has led to the species' current status and, for non-federal activities, those things likely to affect the species in the future. At this point, the biologist sums up the previous analyses done to determine (1) the status of the species, (2) the environmental baseline, (3) all effects of the proposed action, and (4) the cumulative effects of other anticipated actions. The final analysis then looks at whether, given the aggregate effects, the species can be expected to both survive and recover, as those terms are defined above. For the jeopardy analysis, this survival is framed in terms of the species' reproduction, numbers, and distribution in the wild.

The Section 7 Handbook discusses the Service's application of the jeopardy standard to an entire species. According to the Handbook, generally a jeopardy opinion is rendered when the total of the species' status, environmental baseline, effects of the proposed action, and cumulative effects lead to the conclusion that the proposed action is likely to jeopardize the continued existence of the entire species, subspecies, or vertebrate population as listed. The Handbook notes that for some wide-ranging species or those with disjunct or fragmented distributions, however, strict adherence to this general policy can result in significant accumulated losses of habitat and population that may, in total, result in a jeopardy situation. The Handbook explains further that in the past, exceptions from applying the jeopardy standard to an entire species were granted by memorandum for specific populations or "recovery units" of a species. The Handbook states that limiting the exceptions to those populations/recovery units listed in a memorandum is "hereby discontinued and all future exceptions will adhere" to guidance discussed below regarding distinct population segments.[445]

As explained in the Section 7 Handbook, jeopardy analyses may be based on an assessment of impacts to distinct population segments (DPS) of a species documented per the Services' joint policy on DPS (1995) in a final listing rule, or to a DPS as identified in a NMFS recovery plan, or to recovery units when those units are documented as necessary to both the survival and recovery of the species in a final recovery plan, for which a notice of availability has been published in the Federal Register. For species which had recovery plan notices published prior to this guidance, an addendum to the recovery plan, documenting the need to evaluate jeopardy on separate recovery units, can be written, and notice of its availability should be published in the Federal Register.[446]

According to the Service and as described in the Section 7 Handbook, at publication a species' recovery plan lays out the best available scientific information relative to the areas and environmental elements needed for that species to recover. Recovery plans

---

445 Section 7 Handbook at p. 4-38.

446 *Id.*

may geographically describe actual recovery units (e.g., show lines on a map) essential to recovering the species that may or may not have been designated as critical habitat. When an action appreciably impairs or precludes the capability of a recovery unit from providing both the survival and recovery function assigned it, that action may represent jeopardy to the species. When using this type of analysis, the Service should include in the Biological Opinion a description of how the action affects not only the recovery unit's capability, but the relationship of the recovery unit to both the survival and recovery of the listed species as a whole.[447]

The Ninth Circuit Court of Appeals has suggested that although the ESA does not require Biological Opinions to include Incidental Take Statements for listed plant species, the ESA does require the Service to evaluate whether a proposed action would result in jeopardy to listed plant species. In *Center for Biological Diversity v. Bureau of Land Management*,[448] the Ninth Circuit considered the Service's evaluation of a threatened plant species (Peirson's milkvetch) in the context of Section 7 consultation for a BLM proposal to expand access for off-road vehicles in a special management area. The court explained that Section 7 requires action agencies to "insure that any action authorized, funded, or carried out by such agency . . . does not jeopardize the continued existence of any endangered species or threatened species . . . ." and that consultation results in a Biological Opinion summarizing the relevant findings and determining whether the proposed action is "likely to jeopardize the continued existence of the species." Without reaching a holding on the issue, the court suggested that the Service is required under Section 7 to evaluate whether an agency action will result in jeopardy to a listed plant species, even though the Service is not required to issue an Incidental Take Statement for that plant species.[449]

Other court decisions provide additional guidance on the Service's methodology and approach to analyzing jeopardy. As discussed below, certain themes have emerged as a result of this case law.

Using Habitat as a Proxy for Individual Species. The use of habitat as a proxy for evaluating jeopardy of individual species has been upheld by the courts. In certain circumstances, this metric may be the only tool available to evaluate impacts from a proposed action. It may not be possible to identify a precise number of individual species that will be impacted. For example, in *Arizona Cattle Growers' Association v. U.S. Fish & Wildlife Service*,[450] the Ninth Circuit Court of Appeal considered a Biological Opinion that evaluated the impacts associated with cattle allotments on certain fish species. Instead of evaluating the extent of incidental take using a precise number, the Service used ecological conditions for those species. Citing a lower court's finding, the Ninth Circuit explained that "the use of ecological conditions as a surrogate for defining the

Peirson's milkvetch. Photo: Pacific Southwest Region USFW. Public Domain.

447 *Id.*
448 833 F.3d 1136 (9th Cir. 2016).
449 *Id.* at 1141–42.
450 273 F.3d 1229 (9th Cir. 2001).

amount or extent of incidental take is reasonable so long as these conditions are linked to the take of the protected species."[451]

In *Gifford Pinchot Task Force v. U.S. Fish & Wildlife Service,*[452] the court considered challenges to Biological Opinions prepared in connection with certain Forest Service actions and to evaluate impacts to the northern spotted owl. The plaintiffs argued that the Service may not use the changes to the owl's habitat as a proxy for the jeopardy that the owl may face from any given proposed project. The Service argued that predicting species jeopardy based on habitat degradation is within the realm of agency discretion, is scientifically sound, and has been approved by the courts in other contexts. The court explained that the test for whether the habitat proxy is permissible is whether it "reasonably ensures" that the proxy results mirror reality.[453]

Consideration of Actions' Impacts on Species' Chances of Recovery. In *National Wildlife Federation v. National Marine Fisheries Service,*[454] the Ninth Circuit considered challenges brought against a Biological Opinion related to impacts to fish species from operations of the Federal Columbia River Power System. Plaintiffs argued that the Biological Opinion was legally deficient because its jeopardy analysis did not adequately consider the actions' impacts on the listed species' changes of recovery in contravention of the ESA's prohibition against agency action that is "likely to jeopardize the continued existence" of "any listed species," interpreted to mean a prohibition against any agency action "that reasonably would be expected, directly or indirectly, to reduce appreciably the likelihood of both the survival and recovery of a listed species in the wild."[455] NMFS argued that this restriction bars only actions that will both (1) reduce appreciably the likelihood of survival and (2) reduce appreciably the likelihood of recovery. The court explained that this interpretation was improper because it required NMFS to "only consider effects on survival: if there is no appreciable reduction of survival odds, there can never be jeopardy, even if recovery is completely impossible. Because a species can often cling to survival even when recovery is far out of reach, NMFS's interpretation of the jeopardy regulation reads 'and recovery' entirely out of the text."[456] The court explained that this case is similar to its decision in *Gifford Pinchot Task Force v. U.S. Fish & Wildlife Service,* in which the court concluded that the jeopardy regulation requires the Service to consider recovery as well as survival impacts in evaluating adverse modification of critical habitat. In light of its prior decision in *Gifford Pinchot,* the court concluded that the jeopardy regulation requires NMFS to consider both recovery and survival impacts.

---

451 *Id.* at 1250. The court also noted that this approach is consistent with the Section 7 Handbook's discussion regarding the preparation of Incidental Take Statements.

452 378 F.3d 1059 (9th Cir. 2004).

453 *Id.* at 1066 (citing *Idaho Sporting Cong., Inc. v. Rittenhouse,* 305 F.3d 957, 972–73 (9th Cir. 2002) (holding that deference to proxy on proxy approaches is not warranted when the proxy method does not "reasonably ensure" accurate results)).

454 524 F.3d 917 (9th Cir. 2008).

455 *Id.* at 931 (citing 50 C.F.R. § 402.02).

456 *Id.*

Destruction or Adverse Modification of Critical Habitat

Section 7 requires the Service to evaluate during the consultation process whether the agency action is likely to jeopardize the continued existence of listed species or result in the "destruction or adverse modification of critical habitat."[457] The phrase "destruction or adverse modification" has been the subject of intense judicial scrutiny. See the discussion above regarding challenges to the original regulatory definition of this term and the Ninth Circuit Court of Appeals' decision in *Gifford Pinchot Task Force v. U.S. Fish & Wildlife Service.*[458]

As discussed above, the Service issued a final rule in 2016 that revised the definition of "destruction or adverse modification." As a result of this 2016 rule, this phrase is now defined as:

> [A] direct or indirect alteration that appreciably diminishes the value of critical habitat for the conservation of a listed species. Such alterations may include, but are not limited to, those that alter the physical or biological features essential to the conservation of a species or that preclude or significantly delay development of such features.[459]

It can be helpful to understand the import of this definition by defining two other terms used in the definition: "critical habitat" and "conservation." *Critical habitat* is defined as the specific areas within the geographical area occupied by the species, at the time it is listed in accordance with the provisions of Section 4 of the Act, on which are found those physical or biological features (1) essential to the conservation of the species; and (2) which may require special management considerations or protection, as well as specific areas outside the geographical areas occupied by the species at the time it is listed in accordance with the provisions of Section 4 of the Act, upon a determination by the Service that such areas are essential for the conservation of the species.[460] *Conservation* means to use and the use of all methods and procedures that are necessary to bring any endangered species or threatened species to the point at which the measures provided pursuant of the Act are no longer necessary.[461]

The preamble to the 2016 final rule offers some guidance regarding the application of this language. Particularly helpful is the following clarification:

> [T]he "destruction or adverse modification" definition focuses on how Federal actions affect the quantity and quality of the physical or biological features in the designated critical habitat for a listed species and, especially in the case of unoccupied habitat, on any impacts to the critical habitat itself. Specifically, the Services will generally conclude that a Federal action is likely to "destroy or adversely modify" designated critical habitat if the

457 16 U.S.C. § 1536(a)(2).

458 378 F.3d 1059 (9th Cir. 2004).

459 50 C.F.R. § 402.02.

460 16 U.S.C. § 1532(5)(A).

461 *Id.* § 1532(3).

action results in an alteration of the quantity or quality of the essential physical or biological features of designated critical habitat, or that precludes or significantly delays the capacity of that habitat to develop those features over time, and if the effect of the alteration is to appreciably diminish the value of critical habitat for the conservation of the species.

[¶]

[T]he Services may consider other kinds of impacts to designated critical habitat. For example, some areas that are currently in a degraded condition may have been designated as critical habitat for their potential to develop or improve and eventually provide the needed ecological functions to support species' recovery. Under these circumstances, the Services generally conclude that an action is likely to "destroy or adversely modify" the designated critical habitat if the action alters it to prevent it from improving over time relative to its pre-action condition.[462]

Other aspects of the preamble may be helpful in interpreting the application of this revised definition of "destruction or adverse modification."

Although its guidance is dated in light of the *Gifford Pinchot* decision and the Final Rule issued in 2016 re-defining the term "destruction or adverse modification," the Section 7 Handbook provides useful instruction regarding the analysis of destruction or adverse modification of critical habitat. Because it was prepared before these recent changes, however, practitioners should be cautious in relying on this guidance.

As described in the Handbook, critical habitat includes those physical and biological features essential to the conservation of listed species that may require special management considerations or protection. These physical and biological features include:

> space for individual and population growth and for normal behavior
> food, water, air, light, minerals, or other nutritional or physiological requirements
> cover or shelter
> sites for breeding, reproduction, rearing of offspring, germination, or seed dispersal
> habitats protected from disturbance or representative of the historic geographical and ecological distributions of a species

Critical habitat designations must be thorough and accurate, encompassing habitat and its constituent elements which describe an area that is essential to the ultimate survival and recovery of the listed species. However, many critical habitat designations predate the requirement for identification of constituent elements or habitat qualities necessary to allow a species to survive and recover from the threat of extinction. In such cases, the biologist should use the best scientific and commercial data available to

---

462 Interagency Cooperation – Endangered Species Act of 1973, as Amended; Definition of Destruction or Adverse Modification of Critical Habitat, Final Rule, 81 Fed. Reg. 7214, 7216–17 (Feb. 11, 2016).

determine and document those characteristics of the designated critical habitat that support the species' survival and recovery.

The following steps help determine if a proposed action is likely to destroy or adversely modify critical habitat:

(1) Review the status of the critical habitat as designated and the environmental baseline within the action area. The status and environmental baseline for any constituent elements may have been modified by actions considered in earlier Biological Opinions.

(2) Those opinions should be consulted to determine the current baseline.

(3) Evaluate the effects of the proposed action on the constituent elements of critical habitat.

(4) Evaluate the cumulative effects in the action area on the critical habitat and its constituent elements.

(5) Assess whether the aggregate effects of these analyses will appreciably diminish[463] the value of the critical habitat in sustaining its role in both the survival and recovery of the species.

Reasonable and Prudent Alternatives

As described in the Section 7 Handbook, this section of the Biological Opinion lays out reasonable and prudent alternative actions, if any, that the Service believes the action agency or the applicant may take to avoid the likelihood of jeopardy to the species or destruction or adverse modification of designated critical habitat.[464] When a reasonable and prudent alternative consists of multiple activities, the Handbook explains that the Biological Opinion must contain a thorough explanation of how each component of the alternative is essential to avoid jeopardy and/or adverse modification. The action agency and the applicant should be given every opportunity to assist in developing the reasonable and prudent alternatives. Often they are the only ones who can determine if an alternative is within their legal authority and jurisdiction, and if it is economically and technologically feasible.

If adopted by the action agency, the reasonable and prudent alternatives do not undergo subsequent consultation to meet the requirements of Section 7(a)(2). The action agency's acceptance in writing of the Service's reasonable and prudent alternative concludes the consultation process.

The Section 7 regulations limit reasonable and prudent alternatives to:

> alternatives the Service believes will avoid the likelihood of jeopardy or adverse modification

> alternatives that can be implemented in a manner consistent with the intended purpose of the action

---

463 As discussed above, caution should be exercised in applying this guidance in light of the Ninth Circuit's decision in *Gifford Pinchot Task Force v. U.S. Fish & Wildlife Service* and the revised definition of "destruction or adverse modification" in the 2016 Final Rule.

464 Section 7 Handbook at p. 4-43 (citing 50 C.F.R. §402.14(h)(3)).

THE ENDANGERED SPECIES COMMITTEE

In 1978, the Endangered Species Act was amended to establish the Endangered Species Committee, otherwise known as the "God Squad." The God Squad is composed of seven Cabinet-level members: the Administrator of the Environmental Protection Agency, the Administrator of the National Oceanic and Atmospheric Administration, the Chairman of the Council of Economic Advisers, the Secretary of Agriculture, the Secretary of the Army, the Secretary of the Interior, and one representative from the affected state, as determined by the Secretary of the Interior and appointed by the President. (16 U.S.C. § 1536(e).) A federal agency, the governor of the state in which an agency action will occur, or a permit or license applicant may apply for an exemption for an agency action, exempting the action from the requirements of Section 7(a)(2). (16 U.S.C. § 1536(g)(1).) The exemption may only be granted by a vote of not less than five of its seven members, and the Committee may grant the exemption only if it finds that (1) there are no reasonable and prudent alternatives to the agency action; (2) the benefits of such action clearly outweigh the benefits of alternative courses of action consistent with conserving the species or its critical habitat, and such action is in the public interest; (3) the action is of regional or national significance; and (4) neither the action agency nor the exemption applicant made any irreversible or irretrievable commitment of resources. (16 U.S.C. § 1536(h)(1)(A).) The Committee must also establish reasonable mitigation and enhancement measures as are necessary and appropriate to minimize the adverse effects of the action agency. (16 U.S.C. § 1536(h)(1)(B).)

> alternatives that can be implemented consistent with the scope of the action agency's legal authority and jurisdiction

> alternatives that are economically and technologically feasible

If the Service concludes that certain alternatives are available that would avoid jeopardy and adverse modification, but such alternatives fail to meet one of the other three elements in the definition of "reasonable and prudent alternative," the Service should document the alternative in the Biological Opinion to show it was considered during the formal consultation process. This information could prove important during any subsequent proceeding before the Endangered Species Committee (established under Section 7(e) of the Act), which reviews requests for exemptions from the requirements of Section 7(a)(2).

Although a strong effort should always be made to identify reasonable and prudent alternatives, in some cases, no alternatives are available to avoid jeopardy or adverse modification. Examples include cases in which the corrective action relies on:

> an alternative not under consideration (e.g., locating a project in uplands on a site not available to the applicant instead of requiring a Corps permit to fill a wetland)

> actions of a third party not involved in the proposed action (e.g., only the county, which is not a party to the consultation, has the authority to regulate speed limits)

> actions on lands or activities over which the action agency has no jurisdiction or no residual authority to enforce compliance

> data not available on which to base an alternative

In these cases, a statement is included that no reasonable and prudent alternatives are available, along with an explanation. When data are not available to support an alternative, the explanation is that according to the best available scientific and commercial data, there are no reasonable and prudent alternatives to the action undergoing consultation.

The Service is committed to working closely with action agencies and applicants in developing reasonable and prudent alternatives. The Service will, in most cases, defer to the action agency's expertise and judgment as to the feasibility of an alternative. When the agency maintains that the alternative is not reasonable or not prudent, the reasoning for its position is to be provided in writing for the administrative record. The Service retains the final decision on which reasonable and prudent alternatives are included in the Biological Opinion. When necessary, the Service may question the agency's view of the scope of its authorities to implement reasonable and prudent alternatives.

The following standardized paragraphs are used in the Reasonable and Prudent Alternatives section:

Introductory paragraph:

Regulations (50 CFR §402.02) implementing section 7 of the Act define reasonable and prudent alternatives as alternative actions, identified during formal consultation, that: (1) can be implemented in a manner consistent with the intended purpose of the action; (2) can be implemented consistent with the scope of the action agency's legal authority and jurisdiction; (3) are economically and technologically feasible; and (4) would, the Service believes, avoid the likelihood of jeopardizing the continued existence of listed species or resulting in the destruction or adverse modification of critical habitat.

Closing paragraph:

Because this biological opinion has found (jeopardy/destruction or adverse modification of critical habitat), the (agency) is required to notify the Service of its final decision on the implementation of the reasonable and prudent alternatives.

Reasonable and Prudent Measures

According to the Section 7 Handbook, Section 7 requires minimization of the level of take. It is not appropriate to require mitigation for the impacts of incidental take.

Reasonable and prudent measures can include only actions that occur within the action area, involve only minor changes to the project, and reduce the level of take associated with project activities. These measures should minimize the impacts of incidental take to the extent reasonable and prudent.

For example, a measure may call for actions like education of employees about the species, reduction of predation, removal or avoidance of the species, or monitoring. Measures are considered reasonable and prudent when they are consistent with the proposed action's basic design (e.g., narrowing of disturbed right-of-way at known species locations), location (e.g., temporary storage of equipment or other materials), scope, duration, and timing. The test for reasonableness is whether the proposed measure would cause more than a minor change to the project.

The Section 7 Handbook explains that reasonable and prudent measures and terms and conditions should be developed in coordination with the action agency and applicant, if any, to ensure that the measures are reasonable, that they cause only minor changes to the project, and that they are within the legal authority and jurisdiction of the agency or applicant to carry out. For example, the effect of measures costing $10,000 or $100,000 may be critically significant for a single-family boat dock, but minor for a multi-million dollar development complex. An example of an unreasonable measure would be a timing delay to minimize the impacts of incidental take if project timing is critical.[465]

Reasonable and prudent measures serve to minimize impacts on the specific individuals or habitats affected by the action. Activities resulting from these measures must occur within the action area, which may be larger than the footprint of the project itself.[466] Reasonable and prudent measures are not a substitute for a finding of jeopardy or adverse modification. Similarly, discretionary conservation recommendations under Section 7(a)(1) are not a substitute for reasonable and prudent measures as a means of minimizing the impacts of incidental take.[467]

Terms and Conditions

A Biological Opinion sets forth terms and conditions for implementation of the action. As described in the Section 7 Handbook, the terms and conditions set out the specific methods by which the reasonable and prudent measures are to be accomplished, e.g., who is to be educated, when/what/how; the actions necessary to reduce predation; who may remove or how to avoid the species; or the protocol for monitoring.

Terms and conditions of an Incidental Take Statement must include reporting and monitoring requirements that assure adequate action agency oversight of any incidental take.[468] The monitoring must be sufficient to determine if the amount or extent of take

---

465 Section 7 Handbook at p. 4-53.

466 *Id.*

467 *Id.* at p. 4-54.

468 *Id.* (citing 50 C.F.R. § 402.14(i)(1)(iv) & (i)(3)).

is approached or exceeded, and the reporting must assure that the Services will know when that happens.

Conservation Recommendations

Biological Opinions typically include conservation recommendations. The Section 7 Handbook describes the use and purpose of these recommendations. According to the Handbook, when the Service identifies discretionary actions the action agency can implement, relevant to the proposed action and consistent with their Section 7(a)(1) authority, voluntary conservation recommendations may be included as a separate item in the consultation package.[469]

Conservation recommendations serve several purposes. They can suggest how an action agency can assist species conservation in furtherance of their responsibilities under Section 7(a)(1) of the Act. They may further minimize or avoid the adverse effects of a proposed action on listed species or critical habitat—in which case they are applied after the terms and conditions of the Incidental Take Statement are implemented. They may also suggest ways to minimize or avoid the adverse effects of a proposed action on proposed or candidate species. They can recommend studies improving an understanding of a species' biology or ecology. Wherever possible, these actions should be tied to tasks identified in recovery plans.[470]

Conservation recommendations may be provided separately or at the end of the consultation package, but they are not incorporated anywhere in the Biological Opinion or Incidental Take Statement where they may be confused with the opinion or statement itself. These recommendations are never a precondition for a subsequent finding of no jeopardy or to reduce the impacts of anticipated incidental take.[471]

Monitoring and Reporting

The Section 7 regulations require that terms and conditions for a Biological Opinion include provisions for monitoring project activities to determine the actual project effects on listed fish or wildlife species.[472] The Section 7 Handbook elaborates on this requirement further by explaining that project monitoring, carried out by the federal agency or applicant, provides the Service with information essential to assessing the effects of various actions on listed species and designated critical habitat. Monitoring allows the Service to track incidental take levels and to refine Biological Opinions, reasonable and prudent alternatives, reasonable and prudent measures, and terms and conditions. Consequently, monitoring programs should be integral elements of all interagency consultations concluding that an action may adversely affect listed species or critical habitat.

469 Section 7 Handbook at p. 4-62.
470 *Id.* at pp. 4-62 to 4-63.
471 *Id.* at p. 4-63.
472 50 C.F.R. § 402.14(i)(3).

The Handbook notes further that monitoring programs resulting from interagency consultations should be designed to: (1) detect adverse effects resulting from a proposed action, (2) assess the actual level of incidental take in comparison with the anticipated incidental take level documented in the Biological Opinion, (3) detect when the level of anticipated incidental take is exceeded, and (4) determine the effectiveness of reasonable and prudent measures and their implementing terms and conditions.

The Section 7 Handbook suggests that the following objectives/steps should be taken to develop monitoring programs:

> **Develop objectives.** Any monitoring program associated with Section 7 consultations should answer specific questions or lead to specific conclusions, captured in the objectives. If the objectives are well-developed, they will help shape a complete monitoring program.

> **Describe the subject of the monitoring program.** This includes effects on populations of a listed species, effects on the habitat (critical or not) of a listed species, or effects on both.

> **Describe the variables to be measured and how data will be collected.** The success or failure of monitoring programs ultimately depends on the information collected about the variables that demonstrate or refute a position outlined in the objectives. Collection methods should be standardized to ensure comparability with data from studies in other areas.

> **Detail the frequency, timing, and duration of sampling for the variables.** Determining how frequently and how long to collect data is important to the success or failure of the program. If the interval between samples is too long or if the sampling program is too short, the monitoring program may not detect an effect. The frequency, timing, and duration of the sampling regimen should relate to the type of action being evaluated, the organism affected by the action, and the response of the organism to the effects produced by the action.

> **Describe how the data are to be analyzed and who will conduct the analyses.** A monitoring program is more effective when the analytical methods are integrated into the design. For example, parametric and non-parametric statistical analyses require different sample sizes, which will affect the frequency, timing, and duration of sampling.

> **Discuss the relationship between the monitoring program being included in a consultation and other monitoring programs.** At almost any given time, hundreds of environmental monitoring programs are being conducted in every region of the country. Whenever possible, these should be coordinated to eliminate duplication, standardize sampling methods, and/or improve geographic coverage.

SAFE HARBOR AGREEMENTS

Background

Safe Harbor Agreements are another mechanism for private property owners to obtain take authorization for listed species in connection with development or other activities proposed for that property.[473] Similar to Habitat Conservation Plans under Section 10 of the Endangered Species Act, Safe Harbor Agreements provide this take authorization in the context of a planning effort to conserve the species' habitat.

The Service's Safe Harbor Agreement policy emerged in 1997 and was designed to create incentives for non-federal property owners to implement conservation measures for listed species by providing certainty with regard to possible future land, water, or resource use restrictions should the covered species later become more numerous as a result of the property owner's actions.[474]

The overarching concept behind the Safe Harbor Agreement policy is that non-federal property owners, who through a Safe Harbor Agreement commit to implement voluntary conservation measures for a listed species will receive assurances from the Service that additional conservation measures will not be required, and additional land, water, or resource use restrictions will not be imposed should the covered species become more numerous as a result of the property owner's actions.[475]

In summary, the policy is designed to ensure enhancement of a species' propagation or survival, while at the same time protecting the landowner from violating the ESA should a take of such species occur on the property. To that end, the policy includes provisions that protect listed species covered by a Safe Harbor Agreement and occupying a landowner's property at the time of enrollment in the program by including them in the "baseline conditions" for the property. If species were included in the baseline conditions, an incidental take would not be allowed. However, if the numbers or range of those covered species increases because of voluntary conservation measures conducted in accordance with a Safe Harbor Agreement, the landowner would be authorized to incidentally "take" those individuals above the baseline without penalty.[476]

---

473 Yet another mechanism is a Candidate Conservation Agreement with Assurances (CCAA), which is a formal agreement between the Service and one or more parties to address the conservation needs of proposed or candidate species, or species likely to become candidates, before they become listed as endangered or threatened. Landowners voluntarily commit to conservation actions that will help stabilize or restore the species with the goal that listing will become unnecessary. The benefit of using a CCAA is that, if the species is listed, the agreement automatically becomes a permit authorizing the landowner incidental take of the species. Thus, these agreements provide landowners with assurances that their conservation efforts will not result in future regulatory obligations in excess of those they agree to at the time they enter into the CCAA. See 50 C.F.R. § 17.22(d) (application requirements for permits for the enhancement of survival through CCAAs, issuance criteria for CCAAs, permit conditions, and other requirements related to CCAAs). See also U.S. Fish and Wildlife Service Midwest Region website regarding CCAAs for more information (https://www.fws.gov/midwest/endangered/permits/enhancement/ccaa/index.html).

474 64 Fed. Reg. 32,717, 32,717 (June 17, 1999) (citing 62 Fed. Reg. 32,178, which provided notice of the draft Safe Harbor Agreement policy).

475 *Id.*

476 *Id.* at 32,718.

These arrangements are formalized through a streamlined permitting process and an agreement or similar instrument between the landowner and the Service. The policy also includes a streamlined process where the Service issues a blanket permit to an appropriate agency or organization that would in turn issue "Certificates of Inclusion" or "Participation Certificates" to landowners.[477]

According to the Service, "The ultimate goal of the [policy is] to encourage non-Federal landowners to voluntarily implement beneficial management actions for those listed species that occur on their lands or would be attracted as a result of the beneficial management actions."[478]

Substantive and Procedural Requirements

The process to apply for a Safe Harbor Agreement is set forth in the Service's Endangered Wildlife regulations. An applicant begins the process by first submitting an application to the Service for the "enhancement of survival through Safe Harbor Agreements."[479] The Service must publish notice in the Federal Register of the application, and the notice must invite the submission from interested parties, within 30 days after the date of the notice, or written data, views, or arguments with respect to the application.[480]

Before issuing the permit, the Service must consider the following factors:

> the take will be incidental to an otherwise lawful activity and will be in accordance with the terms of the Safe Harbor Agreement

> the implementation of the terms of the Safe Harbor Agreement is reasonably expected to provide a net conservation benefit to the affected listed species by contributing to the recovery of listed species included in the permit, and the Safe Harbor Agreement otherwise complies with the Safe Harbor policy available from the Service

> the probable direct and indirect effects of any authorized take will not appreciably reduce the likelihood of survival and recovery in the wild of any listed species

> implementation of the terms of the Safe Harbor Agreement is consistent with applicable federal, state, and tribal laws and regulations

> implementation of the terms of the Safe Harbor Agreement will not be in conflict with any ongoing conservation or recovery programs for listed species covered by the permit

---

477 *Id.*

478 *Id.*

479 50 C.F.R. § 17.22(c)(1). The Service provides Form 3-200.54 for the application and requires additional information including: (1) the common and scientific names of the listed species for which the applicant requests incidental take authorization; (2) a description of how incidental take of the listed species pursuant to the Safe Harbor Agreement is likely to occur, both as a result of management activities and as a result of the return to baseline; and (3) a Safe Harbor Agreement that complies with the requirements of the Safe Harbor policy available from the Service. *Id.* § 17.22(c)(1)(i)–(iii).

480 *Id.* § 17.22.

> the applicant has shown capability for and commitment to implementing all of the terms of the Safe Harbor Agreement[481]

If the permit is issued, the Service must impose general conditions on the permit. Conditions may include, for example, strict interpretations of permit authorizations,[482] filing of reports,[483] and acceptance of liability for permit holders.[484] In addition, the Service must impose the following special conditions:

> a requirement for the participating property owner to notify the Service of any transfer of lands subject to a Safe Harbor Agreement

> when appropriate, a requirement for the permittee to give the Service reasonable advance notice (generally at least 30 days) of when he or she expects to incidentally take any listed species covered under the permit; such notification will provide the Service with an opportunity to relocate affected individuals of the species, if possible and appropriate

> any additional requirements or conditions the Service deems necessary or appropriate to carry out the purposes of the permit and the Safe Harbor Agreement[485]

Safe Harbor permits become effective the day of issuance for species covered by the Safe Harbor Agreement.[486]

Perhaps most important to the landowner are the assurances that a Safe Harbor permit provides. The Service will maintain these assurances only where the Safe Harbor Agreement is being properly implemented, and they will apply only with respect to species covered by the agreement and the permit.[487] The operative language in the Service's regulations is the following:

> The [Service] and the permittee may agree to revise or modify the management measures set forth in a Safe Harbor Agreement if the Director determines that such revisions or modifications do not change the [Service's] prior determination that the Safe Harbor Agreement is reasonably expected to provide a net conservation benefit to the listed species. However, the

481 50 C.F.R. § 17.22(c)(2). The Service must also consider other general issuance criteria, which specifies that the Service may not issue the permit if (1) the applicant has been assessed a civil penalty or convicted of any criminal provision of any statute or regulation relating to the activity for which the application is filed, if such assessment or conviction evidences a lack of responsibility; (2) the applicant has failed to disclose material information required, or has made false statements as to any material fact, in connection with the application; (3) the applicant has failed to demonstrate a valid justification for the permit and a showing of responsibility; and (4) the Service finds through further inquiry or investigation, or otherwise, that the applicant is not qualified. 50 C.F.R. § 13.21(b). The Service specifically excludes the condition listed in Section 13.21(b)(4) as to potential threats to wildlife or plant populations for Safe Harbor Agreement permits.

482 *Id.* § 13.43.

483 *Id.* § 13.45.

484 *Id.* § 13.50.

485 *Id.* § 17.22(c)(3).

486 *Id.* § 17.22(c)(4).

487 *Id.* § 17.22(c)(5)(i). These assurances apply only to Safe Harbor permits issued after July 19, 1999.

[Service] may not require additional or different management activities to be undertaken by a permittee without the consent of the permittee.[488]

The Service may revoke a Safe Harbor permit if continuation of the permitted activity would either appreciably reduce the likelihood of survival and recovery in the wild of any listed species or directly or indirectly alter designated critical habitat such that it appreciably diminishes the value of that critical habitat for both the survival and recovery of a listed species. Before revoking a permit for either of the latter two reasons, the Service, with the consent of the permittee, will pursue all appropriate options to avoid permit revocation. These options may include but are not limited to: extending or modifying the existing permit, capturing and relocating the species, compensating the landowner to forgo the activity, purchasing an easement or fee simple interest in the property, or arranging for a third-party acquisition of an interest in the property.[489]

The duration of a Safe Harbor permit must be sufficient to provide a net conservation benefit to species covered in the permit. In determining the duration of a permit, the Service will consider the duration of the planned activities, as well as the positive and negative effects associated with permits of the proposed duration on covered species, including the extent to which the conservation activities included in the Safe Harbor Agreement will enhance the survival and contribute to the recovery of listed species included in the permit.[490]

The Service's Final Rule regarding its Safe Harbor Agreement Policy in the Federal Register provides useful information and clarification regarding the substantive and procedural requirements of Safe Harbor Agreements and permits. Particularly noteworthy are the following points of clarification:

Definitions. The Final Rule provides definitions for several terms and phrases used in the Service's regulations. For example, "baseline condition" is defined as "population estimates and distribution and/or habitat characteristics and determined area of the enrolled property that sustain seasonal or permanent use by the covered species at the time the Safe Harbor Agreement is executed between the Service and the property owner. "Net conservation benefit" is defined as the "cumulative benefits of the management activities identified in a Safe Harbor Agreement that provide for an increase in a species' population and/or the enhancement, restoration, or maintenance of covered species' suitable habitat within the enrolled property, taking into account the length of the agreement and any off-setting adverse effects attributable to the incidental taking allowed by the enhancement of survival permit. Net conservation benefits must be

---

488 *Id.* § 17.22(c)(5)(ii).

489 *Id.* § 17.22(c)(7). The Service may also revoke a permit for any of the additional following reasons: (1) the permittee willfully violates any federal or state statute or regulation, or any Indian tribal law or regulation, or any law or regulation of any foreign country, which involves a violation of the conditions of the permit or of the laws or regulations governing the permitted activity; (2) the permittee fails within 60 days to correct deficiencies that were the cause of a permit suspension; (3) the permittee becomes disqualified to hold a permit; or (4) a change occurs in the statute or regulation authorizing the permit that prohibits the continuation of a permit issued by the Service. *Id.* § 13.28(a)(1)–(4).

490 *Id.* § 17.22(c)(8).

sufficient to contribute, either directly or indirectly, to the recovery of the covered species." "Safe Harbor Assurances" is defined as allowing "the property owner to alter or modify enrolled property, even if such alteration or modification results in the incidental take of a listed species to such an extent that it returned the species back to the originally agreed upon baseline conditions."[491]

Application of Net Conservation Benefit. This concept is explained in more detail in the Final Rule. Some of the requirements related to the application of net conservation benefit include the requirement that the Service must make a written finding that all covered species will receive a net conservation benefit from management actions undertaken pursuant to a Safe Harbor Agreement before the Service will enter into the agreement. In addition, the Final Rule explains that net conservation benefits must contribute, directly or indirectly, to the recovery of the covered species. Conservation benefits from Safe Harbor Agreements include, but are not limited to, reduction of habitat fragmentation rates; the maintenance, restoration, or enhancement of habitats; increase in habitat connectivity; maintenance or increase of population numbers or distribution; reduction of the effects of catastrophic events; establishment of buffers for protected areas; and establishment of areas to test and develop new and innovative conservation strategies.[492]

Standards for Preparing a Safe Harbor Agreement. The Final Rule provides additional substantive requirements for an Agreement. An Agreement must:

(1) specify the species and/or habitats covered, including the habitat conditions, and identify the enrolled property covered by the Agreement

(2) include a full description of the agreed upon baseline conditions for each of the covered species within the enrolled property

(3) identify management actions that would be undertaken to accomplish the expected net conservation benefits to the species, where and when the benefits would be achieved, and the agreed upon time frames these management actions will remain in effect to achieve the anticipated net conservation benefits

(4) describe any incidental take associated with the management actions during the term of the Agreement

(5) if appropriate, incorporate a notification requirement to provide the Service or appropriate state agencies with a reasonable opportunity to rescue individuals of a covered species before any authorized incidental taking occurs

(6) describe what activities would be expected to return the enrolled property to baseline conditions and the extent of incidental take that would likely result from such activities

(7) satisfy other requirements of Section 10 of the ESA

---

491 64 Fed. Reg. 32,717, 32,723 (June 17, 1999).

492 *Id.*

(8) identify a schedule for monitoring and the responsible parties who will monitor maintenance of baseline conditions, implementation of terms and conditions of the Agreement, and any incidental take as authorized in the permit[493]

Baseline Conditions. The Final Rule explains how the Service determines baseline conditions, which is generally in terms of the number and location of individual animals (if determinable), existing habitat areas or characteristics that support the species covered at the time of the agreement, and other appropriate attributes. For species that are extremely difficult to survey and quantify, an estimate and an indirect measure (e.g., number of suitable acres of habitat of the species) is acceptable and should be based on the best available techniques and information. In most cases, the baseline conditions will be described as the extent and condition of habitat in the enrolled lands and not the number of individuals of covered species, since the number of individuals could fluctuate over time.[494]

Whether Plants Are Covered by the Safe Harbor Policy. The Final Rule notes that the ESA's take prohibitions generally do not apply to listed plant species on private property, and therefore, the incidental take assurances provided in the Safe Harbor policy are legally not necessary for listed species. However, the Final Rule explains that the Service must review the effects of the Safe Harbor permit on listed plants under Section 7 of the Act, even when those plants are found on private property. In approving a Safe Harbor permit and entering into a Safe Harbor Agreement, the Service must confirm under Section 7 that the Agreement is not likely to "jeopardize the continued existence" of any listed plants.[495]

Assurances to Property Owners. The Final Rule provides additional commentary on the concept of assurances. If the property owner carried out the management actions and complied with the permit and the agreement conditions, the property owner would be authorized to use the property in any manner that does not result in moving the enrolled property to below baseline conditions. These assurances run with the enrolled lands and are valid for as long as the participating landowner is complying with the Safe Harbor Agreement and permit.[496]

Monitoring for Safe Harbor Agreement. The Final Rule indicates that the Service will ensure that adequate monitoring is included in each agreement and permit. In addition, the public will have an opportunity to review the monitoring plan during the public comment period on the issuance of the permit.[497]

Compliance with NEPA. According to the Final Rule, the Service will review each Safe Harbor Agreement and permit for any significant environmental, economic, social, historical, or cultural impact, or for significant controversy pursuant to the National

493 *Id.* at 32,723.

494 *Id.* at 32,723–32,724.

495 *Id.* at 32,724.

496 *Id.*

497 *Id.*

NEPA = National Environmental Policy Act

EIS = Environmental Impact Statement

FONSI = Finding Of No Significant Impact

EA = Environmental Assessment

Environmental Policy Act. If a Safe Harbor Agreement and permit are not expected to individually or cumulatively have a significant impact on the quality of the human environment or other natural resources, the Agreement and permit may be categorically excluded.[498]

Permit Transfer. The Final Rule offers guidance on whether Safe Harbor Agreements can be transferred. If a property owner who is a party to a Safe Harbor Agreement transfers ownership of the enrolled property to a non-federal entity, the Service will regard the new owner as having the same rights and obligations with respect to the enrolled property as the original property owner, if the new property owner agrees to become a party to the original agreement and permit. The new property owner would not be responsible for any provisions of the Agreement and would not receive any assurances relative to take prohibitions, unless the new owner agrees to become a party to the Agreement and permit.[499]

THE RELATIONSHIP BETWEEN THE ESA AND NEPA

The relationship between the ESA and the National Environmental Policy Act (NEPA), particularly whether actions taken by the Service or by private applicants pursuant to the ESA require NEPA environmental clearance, has been tested and explored by the courts in a number of court decisions. Below are significant issues that periodically arise relative to the question of whether NEPA applies to certain ESA actions.

For background, NEPA requires "to the fullest extent possible," that "all agencies of the federal government" comply with NEPA when they take "major federal actions significantly affecting the quality of the human environment."[500] Some decisions require the preparation of an Environmental Impact Statement (EIS), while other decisions that do not trigger the thresholds required for an EIS may be covered by a "categorical exclusion" or result in a Finding of No Significant Impact (FONSI), typically after the federal agency has prepared an Environmental Assessment (EA), thus resulting in what can be called an EA/FONSI.

NEPA's Applicability to Listing Decisions

Although the issue does not appear to have been squarely presented to the Ninth Circuit Court of Appeals, the Sixth Circuit in *Pacific Legal Foundation v. Andrus*[501] has held that NEPA does not apply when the Service lists a species as threatened or endangered under the ESA. However, in dicta the Ninth Circuit has acknowledged without explicit objection that the Sixth Circuit has reached this conclusion.[502]

---

498 *Id.* at 32,725.

499 *Id.*

500 42 U.S.C. § 4332(2)(c).

501 657 F.2d 829 (6th Cir. 1981).

502 *Douglas County v. Babbitt*, 48 F.3d 1495 (9th Cir. 1995).

NEPA's Applicability to Critical Habitat Designations

Whether NEPA applies to the designation of critical habitat under the ESA was a question of first impression in the Ninth Circuit Court of Appeals' case *Douglas County v. Babbitt*.[503] The court in *Douglas County* began its analysis by noting prior court decisions determining that "NEPA was not intended to repeal by implication any other statute."[504] The court then evaluated the legislative history of the ESA, concluding Congress intended that "the ESA procedures for designating a critical habitat replace the NEPA requirements."[505] The court explained that the ESA "has an important mandate that distinguishes it from NEPA." According to the court, "Though the Secretary may exclude from the critical habitat any area, the exclusion of which, would be more beneficial than harmful, he or she must designate any area without which the species would become extinct. This mandate conflicts with the requirements of NEPA because in cases where extinction is at issue, the Secretary has no discretion to consider the environmental impact of his or her actions."[506] The court further found that NEPA does not apply to the designation of a critical habitat because the ESA furthers the goals of NEPA without demanding an EIS. Accordingly, the court held that NEPA does not apply to the Service's decision to designate critical habitat.[507]

NEPA's Applicability to Biological Opinions

Courts have considered the question of whether the Service's issuance of a Biological Opinion is a "major federal action[] significantly affecting the quality of the human environment" imposing on the Service an obligation to comply with NEPA.

For example, in *San Luis & Delta-Mendota Water Authority v. Jewell*,[508] the Ninth Circuit Court of Appeals considered whether the Service's issuance of a Biological Opinion for the continued operation of the Central Valley Project required NEPA review. The Service argued that, in its capacity as a consulting agency under Section 7 of the ESA, it was merely offering its opinions and suggestions to the Bureau of Reclamation, which, as the action agency, ultimately decides whether to adopt or approve the operation plan.

The court found this position persuasive, particularly in light of the fact that prior Ninth Circuit case law confirms that an action agency has some discretion to deviate from Biological Opinions and reasonable and prudent alternatives.[509] The court explained that, "Unlike Reclamation, the [Service] is not responsible for, and will not implement, the [reasonable and prudent alternatives identified in the Biological

---

503 48 F.3d 1495 (9th Cir. 1995).

504 *Id.* at 1501 (citing *Merrell v. Thomas*, 807 F.2d 776 (9th Cir. 1986), *cert. denied,* 484 U.S. 848 (1987)).

505 *Id.* at 1503.

506 *Id.*

507 *Id.* at 1507.

508 747 F.3d 581 (9th Cir. 2014).

509 *Id.* at 643 (citing *Pyramid Lake Paiute Tribe of Indians v. U.S. Dep't of Navy*, 898 F.2d 1410, 1418 (9th Cir. 1990)).

Opinion]. And even if Reclamation felt compelled to implement the [Service's] proposal, we must bear in mind that Reclamation will complete an EIS evaluating the effects of implementing the [Biological Opinion]."[510] The court concluded that under these circumstances, the Service was not required to comply with NEPA in issuing the Biological Opinion.

Although the court determined the Service was not required to comply with NEPA, it reached a different conclusion with respect to the Bureau of Reclamation, i.e., the action agency. The court held that Reclamation's adoption and implementation of the Biological Opinion triggered NEPA compliance and required the preparation of an EIS. Among other things, the court found that "Congress specifically contemplated that an action agency discharging its duties under Section 7 of the ESA would also comply with NEPA by completing an EA and, if necessary, an EIS."[511]

The court in *San Luis* distinguished a case which suggests the Service may be required to comply with NEPA when it issues a Biological Opinion. That case is *Ramsey v. Kantor*,[512] a decision in which the Ninth Circuit Court of Appeals held that the agency issuing a Biological Opinion and an Incidental Take Statement was required to comply with NEPA. In *Ramsey*, NMFS produced a Biological Opinion and Incidental Take Statement in connection with the Columbia River Fish Management Plan, which is a "unique, judicially created, federal-state tribal compact" that "apportions the fishing rights to the state and tribal members."[513] "The states then enact regulations governing fishing in the Columbia River, although they must do so in compliance with the terms of the Columbia River Fish Management Plan."[514] After NMFS completed its Biological Opinion and Incidental Take Statement, the states of Washington and Oregon issued regulations, which "would be illegal, if not for that [incidental take] statement," permitting a specified amount of salmon fishing in the Columbia River.[515] The *Ramsey* court "conclude[d] that the Incidental Take Statement in this case is functionally equivalent to a permit."[516] The Ninth Circuit had already established that "if a federal permit is a prerequisite for a project with adverse impact on the environment, issuance of that permit does constitute major federal action and the federal agency involved must conduct an EA and possibly an EIS before granting it."[517] Thus, the court held "that the issuance of [the incidental take] statement constitutes major federal action for purposes of NEPA."[518]

510 *Id.* at 643.

511 *Id.*

512 96 F.3d 434 (9th Cir. 1996).

513 *Id.* at 438.

514 *Id.*

515 *Id.* at 444.

516 *Id.*

517 *Id.* (citing *Jones v. Gordon*, 792 F.2d 821, 827–29 (9th Cir. 1986); *Port of Astoria v. Hodel*, 595 F.2d 467, 478–79 (9th Cir. 1979)).

518 *Id.* (citing *Port of Astoria*, 595 F.2d at 446).

Notably, the *San Luis* court distinguished *Ramsey* by explaining that the *Ramsey* decision involved the states of Washington and Oregon playing a role typically played by a federal action agency such as Reclamation, because the Biological Opinion and Incidental Take Statement were issued as part of a federal-state-tribal compact.[519] Because NEPA applies only to "federal actions," in that case there was no federal agency essentially involved in the project to complete an EIS. In *Ramsey*, if the consulting agency, NMFS, had not prepared an EIS then the action would have evaded NEPA review altogether even though the action was, in substance, identical to the process for issuing a permit. In *San Luis*, the court noted that by comparison there was "no comparable need to require the [Service] to prepare an EIS because Reclamation stands ready to do so."[520]

JUDICIAL REVIEW

Standard of Review

Courts review the Service's actions pursuant to the ESA under the Administrative Procedure Act,[521] which provides that an agency action may be set aside only if it is "arbitrary, capricious, an abuse of discretion, or otherwise not in accordance with law."[522] This standard of review is "highly deferential, presuming the agency action to be valid and affirming the agency action if a reasonable basis exists for its decision."[523] Generally, the court may not consider information outside the administrative record, and may not "substitute its judgment for that of the agency."[524] The court's task is simply to ensure that the agency considered the relevant factors and articulated a rational connection between the facts found and the choices made."[525]

In other ESA cases, the Ninth Circuit has relied on the following test articulated by the U.S. Supreme Court. An agency decision will survive arbitrary and capricious review if it is:

> rational, based on consideration of the relevant factors and within the scope of the authority delegated to the agency by the statute . . . . Normally, an agency rule would be arbitrary and capricious if the agency has relied on factors which Congress had not intended it to consider, entirely failed to consider an important aspect of the problem, offered an explanation for its decision that runs counter to the evidence before the agency, or is so

519 *San Luis & Delta-Mendota Water Authority*, 747 F.3d at 644.

520 *Id.*

521 See, e.g., *Northwest Ecosystem Alliance v. U.S. Fish & Wildlife Serv.*, 475 F.3d 1136, 1140 (9th Cir. 2007).

522 5 U.S.C. § 706(2)(A).

523 See *Northwest Ecosystem Alliance*, 475 F.3d at 1140.

524 *Id.*

525 *Id.*; see also *Nat'l Ass'n of Home Builders v. Norton*, 340 F.3d 835, 841 (9th Cir. 2003); *Blue Mountains Biodiversity Project v. Blackwood*, 161 F.3d 1208, 1211 (9th Cir. 1998) (court must determine whether the agency decision was "based on a consideration of the relevant factors").

implausible that it could not be ascribed to a difference in view or the product of agency expertise.[526]

This review is based on the "grounds . . . upon which the record discloses that its action was based," not on any post-decision statements or briefing during litigation.[527]

Justiciability Issues

Several unique justiciability issues apply to legal challenges alleging violations of the ESA. Below is a discussion of the most significant issues that practitioners should be aware of when bringing or defending against an ESA challenge.

Ripeness. Courts apply to ESA challenges the same ripeness factors used in other legal contexts.[528] These factors are: (1) whether delayed review would cause hardship to the plaintiffs; (2) whether judicial intervention would inappropriately interfere with further administrative action; and (3) whether the courts would benefit from further factual development of the issues presented.[529]

In *California River Watch v. County of Sonoma*,[530] the Northern District of California applied these factors to conclude that an action against Sonoma County alleging violations of the ESA was not ripe because it did not challenge a specific land development project but rather broadly sought to enjoin the County from issuing any and all land development permits without surveys and mitigation designed to protect the Sonoma County distinct population segment of the endangered California tiger salamander. The court rejected plaintiff's argument that county agencies can be liable for regulatory failures that result in a "taking," even if that taking is directly caused by the action of a regulated party.[531] The court found that, first, delaying review until the plaintiff found a specific, concrete instance of a "take" would not cause hardship but would rather allow for the development of specific facts. Second, immediate judicial review directed at all land use permits would hinder the County's efforts regarding the permitting process. Third, the action would benefit from further factual development.[532]

Standing. An important case regarding standing in the context of the ESA is the U.S. Supreme Court's landmark decision *Bennett v. Spear*.[533] *Bennett* involved a Biological Opinion issued by the Service to the Bureau of Reclamation relative to the Bureau's Klamath Project operations and their effects on two species of endangered suckers. To protect the suckers, the Service recommended higher reservoir levels to

---

526 *Defenders of Wildlife v. U.S. Environmental Protection Agency*, 420 F.3d 946, 959 (9th Cir. 2005).

527 *Id.* at 960.

528 See, e.g., *California River Watch v. County of Sonoma*, 55 F. Supp. 3d 1204 (N.D. Cal. 2014).

529 *Ohio Forestry Ass'n v. Sierra Club*, 523 U.S. 726 (1998) (holding that a generic challenge to a forest plan untethered to any site-specific violation was not ripe for adjudication).

530 55 F. Supp. 3d 1204.

531 *Id.* at 1211 (distinguishing *Strahan v. Coxe*, 127 F.3d 155 (1st Cir. 1997), and *Loggerhead Turtle v. Council of Volusia County*, 148 F.3d 1231 (11th Cir. 1998)).

532 *Id.* at 1210–11.

533 520 U.S. 154 (1997).

protect the suckers, thus reducing the amount of tailwater flow available to downstream irrigation districts and ranchers, who brought suit to redress their injuries under the ESA's citizen suit provisions. The government argued that the landowners did not have standing to bring suit under the ESA, because they were not in the "zone of interests" protected under the statute. Writing for the Court, Justice Scalia reasoned that the language of that provision (which allows "any" person to bring suit) permitted the suit and that a prudential standing analysis was not required. With respect to Article III standing, the Court concluded that a specific injury to the plaintiffs could be presumed from a showing of general injury arising from the reduction in water flows.

Injunctive Relief

In most cases, a party is entitled to a preliminary injunction after clearly demonstrating (1) a likelihood of success on the merits and the possibility of irreparable injury, or (2) sufficiently serious questions going to the merits to make them a fair ground for litigation and a balance of hardships tipping decidedly in favor of the party seeing relief.[534] These are not two independent tests but the extremes of the continuum of equitable discretion.[535]

This is not the test for injunctions under the ESA. The Ninth Circuit Court of Appeals has developed a modified test for injunctions under the Act in light of the U.S. Supreme Court's decision in *Tennessee Valley Authority v. Hill* and its exhortation that Congress made it "abundantly clear that the balance has been struck in favor of affording endangered species the highest of priorities."[536] Under this test, courts must effectively presume that "the balance of hardships and the public interest tip heavily in favor of endangered species."[537] The ESA does not permit courts to consider the hardship an injunction may impose on a project if endangered species' habitat is likely to be destroyed.[538]

Citizen Suit Requirements

The ESA includes a citizen suit provision that allows a private citizen to bring suit to remedy a violation of the Act provided that the private citizen give written notice of the alleged violation or violations upon which the suit is based at least 60 days before the suit is filed.[539]

---

534 *Sierra Club v. Marsh*, 816 F.2d 1376, 1382 (9th Cir. 1987).

535 *Id.* at 1383 (citing *Los Angeles Memorial Coliseum Comm'n v. National Football League*, 634 F.2d 1197, 1200–01 (9th Cir. 1980)).

536 *Id.* (citing *Tennessee Valley Authority v. Hill*, 437 U.S. 153, 173 (1978)). See also *National Wildlife Fed'n v. National Marine Fisheries Service*, 886 F.3d 803, 818–20 (9th Cir. 2018) (holding that extinction-level threat to listed species is not required before an injunction can issue under the ESA); *Cottonwood Envtl. Law Center v. U.S. Forest Serv.*, 789 F.3d 1075, 1090 (9th Cir. 2015) ("There is no question, as firmly recognized by the Supreme Court, that the ESA strips courts of at least some of their equitable discretion in determining whether injunctive relief is warranted.").

537 *Sierra Club*, 816 F.2d at 1383.

538 *Id.* at 1387.

539 16 U.S.C. § 1540(g)(2)(A)(i) ("No action may be commenced . . . prior to sixty days after written notice of the violation has been given to the Secretary, and to any alleged violator . . . .")).

This notice requirements serves two purposes. First, it "allows Government agencies to take responsibility for enforcing environmental regulations, thus obviating the need for citizens suits." Second, it "gives the alleged violator 'an opportunity to bring itself into complete compliance with the act and thus likewise render unnecessary a citizen suit.'" The Supreme Court has concluded that these purposes are best fulfilled by requiring strict compliance with the statute's timeliness and party identification requirements.[540]

The 60-day notice requirement is jurisdictional.[541] A failure to strictly comply with the notice requirement acts as an absolute bar to bringing suit under the ESA.[542]

An important issue that often arises is how specific the 60-day notice must be in order to preserve a plaintiff's ability to sue under the ESA or to sue on certain issues under the ESA. To provide proper notice of an alleged violation, the plaintiff must at a minimum "provide sufficient information . . . so that the [notified parties] could identify and attempt to abate the violation."[543] A citizen "is not required to list every specific aspect or detail of every alleged violation. Nor is the citizen required to describe every ramification of a violation."[544] Rather, the analysis turns on the "overall sufficiency" of the notice.[545] "A reviewing court may examine both the notice itself and the behavior or its recipients to determine whether they understood or reasonably should have understood the alleged violations."[546]

In *Klamath-Siskiyou Wildlands Center v. MacWhorter*, plaintiffs challenged a decision by the U.S. Forest Service to allow suction dredge mining within a river on the National Forest that provided designated critical habitat for coho salmon. The plaintiffs submitted a letter that alleged only in general terms that the Forest Service had failed to consult with NMFS before approving the mining. The plaintiffs argued this letter provided sufficient notice under the ESA's citizen-suit provisions. The court reviewed three prior citizen-suit cases in which the Ninth Circuit allowed plaintiffs to plead alleged violations that were not specifically detailed in a notice letter. The key issue in all three of those cases was whether the notice provided information that allowed the Forest Service to identify and address the alleged violations, considering the Forest Service's ability to access information about its own activities.

---

540 *Klamath-Siskiyou Wildlands Center v. MacWhorter*, 797 F.3d 645, 650 (9th Cir. 2015) (citations omitted).

541 *Southwest Center for Biological Diversity v. U.S. Bureau of Reclamation*, 143 F.3d 515, 520 (9th Cir. 1998); *Save the Yaak Committee v. Block*, 840 F.2d 714, 721 (9th Cir. 1988).

542 *Southwest Center*, 143 F.3d at 520 (citing *Lone Rock Timber Co. v. U.S. Dep't of Interior*, 842 F. Supp. 433, 440 (D. Or. 1994); see also *Hallstrom v. Tillamook County*, 493 U.S. 20, 26–28 (1989) (holding that the citizen suit notice requirements in a RCRA action cannot be avoided by employing a flexible or pragmatic construction and that plaintiff's suit must be dismissed where plaintiff has not strictly complied with the notice requirements).

543 *Southwest Center*, 143 F.3d at 522 (citing *Pub. Interest Grp. of N.J., Inc. v. Hercules, Inc.*, 50 F.3d 1239, 1249 (3d Cir. 1995)).

544 *Cmty. Ass'n for Restoration of the Env't v. Henry Bosma Dairy*, 305 F.3d 943, 951 (9th Cir. 2002).

545 *Id.*; see also *Marbled Murrelet v. Babbitt*, 83 F.3d 1068, 1073 (9th Cir. 1996) (examining "the letter as a whole" for sufficiency of notice).

546 *Klamath-Siskiyou Wildlands Center*, 797 F.3d at 651.

First, in *Ecological Rights Foundation v. Pacific Gas & Electric Co.*,[547] the plaintiff sent PG & E a notice letter alleging it violated the Clean Water Act and the Resources Conservation and Recovery Act by releasing toxic wood preservative from its utility poles during periods of substantial rainfall. PG & E argued that the letter provided insufficient notice because it did not specify the location of each pole covered in the complaint. The court disagreed and explained that "as long as a notice letter is reasonably specific as to the nature and time of the alleged violations, the plaintiff has fulfilled the notice requirement. The letter does not need to describe every detail of every violation; it need only provide enough information that the defendant can identify and correct the problem."[548] According to the court, "The key inquiry was whether the identifying information in the notice letter provided PG & E with enough information, when combined with PG & E's knowledge of its own activities, to allow PG & E to identify the additional poles not specifically identified in the letter."[549]

Second, in *Community Association for Restoration of the Environment v. Henry Bosma Dairy*,[550] the plaintiff sent a notice letter listing 12 specific manure discharges that allegedly violated the Clean Water Act. Each of the discharges was described and identified by particular dates. The plaintiff's complaint alleged, in addition to the 12 discharges identified in its letter, 32 additional discharges, described and identified by particular dates. The court held that the notice was sufficient not only for the 12 violations specified in the notice letter, but also for the 32 additional unspecified violations. The court further held that requiring the plaintiff to list each specific violation in the notice was not necessary because "[t]he purpose of the 60-day notice is to provide the agencies and the defendant with information on the cause and type of environmental laws or orders the defendant is allegedly violating so that the agencies can step in, investigate, and bring the defendant into compliance . . . . Congress did not intend to unduly burden citizens by requiring them to basically carry out the job of the agency."[551]

Third, in *San Francisco BayKeeper v. Tosco Corp.*,[552] the plaintiff sent a notice letter alleging that Tosco had violated the Clean Water Act by spilling petroleum coke into San Francisco Bay waters during ship loading, and by allowing the wind to blow coke into the water from uncovered piles. The letter alleged spilling violations on 14 specified dates when, based on Coast Guard records, ships were moored at Tosco's dock, as well as additional possible violations on unspecified dates. The letter alleged windblown violations without listing any specific dates, saying only that the violations occurred "on each day when the wind has been sufficiently strong to blow coke from the piles into the slough." The court held that sufficient notice had been provided for both kinds of violations. With respect to the additional spilling violations not specifically identified in the

547 713 F.3d 502 (9th Cir. 2013).

548 *Id.* at 651.

549 *Id.* at 652.

550 305 F.3d 943 (9th Cir. 2002).

551 *Id.* at 948.

552 309 F.3d 1153 (9th Cir. 2002).

notice, the court explained that "Tosco is obviously in a better position than BayKeeper to identify the exact dates, or additional dates, of its own ship loading. The notice regulation does not require BayKeeper in such a situation to provide the exact dates of alleged violations . . . ."[553] With respect to the wind-blown violations, the court wrote that the letter's general allegations regarding the mechanism for the violation were sufficient because the notice "'inform[ed] [Tosco] about what it [was] doing wrong'" and gave it "an 'opportunity to correct the problem' by enclosing or covering the coke piles."[554]

The court contrasted these three decisions, in which sufficient notice was provided, with its decision in the case *Southwest Center for Biological Diversity v. U.S. Bureau of Reclamation*,[555] in which such notice was not provided. In *Southwest Center*, the plaintiff sent three letters to the Department of the Interior and the Bureau of Reclamation notifying them "[a]t most" that "Southwest (1) desired consultation over Reclamation's operations in the Lower Colorado River and (2) felt that the [Memorandum of Agreement for Development of a Lower Colorado River Species Conservation Program] contravened the policies and dictates of the ESA."[556] The plaintiff then filed suit under the ESA seeking an order that would protect the southwestern willow flycatcher by requiring a lower water level of Lake Mead, the Colorado River reservoir behind Hoover Dam. The court held that the notice letters were inadequate because "none of [them] informed the [federal defendants] that Southwest had a grievance about the Flycatcher habitat at the Lake Mead delta."[557]

After reviewing this case law, the Ninth Circuit in *Klamath-Siskiyou Wildlands Center* found that the notice in this case was much more akin to the notice in *Ecological Rights Foundation, Bosma Dairy*, and *San Francisco BayKeeper*. The court explained that the plaintiff in this case did not in its notice letter only generally allege violations of the ESA, as the plaintiff did in *Southwest Center*. Rather, the plaintiff specifically alleged a geographically and temporally limited violation of the ESA. As such, the court concluded that the plaintiff's notice letter was sufficient notice under the citizen-suit notice provision of the ESA.[558]

---

553 *Id.* at 1158–59 (quoting 40 C.F.R. § 135.3(a)).

554 *Id.* at 1159 (internal citation omitted and second alteration in original).

555 143 F.3d 515 (9th Cir. 1998).

556 *Id.* at 521.

557 *Id.*

558 *Klamath-Siskiyou Wildlands Center*, 797 F.3d at 653–54.

CHAPTER 2

The California Endangered Species Act

This chapter provides an overview of the California Endangered Species Act, which protects threatened and endangered species in California. This chapter covers the substantive protections of CESA, the permitting program administered by the California Department of Fish and Wildlife, and the listing process administered by the California Fish and Game Commission.

CESA = California Endangered
Species Act

ESA = Endangered Species Act

MBTA = federal Migratory Bird
Treaty Act

CDFW or the "Department" =
California Department of Fish
and Wildlife

HISTORY AND STRUCTURE OF CESA

The California Endangered Species Act (CESA)[1] is one of the earliest comprehensive state laws established for the protection of threatened and endangered species. CESA was passed in 1970, three years prior to passage of the federal Endangered Species Act (ESA). It was not, however, California's first foray into species protections beyond traditional fish and game regulations.

Early Fish and Game Protections

California first protected non-game birds by statute in 1909.[2] The statute was passed due to growing public awareness of the need to protect bird species from human predation from, among other things, the widespread use of bird plumage for hats and other attire. Although California's version predated the federal Migratory Bird Treaty Act (MBTA) by almost a decade, like the later MBTA the new law criminalized the take or needless destruction of wild bird nests or eggs. California later added statutory protections for sea otters in 1913, prohibiting the hunting, pursuit, take, killing, destruction or possession of a sea otter, subject to a fine of up to $1,000 and/or imprisonment up to one year.[3]

In 1957, the state took a step further by adding statutory "fully protected" protections for certain birds and mammals.[4] Fully protected animals were not allowed to be taken at any time. These protections later were expanded to include amphibians, reptiles, and fish as part of the California Species Preservation Act.[5] The species listed under these statutes are not necessarily rare or threatened, and the code offers only limited relief in the form of permitting. Nonetheless, they continue to play a significant role in California.

In 1961, the state adopted a broad set of protections for fish and wildlife resources associated with rivers, streams and lakes, which today is memorialized in Fish and Game Code Section 1600 *et seq.* The modern version of this statute (discussed more fully in Chapter 9) does not limit its protections to any particular species, whether rare or otherwise, but protects *any* fish or wildlife resource that may be impacted by certain activities in and around rivers, streams, and lakes. Unlike the "fully protected" laws, this statute includes a permitting mechanism in the form of "Lake and Streambed Alteration Agreements," and delegates to the California Department of Fish and Wildlife (CDFW) considerable discretion to require the implementation of protective measures for fish and wildlife resources.

---

1   Fish & Game Code § 2050 *et seq.*

2   1909 Cal. Stat., ch. 617.

3   1913 Cal. Stat., ch. 562.

4   1957 Cal. Stat., ch. 1972.

5   Fish & Game Code § 3511 (fully protected birds), § 4700 (fully protected mammals), § 5050 (fully protected reptiles and amphibians), and § 5515 (fully protected fish).

Pre-CESA Protections for Rare and Threatened Species

CSPA = California Species Preservation Act

It was not until 1970 that the California Legislature passed two statutes directed specifically towards the protection of at-risk wildlife.

The first of these, known as the California Species Preservation Act (CSPA),[6] had a relatively light touch. This statute directed the Department of Fish and Game (now the Department of Fish and Wildlife) to "establish criteria" for determining if a species or subspecies of bird, mammal, fish, amphibian, or reptile is endangered or rare. The statute defined the term "endangered" to mean "when [the] prospects for survival and reproduction [of a species] are in immediate jeopardy." It defined the term "rare" to characterize a species which "may become endangered if its present environment worsens."[7]

The California Species Preservation Act further directed the Department to inventory all "threatened" (a term not defined in the statute) birds, mammals, fish, amphibians, and reptiles, and to report biennially to the Governor and Legislature on the status of these animals, including recommendations for (1) preserving, protecting and enhancing the conditions of endangered and rare species of the state; and (2) the addition or deletion of endangered and rare species under the fully protected category where necessary.[8] The CSPA also made additions to the list of fully protected birds and mammals, and established fully protected categories for amphibians, reptiles, and fish.

The second of the 1970 statutes was CESA in its original, rudimentary form. In adopting this statute,[9] the Legislature found that many species and subspecies of birds, mammals, fish, amphibians, and reptiles were endangered "because their habitats are threatened with destruction, adverse modification, or severe curtailment, or because of overexploitation, disease, predation, and other factors."

Like the CSPA, this statute defined the terms "rare" and "endangered," but with somewhat greater precision. In particular, Section 2051(a) defined the term "endangered animal" to mean "an animal of a species or subspecies" of birds, mammals, fish, amphibians or reptiles, "the prospects of survival and reproduction of which are in immediate jeopardy from one or more causes, including loss of habitat, change in habitat, overexploitation, predation, competition, or disease." Section 2051(b) defined "rare" animals to include species and subspecies that, although not presently threatened with extinction, are in such small numbers throughout their range that they may be endangered if their environment worsens.

Most significantly, Section 2053 contained the state's first take prohibition for rare and endangered species. The provision provided that:

> No person shall import into this state, or take, possess, or sell within this
> state, any bird, mammal, fish, amphibian, or reptile, or any part or product

---

6   1970 Cal. Stat., ch. 1036.

7   *Id.* § 901.

8   *Id.* § 903.

9   1970 Cal. Stat., ch. 1510.

CEQA = California
Environmental Quality Act

MOU = Memorandum of
Understanding

thereof, that the commission determines to be an endangered animal or rare animal, except as otherwise provided in this chapter.

The statute criminalized such activities, imposing a fine of not more than $500 or six months in prison, or both, and it provided no permitting mechanism.

The Beginnings of CESA

In 1984, the Legislature undertook a comprehensive modernization of CESA.[10] Among other things, these revisions (1) replaced the "rare" and "endangered" categories with new "endangered," "threatened," and "candidate" categories; (2) established a statutory process for the Fish and Game Commission (Commission) to list threatened and endangered species; (3) updated the list of activities prohibited under CESA; (4) authorized the Department to enter into "permits or memoranda of understanding" to authorize the import, export, take, or possession of listed or candidate species "for scientific, educational, or management purposes"; and (5) established a process for the Department, when consulting with other state agencies under CEQA, to make jeopardy or adverse modification findings and to recommend reasonable and prudent alternatives to prevent jeopardy or adverse modification.

As written in 1984, CESA did not have a clear vehicle for the permitting of incidental take. Nonetheless, to authorize intentional take for development and similar activities, the Department relied on memoranda of understanding based on statutory language authorizing the use of such agreements to permit the take of listed and candidate species "for scientific, educational, or management purposes." This practice was challenged after the Department entered into such an agreement with various parties in San Bernardino County authorizing the take of Stevens kangaroo rat. The agreement permitted the developer of a 3,000-acre development project in Moreno Valley to take kangaroo rats in connection with the construction of that project, so long as mitigation was provided in accordance with a habitat conservation plan prepared for the area. The San Bernardino Valley Audubon Society brought suit, arguing that such agreements could not legally be used to authorize take in connection with a private development project.[11]

In its response, the Department argued that management agreements for private parties properly enable the Department to "manage the populations and habitats of protected species where otherwise lawful activities may affect the species."[12] The Department based this argument on the fact that such agreements require a developer to provide funds for the initial protection and long-term mitigation of habitat to offset the losses associated with a project. According to the Department, as of 1994 about 80 such MOUs had been entered into around the state.[13]

---

10   1984 Cal. Stat., chs. 1162, 1240.

11   *San Bernardino Valley Audubon Society v. City of Moreno Valley*, 44 Cal. App. 4th 593 (1996).

12   *Id.* at 603.

13   *Id.* at 604.

The Court of Appeal dispensed with the Department's argument, noting that CESA defines "scientific resources management activities" to include *only* such activities as research, census, law enforcement, habitat acquisition, restoration, maintenance and propagation. The court also noted that, although CESA was drafted largely and intentionally in parallel with the federal ESA, the California legislature deliberately omitted the inclusion of an incidental take process like those found in the ESA. Accordingly, although the court ultimately did not reach this issue in its opinion, it stated that it would have found that "management MOUs" could not be used to authorize incidental take for activities such as private development projects.

About the time of *San Bernardino Audubon Society,* the Department's authority under CESA was challenged in another context. In early 1995, following a series of significant new-year storms, the Department issued a general permit authorizing affected parties to take listed or candidate species "for management purposes" as needed to prevent or mitigate an emergency or natural disaster in certain counties. The permit also authorized take in accordance with any activity whose purpose was to "restore any property or public or private facility to the condition in which it existed immediately before an emergency or natural disaster."

In *Planning and Conservation League v. Department of Fish and Game,* the Planning and Conservation League brought suit, asserting that the permit did not fall within the scope of the Department's authority to permit take for "management purposes."[14] Again, the Department argued that its authority to issue management permits was analogous to the Service's authority to issue incidental take permits under the federal ESA. This required the Department to argue that the court in *Audubon Society* was incorrect. The court disagreed, arguing that the logic of *Audubon Society*—which addressed permitting authority for private projects—applied equally to public activities such as responding to an emergency. Thus, although the facts of *Planning and Conservation League* might have been more compelling than those in *Audubon Society*, it made no difference to the court.[15]

In 1997, acknowledging the bind in which the Department found itself, the Legislature undertook another overhaul of CESA that, among other things, modified certain aspects of the listing process and established the incidental take permit process that is in use today. Various other changes have been made to CESA since that time, including repeal of the state agency consultation requirements described above.

The Conservation Mandate

CESA is usually viewed in terms of three principal components: (1) the listing process; (2) the take prohibition; and (3) the permit process. These components, however, comprise only the regulatory aspects of CESA. The reach of the statute, and certainly its policy foundation, is actually much broader than this.

---

14 *Planning and Conservation League v. Dept. of Fish and Game,* 67 Cal.Rptr.2d 650 (1997), review granted and dismissed November 25, 1997, S0651521.

15 *Id.* at 656–57.

First, although CESA's take prohibition is focused on the mortality of individual animals, the legislative findings in Section 2051(b) make clear that the broader purpose of the statute is to address the destruction, adverse modification, and curtailment of habitat. In fact, Section 2052 declares that it is the policy of the state to "conserve, protect, restore and enhance" any endangered species or any species and its habitat, and "to acquire lands for habitat of these species."

Second, although the statute's permit mitigation requirements are compensatory in nature (that is, they ensure that mitigation is limited to that which is roughly proportional to the impact), the stated purpose of CESA is not limited to simply mitigating habitat losses. As noted above, the statute is intended to affirmatively "conserve" at-risk species and their habitat. The term "conserve" (along with its cognates, "conserving" and "conservation") is defined in Section 2061 of CESA to mean:

> to use, and the use of, all methods and procedures which are necessary to bring any endangered species or threatened species to the point at which the measures provided pursuant to this chapter are no longer necessary. These methods and procedures include, but are not limited to, all activities associated with scientific resources management, such as research, census, law enforcement, habitat acquisition, restoration and maintenance, propagation, live trapping, and transplantation, and, in the extraordinary case where population pressures within a given ecosystem cannot be otherwise relieved, may include regulated taking.

In 2018, the Legislature took an additional step towards facilitating CESA's recovery-related tools by adding a provision to the Fish and Game Code (Section 2079.1) authorizing the Department, subject to available funding, to develop and implement "nonregulatory" recovery plans for threatened and endangered species, unless the Department finds that such a plan would not actually promote the conservation of the species. Section 2079.1 identifies the required contents of recovery plans and requires that they be developed through a public process including at least one public meeting at which the Department provides landowners, local governments, and interested members of the public with opportunity for input. The Legislature also added definitions of "recover" and "recovery" to mean "to improve, and improvement in, the status of a species to the point at which listing is no longer appropriate . . . and, if the Department has approved a recovery plan, satisfaction of the standards of that plan."[16]

In furtherance of CESA's broad mandate, the Department and the Commission carry out a variety of non-regulatory programs to benefit threatened and endangered species and their habitat. The permit requirements of CESA, however, limit their reach to requiring applicants to minimize and mitigate their own projects without requiring them to contribute affirmatively to recovery.

---

16 Fish & Game Code § 2064.5

CESA and State Agencies

Section 2055 of CESA states that "it is the policy of this state that all *state* agencies, boards, and commissions shall seek to conserve endangered species and threatened species and shall utilize their authority in furtherance of the purposes of" CESA. CESA also declares it to be state policy that *public* agencies (not just state agencies) should not approve projects that would cause jeopardy to protected species, or adverse modification of their essential habitat, if there are "reasonable and prudent alternatives" that would not have these effects.[17] This provision further declares it to be state policy that such reasonable and prudent alternatives shall be "developed by the [D]epartment, together with the project proponent and the state lead agency, consistent with conserving the species, while at the same time maintaining the project purpose to the greatest extent possible."[18] These provisions are structured as a statement of policy, not law. That is, CESA does not impose a direct obligation on public agencies—including local agencies—to reject projects where there are alternatives that do not affect protected species. Public agencies still have the ability under CESA to approve projects and reject alternatives based upon overriding considerations and questions of feasibility arising under CEQA.

Like private entities, however, public agencies are subject to the take prohibitions of CESA. In *Kern County Water Agency v. Watershed Enforcers*,[19] local water agencies argued that CESA did not apply to the California Department of Water Resources because it was not a "person" within the meaning of Section 2080. After analyzing both the statutory structure and language of CESA as well as the Department's own regulations, the court disagreed. In its ruling, the court observed that to exclude state agencies from the take prohibition would lead to the unreasonable result that major actors, whose operations result in the taking of endangered and threatened species, would be free to act without regard to potential impacts on sensitive species.

Organization

CESA is made up of the following general components:

> Article 1 (CESA Sections 2050 through 2069) includes definitions and legislative findings and declarations

> Article 2 covers the listing process (CESA Sections 2070 through 2079)

> Article 3 includes CESA's take prohibition and the permit process (Sections 2080 through 2085)

> Articles 3.5 and 3.7 (CESA Sections 2086 through 2089.26) establish programs to provide relief to agricultural interests affected by CESA

---

17 *Id.* § 2053.

18 The process for permitting incidental take under CESA does not impose such a rigorous alternatives requirement. Instead, the statute merely requires that, where various measures are available to mitigate the impacts of an applicant's project, the measures selected "shall maintain the applicant's objectives" to the greatest extent possible.

19 *Kern County Water Agency v. Watershed Enforcers*, 185 Cal. App. 4th 969 (2010).

DPS = distinct population
segment

> Article 5, largely outdated at this point, establishes funding requirements related to certain renewable energy projects

> The Commission has promulgated a comprehensive set of regulations governing its own activities and those of the Department, which are found at 14 California Code of Regulations, Division 1

THE LISTING PROCESS

Section 2070 of the Fish and Game Code requires the Commission to establish a list of endangered species and a list of threatened species. It must add or remove species from either list if it finds, "upon the receipt of sufficient scientific information," that the action is "warranted."[20] This process begins either with the filing of a listing petition by an "interested person" or a recommendation from the Department that the Commission list or de-list a species.

Sections 2071 and 2071.5 of the Fish and Game Code require the Commission to publish guidelines for the listing process and criteria for making listing determinations. In accordance with these requirements, the Commission has adopted regulations governing the listing process, which are found at 14 California Code of Regulations Section 670.1. This process and the criteria for listing are discussed below. In 2018, Section 2070 was amended to require that the Commission's listing decisions must be based solely upon the best available scientific information.

What Can Be Listed?

Section 2062 CESA defines the term "endangered species" to mean:

> a native species or subspecies of a bird, mammal, fish, amphibian, reptile, or plant which is in serious danger of becoming extinct throughout all, or a significant portion, of its range due to one or more causes, including loss of habitat, change in habitat, overexploitation, predation, competition, or disease.

Section 2067 of CESA defines the term "threatened species" to mean:

> a native species or subspecies of a bird, mammal, fish, amphibian, reptile, or plant that, although not presently threatened with extinction, is likely to become an endangered species in the foreseeable future in the absence of the special protection and management efforts required by this chapter.

These definitions mirror the definitions under the federal ESA in that: (1) both species and subspecies can be listed; (2) virtually any form of threat to the species (anthropogenic or not) can make it subject to listing; and (3) a species may be endangered if the danger of extinction exists only in a significant portion of the species' range.

Under the federal ESA, the term "species" is defined to include any subspecies of fish, wildlife or plants, plus any "distinct population segment" (DPS) of vertebrate fish

In June 2019, the Commission accepted a petition to list certain bumble bees under CESA. This petition will test the common understanding that CESA does not cover insects. The petition is contrary to a 1998 opinion of the Attorney General on this question (98 Ops. Cal. Atty. Gen. 105 (1998)).

20   Fish & Game Code § 2070.

or wildlife which interbreeds when mature. That is, the Service has flexibility to list only certain populations within a subspecies based upon the threats and the status of each such population, or to list different populations at different levels (e.g., one DPS as threatened, another one as endangered). A good example of this in California is the California tiger salamander, which has been divided into different DPS groups, some of which receive different regulatory treatment from the others. NOAA Fisheries commonly exercises this approach when it lists anadromous fish, using the term "evolutionarily significant unit" (ESU) when it does so.

In California, the Commission similarly lists ESUs as endangered, threatened, and candidate species under CESA. A coalition of California corporations challenged this practice in *California Forestry Association v. California Fish & Game Commission*, contending that the Commission erred when it listed two coho salmon ESUs as endangered and threatened under CESA.[21]

The Court of Appeal disagreed, finding that—although the statute is ambiguous—deference to the Commission and the Department's interpretation of "species or subspecies" was appropriate. The court noted that the Commission and the Department's "broad and longstanding interpretation" was based on their scientific expertise and was consistent with the liberal construction accorded to laws providing for the conservation of natural resources. Their interpretation also furthered the conservation, protection, restoration, and enhancement of endangered and threatened species by maintaining the diversity of the species. The court concluded that limiting the term as plaintiffs suggested would frustrate the intent of CESA because it would fail to protect subgroups of a species that are integral to the species' overall survival.[22]

The court in *California Forestry Association* also considered whether the "range" referenced in the definition of endangered and threatened species is a species' *California* range or its *worldwide* range. Finding again that the statutory language was ambiguous, the court found it reasonable to infer that CESA's focus is protecting species within the state, and that limiting the inquiry into a species' likelihood of extinction within California furthers that intent. The court therefore deferred to the Commission and the Department's interpretation that the term "range" as used in Fish and Game Code Section 2060 refers to a species' California range. Accordingly, the government had not erred in considering the coho salmon's risk of extinction in California in determining whether the two coho ESUs were entitled to protection under CESA.[23]

Listing Decisions and CEQA

The California Supreme Court has held that listing decisions are discretionary actions under CEQA.[24] *Mountain Lion Foundation v. Fish and Game Commission* involved a

ESU = evolutionarily significant unit

Service = U.S. Fish and Wildlife Service

NOAA = National Oceanic and Atmospheric Administration

21 *California Forestry Association v. California Fish & Game Commission*, 156 Cal. App. 4th 1535, 1544 (2007).
22 *Id.* at 1544–49.
23 *Id.* at 1549–52.
24 *Mountain Lion Foundation v. Fish and Game Commission*, 16 Cal. 4th 105 (1997).

EIR = Environmental Impact
Report

NEPA = National Environmental
Policy Act

Mojave ground squirrel. Photo:
NC-ND. Licensed under CC 2.0.

challenge to the Commission's removal of the Mojave ground squirrel from the threatened species list in accordance with a petition filed by Kern County. The petitioner in the case asserted that the Commission's failure to prepare an EIR violated CEQA.

Not surprisingly, the Supreme Court found that the Commission exercised sufficient judgment during the listing process that its action was discretionary within the meaning of CEQA. The County nonetheless argued that there is an irreconcilable conflict between CEQA and the Commission's duties under CESA, citing a federal decision[25] that reached this conclusion with respect to NEPA and the federal ESA. The Supreme Court distinguished the reasoning in that case, however, in which the federal court concluded that conducting NEPA in the context of a federal listing would be a "waste of time." Instead, the court concluded that CEQA *would* serve an important purpose in the listing process and that the two statutes ought to be reconciled.[26]

The court also rejected the County's argument that the delisting process should be considered categorically exempt from CEQA. The court did conclude, however, that the Commission's "certified regulatory program" under CEQA covered its decision to delist the Mojave ground squirrel, and that the Department was entitled to an exemption from the EIR process as provided in Public Resources Code Section 21080.5 by adhering to that program when carrying out a delisting. In so concluding, the Supreme Court expressly disagreed with the Court of Appeal, which had found that the certified regulatory program only applied to the Commission's establishment of hunting and fishing seasons and issuance of licenses.

The Supreme Court nonetheless concluded that the Commission had failed to satisfy the requirements of its own certified regulatory program. The Commission did not, for example, respond to significant environmental concerns or assess feasible project alternatives and mitigation measures. Accordingly, because the Commission did not proceed in accordance with these procedures, the court found that the Commission had abused its discretion in delisting the ground squirrel.

Initial Steps in Listing

CESA requires a listing petition to be written, clearly identified as a petition, and clearly indicate the administrative measure recommended (e.g., listing, delisting, change in status).[27] Procedures governing the submission and review of petitions for listing, uplisting, downlisting, and delisting of endangered and threatened species of plants and animals are described in Section 670.1, Title 14, of the California Code of Regulations.[28] To be accepted, a petition must at a minimum include sufficient scientific information

25   *Pacific Legal Foundation v. Andrus*, 657 F.2d 829 (6th Cir. 1981).

26   *Mountain Lion Foundation*, 16 Cal. 4th at 122–23.

27   Fish & Game Code § 2072.

28   A list of California's listed animal species can be found at https://nrm.dfg.ca.gov/FileHandler.ashx?DocumentID=109405&inline.

that a petitioned action "may be warranted." The requisite scientific information must include information regarding:

> population trend

> range

> distribution

> abundance

> life history

> kind of habitat necessary for survival

> factors affecting the ability to survive and reproduce

> degree and immediacy of threat

> impact of existing management efforts

> suggestions for future management[29]

The petition must also identify the availability and sources of information regarding the species and include a detailed distribution map, as well as any other information that the petitioner deems relevant.[30]

A petition will be deemed incomplete if it is not submitted on the Commission's prescribed form or fails to contain information on each of the categories described above.[31] An incomplete petition must be returned to the petitioner by Commission staff within 10 days of receipt.[32]

Once the Commission has accepted a petition as complete, it must refer the petition to the Department and publish a notice of receipt in the California Regulatory Notice Register.[33] That notice must include the scientific and common name of the species, its habitat type, and the location where interested parties may submit information on the petition.[34] Any person may submit relevant information to the Department during the initial 90-day review period (discussed below), and that information must be forwarded by the Department to the petitioner within 30 days of receiving such information.[35]

A petitioner may amend his or her petition at any time prior to the Commission's initial hearing on the petition but, if it determines that the amendment is substantive, the Commission may resubmit the petition to the Department, publish notice of the amendment, and re-notice or continue any scheduled hearing.[36]

---

29   Fish & Game Code § 2072.3; 14 Cal. Code Regs. § 670.1(d).

30   14 Cal. Code Regs. § 670.1(d).

31   *Id.* § 670.1(b).

32   *Id.*

33   Fish & Game Code §§ 2073, 2073.3.

34   *Id.* § 2073.3.

35   *Id.* § 2073.4.

36   *Id.* § 2073.7.

CALIFORNIA'S PARRY TO THE TRUMP ADMINISTRATION

The California Legislature has advanced a number of bills to fill any gap that may be left by relaxation of federal environmental standards under President Trump. Most notable of these is Senate Bill 1 (SB 1) (2019), which addresses air quality, water quality, and species protections. Under the CESA provisions of SB 1 (as amended by the Senate through May 2019), the California Fish and Game Commission (Commission) would be required to initiate a listing process upon either:

> the federal delisting of a species, subspecies or distinct population segment that is eligible for listing under CESA and was federally listed as of January 2017; or

> any change in the legal status of a federally listed species, including (1) a down-listing, (2) the adoption of a 4(d) rule for a threatened species; or (3) any amendment to a "federal baseline standard"

The term "federal baseline standard" includes any federal incidental take statement or permit or biological opinion in effect as of January 2017. Thus, any amendment of any federal ESA permit issued in California before January 2019 would automatically trigger a state-wide listing process for the covered species.

The Commission is required to list the species (or subspecies or DPS) at the earlier to occur of its second upcoming meeting within three months of the triggering event. The Commission is prohibited from following "the regular listing process" set forth in CESA. The listing must occur within the specified timeframe except where (1) the Commission determines that the listing is not warranted under CESA; or (2) the Department recommends that the listing undergo the normal process established under CESA.

If the Department recommends that the species undergo the regular process, the Commission must either (1) accept the Department's recommendation, in which case the species immediately becomes a "candidate" species subject to CESA's take prohibition (i.e., listing will be legally deemed as "may be warranted"), presumably giving the Commission authority ultimately to reject the listing if it is not justified under CESA; or (2) reject the Department's recommendation and list the species immediately. Although there is a flaw in the language, the bill appears to say that any listing is exempt from California's Administrative Procedure Act.

SB 1 allows the Commission or the Department to issue take authorizations as allowed by CESA. In lieu of issuing a standard CESA authorization, the Commission or the Department may simply adopt the terms of any 4(d) rule, or any incidental take statement, permit, or biological opinion in effect as of the federal baseline date. The statute does not appear to require that the adopted federal permit be consistent with CESA under Section 2080.1.

SB 1 requires the Department to "ensure that" protections remain in place pursuant to regulation, or CESA incidental take permit or consistency determination, that are at least as protective of public health and safety, the environment, or natural resources as are the federal baseline standards (according to best available science).

Ninety-Day Review by the Department

Within 90 days of receipt of a petition (plus an additional 30 days if an extension is requested by the Department and granted by the Commission), the Department must evaluate the petition "on its face" and in relation to other information the Department possesses or receives. The Department then submits to the Commission a written evaluation, based upon the information in the petition, with one of the following recommendations: (1) that there is not sufficient information in the petition to indicate that the petitioned action "may be warranted" and that the petition should be rejected; or (2) there is sufficient information that the petitioned action "may be warranted," and that the petition should be accepted and considered.[37] The Department's evaluation report must include all information submitted to the Department during its review or indicate where that information is available for review.

Commission Consideration of Petition and Evaluation Report

Once it receives the Department's evaluation report, the Commission must schedule the petition for evaluation at its next available meeting (but not sooner than 30 days after receipt of the petition and public release of the evaluation report).[38] The Commission must distribute its agenda to persons who have requested to receive them and must make the petition, evaluation report, and other information available for review.[39]

At its scheduled meeting, the Commission must hold a public hearing on the petition and receive information, written or otherwise, and oral testimony. After the conclusion of testimony from Commission and Department staff, the petitioner, and other persons, the Commission may close the public hearing *and* the administrative record.[40] After this point, no person may submit additional information to the Commission, nor may the Commission accept any additional information, except in either of the following circumstances:

> There is a change in state or federal law or regulation that "has a direct and significant impact" on the Commission's determination as to whether the action may be warranted; or

> The Commission determines that it needs further information to evaluate whether the petition contains sufficient information to determine whether the petitioned action may be warranted.[41]

If the Commission determines that it needs further information, the Commission may request such information, specifying a date by which such information must be submitted to the Commission. In this case the administrative record is deemed to be reopened for the limited purpose of receiving the information requested by the

---

37   *Id.* § 2073.5.

38   *Id.* § 2074.

39   *Id.* §§ 2074, 2078.

40   *Id.* § 2074.2(a).

41   *Id.* §§ 2074.2(b), (c).

Commission.[42] If this occurs, any person may submit responsive information, and the Commission must provide an opportunity for public comment on the submitted information prior to issuance of its decision.

The Commission has discretion to either (1) close the public hearing and continue the meeting for the purpose of deliberation, or (2) continue both the public hearing and the meeting to a subsequent date that is no more than 90 days following the originally scheduled meeting.[43] At its original or continued meeting, the Commission must consider the petition, the Department's evaluation report, written comments received, and oral testimony provided during the public hearing, and make and enter into the record one of the following findings:

> that the petition does not provide sufficient information to indicate that the petitioned action "may be warranted," in which case the Commission must publish in the California Regulatory Notice Register a notice of finding that the petition is rejected, including the reasons why the petition is insufficient

> that the petition provides sufficient information to indicate that the petitioned action "may be warranted," in which case the Commission must publish and distribute a notice of finding that the petition is accepted for consideration[44]

If the Commission accepts the petition, it must declare the species under consideration to be a "candidate species." A candidate species is defined by the statute as "a native species or subspecies of a bird, mammal, fish, amphibian, reptile, or plant that the commission has formally noticed as being under review by the department for addition to either the list of endangered species or the list of threatened species, or a species for which the commission has published a notice of proposed regulation to add the species to either list."[45]

The declaration of a candidate species has significant legal consequences, even though the rulemaking process has just been initiated. This is because, under Fish and Game Code Section 2085, the take prohibitions of Section 2080 apply to candidate species if notice has been given pursuant to Section 2074.4. Under Section 2084(a) of the Fish and Game Code, the Commission is permitted to authorize, "subject to terms and conditions it prescribes," the taking of any candidate species, which gives the Commission flexibility to fashion the nature and extent of any take prohibition applicable to a candidate species prior to its actual listing. Under Section 2084(b), the Department may recommend to the Commission that the Commission authorize, or not authorize, the taking of a candidate species (in addition to threatened and endangered species). The legal consequences of a "may be warranted" finding under CESA typically make the finding subject to a high degree of active public involvement, often including litigation.

42   *Id.* § 2074.2(c)(2).

43   *Id.* § 2074.2(d).

44   *Id.* § 2074.2(e); 14 Cal. Code Regs. § 670.1(e).

45   Fish & Game Code § 2068.

The "May Be Warranted" Finding

The cases below explore the burdens of proof associated with whether the Commission has properly made or failed to make a "may be warranted" finding. Suffice it to say, the standard is fairly low once there has been a *prima facie* showing of some affirmative potential for listing, to wit:

In *Natural Resources Defense Council v. California Fish and Game Commission*,[46] NRDC filed a petition and complaint challenging a decision by the Commission to reject a petition for the listing of a gnatcatcher species. On appeal, the court rejected NRDC's argument that a "fair argument" standard (i.e., a standard analogous to CEQA's standard for preparation of an EIR) should apply to the Commission's initial determination as to whether a listing "may be warranted."

Instead, the court interpreted CESA's language requiring "sufficient information" to determine whether a petition may be warranted to mean, when considered in light of the Department's written report and comments received, that amount of information that "would lead a reasonable person to conclude that there is a substantial possibility the requested listing could occur." In reaching this conclusion, the court rejected a "reasonable possibility" standard as being too low and a "reasonably probable" standard as being too high. As noted by the court, "these two standards are helpful in delineating the spectrum of meaning and point to a standard located between them." Having established this rule, the court remanded the proceedings back to the Commission, which ultimately listed the gnatcatcher.

Just a few years later, in *Center for Biological Diversity v. California Fish and Game Commission*,[47] applying the standard established in *NRDC*, the Court of Appeal held that the Commission had erred in rejecting a petition to list the California tiger salamander (CTS) as an endangered species.

The Department's evaluation report had concluded that the primary threat to CTS was the destruction and modification of habitat for various reasons. Other threats included competition, predation and hybridization. At the Commission's hearing, an expert herpetologist testified that CTS require significant areas of terrestrial habitat surrounding CTS breeding ponds, particularly around vernal pools. The Department's report included maps showing areas of CTS in the Bay Area and Central Valley that were under threat from urban development.

A coalition of business interests opposed the listing, arguing that the Department's maps showed an abundance of CTS habitat and that the CTS' status as a federally listed species obviated the need for its listing. Ultimately, the Commission rejected the petition as not satisfying the "may be warranted" standard. The trial court overturned the Commission's decision, and the matter was appealed.

Quoting *NRDC*, the court stated that the phrase "may be warranted" is appropriately characterized as a "substantial possibility that listing could occur," and further

NRDC = Natural Resources Defense Council

CEQA = California Environmental Quality Act

EIR = Environmental Impact Report

CTS = California tiger salamander

California tiger salamander. Photo: Pacific Southwest Region USFWS. Licensed under CC 2.0.

---

46   28 Cal. App. 4th 1104 (1994).

47   166 Cal. App. 4th 597 (2008).

EIR = Environmental Impact Report

characterized the term "substantial possibility" as meaning "something more than the one-sided 'reasonable possibility' test for an [EIR] but does not require that listing be more likely than not."[48]

As stated by the court:

> When this degree of information is adduced in support of a petition, an objective, reasonable person clearly would conclude there is a substantial possibility that listing could occur, unless the countervailing information and logic persuasively, wholly undercut some important component of that *prima facie* showing . . . . All that is required is a substantial possibility that the requested listing could occur . . . . A counter showing or argument that raises only a conflicting inference about a portion of the showing in favor of the petition, unless that counter inference is very strong, will not, for an objective, reasonable person, diminish the possibility that listing could occur to an "insubstantial" level.[49]

Applying this standard, the court found sufficient evidence to support a "may be warranted" finding. It found that the evidence submitted by the business coalition—relative to the abundance of CTS sites and its listed status under the federal ESA—was insufficient to counter the *prima facie* showing of threat reflected in the administrative record.

Petitions to Revisit Earlier Listing Decisions

In 2017, the California Supreme Court considered the Commission's rejection of a petition by an association of timber companies to delist coho salmon in certain coastal streams south of San Francisco.[50] The association argued that, because coho in these areas were "artificially introduced" into the area and thereafter supported by hatchery operations, they do not qualify for listing because they are not "native" within the meaning of CESA and therefore do not qualify for listing.

Coho salmon spawning on the Salmon River. Photo: BLM. Licensed under CC 2.0.

As noted above, in a *delisting* context the Commission must apply the same "may be warranted" standard as it applies in the context of a proposed listing. Applying this standard, the Commission rejected the petition, finding that the fact that the coho were hatchery-raised did mean they were not "native" within the meaning of CESA. The Commission also found that it did not have authority to protect less than the entire range of the taxonomic species (i.e., for just those populations located south of San Francisco).

The trial court disagreed, ordering the Commission to vacate its decision and proceed with further review under CESA. The Court of Appeal, however, found the listing petition to be invalid because it sought to revisit earlier decisions to *list* the coho (which association members had opposed) without any new scientific information about events transpiring *after* the original listing. That is, the court viewed the association's petition as an attempt to re-litigate the battle its members had already lost.

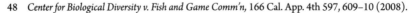

48   *Center for Biological Diversity v. Fish and Game Comm'n*, 166 Cal. App. 4th 597, 609–10 (2008).

49   *Id.* at 612 (citation omitted).

50   *Central Coast Forest Assoc. v. California Fish and Game Comm.*, 2 Cal.5th 594 (2017).

Both the Commission and the association argued before the California Supreme Court that a listing decision should be subject to reconsideration based upon new evidence that constitutes the best available information. The Supreme Court agreed and also found nothing in the statute or regulations limiting a delisting decision to changes in a species' status following the original listing decision.

In particular, the Supreme Court found support in Fish and Game Code Sections 2071 and 2072.7, which allow the Commission or the Department to review a species at any time based upon a petition *or* upon other data available to the Commission or the Department. This, among other things, showed the Legislature's acknowledgment that "information and scientific information are subject to change," and that "the Commission's decisions ought to evolve along with scientific understanding."

Department Review of Candidate Species

Once the Commission has accepted a petition and declared a species to be a candidate species, the Department must promptly initiate a 12-month review of the status of the species.[51] The Commission may grant an extension of up to six months if the Department determines that an extension is necessary to complete its review together with the peer review required under Section 2074.6.

In conducting its review, the Department may rely upon the information contained in the administrative record. CESA does not "impose any duty or obligation for, or otherwise require," the Commission or the Department to "undertake independent studies or other assessments of any species when reviewing a petition and its attendant documents and comments."[52]

During this process, the Department nonetheless must make "all reasonable attempts" to notify interested and affected parties and solicit data (including existing data on the candidate species from independent sources) and comments from as many people as is practicable, including distribution of the agenda and minutes, letters, newspaper notices, and press releases.[53]

The Department is required to seek independent and competent peer review of its status report whenever possible.[54] Peer review is defined to mean "the analysis of a scientific report by persons of the scientific/academic community commonly acknowledged to be experts on the subject under consideration, possessing the knowledge and expertise to critique the scientific validity of the report." The Department also must include in its report a listing of the individuals and agencies that were given an opportunity to review the report prior to its submission to the Commission.

Significantly, the Department must endeavor to provide specific notice to owners of land that may provide habitat essential to the continued existence of the species, unless

---

51   Fish & Game Code § 2074.6; 14 Cal. Code Regs. § 670.1(f).

52   Fish & Game Code § 2074.8.

53   *Id.* § 2074.4; 14 Cal. Code Regs. § 670.1(f).

54   See 14 Cal. Code Regs. § 670.1(f).

the director determines that ownership is so widespread, fragmented, or complex as to make individual notice impractical.[55]

Upon completion of its 12-month review, the Department must produce and make publicly available on the Department's web site a final written peer-reviewed report based upon the best scientific information available to the Department. This report must indicate whether or not the petitioned action is warranted.[56] Among other things, the report must: (1) contain a preliminary identification of the habitat that may be essential to the continued existence of the species; and (2) recommend management activities and other strategies for recovery of the species.

Prior to releasing its final report, the Department must have a draft status review report prepared and independently peer-reviewed. Upon receiving the peer reviewer's input, the Department must evaluate and respond in writing to the independent peer review and amend the draft report "as appropriate."[57] The revised report must be published on the Department's web site for 30 days prior to the Commission's subsequent hearing.

Final Consideration by the Commission

The Commission must schedule a petition for consideration at its next available meeting after receipt of the Department's report (but no sooner than 90 days from the date the candidate species notice was published), distribute an agenda, and make its report available for review.[58]

Public comments, including critiques, rebuttals, or comments on the petition or the Department's status report, may be submitted in writing to the Commission's office or presented as written or oral testimony at the finding hearing. However, parties who wish to submit a "detailed written scientific report" to the Commission must do so before the Department submits its status report. These reports may be peer reviewed and, if so, the peer review must be included with the submission to the Commission. Failure by an interested party to seek peer review of his or her detailed scientific report may be a factor considered by the Commission in its final determination. To assist interested parties with respect to the timing of their efforts, the Department is obligated to provide those who request them estimates as to the timing of the Department's report.[59]

At its meeting, the Commission must open and hold a public hearing on the petition and receive information, written or otherwise, and oral testimony.[60] At the conclusion of the hearing, the Commission may close both the hearing and the administrative record for the Commission's decision. Once the administrative record

55 Fish & Game Code § 2074.4.
56 *Id.* § 2074.6;14 Cal. Code Regs. § 670.1(f).
57 Fish & Game Code § 2074.6.
58 *Id.* § 2075; 14 Cal. Code Regs. § 670.1(f).
59 14 Cal. Code Regs. § 670.1(h).
60 Fish & Game Code § 2075.5(a).

has been closed, it may not be reopened unless (1) there is a change in law that has a direct and significant impact on the Commission's determination; or (2) the Commission itself decides that it requires further information to make its determination.[61] In this instance, the Commission must specify a date by which any additional information must be submitted, and the hearing will be reopened for this limited purpose.[62] Section 2075.5(d) includes additional requirements for continuances of the Commission's hearing.

At its meeting, the Commission must make one of the two following findings:

> that the petitioned action is not warranted, in which case the petitioned species is removed from the list of candidate species

> the petitioned action is warranted, in which case the Commission must publish a notice of proposed rulemaking to add the species to, or remove it from, the list of endangered or threatened species, as appropriate, and must submit the change in status to the Office of Administrative Law for filing with the Secretary of State and publication in the California Code of Regulations[63]

The Commission's regulations specify that a species "shall be listed as endangered or threatened . . . if the Commission determines that its continued existence is in serious danger or is threatened by any one or any combination of the following factors:"

> present or threatened modification or destruction of its habitat

> overexploitation

> predation

> competition

> disease

> other natural occurrences or human-related activities[64]

A species may be *delisted* as endangered or threatened if the Commission determines that its continued existence is no longer threatened by any one of or combination of these same factors.

Following publication of the notice of proposed rulemaking, the process established under the California Administrative Procedure Act,[65] the Commission may proceed to a final rulemaking under that statute. As a first step in this process, the Commission's regulations require the Department to prepare an "Initial Statement of Reasons for Regulation Change" in accordance with Government Code Sections 11346.5, which statement must be delivered to the Commission at its next available meeting.

Under Section 2076 of the Fish and Game Code, any finding made during the listing process is subject to judicial review under Section 1094.5 of the Code of Civil Procedure (i.e., administrative mandamus).

---

61 *Id.* § 2075.5(a),(b).

62 *Id.* § 2075.5(b),(c).

63 *Id.* § 2075.5(e).

64 14 Cal. Code Regs. § 670.1(i).

65 Gov't Code § 11340 *et seq.*

Emergency Listings

Notwithstanding the procedural requirements of Sections 2071 through 2075.5, the Commission may adopt a regulation that adds a species to the list of endangered species or threatened species as an emergency regulation in accordance with Fish and Game Code Section 399 if the Commission finds that "there is any emergency posing a significant threat to the continued existence of the species."[66] Fish and Game Code Section 399 allows the Commission, when adopting, amending, or repealing a regulation, to do so on an emergency basis (in accordance with Government Code Section 11346.1) if it makes either of the following findings:

> that the action is necessary for the immediate conservation, preservation, or protection of birds, mammals, fish, amphibians, or reptiles, including their nests or eggs

> that the action is necessary for the immediate preservation of the public peace, health and safety, or general welfare[67]

If the Commission takes emergency action under Section 2076.5, it must notify affected or interested persons in accordance with the requirements of Section 2074.4.

Periodic Review of Listed Species

Subject to available funding, Section 2077 of CESA requires the Department to review listed threatened and endangered species every five years to determine if the conditions that led to the original listing are still present. This review must be conducted based upon information that is consistent with the information required to be included in a listing petition under Section 2072.3 and which is the best scientific information available to the Department.

Similar to the Department's 12-month status review under Fish and Game Code Section 2074.6, this evaluation must include: (1) a review of the habitat that may be essential to the continued existence of the species; and (2) the Department's recommendations for management activities and other recommendations for recovery of the species. To the extent any species under review are federally listed by the Service, the Department's review must be coordinated with that agency. If the Department's report contains a recommendation to add or remove a species from the list of threatened or endangered species, the Commission must treat that recommendation as a petition in accordance with Section 2072.7. The deadlines specified in Section 2077 do not preclude the Commission or the Department from reviewing a species at any time based upon a petition or other information available to the Department and the Commission.

In addition to the five-year status review required under Section 2077, by January 30 of every third year the Department is required to prepare a report summarizing the status of all state-listed endangered, threatened, and candidate species.[68] That report

---

66 Fish & Game Code § 2076.5.

67 *Id.* § 399.

68 Fish & Game Code § 2079.

will be posted on the Commission's web site and must include, but is not limited to, a listing of those species designated as endangered, threatened, and candidate species, a discussion of the current status of endangered, threatened, and candidate species, and the timeframes for the review of listed species.

THE TAKE PROHIBITION

The Basic Prohibition

CESA prohibits the import, export, taking, possession, purchase, or sale of any endangered species, threatened species, or part or product of an endangered or threatened species, unless otherwise duly authorized under CESA, the Natural Community Conservation Planning Act or, with respect to plants, the Native Plant Protection Act or the Desert Native Plants Act.[69] Unlike the federal ESA, CESA's take prohibition applies not only to listed endangered and threatened species, but also to candidate species that are the subject of a listing petition. CESA does not, however, prohibit the take of insects or other invertebrates that are not fish.[70] CESA's take prohibition does not apply to possession or take by Department employees and agents for scientific, educational, management, or law enforcement purposes.[71]

Definition of Take

CESA prohibits not just *take* of listed and candidate species, but also the *possession, purchase or sale* of such species (or any attempt to do any of the foregoing).[72] The term "take" is defined in Section 86 of the Fish and Game Code to mean "hunt, pursue, catch, capture, or kill, or attempt to hunt, pursue, catch, capture or kill." This definition was incorporated into the Fish and Game Code in 1957, long before CESA was enacted, and was therefore originally intended to govern traditional hunting and fishing activities.

Anderson-Cottonwood and the Hunting and Fishing Question

The first case to interpret these definitions was the 1992 case, *Department of Fish and Game v. Anderson-Cottonwood Irrigation District*.[73] This case involved the operation by the Anderson-Cottonwood Irrigation District (ACID) of a pump diversion facility on the Sacramento River. These pumps were known to entrain and kill endangered winter-run chinook salmon. The trial court denied an application for preliminary injunction on the basis that the prohibitions against take and possession pertained only to hunting and fishing activity and required a specific intent to kill. The Court of Appeal, however, did not agree.

---

69   *Id.* § 2080; 14 Cal. Code Regs. § 783.1.

70   14 Cal. Code Regs. § 783.1.

71   *Id.* § 783.1.

72   Fish & Game Code § 2080.

73   8 Cal. App. 4th 1554 (1992).

With respect to "possession," the court relied on plain language to conclude that, by entraining salmon, ACID necessarily possessed them.[74] The court also easily concluded that the Section 86 definition of "take" did not specifically limit the term "kill" to that which occurs in hunting or fishing activities. The court also found persuasive that CESA prohibits the killing of listed plants, which of course is not the result of fishing or hunting. Ultimately, however, it appears the court was primarily guided by the legislative findings and declarations contained in CESA. As stated by the court, these provisions make it clear that the intent of CESA "is to protect fish, not punish fishermen. It is inconceivable that a statutory scheme, the purpose of which is to protect natural resources, should be construed to allow the wholesale killing of endangered species simply because the mode of death does not involve hunting or fishing."[75]

Indirect Harm under CESA

A few years later, in 1995, the California Attorney General opined on whether CESA's take prohibition covers *indirect* harm through habitat modification, even if that modification "actually kills or injures one or more members of an endangered or threatened species by impairing essential behavioral patterns, including breeding, feeding, or sheltering . . . ."[76]

The question was timely because the U.S. Supreme Court was also confronting this issue in the context of the federal ESA. The federal ESA makes it unlawful for any person to "take" endangered or threatened species, and in turn defines "take" to mean "harass, harm, pursue," "wound," or "kill."[77] The Secretary of the Interior had further defined "harm" in the regulations to include "significant habitat modification or degradation where it actually kills or injures wildlife."[78] That definition was challenged by various parties involved in the forest product industry in *Babbitt v. Sweet Home Chapter of Communities for a Great Oregon*,[79] who claimed that Congress did not intend the word "take" to include habitat modification. The U.S. Supreme Court ultimately disagreed, however, finding that the Secretary had reasonably construed "harm" to include habitat modification where it may actually kill or injure wildlife.[80]

In his opinion, the California Attorney General began by citing *Anderson-Cottonwood* for the proposition that "take" does not require a specific intent to kill. He continued by observing: "That is not to say, however, that a violation of the Act may be proved without a direct act of killing within the meaning of Section 86." Like the court in *Anderson-Cottonwood*, the Attorney General found it significant that, when adopting the 1984 amendments, the California Legislature was aware that the federal ESA

74 *Id.* at 1562.

75 *Id.* at 1563–64.

76 78 Ops. Cal. Atty. Gen. 137 (1995).

77 16 U.S.C. § 1532(19).

78 50 C.F.R. § 17.3.

79 *Babbitt v. Sweet Home Chapter of Communities for a Great Oregon*, 515 U.S. 687 (1995).

80 *Id.* at 708.

contained a much broader take prohibition through the notion of "harm." The Attorney General relied upon legislative history to confirm that the term "harm" was "designedly excluded" from CESA.

ITP = Incidental Take Permit

Pursue, Catch, and Capture

In 2015, in *Center for Biological Diversity v. California Department of Fish and Wildlife* (2015),[81] the California Supreme Court considered whether the term "take" includes certain actions carried out for the purpose of conserving a protected species. This question arose in connection with a "fully protected" fish, the unarmored threespine stickleback.

In its CEQA review of the Newhall Ranch project, the Department had imposed a number of mitigation measures providing for the collection and relocation of stickleback to minimize impacts associated with construction in, or temporary diversions of, the Santa Clara River. Despite the strong policy arguments made by the Department that conservation-related activities should not be prohibited under CESA, the court had no difficulty reaching the conclusion that clear language of the statute made clear that these activities constituted take in the form of pursuit, catch, and capture.

INCIDENTAL TAKE PERMITS UNDER SECTION 2081

There are a number of vehicles for securing incidental take authorization for candidate and listed species. As noted above, in 1997 the Legislature created broad authority for issuance of permits by the Department for the incidental take of endangered, threatened, and candidate species. These permits are known as incidental take permits or, more simply, "ITPs."

There are, however, other avenues of permitting authority, including "consistency determinations" under CESA Section 2080.1 (discussed below), the Commission's flexible authority under CESA Section 2084 relative to candidate species (which is analogous to the Service's "4(d)" authority under the ESA), the Natural Community Conservation Planning Act and certain specialized forms of relief for routine and ongoing agricultural activities, as well as for scientific, educational or management purposes (also discussed below).

In General

Under CESA Section 2081(b), the Department may issue an ITP if all of the following conditions are met:

> the take is incidental to an otherwise lawful activity
> the impacts of the authorized take are "minimized and fully mitigated"
> the permit is consistent with any regulations adopted pursuant to Fish and Game Code Sections 2112 and 2114 (now repealed)

---

81   62 Cal. 4th 204, 231–37 (2015).

> the applicant has ensured "adequate funding" to implement the minimization and mitigation measures required under the ITP, and for monitoring compliance with, and effectiveness of, those measures

No permit may be issued by the Department if the permit would jeopardize the continued existence of the species.[82] This determination must be based upon the best scientific information that is reasonably available, and must include consideration of the species' capability to survive and reproduce, and any adverse impacts of the taking on those abilities in light of:

> known population trends
> known threats to the species
> reasonably foreseeable impacts on the species from other "related projects and activities"

Each of these criteria and the way they are applied are discussed further below.

Take Must Be Incidental

Take may be permitted only if it is incidental to an otherwise legal activity. There has been little jurisprudence on this question in California, although the *EPIC* decision, discussed further below, provides helpful context. The issue has been litigated more heavily in the context of the Migratory Bird Treaty Act and the federal ESA, and the discussions of this question are treated more fully in those chapters.

Minimization and Full Mitigation

Consistent with Section 2081(b)(2) of the Fish and Game Code, the Department's regulations require that the applicant "minimize and fully mitigate the impacts of the take authorized under the permit."[83]

CESA's "full mitigation" standard is different from the federal ESA's standard under Section 10, which requires the impacts of take to be minimized and mitigated "to the maximum extent practicable."[84] CESA has no statutory practicability standard (although there are some protections built into the regulations as described below), but it does limit the minimization and mitigation obligation to that which is "roughly proportional in extent to the impact of the authorized taking on the species."[85]

As described by the California Supreme Court in *Environmental Protection Information Center v. California Department of Fish and Wildlife* (EPIC),

> the "roughly proportional" language [in CESA] mirrors the constitutional standard for what constitutes the taking of property set forth in *Dolan v. City of Tigard* (1994) 512 U.S. 374. . . . As we stated in a case that applied *Dolan's* rationale to development fees, *Dolan* was concerned with implementing one

82 Fish & Game Code § 2081(c).
83 14 Cal. Code Regs. § 783.4(a)(2).
84 See 16 U.S.C. § 1539(a)(2)(B)(ii).
85 Fish & Game Code § 2081(b)(2).

of the fundamental principles of modern takings jurisprudence—to bar Government from forcing some people alone to bear public burdens which, in all fairness and justice, should be borne by the public as a whole.[86]

NCCP = Natural Community Conservation Plan

The "rough proportionality" standard therefore acts as a guard against any undue obligation that the Department may seek to impose on private parties to advance the broader purpose of CESA to "conserve" at-risk species. As noted above, under Fish and Game Code Section 2061 the term "conserve" means "to use, and the use of, all methods and procedures which are necessary to bring any endangered species or threatened species to the point at which the measures provided pursuant to this chapter are no longer necessary." That is, while private parties may be required to mitigate their impacts, it is the government's responsibility to take the next steps towards actual recovery.

As stated by the California Supreme Court in *EPIC*:

> In other words, reading the "roughly proportional" language together with the "fully mitigate" language leads to the conclusion the Legislature intended that a landowner bear no more—but also no less—than the costs incurred from the impact of its activity on listed species.[87]

Although a "conservation" or "recovery standard" is required to be met in the context of a Natural Community Conservation Plan (NCCP) under Fish and Game Code Section 2800 *et seq.*, and any adverse modification of federally designated critical habitat may result in a conservation obligation under Section 7 of the federal ESA, this obligation does not exist under Section 2081 of CESA.

The rough proportionality standard is not CESA's only significant substantive protection for applicants. For example, Fish and Game Code Section 2081(b)(2) provides that, "[w]here various measures are available to meet [the minimization and mitigation] obligation, the measures required shall maintain the applicant's objectives to the greatest extent possible." The California Supreme Court has stated that this language "does not diminish a landowner's obligation under CESA . . . but merely provides that when that obligation can be met in several ways, the way most consistent with a landowner's objectives should be chosen. It does not relieve the landowner of the obligation to fully mitigate its own impacts."[88]

Moreover, as noted below, the Department's regulations provide that, in determining what measures might successfully be imposed on a permit, the Department shall consider whether the measures are legally, technologically, economically, and biologically practicable.[89] That is, there is a feasibility standard built into mitigation under CESA much in the same way that it exists under CEQA.

---

86 *Environmental Protection Information Center v. California Department of Forestry and Fire Protection,* 44 Cal. 4th 459, 510 (2008) (*EPIC*) (internal quotation marks omitted and citing *Ehrlich v. City of Culver City,* 12 Cal. 4th 854, 880 (1996)).

87 *Id.* at 511.

88 *Id.* at 512.

89 14 Cal. Code Regs. § 783.4(c).

Notwithstanding the limitations on minimization and mitigation described above, CESA does include a rather unusual provision that the Department relies on to require mitigation for species-related impacts other than the take itself. Under Fish and Game Code Section 2081(b)(2) and Section 783.4(a)(2) of the Department's regulations, the impacts of taking to be minimized and mitigated include "all impacts on the species that result from any act that would cause the proposed taking." If there are other, non-lethal impacts to the species associated with the activity causing take, then the Department will require those also to be mitigated. The Department will occasionally insist that this provision requires the mitigation to address all species-related impacts arising from a development project in general (e.g., long-term restriction of a migratory corridor that does not cause specific mortality), rather than the specific act causing take (e.g., destruction of a kit fox burrow).

Efficacy of Mitigation

The Department's regulations require that "[a]ll required measures shall be capable of successful implementation."[90] They further require that:

> Every permit issued under this article shall contain such terms and conditions as the Director deems necessary or appropriate to meet the standards in this section. In determining whether measures are capable of successful implementation, the Director shall consider whether the measures are legally, technologically, economically and biologically practicable. This provision does not preclude the use of new measures or other measures without an as-yet established record of success which have reasonable basis for utilization and a reasonable prospect for success.

This language bears some relationship to CEQA's requirement that mitigation imposed by the agency must be: (1) incorporated into the design of the project or fully enforceable through conditions, agreements, or other means; and (2) feasible to implement.[91]

There has been little reported case law under CESA relative to the efficacy of measures imposed by the Department. The issue was presented somewhat obliquely, however, in *Environmental Council of Sacramento v. City of Sacramento (Natomas)*.[92]

Natomas was the state court proceeding that evaluated the legality of the Natomas Basin Habitat Conservation Plan (NBHCP). The NBHCP is a regional HCP covering a large region north of Sacramento and which establishes a mitigation program for Swainson's hawk and giant garter snake. The NBHCP authorizes over 17,000 acres of urban development and, given its size, was an inevitable target for environmental litigation. The NBHCP was the subject of successful federal litigation that ultimately was settled. The revised NBHCP that arose from that settlement drew litigation in state

90 *Id.* § 783.4(a)(2).

91 See 14 Cal. Code Regs. § 15126.4.

92 *Environmental Council of Sacramento v. City of Sacramento*, 142 Cal. App. 4th 1018 (2006).

court, which was focused on CEQA and CESA compliance specifically related to the state-listed Swainson's hawk.

HCP = Habitat Conservation Plan

The NBHCP made certain assumptions about baseline conditions, and the HCP's conservation strategy was based upon the viability of these assumptions. For example, the NBHCP assumed that approximately 15,000 acres in the Natomas Basin would remain in agricultural uses friendly to the giant garter snake and Swainson's hawk, that connectivity among various irrigation channels and ditches would remain, and that certain setbacks assumed in the HCP would remain intact and not be lost to urban encroachment.

The plaintiffs in *Natomas* insisted that these various assumptions should be treated as *mitigation* with the consequent requirements for funding and enforceability under both CESA and CEQA. The court found that the plaintiffs had confused the concepts of mitigation and baseline assumptions, and that the Department's reliance on assumptions would be upheld if based upon substantial evidence. In the case of the NBHCP, the court found those assumptions to be sustainable.

Use of Mitigation Ratios

The NBHCP required all developers within the permit area to mitigate at a 0.5:1 ratio. That is, each developer was required to fund the equivalent of ½ acre of mitigation for every acre developed. Although this might seem like less than "full mitigation," the requirement was imposed on all landowners regardless of whether their properties actually provided habitat for the Swainson's hawk or giant garter snake. Taken together, therefore, the aggregate mitigation provided under the NBHCP for *habitat* converted to urban use exceeded what would be considered full mitigation. Moreover, the NBHCP contained a number of additional measures to augment the mitigation ratios themselves (e.g., requirements for managed marsh, minimum preserve sizes and other measures).

Plaintiffs asserted that full mitigation could only be accomplished through mitigation at a 1:1 ratio. The court recognized, however, that because the mitigation was imposed on all landowners regardless of habitat value (and in many cases probably exceeded the "rough proportionality" limitation), they concluded that the 0.5:1 ratio was probably more than generous. The court also found that there was substantial evidence to support the notion that the mitigation imposed was financially feasible.[93]

The assumption in the petitioner's arguments, and the court's analysis, is that a 1:1 mitigation ratio normally would be considered adequate mitigation under CESA. The practitioner should be aware, however, that the Department typically will insist on multiple levels of mitigation (e.g., 3:1 for the California tiger salamander) under the theory that, even with a multiplied ratio, there is still a net loss of habitat. For example, if a project causes the loss of 10 acres of habitat and preserves 30 acres of habitat, that preservation action still results in an overall 25 percent loss of habitat.

---

93 *Environmental Council of Sacramento*, 142 Cal. App. 4th at 1038–41.

This position is not consistent with the assumption in *Natomas,* and is also inconsistent with standard environmental practice in California under CEQA, in which "replacement" is considered an adequate form of mitigation. In *Masonite Corp. v. County of Mendocino,*[94] for example, the court rejected an argument that mitigation of agricultural impacts through an agricultural conservation easement is legally infeasible because it does not actually create new farmland. Moreover, in *Save Panoche Valley v. San Benito County,*[95] the court specifically upheld such measures as part of a suite of mitigation in the agricultural context.

Ensured and Adequate Funding

Natomas is instructive also with respect to the requirement that the applicant "ensure" adequate funding of mitigation. The court found that this standard had been met in *Natomas* because the HCP required fees to be imposed on developers, which fees would be reviewed annually and adjusted to reflect the actual costs of the HCP. The plan had no cap on mitigation fees and allowed developers, if land prices became exorbitant, to contribute land instead of paying fees to satisfy their mitigation requirements. Most importantly—and this has since become a feature of almost all regional habitat conservation plans—the NBHCP contained a "get-ahead-stay-ahead" provision prohibiting the issuance of grading permits until the HCP manager had established (and thereafter maintained) a 200-acre mitigation "cushion" to assure that the establishment of adequate mitigation actually *preceded* at all times the development that generated the need for that mitigation.[96]

Despite the limited case law addressing CESA's "ensured funding" requirement, the Department has developed over the last decade a number of policies related to the implementation of mitigation. These policies are intended to address Fish and Game Code Section 2081(b)(4), which requires ensured funding not only for the minimization and mitigation measures required under the ITP but also for monitoring compliance with, and effectiveness of, the measures imposed. These important policies, which include the posting of endowments and other financial security all to be managed in accordance with certain established Probate Code requirements, are described more fully below.

No Jeopardy

Consistent with Section 2081(c) of CESA, the Department's regulations provide:

> No incidental take permit shall be issued . . . if issuance of the permit would jeopardize the continued existence of the species. The Department shall make this determination based on the best scientific and other information that is reasonably available, and shall include consideration of the species' capability to survive and reproduce, and any adverse impacts of the taking

94   218 Cal. App. 4th 230, 238 (2013).

95   217 Cal. App. 4th 503, 529 (2013).

96   *Environmental Council of Sacramento,* 142 Cal. App. 4th at 1044.

on those abilities in light of (1) known population trends; (2) known threats to the species; and (3) reasonably foreseeable impacts on the species from other related projects and activities.[97]

There has been little California case law on the meaning of jeopardy under CESA, including the background information required to be considered by the Department in conducting that evaluation under Fish and Game Code Section 2081(c) (i.e., known population trends, known threats, and reasonably foreseeable impacts from related projects and activities). The "related projects and activities" prong was, however, considered in *Natomas.*

The petitioners in *Natomas* argued that the Department had failed to consider the potential for future development under a memorandum of understanding between certain local agencies (known as the "Joint Vision MOU") as to how to address future development pressures in the Natomas Basin. The Joint Vision MOU discussed the potential for future development in a 10,000-acre area that was assumed in the NBHCP to remain in agricultural use (i.e., and would have exceeded the 17,500-acre development cap assumed in the NBHCP). But the MOU was conceptual in nature, and it acknowledged that a myriad of permits (including endangered species permits) would be required if any further development were to be considered in the future.

Although the federal court had dismissed the MOU as purely conceptual, the petitioners argued in state court that it constituted a "related project" and "known threat" that should have been addressed in the Department's jeopardy analysis (and as a "cumulative project" under CEQA).

Ultimately, the Court of Appeal agreed with the trial court and the federal district court that:

> an environmental analysis now of the unspecified and uncertain development that might be approved in the future under the Joint Vision MOU would be speculative, wasteful, and of little value to the consumers of the EIR. Far too little is known about the scope, the location, or the types of projects that might be proposed in the future to assist decision makers in evaluating any potential environmental tradeoffs.[98]

With respect to CESA specifically, the court stated:

> Plaintiffs have cited no cases, and we have not found any, to support their counterintuitive proposition that a vague planning document that does not qualify as a project under CEQA nonetheless constitutes a known threat to a species or a related project with reasonably foreseeable impacts on hawks and snakes.[99]

---

97 14 Cal. Code Regs. § 783.4(b).

98 *Environmental Council of Sacramento,* 142 Cal. App.4th at 1032.

99 *Environmental Council of Sacramento,* 142 Cal. App.4th at 1034.

Although the court engaged in no discussion about the jeopardy standard itself, it found that the Joint Vision MOU did not establish a "known threat" or a "related project" under CESA.

"No Surprises" and 2081 Permits

As described in Chapter 11 (Conservation Planning), the Department has the ability, in the context of an NCCP, to offer "no surprises" assurances (commonly referred to as "regulatory assurances" to plan participants). In particular, Fish and Game Code Section 2820(f)(2) provides that:

> If there are unforeseen circumstances, additional land, water, or financial compensation or additional restrictions on the use of land, water, or other natural resources shall not be required without the consent of plan participants for a period of time specified in the implementation agreement, unless the department determines that the plan is not being implemented consistent with the substantive terms of the implementation agreement.

The availability of "no surprises" assurances is not the only difference between the NCCP Act and ordinary permitting under 2081. Unlike a 2081 permit, an NCCP permit can provide take authority for both unlisted species and fully protected species.

In the *EPIC* decision discussed above,[100] the California Supreme Court evaluated, among other things, whether the Department may similarly include regulatory assurances in ITPs issued under Fish and Game Code Section 2081, despite the lack of specific statutory authority to do so. After considering the language and structure of CESA, the court ultimately concluded that the Department could not include such assurances under Section 2081.

The case arose from the "Headwaters Agreement" consummated by the Pacific Lumber Company and the state and federal governments. The agreement was intended to settle matters of litigation and public controversy surrounding the intensive logging of old growth redwoods and other trees on Pacific Lumber's property in Humboldt County. In addition to the state and federal governments' purchase of a relatively small portion of Pacific Lumber's property for conservation purposes, it was agreed that Pacific Lumber could log the rest of its property, provided that it obtain certain regulatory approvals from state and federal agencies. One of these approvals was an ITP under CESA.

Following execution of the Headwaters Agreement, an ITP was issued to Pacific Lumber authorizing the incidental take of the marbled murrelet, an endangered bird, and the bank swallow, a threatened bird. Among other things, the ITP contained certain regulatory assurances for potential "changed circumstances" and "unforeseen circumstances." In the case of changed circumstances, the landowner would be required to implement only certain prescribed measures, and no others. In the case of unforeseen circumstances, the government agreed not to require the commitment by the landowner of additional land, water, or financial compensation, or additional restrictions on the use of the land, water, or other natural resources, unless the landowner consented. EPIC

---

100 *Environmental Protection Information Center v. California Department of Forestry and Fire Protection*, 44 Cal. 4th 459, 507 (2008).

contended that these provisions constituted unlawful "no surprises" clauses under Section 2081 because they failed to "fully mitigate" the impacts of the authorized take.

In response, the Department argued that the no surprises rule is the established policy of federal wildlife agencies and, because CESA and the NCCP Act are distinct statutory schemes, the explicit provision for regulatory assurances in the NCCP Act should not imply a lack of authority to grant regulatory assurances under CESA. The California Supreme Court disagreed, finding that, while CESA and the NCCP Act share the common objective of authorizing incidental take in a way that minimizes impacts on listed species, they do so in alternative ways. Moreover, the court noted, CESA had been amended several times either contemporaneously with or subsequent to the 2002 amendment of the NCCP Act, and the natural inference therefore is that the Legislature did not intend the same assurances to be provided in the other scheme.

California redwood forest. Photo: Bonnie Peterson. Licensed under CC 2.0.

In addition, the court further noted that reading the "roughly proportional" language of Fish and Game Code Section 2081 together with the "fully mitigate" language in that section leads to the conclusion that the Legislature intended the landowner to bear no more—but also no less—than the costs incurred from the impact of its activity on listed species. Thus, to the extent that the changed and unforeseen circumstances provisions of the ITP would exempt landowners from this obligation, they exceeded the Department's statutory authority under CESA. On this basis, the court concluded that the ITP approvals were invalid and remanded for further proceedings consistent with its opinion.[101]

THE PERMIT PROCESS

Section 2081(d) requires the Department to adopt regulations to aid in the implementation of the ITP process as well as the California Environmental Quality Act. These regulations are found at California Code Regulations, title 14, Sections 783.2 through 783.8. Section 2081(d) also authorizes the Department to seek certification of its ITP program as a certified regulatory program under Public Resources Code Section 21080.5. In fact, the ITP program has been certified as such, which is why the Department's CESA regulations include CEQA-related requirements that apply when the Department is acting in the capacity of a lead agency.

In 2018, the Legislature authorized the Department to implement a new fee program for the processing of incidental take permits. The basis of fee calculations, and exceptions to the fee, can be found in Section 2081.2 of CESA.

ITP Applications

ITP applications must be submitted to the Department's Regional Manager for the geographic area in which the project is located. ITP applications are required to include:

> the applicant's identifying information (name, address, etc.)

> the common and scientific names of the species proposed to be covered by the ITP and their status under CESA

> a complete description of the project for which the ITP is being sought

> the location where the project will occur

101 *Id.* at 511–14, 526–27.

> an analysis of whether and to what extent the project could result in the taking of a species to be covered by the ITP

> an analysis of the impacts of the proposed taking on the species

> an analysis of whether issuance of the ITP would jeopardize the continued existence of the species, which must consider the species' ability to survive and reproduce in light of known population trends and threats to the species as well as reasonably foreseeable impacts

> proposed mitigation measures to minimize or eliminate impacts of the taking

> a proposed mitigation monitoring plan to assess compliance with and effectiveness of the mitigation measures

> a description of the funding source and availability of funding to implement the mitigation measures

All applications must be based upon the best information, scientific or otherwise, that is reasonably available to the applicant, and the applicant must certify the information contained in the application under penalty of civil and criminal prosecution. Where an analysis meeting these requirements is prepared pursuant to another state or federal law—for example, the federal ESA—it may be used for an ITP application as well. To ensure an ITP application will satisfy the Department's requirements, an applicant may request a consultation with the Department to review the application in advance of submission. When such a consultation is requested, the Department is obligated to consult with the applicant to the greatest extent practicable.[102]

CEQA Considerations

The Department's issuance of an ITP is considered a discretionary action under CEQA. In most cases the Department serves as the CEQA responsible agency for purposes of issuing an ITP where another public agency has taken on the CEQA lead agency role for the overall project. When the Department is acting as a CEQA responsible agency, the ITP application must also include:

> contact information of the lead agency

> a statement as to whether an Environmental Impact Report, Negative Declaration, Mitigated Negative Declaration, or initial study has been prepared or is being considered

The applicant may also elect to attach any notice of preparation, notice of determination, or draft or final environmental document that may be available to the ITP application.

In cases where issuance of the ITP is the only public agency action subject to CEQA for a project, the Department will assume the CEQA lead agency role.[103] The Department has adopted a set of CEQA guidelines governing the Department's role as lead agency.[104]

---

102 14 Cal. Code Regs. § 783.2(b).

103 14 Cal. Code Regs. § 783.3(b).

104 *Id.* § 754–757.

For the most part, these guidelines echo the provisions of the state's CEQA Guidelines as promulgated by the Governor's Office of Planning and Research.[105]

Under the Department's CESA regulations, where the Department is acting as lead agency the ITP application must provide enough information for the Department to be able to determine whether the proposed project will result in significant adverse environmental effects *in addition to* the impacts of the proposed taking, and whether any feasible alternatives or mitigation measures would avoid or substantially lessen those adverse effects.[106]

This requires the ITP applicant to analyze all potentially significant adverse effects of the project, and to provide either:

> a discussion of feasible alternatives and mitigation measures to avoid or substantially lessen any adverse environmental effects

> a statement that the applicant's analysis showed the project would not have any significant or potentially significant effects on the environment, and accordingly mitigation measures and alternatives are not proposed

If the applicant's analysis identifies significant environmental effects that cannot be mitigated, the application must describe any specific environmental, economic, legal, social, technological, or other benefits that justify the project's significant adverse effects. An analysis that satisfies CEQA requirements must be provided as soon as practicable after the application is submitted.[107]

Because the Department acts as responsible agency in most permit situations, its CEQA obligations in that capacity are couched in the following discussion of the ITP review process.

Initial Review

Once an ITP application is submitted, the Department will complete an initial review within 30 days.[108] This initial review only assesses the completeness of the application, not its merits. If the Department determines the application is complete, it will proceed to assessing the merits of the application. If the Department believes the application is incomplete, it will return the application with a description of the deficiency, providing the applicant 30 days to correct and resubmit the application. The Department reserves the right to request supplemental information from an applicant even after a completeness determination has been made, and to require an on-site inspection of the project before a final decision on the ITP.

105 *Id.* § 15000 *et seq.*
106 *Id.* § 783.3(b).
107 *Id.*
108 *Id.* § 783.5(b).

PSA = Permit Streamlining Act

Department as Responsible Agency

If the Department is acting as a responsible agency, it must follow Section 15096 of the CEQA Guidelines, which outline the responsibilities of a responsible agency. Although this provision requires the Department to review and comment on notices of preparation and draft environmental documents,[109] it often fails to do so. This often leads to consternation on behalf of local lead agencies and applicants when, in response to ITP applications, the Department raises issues that were most appropriately raised during the lead agency's CEQA process.

Regardless of whether it participated in the lead agency's CEQA process, as a matter of law the Department will be deemed to have waived any objection to the adequacy of the lead agency's environmental document unless the Department brings a CEQA action against the lead agency within the applicable statute of limitations.[110] If the Department fails to initiate such an action, it may prepare additional CEQA documentation only if a subsequent EIR is justified under Section 15162 of the CEQA Guidelines or the Department is authorized to assume lead agency status under Section 15052 of the CEQA Guidelines. A failure by the Department to respond to a lead agency's environmental document or bring suit as described above may act to limit the Department's discretion under CEQA when considering an ITP application. This is because the Department is required, prior to reaching a decision on an application, to consider the environmental effects of the project "as shown in the [lead agency's] EIR or Negative Declaration."[111]

Once an application is filed, the Department will decide whether the ITP can be issued based on a review of the ITP application and the CEQA documentation for the project, as well as any other relevant information in the administrative record.[112] The Department's regulations also require the Department to consider the lead agency's CEQA findings. Although the regulations do not explicitly state the extent to which the Department must defer to the lead agency's findings, clearly those findings carry some legal weight even if the Department may disagree with them.

Assuming the Department has waived any objection to the lead agency's EIR and no further CEQA review is justified under the CEQA provisions cited above, the Department is required to either approve and issue an ITP or deny the ITP no later than the latest of 90 days from either (1) the date on which the lead agency approved the project or (2) the date on which the ITP application was accepted as complete by the Department. Under unique circumstances where an application is particularly complex, the Department may extend this timeframe by up to 60 days, to a total of 150 days.

If the Department approves the ITP, it must make the findings required by CEQA— namely, that any significant adverse environmental effects of the project have been

---

109 14 Cal. Code Regs. § 15096(b)(d).

110 *Id.* § 15096(e).

111 *Id.* § 15096(f).

112 14 Cal. Code Regs. § 783.5(c).

avoided or substantially lessened, or that there are specific economic, legal, social, technological, or other considerations that make mitigation infeasible—and then issue the ITP and file a notice of determination. If the Department denies the ITP, the application is returned with a written statement explaining the denial and any measures the Department considers necessary for the application to be approved.

PSA = Permit Streamlining Act

Unlike the process for a Lake and Streambed Alteration Agreement under Section 1600 of the Fish and Game Code, the Department's failure to approve or deny a permit within the requisite 90 days will not result in a deemed approval of the permit. However, an ITP falls within the ambit of California's Permit Streamlining Act (PSA), which establishes timelines for state and local agency decisionmaking on any application for a "development project."[113] The term "development project" is defined broadly to include "any project undertaken for the purpose of development," which includes, among other things, the placement of any solid material or structure, the discharge of fill material, and the grading or removal of any materials.[114]

The PSA establishes the same 30-day window for determining completeness as is set forth in CESA. Under the PSA, however, if a determination of completeness is not made by the Department by this date, the ITP application will be deemed complete as a matter of law, although this does not preclude the Department from requesting additional information within certain limits.[115]

The application completeness date is important under the PSA because it triggers the deadlines for agency action on the permit. Once the application has been accepted as or deemed complete, the Department must approve or disapprove the project within the *later* to occur of (1) 180 days from the lead agency's approval of the project; or (2) 180 days from the date the application was accepted as or deemed complete.[116] If the agency fails to act within this time period, the permit is deemed approved by operation of law.[117]

Department as Lead Agency

If the Department is acting as the CEQA lead agency, it must either approve or deny the ITP within 120 days of accepting the application as complete. Under the Department's regulation regarding its lead agency process under CESA, which are set forth in Section 783.5(d) of Title 14, the Department may extend that timeframe by up to 60 days (the maximum allowed under the PSA) by making a written finding that the application's complexity or scope warrants additional consideration.

Upon receiving the completed application, the Department will review it for consistency with CEQA and make any revisions it deems necessary for CEQA compliance.

---

113 Cal. Gov't Code § 65920 *et seq.*

114 *Id.* § 65927.

115 *Id.* § 65944(a).

116 *Id.* § 65956.

117 *Palmer v. City of Ojai*, 178 Cal. App. 3d 280, 293 (1986); *Orsi v. City Council*, 219 Cal. App. 3d 1576, 1584 fn. 5 (1990).

After those revisions are made, the Department must make both the application and the CEQA analysis available for public review and comment by publishing a Notice of Public Availability and allowing at least 30 days for public comment. Concurrent with the distribution of the Notice of Public Availability, the Department must also consult with any other public agencies that have jurisdiction over the project for which the ITP is sought.

Once comments have been received, the Department will respond to all significant environmental points raised by the comments, and then proceed to a decision on the ITP based on the application and CEQA analysis, public comments and responses, and any other relevant information in the administrative record. As lead agency, the Department will decide not only whether to issue the ITP, but whether the project will result in any significant adverse environmental effects and, if so, whether mitigation or alternatives could avoid or lessen those effects. If significant adverse effects are likely to result even after inclusion of alternatives or mitigation measures, the Department may still approve the ITP, but must find that there are specific economic, legal, social, technological, or other considerations that make mitigation infeasible.

Regardless of whether the Department issues or denies the ITP, it must file a notice of decision within five days. If the Department denies the ITP, the application is returned with a written statement explaining the denial and any measures the Department considers necessary for the application to be approved. Any permit issued after January 1, 2019 must be posted on the Department's internet website within 15 days of the effective date of the permit.[118]

Reconsideration and Appeal

The Department's processes for reconsideration and appeal are set forth in Section 783.8 of Title 14. Under these provisions, if an ITP applicant is denied issuance of an ITP or is issued an ITP subject to certain limitations—for example, the applicant cannot perform all requested activities under the ITP, or the ITP requires mitigation measures other than those proposed by the applicant—the applicant can request that the Department reconsider its decision.

Requests for reconsideration must be made in writing to the Regional Manager within 30 days of notification of the Department's decision. The written request must state the decision to be reconsidered and the reasons for reconsideration, including any new information pertinent to the request, and must be certified under penalty of civil and criminal liability. The Department itself may separately initiate an inquiry into the matter.

Within 45 days of receiving a reconsideration request, the Department must notify the applicant in writing of its decision, including the reasons for the decision and the evidence relied upon by the Department. Appeal from an adverse decision on reconsideration must be submitted to the Director of the Department within 30 days of

---

118 Fish & Game Code § 2081(e).

notification of the reconsideration decision. The appeal must state the reasons and issues upon which the appeal is based; an applicant may submit additional evidence and arguments in support of the appeal.

Under some circumstances, the Director may determine that oral argument is necessary to clarify the issues raised in the written record; otherwise, a decision on appeal will be made by considering the written record. The decision on appeal must be rendered within 30 days unless the Department elects to extend the timeframe by 30 days for good cause and notifies the appellant of that extension. The Director's decision on appeal is the final administrative decision of the Department, and may be appealed to California superior court.

POST-PERMIT CONSIDERATIONS

Assignments and Transfers

The Department's regulation establishing general conditions required for ITPs are set forth in Section 783.6 of Title 14. Under these provisions, ITPs cannot be assigned or transferred without the written consent of the Department, although the regulations provide that such consent "shall not be unreasonably withheld." An ITP may be assigned or transferred, without written notice, under the following circumstances:

> sale, merger, annexation, consolidation, or other acquisition of a corporate, public, or institutional permit holder by another entity

> transfer of a permit from a person to the individual's employer

> as security for debt for a mortgage, deed of trust, indenture, bank credit agreement, or other similar instrument

Renewal of Permits

To renew an ITP under Section 783.6, a written application must be submitted to the Regional Manager at least 60 days before the ITP expires. The applicant must certify that all of the statements in the original application remain current or correct, or provide corrected information if changes must be made. If the application continues to meet the standards for issuance of an ITP, the ITP will be renewed. As long as a permittee has submitted a timely application for renewal of its ITP, it may continue to conduct the activities authorized by the expired ITP while the renewal application is pending. Should the Department renew the ITP subject to conditions, such as additional mitigation measures not proposed by the applicant or limitation on the permittee's ability to perform all requested activities under the ITP, the permittee may appeal the renewal decision through the same reconsideration and appeal mechanism used to challenge initial permit decisions.

Amendments

Also under Section 783.6, if circumstances change and a permittee wishes to modify the terms of its ITP, it must submit an application and supporting information to the

Department. The Department may also, of its own volition, amend any ITP at any time during its term as long as the permittee concurs, or, if the amendment is required by law, regardless of the permittee's concurrence.

Minor permit amendments—amendments that do not significantly modify the scope of the project or the mitigation measures set forth in the ITP—are to be approved and incorporated or denied within 60 days of submission of an application. The Department cannot impose a new or modified permit condition upon minor amendment unless it relates solely to the minor amendment, is required by law, or is needed to make existing permit conditions consistent with the amendment.

Major permit amendments—amendments that would significantly change the scope of the project or mitigation measures, or that require additional CEQA review—will be reviewed according to the process for an initial ITP application. Information and analysis provided to support the application for a major amendment may rely on and supplement the information from the original ITP application for the project.

The Department must approve any minor or major permit amendment if the amended ITP would continue to meet the standards for issuance of an ITP. Should the Department deny the amendment request, the permittee may appeal the denial through the same reconsideration and appeal mechanism used to challenge initial permit decisions.

While a permittee is not required to amend an ITP upon a change of business name or address, the Department must be notified within 10 days of such a change.

Permit Suspension and Revocation

The Department's procedures for permit suspension and revocation are set forth in Section 783.7 of Title 14. Under these provisions, if a permittee fails to comply with the terms of its ITP, the Department may suspend some or all of the permittee's privileges under its ITP. Suspension of privileges must be limited to address the action or inaction that resulted in the suspension. A permittee will be notified in writing of the suspension, the reasons for the suspension, and the actions necessary to correct the deficiencies in compliance.

If the permittee does not correct the conditions that lead to suspension within 60 days, the Department may begin procedures to revoke its ITP. The Department may also act to revoke an ITP if subsequently enacted laws prohibit the continuation of the ITP or the project covered by the ITP. As with suspension, revocation actions must be tailored to address the specific compliance deficiencies or legal prohibitions.

A permittee may object to the Department's decision to suspend or revoke its ITP within 45 days of receiving a suspension or revocation notice. Such an objection must be made in writing and state the reasons why the permittee objects to the Department's action, including any supporting documentation. The Department must make a decision on the permittee's objection within 45 days of the end of the objection period, and it must notify the permittee of its decision and the reasons for the decision in writing.

After a decision on an objection to suspension or revocation is issued, an ITP suspension or revocation may be appealed through the same reconsideration and appeal mechanism used to challenge initial permit decisions. The challenged ITP will remain valid and in effect pending final action by the Department unless immediate suspension is required because the project or activity covered by the ITP is prohibited by a new law.

CONSISTENCY DETERMINATIONS UNDER SECTION 2080.1

Fish and Game Code Section 2080.1 establishes a form of permit streamlining for incidental take of species that are both state-listed and federally listed. Under this provision, if any person secures an incidental take statement or permit (collectively, an "ITP") from the Service or NOAA Fisheries under Section 7 or Section 10 of the federal ESA and that statement or permit authorizes take of a federally listed species that is also listed under CESA as an endangered, threatened, or candidate species, then no further authorization is required under CESA if:

> that person notifies the Director that he or she has received an ITP and includes a copy of the permit or statement with such notice

> the Director does not determine that the ITP is inconsistent with CESA[119]

Section 2080.1(b) requires the Director immediately to publish, in the California Regulatory Notice Register, notice of receipt of a consistency determination request. Within 30 days after receipt of such a request, the Director must determine whether the ITP is consistent with CESA. If the Director determines, based upon substantial evidence, that the ITP is *not* consistent with CESA, then the proposed incidental taking may occur only in accordance with an authorization from the Department.[120] The Director's determination must be published in the California Regulatory Notice Register.[121]

Section 2080.1 does not provide any guidance as to what criteria must be employed by the Director in making a consistency determination. Typically, however, the Director will evaluate whether the activity (including any mitigation) complies with the permit criteria for incidental take permits under Section 2081 of the Fish and Game. More information can be found on the Department's website at https://www.wildlife.ca.gov/Conservation/CESA/Consistency-Determinations.

In recent years, the Department has relied on consistency determinations rather infrequently, usually suggesting to applicants that the Section 2081 ITP process is preferable. This is due largely to concerns of the Department that a USFWS-issued Biological Opinion is not required to satisfy the more rigorous permit standards under CESA. For example, the threshold question in a Biological Opinion is whether a particular action would cause jeopardy to a federally listed species, which is only one of the standards contained in Section 2081 for issuance of an ITP. Although a

119 Fish & Game Code §§ 2080.1(a)–(c).

120 *Id.* § 2080.1(c).

121 *Id.* § 2080.1(d).

USFWS or the "Service" = U.S.
Fish and Wildlife Service

Biological Opinion must identify "reasonable and prudent" measures to mitigate the impacts of take, the Department typically takes the position that the Service's requirements for financial assurances often are not adequate under California law. Although the Department encourages federal permit applicants to involve the Department in the federal permitting process to assure consistency with CESA, this does not always happen in practice.

SCIENTIFIC, EDUCATIONAL AND MANAGEMENT AUTHORIZATIONS

Although the courts rejected the Department's use of management agreements to authorize incidental take, they are still used for other purposes. In particular, under Section 2081(a) of CESA, the Department is authorized to issue permits or memoranda of understanding to permit "individuals, public agencies, universities, zoological gardens, and scientific or educational institutions" to import, export, take or possess protected species for scientific, educational or management purposes.

PROVISIONS GOVERNING AGRICULTURAL ACTIVITIES

Accidental Take

Section 2087 of CESA states that "accidental take" of a species protected under CESA in the course of otherwise lawful routine and ongoing agricultural activities is not prohibited. The statute defines the term "accidental" as meaning "unintended or unforeseen." This exemption is currently scheduled to sunset as of January 1, 2020.

Voluntary Local Programs

CESA Section 2086 provides some relief to the agricultural community. Section 2086(a) requires the Department to adopt regulations authorizing locally designed voluntary programs on farms or ranches that encourage habitat for species protected under CESA and for wildlife generally. Such programs may be presented to the Department by agricultural experts, extension agents, farmers, ranchers, or other agricultural experts, in cooperation with environmental groups. Any take that occurs incidental to routine and ongoing agricultural activities (other than the take of fish species) while the management practices included in a voluntary program are followed, is exempt from the provisions of CESA.[122]

Routine and ongoing agricultural activities include soil cultivation and tillage; crop rotation; fallowing; dairying; the production of any agricultural commodity including viticulture, vermiculture, apiculture, or horticulture; the raising of livestock, furbearers, fish or poultry; and any practice performed by a farmer on a farm as incidental to or in conjunction with any of the foregoing activities subject to certain conditions. The term also includes ordinary pasture maintenance and renovation and dry land farming

---

122 Fish & Game Code § 2086(c).

operations "consistent with rangeland management."[123] Importantly, permitted activities do not include the conversion of agricultural land to non-agricultural use, timber harvesting activities governed by the State Board of Forestry or activities that intentionally reduce habitat and wildlife to facilitate conversion to a non-agricultural use. Moreover, the conversion of rangeland to more intensive agricultural uses is not considered a routing and ongoing agricultural activity.[124]

Under the statute, such programs must:

> include management practices that, to the maximum extent feasible, avoid and minimize take of protected species while encouraging the enhancement of habitat

> be supported by the best available scientific information for both agricultural and conservation practices

> be consistent with the goals and policies of CESA

> be designed to provide sufficient flexibility to maximize participation and to gain the maximum wildlife benefits without compromising the economics of agricultural operations

> include terms and conditions to allow farmers or ranchers to cease participation in a program without penalty, including reasonable measures to minimize take during withdrawal from the program[125]

The term "management practices" is defined as "practical, achievable agricultural practices that, to the maximum extent practicable, avoid and minimize the take of [protected] species," but without compromising the economics of the agricultural operations. Examples include the establishment of brood ponds, installing artificial nesting structures, reducing harvester speed, integrated pest management techniques, planting fallow fields, delaying fall tillage, flooding harvested fields and establishing wildlife refugia at the margins of fields.

The Department is required to post a report every five years regarding the effect of voluntary programs. In consultation with the Department of Food and Agriculture, the Department must address such factors as the temporary and permanent acreage benefiting from the programs, an estimate of the amount of land enrolled, examples of farmer and rancher cooperation, and recommendations as to how to improve participation.[126] The statute also authorizes the Department to work with agricultural and other nonprofits to initiate public education and outreach activities to promote the use of voluntary programs.[127]

---

123 14 Cal. Code Regs. § 786.1.

124 Fish & Game Code § 2089.

125 *Id.* § 2086(b).

126 *Id.* § 2086(d)(2).

127 *Id.* § 2086(f).

The Department's voluntary local program provisions have not been used to a considerable extent, but there are a few examples, including one program established in Alameda County.

The Department's regulations establish a process for the development of a voluntary program, with a view towards having such programs emerge from local agricultural interests rather than from the Department itself. That process can be found at 14 California Code Regulations Sections 786.2 through 786.4.

Safe Harbor Agreements

CESA includes provisions authorizing the use of safe harbor agreements.[128] Like the voluntary local programs described above, safe harbor agreements allow a landowner to secure limited protection against incidental take liability when the landowner undertakes habitat enhancement or other activities that result in a "net conservation benefit." This program, which was reauthorized in 2018, is a companion to the safe harbor program run by the federal government under the federal ESA, which is discussed more fully in Chapter 1 above.

As stated in Section 2089.2, the purpose of the safe harbor program is to "encourage landowners to manage their lands voluntarily to benefit endangered, threatened, or candidate species, or declining or vulnerable species, and not be subject to additional regulatory restrictions as a result of their conservation efforts." The Department's website reported the completion of seven safe harbor agreements between 2012 and 2016.

In order to enter into a safe harbor agreement, the Department must find that the agreement is reasonably expected to provide a "net conservation benefit" to the species listed in the application, which finding must be based, at a minimum, upon a determination that the agreement is of sufficient duration and has appropriate assurances to realize those benefits.[129] In addition, the take must be incidental to an otherwise lawful activity and must not result in jeopardy; the landowner must agree to avoid or minimize take to the maximum extent practicable; and certain requirements regarding funding and monitoring must be satisfied.[130] If the safe harbor covers only a "declining or vulnerable" species (i.e., the species is not a candidate, threatened or endangered species), then no further action is required if the species is up-listed at a later date.[131] Note also that the Department can employ its powers under Section 2080.1 (consistency determinations) to authorize take based upon a federal safe harbor agreement.[132]

More information on the Department's safe harbor program can be found at https://www.wildlife.ca.gov/Conservation/CESA/Safe-Harbor-Agreements.

128 *Id.* § 2089.2.

129 Fish & Game Code § 2096(a).

130 *Id.*

131 *Id.* § 2089.6(b).

132 *Id.* § 2089.22(a).

PENALTIES AND ENFORCEMENT

Division 9 of the Fish and Game Code[133] establishes a system of statutory fines and penalties for violations of CESA and other code provisions. With some exceptions, most violations of the Fish and Game Code are misdemeanors punishable by a fine of not more than $1,000, imprisonment in the county jail for a period not exceeding six months, or both.[134] CESA violations, however, are punishable by a fine of not more than $5,000, or imprisonment in the county jail for not more than one year, or both.[135] Practitioners should note that violations of the take prohibitions for endangered, threatened, and candidate species listed under CESA can result in a fine of not less than $25,000 or more than $50,000 for each violation or imprisonment in the county jail for not more than one year, or both that fine and imprisonment.[136] Many CESA violations may involve activities that violate other provisions of the Fish and Game Code, and in some instances, may provide the Department with a tool to implement code provisions for authorization of forfeitures and seizures.[137]

Fish and Game wardens have broad investigative authority, including the authority to enter private property for inspections on a routine basis without a warrant or probable cause. (*Betchart v. Department of Fish and Game*, 158 Cal. App. 3d 1104 (1984).) Wardens may also conduct personal searches based upon fairly limited evidence. (*People v. Maikhio* 51 Cal. 4th 1074 (2011).)

133 *Id.* § 12000 *et seq.*

134 *Id.* § 12002.

135 *Id.* § 12008.

136 *Id.* § 12008.1(a).

137 *Id.* § 12150 *et seq.*

CHAPTER 3

State and Federal Avian Protections

This chapter provides an overview of state and federal protections for avian species in California. At the federal level, this chapter covers the Migratory Bird Treaty Act and the Bald and Golden Eagle Protection Act, which are administered by the U.S. Fish and Wildlife Service. It also covers California Fish and Game Code protections for avian species in general, which are enforced by the California Department of Fish and Wildlife.

MBTA = Migratory Bird Treaty Act

MIGRATORY BIRD TREATY ACT

History and Background

The Migratory Bird Treaty Act of 1918 (MBTA)[1] is one of the nation's earliest wildlife protection statutes. It finds its origin in a 1916 treaty, the Convention Between the United States and Great Britain for the Protection of Migratory Birds[2] which was established for the protection of the "[m]any species of birds [which] in their annual migration traverse certain parts of the United States and . . . Canada." The convention itself found its origin in public concerns, fueled by the writings of James Audubon and other American conservationists, over the extensive hunting, on many continents, of exotic birds for their fashionable plumage.

The convention found that migratory bird species "are of great value as a source of food or in destroying insects which are injurious to forest and forage plants on the public domain . . . but are nevertheless in danger of extermination through lack of adequate protection during the nesting season or while on their way to and from their breeding grounds." The convention sought to adopt "some uniform system of protection" to "[save] from indiscriminate slaughter and [insure] the preservation of such migratory birds as are either useful to man or are harmless . . ."

The MBTA was enacted to implement this convention, and later amended to incorporate similar treaties with Mexico (1936), Japan (1972) and the Soviet Union (1976). Although the take prohibitions in the MBTA differ from those described in the original treaty, it incorporates the treaty's prohibition against the "taking of nests or eggs of migratory game or insectivorous or nongame birds . . . except for scientific or propagating purposes under such laws as the [contracting powers] may severally deem appropriate."

Soon after its enactment, the State of Missouri challenged the constitutionality of the MBTA in a case seeking to enjoin the federal government from enforcing its provisions.[3] The State of Missouri relied upon earlier District Court decisions holding that a statutory predecessor of the MBTA (enacted prior to the convention with Canada) was invalid because migratory birds were owned by the *states* in their sovereign capacity as trustees for their people.

In an opinion authored by Justice Oliver Wendell Holmes, the Supreme Court rejected this legal theory, holding that the constitutionality of the MBTA could *not* be addressed solely by reference to the Tenth Amendment, which reserves to the states powers not specifically delegated to the United States. Although the Court recognized that, as between a state and its inhabitants, a state may regulate the killing and sale of protected birds, it found that the states' authority is not exclusive of the federal government's paramount powers.

As stated by Justice Holmes:

An informative history of the Migratory Bird Treaty Act can be found in Chapter 4 of *The Feather Thief,* by Kirk Wallace Johnson (Viking, 2018). *The Feather Thief* is an entertaining fictional account of the true story of Edwin Rist, an American music student who stole a suitcase of stuffed rare birds from the British Museum of Natural History and sold them illegally across the globe to tiers of salmon flies.

Stuffed passenger pigeon (extinct). Photo: James St. John. Licensed under CC 2.0.

1   16 U.S.C. §§ 703–11.

2   39 Stat. 1702.

3   *Missouri v. Holland,* 252 U.S. 416 (1920).

To put the claim of the State upon title is to lean upon a slender reed. Wild birds are not in the possession of anyone, and possession is the beginning of ownership. The whole foundation of the State's rights is the presence within their jurisdiction of birds that yesterday had not arrived, tomorrow may be in another State, and, in a week, a thousand miles away . . . . The subject matter is only transitorily within the State, and has no permanent habitat therein. But for the treaty and the statute, there soon might be no birds for any powers to deal with. We see nothing in the Constitution that compels the Government to sit by while a food supply is cut off and the protectors of our forests and our crops are destroyed.[4]

ESA = Endangered Species Act

USFWS or the "Service" = U.S. Fish and Wildlife Service

DOI = Department of the Interior

The Court held that the combined effect of the treaty power[5] and the Supremacy Clause under the Constitution[6] was sufficient to render the enactment of the MBTA within the scope of federal authority under the "necessary and proper" clause of Article I, Section 6 of the Constitution. Subsequent Supreme Court jurisdiction has further limited state claims to ownership of wildlife, although the Court has continued to recognize the right of the states to enact and enforce wildlife-related legislation.[7]

Scope of Protections

The MBTA offers protection to more than one thousand bird species, of which less than 10 percent are listed as threatened or endangered under the federal ESA, and only about 25 percent are designated by USFWS as "Birds of Conservation Concern" (i.e., likely to become candidates for listing under the ESA).[8] This is to say that the MBTA protects migratory birds regardless of their relative level of rarity.

Bird species protected under the MBTA are listed in regulations adopted by the Department of the Interior (DOI). These regulations[9] define "migratory bird" as "any bird, whatever its origin and whether or not raised in captivity, which belongs to [an MBTA-listed species], or which is a mutation or hybrid of any such species."[10] The MBTA protects these species regardless of whether they migrate.

Much like California's statutory protections for bird species, the MBTA protects not only the birds themselves, but also the nests, eggs and parts of protected birds. The MBTA regulations further protect not only "any part, nest or egg" of a protected bird, but also "any product, whether or not manufactured, which consists, or is composed in whole or part, of any [protected] bird or any part, nest, or egg thereof."[11] The regulations further define the

4 *Id.* at 434–35.

5 U.S. Constitution, Article II, § 6.

6 U.S. Constitution, Article VI.

7 *Kleppe v. New Mexico*, 426 U.S. 529 (1976); *Hughes v. Oklahoma*, 441 U.S. 322 (1979).

8 See Migratory Bird Permits; Programmatic Environmental Impact Statement, 80 Fed. Reg. 30,032 (May 26, 2015).

9 50 C.F.R. Part 10.

10 50 C.F.R. § 10.12.

11 16 U.S.C. § 703; 50 C.F.R. § 10.12.

term "bird" to include "the dead body or parts thereof (excluding fossils), whether or not included in a manufactured product or in a processed food product."[12]

Prohibited Acts

The fundamental prohibition of the MBTA is found in Section 703, which states that—except as permitted by regulations authorized under the MBTA—it shall be unlawful "at any time, by any means or in any manner," to:

> > pursue, hunt, take, capture, kill
> > attempt to take, capture, or kill
> > possess, offer for sale, sell, offer to barter, offer to purchase, purchase
> > deliver for shipment, ship, export, import
> > deliver for transportation, transport or cause to be transported
> > carry or cause to be carried, or receive for shipment, transportation or carriage or export

any migratory bird, any part, nest or egg of any such bird, or any product, whether or not manufactured, which consists, or is composed in whole or part, of any such bird or any part, nest, or egg thereof.[13]

The broad range of prohibited activities mirrors similar provisions found in other federal laws regulating the sale or transport of protected species, including the MBTA's predecessor, the Lacey Act of 1900,[14] which prohibits the transportation or sale of illegally-taken wildlife.[15] As discussed further below, the phrase "by any means or in any manner" has led to an ongoing debate as to whether otherwise legal acts that are not *intended* to kill migratory birds (e.g., windfarm or solar operations) are criminalized under the MBTA.

The MBTA itself does not define the term "take." The USFWS has defined the term, however, to mean "pursue, hunt, shoot, wound, kill, trap, capture or collect . . ." (several of which actions are described in the statute itself as something other than take), or to attempt to do any of these things.[16] Although the MBTA's definition of "take" does not include either "harm" or "harassment" as does the definition of this term under the federal ESA, the breadth of the MBTA is significant. This is due in part to the large number of birds listed under the MBTA, the strict liability potentially imposed under the statute, and the fact that the USFWS—at least until the current Administration—has historically taken the position that the MBTA criminalizes many innocent activities that incidentally cause the take of listed birds.

---

12   50 C.F.R. § 10.12.

13   16 U.S.C. § 703(a); 50 C.F.R. § 21.11.

14   16 U.S.C. §§ 701, 3371–78; 18 U.S.C. § 42.

15   We have generally excluded from this book federal laws governing the sale, transportation, export, import, sale or barter of fish, wildlife and plants or their parts, including the Lacey Act, the Convention on International Trade in Endangered Species of Wild Fauna and Flora (CITES) and other similar laws.

16   50 C.F.R. § 10.12.

USFWS has not adopted a permitting structure to authorize *incidental* take under the MBTA. The MBTA Regulations do authorize permits for certain types of *intentional* take, including hunting, bird banding and marking, scientific research, bird rehabilitation, raptor propagation and falconry.[17] The regulations also authorize the issuance of "special purpose permits," i.e., permits "for activities that fall outside the scope of specific MBTA permit types."[18] These permits have not been used widely for private activities, but the USFWS has issued a number of special purpose permits to federal agencies, primarily in the context of projects for the eradication of exotic species.[19]

Liability for Incidental Take?

The most important legal question under the MBTA is whether its prohibitions are limited to acts specifically directed against migratory birds. That is, must take be intentional to be covered by the MBTA? When one looks at the list of actions that qualify as "take" (i.e., to "pursue, hunt, shoot, wound, kill, trap, capture or collect"), it would appear that the MBTA was enacted to prohibit deliberate action against birds. The only logical exception in this list is the word "kill," which is something that can occur accidentally. Proponents of a narrow reading of the word "take" refer to the legal doctrine *noscitur a sociis*, in which the meaning of an ambiguous word may be determined by reference to the words around it. Under this theory, one would conclude that "kill" within the meaning of the MBTA requires intent, as do the other forms of take identified in the MGTA regulations.

Some courts and, until recently the USFWS, have not read the statute to include this limitation. Under this "incidental take" theory, liability does not depend (except in felony cases) upon the mental state of the acting party. Advocates of the incidental take theory also cite to the MBTA's proscription of take "by any means and in any manner."

Historically, the USFWS applied the MBTA to incidental take.[20] In January 2017, just 10 days before the inauguration of Donald Trump as president, the Solicitor of DOI under the Obama Administration issued a reasoned opinion (as described above, "Solicitor's Opinion M-37041") entitled *Incidental Take Prohibited Under the Migratory Bird Treaty Act*, taking precisely this position and cementing (at least temporarily) views long held within the agency.

The January 2017 Solicitor's Opinion M-37041 relied heavily on the generally conceded theory that the MBTA is a strict liability statute (except in the case of felonies, which require a "knowing" violation of the MBTA). The opinion also cited to the purpose of the treaties that the MBTA was intended to implement; arguments based upon the legislative history of the MBTA; and the argument that USFWS has long asserted that the MBTA prohibits incidental take. Solicitor's Opinion M-37041 also relied as

---

17 See 50 C.F.R. Part 21.

18 *Id.* § 21.27.

19 See Opinion of the Office of the Solicitor, U.S. Department of the Interior, January 10, 2017 ("Solicitor's Opinion M-37041") (discussed further below).

20 See Migratory Bird Permits; Programmatic Environmental Impact Statement, 80 Fed. Reg. 30,032 (May 26, 2015).

authority on a January 10, 2001 executive order issued by President Clinton asserting the MBTA prohibits the unpermitted incidental take of migratory birds.

None of the foregoing arguments cited by the Solicitor in Solicitor's Opinion M-37041 are particularly compelling, other than the fact that the MBTA prohibits take "by any means and in any manner." While this argument may have some appeal, the courts are divided on it, because it seems to avoid the predicate question as to whether an activity constitutes "take" in the first place. As stated by one court, the question of whether a person has acted with the requisite mental state (i.e., *mens rea*) must be distinguished from the question of whether the person has committed the prohibited act itself (i.e., *actus reus*).[21]

The "Obama opinion" was short-lived. On February 6, 2017, the Trump Administration suspended Solicitor's Opinion M-37041 pending further review. Subsequently, on December 22, 2017, the Solicitor of DOI issued a 41-page opinion entitled *The Migratory Bird Treaty Act Does Not Prohibit Incidental Take* ("Solicitor's Opinion M-37050") withdrawing and reversing Solicitor's Opinion M-37041 and concluding that "[i]nterpreting the MBTA to apply to incidental or accidental actions hangs the sword of Damocles over a host of otherwise lawful and protective actions . . ."[22]

Solicitor's Opinion M-37050 takes the position that Solicitor's Opinion M-37041's reliance on the MTBA's strict liability provisions improperly conflated the issues of intent and the nature of the prohibited acts themselves. Relying on a detailed review of the MBTA's legislative history, Solicitor's Opinion M-37050 concludes that the original purpose of the MBTA was to target affirmative actions to kill or take migratory birds, and that the operative language effectuating this purpose has changed little since the MBTA's enactment. Solicitor's Opinion M-37050 also cites due process concerns, arguing that the scope of liability contemplated by Solicitor's Opinion M-37041 was so vague and overbroad that criminal liability under the statute would be virtually limitless, a concern that could not be mitigated through prosecutorial discretion. Calling the MBTA "the epitome of vague law," Solicitor's Opinion M-37050 concludes that a narrow interpretation of liability is necessary to avoid constitutional deficiencies.

> Opinion M-37050 was challenged in three separate lawsuits, including one joined by the California Attorney General. This litigation was pending as of the time this manuscript was submitted for publication.

In rendering Opinion M-37050, the Solicitor acknowledged that these issues remain the subject of disagreement among courts, noting that "courts have adopted different views on whether Section 2 of the MBTA prohibits incidental take, and, if so, to what extent." Thus, although the Solicitor's views on the MBTA appear to change from time to time, ultimately this will be a question for the courts to decide.

The positions taken by the various U.S. Circuit Courts of Appeal are described below.

Courts Rejecting Incidental Take Theory (Fifth, Eighth, and Ninth Circuits)

The Fifth, Eighth, and Ninth Circuits generally have interpreted the MBTA to apply only to acts done directly and intentionally to migratory birds. These courts have placed

---

21 *United States v. Citgo Petroleum Corp.*, 801 F.3d 477 (5th Cir. 2015).

22 See Opinion of the Office of the Solicitor, U.S. Department of the Interior, December 22, 2017.

decisive weight on, among other things, the common law meaning of "take" and the doctrine *noscitur a sociis*.

In *Seattle Audubon Society v. Evans*, the Ninth Circuit found that the MBTA did not preclude the logging timber of lands that might provide habitat for the northern spotted owl.[23] In rejecting plaintiffs' claims, the Ninth Circuit first characterized a "take" under the MBTA as describing "physical conduct of the sort engaged in by hunters and poachers, conduct which was undoubtedly a concern at the time of the statute's enactment in 1918."[24]

Logging activity. Photo: Mussi Katz. Licensed under CC 1.0.

The court then contrasted the definition of "take" under the MBTA with the definition of "take" under the Endangered Species Act, which includes "harass" and "harm" in addition to the verbs included in the MBTA.[25] The court called attention to the fact that "harm" is defined under the ESA's regulations to include "habitat modification or degradation," citing to the U.S. Supreme Court's ESA holding in *Babbitt v. Sweet Home Chapter of Communities for a Great Oregon*.[26] The MBTA, by contrast, makes no mention of "indirect take" through habitat modification or degradation. Thus, the court reasoned, while habitat destruction may cause "harm" to the owls under the ESA, it does not "take" them within the meaning of the MBTA.[27]

In *Newton County Wildlife Association v. United States Forest Service*,[28] also a logging case, the Eighth Circuit agreed with the Ninth Circuit. Citing *Seattle Audubon Society*, the court found that while "[s]trict liability may be appropriate when dealing with hunters and poachers," it would stretch the MBTA "far beyond the bounds of reason to construe it as an absolute criminal prohibition on conduct, such as timber harvesting, that *indirectly* results in the death of migratory birds."[29] Notably, however, while both the Eighth and Ninth Circuits have characterized the MBTA as applying only to the direct take of migratory birds, both have considered this question only in the limited context of determining whether *habitat destruction* constitutes "take."

More recently, in *United States v. Brigham Oil & Gas, L.P.*,[30] a district court in the Eighth Circuit followed *Newton County Wildlife Association* and held that oil and gas companies' use of oil "reserve pits," which resulted in the death of migratory birds, did not violate the MBTA where death or injury of migratory birds was unintentional. Explaining that the MBTA does not define the term "take," the court first determined that, when applied to wildlife, "take" requires an intentional reduction of wildlife to

23   952 F.2d 297 (9th Cir. 1991).

24   *Id.* at 302.

25   16 U.S.C. § 1532(19).

26   515 U.S. 687 (1995).

27   *Seattle Audubon Society*, 952 F.2d at 302–03; *Accord Citizens Interested in Bull Run, Inc. v. Edrington*, 781 F. Supp. 1502 (D. Or. 1991) (holding that loss of owl habitat under proposed timber sale would not result in "take" under the MBTA). That is, the Court focused primarily on whether the prohibited take is "direct" (as under the MBTA) or may be "indirect" (as under the ESA).

28   113 F.3d 110 (8th Cir. 1997).

29   *Id.* at 115 (emphasis in original).

30   840 F. Supp. 2d 1202 (D. N.D. 2012).

MMPA = Marine Mammal Protection Act

possession. This definition, the court reasoned, involves deliberate—not accidental—conduct and "refers to a purposeful attempt to possess wildlife through capture, not incidental or accidental taking through lawful commercial activity."[31]

The court further stated that to include unintentional "take" arising from otherwise lawful activity would be unworkable and offer "unlimited potential for criminal prosecutions." Under such a standard, for example, many everyday activities—such as driving a vehicle, owning a building with windows, or owning a cat—would be unlawful and subject to criminal sanctions. The court reasoned that it was required to construe a criminal statute narrowly, and that if Congress intended to criminalize activity that incidentally injures migratory birds, the law must be clear and certain.[32]

Most recently, in *United States v. CITGO Petroleum Corp.*,[33] the Fifth Circuit found that a CITGO oil refinery's use of two large, uncovered "equalization tanks" containing oil did not violate the MBTA. Consistent with both the Eighth and Ninth Circuit, the Fifth Circuit found that, as applied to wildlife, the common law meaning of "take" is to "reduce those animals, by killing or capturing, to human control" and that "[o]ne does not reduce an animal to human control accidentally or by omission."[34] Similar to the Ninth Circuit, the court then contrasted the language of the MBTA with the ESA and the Marine Mammal Protection Act (MMPA), both of which departed from the common law definition of "take" by inclusion of words such as "harm" and "harass." The absence of these additional terms in the MBTA, or any other language signaling Congress' intent to modify the common law definition, the court reasoned, supports a reading of "take" consistent with its common law meaning.

As noted above, the *CITGO* court criticized decisions that have extended the MBTA to incidental take, finding that those decisions confuse the *mens rea* and the *actus reus* requirements under the MBTA. While strict liability crimes dispense with the *mens rea* element of a crime, for instance, the court explained that a defendant still must commit the criminal act to be found guilty. Under the MBTA, the court reasoned, that act is "to take," which, even without a *mens rea*, is not something that can be done unknowingly or involuntarily. Thus, the court described, the owners of electrical lines do not "take" migratory birds that run into those lines.[35]

Courts Accepting Incidental Take Theory (Second and Tenth Circuits)

By contrast, the Second and Tenth Circuits have interpreted the MBTA to prohibit any activity that may proximately cause the death of a migratory bird. In short, these courts have largely focused on the MBTA's status as a strict liability offense and the fact that it proscribes "taking" and "killing" of migratory birds "by any means or in any manner."

---

31 *Id.* at 1209.

32 *Id.* at 1212–14.

33 801 F.3d 477 (5th Cir. 2015).

34 *Id.* at 489.

35 *Id.* at 493.

Notably, most of the courts adopting this position have struggled with the potential that some truly innocent activities (e.g., cat ownership) might lead to criminal convictions under the MBTA under this theory.

In *United States v. FMC Corporation*, the Second Circuit upheld the conviction of a pesticide manufacturer for deaths to migratory birds associated with use of a wastewater pond.[36] Analogizing to cases imposing strict liability for ultra-hazardous activities, the court reasoned that FMC engaged in an activity involving the manufacture of a highly toxic chemical, and FMC failed to prevent that chemical from escaping into the pond and killing migratory birds. "This," the court concluded, "is sufficient to impose strict liability on FMC."[37]

The Second Circuit, however, rejected the contention that liability under the MBTA is without limitation. "Certainly construction that would bring every killing within the statute, such as deaths caused by automobiles, airplanes, plate glass modern office buildings or picture windows in residential dwellings into which birds fly," the court found, "would offend reason and common sense." Such situations, the court reasoned, could be left to "the sound discretion of prosecutors and the courts."[38]

In *United States v. Moon Lake Electric Association, Inc.*,[39] a Tenth Circuit district court denied Moon Lake's motion to dismiss charges under the MBTA and found that the MBTA extends to any activity that proximately causes the death of a migratory bird. At issue in the case was Moon Lake's supply of electricity to an oil field. The government alleged that Moon Lake failed to install equipment on certain power poles, causing the death of migratory birds.

The court first found that, because the MBTA is a strict liability crime, it was not necessary to prove that Moon Lake intended to cause the deaths of migratory birds. The court then rejected Moon Lake's assertion that the MBTA prohibits only physical conduct normally exhibited by hunters and poachers. Instead, the court found that by prohibiting "taking" and "killing" of migratory birds "by any means or in any manner," in addition to the acts of hunting, capturing, shooting, and trapping, the MBTA "does not seem overly concerned with how captivity, injury, or death occurs." By contrast, by focusing on whether a taking is "direct" or "indirect," the court concluded that other courts have read into the MBTA a *mens rea* requirement and ignored the strict liability nature of the MBTA.[40]

The Moon Lake court also responded to the contention that its interpretation of the MBTA would lead to absurd results. Specifically, the court relied on the argument that, to obtain a guilty verdict, the government must prove proximate causation beyond a

36 572 F.2d 902 (2d Cir. 1978).

37 *Id.* at 908.

38 *Id.* at 905; see also *United States v. Corbin Farm Service*, 444 F. Supp. 510 (E.D. Cal. 1978) (contemporaneous case, finding that the MBTA applied to death of migratory birds from pesticide application, even if deaths were unintentional).

39 45 F. Supp. 2d 1070 (D. Colo. 1999).

40 *Id.* at 1073–74.

reasonable doubt. Thus, the death of any migratory bird must be reasonably anticipated or foreseen as a natural consequence of a wrongful fact. "Because the death of a protected bird is generally not a probable consequence of driving an automobile, piloting an airplane, maintaining an office building, or living in a residential dwelling with a picture window," the court reasoned, "such activities would not normally result in liability under [the MBTA], even if such activities would cause the death of protected birds." "Proper application of the law," the court therefore concluded, "should not lead to absurd results."[41]

Most recently, in *United States v. Apollo Energies, Inc.*, the Tenth Circuit agreed with the broad holding reached in *Moon Lake*.[42] The defendants in this case were two Kansas oil drilling operators charged with violating the MBTA after dead migratory birds were discovered lodged in a piece of their oil drilling equipment referred to as a "heater-treater."

The court first dispensed with defendants' assertion that the MBTA is not a strict liability statute, finding this argument to be foreclosed by the Tenth Circuit's earlier holding in *United States v. Corrow*.[43] The court then addressed defendants' contention that the MBTA violated their due process rights because, among other things, it did not provide fair notice that their conduct violated the MBTA. Conceptually, the court reasoned that the question of whether a defendant was *on notice* that a certain act could lead to a crime was indistinct from the question of whether a defendant *caused* a crime. The court therefore concluded that, to satisfy due process and be found guilty under the MBTA, a defendant must proximately cause the death of a migratory bird.

Applying that standard, the court then held that defendants could be found guilty under the MBTA once the Service had put them on notice that the heater-treaters could lead to the death of migratory birds. Prior to such notice from the Service, however, the court found that no reasonable person would have concluded that the heater-treaters would lead to the deaths of migratory birds and therefore no violation of the MBTA had occurred.

Given the split in the circuits, we must wait for either the U.S. Supreme Court or Congress to act. In the meantime, as expressed in Solicitor's Opinion M-37050, the Service will no longer initiate enforcement actions based upon an incidental take theory.

Penalties

Penalties under the MBTA are established in 16 U.S.C. Section 707, as amended by 18 U.S.C. Sections 3559 and 3571, and they include both criminal penalties and forfeitures. Under these provisions, it is a misdemeanor to violate any provision of the MBTA, with punishment of a maximum fine of $15,000 or imprisonment up to six months, or both.[44] It is a felony, however, to "knowingly" take a protected bird with *intent* to sell, offer to sell,

---

41   *Id.* at 1085.

42   611 F.3d 679 (10th Cir. 2010).

43   *Id.* at 684 (citing *United States v. Corrow*, 119 F.3d 796 (10th Cir. 1997)).

44   16 U.S.C. § 707(a).

barter, or offer to barter, or to *actually* sell, offer to sell, barter, or offer to barter, with punishment of a maximum fine of $2,000 or imprisonment up to two years, or both.[45] There is a question as to whether the take of multiple birds would result in a conviction for each bird taken. At least one court has answered this question in the negative.[46]

In addition, the United States may seize all guns, traps, nets, vessels, vehicles, and other equipment used in pursuing, hunting, taking, trapping, ensnaring, capturing, killing, or attempting to take, capture, or kill a migratory bird with the intent to offer to sell, sell, offer to barter, or barter, and may be held pending prosecution. Upon conviction, a court may require that these items be forfeited in addition to any other assigned penalties.[47]

Enforcement

Generally, the Service has focused its enforcement efforts on industries and other activities that "chronically kill birds," and has pursued criminal prosecution only after notifying entities of its concerns with avian mortality and working to find solutions.[48] In recent years, the Service entered into agreements with a number of wind energy providers, some of which came during pending criminal proceedings, requiring the companies to implement certain avian protection measures in lieu of criminal penalties.

With respect to private enforcement, the MBTA does not contain an explicit citizen suit provision. Under certain circumstances, however, the courts have allowed organizations and individuals to seek civil injunctions against federal agencies under the Administrative Procedure Act for alleged violations of the MBTA.

In *Humane Society of the United States v. Glickman*, for example, the D.C. Circuit affirmed a district court injunction requiring the U.S. Department of Agriculture to obtain a permit from the Department of the Interior prior to implementing a management plan that would take and kill Canada Geese.[49] By contrast, in *Friends of Boundary v. Army Corps of Engineers*,[50] the court refused to set aside a Corps permit issued to a wind farm developer on the basis that the wind farm operations would take migratory birds. The court reasoned that "[t]he relationship between the Corps' regulatory permitting activity and any potential harm to migratory birds appears to be too attenuated to support a direction action against the Corps to enforce the MBTA's prohibition on 'takes.'" The court further noted that the Corps "simply exercised its authority to permit

Wind farm, San Gorgonio Pass, Palm Springs. Photo: Ken. Licensed under CC 2.0.

---

45   *Id.* § 707(b).

46   *United States v. Corbin Farm Service*, 444 F. Supp. 510 (E.D. Cal. 1978).

47   16 U.S.C. § 707(d).

48   See Migratory Bird Permits; Programmatic Environmental Impact Statement, 80 Fed. Reg. 30,032, 30,034 (May 26, 2015); see also *United States v. Apollo Energies, LLC*, 611 F.3d 679 (10th Cir. 2010) (initiating enforcement proceedings only after engaging in education campaign).

49   217 F.3d 882 (D.C. Cir. 2000); see also *Public Employees for Environmental Responsibility v. Beaudreau*, 25 F. Supp. 3d 67 (D.D.C. 2014) (considering claims by individuals and environmental groups seeking to challenge federal agencies' approval of off-shore wind energy project); *Center for Biological Diversity v. Pirie*, 191 F. Supp. 2d 161 (D.D.C. 2002), and 201 F. Supp. 2d 113, *vacated as moot*, 2003 WL 179848 (D.C. Cir. 2003) (considering suit by environmental group seeking to prevent military's use of live fire training exercises allegedly in violation of the MBTA).

50   24 F. Supp. 3d 105 (D. Maine 2014).

NEPA = National Environmental
Policy Act

MOU = Memorandum of
Understanding

MOA = Memorandum of
Agreement

NOI = Notice of Intent

dredging and fill activity; the Corps will not construct the project or operate the project when it is completed . . . ."[51]

The Ninth Circuit has found that a city had standing to challenge a federal agency's redevelopment plan for a former military base for allegedly violating the MBTA, although it rejected the city's claims on the merits.[52] This practice, however, does not appear to be followed in all jurisdictions.[53]

Permitting

As mentioned above, there is no regulatory scheme authorizing the issuance of incidental take permits for migratory birds except in limited contexts. Until the Trump Administration issued its interpretation of the MBTA, the USFWS continued to assert that various industries (particularly the wind industry) were at risk of prosecution under the MBTA for incidental take, despite the lack of clarity provided by the courts. Accordingly, government and industry sought to find ways of identifying best management practices that might be employed by industry to *minimize* incidental take and thereby avoid becoming the target of federal prosecutorial discretion. In the case of wind, this resulted in the development of various "voluntary" tools that might be employed to avoid prosecution. Most notable of these are the *Land-Based Wind Energy Guidelines* (2012) and the APLIC/USFWS *Avian Protection Plan Guidelines* (2005).

In May 2015, the USFWS announced its intent to prepare a programmatic Environmental Impact Statement under the National Environmental Policy Act (NEPA) for use in evaluating the creation of a permitting program to authorize incidental take.[54] Although the notice requested public comment on a variety of questions that might arise in the permitting context, it did not request public comment on whether incidental take is covered by the MBTA in the first place.

According to the Notice of Intent (NOI), the purposes of the proposed permit program were to (1) create greater clarity about the scope of the MBTA and (2) create a regulatory mechanism to obtain compensatory mitigation for bird mortality that cannot be avoided through best practices, risk management processes, or technologies. The USFWS offered a variety of regulatory options, including a general permit program for various industries most affected by the MBTA; an individual permit program that includes standards for avoidance, minimization and mitigation; MOUs or MOAs with other governmental agencies; and voluntary programs for individual industry sectors to address impacts on migratory birds (e.g., similar to the *Land-Based Wind Energy Guidelines* described above). The specific industries or activities which received special attention in the NOI include

---

51 *Id.* at 114.

52 See *City of Sausalito v. O'Neill*, 386 F.3d 1186 (9th Cir. 2004).

53 See, e.g., *Newton County Wildlife Association v. United States Forest Service*, 113 F.3d 110, 115 (8th Cir. 1997) (stating that the MBTA does not appear to apply to the actions of federal government agencies); *Sierra Club v. Martin*, 110 F.3d 1551 (11th Cir. 1997) (finding that the MBTA does not apply to the federal government).

54 Migratory Bird Permits; Programmatic Environmental Impact Statement, 80 Fed. Reg. 30,032 (May 26, 2015).

methane or other gas burner pipes at oil production sites; communication towers; electric transmission and distribution lines; and wind industry generation.

Given Solicitor's Opinion M-37050, it is unlikely that the Trump Administration will pursue this permitting program to completion. Solicitor's Opinion M-37041 was intended precisely to establish an enforcement "placeholder" in the event incidental take regulations are stalled or abandoned.

In the meantime, the USFWS' updated *HCP Handbook* (2016) provides guidance on how to manage MBTA issues in other regulatory contexts. In Section 7.4.1, the Handbook indicates that, if a migratory bird is listed under the ESA, the issuance of an ESA incidental take permit can authorize take of that species for the purposes of both statutes. If the migratory bird is not listed under the ESA, however, the USFWS has no way of authorizing incidental take. In the latter circumstances, USFWS suggests two approaches to dealing with non-listed birds.

The first is to cover them in the HCP (like any other non-listed but covered species) to demonstrate the applicant's "good faith efforts" to comply with the MBTA. The Handbook notes that the USFWS Office of Law Enforcement "may take into consideration the good faith effort should unintentional MBTA violations occur." The second is to develop a "Bird and Bat Conservation Strategy," which is a program of avoidance and minimization measures that an applicant will take to reduce impacts on MBTA species and bats. In the case of wind, this resulted in the development of various voluntary tools that might be used to limit the impacts of wind energy facilities, including transmission lines. These include the Land-Based Wind Energy Guidelines (USFWS, 2012), the California Wind Energy Guidelines (CDFW, CEC, 2007) and the Avian Protection Plan Guidelines (USFWS, APLIC, 2005). Although voluntary, these various guidelines have tended to find their way into the environmental review and permitting processes for wind projects.

BALD AND GOLDEN EAGLE PROTECTION ACT

History and Background

It is said that, when the Continental Congress adopted the bald eagle as the national bird in 1782, Benjamin Franklin objected, claiming that the bald eagle is a bird of "bad moral character . . . and very lousy."[55] Nonetheless, the eagle became an enduring national symbol and, in 1940, Congress enacted the Bald Eagle Protection Act[56] to protect the bird from extinction. In 1962, Congress amended the act to include protection for the golden eagle, and the statute became known as the Bald and Golden Eagle Protection Act (BGEPA).[57]

BGEPA = Bald and Golden Eagle Protection Act

Bald eagle. Photo: Oregon Department of Fish and Wildlife. Licensed under CC 2.0.

55   Littel, Endangered and Other Species, Bureau of National Affairs (1992), citing *United States v. Hetzel*, 385 F. Supp. 1311, 1315 n.1 (W.D. Mo. 1974).

56   54 Stat. 250, ch. 278 (1940).

57   16 U.S.C. §§ 668–668d.

Golden eagle. Photo: Mr. Leeds. Licensed under CC 2.0.

When golden eagles were added to the Act,[58] Congress authorized the issuance of permits for certain acts associated with the religious purposes of Indian tribes and included protections for the protection of livestock. Additional exemptions were added in 1972 for grazing and falconry,[59] and again in 1978 for the taking of *golden* eagle nests which interfere with "resource development and recovery operations."[60] During these years, the Act was amended to increase the original criminal penalties, add civil penalties, and change the *mens rea* requirement—which originally covered only willful acts—to prohibit take that occurs "knowingly, or with wanton disregard of the consequences," of the act in question.

Since 1978 and until the substantial growth of wind power production projects during the Obama Administration, little has happened with BGEPA and it did not often present itself as an issue in the development context. There were, however, numerous cases that addressed the scope and enforceability of BGEPA in the tribal context. In 1996, BGEPA was upheld in a commerce clause challenge in the Ninth Circuit. In that case, *United States v. Bramble*,[61] the court held that the potential extinction of eagles would substantially affect interstate commerce by "foreclosing . . . several types of commercial activity; future commerce in eagles or their parts; future interstate travel for the purpose of observing or studying eagles; or future commerce in beneficial products derived either from eagles or from analysis of their genetic material."[62]

It should be kept in mind that BGEPA is not the only statutory protection for eagles. Although the bald eagle was delisted under the ESA in 2007, both eagles are still protected by the Lacey Act and the MBTA. Moreover, the bald eagle is listed as endangered species under the California Endangered Species Act, and both eagles are listed as "fully protected birds" in California.

Prohibited Acts

BGEPA makes it illegal for any person, acting without a permit and either knowingly or with wanton disregard for the consequences of that act, to "take, possess, sell, purchase, barter, offer to sell, purchase or barter, transport, export or import, at any time or in any manner, any bald eagle . . . or golden eagle, alive or dead, or any part, nest, or egg thereof . . ."[63] Although this list is similar to the MBTA's list of prohibitions, BGEPA contains a *statutory* definition of "take" that is absent from the MBTA. Under Section 668(c) of the act, "take" is defined to include "pursue, shoot, shoot at, poison, wound, kill, capture, trap, collect, molest or *disturb*."[64]

---

58 Pub. L. No. 87-884, 76 Stat. 1246.

59 Pub. L. No. 92-535, 86 Stat. 1064.

60 Pub. L. No. 95-616, 92 Stat. 3114.

61 103 F.3d 1475 (9th Cir. 1996).

62 *Id.* at 1481.

63 16 U.S.C. § 668(a).

64 *Id.* § 668(c) (emphasis added).

The inclusion of "disturbance" as a form of take under BGEPA is important. As defined in the Service's BGEPA regulations,[65] the term "disturb" means "to agitate or bother a bald or golden eagle to a degree that causes, or is likely to cause, based upon the best scientific information available, (1) injury to an eagle, (2) a decrease in its productivity by substantially interfering with normal breeding, feeding, or sheltering behavior, or (3) nest abandonment, by substantially interfering with normal breeding, feeding, or sheltering behavior."

MBTA = Migratory Bird Treaty Act

This definition of "disturbance" take is roughly analogous to ESA's prohibition of take by "harm" as described by the U.S. Supreme Court in *Babbitt v. Sweet Home Chapter of Communities for a Great Oregon*.[66] In particular, both BGEPA's "disturbance" take and ESA's "harm" include what is often referred to as "indirect" take (i.e., through activities that do not involve direct physical contact with an eagle but which nonetheless have significant impacts on a bird's behavior). The most common examples in the development context are habitat modifications (e.g., loss of foraging or nesting habitat) or construction-related activities in proximity to an established nest. In this sense both BGEPA's and ESA's definitions of take are broader than those contained in the MBTA, even as broadly defined.

Liability for Incidental Take

Originally, BGEPA imposed liability only if a person willfully molested or disturbed an eagle.[67] In the 1972 amendments, however, Congress lowered this standard to its present level. Today, unlike the MBTA (at least as it is interpreted in the Second and Tenth Circuits), BGEPA does not create liability for wholly unintentional take of eagles. On the other hand, BGEPA can create minimal liability for acts that were not intended to injure protected birds. This is because BGEPA prohibits acts that either (1) "knowingly" cause take; or (2) which are undertaken by a person with "wanton disregard for their consequences." In either case, the take may occur as a result of otherwise legal activity.

But what is it the person must "know" before liability can be imposed under BGEPA? In *United States v. Zak*,[68] the court considered the culpability of the owner of a fish hatchery who routinely shot herons and egrets from a tree on his property to prevent predation on his crop. Among the many dead birds found below the "hanging tree"—as it was called by hatchery employees—was a juvenile bald eagle that had been killed with a .22 caliber shell. The defendant argued that he had not violated BGEPA because he thought the eagle was a "big brown hawk," and thus he had not "knowingly" violated the act. The court concluded otherwise, reasoning that it was sufficient that he "knew" he was shooting the bird, regardless of whether he thought it was an eagle or a "big brown hawk."

---

65   50 C.F.R. § 22.2.

66   515 U.S. 687 (1995).

67   See *United States v. Hetzel*, 385 F. Supp. 1311 (W.D. Mo. 1974).

68   486 F. Supp. 2d 208 (D. Mass. 2007).

DOI = Department of the
Interior

In reaching this conclusion, the court cited prior case law for the proposition that "[t]he courts have consistently rejected arguments . . . which posit that the term 'knowingly,' standing alone, requires the prosecution to show that the defendant knew his behavior was unlawful, instead interpreting 'knowingly' . . . to require no more than that the defendant know he was engaging in the prohibited conduct . . ."[69]

This distinction is important in the development context. Consider, for example, a developer who engages in construction activities in proximity to an inactive eagle nest that turns out—that year at least but without actual knowledge on the developer's part—not to have been so inactive. Or consider the wind farm developer, who knows that his or her project will take avian species but has no specific knowledge that an eagle nest has recently been established within a few miles of his or her project.

Penalties and Enforcement

Criminal Penalties

For a first offense, BGEPA prescribes a penalty of not more than $5,000 or one year of imprisonment, or both.[70] In the case of a second or subsequent conviction, the penalty is not more than $10,000 or two years of imprisonment, or both. BGEPA establishes a reward of $2,500 (half the fine) be paid to any person giving information that leads to a conviction.

Section 668(b) gives DOI the authority to arrest without warrant any person violating the Act in the presence or view of an officer and take such person "immediately" for examination or trial. The statute also gives DOI the authority to execute any warrant or other process issued by an officer or court of competent jurisdiction, as well as the authority to search any place with or without a warrant.

Civil and Other Penalties

Unlike the MBTA, BGEPA contains a civil penalty provision.[71] Because it establishes civil rather than criminal penalties, this provision does *not* require the offender to have acted with knowledge or wanton disregard. Moreover, it applies not only to takes, but also to the violation of any permit or regulation. The civil penalty is $5,000 per violation, and it may be imposed only after notice to the offender and a hearing, during which the hearing officer must consider the gravity of the violation and the good faith of the offender. If an offender fails to pay the penalty, an enforcement action may be instituted in district court. In this case the government's determination will be upheld if based upon substantial evidence.

All eagles or eagle parts, nests or eggs, and any equipment used in violating the act (including guns, traps, nets, and other equipment, vessels, vehicles, aircraft and other

---

69 *Id.* at 219 (citing and quoting *United States v. Pitrone*, 115 F.3rd 1, 6 (1st Cir. 1997)).

70 16 U.S.C. § 668(a).

71 *Id.* § 668(b).

means of transportation used to aid in the taking) are subject to forfeiture. Moreover, if any violator holds a federal grazing lease, that lease may be canceled in the event of conviction.

Citizen Suits

Like the MBTA, BGEPA does not include an explicit citizen enforcement provision. Noting this fact, one court refused to set aside a Corps of Engineers permit on the basis that the approved wind project would take eagles, noting that the BGEPA incidental take permit matter is a matter for the Service to monitor through its independent regulatory authority.[72] However, the Ninth Circuit has decided that a citizen suit may be brought to prevent violations of the MBTA.[73]

Permitting

Background

BGEPA authorizes the Secretary of the Interior to issue permits for the taking of eagles for various purposes, provided the taking is compatible with the preservation of eagles.[74] While BGEPA and the "Eagle Rule" (described below) authorize the issuance of permits for Indian religious purposes, protection of livestock or domestic animals, falconry, and scientific and exhibition purposes, the permit most relevant to the development context is that which is authorized to "protect the interests in a particular locality." As described by USFWS in its original rule establishing an incidental take permit program under BGEPA, "[t]his statutory language accommodates a broad spectrum of public and private interests (such as utility infrastructure development and maintenance, road construction, operation of airports, commercial or residential construction, resource recovery, recreational use, etc.) that might 'take' eagles as defined under [BGEPA]."[75]

In 2009, USFWS issued a set of regulations for the issuance of permits for the "non–purposeful" (i.e., incidental) take of bald and golden eagles, as well as permits for the take of *golden* eagle nests (the "Eagle Rule").[76] These permits (other than the nest permits) are limited to incidental take and do not authorize non-tribal permits for the import, export, purchase, sale, trade or barter of eagles or their parts, nests or eggs.[77]

As originally written, the Eagle Rule provided for the issuance of two types of incidental take permits—"standard" and "programmatic"—and established, among other things, a maximum five-year life for eagle take permits. Because wind turbines, transmission lines, and other activities that cause ongoing take typically have a life of more than five years, the limited shelf life of eagle take permits provided little incentive for industry (particularly

---

72   *Friends of Boundary v. Army Corps of Engineers*, 24 F. Supp. 3d 105 (D. Maine 2014).

73   See *City of Sausalito v. O'Neill*, 386 F.3d 1186 (9th Cir. 2004) (involving suit by city to prevent implementation of federal redevelopment plan with the potential to take migratory birds).

74   16 U.S.C. § 668.

75   74 Fed. Reg. 46,837–38.

76   50 C.F.R. Part 22.

77   *Id.* §§ 22.1, 22.12.

EMU = Eagle Management Unit

LAP = Local Area Population

wind) to apply for permits. Between 2009 and 2017, only two eagle take permits were issued nationwide.

To address this problem, in 2016 the USFWS updated the Eagle Rule to authorize the issuance of 30-year eagle take permits and otherwise make permit processing easier and more defined.[78] As stated in the preamble to the updated Eagle Rule, "[t]he 2009 permit regulations have not provided an optimal framework for authorizing incidental take . . . , particularly for incidental take resulting from long-term, ongoing activities . . . . One of [the] challenges has been a general perception that the 2009 permitting framework did not provide enough flexibility to issue eagle take permits in a timely manner . . . . When projects go forward without permit authorization, the opportunity to obtain benefits to eagles in the form of required conservation measures is lost and project operators put themselves at risk of violating the law."[79]

The Preservation Standard

BGEPA allows the issuance of permits only if "compatible with the preservation of eagles."[80] The Eagle Rule defines this phrase—referred to as the "preservation standard"—to mean "consistent with the goals of maintaining stable or increasing breeding populations in all *eagle management units* and the persistence of *local populations* throughout the geographic range of each species."[81]

The "preservation standard" is intended to assure preservation at both a national as well as a local or regional scale. At a national level, the USFWS has designated a number of large-scale "Eagle Management Units" (EMUs), each of which represents all or a portion of the Mississippi/Atlantic, Central or Pacific flyways, respectively. At a local or regional level, the Eagle Rule offers protection for Local Area Populations (LAPs) within each EMU, primarily through the establishment of take limits for the various LAPs.

The term EMU is defined to mean "a geographically bounded region within which permitted take is regulated to meet the management goal of maintaining stable or increasing breeding populations of bald or golden eagles."[82] An LAP is defined to mean "the bald or golden eagle population within the area of a human activity or project bounded by the natal dispersal distance for the respective species." The eagle population within each LAP is estimated using the "average eagle density of the EMU or EMUs where the activity or project is located."[83]

The Eagle Rule allows some unmitigated take of bald eagles but—at least according to the preamble to the rule—has limited tolerance for the unmitigated take of golden

---

78 81 Fed. Reg. 91,494 *et seq.*

79 *Id.* at 91,495.

80 16 U.S.C. § 668a.

81 81 Fed. Reg. at 91,497 (emphasis added).

82 50 C.F.R. § 22.3.

83 *Id.*

eagles.[84] The Eagle Rule indicates that compensatory mitigation may be required for any permit when (1) take authorized under the permit would result in an exceedance of the applicable EMU unit take limit (although the rule does not specify what the take limits are for EMUs in general or for any particular EMU); (2) when cumulative *authorized* take, including the proposed take, would exceed five percent of the LAP; or (2) when available data indicates that *cumulative unauthorized mortality* would exceed ten percent of the LAP.[85] The compensatory mitigation ratio for eagle take is not established in the rule per se.

Incidental Take Permits under the Eagle Rule

The Eagle Rule authorizes take of bald and golden eagles where the take is (1) compatible with the preservation of the bald eagle and golden eagle; (2) necessary to protect an interest in a particular locality; (3) associated with, but not the purpose of, the activity (i.e., the take is "incidental"); and (4) cannot *practicably* be avoided.[86]

Under the original Eagle Rule, a permit could be issued only if take was unavoidable. The 2016 version added the qualification that avoidance is required only to the extent "practicable."[87] The Eagle Rule defines the term "practicable" by borrowing roughly from the Clean Water Act Section 404(b)(1) Guidelines, to wit: "Practicable means available and capable of being done after taking into consideration existing technology, logistics, and cost in light of a mitigation measure's beneficial value to eagles and the activity's overall purpose, scope, and scale."[88] Note, however, that, unlike the definition of practicability under the Section 404(b)(1) Guidelines, the Eagle Rule's definition specifically allows consideration of the efficacy of proposed mitigation measures, albeit in rather vague language.

Where required, compensatory mitigation must be "scaled to project impacts" and must ensure the preservation of the affected eagle species "by reducing another ongoing form of mortality by an amount equal to or greater than the unavoidable mortality, or increasing the eagle population by an equal or greater amount."[89] The preamble to the Eagle Rule suggests that mitigation generally will be set at a 1.2:1 ratio, although in practice this ratio likely will differ from situation to situation and, given the healthier status of nationwide bald eagle populations as compared to golden eagles, between the two eagle species.

Under the Eagle Rule, all required compensatory mitigation must:

> be determined based on application of all practicable avoidance and minimization measures

---

84 81 Fed. Reg. at 91,498.

85 50 C.F.R. § 22.26.

86 50 C.F.R. § 22.26.

87 *Id.*

88 *Id.* § 22.3.

89 *Id.* § 22.26(c)(1)(i).

> be sited within the same EMU where the permitted take will occur, unless the Service finds that the affected population includes individuals that are reasonably likely to use another EMU during part of their seasonal migration

> use the best available science in formulating and monitoring the long-term effectiveness of mitigation measures and use rigorous compliance and effectiveness monitoring and evaluation to make certain that mitigation measures achieve their intended outcomes (or that necessary changes are implemented to achieve them)

> be "additional" and "improve upon the baseline conditions of the affected eagle species" in a manner that is demonstrably "new" and would not have occurred without the compensatory mitigation (except for voluntary measures undertaken in anticipation of mitigation that might be required under a yet-to-be issued permit)

> be "durable" and, at a minimum, maintain the intended purpose for as long as the impacts of the authorized take persist (e.g., 30 plus years for a wind generation project)

> include mechanisms to account for and address the uncertainty and risk of failure of a compensatory mitigation measure[90]

Compensatory mitigation may be provided through conservation banks, in-lieu fee programs, other third-party mitigation projects, and, in some circumstances, permittee-responsible projects.[91]

The issue of quantifying the efficacy of mitigation for eagle take is a developing science. For wind projects, the most widely used measure has been power-pole retrofits to reduce electrocution of eagles using probability models to quantify take reductions. Other measures include the preservation of nest or foraging habitat; removal of lead ammunition from the environment; and even methods of reducing road kill. The Eagle Rule does not address these methods specifically, although the USFWS has indicated that it intends to develop further guidance on compensatory mitigation projects, including methods and standards for determining credits, mitigation ratios based on temporal loss and other factors, durability assurance requirements, compliance and effective monitoring, and other considerations.

In determining whether to issue a permit, the USFWS will evaluate a variety of factors, including whether the take is:

> likely to occur based on the magnitude and nature of the impacts

> compatible with the preservation of the bald eagle and the golden eagle, including consideration of indirect effects and the cumulative effects of other permitted take and other additional factors affecting eagle populations

> associated with the permanent loss of an important eagle use area

> necessary to protect a legitimate interest in a particular locality

90   *Id.* § 22.26(c)(1)(iii).
91   *Id.* § 22.26(c)(1)(iv).

> associated with, but not the purpose of, the activity[92]

In addition, the USFWS will consider:

> whether the cumulative *authorized* take (including the proposed take) would exceed five percent of the LAP

> any available data indicating that *unauthorized* take may exceed ten percent of the LAP

> whether the applicant has proposed all avoidance and minimization measures to reduce take to the maximum degree practicable relative to the magnitude of impacts

> whether the applicant has proposed compensatory mitigation to compensate for unavoidable impacts remaining after all appropriate and practicable avoidance and minimization measures have been applied

> whether the permit would preclude the USFWS from authorizing another take needed to protect "an interest of higher priority," such as safety emergencies, tribal needs, and non-emergency activities necessary to ensure public health and safety

> whether past unpermitted takes by the applicant have been or are in the process of being resolved in an enforcement context

> other additional relevant factors that may be relevant, including, but not limited to, the cultural significance of a local eagle population[93]

When issuing an eagle take permit, the USFWS must make a variety of findings, including the following:

> the direct and indirect effects of the take and required mitigation, together with the cumulative effects of other permitted take and additional factors affecting the eagle populations within the EMU and the LAP, are compatible with the preservation of bald and golden eagles

> the taking is necessary to protect an interest in a particular locality

> the taking is associated with, but not the purpose of, the activity

> the applicant has applied all appropriate and practicable avoidance and minimization measures to reduce impacts to eagles

> the applicant has applied all appropriate and practicable compensatory mitigation measures, as required, to compensate for remaining unavoidable impacts after all appropriate and practicable avoidance and minimization measures have been applied

> issue of the permit will not preclude issuance of another permit necessary to protect an interest of higher priority as set forth in 50 Code of Federal Regulations § 22.26(e)(7)

---

92   *Id.* § 22.26(e)(1)–(2).

93   *Id.* § 22.26(e)(3)–(9).

> issuance of the permit will not interfere with an ongoing civil or criminal action concerning unpermitted past eagle take at the project[94]

Monitoring and Adaptive Management

As noted above, given industry's lack of interest in pursuing eagle take permits under the original Eagle Rule, the USFWS extended the authorized life of take permits from 5 to up to 30 years.[95] The exact duration of each permit will be based on the duration of the proposed activities, the period of time for which take will occur, the level of impacts to eagles, and the nature and extent of mitigation measures incorporated into the terms and conditions of the permit.[96]

While this longer permit term is intended to provide industry with greater predictability by assuring that, once secured, an eagle take permit will last for the life of a project, this does not mean that the rules will not change significantly from time to time, thereby undercutting to some extent the certainty sought to be achieved through the new long-term permits. This is because every permitted project is subject to ongoing monitoring and adaptive management and, if the amount of take exceeds the levels even under adaptive management, additional measures might be imposed by the USFWS.

Under Sections 22.26(c)(2)–(7) of the Eagle Rule, a permittee may be required to monitor impacts to eagles for the life of the project and up to three years after completion, or as otherwise set forth in an approved management plan. The frequency and duration of the monitoring—including annual reporting—will "depend on the form and magnitude of the anticipated take and the objectives of associated avoidance, minimization, or other mitigation measures, not to exceed what is reasonable to meet the primary purpose of the monitoring, which is to provide data needed by the [USFWS] regarding the impacts of the activity on eagles for purposes of adaptive management."[97]

For permits with durations longer than five years, monitoring to assess impacts to eagles and the effectiveness of avoidance and minimization measures must be conducted only by qualified, independent third parties approved by the USFWS. These monitors must report directly to the USFWS with copies of reports and materials to the permittee.[98] Long-term permits also must "specify circumstances under which modifications to avoidance, minimization, or compensatory mitigation measures or monitoring protocols will be required," which circumstances may include the project's actual take levels, location of take, and changes in eagle use of the area surrounding the project.[99]

Under the rule's adaptive management provisions, a permit must specify actions to be taken if take approaches or reaches the amount of take authorized within time

94 *Id.* § 22.26(f).
95 *Id.* § 22.26(h).
96 *Id.*
97 *Id.* § 22.26(c)(2).
98 *Id.* § 22.26(c)(7).
99 *Id.*

frames specified in the permit. The Eagle Rule requires that each long-term permit be reviewed every five years and may require "prompt action" upon reaching specified conditions at any time during the review period. The USFWS will review the information provided by the permittee and independent monitors and determine whether the permittee has complied with permit terms and whether actual eagle take exceeded the authorized levels. Based on the permit review, the USFWS also will update fatality predictions, authorized take levels, and compensatory mitigation requirements for future years.[100]

If authorized take levels for the review period are exceeded "in a manner or to a degree not addressed in the adaptive management provisions of the permit," the USFWS may require additional actions, including but not limited to:

> adding, removing, or adjusting avoidance, minimization, or compensatory mitigation measures

> modifying adaptive management conditions

> modifying monitoring requirements

> suspending or revoking the permit in accordance with the USFWS' "General Permit Procedures," as set forth in 50 C.F.R. Part 13[101]

Fortunately, the Eagle Rule also allows some credit if actual take comes in below estimates. If the observed levels of take, "using approved protocols for monitoring and estimating total take," are below authorized take levels, the USFWS "will" proportionately revise the amount of compensatory mitigation required for the next review period, including crediting excess compensatory mitigation already provided by applying it to the next review period.[102]

In light of these five-year reviews, there is some question as to whether would-be applicants will consider the long-term permit conditions sufficiently certain to seek permits. To address this question, the Eagle Rule does provide a limited form of "no surprises" assurance. That is, if the "permittee implements all required actions and remains compliant with the terms and conditions of the permit" (presumably including take limits), then "no other action is required" as a result of the five-year review. However, *with the consent of the permittee*, the USFWS may make additional changes to avoidance or minimization measures or monitoring requirements. If such voluntary measures are adopted and have been shown to be effective in reducing risk to eagles, "appropriate adjustments will be made in fatality predictions, take estimates, and compensatory mitigation."[103] That is, while the five-year review may result in more stringent permit requirements if take exceeds expectations, an applicant may seek *reduced* restrictions if take levels do not exceed permit limits or the applicant agrees to other take-reducing measures.

100 *Id.*
101 *Id.*
102 *Id.*
103 *Id.* § 22.26(c)(7)(iv)(D).

Early Consultation and Survey Protocols

The Eagle Rule encourages early consultation between applicants and the agency. Among other things, the rule requires an applicant to coordinate with USFWS to "develop project-specific monitoring and survey protocols, take probability models, and any other applicable data quality standards."[104] Moreover, the rule requires that, if the USFWS has "officially" issued or endorsed survey, modeling, or other data quality standards for an activity that will take eagles, an applicant "must" follow them and include them in the application unless waived by the USFWS. For wind projects, the Eagle Rule prescribes certain specific protocols that must be followed.

Golden Eagle Nest Permits

Section 22.25 of the Eagle Rule establishes a permit program specifically for the take of *golden* eagle nests allowing for the take of "alternate golden eagle nests" during a "resource development or recovery operation" if the taking is compatible with the preservation of golden eagles. Resource development and recovery operations include, but are not limited to, "mining, timbering, extracting oil, natural gas, and geothermal energy, construction of roads, dams, reservoirs, power plants, power transmission lines, and pipelines, as well as facilities and access routes essential to these operations, and reclamation following any of these operations."[105]

Golden eagle on nest. Photo: Rhona Anderson. Licensed under CC BY-ND 2.

An "alternate nest" is defined as "one of potentially several nests within a nesting territory that is not an in-use nest at the current time. When there is no in-use nest, all nests in the territory are alternate nests." "Nesting territory" in turn means "the area that contains one or more eagle nests within the home range of a mated pair of eagles, regardless of whether such nests were built by the current resident pair." An "in-use nest" is "characterized by the presence of one or more eggs, dependent young, or adult eagles on the nest in the past 10 days during the breeding season." So what is a nest? An eagle nest is "any assemblage or materials built, maintained, or used by bald eagles or golden eagles for the purpose of reproduction."[106]

Golden eagle nest permits are subject to certain specific conditions (in addition to the general conditions set forth in the USFWS' General Permit), including the following:

> only "alternate" nests may be taken
> a report of activities must be submitted to the USFWS within 10 days following permit expiration
> the permittee must notify the USFWS at least 10 days, but not more than 30 days, before a nest is taken

---

104 *Id.* § 22.26(d)(3).

105 *Id.* § 22.3.

106 *Id.*

> the permittee must comply with any mitigation and monitoring measures determined by USFWS to be practicable and compatible with the resource development or recovery operation

> any permit issued before commencement of a resource recovery or recovery operation is invalid if the activity which required a permit is not performed[107]

The USFWS will not issue a golden eagle nest permit unless the taking is compatible with the preservation of golden eagles. In making this determination, the USFWS must consider the following:

> whether the applicant can "reasonably" conduct the operation in a manner that avoids taking any golden eagle nest

> the total number of nests proposed to be taken

> whether suitable golden eagle nesting and foraging habitat that is *unaffected* by the operation is available to accommodate any displaced golden eagles

> whether practicable mitigation measures compatible with the operation are available to encourage reoccupation by golden eagles of the project site; these measures may include, but are not limited to, reclaiming disturbed land to enhance nesting and foraging habitat, relocating the taken eagle nest in suitable habitat, or establishing one or more suitable nest sites[108]

Applications for golden eagle nest take permits must be submitted to the appropriate Regional Director (rather than a USFWS field office), attention of the Migratory Bird Permit Office. Permits will only be considered if an applicant is actually conducting a resource recovery or development operation, or is in the planning or permitting stage of such an operation. The Eagle Rule identifies a list of materials to be included in an eagle nest take permit application including, among other things, (1) a description of the monitoring completed to verify that eagles are not "attending" the nest for breeding purpose; and (2) a description of proposed mitigation measures.[109] Nest permits are valid for a maximum period of two years from permit issuance.[110]

Relationship to Permitting under Other Statutes

No person may take, possess, or transport any bald eagle or golden eagle except as allowed by a valid permit issued under the Eagle Rule, 50 C.F.R. Part 13 (General Permit Procedures), 50 C.F.R. Part 17 (Endangered Species) and/or 50 C.F.R. Part 21 (Migratory Bird Permits) as provided in Section 21.2 of that part. A permit issued under the Eagle Rule does not provide coverage under either the ESA or the MBTA.[111]

---

107 *Id.* § 22.25(b).

108 *Id.* § 22.25(c).

109 *Id.* § 22.25(a).

110 *Id.* § 22.25(d).

111 *Id.* § 22.11.

However, a permit issued under the ESA[112] for bald or golden eagles does constitute a permit for purposes of the Eagle Rule provided that the permittee is in full compliance with the ESA permit. In fact, in February 1996, relying upon a legal opinion from the Office of the Solicitor (also February 1996), the Director of USFWS issued a memorandum to the agency indicating that incidental take statements under Sections 7 and 10 of ESA should contain provisions indicating that the agency will not prosecute violations of BGEPA if the bird in question is covered by the incidental take statement. The efficiencies associated with and processes for such joint permitting have been outlined more recently in a May 10, 2011 memorandum entitled *Use of Endangered Species Act Section 10 Permits to Provide Bald and Golden Eagle Protection Act Authorization for Incidental Take of Bald Eagles and Golden Eagles.*[113]

AVIAN PROTECTIONS UNDER CALIFORNIA LAW

Fish and Game Code Protections

The California Fish and Game Code contains its own specific protections for avian species. Although most of these provisions probably were applied in situations involving intentional take, over the years they have become more commonly applied in the development context, particularly in California Environmental Quality Act (CEQA) documents. Because California's laws (other than CESA) regarding avian take tend to protect the birds, their nest and eggs, including incidental take under Section 86 of the Fish and Game Code, they are not specifically directed at broader habitat protection (e.g., protection of foraging habitat). Moreover, these laws are sweeping in their scope in the sense that they protect virtually all birds, not just those considered rare, threatened or endangered. Accordingly, in the development context, mitigation measures are typically targeted at avoidance measures, particularly during the nesting season.

In response to the Trump Administration's position that the MBTA does not regulate incidental take, California's Attorney General has weighed in to remind the public that the federal rollback does not change the law in California. In November 2018, Attorney General Xavier Becerra issued an "advisory" outlining his position relative to the protection for migratory birds, although the advisory is relevant to all birds in California, whether listed under the MBTA or not.

The broadest of California's statutes, which are overlapping and not necessarily coordinated with each other, are Fish and Game Code § 2000, which makes it unlawful to take a bird (or a mammal, fish, reptile or amphibian), and Fish and Game Code § 3800, which makes it unlawful to take any non-game bird (i.e., bird that is naturally occurring in California that is not a gamebird, migratory gamebird, or fully protected bird). Despite the breadth of these very brief statutory provisions, CEQA analyses tend to focus on Sections 3503 and 3503.5 of the Fish and Game Code, as well as the MBTA and its application in California.

112 *Id.* Part 17.

113 See also HCP Handbook, Section 7.4.2.

Fish and Game Code Section 3503 makes it unlawful "to take, possess, or needlessly destroy the nest or eggs of any bird, except as otherwise provided by this code or any regulation made pursuant thereto." Fish and Game Code Section 3503.5 makes it unlawful to "take, possess or destroy any birds in the orders Falconiformes or Strigiformes (birds of prey) or to take, possess or destroy the nest or eggs of any such bird except as otherwise provided by this code or any regulation adopted pursuant thereto."

Note the minor differences between these two provisions. Section 3503, which relates to birds generally, does not prohibit the take of birds. Its prohibitions are limited to nests and eggs. This gap is filled, however, by Section 3513 of the Fish and Game Code, which makes it unlawful to take or possess any migratory *nongame* bird listed under the MBTA.

More significantly, Section 3503 appears to allow the *destruction* of nests or eggs if the destruction is not "needless" (i.e., nests or eggs may be destroyed if there is a "need" for it), although the prohibitions against *take* and *possession* do not contain this limitation. Section 3503.5 is limited to birds of prey, but it prohibits the take, possession and destruction of the birds, nests and eggs (without the "needless" qualification).

The Fish and Game Code's generally applicable definition of "take" applies to Sections 3503 and 3503.5. Section 86 of the Fish and Game Code defines "take" to mean hunt, pursue, catch, capture, or kill, or attempt to hunt, pursue, catch, capture, or kill."[114] As described in Chapter 2, the term "take" under the Fish and Game Code is much narrower than the definition of the term under the ESA. This is because the California definition does not include the "harm" and "harassment" components contained in the federal definition. As stated by one court, "We reject any insinuation that the definition of 'take' . . . encompasses the taking of habitat alone or the impacts of the taking. As Section 86 of the Fish and Game Code makes clear, proscribed taking involves mortality."[115] Although the State definition of take is narrower than that found in the federal ESA, it does include incidental take which, at least as currently interpreted by the federal government, is not a prohibited act under the Migratory Bird Treaty Act.

Section 3513 of the Fish and Game Code makes it illegal to take or possess any migratory non-game bird as designated in the MBTA except as provided under federal regulations. As of March 2019, the California Legislature was considering legislation to fill the regulatory gap left by Solicitor's Opinion M-37050. This legislation (AB 454) would prohibit the take of MBTA-listed species except as authorized under *California* (rather than federal) law.

As noted above, the foregoing avian protections are often raised in the CEQA context, either by CDFW in its capacity as a responsible or trustee agency, or by the lead agency preparing the CEQA document. The primary concern typically is disturbance from construction activities occurring in close proximity to a nest during nesting season.

---

114 See also 14 Cal. Code Regs. § 1.80.

115 *Environmental Council of Sacramento v. City of Sacramento*, 142 Cal.App.4th 418, 559–60 (2006). See also *Department of Fish & Game v. Anderson-Cottonwood Irrigation Dist.*, 8 Cal.App.4th 1554 (1992).

CDFW or the "Department" = California Department of Fish and Wildlife

NCCP = Natural Community Conservation Plan

Assemby Bill 454 is an Audubon-backed bill intended to stopgap further erosion of federal protections under the MBTA. AB 454 would amend Section 3513 of the Fish and Game Code to eliminate its provision allowing the take of MBTA-designated species in accordance with *federal* law. Instead, take of an MBTA species in California would only be authorized if otherwise allowed under *California* law, and only if such a state law (including any rule, regulation or order) is consistent with or more protective than federal rules or regulations promulgated under the MBTA.

Mitigation measures typically imposed to avoid these impacts include pre-construction surveys, buffers for any construction occurring during the nesting season, and monitoring by a qualified biologist during construction. In the case of ground-nesting birds such as burrowing owls, mitigation protocol may also include passive relocation of birds during the non-nesting season.

Because these measures are typically formulated on a case-by-case basis, CDFW proposed in 2015 a rule to establish uniform standards and definitions to deal with construction-related impacts to nesting birds. The proposed rule contained the following helpful definitions, among others:

> *Destroy* is defined as "any action that physically modifies a nest from its previous condition and adversely affects the survival or a bird of prey or its eggs."

> *Needlessly destroy* is defined as any action falling within the definition of destroy "when it is feasible to avoid such effect until eggs, nestlings, or juvenile birds no longer require the nest for survival."

> *Nest* is defined as "a site or a structure built, maintained or used by a native bird, which is occupied by eggs or nestlings, or is otherwise essential to the survival of a juvenile bird."

> *Feasible* has the meaning assigned to that term under Section 15364 of the CEQA Guidelines (i.e., "capable of being accomplished in a successful manner within a reasonable period of time, taking into account economic, environmental, legal, social and technological factors").

Significantly, the proposed rule sought to establish certain helpful exemptions from the statute, including:

> actions meeting the criteria set forth in the rule and which have been authorized by the USFWS under the terms of the MBTA

> actions authorized under CESA, the NCCP Act or other programs including approved "Voluntary Local Programs" or "Safe Harbor Agreements"

> actions authorized under a Lake and Streambed Alteration Agreement under Section 1602 of the California Fish and Game Code

Unfortunately, on August 5, 2016, CDFW issued a notice of its decision not to proceed with the proposed nest regulations. Nonetheless, the definitions contained in the proposed rule can be used as a rule of thumb in the field, and one might expect CDFW personnel to do the same. It is unclear, however, whether CDFW will—without statutory authorization—continue to offer the exemptions articulated in the proposed rule.

Notwithstanding the demise of the nest regulations, the issuance of Solicitor's Opinion M-37050 in December 2017 continues to put California's bird protections in the spotlight. In November 2018, California's Attorney General issued an advisory, entitled *Affirming California's Protections for Migratory Birds,* which outlined the statutory provisions above and serves as a reminder that the State's definition of take, under Section 86 of the Fish and Game Code, includes incidental take. This advisory can be found at https://oag.ca.gov/system/files/attachments/press-docs/20181129mbta-advisory3.pdf.

California Environmental Quality Act

CEQA = California
Environmental Quality Act

In General

Although birds protected under the MBTA, and Sections 3503 and 3503.5 of the Fish and Game Code, occasionally are treated categorically as "special status species" within the meaning of the California Environmental Quality Act (CEQA), it is not clear that this is appropriate under all circumstances. As acknowledged by CDFW in its proposed rule in 2015, impacts on a bird species should be considered significant if the species meets the standards of Section 15380 of the CEQA Guidelines, which itself defines when a species should be treated as "endangered, rare or threatened."

Note, however, that if an unlisted migratory or native bird species is affected by a proposed project under CEQA, the analysis is not limited to the question of whether a bird or nest will be "taken" within the meaning of the Fish and Game Code or the MBTA. In its proposed rule, CDFW recommended that a CEQA document employ the following findings of significance, which reflect an amalgam of standards found in both CEQA Section 15065 (i.e., mandatory findings of significance) and Appendix G of the CEQA Guidelines:

> the project has a substantially adverse effect, either directly or through habitat modifications, on any species meeting the standards set forth in Section 15380 of the CEQA Guidelines

> the project has the potential to substantially reduce the habitat, restrict the range or cause a population of a native bird species to drop below self-sustaining levels

> the project is likely to have long-term adverse consequences for one of more populations of native bird species

> the project has direct or indirect environmental effects on native bird species that are individually limited but cumulatively considerable

As noted above, CDFW declined to publish its "nest and egg" rule, so these recommendations do not have the force of law. Nonetheless, they do provide some evidence as to how the Department views its role as a responsible or trustee agency under CEQA.

In 2018, California enacted legislation (AB 2640) exempting Northern California condors from the take protections established under Fish and Game Code Section 3511 where (1) the take has been authorized under a federal "enhancement and survival permit" or through a federal experimental population designation and (2) California's Director of Fish and Wildlife has found the federal program to be consistent with the Northern California Condor Restoration Program associated with the Service's 1996 California Condor Recovery Plan.

Specific Species

CDFW has on occasion issued guidance on how particular species ought to be treated under CEQA. Most notable among these are CDFW's *Staff Report on Burrowing Owl Mitigation* (updated in 2012), and the 2010 report issued by CDFW and the California Energy Commission, entitled *Swainson's Hawk Survey Protocols, Impact Avoidance, and Minimization Measures for Renewable Energy Projects in the Antelope Valley of Los Angeles and Kern Counties, California.*

These documents provide technical information on how to evaluate impacts to burrowing owls and Swainson's hawks, respectively; buffer requirements for construction activities during the breeding season; and proposed mitigation methods and ratios. Particularly helpful, in the burrowing owl report, are the Department's protocols for

Brown pelican. Photo: Tracie Hall.
Licensed under CC 2.0.

burrowing owl exclusion and relocation plans during the non-nesting season which are used widely throughout the species' range in California.

Fully Protected Birds

California has established a statutory list of "fully protected" animals that may not be taken under any circumstances except to the extent such a species is covered under a Natural Community Conservation Plan. The list of fully protected birds includes the following species:

> American peregrine falcon (Falco peregrinus anatum)
> brown pelican (=California brown pelican) (Pelecanus occidentalis) (=P. o. occidentalis)
> California black rail (Laterallus jamaicensis coturniculus)
> California clapper rail (Rallus longirostris obsoletus)
> California condor (Gymnogyps califonianus)
> California least tern (Sterna albifrons brown) (=Sterna antillarum browni)
> golden eagle (Aquila chrysaetos)
> greater sandhill crane (Grus candadensis tabida)
> light-footed clapper rail (Rallyus longirostris levipes)
> southern bald eagle (=bald eagle) (Haliaeetus leucocephalus leucocephalus) (=Haliaeetus leucocephalus)
> trumpeter swan (Cygnus buccinator)
> white-tailed kite (Elanus leucurus)
> Yuma clapper rail (Rallus longirostris ymanensis)

CHAPTER 4

State and Federal Plant Protections

This chapter covers state and federal protections for plant species. At the federal level, it discusses the scope of limited protections applicable to plant species under the federal Endangered Species Act. At the state level, it explores the complicated relationship between the California Endangered Species Act, the Native Plant Protection Act, the Natural Community Conservation Planning Act, the California Desert Native Plants Act, and the California Environmental Quality Act.

INTRODUCTION TO PLANT PROTECTIONS

The federal ESA was passed in 1973 to provide a legal mechanism for the conservation of endangered and threatened species and their ecosystems, including plants. The federal ESA was, in fact, the first comprehensive federal legislation to protect plants. As of April 2018, there were 949 plant species listed under the federal ESA.[1] As more fully described below, however, plants receive more limited protection under the federal ESA than do other types of fish and wildlife resources.

In addition to the federal ESA, four distinct but related laws form the legal framework for protecting plant species in California. These include the California Endangered Species Act (CESA), the Native Plant Protection Act (NPPA), the Natural Community Conservation Planning Act (NCCPA), and the California Desert Native Plants Act (CDNPA). Each of these laws and the relationship between their permitting structures is discussed more fully below.

CLASSIFICATIONS OF PLANT SPECIES

When it comes to plants, an explanatory note about nomenclature is in order, because the state laws collectively employ not only the usual "threatened" and "endangered" categories, but also a category called "rare" species.

The federal ESA characterizes species, including plants, as either threatened or endangered.[2] "Threatened" species means:

> Any species which is likely to become an endangered species within the foreseeable future throughout all or a significant portion of its range.[3]

And "endangered" species is defined to include:

> Any species which is in danger of extinction throughout all or a significant portion of its range.[4]

The definitions of "threatened" and "endangered" under CESA and the federal ESA closely mirror each other. Neither CESA nor the federal ESA use the term "rare" when referring to plant species. By contrast, however, the NPPA does not use the "threatened" classification, instead providing protections for plants that it classifies as "rare" or "endangered." Moreover, the NPPA's definition of "endangered" is different from that found under either CESA or the federal ESA. Under the NPPA, "endangered" means that a plant's "prospects of survival and reproduction are in immediate jeopardy from one or more causes."[5]

---

1   USFWS, Environmental Conservation Online System, available at: https://ecos.fws.gov/ecp0/reports/ ad-hoc-species-report?kingdom=P&status=E&status=T&status=EmE&status=EmT&status=EXPE&status=- EXPN&status=SAE&status=SAT&mapstatus=3&fcrithab=on&fstatus=on&fspecrule=on&finvpop= on&fgroup=on&ffamily=on&header=Listed+Plants.

2   See 50 C.F.R. §§ 17.11, 17.12.

3   16 U.S.C. § 1532 (20); 50 C.F.R. § 17.3.

4   16 U.S.C. § 1532 (6); 50 C.F.R. § 17.3.

5   Fish & Game Code § 1901.

Although the NPPA does not use the term "threatened," its definition of "rare" roughly mirrors the definition of "threatened" under CESA and the federal ESA. In particular, the NPPA defines a rare plant as one that, "although not presently threatened with extinction, [] is in such small numbers throughout its range that it may become endangered."[6] Because CESA has not historically authorized the California Department of Fish and Wildlife (CDFW) to issue incidental take permits for species other than those listed as threatened or endangered, in 2015 CDFW promulgated regulations specifically authorizing the CDFW to issue take permits for plants designated as rare under the NPPA in the same manner as for endangered and threatened plants under CESA.[7]

The California Environmental Quality Act (CEQA) contains an even different method of classifying plants based upon their relative level of abundance. In particular, like the NPPA, CEQA defines plants as either "rare" or "endangered," but refers to the federal ESA definition of "threatened" to define what it means to be "rare." However, CEQA's definition of rare species is not limited to those that have been formally listed as threatened. CEQA's definitions are found in Section 15380(b) of the CEQA Guidelines.

Under CEQA, a species is "endangered" when:

> its survival and reproduction in the wild are in immediate jeopardy from one or more causes, including loss of habitat, change in habitat, overexploitation, predation, competition, disease, or other factors.

CEQA defines a species as "rare" when:

> Although not presently threatened with extinction, the species is existing in such small numbers throughout all or a significant portion of its range that it may become endangered if its environment worsens; or

> The species is likely to become endangered within the foreseeable future throughout all or a significant portion of its range and may be considered "threatened" as that term is used in the federal Endangered Species Act.

CEQA also presumes a plant species to be endangered, rare, or threatened if it is listed as such under the federal ESA or CESA.[8]

In addition to species lists prepared pursuant to the above-listed authorities, the California Native Plant Society (CNPS) publishes its own list, the *CNPS Inventory of Rare and Endangered Plants*, which can be found at http://rareplants.cnps.org/. CNPS is a nonprofit environmental organization and not a governmental agency, and as such, the CNPS lists are not based in any regulatory authority or subject to any governmental oversight. As described below, however, the lists maintained by CNPS are routinely used during the environmental review process (i.e., CEQA) in California. In the authors' view, practitioners should be aware that although the CNPS lists sometimes are

CDFW or the "Department" = California Department of Fish and Wildlife

CEQA = California Environmental Quality Act

CNPS = California Native Plant Society

---

6   Fish & Game Code § 1901.

7   14 Cal. Code Regs. § 768.9.

8   *Id.* § 15380(c).

perceived as having regulatory effect, legally their role in anything other than the CEQA process is essentially advisory.[9]

CNPS places sensitive native plants into categories or ranks reflecting degrees of concern. The resulting list is more inclusive than the federal and state lists. The CNPS list, referred to as the "Rare Plant Ranks," uses the following ranking system:

California Rare Plant Rank 1A—Plants presumed extirpated in California and either rare or extinct elsewhere. According to CNPS, these plants species have not been seen or collected in the wild in California "for many years."[10]

California Rare Plant Rank 1B—Plants rare, threatened, or endangered in California and elsewhere. As CNPS explains, "Most of the plants that are ranked 1B have declined significantly over the last century."[11]

California Rare Plant Rank 2A—Plants presumed extirpated in California but common elsewhere. These plants are "presumed extirpated because they have not been observed or documented in California for many years."[12]

California Rare Plant Rank 2B—Plants rare, threatened, or endangered in California but more common elsewhere. "Except for being common beyond the boundaries of California, plants with a California Rare Plant Rank of 2B would have been ranked 1B. From the federal perspective, plants common in other states or countries are not eligible for consideration under the provisions of the federal Endangered Species Act."[13]

California Rare Plant Rank 3—Review List: Plants about which more information is needed. "Plants with a California Rare Plant Rank of 3 are united by one common theme—we lack the necessary information to assign them to one of the other ranks or to reject them."[14]

California Rare Plant Rank 4—Watch List: Plants of limited distribution. "Plants with a California Rare Plant Rank of 4 are of limited distribution or infrequent throughout a broader area in California, and their status should be monitored regularly."[15]

Ranks at each level also include a threat rank (e.g., CRPR 4.3) and are determined as follows:

0.1—Seriously threatened in California (over 80 percent of occurrences threatened/high degree and immediacy of threat)

0.2—Moderately threatened in California (20–80 percent of occurrences threatened/moderate degree and immediacy of threat)

9   CNPS describes itself as a "501(c)3 non-profit dedicated to conserving California native plants and their natural habitats, while increasing the understanding, enjoyment, and horticultural use of native plants." Its mission is "to conserve California native plants and their natural habitats, and increase understanding, appreciation, and horticultural use of native plants." CNPS is often actively opposed to development. See https://www.cnps.org.

10   See CNPS website regarding the ranking of plant species. Available at https://www.cnps.org/rare-plants/cnps-rare-plant-ranks.

11   *Id.*

12   *Id.*

13   *Id.*

14   *Id.*

15   *Id.*

0.3—Not very threatened in California (less than 20 percent of occurrences threatened/low degree and immediacy of threat or no current threats known)

Practitioners should be aware that the CNPS ranking system does not correspond, except only roughly, to the list of protected plant species maintained pursuant to the federal or California Endangered Species Acts. For example, Congdon's tarplant is a CNPS Rare Plant Rank 1B species because CNPS considers it rare in California. However, this plant is not listed as threatened or endangered under either the federal or the California Endangered Species Act.

Congdon's tarplant. Photo: Bonnie Peterson. Licensed under CC 2.0.

Although the CNPS list has no regulatory authority or governmental imprimatur, CDFW often takes into consideration CNPS Rankings when providing comments on CEQA documents. By extension, CDFW and most environmental consultants often take the position that a plant species with a CNPS Ranking of "rare" must be treated as "rare" for purposes of the CEQA. This is because the CEQA Guidelines lists certain conditions that trigger "mandatory findings of significance," one of which is whether the project "has the potential to . . . substantially reduce the number or restrict the range of an endangered, rare, or threatened species."[16] Moreover, the CEQA Guidelines define the term "species" to mean an "endangered," "threatened," or "rare" species.[17] Thus, often these lead agencies use the CNPS Rankings for "rare" species to justify treating them as "rare" for purposes of CEQA. In the authors' view, although this is widespread and common practice, there is no legal authority actually *requiring* CDFW or any CEQA lead agency to treat the CNPS Rankings list in such a way.

FEDERAL ENDANGERED SPECIES ACT

Limited Scope of Section 9 Protections

Although listed plants are not specified as protected under the general take prohibitions in the federal ESA, Section 9 includes a set of narrow protections for listed plant species.[18] With respect to *endangered* species of plants, Section 9 makes it illegal for any person to:

> import or export any such species (into, out of, or through the United States)

> remove and reduce to possession any such species from areas under federal jurisdiction; maliciously damage or destroy any such species on any such area; or remove, cut, dig up, or damage or destroy any such species on any other area in knowing violation of any law or regulation of any state or in the course of any violation of a state criminal trespass law

> deliver, receive, carry, transport, or ship in interstate or foreign commerce, by any means whatsoever and in the course of a commercial activity, any such species

> sell or offer for sale in interstate or foreign commerce any such species

16 14 Cal. Code Regs. § 15065(a).

17 *Id.* § 15380.

18 16 U.S.C. § 1538(a)(2).

> violate any regulation pertaining to such species or to any threatened species of plants[19]

Protections for *threatened* plants are similar to those for endangered plants, except that seeds of cultivated specimens of threatened plant species are exempt from the prohibitions, provided that a statement that the seeds are of "cultivated origin" accompanies the seeds or their container during the course of any activity otherwise prohibited.[20]

As noted above, Section 9 of the federal ESA regulates the destruction of listed plants if the activities involve a species *on federal land*, or if the action would violate state laws. Thus, if a person wishes to develop *private land* in accordance with state law, the potential destruction, damage, or movement of endangered or threatened plants should not be a violation of the federal ESA. Theoretically, such a situation might arise if a person wishes to take a listed plant species located solely on private property, and the take of that species does not violate state law, such as any take prohibition under CESA or other controlling state statute and in the absence of any applicable take authorization.

In 2011, the Ninth Circuit Court of Appeals clarified that "areas under federal jurisdiction" for purposes of Section 9 means "federal land," and does not include privately owned land, even if that land is *subject to* federal regulation, such as wetlands pursuant to the Clean Water Act. In *Northern California River Watch v. Wilcox*,[21] a CDFW conservation manager, for the purposes of examination, removed an endangered plant from federally jurisdictional wetlands located on private property. An environmental organization sued CDFW, alleging federal ESA violations due to the plant's removal on the theory that the wetlands from which the plant was taken was an "area under federal jurisdiction." In ruling against the organization, the court stated that to rule otherwise would "arguably [expand the federal ESA] to apply to private lands which are subject to any sort of federal regulatory jurisdiction by any federal statute."[22]

Section 10 Permitting

Section 10 of the federal ESA describes conditions under which the U.S. Fish and Wildlife Service (USFWS) will grant permits to allow for otherwise prohibited acts relating to plants. For endangered plant species, permits may be obtained for scientific study or to enhance the propagation or survival of the species.[23] Permits also may be issued with respect to threatened plant species for the following activities: scientific purposes, the enhancement of the propagation or survival of threatened species, economic hardship, botanical or horticultural exhibition, educational purposes, or other activities consistent with the purposes and policy of the Act.[24] In light of the Ninth

---

19 16 U.S.C. § 1538(a)(2); 50 C.F.R. § 17.61.

20 50 C.F.R. § 17.71(a).

21 *N. California River Watch v. Wilcox*, 633 F.3d 766, 770, 781–82 (9th Cir. 2011).

22 *Id.* at 781.

23 16 U.S.C. § 1539(a)(1); 50 C.F.R. § 17.62.

24 50 C.F.R. § 17.72(a).

Circuit Court of Appeals decision in *Northern California River Watch v. Wilcox*,[25] presumably a Section 10 incidental take permit would be necessary only for the take of listed plant species that are located on "areas under federal jurisdiction" and not on private land or within a federally jurisdictional water located on that private land.

BLM = Bureau of Land Management

Section 7 Consultations

A Biological Opinion prepared by the USFWS under Section 7 must consider whether jeopardy of a listed plant species or adverse modification of a listed plant species' critical habitat would result from a proposed federal action. In *Center for Biological Diversity v. Bureau of Land Management*,[26] the Bureau of Land Management (BLM) and USFWS prepared a Biological Opinion regarding BLM's proposal to expand access for off-road vehicle recreation in the Imperial Sand Dunes Special Recreation Management Area. Although the Biological Opinion included a jeopardy analysis for affected listed plants, the Center for Biological Diversity alleged that the BLM and USFWS also were required to include an Incidental Take Statement in the Biological Opinion. In holding that the federal ESA contains no such requirement for plants, the court suggested that, although a Section 10 incidental take permit may not be required for the take of a listed plant, a Biological Opinion prepared by the Service under Section 7 must still consider whether jeopardy of a listed plant species or adverse modification of a listed plant species' critical habitat would result from a proposed federal action.[27]

The U.S. Fish and Wildlife Service's Final ESA Section 7 Consultation Handbook (Mar. 1998) ("Section 7 Handbook") provides additional guidance on the treatment of plants in the context of Section 7. The Section 7 Handbook explains that, "[w]hen the consultation involves listed plants, the [action] agency is advised that the [Endangered Species Act] does not prohibit incidental take of these species. However, cautions may be provided on prohibitions against certain deliberate removal or disturbance of plants."[28]

According to the Section 7 Handbook, if listed plant species are present in the action area, the following special provision should be included within the Service's Biological Opinion for the action:

> Sections 7(b)(4) and 7(o)(2) of the Act generally do not apply to listed
> plant species. However, limited protection of listed plants from take is pro-
> vided to the extent that the Act prohibits the removal and reduction to

---

25   633 F.3d at 770, 781–82.

26   833 F.3d 1136 (9th Cir. 2016).

27   *Id.* at 1145 ("The Endangered Species Act does not require Biological Opinions [prepared pursuant to Section 7] to contain Incidental Take Statements for threatened plants."); see also, e.g., *Cal. Native Plant Soc'y v. Norton*, No. 01CV1742 DMS (JMA), 2004 WL 1118537, at *8 (S.D. Cal. Feb. 10, 2004) ("In the absence of a prohibition on the 'take' of plant species, Defendants are correct that 'such take cannot occur, and no incidental take statement is needed.'"); *N. Cal. River Watch v. Wilcox*, 547 F. Supp. 2d 1071, 1075 (N.D. Cal. 2008), aff'd, 633 F.3d 766 (9th Cir. 2010) ("[S]ection 10—allowing a private party to apply for an incidental take permit—applies only to fish and wildlife; there is no section 10 incidental take permit provision for endangered plants.").

28   Section 7 Handbook at p. 4-46.

NPPA = Native Plant Protection Act

NCCPA = Natural Community Conservation Planning Act

CDNPA = California Desert Native Plants Act

possession of federally listed endangered plants or the malicious damage of such plants on areas under federal jurisdiction, or the destruction of endangered plants on non-federal areas in violation of state law or regulation or in the course of any violation of a state criminal trespass law.[29]

CALIFORNIA ENDANGERED SPECIES ACT

Special-status plant species are governed by the California Endangered Species Act in light of CESA's take prohibition in Section 2080 of the Fish and Game Code and CESA's incidental take authorization mechanisms in Sections 2081 and 2080.1 of the Fish and Game Code.

Take Prohibition

Section 9 of the federal ESA establishes take prohibitions for listed plant species that are more limited than its take prohibitions for listed fish and wildlife species. By contrast, CESA prohibits the take of "any endangered species, threatened species, or part or product thereof," which on its face extends to plant species. However, CESA includes an exception with respect to plants that creates some complexity with respect to how this prohibition applies under certain other state laws.

Section 2080 of CESA prohibits the importation or exportation, take, possession, purchase or sale of any threatened or endangered species *except as otherwise provided in this chapter, the Native Plant Protection Act, or the California Desert Native Plants Act.*[30] In other words, the take of any listed plant species is prohibited *unless* that take is authorized by one of the three identified statutes. Each of these statutes has its own provisions authorizing the take of certain plants in different circumstances.

First, Sections 2081 and 2080.1 of the California Fish and Game Code establish processes to authorize the incidental take of threatened and endangered plants, and these processes have been extended by regulation to plants listed as rare under the NPPA. These sections refer broadly to "species" and therefore authorize the take of protected plant species, as well as fish and wildlife species.

Second, the NPPA carves out several activities that are not subject to its take prohibitions. As discussed in more detail below, these activities include agricultural

---

29 Section 7 Handbook at pp. 4-49 to 4-50.

30 The CDFW regulations implementing CESA add one additional statute: the Natural Community Conservation Planning Act (NCCPA). Below in its entirety is the take prohibition from the regulations:
    No person shall import into this State, export out of this State or take, possess, purchase, or sell within this State, any endangered species, threatened species, or part or product thereof, or attempt any of those acts, except as otherwise provided in the California Endangered Species Act, . . . the Native Plant Protection Act, the Natural Community Conservation Planning Act, the California Desert Native Plants Act, or as authorized under this article in an incidental take permit. 14 Cal. Code Regs. § 783.1(a).
    In the authors' view, the added reference to the NCCPA in the CDFW regulations makes sense given that this act, like the other statutes identified in the exception language of Section 2080, includes an exception for incidental take of species listed as threatened and endangered under the California Endangered Species Act and species that have been designated as "fully protected species" pursuant to certain sections in the California Fish & Game Code. See Chapter 11 for further information regarding the NCCPA.

operations or management practices, including the clearing of land for agricultural practices or fire control measures, timber operations in accordance with an official timber
harvesting plan, required mining assessment work, or "the removal of endangered or
rare native plants from a canal, lateral ditch, building site, or road, or other right-of-way
by the owner of the land or his agent," or the "performance by a public agency or a publicly or privately owned public utility of its obligation to provide service to the
public."[31]

These carve-outs from the take prohibitions of the NPPA are fairly broad. Perhaps
most significant is the one related to "the removal of endangered or rare native plants
from a canal, lateral, ditch, building site, or road, or other right-of-way by the owner of
the land or his agent." Focusing on the term "building site," for example, this language
suggests that the NPPA exempts the take of protected plants associated with construction activities so long as the work is performed by the landowner or his agent.

Given that CESA states that no listed plant may be taken except as provided by the
NPPA, this gives rise to the question of whether a CESA take authorization is required
for an activity that may take a threatened or endangered plant but which is exempt from
the provisions of the NPPA. The answer to this question, according to the California
Attorney General, is "no."

This issue, and more generally the relationship between CESA and the NPPA, was
addressed in an Opinion by the California Attorney General in 1998.[32] In this Opinion,
the Attorney General responds to a set of questions pertaining to certain interpretations
of CESA. One of these questions asks: "Under what circumstances may a landowner
destroy a plant on his property that is listed as threatened or endangered under the
California Endangered Species Act?"

To analyze this question, the Attorney General begins by quoting Section 2080 of
the California Fish and Game Code. The Attorney General then explains that with reference to plants, "the term 'take' as used in section 2080 means to destroy," and "a plant
listed under [the California Endangered Species Act] may only be destroyed as authorized by [the California Endangered Species Act] or [the Native Plant Protection Act]."

From this starting point, the Attorney General analyzes each statute in turn, evaluating the extent to which these statutes authorize the take, i.e., destruction, of protected
plant species. The Attorney General summarizes the two key statutory provisions in
CESA that provide incidental take authorization: a Section 2080.1 "consistency determination" and a Section 2081 incidental take permit.

The Attorney General then explains that, based on the exception language in
Section 2080, a plant listed under CESA "may be destroyed if such destruction is
allowed under [the Native Plant Protection Act]." As the Attorney General explains,

> [The Native Plant Protection Act] . . . allows destruction of a listed plant
> with respect to "agricultural operations or management practices, including

---

31 Fish & Game Code § 1913(a) & (b).

32 81 Ops.Cal.Atty.Gen. 222 (1998).

To date no court has addressed the extent of the Native Plant Protection Act's exemption for activities on building sites. From the authors' perspective, the NPPA should mean what it says, namely that the removal of protected plants from building sites developed by landowners on private property is not regulated by the NPPA. Assuming this is true, then, *a fortiori,* the exception language in Section 2080 of the California Endangered Species Act should in those circumstances exempt the take of plants regulated by the NPPA. The authors understand that CDFW has taken the position that the reference to "building sites" and other such development in the NPPA is a reference to existing, not proposed, development. In other words, CDFW appears to interpret this exemption language as applying only to the take of plants regulated by the Act from sites that have already been developed as "building sites" or other developments identified in the Act.

the clearing of land for agricultural practices or fire control measures" and "timber operations in accordance with a timber harvesting plan . . . or required mining assessment work pursuant to federal or state mining laws, or the removal of endangered or rare native plants from a canal, lateral ditch, building site, or road, or other right-of-way."

Because of the exception language in Section 2080, the Attorney General concluded:

> [A] landowner may destroy a plant on his property that is listed as threatened or endangered under [the California Endangered Species Act] when (1) federal approval has been given, (2) approval by [CDFW] has been given, (3) incidental to a properly permitted surface mining operation, (4) incidental to routine and ongoing agricultural activities that occur while specified management practices are followed, (5) due to inadvertent or ordinarily negligent acts during lawful, routine, and ongoing agricultural operations, (6) incidental to state agency projects under findings of [CDFW], (7) incidental to specified emergency projects, or (8) incidental to certain agricultural operations, timber operations, mining assessment work, and the clearing of certain property under the provisions of [the Native Plant Protection Act].

Practitioners should note that this Opinion does not elaborate on the last category and in particular the circumstance in which a project involves "the clearing of certain property under the provisions of [the Native Plant Protection Act]." It appears, however, that because Section 2080 of the California Endangered Species Act exempts the take of plants allowed under the NPPA, and because the NPPA allows the take of plants for "the removal of endangered or rare native plants from a canal, lateral ditch, building site, or road, or other right-of-way," Section 2080 on its face exempts the take of protected plant species without the need for a Section 2080.1 "consistency determination" or a Section 2081 incidental take permit.

Third, with respect to the California Desert Native Plants Act, this Act also includes a set of provisions allowing for the take of certain protected species. See discussion below regarding the take authorization mechanisms relevant to this Act.

Incidental Take Authorization Mechanisms for Protected Plants

CDFW may authorize the take of endangered and threatened plant species through two mechanisms: a Section 2081 incidental take permit and a Section 2080.1 "consistency determination." See Chapter 2 for more information regarding these procedures. In 2015, CDFW created a permitting mechanism for the take of *rare* plants under the NPPA. This mechanism uses the process already established for Section 2081 incidental take permits. This issue is discussed in more detail below. Practitioners should note the discussion above regarding the possibility—thus far untested—that certain plants may be exempt from CESA take prohibitions depending upon the proposed work activity and the location of the plant to be removed.

NPPA = Native Plant Protection Act

NATIVE PLANT PROTECTION ACT

The Native Plant Protection Act of 1977 (NPPA)[33] authorizes the Fish and Game Commission to designate plants as rare and endangered. "Native plant" means "a plant growing in a wild uncultivated state which is normally found native to the plant life of the state."[34] The Commission currently has designated 64 species, subspecies, and varieties of plants to be protected as rare under the NPPA. The NPPA generally prohibits the take of endangered or rare native plants, with exceptions for certain agricultural and nursery operations, emergencies, and following proper notification to CDFW for removal of vegetation from canals, lateral ditches, building sites, or roads, and other rights of way.

Designation of Plants as Rare or Endangered

The Commission may designate a native plant as rare or endangered following a public hearing. After such designation, CDFW must notify affected landowners that an endangered or rare native plant is present, and it must provide the landowner with information regarding protection of the plant.[35] The NPPA does not provide for the same petition procedures for listing as under CESA and appears to require only an evaluation against CDFW-developed criteria for listing under the NPPA. CDFW maintains an official list of rare plants in the California Code of Regulations.[36]

Prohibitions under the NPPA

No person may import into the state, take, possess, or sell within the state of California any native plant or part thereof that has been designated as rare or endangered. This prohibition does not apply to the sale of real property on which such native plants are located.[37]

Discussed in more detail above, the NPPA's take prohibition is not absolute. For example, a landowner may destroy an endangered or rare plant on its property when the landowner is conducting an activity that is otherwise authorized under the NPPA. As discussed above, based on an Attorney General Opinion interpreting the relationship between CESA and the NPPA, arguably this and other exceptions to the NPPA's take prohibitions apply to plant species listed under CESA and would not require a separate CESA permit. Notably, the NPPA includes take exceptions as to endangered and rare plants, not threatened plants. Thus, these exceptions create some ambiguity as to plant species that

---

33   Fish & Game Code § 1900 *et seq.*

34   *Id.* § 1901.

35   *Id.* § 1904.

36   14 Cal. Code Regs. § 670.2(c).

37   Fish & Game Code § 1908.

are not listed as endangered or as rare, but are listed as threatened under CESA. In the authors' opinion, threatened species should be treated the same.

Persons engaged in the production, storage, sale, delivery of transportation of nursery grown stock, or those purchasing nursery grown stock, generally are not required to obtain a permit pursuant to the NPPA, unless that stock consists of rare or endangered native plants.[38] The provisions of the NPPA do not apply to emergency work necessary to protect life or property as long as the person performing such emergency work provides notice to CDFW within 14 days of the commencement of such work.[39] The NPPA also does not apply to agricultural operations or management practices, including the clearing of land for agricultural purposes or fire control measures.[40]

The provisions of the NPPA do not apply to the following activities: timber harvesting conducted pursuant to an approved timber harvesting plan under the provisions of the Z'berg-Nejedly Forest Protection Act of 1973; mining assessment work pursuant to federal or state mining laws; the removal of rare or endangered plants from a canal, road, lateral ditch, or building site; or by a publicly or privately owned public utility for the purpose of providing service to the public also are not restricted under the NPPA.[41] See the discussion above for interpretations as to the applicability of these exceptions.

There is no affirmative obligation of a landowner to notify CDFW prior to destroying a rare or endangered plant unless CDFW has first notified the landowner of the presence of the plant on the owner's land. In the above-listed circumstances, where CDFW has notified the landowner of the presence of a rare or endangered native plant on the affected land, the owner must notify CDFW at least 10 days prior to removal of the native plant to allow CDFW an opportunity to salvage the plant.[42] The failure of CDFW to salvage the plant within 10 days of notification by the landowner entitles the landowner to proceed with the work. For purposes of this provision, the conversion of an agricultural use to another agricultural use does not constitute notice.[43]

Take and Permitting

The NPPA does not provide any statutory mechanism for permitting the take of endangered or rare plant species. In the case of endangered plant species, because the plant species identified as endangered for purposes of the NPPA coincide with the plant species identified as endangered for purposes of CESA, an applicant seeking to take an

---

38   *Id.* § 1907.

39   *Id.* § 1912.

40   *Id.* § 1913(a).

41   *Id.* § 1913(b).

42   *Id.* § 1913(c).

43   In 81 Ops.Cal.Atty.Gen. 222 (1998), the California Attorney General considered whether a landowner is required to give notice of his intention to destroy a rare or endangered native plant in connection with an activity authorized under the NPPA (§ 1913(a), (b)) if the landowner has not been previously notified by CDFW of the presence of the plant on the property. The Attorney General concluded that the landowner has no such obligation.

endangered plant species would utilize the incidental take mechanisms provided by CESA, i.e., either Section 2081 or Section 2080.1 of the California Fish and Game Code.

Prior to 2015, the NPPA did not include provisions regarding take authorization for rare plants. To address this gap in CDFW's permitting authority, and as noted above, in 2015 the Fish and Game Commission adopted new regulations allowing CDFW to authorize the take of rare plants as if they were listed as endangered, threatened or candidate species under CESA. Pursuant to those regulations, CDFW may issue take permits for "rare plants," pursuant to the regulations relating to Section 2081 incidental take permits, Natural Community Conservation Plans, and other authorities.[44]

CALIFORNIA DESERT NATIVE PLANTS ACT

The California Desert Native Plants Act[45] (CDNPA) is intended to protect California desert native plants from unlawful harvesting on both public and private lands. The CDNPA applies only within the boundaries of the Counties of Imperial, Inyo, Kern, Los Angeles, Mono, Riverside, San Bernardino, and San Diego.[46] Within these counties, the CDNPA prohibits the harvest, transport, sale, or possession of specific native desert plants unless a person has a valid permit or wood receipt.

Unlike the NPPA, the CDNPA does not overlap with other laws protecting plants. The CDNPA does not apply to native plants that are declared to be a rare, endangered, or threatened species by federal or state law or regulations (such as the federal ESA, CESA, or the NPPA). Such native plants instead are protected pursuant to the terms of those laws or regulations.[47]

Protected Plants

Under the CDNPA, no person may destroy, dig up, mutilate, or harvest any living native plant, or the living or dead parts of any native plant, without obtaining written permission from the landowner, and a permit and any required wood receipts or tags and seals from the county agricultural commissioner or sheriff.[48]

Native plants protected under the CDNPA are:

> all species of the family Agavaceae (century plants, nolinas, yuccas)

> all species of the family Cactaceae (cacti), except for the plants listed in Section 80072 of the Food and Agricultural Code, which may be harvested for scientific or educational purposes, upon issuance of a permit

> all species of the family Fouquieriaceae (ocotillo, candlewood)

> all species of the genus Prosopis (mesquites)

A peace officer or a CDFW employee or agent may make arrests without a warrant for violations of the NPPA that the officer, agent, or employee witnesses, and may confiscate plants or parts thereof when unlawfully taken, transported, possessed, or sold in violation of the NPPA (Fish & Game Code § 1910). Other penalties under the California Penal Code may apply.

Joshua tree (Yucca brevifolia). Photo: Bonnie Peterson. Licensed under CC 2.0.

44 14 Cal. Code Regs. § 786.9(b).

45 Food & Ag. Code § 80001 *et seq.*

46 *Id.* § 80003.

47 *Id.* § 80075 ("Any native plant that is declared to be a rare, endangered, or threatened species by federal or state law or regulations, including, but not limited to, the Fish and Game Code, is exempt from this division."). For this reason, the interpretations raised above in connection with the NPPA creating exceptions to the CESA do not necessarily apply in the context of the CDNPA.

48 *Id.* § 80111.

> all species of the genus Cercidium (palos verdes)
> Acacia greggii (catclaw)
> Atriplex hymenelytra (desert-holly)
> Dalea spinosa (smoke tree)
> Olneya tesota (desert ironwood), including both dead and live desert ironwood[49]

The fruit from the above-listed native plants may be harvested without a permit.

Certain other protected plants may only be harvested for scientific or educational purposes, upon issuance of a permit by the commissioner or sheriff of the county in which the plant is growing. These plants are:

> all species of Burseraceae family (elephant tree)
> Carnegiea gigantea (saguaro cactus)
> Ferocactus acanthodes (barrel cactus)
> Castela emoryi (crucifixion thorn)
> Dudleya saxosa (panamint dudleya)
> Pinus longaeva (bristlecone pine)
> Washingtonia filifera (fan palm)[50]

Permits, Receipts, Tags, and Seals

An application for a permit must specify, among other things, the species of native plants to be harvested, the area from which the plant will be harvested, and the manner of harvesting.[51]

Permits are valid only for the period of time stated on the permit to allow the permittee to remove the specified number of plants or wood, or the period of time stated by the landowner as part of the landowner's permission, whichever is shorter, but in no case for more than one year.[52] The permit will otherwise expire once the tags or seals are attached to the plants and the plants are no longer in the possession of the permittee.[53]

Upon issuance of a permit, any person who wishes to harvest, transport, offer for sale, or possess a protected plant must attach the required wood receipt, tag or seal to the native plant at the time of harvesting and before transport. Once tagged and harvested, the wood receipt, tag or seal may not be removed until the plant has been transplanted to its ultimate destination.[54] The wood receipt, tag or seal should be retained as proof of legal ownership.

49 *Id.* § 80073.
50 *Id.* § 80072.
51 *Id.* §§ 80101, 80114.
52 *Id.* § 80113.
53 *Id.* § 80115.
54 *Id.* § 80102.

Applicability of the CDNPA and Exemptions

The CNDPA does not apply to the cutting, removing, harvesting or possessing, for purposes other than resale, of five or fewer native plants.[55] Further, the CDNPA does not prevent the following activities:

> the clearing of land for agricultural purposes, fire control measures, or required mining assessment work pursuant to federal or state mining laws

> the holding of a recreational event sanctioned by the Bureau of Land Management

> the clearing or removal of native plants from a canal, lateral ditch, survey line, building site, or road or other right-of-way by the landowner, if the native plants are not to be transported from the land or offered for sale and if the commissioner or sheriff is given at least 10 days' notice[56]

The CDNPA also does not apply to a public agency or to a publicly or privately owned public utility when acting in the performance of its obligation to provide service to the public.

A permit also is not required to remove dead plants or wood if the person undertaking the removal is in possession of a valid permit issued by the U.S. Forest Service, the National Park Service, or the Bureau of Land Management; or the person undertaking the removal is complying with appropriate federal regulations and policies allowing the removal of dead plants or wood from lands administered by the Bureau of Land Management.[57]

Enforcement and Penalties

Violations of the CDNPA constitute a misdemeanor punishable by a fine of between $1,500 or more than $2,500 for each violation upon the first conviction, of between $300 and $5,000 for each violation upon the second conviction, or by imprisonment in the county jail not to exceed one year, or both, and each violation constitutes a separate offense.[58] If convicted of a violation, all permits are revoked and wood receipts, tags, and/or seals are confiscated. No new permits may be issued for at least one year from the date of the conviction.[59] If a person is convicted a second time, no new permits may be issued to that person.[60]

---

55   *Id.* § 80118.

56   *Id.* § 80117.

57   *Id.* § 80104.

58   *Id.* §§ 80172, 80174.

59   *Id.* § 80173.

60   *Id.* § 80174.

NCCP = Natural Community
Conservation Plan

CEQA = California
Environmental Quality Act

CALIFORNIA ENVIRONMENTAL QUALITY ACT

Protection of Plants

In addition to other environmental impact categories, CEQA requires the evaluation of impacts to plant species and the incorporation of feasible mitigation measures to reduce impacts identified as significant. Specifically, CEQA requires an evaluation of conflicts with an adopted NCCP or other local, regional, or state habitat conservation plan; and of impacts to any candidate, sensitive, or special status species in local plans, policies, or regulations of CDFW or of the U.S. Fish and Wildlife Service. Thus, this would encompass impacts to any plant species protected under CESA, the NPPA, the NCCPA, or the CDNPA. Other impacts to plant species that should be evaluated include impacts related to whether the project may adversely affect plants or animals because it has the potential to: (1) threaten to eliminate a plant or animal community; or (2) substantially reduce the number or restrict the range of an endangered, rare, or threatened species.[61]

Protection of Oak Woodlands

In addition to providing for environmental review and public disclosure of impacts to species and habitat, among other impacts resulting from development, CEQA also includes certain requirements regarding impacts to oak woodlands.[62] For purposes of Section 21083.4, "oak" means a native tree species in the genus Quercus, not designated as Group A or Group B commercial species under regulations adopted by the State Board of Forestry and Fire Protection pursuant to Section 4526 of the Fish and Game Code, and that is five inches or more in diameter at breast height.

Mitigation Requirements

If CEQA review by a county discloses that a project may result in a conversion of oak woodlands that will have a significant effect on the environment, in order to approve the project counties acting as lead agencies must require one or more of the following oak woodlands mitigation alternatives to mitigate the significant effect of the conversion of oak woodlands:[63]

> conserve oak woodlands, through the use of conservation easements
> plant an appropriate number of trees, including maintaining plantings and replacing dead or diseased trees, as follows:
  • the requirement to maintain trees terminates seven years after the trees are planted

61 Pub. Res. Code § 21083(b); 14 Cal. Code Regs. § 15065(a).

62 Pub. Res. Code § 21083.4. In 2016, the California Legislature introduced the Oak Woodlands Protection Act (AB 2162), which would have prohibited a person from removing from an oak woodland specified oak trees, unless an oak removal plan and oak removal permit application for the oak tree removal was submitted to and approved by the Director of Fish and Wildlife. However, the proposed legislation was not enacted.

63 Practitioners should note that these provisions apply only to counties, not cities or state agencies that also assume the role of lead agency under CEQA.

- this mitigation must not fulfill more than one-half of the mitigation requirement for the project
- these mitigation requirements also may be used to restore former oak woodlands
> contribute funds to the Oak Woodlands Conservation Fund, as established under Subdivision (a) of Section 1363 of the Fish and Game Code, for the purpose of purchasing oak woodlands conservation easements, as specified under paragraph (1) of Subdivision (d) of that section and the guidelines and criteria of the Wildlife Conservation Board. A project applicant that contributes funds for these purposes must not receive a grant from the Oak Woodlands Conservation Fund as part of the mitigation for the project
> other mitigation measures developed by the county[64]

Sonoma Oak woodland. Photo: Bo Gould. Licensed under CC 2.0.

Exemptions

CEQA provides exemptions from the oak woodland mitigation requirements for the following:
> projects undertaken pursuant to an approved NCCP
> affordable housing projects within an urbanized area or sphere of influence
> conversion of oak woodlands on agricultural land that includes land that is used to produce or process plant and animal products for commercial purposes
> projects undertaken pursuant to a state regulatory program pursuant to Public Resources Code Section 21080.5

64   *Id.* § 21083.4(b).

CHAPTER 5

State and Federal Fish Protections

This chapter covers state and federal protections for fish species. Because most of these protections can be found in other chapters of this book (in particular, the chapters on the California and federal Endangered Species Acts), this chapter focuses primarily on the Magnuson-Stevens Act administered by the National Marine Fisheries Service within the Department of Commerce.

NOAA = National Oceanic and Atmospheric Administration

NMFS = National Marine Fisheries Service

USFWS = U.S. Fish and Wildlife Service

ESA = Endangered Species Act

ESU = evolutionarily significant unit

FEDERAL ENDANGERED SPECIES ACT

The federal Endangered Species Act protects listed fish species. Those protections are administered by two different agencies depending on the biology and habitat of the fish species. As a general rule, anadromous fish (i.e., fish that spend at least some portion of their lifecycle in the ocean, such as salmon and steelhead) are generally subject to the jurisdiction of the Department of Commerce through NOAA's National Marine Fisheries Service (NOAA Fisheries or NMFS). Fish that do not exhibit any anadromy (i.e., fish that do not spend any portion of their lifecycle in the ocean, such as delta smelt and desert pupfish) are generally subject to the jurisdiction of the U.S. Fish and Wildlife Service.

NMFS or the USFWS's administration of the federal ESA for listed fish species generally is no different from these agencies' administration of the federal ESA for any other species. Thus, these agencies are responsible under the federal ESA for the listing and de-listing of fish species, conducting consultations and issuing Biological Opinions under Section 7, and issuing Section 10 incidental take permits under the provisions of approved habitat conservation plans covering such species.

One thing that is unique to the regulation of fish species under the Endangered Species Act is the concept of the "evolutionarily significant unit." Because of their natural history, NMFS regulates certain populations of anadromous fish species, namely salmon and steelhead, based on concepts derived from the "distinct population segment" approach to applying ESA mandates. These populations are referred to as "evolutionarily significant units" (ESUs). For all practical purposes, the ESUs, although not a species per se, are treated as if they are protected under the Endangered Species Act.

Adams River salmon run. Photo: Lee Shoal. Licensed under CC 2.0.

MAGNUSON-STEVENS FISHERY CONSERVATION AND MANAGEMENT ACT

Unlike the Endangered Species Act, the Magnuson-Stevens Fishery Conservation and Management Act specifically applies to the conservation and management of fish species.

Overview

The Magnuson-Stevens Fishery Conservation and Management Act[1] establishes protections for what the Act defines as "essential fish habitat." Although the majority of Magnuson-Stevens focuses on the regulation of marine fisheries within a claimed "exclusive economic zone" for the United States, certain provisions require the Act's "fishery management councils" to consider "essential fish habitat." These provisions also require federal agencies (e.g., the Corps of Engineers when issuing permits under Section 404 of the Clean Water Act or Section 10 of the Rivers and Harbors Act) to consult with NMFS when the actions of those agencies may adversely affect such habitat. The scope and structure of these consultations is discussed below. More information regarding this program can be found at https://www.fisheries.noaa.gov/resource/document/magnuson-stevens-fishery-conservation-and-management-act.

1   16 U.S.C. § 1801 *et seq.*

First passed in 1976, the Magnuson-Stevens Act is the primary law governing the management of marine fisheries within waters along the U.S. coastline. The stated objectives of the Act are to:

> prevent overfishing

> rebuild overfished stocks

> increase long-term economic and social benefits

> use reliable data and sound science

> conserve essential fish habitat

> ensure a safe and sustainable supply of seafood

To implement these goals, the Act provides management jurisdiction to eight, regional "fishery management councils," which act under the oversight of NMFS. The members of these councils include representatives from regional states, treaty fishing tribes, fishery and ocean stakeholders, and the federal government. As discussed below, these councils are required to create a "fishery management plan" for each fishery in need of conservation and management. These plans must comply with various conservation and management requirements, including 10 national standards identified in the accompanying regulations, which are briefly summarized below.[2]

History

Prior to passage of the Magnuson-Stevens Act in 1976, international waters began at just 12 miles from shore and were commonly fished by unregulated foreign fleets. The Legislature acted to promote U.S. commercial fishing off the coast of the United States by "consolidating control over territorial waters" after widespread intrusion by foreign fishing vessels.

Under Magnuson-Stevens, the United States claims sovereign rights and exclusive fishery management authority over all fish and continental shelf fishery resources (with certain exceptions) within an "exclusive economic zone," which begins in most instances at three nautical miles from the shoreline and extends out to 200 miles.[3] The protections of Magnuson-Stevens, described more fully below, are intended to apply to this zone.[4]

---

2   A notable aspect of the Magnuson-Stevens Act that sets it apart from other resource management statutes such as the National Forest Management Act and the Federal Land Policy and Management Act is that, absent some affirmative agency action, fisheries in federal waters go unregulated. The default status of fisheries within the federal government's jurisdiction is open, thereby allowing unrestricted harvests. Thus, when NMFS takes an action pursuant to the Magnuson-Stevens Act, it imposes a restriction that otherwise would not exist. In contrast, public lands are considered to be "owned" by the United States, and the federal agencies charged with managing them must take an action to authorize consumptive use.

3   This jurisdictional claim is consistent with the definition of "exclusive economic zone" included in the United Nations Convention on the Law of the Sea. United Nations Convention on the Law of the Sea, Dec. 10, 1982, 1833 U.N.T.S. 419.

4   16 U.S.C. §§ 1802(6) & (7) (defining "continental shelf"), 1802(11) (defining "exclusive economic zone"), 1811(a), 1812 (highly migratory species); see also Presidential Proclamation No. 5030 (Mar. 10, 1983). Under the Magnuson-Stevens Act, the United States also claims exclusive fishery management authority over: (1) all anadromous species throughout the migratory range of each such species beyond the exclusive economic zone, aside from any time they are found within any waters of a foreign nation; and (2) all continental shelf fishery resources beyond the exclusive economic zone. 16 U.S.C. § 1811(b).

In 1996, Congress passed the Sustainable Fisheries Act which amended the Magnuson-Stevens Act to, among other things, strengthen requirements to prevent overfishing and rebuild overfished fisheries; set standards for fishery management plans to specify objective and measurable criteria for determining stock status; add three new national standards to address fishing vessel safety, fishing communities, and bycatch; and introduce fish habitat as a key component in fisheries management.

Subsequently, in 2007 Congress passed the Magnuson-Stevens Reauthorization Act, which, among other things: established annual catch limits and accountability measures; promoted market-based management strategies, including limited access privilege programs, such as catch shares; strengthened the role of science through peer review, the scientific and statistical committees, and the Marine Recreational Information Program; and enhanced international cooperation by addressing illegal, unregulated, and unreported fishing and bycatch.

Fisheries Management Councils and Plans

As mentioned above, Magnuson-Stevens establishes eight regional fishery management councils comprised of fishing representatives and government and tribal officials.[5] These eight councils are as follows: New England Council; Mid-Atlantic Council; South Atlantic Council; Caribbean Council; Gulf Council; Pacific Council; North Pacific Council; and Western Pacific Council.[6] Councils are in turn overseen by the U.S. Secretary of Commerce, who has delegated much of this authority to NOAA Fisheries. To see more information published by NMFS' West Coast region, you can find it at https://www.westcoast.fisheries.noaa.gov/.

California is included within the Pacific Fishery Management Council, which also includes Oregon, Washington, and Idaho. In total, the Pacific Council consists of 14 voting members, including: eight appointed by the Secretary of Commerce under 16 U.S.C. Section 1852(b)(2) (at least one of whom is appointed from each state); one appointed from an Indian tribe with federally recognized fishing rights from California, Oregon, Washington, or Idaho in accordance with 16 U.S.C. Section 1852(b)(5); one representative of each states' marine fisheries management agency; and one NOAA Fisheries representative.[7] There are also five nonvoting members representing U.S. Fish and Wildlife Service, Pacific States Marine Fisheries Commission, U.S. Coast Guard, the State of Alaska, and the Department of State.[8] The Pacific Council also has a scientific and statistical committee as well as a number of advisory committees.[9]

Each regional fishery management council is charged with preparing fishery management plans for the fisheries under its authority and which need "conservation and

---

5   16 U.S.C. § 1852.

6   *Id.* § 1852(a)(1).

7   *Id.* § 1852(b).

8   *Id.* § 1852(c).

9   *Id.* § 1852(g).

management."[10] Any stocks that are predominately caught in federal waters and are overfished or subject to overfishing, or likely to become overfished or subject to over-fishing, are considered to require conservation and management within the meaning of the Act. Based on certain criteria, councils may determine that additional stocks require conservation and management.[11]

Fishery management plans must be consistent with ten established national stand-ards for fishery conservation and management.[12] These plans also contain certain required provisions,[13] including requirements to:

> describe the fishery

> specify the conservation and management measures necessary to prevent over-fishing and rebuild overfished stocks

> assess and specify, among other things, the optimum yield from the fishery[14]

> assess and specify, among other things, the extent to which U.S. fishing vessels, on an annual basis, will harvest the optimum yield, and the portion of such yield that can be made available for foreign fishing

> describe and identify essential fish habitat for the fishery

> specify objective and measurable criteria for identifying when the fishery is overfished

> establish a standardized reporting methodology to assess the amount and type of bycatch occurring in the fishery and include relevant conservation and man-agement measures

> to the extent that measures are necessary to reduce overall harvest to prevent overfishing, allocate any harvest restrictions fairly and equitably among the fish-ing sectors that participate in the fishery

> establish a mechanism for specifying annual catch limits

Fishery management plans may also include certain additional provisions at the discretion of the council preparing the plan, including: creation of a fee permit system; restrictions on fish catch or fishing gear types; creation of a limited access system in order to achieve optimum yield; or any other measures determined to be necessary and appropriate for the conservation and management of the fishery.[15]

Once completed, fisheries management plans are submitted to NOAA Fisheries, acting on behalf of the Secretary of Commerce, and the public for review.[16] The coun-cils and NOAA Fisheries follow the same process for regulations to implement a given plan.[17] In certain instances, the Secretary of Commerce may prepare a fishery

10   *Id.* § 1852(h)(1).

11   50 C.F.R. § 600.305(c).

12   16 U.S.C. § 1851(a); see also 50 C.F.R. §§ 600.310–355 (implementing regulations).

13   16 U.S.C. § 1853(a).

14   See also 50 C.F.R. § 600.10 (defining "optimum yield").

15   16 U.S.C. § 1853(b).

16   *Id.* § 1854(a).

17   *Id.* §§ 1853(c), 1854.

management plan where the regional council either fails to develop a plan within a reasonable amount of time or otherwise prepares an insufficient plan.[18]

Essential Fish Habitat

> For purposes of the Act, "essential fish habitat" means "those waters and substrate necessary to fish for spawning, breeding, feeding or growth to maturity" (16 U.S.C. § 1802(10); see also 50 C.F.R. § 600.10).

As noted above, the Magnuson-Stevens Act was amended in 1996 to, among other things, introduce the concept of "essential fish habitat" and require all fishery management plans to: (1) describe and identify such habitat for each fishery (including adverse impacts on such habitat); (2) minimize to the extent practicable adverse effects on such habitat caused by fishing; and (3) identify other actions to encourage the conservation and enhancement of such habitat.[19] To this end, NOAA Fisheries must coordinate with and provide information to other federal agencies to further the conservation and enhancement of essential fish habitat. Federal action agencies also must consult with NOAA Fisheries on activities that may adversely affect essential fish habitat.[20]

In January 2002, NOAA Fisheries issued a final rule establishing guidelines to implement the statutory provisions for essential fish habitat under Magnuson-Stevens. Act Provisions.[21] Under these regulations, an essential fish habitat provision in a fishery management plan must include all fish species in the fishery management unit.[22] Essential fish habitat may be described and identified in waters of the United States as defined in regulations promulgated by the Army Corps of Engineers,[23] and in the exclusive economic zone as defined in 50 Code of Federal Regulations Section 600.10. As noted above, fishery management plans in turn are required to include the components identified below.[24]

Contents of Fishery Management Plans

Description and Identification of Essential Fish Habitat

Fishery management plans must describe and identify essential fish habitat in text that clearly states the habitats or habitat types determined to be such habitat for each life stage of the managed species. Plans should explain the physical, biological, and chemical characteristics of essential fish habitat and, if known, how these characteristics influence the use of essential fish habitat by the species/life stage. Plans must identify the specific geographic location or extent of habitats described as essential fish habitat. Plans must also identify maps of the geographic locations of essential fish habitat or the geographic boundaries within which essential fish habitat for each species and life stage is found.

---

18   *Id.* § 1854(c).

19   *Id.* § 1853(a)(7); see also *id.* § 1855(b)(1)(A).

20   *Id.* § 1855(b).

21   67 Fed. Reg. 2343 (Jan. 17, 2002) (codified at 50 C.F.R. pt. 600).

22   50 C.F.R. § 600.805.

23   33 C.F.R. § 328.3.

24   50 C.F.R. § 600.815.

Fishing Activities That May Adversely Affect Essential Fish Habitat

Plans must contain an evaluation of the potential adverse effects of fishing on essential fish habitat designated under the plan, including the effects of each fishing activity regulated under the plan or other federal fish management plans. Each plan also must identify measures to minimize to the extent practicable adverse effects from fishing on essential fish habitat, including such habitat designated under other federal fish management plans. Options for managing adverse effects from fishing include, but are not limited to, fishing equipment restrictions, time/area closures, and harvest limits.

Non-Magnuson-Stevens Act Fishing Activities That May Adversely Affect Essential Fish Habitat

Plans must identify any fishing activities that are not managed under the Magnuson-Stevens Act that may adversely affect essential fish habitat. Such activities may include fishing managed by state agencies or other authorities.

Non-Fishing Related Activities That May Adversely Affect Essential Fish Habitat

Plans must identify activities other than fishing that may adversely affect essential fish habitat. Such activities may include, but are not limited to: dredging, filling, excavation, mining, impoundment, discharge, water diversions, and thermal additions. For each activity, the plan should describe known and potential adverse effects to essential fish habitat.

Cumulative Impacts Analysis

To the extent feasible and practicable, plans should analyze how the cumulative impacts of fishing and non-fishing activities influence the function of essential fish habitat on an ecosystem or watershed scale. An assessment of the cumulative and synergistic effects of multiple threats, including the effects of natural stresses (e.g., storm damage or climate-based environmental shifts) and an assessment of the ecological risks resulting from the impact of those threats on essential fish habitat, also should be included.

Conservation and Enhancement

Plans must identify actions to encourage the conservation and enhancement of essential fish habitat, including recommended options to avoid, minimize, or compensate for any identified adverse effects, especially in habitat areas of particular concern.

Prey Species

Under the regulations, actions that reduce the availability of a major prey species, either through direct harm or capture, or through adverse impacts to the prey species' habitat that are known to cause a reduction in the population of the prey species, may be considered adverse effects on essential fish habitat if such actions reduce the quality of essential fish habitat. Plans should list the major prey species for the species in the fishery management unit and discuss the location of prey species' habitat. Adverse effects on prey species and their habitats may result from fishing and non-fishing activities.

Concern

Plans should identify specific types or areas of habitat within essential fish habitat as habitat areas of particular concern based on one or more of the following considerations: (1) the importance of the ecological function provided by the habitat; (2) the extent to which the habitat is sensitive to human-induced environmental degradation; (3) whether, and to what extent, development activities are, or will be, stressing the habitat type; and (4) the rarity of the habitat type.

Research and Information Needs

Plans should contain recommendations, preferably in priority order, for research efforts that the fishery management councils and NOAA Fisheries view as necessary to improve upon the description and identification of essential fish habitat, the identification of threats to essential fish habitat from fishing and other activities, and the development of conservation and enhancement measures for essential fish habitat.

Review and Revision of Essential Fish Habitat Component of Fish Management Plans

Councils and NOAA Fisheries should periodically review the essential fish habitat provisions of plans and revise or amend essential fish habitat provisions as warranted based on available information. Plans should outline the procedures the council will follow to review and update essential fish habitat information. A complete review should be conducted as recommended by NOAA Fisheries, but at least once every five years.

General Coordination with Other Federal Agencies

Under the Magnuson-Stevens Act, NOAA Fisheries must "coordinate with and provide information to other federal agencies to further conservation and enhancement of essential fish habitat."[25] To this end, the implementing regulations require NOAA Fisheries to compile and make available to other federal and state agencies (as well as the general public) information on the locations of essential fish habitat, including maps and narrative descriptions.[26] Consistent with this requirement, NOAA Fisheries has provided an "Essential Fish Habitat Mapper" on its website, which displays maps for essential fish habitat, habitat areas of particular concern, and essential fish habitat areas protected from fishing.

Under the regulations, NOAA Fisheries also must provide information on ways to improve ongoing federal operations to promote the conservation and enhancement of

25   16 U.S.C. § 1855(b)(1)(D).
26   50 C.F.R. § 600.915.

essential fish habitat. Federal and state agencies empowered to authorize, fund, or undertake actions that may adversely affect essential fish habitat are encouraged to contact NOAA Fisheries and the relevant fishery management councils to become familiar with areas designated as essential fish habitat, potential threats to essential fish habitat, and opportunities to promote the conservation and enhancement of such habitat.

EFH = essential fish habitat

Consultations under Magnuson-Stevens

Under the Magnuson-Stevens Act, a federal agency is required to consult with NOAA Fisheries on any action "that may adversely affect" essential fish habitat.[27] Not coincidentally, this "may adversely affect" standard is essentially identical to the standard triggering formal consultation under the federal ESA. Because of this, consultations under Magnuson-Stevens typically are carried out in the context of formal consultations under the federal ESA.

Magnuson-Stevens requires NOAA Fisheries to review the project and provide non-prescriptive "conservation recommendations" to the agency. In connection with this process, NOAA Fisheries and the lead federal agency must use the best scientific information available to assess the potential effects of a proposed action on essential fish habitat, although they also may consider other appropriate sources of information.[28]

As under the federal ESA, consultations under Magnuson-Stevens must be performed by federal agencies not only for actions undertaken by that agency but also for actions authorized or funded by the agency, when such actions may adversely affect essential fish habitat.[29] A federal agency also must consult on renewals, reviews, or substantial revisions to actions that may adversely affect essential fish habitat.

Generally, consultation is initiated when a federal agency provides to NOAA Fisheries notification of a proposed action together with an Essential Fish Habitat Assessment, or "EFH Assessment" that is analogous to a Biological Assessment under the federal ESA. Federal agencies are encouraged to notify NOAA Fisheries in writing as early as practicable regarding actions that may adversely affect essential fish habitat.[30] Such early coordination is encouraged to occur during pre-application planning for projects subject to a federal permit or license or during preliminary planning for projects to be funded or undertaken directly by a federal agency. If, by contrast, NOAA Fisheries receives information regarding a federal action that may adversely affect EFH but the "action agency" has not initiated consultation under the Act, NOAA Fisheries may inform the action agency of the requirement to consult on the proposed action.

---

27 For purposes of the Act, "adversely affect" means "any impact that reduces quality and/or quantity" of essential fish habitat. 50 C.F.R. § 600.810(a). This may include, but is not limited to, direct or indirect physical, chemical, or biological alterations of the waters or substrate and loss of, or injury to, benthic organisms, prey species, and their habitat, and other ecosystem components. Adverse effects may result from actions occurring with essential fish habitat or outside of such habitat and may include site-specific or habitat-wide impacts, including individual, cumulative, or synergistic consequences of actions. *Id.*

28 *Id.* § 600.920(d).

29 *Id.* § 600.920(a)(1).

30 *Id.* § 600.920(a)(3).

NEPA = National Environmental
Policy Act

EFH Assessments

As mentioned above, in conjunction with any consultation, under Magnuson-Stevens, federal "action agencies" must provide NOAA Fisheries with a written assessment of the potential effects of the action on essential fish habitat.[31] In certain instances, federal agencies may incorporate these assessments into documents prepared for other purposes, including Biological Assessments under the federal ESA[32] and certain National Environmental Policy Act (NEPA) documents.[33] If an EFH Assessment is contained in another such regulatory document, it must still include all of the information required under the Act and identified clearly as an EFH Assessment.

Under the implementing regulations, EFH Assessments must include: (1) a description of the action; (2) an analysis of the potential adverse effects of the action on essential fish habitat and the managed species; (3) the federal agency's conclusions regarding the effects of the action on essential fish habitat; and (4) proposed mitigation, if applicable.[34] As necessary, assessments also should include: (1) the results of an on-site inspection to evaluate the habitat and the site-specific effects of the project; (2) the views of recognized experts on the habitat or species that may be affected; (3) a review of pertinent literature and related information; (4) an analysis of alternatives to the action; and (5) other relevant information.[35] An assessment also may incorporate by reference a completed assessment prepared for a similar action, supplemented with any relevant new project specific information, as well as other relevant Environmental Assessment documents if those documents are provided to NOAA Fisheries.[36]

Consultation Procedures

The implementing regulations encourage NOAA Fisheries and other federal agencies to consolidate any essential fish habitat consultation with any interagency consultation, coordination, and environmental review procedures required by other statutes, such as NEPA, the federal ESA, the Fish and Wildlife Coordination Act, the Clean Water Act, and the Federal Power Act. Such consolidation is considered appropriate where the following three criteria can be met:

> The existing process must provide NOAA Fisheries with timely notification of actions that may adversely affect essential fish habitat. Generally, NOAA Fisheries requests at least 60 days' notice prior to a final decision on an action, or at least 90 days if the action would result in substantial adverse impacts.

---

31   *Id.* § 600.920(e).

32   *Id.* part 402.

33   40 C.F.R. part 1500.

34   50 C.F.R. § 600.920(e)(3).

35   *Id.* § 600.920(e)(4).

36   *Id.* § 600.920(e)(5).

> An assessment of the impacts on essential fish habitat must be prepared that meets the requirements for EFH Assessments.[37] If the assessment is contained in another document, the federal agency must identify that section of the document as the EFH Assessment.

> NOAA Fisheries must make a finding that the existing consultation or environmental review process meets the statutory requirements under the Magnuson-Stevens Act.[38]

According to NOAA Fisheries, the vast majority of essential fish habitat consultations are project-specific consultations incorporated into existing environmental review procedures, where consultation and coordination already is required by other statutes.[39] Some of the most commonly used existing processes include the following.

National Environmental Policy Act

In many instances, an essential fish habitat consultation can be accommodated through the environmental review process required under NEPA, either through an Environmental Impact Statement or an Environmental Assessment. Generally, notification occurs when NOAA Fisheries receives a draft EIS or EA that includes an EFH Assessment satisfying all of the regulatory requirements of the Act. In this case, NOAA Fisheries provides conservation recommendations as part of its overall comments on the draft document.

Endangered Species Act

There are many situations where designated essential fish habitat overlaps with the habitat (including critical habitat) of a species listed under the federal ESA. Thus, a proposed federal action therefore might affect both a listed species (including any designated critical habitat) *and* essential fish habitat, thereby requiring consultation under both Section 7 of the federal ESA and the essential fish habitat provisions of Magnuson-Stevens. Generally, essential fish habitat consultations can be completed using the Section 7 consultation process provided that the federal action agency supplies the information required for an EFH Assessment and NOAA Fisheries clearly distinguishes its essential fish habitat conservation recommendations from its federal ESA recommendations under 50 Code of Federal Regulations Section 402.14(j) (or any other measures or conditions under the federal ESA). To this end, NOAA Fisheries published guidance for integrating these consultation procedures in January 2001.[40]

EIS = Environmental Impact Statement

EA = Environmental Assessment

---

37   See *id.* § 600.920(e).

38   *Id.* § 600.920(f).

39   See NOAA Fisheries, *What is an Essential Fish Habitat Consultation* (Aug. 2013), available at http://sero.nmfs.noaa.gov/habitat_conservation/documents/efh_consultation_101_ver082013.pdf.

40   See NOAA Fisheries, Guidance for Integrating Magnuson-Stevens Fishery Conservation and Management Act EFH Consultations With Endangered Species Act Section 7 Consultations (Jan. 2001), available at http://www.dodworkshops.org/files/Training/References/10_NMFS_Appendix_C_EFH_Consultation_Guidance.pdf.

FERC = Federal Energy
Regulatory Commission

Corps Permitting

The individual permit process used by the Army Corps of Engineers to authorize projects under Section 404 of the Clean Water Act and Section 10 of the Rivers and Harbors Act (as well as Section 103 of the Marine Protection, Research, and Sanctuaries Act) also can be used to meet the essential fish habitat consultation requirements under Magnuson-Stevens. Generally, notification occurs when NOAA Fisheries receives a public notice from the Corps on a proposed action. For projects that require abbreviated consultation, the Corps will put a brief EFH Assessment in the public notice. For projects that require expanded consultation, the Army Corps may provide NOAA Fisheries with a detailed EFH Assessment, which may be a separate document or it may be a component of another document (e.g., a draft Statement of Findings), and which will be provided to NOAA Fisheries in a time frame sufficient for developing conservation recommendations. In these instances, NOAA Fisheries will provide conservation recommendations in response to the public notice and the Army Corps will respond to the conservation recommendations in either a letter or other document (e.g., a Statement of Findings or an EA) at least 10 days before the permit is issued.

Federal Power Act

The Federal Power Act authorizes NOAA Fisheries to provide mandatory fishway prescriptions and recommendations when non-federal hydropower projects receive a new license from the Federal Energy Regulatory Commission (FERC). In most instances, FERC and the applicant coordinate the process with extensive consultation among federal and state agencies, tribes, and other stakeholders.

If a post-licensing activity may adversely affect essential fish habitat, the need for consultation will depend on whether consultation already has been conducted, and whether the action was anticipated during the original licensing. If possible adverse effects on essential fish habitat already have been analyzed and addressed in the consultation completed for the existing licensing, additional consultation may not be required. If possible adverse effects on essential fish habitat have not previously been analyzed, FERC will complete consultation following the same general procedures for licensing, with certain modifications.

Fish and Wildlife Coordination Act

The Fish and Wildlife Coordination Act[41] requires that fish and other wildlife receive equal consideration and be coordinated with other aspects of water resource development. This is accomplished by requiring consultation with the U.S. Fish and Wildlife Service, NOAA Fisheries, and appropriate state agencies whenever any body of water is proposed to be modified in any way and a federal permit or license is required. In connection with this process, NOAA Fisheries submits comments to federal licensing and

41   16 U.S.C. §§ 661–667e.

permitting agencies on the potential harm to living marine resources caused by the proposed water development project and recommendations to prevent harm. Generally, comments submitted under the authority of the Fish and Wildlife Coordination Act may be integrated with the essential fish habitat consultation process.

Programmatic Consultation

Programmatic consultation provides a means for NOAA Fisheries and a federal agency to consult regarding a potentially large number of individual actions that may adversely affect essential fish habitat. Programmatic consultation will generally be the most appropriate option to address funding programs, large-scale planning efforts, and other instances where sufficient information is available to address all reasonably foreseeable adverse effect on essential fish habitat of an entire program, parts of a program, or a number of similar individual actions occurring within a given geographic area.[42] Any size program may be addressed through a programmatic consultation, however, depending on the nature of the actions conducted in the program. Whether a particular program should be subdivided, or whether some programs should be lumped together for the consultation, generally will be determined jointly by NOAA Fisheries and the federal action agency.

Generally, a federal agency will request programmatic consultation by providing NOAA Fisheries with an EFH Assessment. The description of the proposed action in the assessment will describe the program and the nature and approximate number (annually or some other appropriate time frame) of the actions.[43] NOAA Fisheries will then respond to the federal agency with programmatic conservation recommendations and, if applicable, will identify any potential adverse effects that could not be addressed programmatically and require project-specific consultation.[44] Alternatively, NOAA Fisheries may determine that programmatic consultation is not appropriate, in which case project-specific consultations will be required. Where appropriate, NOAA Fisheries' response may include a general concurrence for certain activities.

General Concurrence

The general concurrence process is used to identify specific types of federal actions that may adversely affect essential fish habitat, but for which no further consultation generally is required because NOAA Fisheries has determined that the identified types of actions likely will result in no more than minimal adverse effects to essential fish habitat individually and cumulatively.[45] Concurrences may be national or regional in scope.

---

42   50 C.F.R. § 600.920(j)(1).

43   *Id.* § 600.920(j)(2).

44   *Id.* § 600.920(j)(3).

45   *Id.* § 600.920(g)(1).

In order for federal actions to qualify under a general concurrence, NOAA Fisheries must determine that the actions meet all of the following criteria:[46]

> the actions must be similar in nature and similar in their impact on essential fish habitat

> the actions must not cause greater than minimal adverse effects on essential fish habitat when implemented individually

> the actions must not cause greater than minimal cumulative adverse effects on essential fish habitat[47]

NOAA Fisheries also may determine that certain categories of federal actions meet the required criteria if modified by appropriate conditions, including, for example, project size limitations, seasonal restrictions, or other conditions necessary to ensure that the effects on essential fish habitat will be minimal individually and cumulatively.[48] In addition, a higher level of scrutiny may be warranted if a general concurrence is proposed for actions that may adversely affect habitat areas of particular concern.[49]

A federal agency may request that NOAA Fisheries develop a general concurrence for specific types of agency actions, or NOAA Fisheries may develop a general concurrence on its own initiative. Where a federal agency requests a general concurrence, the agency should provide NOAA Fisheries with an EFH Assessment including a written description of the nature and approximate number of the proposed actions, an analysis of the effects of the actions on essential fish habitat, including cumulative effects, and the federal agency's conclusions regarding the magnitude of such effects.[50]

If NOAA Fisheries determines that the actions fit the criteria for a general concurrence, it will provide the federal agency with a written statement of general concurrence that further consultation is not required.[51] If NOAA Fisheries does not agree that the actions fit the required criteria, it will instead notify the federal agency that a general concurrence will not be issued and that another type of consultation will be required.

NOAA Fisheries also may request notification for actions covered under a general concurrence if it concludes there are circumstances under which such actions could result in more than a minimal impact on essential fish habitat, or if it determines that there is no process in place to adequately assess the cumulative impacts of actions covered under the general concurrence.[52] NOAA Fisheries also may request further consultation for these actions on a case-by-case basis. As appropriate, a general concurrence will establish specific procedures for further consultation. Once issued, NOAA Fisheries will provide a copy to the appropriate fishery management council(s) and will make the

---

46 The criteria for development of a general concurrence are very similar to the criteria for Nationwide Permits under Section 404(e) of the Clean Water Act. See 33 U.S.C. § 1344(e).

47 50 C.F.R. § 600.920(g)(2)(i).

48 *Id.* § 600.920(g)(2)(iii).

49 *Id.* § 600.920(g)(2)(iv).

50 *Id.* § 600.920(g)(3).

51 *Id.*

52 *Id.* § 600.920(g)(4).

general concurrence available to the public by posting the document on the internet or through other appropriate means.[53]

Although activities that qualify for a general concurrence do not require EFH Assessments, qualifying actions must be tracked to ensure that their cumulative effects are no more than minimal.[54] In most cases, tracking actions covered by a general concurrence will be the responsibility of the federal agency because the information is most readily available to that agency. NOAA Fisheries may agree to track actions covered by a general concurrence if the concurrence includes a requirement for the agency to notify NOAA Fisheries of individual actions. Tracking should include numbers of actions and the amount and type of habitat adversely affected and should specify the baseline against which the actions will be tracked. The agency responsible for tracking such actions should make the information available to NOAA Fisheries, the applicable fishery management council, and the public on an annual basis.

Abbreviated and Expanded Consultation

Where a specific federal action may adversely affect essential fish habitat, but no existing environmental review process is available, and no general concurrence or programmatic consultation has been completed, an individual consultation must be completed. Individual consultations can be either abbreviated[55] or expanded,[56] depending on the extent of the anticipated adverse effects. Both of these consultation procedures begin with submission of an EFH Assessment to NOAA Fisheries by the federal action agency.[57]

Generally, an abbreviated consultation allows NOAA Fisheries to quickly determine whether, and to what degree, a federal action may adversely affect essential fish habitat. Abbreviated consultation procedures should be used when the adverse effects of an action can be alleviated through minor modifications to the action.[58] Expanded consultation, by contrast, allows maximum opportunity for NOAA Fisheries and the federal agency to work together to review the action's impacts on essential fish habitat and to develop conservation recommendations.[59] Expanded consultation procedures must be used for federal actions that would result in substantial adverse effects to essential fish habitat.

In most instances, the federal action agency determines the appropriate level of consultation, but if NOAA Fisheries determines that a proposed action will have substantial adverse effects on essential fish habitat, NOAA Fisheries may request expanded

---

53 *Id.* § 600.920(g)(5).

54 *Id.* § 600.920(g)(2)(ii).

55 *Id.* § 600.920(h).

56 *Id.* § 600.920(i).

57 *Id.* §§ 600.920(h)(2), 600.920(i)(2).

58 *Id.* § 600.920(h)(1).

59 *Id.* § 600.920(i)(1).

consultation.[60] Any such request will be in writing and will explain why NOAA Fisheries believes expanded consultation is warranted. Alternatively, if NOAA Fisheries determines that an action would not adversely affect essential fish habitat, or it determines that no conservation recommendations are needed, it will notify the federal agency either informally or in writing of its determination.

The implementing regulations provide specific schedules for completion of abbreviated and expanded consultations.[61] Under the abbreviated procedures, a federal agency must submit its EFH Assessment to NOAA Fisheries as soon as practicable, but at least 60 days prior to a final decision on the action.[62] NOAA Fisheries then must respond within 30 days.

Under the expanded consultation procedures, the federal agency must submit its EFH Assessment at least 90 days prior to a final decision on the action.[63] NOAA Fisheries must then respond within 60 days unless consultation is extended by agreement. Under either procedure, however, NOAA Fisheries and the federal agency may agree to a compressed schedule in cases where regulatory approvals or emergency situations cannot accommodate the presumptive timeframe. They also may agree to conduct consultation earlier in the planning cycle for actions with lengthy approval processes.[64]

Conservation Recommendations to Federal and State Agencies

As part of any consultation process, NOAA Fisheries is required to provide non-prescriptive conservation recommendations to federal and state agencies for actions that would adversely affect essential fish habitat.[65] For federal actions, these recommendations are provided to federal agencies as part of the consultation process. If NOAA Fisheries becomes aware of a federal action that would adversely affect essential fish habitat, but for which a federal agency has not initiated a consultation, it may request that the federal agency initiate consultation, or it may provide conservation recommendations based on the information available.[66]

The Magnuson-Stevens Act, however, does not require state agencies to consult with NOAA Fisheries.[67] NOAA Fisheries will instead use various procedures to identify state actions that may adversely affect essential fish habitat and to determine the most appropriate method for providing conservation recommendations to state agencies. Where an action that would adversely affect essential fish habitat is authorized, funded, or undertaken by both federal and state agencies, NOAA Fisheries will provide the

---

60   *Id.* § 600.920(h)(3).

61   *Id.* §§ 600.920(h)(4), 600.920(i)(4)–(5).

62   *Id.* § 600.920(h)(4).

63   *Id.* § 600.920(i)(4).

64   *Id.* §§ 600.920(h)(4), 600.920(i)(4).

65   16 U.S.C. §1855(b)(4)(A); 50 C.F.R. § 600.925(a).

66   50 C.F.R. § 600.925(b).

67   *Id.* § 600.925(c)(1).

appropriate state agencies with copies of the conservation recommendations developed as part of the federal consultation process.[68]

Fishery management councils also may comment on and make recommendations to NOAA Fisheries and any federal or state agency concerning any activity or proposed activity authorized, funded, or undertaken by the agency that, in the view of the council, may affect the habitat, including essential fish habitat, of a fishery resource under its authority.[69] Councils must provide such comments and recommendations concerning any activity that, in the view of the council, is likely to substantially affect the habitat, including essential fish habitat, of an anadromous fishery resource under council authority. Accordingly, NOAA Fisheries will coordinate with each council to identify the types of actions on which the councils intend to comment.[70] For such actions, NOAA Fisheries will share pertinent information with the council, including copies of its conservation recommendations.

In any event, the federal action agency must in turn provide a detailed response in writing to NOAA Fisheries and any council commenting on an action within 30 days.[71] This response must be provided at least 10 days prior to final approval of the action if the response is inconsistent with any of the conservation recommendations, unless NOAA Fisheries and the agency have agreed to use alternative time frames for the federal agency response. At a minimum, the response must include a description of the measures proposed by the agency for avoiding, mitigating, or offsetting the impact of the activity on essential fish habitat. If the agency's response is inconsistent with the conservation recommendations, the agency must explain its reasons for not following the recommendations, including the scientific justification for any disagreements with NOAA Fisheries over the anticipated effects of the proposed action and the measures needed to avoid, minimize, mitigate, or offset such effects.

To the extent a federal agency decision is inconsistent with any conservation recommendation, NOAA Fisheries may request a meeting with the head of the federal agency, as well as with any other agencies involved, to discuss the action and opportunities for resolving any disagreements.[72] If such a decision also is inconsistent with a recommendation from a fishery management council, the council may request that NOAA Fisheries initiate further review of the federal agency's decision and involve the council in any interagency discussion to resolve disagreements with the federal agency.[73]

> In the event that a federal agency substantially revises its plans for an action in a manner that may adversely affect essential fish habitat, or if new information becomes available that affects the basis for any conservation recommendations, the federal agency must reinitiate consultation with NOAA Fisheries (50 C.F.R. § 600.920(l)).

OTHER CALIFORNIA PROTECTIONS FOR FISH

Much of California's statutory and regulatory protections related to fish species pertain to commercial fishing and fishery operations. Some provisions in the California Fish

68 *Id.* § 600.925(c).

69 16 U.S.C. § 1855(b)(3); 50 C.F.R. § 600.930.

70 50 C.F.R. § 600.925(d).

71 *Id.* § 600.920(k)(1).

72 *Id.* § 600.920(k)(2).

73 *Id.*

The California Endangered Species Act (Fish & Game Code § 2050 *et seq.)* does not treat fish species in a manner different from all other species. The same set of procedural and substantive requirements apply to fish species. See Chapter 2 for more details regarding the California Endangered Species Act.

and Game Code protect fish indirectly by regulating structures that can be placed within waters, such as dams or other diversions. An example of this is the California Department of Fish and Wildlife's Lake and Streambed Alteration Program pursuant to California Fish and Game Code Section 1600.[74] The primary statutes in California governing the protection of fish species in California are the California Endangered Species Act and the fully protected fish species statute.

Fully Protected Species

Section 5515 of the California Fish and Game Code identifies "fully protected" fish species, which include the following:[75]

> Colorado River squawfish
> thicktail chub
> Mohave chub (=Mohave tui chub)
> Lost River sucker
> Modoc sucker
> shortnose sucker
> humpback sucker (=razorback sucker)
> Owens River pupfish (=Owens pupfish)
> unarmored threespine stickleback
> rough sculpin

See Chapter 6 for more details regarding fully protected species.

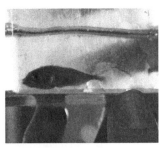

Unarmored threespine stickleback. Photo: Pacific Southwest Region USFWS. Licensed under CC 2.0.

---

74 Under this program, any entity is required to notify the California Department of Fish and Wildlife before beginning any activity that may substantially divert or obstruct the natural flow of, or substantially change or use any material from the bed, channel, or bank of any river, stream, or lake. If the Department determines that the activity may substantially adversely affect fish and wildlife resources, a Lake and Streambed Alteration Agreement will be required. See Chapter 9 for more details regarding this program.

75 Legislation enacted in 2018 provides that CDFW may authorize the take of Lost River sucker and shortnose sucker resulting from impacts attributable or otherwise related to the decommissioning and removal of the Iron Gate Dam, the Copco 1 Dam, the Copco 2 Dam, or the J.C. Boyle Dam, each located on the Klamath River, consistent with the Klamath Hydroelectric Settlement Agreement, provided that CDFW finds the take will not jeopardize the continued existence of these species, the impacts of the take are minimized, and the take authorization requires CDFW approval of a sampling, salvage, and relocation plan. Fish & Game Code § 2081.11(a).

CHAPTER 6

Fully Protected
and Other
Special Status Species

This chapter discusses California's statutory protections for "fully protected species." It also discusses certain other species-related classifications maintained by the Department of Fish and Wildlife and which guide agency decision-making under CEQA and other laws. These include species of special concern, special status species, at-risk species, and special animals.

FULLY PROTECTED SPECIES

Background

California law prohibits the take of certain species of mammals, birds, fish, reptiles and amphibians, and the parts of such animals. These species are generally referred to as "Fully Protected Species." Except in limited instances as set forth below, the California Department of Fish and Wildlife is not authorized to issue permits for the take of Fully Protected Species. Accordingly, these protections are analogous to the protections for birds found in Sections 3503 and 3503.5 of the Fish and Game Code.

Fully Protected Mammals (Fish and Game Code Section 4700)

The state's fully protected mammals are:

> Morro Bay kangaroo rat (Dipodomys heermanni morroensis)

> bighorn sheep (Orvis canadenis) other than Nelson bighorn sheep

> northern elephant seal (Mirounga angustirostris)

> Guadalupe fur seal (Arctocephalus townsendi)

> ring-tailed cat (genus Bassariscus)

> Pacific right whale (Eubalaena sieboldin)

> salt-marsh harvest mouse (Reithrodontomys raviventris)

> southern sea otter (Enhydra lutris nereis)

> wolverine (Gulo luscus)

Fully Protected Birds (Fish and Game Code Section 3511)

The state's fully protected birds are:

> American peregrine falcon (Falco peregrinus anatum)

> brown pelican

> California black rail (Laterallus jamaicensis coturniculus)

> California clapper rail (Rallus longirostris obsoletus)

> California condor (Gymnogyps californianus)

> California least tern (Sterna albifrons browni)

> golden eagle

> greater sandhill crane (Grus Canadensis tabida)

> light-footed clapper rail (Rallus longirostris levipes)

> southern bald eagle (Haliaeetus leucocephalus leucocephalus)

> white-tailed kite (Elanus leucurus)

California condor. Photo: Bonnie Peterson. Licensed under CC 2.0.

Fully Protected Fish (Fish and Game Code Section 5515)

The state's fully protected fish are:

> Colorado River squawfish (Ptychocheilus lucius)

> thicktail chub (Gila crassicauda)

> Mohave chub (Gila mohavensis)

> Lost River sucker (Catostomus luxatus)

> Modoc sucker (Catostomus microps)

> shortnose sucker (Chasmistes brevirostris)

> humpback sucker (Xyrauchen texanus)

> Owens River pupfish (Cyprinoden radiosus)

> unarmored threespine stickleback (Gasterosteus aculeatus williamsoni)

> rough sculpin (Cottus asperrimus)

CEQA = California
Environmental Quality Act

Fully Protected Reptiles and Amphibians (Fish and Game Code Section 5050)

The state's fully protected reptiles and amphibians are:

> blunt-nosed leopard lizard (Crotaphytus wislezenii silus)

> San Francisco garter snake (Thamnophis sitralis tetrataenia)

> Santa Cruz long-toed salamander (Ambystoma macrodactylum croceum)

> limestone salamander (Hydromantes brunus)

> black toad (Bufo boreas exsul)

San Francisco garter snake. Photo: John Kunna.

Authority to Take Fully Protected Species

Generally speaking, incidental take authority for Fully Protected Species may be issued only in accordance with a Natural Community Conservation Plan. In particular, Section 2835 of the Fish and Game Code states that the Department may "authorize by permit the taking of any . . . species designated as fully protected species . . . whose conservation and management is provided for in a natural community conservation plan" approved by the Department. The Legislature has also authorized the take of certain Fully Protected Species under the Salton Sea Restoration Act, and in connection with the removal of dams from the Klamath River. The Department is also authorized under the fully protected statutes to issue permits to possess legally imported fully protected mammals. The Department may authorize the direct take or possession of Fully Protected Species for "necessary scientific research," including efforts to recover the designated species.

The Fish and Game code explicitly excludes from the definition of scientific activities, however, any actions taken as part of specified mitigation for a "project" as defined in Section 21065 of CEQA. The meaning of this limitation was addressed by the California Supreme Court in 2015. In *Center for Biological Diversity v. California*

DFW = Department of Fish and
Wildlife

EIR = Environmental Impact
Report

Department of Fish and Wildlife[1] the California Supreme Court considered whether the translocation of unarmored threespine stickleback—as a take avoidance and minimization measure for the Newhall Ranch project in Ventura County—constituted scientific research or, on the other hand, mitigation for a project.

As stated by the court:

> We must reject the claim DFW may authorize, as CEQA mitigation, actions to protect a fully protected species from harm when, as here, those actions are otherwise prohibited as takings. The Legislature has expressly precluded this interpretation of the statutes by providing, in Fish and Game Code section 5515, subdivision (a), that permitted taking of a fully protected species for "scientific research" may include "efforts to recover" the species but that such "scientific research" does not include "any actions taken as part of specified mitigation for a project" as defined in CEQA. We cannot give effect to this provision and at the same time hold that DFW may, as CEQA mitigation, authorize the trapping and transplantation of stickleback—actions that plainly call for the fish's "catch," or "capture" (Fish & Game Code § 86). That such catch or capture is intended to protect the stickleback from harm caused by the project's construction is inherent in its adoption as CEQA mitigation and is expressly barred under section 5515.[2]

The court further stated:

> DFW urges deference to its interpretation of Fish and Game Code provisions, an area in which it has both expertise and substantial administrative responsibility. We consider an agency's interpretation of statutes and regulations in light of the circumstances, giving greater weight where the interpretation concerns technical and complex matters within the scope of the agency's expertise . . . . Even in substantive areas of the agency's expertise, however, our deference to an agency's statutory interpretation is limited; determining statutes' meaning and effect is a matter "lying within the constitutional domain of the courts." . . . That said, we acknowledge DFW's superior expertise in the administration of the Fish and Game Code, and we would not lightly adopt an interpretation of that code's provisions the department persuasively argued would defeat its ability to pursue species conservation and recovery. Again, however, we do not hold trapping and transplantation of fully protected fish species is prohibited as part of a species recovery effort. We hold only that such actions may not be specified as project mitigation measures in an EIR or other CEQA document. Nothing we say precludes DFW from using its expertise and judgment in

---

1   62 Cal. 4th 204 (2015).

2   *Id.* at 233.

determining, at any time, how best to protect a fully protected species from an imminent threat to its habitat.[3]

SSC = Species of Special Concern

SPECIES OF SPECIAL CONCERN

The Department maintains a list of "Species of Special Concern," which is an administrative designation and carries no formal legal status. However, impacts to species of special concern are typically considered significant impacts under CEQA. According to the Department's website, a Species of Special Concern is "a species, subspecies, or distinct population of an animal native to California" that satisfies one or more of the following criteria:

More information on this category of animals can be found at https://www.wildlife.ca.gov/Conservation.

> is extirpated from the state or, in the case of birds, is extirpated in its primary season or breeding role

> is listed as federally but not state-threatened or endangered; meets the state definition of threatened or endangered but has not formally been listed

> is experiencing, or formerly experienced, serious (noncyclical) population declines or range retractions (not reversed) that, if continued or resumed, could qualify it for state threatened or endangered status

> has naturally small populations exhibiting high susceptibility to risk from any factor(s), that if realized, could lead to declines that would qualify it for state threatened or endangered status

The Department indicates on its website that Species of Special Concern have a number of things in common. In particular, Species of Special Concern:

> occur in small, isolated populations or in fragmented habitat, and are threatened by further isolation and population reduction

> show marked population declines. Taxa that show a marked population decline, yet are still abundant, may not meet the SSC definition, whereas marked population decline in uncommon or rare species may meet the SSC definition. Note that population estimates are unavailable for the vast majority of California taxa.

> depend on a habitat that has shown substantial historical or recent declines in size and/or quality or integrity. This criterion infers the population viability of a species based on trends in the habitats in which it specializes. Coastal wetlands, particularly in the urbanized San Francisco Bay and along the southern coast, alluvial fan sage scrub and coastal sage scrub in the southern coastal basins, vernal pools in the Central Valley, arid scrub in the San Joaquin Valley, and riparian habitat statewide, are examples of California habitats that have seen dramatic reductions in size in recent history.

> occur only or primarily in or adjacent to an area where habitat is being converted to uses incompatible with the animal's survival

3   *Id.* at 236 (citations omitted).

CNDDB = California Natural Diversity Database

ESU = evolutionarily significant unit

CESA = California Endangered Species Act

ESA = Endangered Species Act

NGO = non-governmental organization

> have few California records, or which historically occurred in the state but for which there are no recent records
> occur largely in areas where current management practices are inconsistent with the animal's persistence

It should be kept in mind that this category of species should be distinguished from the much broader list of special status species, at-risk species, and special animals identified in the California Natural Diversity Database (discussed below).

SPECIAL STATUS SPECIES, AT-RISK SPECIES, AND SPECIAL ANIMALS

In addition to its list of Species of Special Concern, the Department maintains a GIS database for tracking a very broad range of species. This database is known as the "California Natural Diversity Database" (CNDDB) and is used by the Department and biologists to record occurrences of these species. As of 2017, CNDDB tracked 914 different taxa, the distribution of which are published on the Department's website.

The Department describes the CNDDB program as follows:

The CNDDB is a "natural heritage program" and is part of a nationwide network of similar programs overseen by NatureServe (formerly part of The Nature Conservancy). All natural heritage programs provide location and natural history information on special status plants, animals, and natural communities to the public, other agencies, and conservation organizations. The data help drive conservation decisions, aid in the environmental review of projects and land use changes, and provide baseline data helpful in recovering endangered species and for research projects.

The terms "Special Animals," "Special Status Species," and "Species at Risk" typically are used to refer to taxa tracked by CNDDB, regardless of their listing status. This list includes species, subspecies and "evolutionarily significant units" (ESUs) where at least one of the following applies:

> listed or proposed for listing under either CESA or the federal ESA
> taxa identified as Species of Special Concern
> taxa which meet the criteria for listing as described in Section 15380 of the CEQA Guidelines
> taxa that are biologically rare, very restricted in distribution, or declining throughout their range but not currently threatened with extirpation
> taxa closely associated with a habitat that is declining in California at a significant rate (e.g., wetlands, riparian, vernal pools, old growth forests, desert aquatic systems, native grasslands, valley shrubland habitat
> taxa designated as a special status, sensitive or declining species by other state or federal agencies, or a non-governmental organization (NGO) and determined

by the CNDDB to be rare, restricted, declining or threatened across their range in California

Information from CNDDB is typically used in various types of biological resource reports, including Environmental Impact Reports and other CEQA documents. Note that, while CNDDB shows the locations of various species occurrences, it is not itself a reliable predictor of species presence or absence on a given property. This is because most entries shown on CNDDB are the result of focused biological surveys in a particular area. If there have been no surveys, there will be no data. Accordingly, in the permitting and development context, CNDDB is just a starting point and should be supplemented with site-specific information and other sources relative to the distribution of the species in question.

RARE SPECIES

Except for plants (as described in Chapter 4), the term "rare species" does not refer to any legally designated category of animals, although the term did appear in earlier versions of CESA and is now used by Department in administrative contexts (e.g., the California Natural Diversity Database).

Although not discussed in detail in this book, the term "rare species" is used in CEQA and is defined in Section 15380 of the CEQA Guidelines to mean a species that:

> although not presently threatened with extinction, is existing in such small numbers throughout all or a significant portion of its range that it may become endangered if its environment worsens

> is likely to become endangered in the foreseeable future throughout all or a significant portion of its range and may be considered "threatened" as that term is defined in the federal ESA

If a species satisfies this definition, it may be included in the list of species tracked by the California Natural Diversity Database.

WETLANDS AND OTHER AQUATIC RESOURCES

CHAPTER 7

Wetlands and Other Waters of the United States

This chapter discusses the protection of wetlands and other waters of the United States. The chapter is focused primarily on regulation by the U.S. Army Corps of Engineers of the disposal of dredged and fill material into wetlands and other waters of the United States under the Clean Water Act. The chapter also covers the regulations of navigable waters by the Corps under the Rivers and Harbors Act of 1899. The chapter focuses on Clean Water Act Section 404 permitting approaches, requirements, and mitigation mechanisms.

HISTORY AND BACKGROUND

As its name suggests, the U.S. Army Corps of Engineers is a sub-branch of the U.S. Army, and the Corps' civil program (as opposed to its military program) is the program that regulates wetlands and waterways. The Corps' original mission was to regulate the placement of structures that might affect navigation of waterways in the United States. In 1899, Congress enacted the Rivers and Harbors Act which gave the Corps authorization to issue permits for the placement of structures and for other activities in "navigable waters of the United States."[1] This program is still in existence today, and the permit associated with that kind of work is referred to as a Section 10 Rivers and Harbors Act permit.[2]

Over the years, the Corps' mission began to include the discharge of fill or dredged material within these waterways. Today's modern Corps permitting process, designed to protect the environmental values associated with wetlands and other waters, began to emerge in the 1960s and 1970s as the Corps promulgated regulations giving it authority under the Rivers and Harbors Act to regulate these activities based on environmental effects. The enactment of the Clean Water Act in 1972 made the Corps the primary agency responsible for regulating the fill of wetlands, streams, and other waters identified as "waters of the United States."

Organizationally, the Corps is divided into several different geographic divisions. The South Pacific Division covers California, as well as other states and portions of states located in the southwestern United States, and the South Pacific Division Headquarters is located in San Francisco. Within California, the Corps is comprised of three districts: San Francisco District, Los Angeles District, and Sacramento District. Permit applications and correspondence to the Corps regarding a project depends on that project's location within the state. For example, a permit for a project along the northern coastline of California likely will be processed by the San Francisco District, a permit for a project in the Sacramento Valley will be processed by the Sacramento District, and a permit for a project in southern California or along the eastern flanks of the Sierra Nevada will be processed by the Los Angeles District.[3]

OVERVIEW OF FEDERAL STATUTES REGULATING WETLANDS AND OTHER WATERS

A number of federal statutes and permitting regimes may apply to projects that result in the fill of wetlands and other waters.

Clean Water Act Section 404

The primary federal statute regulating the fill of wetlands or streams is the Clean Water Act.[4] The Clean Water Act emerged in 1948 as the Federal Water Pollution Control Act.

---

1   33 U.S.C. §§ 401–413.

2   *Id.* § 406(13).

3   For each District's geographic boundary, see http://www.usace.army.mil/Locations.aspx.

4   33 U.S.C. § 1251 *et seq.*

The Act was significantly reorganized and expanded in 1972, and with those amendments the Act has since been commonly referred to as the "Clean Water Act."

EPA = Environmental Protection
Agency

Section 404 of the Clean Water Act is the primary statutory driver for the federal
government's wetland regulation program. Section 404 provides:

> The [U.S. Army Corps of Engineers] may issue permits, after notice and
> opportunity for public hearings for the discharge of dredged or fill material
> into the navigable waters at specified disposal sites.[5]

Both the Corps and the U.S. Environmental Protection Agency are authorized to
implement various provisions of Section 404 and the regulation of wetland fills. For
example, Section 404(b) authorizes both agencies to develop guidelines regulating the
location of disposal sites.[6] The regulations promulgated under this authority are commonly referred to as the "Section 404(b)(1) Guidelines." In addition, Section 404(c)
authorizes the Environmental Protection Agency to prohibit "the specification (including the withdrawal of specification) of any defined area as a disposal site" after consulting with the Corps.[7] This is commonly referred to as a Section 404(c) "veto" by EPA.
EPA also has the authority to elevate proposed Corps decisions for consideration at the
headquarters level.[8] EPA also has a significant enforcement role under Section 404.[9]

Rivers and Harbors Act Section 10

The Corps administers another statute relevant to the fill of wetlands and streams that
are navigable. Section 10 of the Rivers and Harbors Act of 1899 requires authorization
from the Secretary of the Army, acting through the Corps, for the construction of any
structure in or over any navigable water of the United States.[10] Structures or work
outside the limits defined for navigable waters of the United States require a Section
10 permit if the structure or work affects the course, location, or condition of the
water body.[11] The law applies to any dredging or disposal of dredged materials, excavation, filling, re-channelization, or any other modification of a navigable water of the
United States, and applies to all structures, from the smallest floating dock to the largest commercial undertaking. It further includes, without limitation, any wharf, pier,
dolphin, boom, weir, breakwater, bulkhead, jetty, or other structures in any port, road-
stead, haven, harbor, canal, navigable river, or other water of the United States.
Authorization under this statute is commonly referred to as a Rivers and Harbors Act
Section 10 permit.

5   *Id.* § 1344(a).

6   *Id.* § 1344(b).

7   *Id.* § 1344(c).

8   Clean Water Act Section 404(q) Memorandum of Agreement Between the Environmental Protection
Agency and the Department of the Army (Aug. 11, 1992).

9   Federal Enforcement for the Section 404 Program of the Clean Water Act Memorandum Between the
Department of the Army and the Environmental Protection Agency (Jan. 1989).

10   33 U.S.C. § 403.

11   *Id.*

Food Security Act of 1985

The Food Security Act of 1985 was a five-year omnibus farm bill that included provisions commonly referred to as the "swampbuster" provisions.[12] Similar to the Section 404 program, the "swampbuster program" generally allows the continuation of most farming practices so long as wetlands are not converted or wetland drainage increased. However, certain activities such as clearing, draining, or otherwise converting a wetland are activities addressed by the swampbuster program. The program discourages farmers from altering wetlands by withholding federal farm program benefits from any person who plants an agricultural commodity on a converted wetland that was converted by drainage, dredging, leveling, or any other means (after December 23, 1985); or converts a wetland for the purpose of or to make agricultural commodity production possible (after November 28, 1990).

Coastal Zone Management Act

The Coastal Zone Management Act of 1972[13] was enacted in recognition of the "importance of meeting the challenge of continued growth in the coastal zone." Two national programs were created under this act: the National Coastal Zone Management Program and the National Estuarine Research Reserve System. The Coastal Management Program for the state of California was approved by NOAA in 1978. California's program is administered by three state agencies. As described in Chapter 13, primary among these are the California Coastal Commission. Development within the San Francisco Bay is administered by the San Francisco Bay Conservation and Development Commission, or "BCDC". The California Coastal Conservancy purchases, protects, restores, and enhances coastal resources, and provides access to the shore. The primary authorities for the California Coastal Management Program are the California Coastal Act, McAteer-Petris Act, and Suisan Marsh Preservation Act.

GUIDANCE RELIED UPON BY THE CORPS

Like most federal agencies, the Corps relies upon a number of guidance documents to implement its permitting programs under both Section 404 of the Clean Water Act and Section 10 of the Rivers and Harbors Act of 1899. In addition to the Clean Water Act statute and its implementing regulations in Title 33 of the Code of Federal Regulations, the Corps relies on Regulatory Guidance Letters, or "RGLs," and various memoranda of agreement and understandings with other federal agencies in order to implement these permitting programs.

As described by the Corps, Regulatory Guidance Letters were developed by the Corps as a system to organize and track written guidance issued to its field agencies.[14]

---

12   Pub. Law 99–198 (1985).

13   16 U.S.C. §§ 1451–1464.

14   U.S. Army Corps of Engineers, Regulatory Guidance Letters, available at https://www.usace.army.mil/Missions/Civil-Works/Regulatory-Program-and-Permits/Guidance-Letters/. This website also includes an archive of all RGLs issued since 1981.

RGLs are normally issued as a result of evolving policy and judicial decisions, and changes to the Corps regulations or another agency's regulations which affect the permit program. RGLs are used only to interpret or clarify existing Regulatory Program policy, but according to the Corps, they do "provide mandatory guidance to the Corps district offices."[15] RGLs are sequentially numbered and expire on a specified date. However, unless superseded by specific provisions of subsequently issued regulations or guidance, the content provided in RGLs generally remains valid after the expiration date.[16] The Corps incorporates most of the guidance provided by RGLs whenever it revises its permit regulations.

The Corps began issuing RGLs in 1981, but the Corps does not issue RGLs every year. For example, the Corps issued no new RGLs between 2008 and 2016.

In addition to the RGLs, the Corps also relies upon a number of memoranda to the field, and memoranda of understanding and agreement, which are cited where relevant in this chapter. The Corps also relies upon other guidance materials for other aspects of its permitting programs under Section 404 and Section 10.[17] Practitioners should be aware that these materials exist and become familiar with them because they supplement or provide clarifying guidance as to the Corps' statutory and regulatory requirements.

WETLANDS AND OTHER WATERS REGULATED BY THE CLEAN WATER ACT

Navigability and "Waters of the United States"

Section 404 of the Clean Water Act regulates the discharge of dredged or fill material into navigable waters.[18] "Navigable waters" is defined in the Clean Water Act as "waters of the United States." This definition fails to give the phrase "navigable waters" all of its historic nuance and color, however, which may be helpful to the practitioner seeking to understand the scope of the Act.

Traditional navigability is the touchstone for the meaning of "navigable waters." The definitive case on navigability is the 1887 U.S. Supreme Court decision, *The Daniel Ball*.[19] In *The Daniel Ball*, the Court defined navigable waters in relation to Congress' power to regulate interstate commerce:

> Those rivers must be regarded as public navigable rivers in law which are navigable in fact. And they are navigable in fact when they are used, or are

---

15   As described in the description of Regulatory Guidance Letters on the Corps' website at https://www.usace.army.mil/Missions/Civil-Works/Regulatory-Program-and-Permits/Guidance-Letters/.

16   See Regulatory Guidance Letter No. 05-06 (Dec. 7, 2005) (explaining that expired RGLs generally remain valid after the expiration date, unless superseded by regulations or another RGL, and identifying specific expired RGLs that remain generally applicable).

17   The website for the Corps' Civil Works Regulatory Program includes a helpful archive of most of this material. For more, see https://www.usace.army.mil/Missions/Civil-Works/Regulatory-Program-and-Permits/MOU-MOAs/.

18   33 U.S.C. § 1344(a).

19   77 U.S. (10 Wall.) 557 (1871).

susceptible of being used, in their ordinary condition, as highways for commerce, over which trade and travel are or may be conducted in the customary modes of trade and travel on water.[20]

Other early case law concerning navigability turns on whether the watercourse allows for "customary modes of trade and travel" along the "highway of commerce."[21] The mere fact that a watercourse may support a floating craft of some sort is not necessarily sufficient for navigability. Instead, "it must be generally and commonly useful to some purpose of trade or agriculture."[22]

More recent case law similarly indicates that navigability is fundamental to Clean Water Act jurisdiction. For example, the Supreme Court in *Solid Waste Agency of Northern Cook County v. United States Army Corps of Engineers* (*SWANCC*)[23] held that the focus of Clean Water Act jurisdiction should be on navigability. The *SWANCC* court found that although "the term 'navigable' is of 'limited import'," navigability is an important factor in evaluating whether the Corps has jurisdiction over a water feature: "The term 'navigable' has at least the import of showing us what Congress had in mind as its authority for enacting the Clean Water Act: its traditional jurisdiction over waters that were or had been navigable in fact or which could reasonably be so made." "Navigable" cannot be read out of the statute: "[I]t is one thing to give a word limited effect and quite another to give it no effect whatever."[24]

Although "navigable" is defined in the Clean Water Act, the phrase "waters of the United States" itself is not further defined in the statute. Instead, this phrase is defined by regulations established by the Environmental Protection Agency and the Corps. Because the Section 404 Clean Water Act permitting requirements apply only to waters of the United States, this phrase has been the subject of much controversy by both environmental organizations and the regulated community.

Currently, waters of the United States include both wetland and non-wetland aquatic features, such as streams, rivers, lakes, ponds, bays, and oceans, and the Corps and EPA regulations define waters of the United States as:

(1) all waters that are currently used, or were used in the past, or may be susceptible to use in interstate or foreign commerce, including all waters that are subject to the ebb and flow of the tide

(2) all interstate waters including interstate wetlands

(3) all other waters such as intrastate lakes, rivers, streams (including intermittent streams), mudflats, sandflats, wetlands, sloughs, prairie potholes, wet meadows,

---

20 *Id.* at 563.

21 E.g., *The Montello*, 87 U.S. (20 Wall.) 430 (1874); *The Daniel Ball*, 77 U.S. (10 Wall.) 557 (1871); *The Propeller Genesee Chief*, 53 U.S. (12 How.) 443 (1852).

22 *The Montello*, 87 U.S. (20 Wall.) at 442 (a navigable watercourse is not "'every small creek in which a fishing skiff or gunning canoe can be made to float at high water . . . in order to give it the character of a navigable stream, it must be generally and commonly useful to some purpose of trade or agriculture.").

23 531 U.S. 159 (2001).

24 *Id.* at 172.

playa lakes, or natural ponds, the use, degradation or destruction of which could affect interstate or foreign commerce including any such waters:

(i)   that are or could be used by interstate or foreign travelers for recreational or other purposes; or

(ii)   from which fish or shellfish are or could be taken and sold in interstate or foreign commerce; or

(iii)   that are used or could be used for industrial purpose by industries in interstate commerce

(4) all impoundments of waters otherwise defined as waters of the United States under the definition

(5) tributaries of waters identified in paragraphs (1) through (4) of this section

(6) the territorial seas

(7) wetlands adjacent to waters (other than waters that are themselves wetlands) identified in paragraphs (1) through (6) of this section. Waste treatment systems, including treatment ponds or lagoons designed to meet the requirements of the Clean Water Act (other than cooling ponds as defined in 40 C.F.R. § 123.11(m) which also meet the criteria of this definition) are not waters of the United States

(8) waters of the United States do not include prior converted croplands; notwithstanding the determination of an area's status as prior cropland by any other agency, for the purposes of the Clean Water Act, the final authority regarding Clean Water Act jurisdiction remains with EPA[25]

The meaning of "waters of the United States" has been heavily scrutinized by the courts. Since the passage of the Clean Water Act, the courts have been called on many times to determine the appropriate scope of federal jurisdiction over waters covered by that statute. Most of these cases have arisen in the context of Section 404.[26] The recurring issue in these cases is the extent to which a water must be "navigable" to be governed by Section 404.

This question about navigability is present in the very language of the statute. Although the statute prohibits discharges into "navigable waters," it defines this term without any reference to navigability whatsoever. That is, the Clean Water Act defines the term "navigable waters" to mean "the waters of the United States, including the territorial seas."[27] So, at its most basic level, the vexing question is whether a "navigable water" must be "navigable" at all.

Although the Corps initially viewed its jurisdiction as extending only to waters that were navigable-in-fact, in 1975 the Corps issued regulations redefining waters of the United States to include not just navigable waters, but also tributaries, interstate waters and their tributaries, and non-navigable intrastate waters whose use or misuse could

---

25   33 C.F.R. § 328.3(a); 40 C.F.R. § 230.3(s).

26   33 U.S.C. § 1344.

27   *Id.* § 1352(7); 33 C.F.R. § 328.3(a).

affect interstate commerce.[28] These regulations also covered "freshwater wetlands" that were "adjacent" to other waters (and without any specific requirement that those wetlands be navigable or have some connection to interstate commerce).[29]

The first major case to test the validity of these regulations was *United States v. Riverside Bayview Homes, Inc.,*[30] in which the Supreme Court considered whether the Corps' assertion of jurisdiction of "adjacent wetlands"[31] was valid under the Clean Water Act. In this case, the Sixth Circuit[32] held that the wetlands in question were not "adjacent" because they were not subject to actual flooding by nearby navigable waters. That is, the court was looking for some hydrologic connection sufficient to support jurisdiction. The Supreme Court reversed, holding that it was not unreasonable for the Corps to find that, as a general matter, adjacent wetlands are sufficiently "bound up" with nearby navigable waters to justify the assertion of jurisdiction without any fact-specific showing of that connection.[33]

In its analysis, the Court specifically considered the extent to which a water must actually be navigable to be subject to the Clean Water Act. Citing a Senate report, the Court stated that "[a]lthough the Act prohibits discharges into 'navigable waters,' . . . the Act's definition of 'navigable waters' as 'waters of the United States' make it clear that *the term 'navigable' as used in the Act is of limited import.*"[34]

Riverside Bayview Homes was followed several years later by the Supreme Court's decision in *SWANCC.*[35] *SWANCC* involved a non-navigable water-filled mining pit that was isolated from (and not adjacent to) any other body of water.[36] In asserting jurisdiction, the Corps relied on 33 Code of Federal Regulations Section 328.3(a)(3), which covers "[a]ll other waters such as intrastate lakes, rivers, streams . . . , mudflats, sandflats, wetlands, sloughs, prairie potholes, wet meadows, playa lakes, or natural ponds, the use, degradation, or destruction of which could affect interstate commerce." The Corps had asserted a Commerce Clause connection over the mining pit based upon its "Migratory Bird Rule," which posited that a Commerce Clause connection exists for any non-navigable isolated water "which are or would be used by . . . migratory birds that cross state lines."[37]

---

28 40 Fed. Reg. 31,320.

29 *Id.*

30 474 U.S. 121 (1985).

31 The term "wetlands" is defined in the Corps regulations to mean "those areas that are inundated or saturated by surface or ground water at a frequency and duration sufficient to support, and that under normal circumstances do support, a prevalence of vegetation typically adapted for life in saturated soil conditions. Wetlands generally include swamps, marshes, bogs and similar areas." 33 C.F.R. § 323.2(c).

32 729 F.2d 391 (1984).

33 *Riverside Bayview Homes,* 474 U.S. at 134.

34 *Id.* at 133 (internal citations omitted, emphasis added).

35 531 U.S. 159.

36 *Id.* at 163.

37 51 Fed. Reg. 41,206, 41,217 (1986) (Preamble).

Given the attenuated Commerce Clause connection asserted by the Migratory Bird Rule, it was an easy target. In striking down the rule, the Court—in an opinion authored by Justice Rehnquist—struggled again with the import of the term "navigability" in the Clean Water Act. Distinguishing *Riverside Bayview Homes*, the Court reasoned:

> We cannot agree that Congress' separate definitional use of the phrase 'waters of the United States' constitutes a basis for reading the term 'navigable water' out of the statute. We said in *Riverside Bayview Homes* that the word 'navigable' in the statute was of 'limited effect' . . . . But it is one thing to give a word limited effect and quite another to give it no effect whatsoever.[38]

The U.S. Supreme Court in *Rapanos v. United States*[39] also addressed the scope of the federal government's jurisdiction under the Clean Water Act by determining whether a wetland or tributary is a "water of the United States" such that it would be subject to federal jurisdiction. The *Rapanos* decision is comprised of a plurality opinion written by Justice Scalia, an opinion concurring in judgment written by Justice Kennedy, and a dissenting opinion written by Justice Stevens.

Four justices, in the plurality opinion authored by Justice Scalia, rejected the argument that the term "waters of the United States" is limited to only those waters that are navigable in the traditional sense and their abutting wetlands. However, the plurality concluded that the Corps' regulatory authority should extend only to "relatively permanent, standing or continuously flowing bodies of water" connected to traditional navigable waters, and to "wetlands with a continuous surface connection to" such relatively permanent waters. In terms of adjacency, Justice Scalia's opinion explained that "only those wetlands with a continuous surface connection to bodies that are 'waters of the United States' in their own right, so that there is no clear demarcation between 'waters' and wetlands, are 'adjacent to' such waters and covered by the [Clean Water Act]."[40]

Justice Kennedy's opinion confirmed that "[w]hen the Corps seeks to regulate wetlands adjacent to navigable-in-fact waters, it may rely on adjacency to establish its jurisdiction."[41] This rule has been interpreted to be limited to adjacent wetlands. The Ninth Circuit in *San Francisco Baykeeper v. Cargill Salt Division*[42] determined that adjacency to a navigable waterway is not sufficient to establish federal jurisdiction over a waterbody that is not a wetland. In that case, the court rejected the contention that a pond adjacent to a slough was a water of the United States, relying on the fact that *Rapanos* considered only wetlands. The court also relied on the Supreme Court's determination in *Riverside Bayview Homes* that "wetlands adjacent to lakes, rivers, streams, and other bodies of

---

38   531 U.S. at 172.

39   547 U.S. 715 (2006).

40   *Id.* at 742.

41   *Id.* at 782.

42   481 F.3d 700 (9th Cir. 2007).

water may function as integral parts of the aquatic environment even when the moisture creating the wetlands does not find its source in adjacent bodies of water."[43]

In addition, Justice Kennedy's opinion elaborates on the concept of "significant nexus," originally mentioned in the *SWANCC* decision. Where wetlands are not adjacent to a navigable-in-fact waterway, or where wetlands are adjacent to tributaries to navigable waters, a "significant nexus" with the navigable waterway is required for it to be subject to federal jurisdiction.[44] A "significant nexus" to navigable waters will be found where, "either alone or in combination with similarly situated lands in the region, [wetlands] significantly affect the chemical, physical, and biological integrity of other covered waters more readily understood as 'navigable.' When, in contrast, the wetlands' effects on water quality are speculative or insubstantial, they fall outside the zone fairly encompassed by the statutory term 'navigable waters.'"[45]

In *Northern California River Watch v. City of Healdsburg*,[46] the court determined that the Corps had jurisdiction over a pond that was separated from the Russian River by wetlands and a levee because the pond had a "significant nexus" to the river. The pond had a clear hydrological and physical connection to the river because it seeped into the river through both surface wetlands and an underground aquifer. At least 26 percent of the pond's volume annually reached the river. The pond also had a significant ecological connection to the river. The pond supported substantial bird, mammal, and fish populations that were an integral part of and indistinguishable from the rest of the Russian River ecosystem. Finally, the pond also affected the chemical integrity of the river by increasing its chloride levels.[47]

By contrast, in *San Francisco Baykeeper v. Cargill Salt Division*,[48] the Ninth Circuit found that the requisite nexus was not present with respect to a pond that is adjacent to a slough because the effects of the pond on the slough were "speculative and insubstantial." Specifically, there was no evidence that any water ever flowed from the pond to the slough. Evidence that the slough in some situations flowed into the pond did not establish that the pond affected the slough. The court, therefore, rejected the so-called "adjacent-plus-nexus" argument to establish federal jurisdiction over the pond.[49]

Justice Kennedy's opinion in *Rapanos* also noted that seasonal waters can still be waters of the United States. A stream or tributary that connects to a water of the United

43 *United States v. Riverside Bayview Homes, Inc.*, 474 U.S. 121 (1985); see also *Baccarat Fremont Developers, LLC v. U.S. Army Corps of Engineers*, 425 F.3d 1150, 1156–57 (9th Cir. 2005) (significant hydrological or ecological connection not required for jurisdiction over adjacent wetland); *Northern California River Watch v. City of Healdsburg*, 496 F.3d 993, 1000 (9th Cir. 2007) (pond was part of wetlands that were adjacent to Russian River; significant nexus inferred when wetlands are adjacent to navigable waters).

44 *Rapanos*, 547 U.S. at 779–80, 781–82.

45 *Id.* at 780.

46 457 F.3d 993 (9th Cir. 2007).

47 *Id.* at 1000–01.

48 481 F.3d 700 (9th Cir. 2007).

49 *Id.* at 708.

States is itself a water of the United States even if its flows are seasonal.[50] In *United States v. Moses*,[51] the court relied on *Rapanos* and determined that a creek that was dry during much of the year, but which became a "rampaging torrent" during seasonal runoff periods such that it then joined with various rivers, was subject to Corps jurisdiction as waters of the United States.[52]

In December 2008, EPA and the Corps issued guidance on implementing (and interpreting somewhat broadly) the *Rapanos* decision.[53] According to the summary provided in the guidance:

(1) The agencies will assert jurisdiction over the following waters:
   - traditional navigable waters
   - wetlands adjacent to traditional navigable waters
   - non-navigable tributaries of traditional navigable waters that are relatively permanent where the tributaries typically flow year-round or have continuous flow at least seasonally (e.g., typically three months)
   - wetlands that directly abut such tributaries

(2) The agencies will decide jurisdiction over the following waters based on a fact-specific analysis to determine whether they have a significant nexus with a traditional navigable water:
   - non-navigable tributaries that are not relatively permanent
   - wetlands adjacent to non-navigable tributaries that are not relatively permanent
   - wetlands adjacent to but that do not directly abut a relatively permanent non-navigable tributary

(3) The agencies generally will not assert jurisdiction over the following features:
   - swales or erosional features (e.g., gullies, small washes characterized by low volume, infrequent, or short duration flow)
   - ditches (including roadside ditches) excavated wholly in and draining only uplands and that do not carry a relatively permanent flow of water

(4) The agencies will apply the significant nexus standard as follows:
   - a significant nexus analysis will assess the flow characteristics and functions of the tributary itself and the functions performed by all wetlands adjacent to the tributary to determine if they significantly affect the chemical, physical, and biological integrity of downstream traditional navigable waters
   - significant nexus includes consideration of hydrologic and ecologic factors

---

50 *Rapanos*, 547 U.S. at 770–71.

51 496 F.3d 984 (9th Cir. 2007).

52 *Id.* at 990–91.

53 U.S. Environmental Protection Agency & U.S. Army Corps of Engineers, Clean Water Act Jurisdiction Following the U.S. Supreme Court's decision in *Rapanos v. United States* & *Carabell v. United States* (Dec. 2, 2008).

In 2015, EPA and the Corps published a regulation that was intended to help clarify the scope of waters of the United States in light of this fractious case law.[54] This regulation became known as the Clean Water Rule, and it revised the definition of "waters of the United States" by grouping waters and features into three categories: (1) waters that are jurisdictional by rule; (2) waters that will be found jurisdictional only upon a case-specific showing of a significant nexus with a primary water; and (3) waters and aquatic features that are expressly excluded from jurisdiction.[55] The Clean Water Rule did not modify the regulatory text from the 1986 regulation for traditional navigable waters, interstate waters, the territorial seas, or impoundments of jurisdictional waters.[56] Unlike prior regulations, the Clean Water Rule attempted to create bright-line jurisdictional boundaries. For example, the Clean Water Rule promulgated a new definition for "neighboring," interpreting that term to encompass all waters located within 100 feet of the ordinary high water mark and all waters located within 1,500 feet of the high tide line of a "primary water."[57]

Following publication of the Clean Water Rule, several states and other non-state parties filed complaints and petitions for review in multiple federal district and appellate courts challenging the Clean Water Rule. The day before the Clean Water Rule's effective date, the U.S. District Court for the District of North Dakota preliminarily enjoined the Clean Water Rule in the 13 states that challenged the rule in that court.[58] The numerous petitions for review filed in the courts of appeals were consolidated in the U.S. Court of Appeals for the Sixth Circuit, and the Sixth Circuit stayed the Clean Water Rule nationwide.[59] The U.S. Supreme Court granted certiorari on the question of whether the courts of appeals have original jurisdiction to review challenge to the Clean Water Rule. In January 2018, the Supreme Court held that the Clean Water Rule is subject to direct review in the district courts.[60]

Since the Supreme Court's jurisdictional ruling, district court litigation regarding the Clean Water Rule has resumed. The Clean Water Rule continues to be subject to a preliminary injunction issued by the District of North Dakota as to 14 states: Alaska, Arizona, Arkansas, Colorado, Idaho, Iowa, Missouri, Montana, Nebraska, Nevada, North Dakota, South Dakota, Wyoming, and New Mexico. The Clean Water Rule is also subject to a preliminary injunction issued by the U.S. District Court for the Southern District of Georgia as to 11 more states: Georgia, Alabama, Florida, Indiana, Kansas, Kentucky, North Carolina, South Carolina, Utah, West Virginia, and Wisconsin.[61] In

---

54   80 Fed. Reg. 37,054 (June 29, 2015).

55   *Id.* at 37,057.

56   *Id.* at 37,058.

57   *Id.* at 37,105.

58   Alaska, Arizona, Arkansas, Colorado, Idaho, Missouri, Montana, Nebraska, Nevada, New Mexico, North Dakota, South Dakota, and Wyoming. See *North Dakota v. E.P.A.*, 127 F. Supp. 3d 1047 (D.N.D. 2015).

59   *In re EPA & Dep't of Def. Final Rule*, 803 F.3d 804 (6th Cir. 2015).

60   *Nat'l Ass'n of Mfrs. v. Dep't of Def.*, 138 S. Ct. 617, 624 (2018).

61   *Georgia v. Pruitt*, No. 15-cv-79 (S.D. Ga. June 8, 2018).

September 2018, the U.S. District Court for the Southern District of Texas issued a preliminary injunction against the Clean Water Rule in response to motions filed by the states of Texas, Louisiana, and Mississippi.[62] As of publication of this book, the Clean Water Rule is enjoined in 28 states and remains in effect following the lift of the Sixth Circuit stay in 22 states, the District of Columbia, and U.S. Territories. Although the Clean Water Rule remains in effect in California, as a practical matter the Corps has not been implementing the Rule in California, relying instead on the 2008 guidance after the *Rapanos* decision.

On February 28, 2017, the president issued Executive Order 13,778 entitled "Restoring the Rule of Law, Federalism, and Economic Growth by Reviewing the 'Waters of the United States' Rule." Section 1 of the Executive Order states, "It is in the national interest to ensure the Nation's navigable waters are kept free from pollution, while at the same time promoting economic growth, minimizing regulatory uncertainty, and showing due regard for the roles of the Congress and the States under the Constitution." The Executive Order directs EPA and the Corps to review the Clean Water Rule for consistency with the policy outlined in Section 1 of the Order and to issue a proposed rule rescinding or revising the Clean Water Rule as appropriate and consistent with law. The Executive Order also directs the agencies to "consider interpreting the term 'navigable waters' . . . in a manner consistent with" Justice Scalia's plurality opinion in *Rapanos v. United States*. Since the issuance of the Executive Order, the Administration has taken several steps to implement these directives.

Most importantly, the Administration issued a proposed rule in December 2018 to revise the definition of "waters of the United States."[63] The proposed rule could be significantly revised during the rule-making process, but as of this writing, key features of the proposed definition include: (1) the guiding concept that "waters of the United States" are waters within the ordinary meaning of the term, such as oceans, rivers, streams, lakes, ponds, and wetlands; (2) the view that tributaries are rivers, streams, or similarly naturally occurring surface water channels that contribute perennial or intermittent flow to a traditional navigable water in a typical year either directly or indirectly; (3) the elimination of ditches as "waters of the United States" unless they meet certain criteria, such as functioning as traditional navigable waters, if they are constructed in a tributary and also satisfy the conditions of the proposed "tributary" definition, or if they are constructed in an adjacent wetland and also satisfy the conditions of the proposed "tributary" definition; (4) the elimination of ephemeral waters (i.e., features that flow only in response to precipitation) from consideration as "waters of the United States," which is consistent with the plurality opinion's view in *Rapanos* that "waters of the United States" should be considered waters within the ordinary meaning of the term;

---

62   *Texas v. EPA*, No. 3:15-cv-162, 2018 U.S. Dist. LEXIS 160443, at *4 (S.D. Tex. Sept. 12, 2018).

63   Available at https://www.epa.gov/wotus-rule/revised-definition-waters-united-states-proposed-rule. The Administration is proposing to amend the definition of "waters of the United States" as it occurs in various portions of the Code of Federal Regulations. These include 33 C.F.R. Pt. 328 and 40 C.F.R. Pts. 110, 116, 117, 122, 230, 232, 300, 302, 401.

(5) a sharp departure from the "significant nexus" test articulated by Justice Kennedy in the *Rapanos* decision; (6) a definition of "adjacent wetlands" as wetlands that abut or have a direct hydrological surface connection to other "waters of the United States" in a typical year.

The Definition of Wetland

As described above, Section 404 of the Clean Water Act regulates "navigable waters," which in turned is defined more broadly in the Act as "waters of the United States." The meaning of this phrase can be found in the Code of Federal Regulations implementing the Act. Those Regulations define "waters of the United States" broadly to include certain aquatic features, such as "intrastate lakes, rivers, streams (including intermittent streams), mudflats, sandflats, *wetlands*, sloughs, prairie potholes, wet meadows, playa lakes, or natural ponds, the use, degradation or destruction of which could affect interstate or foreign commerce . . . ."[64] The term "wetland" itself is defined in the Corps regulations:

> The term wetlands means those areas that are inundated or saturated by surface or groundwater at a frequency and duration sufficient to support, and that under normal circumstances do support, a prevalence of vegetation typically adapted for life in saturated soil conditions. Wetlands generally include swamps, marshes, bogs, and similar areas.[65]

Regulations adopted by EPA to implement the Section 404 permitting program use an almost identical definition. These regulations further elaborate on the vegetative, hydrological, and physical characteristics associated with wetlands.[66] The regulations also provide detailed examples of the possible loss of values associated with the discharge of dredged or fill material in wetlands.[67]

This regulatory definition, however, is only the beginning of the analysis for what the Corps will actually treat as a wetland. The Corps also turns to a field manual applicable to most of California—the Corps' *Regional Supplement to the Corps of Engineers Wetland Delineation Manual: Arid West Region* (Version 2.0) (Sept. 2008). This Manual is a regional supplement to the 1987 USACE (U.S. Army Corps of Engineers) Wetland Delineation Manual. Those portions of the state that are excluded from the Manual include the Sierra Nevada Mountains and that portion of the state where the Cascade Mountains are located.

---

64 33 C.F.R. § 328.3 (emphasis added).

65 *Id.*; 40 C.F.R. § 230.3(o)(iv).

66 40 C.F.R. § 230.41(a).

67 *Id.* § 230.41(b). By way of example, the regulations state: "The discharge of dredged or fill material in wetlands is likely to damage or destroy habitat and adversely affect the biological productivity of wetlands ecosystems by smothering, by dewatering, by permanently flooding, or by altering substrate elevation or periodicity of water movement. The addition of dredged or fill material may destroy wetland vegetation or result in advancement of succession to dry land species. It may reduce or eliminate nutrient exchange by a reduction of the system's productivity, or by altering current patterns and velocities . . . ." *Id.*

PROPOSED REVISION TO DEFINITION OF "WATERS OF THE UNITED STATES"

On February 14, 2019, the U.S. Environmental Protection Agency and the Army Corps of Engineers issued a proposed rule redefining "waters of the United States." (84 Fed. Reg. 4154.) This proposal was in keeping with Executive Order 13778, signed on February 28, 2017, which requested these agencies to repeal regulations issued in 2015 during the Obama Administration, commonly referred to as the Clean Water Rule, that would have modified the definition of "waters of the United States" to expand upon their jurisdiction. The Executive Order further requested the agencies to consider re-defining the term "waters of the United States" in a manner consistent with Justice Scalia's interpretation in the *Rapanos* decision.

The guiding concept underlying the proposed rule is that "waters of the United States" are waters within the ordinary meaning of the term, such as oceans, rivers, streams, lakes, ponds, and wetlands, and that not all waters are "waters of the United States." The proposed rule interprets the term "waters of the United States" to encompass: traditional navigable waters, including the territorial seas; tributaries that contribute perennial or intermittent flow to such waters; certain ditches; certain lakes and ponds; impoundments of otherwise jurisdictional waters; and wetlands adjacent to other jurisdictional waters.

Under the proposed rule, a tributary is defined as a river, stream, or similar naturally occurring surface water channel that contributes perennial or intermittent flow to a traditional navigable water or territorial sea in a typical year either directly or indirectly through other tributaries, jurisdictional ditches, jurisdictional lakes and ponds, jurisdictional impoundments, and adjacent wetlands or through certain water features so long as those water features convey perennial or intermittent flow downstream.

The proposal defines "adjacent wetlands" as wetlands that abut or have a direct hydrological surface connection to other "waters of the United States" in a typical year. "Abut" is proposed to mean when a wetland touches an otherwise jurisdictional water at either a point or side. A "direct hydrologic surface connection" as proposed occurs as a result of inundation from a jurisdictional water to a wetland or via perennial or intermittent flow between a wetland and jurisdictional water. Wetlands physically separated from other waters of the United States by upland or by dikes, barriers, or similar structures and also lacking a direct hydrologic surface connection to such waters are not adjacent under this proposal.

The proposal would exclude from the definition of "waters of the United States" waters or water features not mentioned above. The proposed definition specifically clarifies that "waters of the United States" do not include features that flow only in response to precipitation; groundwater, including groundwater drained through subsurface drainage systems; certain ditches; prior converted cropland; artificially irrigated areas that would revert to upland if artificial irrigation ceases; certain artificial lakes and ponds constructed in upland; water-filled depressions created in upland incidental to mining or construction activity; storm water control features excavated or constructed in upland to convey, treat, infiltrate, or store storm water run-off; wastewater recycling structures constructed in upland; and waste treatment systems.

Delineating wetlands. Photo: Lindsay Teunis.

The 1987 USACE Wetland Delineation Manual, as supplemented by the Arid West Region manual, provides guidance to the Corps on whether a water feature is a water of the United States. According to the Corps' Manual, identification of wetlands is based on a three-factor approach involving indicators of hydrophytic vegetation, hydric soil, and wetland hydrology.[68] All three of these indicators must be present for the Corps to identify a water feature as a wetland subject to the Corps' jurisdiction. Most practitioners refer to this colloquially as the "three-parameter test." Once a feature is identified as a jurisdictional wetland, any discharge into that feature is regulated pursuant to Section 404, as described in more detail below.

The specific question of whether a water feature satisfies the regulatory definition of "wetlands," as opposed to the more involved and highly nuanced question of whether a wetland is "adjacent" to a navigable water or water of the United States, or has a "significant nexus" to those waters, emerges from time to time.

The Ninth Circuit Court of Appeals considered this issue in *Northern California River Watch v. City of Healdsburg.*[69] That case involved a pit that had been excavated for gravel and sand on land near the Russian River in California. The pit naturally filled with water up to the line of the water table of surrounding aquifer. Eventually, the City of Healdsburg began discharging water from a secondary waste-treatment plant into the pond that had been created. The pond drained into the surrounding aquifer, which in turn drained into the Russian River. The main question for the court was whether the pond constituted an "isolated water" or instead was "adjacent" to the Russian River and, therefore, subject to Section 404 jurisdiction.

Before the court reached that question, though, it considered whether the pond was a wetland. Citing the regulatory definition of "wetland," and specifically the language "those areas that are inundated or saturated by surface or groundwater," the court explained that the record demonstrated that both the River and the pond rested on top of a vast gravel bed extending as much as 60 feet into the earth. The court noted that the

---

68 Notably, in 1989 the Corps adopted a new manual to supersede the 1987 Manual. This manual was referred to as the Federal Manual for Identifying and Delineating Jurisdictional Wetlands, and it employed less stringent methods for delineating wetlands than the 1987 Manual. In response to complaints from business groups and legislators, Congress limited the use of the 1989 Manual in the Energy and Water Development Appropriations Act of 1992, Pub. L. No. 102-104, 105 Stat. 510 (Aug. 17, 1991). This 1992 Act prohibited the use of funds to delineate wetlands under the 1989 Manual "or any subsequent manual not adopted in accordance with the requirements for notice and public comment of the rule-making process of the Administrative Procedure Act." 105 Stat. at 518. The 1992 Act also required the Corps to use the 1987 Manual to delineate any wetlands in ongoing enforcement actions or permit application reviews. The following year, Congress enacted the Energy and Water Development Appropriations Act of 1993, Pub. L. No. 102-377, 106 Stat. 1315 (Oct. 2, 1992), which specified that the Corps would continue to use the 1987 Manual "until a final wetlands delineation manual is adopted." 106 Stat. at 1324. The Corps has not yet adopted a final wetlands delineation manual, and thus the 1987 manual has been used since then. To adjust for regional variations in delineation methodologies, the Corps has prepared regional "supplements," such as the Arid West Region Supplement. In 2018, the Ninth Circuit called into question the Corps' continuing use of the 1987 Manual. In *Tin Cup, LLC v. U.S. Army Corps of Eng'rs,* 904 F.3d 1068 (9th Cir. 2018), the Ninth Circuit held that the 1993 Act does not require the Corps to continue to use the 1987 Manual's guidelines to delineate wetlands. It based its decision on interpretive principles regarding appropriations acts. According to the court, "There is . . . 'a very strong presumption' that if an appropriations act changes substantive law, it does so only for the fiscal year for which the bill was passed." *Id.* at 1073 (citing *Bldg. & Constr. Trades Dep't, AFL-CIO v. Martin,* 961 F.2d 269, 273 (D.C. Cir. 1992)).

69 496 F.3d 993 (9th Cir. 2007).

gravel bed is a porous medium, saturated with water, and through it flows an equally vast underground aquifer. "Beneath the surface, water soaks in and out of the Pond via the underground aquifer. This action is continuous, 24 hours a day, seven days a week, 365 days a year." As such, the court concluded that the pond qualified as a wetland under the regulatory definition.[70]

The determination that an aquatic feature is a wetland under the regulations can be of critical importance. The *Section 404(b)(1) Guidelines for Specification of Disposal Sites for Dredged or Fill Material*, discussed in more detail below, refers to "special aquatic sites," which are defined as "geographic areas, large or small, possessing special ecological characteristics of productivity, habitat, wildlife protection, or other important and easily disrupted ecological values."[71] Wetlands are included in the list of aquatic features identified as "special aquatic sites."[72] For that reason, the discharge of dredged or fill material into wetlands is subject to specific provisions in the Section 404(b)(1) Guidelines.

These specific provisions create presumptions that must be addressed before the Corps may authorize the discharge of dredged or fill material into special aquatic sites. The Section 404(b)(1) Guidelines identify two presumptions.

First,

> Where the activity associated with a discharge which is proposed for a special aquatic site . . . does not require access or proximity to or siting within the special aquatic site in question to fulfill its basic purpose (i.e., is not "water dependent"), practicable alternatives that do not involve special aquatic sites are presumed to be available, unless clearly demonstrated otherwise.[73]

Second,

> [W]here a discharge is proposed for a special aquatic site, all practicable alternatives to the proposed discharge which do not involve a discharge into a special aquatic site are presumed to have less adverse impact on the aquatic ecosystem, unless clearly demonstrated otherwise.[74]

These presumptions are discussed in more detail below in connection with the Section 404(b)(1) Guidelines.

---

70   *Id.* at 997–98.

71   40 C.F.R. § 230.3(m). This section further provides: "These areas are generally recognized as significantly influencing or positively contributing to the general overall environmental health or vitality of the entire ecosystem of a region." *Id.*

72   *Id.* § 230.41. Five other water features are identified as special aquatic sites. These include sanctuaries and refuges (*id.* § 230.40), mud flats (*id.* § 230.42), vegetated shallows (*id.* § 230.43), coral reefs (*id.* § 230.44), and riffle and pool complexes (*id.* § 230.45).

73   *Id.* § 230.10(a)(3).

74   *Id.*

Features Excluded from Jurisdiction under Section 404

Certain aquatic features are expressly excluded from the Corps' jurisdiction under Section 404 of the Clean Water Act. Interestingly, Section 404 of the Act itself does not expressly exclude any features. The Corps regulations, however, expressly carve out from the Corps' jurisdiction two features: prior converted cropland and waste treatment systems. See the discussion below for more information regarding the prior converted cropland exclusion.[75] The regulations also exclude waste treatment systems, including treatment ponds or lagoons designed to meet the requirements of the Clean Water Act.[76]

Although not binding authority, the Corps' preamble to its 1986 Final Rule for Section 404 Regulations provides guidance on other water features the Corps "generally [does] not consider" to be a water of the United States.[77] These features include:

> non-tidal drainage and irrigation ditches excavated on dry land

> artificially irrigated areas which would revert to upland if the irrigation ceased

> artificial lakes or ponds created by excavating and/or diking dry land to collect and retain water and which are used exclusively for such purposes as stock watering, irrigation, settling basins, or rice growing

> artificial reflecting or swimming pools or other small ornamental bodies of water created by excavating and/or diking dry land to retain water for primarily aesthetic reasons

> water-filled depressions created in dry land incidental to construction activity and pits excavated in dry land for the purpose of obtaining fill, sand, or gravel unless and until the construction or excavation operation is abandoned and the resulting body of water meets the definition of waters of the United States[78]

Practitioners should not simply assume the Corps or EPA will disclaim jurisdiction over these features. The preamble cautions that "the Corps reserves the right on a case-by-case basis to determine that a particular waterbody within these categories of waters is a water of the United States. EPA also has the right to determine on a case-by-case basis if any of these waters are 'waters of the United States.'"[79]

---

75 33 C.F.R. § 328.3(a)(8) ("Waters of the United States do not include prior converted cropland. Notwithstanding the determination of an area's status as prior converted cropland by any other Federal agency, for the purposes of the Clean Water Act, the final authority regarding Clean Water Act jurisdiction remains with EPA.").

76 *Id.* This exclusion does not apply to cooling ponds, which is a term of art that had been defined in Section 423.11 of Title 40 of the Code of Federal Regulations. This section has been amended since publication of the Corps regulations, and this term is no longer defined in this section.

77 Final Rule for Regulatory Programs of the Corps of Engineers, 51 Fed. Reg. 41,206 (Nov. 13, 1986).

78 *Id.* at 41,217.

79 *Id.*

WATERS REGULATED BY THE RIVERS AND HARBORS ACT OF 1899

The Rivers and Harbors Act of 1899 primarily concerns obstructions created by work that takes place in navigable waters.

Section 10 Jurisdiction and Permitting Requirements

Under the Rivers and Harbors Act, the Corps regulates only navigable waters (which under this statute are not defined to include some non-navigable waters). Section 10 of the Act requires Corps authorization for certain work within navigable waters. This section provides:

> The creation of any obstruction not affirmatively authorized by Congress, to the navigable capacity of any of the waters of the United States is prohibited; and it shall not be lawful to build or commence the building of any wharf, pier, dolphin, boom, weir, breakwater, bulkhead, jetty, or other structures in any port, roadstead, haven, harbor, canal, navigable river, or other water of the United States, outside established harbor lines, or where no harbor lines have been established, except on plans recommended by the Chief of Engineers and authorized by the Secretary of the Army; and it shall not be lawful to excavate or fill, or in any manner to alter or modify the course, location, condition, or capacity of, any port, roadstead, haven, harbor, canal, lake, harbor or refuge, or enclosure within the limits of any breakwater, or of the channel of any navigable water of the United States, unless the work has been recommended by the Chief of Engineers and authorized by the Secretary of the Army prior to beginning the same.[80]

The Corps regulations explain that "navigable" waters in the context of this provision are those "waters that are navigable in a traditional sense where permits are required for certain work or structures pursuant to Section 9 and Section 10 of the Rivers and Harbors Act of 1899."[81] The term "structure" includes "any pier, boat, dock, boat ramp, wharf, dolphin, weir, boom, breakwater, bulkhead, revetment, riprap, jetty, artificial island, artificial reef, permanent mooring structure, power transmission line, permanently moored floating vessel, piling, aid to navigation, or any other obstacle or obstruction."[82] Also relevant is the Corps' definition of "work," which includes "any dredging or disposal of dredged material, excavation, filling, or other modification of a navigable water of the United States."[83]

---

80 33 U.S.C. § 403.

81 33 C.F.R. § 320.1(d).

82 *Id.* § 322.2(b).

83 *Id.* § 322.2(c).

The Corps regulations use a definition of "navigable waters of the United States" that is specific to the Section 10 permitting process.[84] This definition states:

> Navigable waters of the United States are those waters that are subject to the ebb and flow of the tide and/or are presently used, or have been used in the past, or may be susceptible for use to transport interstate or foreign commerce. A determination of navigability, once made, applies laterally over the entire surface of the waterbody, and is not extinguished by later actions or events which impede or destroy navigable capacity.[85]

Generally, the following conditions must be satisfied when the Corps makes a determination whether a waterbody is a navigable water of the United States: (1) past, present, or potential presence of interstate or foreign commerce; (2) physical capabilities for use by commerce; and (3) defined geographic limits of the waterbody.[86] The regulations provide that the determinative factor is the waterbody's capability of use by the public for purposes of transportation of commerce, and not the time, extent, or manner of that use. "[S]ufficient commerce may be shown by historical use of canoes, bateaux, or other frontier craft, as long as that type of boat was common or well-suited to the place and period."[87] The regulations also provide that a waterbody may be entirely within a state, yet still be capable of carrying interstate commerce. "Where a waterbody extends through one or more states, but substantial portions, which are capable of bearing interstate commerce, are located in only one of the states, the entirety of the waterway up to the head (upper limit) of navigation is subject to federal jurisdiction."[88]

One question that often arises regarding the Corps' jurisdiction over navigable waters is whether the extent to which the water channel is artificial has any bearing on the Corps' scope of jurisdiction for purposes of Section 10. The Corps regulations provide that an "artificial channel may often constitute a navigable water of the United States, even though it has been privately developed and maintained, or passes through private property. The test is . . . whether the waterbody is capable of use to transport interstate commerce." The regulations further state that a "canal open to navigable waters of the United States on only one end is itself navigable where it in fact supports interstate commerce." An artificial body, such as a canal, that is subject to ebb and flow of the tide is also a navigable water of the United States.[89]

Further, a waterbody may also be considered a navigable water of the United States depending on the feasibility of its use to transport interstate commerce after the

---

84 *Id.* § 329.1. The regulations specifically state that the definition of "navigable waters of the United States" used for Section 10 of the Rivers and Harbors Act does not apply to the Corps' exercise of authority under the Clean Water Act.

85 *Id.* § 329.4.

86 *Id.* § 329.5.

87 *Id.* § 329.6(a).

88 *Id.* § 329.7.

89 *Id.* § 329.8(a)(1).

construction of what "reasonable" improvements may potentially be made.[90] According to the Corps regulations, the improvement need not exist, be planned, nor even authorized; it is enough that potentially it could be made.[91]

Another critical factor for the Corps' analysis of interstate commerce is the time at which commerce exists or when a determination as to its existence is made. A waterbody which was navigable in its natural or improved state, or which was susceptible to reasonable improvement, is still considered navigable in a legal capacity, even though it is not presently used for commerce, or is presently incapable of such use because of changed conditions or the presence of obstructions.[92] As to future or potential use, a waterway may be considered navigable if it is susceptible to use in its ordinary condition or by reasonable improvement to transport interstate commerce.[93]

In addition to interstate commerce factors, the Corps' Section 10 jurisdiction is subject to certain geographic and topographic constraints for rivers and lakes. In particular, this jurisdiction extends laterally to the entire water surface and bed of a navigable waterbody, which includes all the land and waters below the ordinary high water mark.[94] With respect to non-tidal rivers, the ordinary high water mark on non-tidal rivers is "the line on the shore established by the fluctuations of water and indicated by physical characteristics such as a clear, natural line impressed on the bank; shelving; changes in the character of soil; destruction of terrestrial vegetation; the presence of litter and debris; or other appropriate means that consider the characteristics of the surrounding areas."[95]

The Corps' Section 10 jurisdiction is also subject to certain geographic and topographic constraints for oceanic and tidal waters. Navigable waters of the United States include all ocean and coastal waters within three geographic (nautical) miles seaward from the "baseline,"[96] which is defined as the line on the shore reached by the ordinary low tides, where the shore directly contacts the open sea.[97] The Corps' jurisdiction in coastal areas extends to the line on the shore reached by the plane of the mean (average) high water.[98] Where the precise determination of that location is required, the Corps specifies that it be established by survey with reference to the available tidal datum, preferably averaged over a period of 18.6 years. The Corps authorizes the use of less precise methods only where an estimate is needed of the line reached by the mean high water. Those methods can include observation of the "apparent shoreline"

90 Id. § 329.8(b).
91 Id.
92 Id. § 329.9(a).
93 Id. § 329.9(b).
94 Id. § 329.11(a).
95 Id. § 329.11(a)(2).
96 Id. § 329.12(a).
97 Id. § 329.12(a)(1).
98 Id. § 329.12(a)(2).

which is determined by reference to physical markings, lines of vegetation, or changes in type of vegetation.[99]

The Corps regulations note that conclusive determinations of navigability can be made only by federal courts.[100] Nevertheless, the regulations specify a process for the Corps to use in determining whether a waterbody is a navigable water. This process starts with the relevant Corps district preparing a report of findings, accompanied by an opinion of the district's legal counsel, and forwarded to the division engineer for final determination.[101] The regulations include a suggested format for the report's findings, which include items such as the name of the waterbody, its physical characteristics, its past or present interstate commerce uses, and its potential use for interstate commerce, if applicable.[102]

It can often be helpful to review the Corps' lists of navigable determinations, which are maintained for those waterbodies for which determinations have been made.[103] The absence of a waterbody from these lists does not mean that the waterbody is not navigable.[104]

A Section 10 permit can take the form of a Letter of Permission, Individual Permit, or a General Permit issued on a nationwide basis (i.e., a Nationwide Permit) or issued on a regional basis.[105] However, the practitioner should be aware that certain activities are specifically carved out by the Corps regulations from Section 10 permitting requirements. Activities that were commenced or completed shoreward of established federal harbor lines before May 27, 1970 do not require Section 10 permits.[106] A Section 10 permit is also not required to construct wharves and piers in any waterbody, located entirely within one state, that is a navigable water of the United States solely on the basis of its historical use to transport interstate commerce.[107]

Section 9 Jurisdiction and Permitting Requirements

Section 9 of the Rivers and Harbors Act[108] prohibits the construction of any dam or dike across any navigable water of the United States in the absence of Congressional

99 *Id.*

100 *Id.* § 329.14(a).

101 *Id.* § 329.14(b).

102 *Id.* § 329.14(c).

103 *Id.* § 329.16(a). Each of the Corps Districts in California maintain a list of navigable waterways on their respective websites: Sacramento District, interactive graphic available at https://www.spk.usace.army.mil/Missions/Regulatory/Jurisdiction/Navigable-Waters-of-the-US/; San Francisco District, list available at https://www.spn.usace.army.mil/Portals/68/docs/regulatory/1%20-%20Sect10waters.pdf; Los Angeles District, list available at https://www.spl.usace.army.mil/Missions/Regulatory/Jurisdictional-Determination/Navigable-Waterways/.

104 *Id.* § 329.16(b).

105 *Id.* § 322.2(d), (e), (f).

106 *Id.* § 322.4(a). However, if those activities involve the discharge of dredged or fill material into waters of the United States after October 18, 1972, a Section 404 permit is required.

107 *Id.* § 322.4(b).

108 33 U.S.C. § 401.

consent and approval by the Corps. Where the navigable portions of the waterbody lie wholly within the limits of a single state, the structure may be built under authority of the legislature of that state if approved by the Corps. Section 9 also pertains to bridges and causeways but the authority of the Corps with respect to these structures was transferred to the Secretary of Transportation under the Department of Transportation Act of October 15, 1966.[109]

Section 408 Permission

Some projects in California affect or are located near levees or wharves built by the United States, such as those projects located along the Pacific Ocean or in the San Joaquin-Sacramento Delta. Section 14 of the Rivers and Harbors Act[110] (codified as Section 408 of the Act) provides that the Corps may grant permission for the temporary occupation or use of any sea wall, bulkhead, jetty, dike, levee, wharf, pier, or other work built by the United States.[111]

For some development projects, it may be necessary to make modifications, alterations, or improvements to Corps civil works projects such as levees and other flood risk management, navigation, recreation, or infrastructure improvements. Section 14 of the Rivers and Harbors Act of 1899 provides that the Secretary of the Army may, upon the recommendation of the Chief of Engineers, grant permission to other entities for the permanent or temporary alteration or use of any Corps' civil works project. This requires a determination that the requested alteration[112] is "not injurious to the public interest" and "will not affect the [Corps] project's ability to meet its authorized purpose."

This means that the Corps has the authority to review, evaluate, and approve all alterations to federally authorized civil works projects to make sure that those activities are not harmful to the public and still meet the federal project's intended purposes mandated by congressional authorization. Because Section 14 of the Rivers and Harbors Act corresponds to Section 408 of the U.S. Code, this authorization process and requirement is often referred to as Section 408 review or a Section 408 permission.

The overall Corps review process for Section 408 requests involves four main steps: completeness determination; review and decision; final decision notification; and construction oversight.[113]

---

109 33 C.F.R. § 320.2(a).

110 33 U.S.C. § 408.

111 33 C.F.R. § 320.2(e).

112 The Corps' Engineer Circular (EC) 1165-2-216 (June 21, 2016) defines what the Corps considers an alteration: "Alterations or alter refers to any action by any entity other than [the Corps] that builds upon, alters, improves, moves, occupies, or otherwise affects the usefulness or the structural or ecological integrity, of a [Corps] project. Alterations also include actions approved as 'encroachments' pursuant to 33 C.F.R. 208.10." This document also defined the Corps' jurisdictional reach, explaining that "408 permissions" are only required for alterations proposed within the lands and real property interests identified and acquired for the Corps project and to lands available for Corps projects under the navigation servitude. Routine operations and maintenance do not require "408 permissions."

113 This review process is described in detail in the Corps Engineering Circular (EC) 1165-2-220 (Sept. 10, 2018), available at https://www.publications.usace.army.mil/Portals/76/Publications/EngineerCirculars/EC_1165-2-220.pdf?ver=2018-09-07-115729-890. This EC is set to expire September 30, 2020.

> **Step 1: Completeness Determination.** The first part of the process involves the requestor providing information to the Corps or more submittals in order to satisfy all the basic requirements of a complete Section 408 request. When a requestor submits information to a district office, the districts are expected to provide a written completeness determination within 30 days of receipt. If the district determines a submittal is not complete, the district will provide the requestor a written notification within 30 days of receipt, providing a description of what information is required in order for the submittal to be complete. The 30-day timeline for a completeness determination is then restarted upon any subsequent submittals of information.

> **Step 2: Corps Review and Decision.** During this step, the Corps will evaluate the information provided for the completeness determination following certain review requirements. This second step results in the Corps providing a final decision for either validating use of a categorical permission; a specific milestone; or a complete Section 408 request. A final decision generally will be provided by the Corps to the requester within 90 days from the date the completeness determination was made by the district. The district will create a Summary of Findings to serve as the decision document to summarize the administrative record, including the review findings and basis for the final Section 408 decision.

> **Step 3: Final Decision Notification.** The district is responsible for providing a written decision signed by the Corps deciding official to the requestor for all final Section 408 decisions, regardless of the decision level. This written decision must be issued within the 90-day review and decision timeline. At a minimum, certain standard terms and conditions must be included in all Section 408 approval notifications. These standard terms and conditions include, for example, provisions related to the limits of the authorization, indemnification and hold harmless requirements, reevaluation of the permission procedures, and conduct of work under the permission. Districts and divisions may also include any necessary special conditions as requirements for approval.

> **Step 4: Construction Oversight.** The Corps is authorized to incorporate district costs for construction oversight and closeout as part of the review costs for the Section 408 request. During this step, the district may develop procedures for monitoring construction activities. Plans and specifications with amendments during construction showing alterations as finally constructed must be furnished by the requestor after completion of the work if required by the district. The requestor is also required to provide the district with sufficient information to update the portions of the Corps issued Operations & Maintenance Manual to reflect changes as a result of the constructed alteration if necessary. The district may need to conduct a post-construction on-site inspection of the completed alteration to document final condition of the project.

Practitioners should be aware that policies adopted by the Corps in 2016 provided that Section 408 permission must be granted before the Corps will issue a Clean Water Act Section 404 permit or a Rivers and Harbors Act Section 10 permit.[114] In the authors' experience, Corps staff continue to take this position even though more recent policies regarding the Section 408 process rely on coordination efforts between Corps staff managing the Section 404 and Section 10 program, and Corps staff managing the Section 408 program, rather than a sequencing of these authorizations.[115]

DELINEATIONS AND JURISDICTIONAL DETERMINATIONS

A key component of determining the extent to which the Corps has jurisdictional authority over waters on a project site is the wetland delineation process. These are known as Jurisdictional Determinations, and a wetland delineation is the analysis typically performed to prepare a Jurisdictional Determination.

The Corps regulations introduce the concept of Jurisdictional Determination when they "authorize[] its district engineers to issue formal determinations of the applicability of the Clean Water Act to . . . tracts of land."[116] Over the years, the Corps has provided guidance on the use of Jurisdictional Determinations, most recently with Regulatory Guidance Letter No. 16-01. This Guidance notes that the use of Jurisdictional Determinations was not addressed by either the Clean Water Act or the Rivers and Harbors Act, and that the regulations make their use discretionary and do not create a right to a Jurisdictional Determination.

It is important to note that Regulatory Guidance Letter No. 16-01 explains that in certain circumstances, no Jurisdictional Determination is required. Under the heading "No JD Whatsoever," the Guidance states that some jurisdictional inquiries may be resolved without a Jurisdictional Determination. "The Corps generally does not issue a [Jurisdictional Determination] of any type where no [Jurisdictional Determination] has been requested and there are certain circumstances where a [Jurisdictional Determination] would not be necessary (such as authorizations by non-reporting nationwide general permits)." The Guidance further explains: "In some circumstances, including where the Corps verifies general permits or issues letters of permission and/or standard permits, jurisdictional questions may not arise."[117] This suggests that the Corps will waive the requirement for a Jurisdictional Determination in certain circumstances.

The regulations define a Jurisdictional Determination as a "written Corps determination that a wetland and/or waterbody is subject to regulatory jurisdiction under Section 404 of the Clean Water Act or a written determination that a waterbody is

---

114 Army Corps Engineering Circular (EC) 1165-2-216 (June 21, 2016) at p. 5 ("The decision on a Department of Army permit application pursuant to Section 10/404/103 cannot and will not be rendered prior to the decision on the Section 408 request.").

115 Army Corps Engineering Circular (EC) 1165-2-220 (September 10, 2018) at pp. 5–8.

116 33 C.F.R. § 320.1(a)(6).

117 Regulatory Guidance Letter No. 16-01 (Oct. 2016) at p. 3.

JD = Jurisdictional
Determination

AJD = Approved Jurisdictional
Determination

PJD = Preliminary Jurisdictional
Determination

RGL = Regulatory Guidance
Letter

subject to regulatory jurisdiction under Section 9 or 10 of the Rivers and Harbors Act of 1899."[118] According to the Guidance, the regulations authorize their use as a service to the public, and the Corps has developed a practice of providing them when requested.

Jurisdictional determinations come in two varieties: "preliminary" and "approved." A Preliminary Jurisdictional Determination, often referred to as a "PJD," is defined in the Corps regulations as a written indication "that there may be waters of the United States on a parcel or indications of the approximate location(s) of waters of the United States on a parcel."[119] PJDs are advisory and may not be appealed. An Approved Jurisdictional Determination, or "AJD," is defined in the Corps regulations as a "Corps document stating the presence or absence of waters of the United States on a parcel or a written statement and map identifying the limits of waters of the United States on a parcel." According to the Regulations, AJDs are appealable actions.[120]

Regulatory Guidance Letter No. 16-01 provides additional guidance on the distinction between these two kinds of Jurisdictional Determinations. When the Corps provides a PJD, or authorizes an activity through a general or individual permit relying on an issued PJD, the Corps is making no legally binding determination of any type regarding whether jurisdiction exists over the particular aquatic resource in question. A PJD is "preliminary" in the sense that a recipient of a PJD can later request and obtain an AJD if that becomes necessary or appropriate during the permit process or during the administrative appeal process. In addition, a PJD:

> may be requested in order to move ahead expeditiously to obtain a Corps permit authorization where the requestor determines that it is in his or her best interest to do so

> may be requested even where initial indications are that the aquatic resources on a parcel may not be jurisdictional, if the requestor makes an informed, voluntary decision that it is in his or her best interest not to request and obtain an AJD

> may be used as the basis for a permit decision; however, for purposes of computation of impacts, compensatory mitigation requirements, and other resource protection measures, a permit decision made on the basis of a PJD will treat all aquatic resources that would be affected in any way by the permitted activity on the parcel as jurisdictional

> may include the delineation limits of all aquatic resources on a parcel, without determining the jurisdictional status of such aquatic resources

> may be requested through the use of a form provided by the Corps with this Regulatory Guidance Letter

With respect to AJDs, the Regulatory Guidance Letter describes an AJD as a definitive, official determination that there are, or that there are not, jurisdictional aquatic resources on a parcel and the identification of the geographic limits of jurisdictional

118 33 C.F.R. § 331.2.

119 *Id.*

120 *Id.*

aquatic resources on a parcel can only be made by means of an AJD. AJDs may be either "stand-alone" AJDs or AJDs associated with permit actions. Some "stand-alone" AJDs may later be associated with permit actions, but at the time of issuance are not related to a permit application. A "stand-alone" AJD may be requested so that impacts to jurisdictional aquatic resources may be avoided or minimized during the planning stages of a project, or it may be requested in order to fulfill a local/state authorization requirement.

In addition, an AJD:

> will be used if the Corps is determining the presence or absence of jurisdictional aquatic resources on a parcel

> will be used if the Corps is identifying the geographic limits of jurisdictional aquatic resources on a parcel

> will remain valid for a period of five years, subject to certain limited exceptions

> can be administratively appealed through the Corps administrative appeal process

> may be requested through the use of a form provided by the Corps with the Regulatory Guidance Letter

The Corps regulations include policies and procedures for an affected party to administratively appeal an AJD. Notably, the Corps regulations are specific as to who is allowed to pursue an administrative appeal. "The appeal process will allow the affected party to pursue an administrative appeal of certain [Corps] decisions with which they disagree."[121] The term "affected party" is specifically defined in the regulations as "a permit applicant, landowner, a lease, easement or option holder (i.e., an individual who has an identifiable and substantial legal interest in the property) who has received" the Approved Jurisdictional Determination.[122] This suggests that third parties do not have the right to administratively appeal an AJD.

Practitioners should be aware that other terms used in the regulations regarding the administrative appeal process also have definitions that may be relevant. The term "Jurisdictional Determination," or "JD," means:

a written Corps determination that a wetland and/or waterbody is subject to regulatory jurisdiction under Section 404 of the Clean Water Act or a written determination that a waterbody is subject to regulatory jurisdiction under Section 9 or Section 10 of the Rivers and Harbors Act of 1899. Additionally, the term includes a written reverification of expired JDs and a written reverification of JDs where new information has become available that may affect the previously written determination. For example, such geographic JDs may include, but are not limited to, one or more of the following determinations: the presence or absence of wetlands; the location(s) of the wetland boundary, ordinary high water mark, mean high water mark, and/or high tide line; interstate commerce nexus for isolated

---

121 *Id.* § 331.1.

122 *Id.* § 331.2.

waters; and adjacency of wetlands to other waters of the United States. All JDs will be in writing and will be identified as either preliminary or approved. JDs do not include determinations that a particular activity requires a DA permit.[123]

"Approved Jurisdictional Determination" is defined as a "Corps document stating the presence or absence of waters of the United States on a parcel or a written statement and map identifying the limits of waters of the United States on a parcel."[124] By contrast, the definition of "preliminary JDs" makes clear that a PJD cannot be appealed because it is advisory in nature. The term "preliminary JD" is defined as "written indications that there may be waters of the United States on a parcel or indications of the approximate location(s) of waters of the United States on a parcel. Preliminary JDs include compliance orders that have an implicit JD, but no approved JD."[125]

The Corps regulations specify actions regarding JDs that are not appealable. Those actions include any request for the appeal of an AJD where the Request for Appeal has not been received by the division engineer within 60 days of the date of the Notification of Appeal Process; a previously approved JD that has been superseded by another approved JD based on new information or data submitted by the applicant (the new AJD is an appealable action); an approved JD associated with an individual permit where the permit has been accepted and signed by the permittee; a preliminary JD; or a JD associated with unauthorized activities except as otherwise provided.[126]

The Corps regulations specify the chain of command for reviewing JDs. For the administrative appeal of AJDs, the division engineer acts as the review officer and may delegate the final appeal decision to an official that is at the same or higher grade level than the grade level of the official that signed the AJD.[127]

The process for an administrative appeal is described in detail in the Corps regulations. Generally, affected parties are first notified in writing of the Corps' decision on the AJD. The notification must include a Notification of Appeal Process fact sheet that explains the criteria and procedures for the administrative appeal process, a Request for Appeal form, and a "basis of Jurisdictional Determination."[128] The phrase "basis of Jurisdictional Determination" is specifically defined in the Corps regulations. It means:

> a summary of the indicators that support the Corps approved JD. Indicators supporting the Corps approved JD can include, but are not limited to: indicators of wetland hydrology, hydric soils, and hydrophytic plant communities; indicators of ordinary high water marks, high tide lines, or mean high water marks; indicators of adjacency to navigable or interstate

123 *Id.*
124 *Id.*
125 *Id.*
126 *Id.* § 331.5(b).
127 *Id.* § 331.3(a)(1).
128 *Id.* § 331.4.

waters; indicators that the wetland or waterbody is of part of a tributary system; or indicators of linkages between isolated water bodies and inter-state or foreign commerce.[129]

The affected party has the right to obtain a copy of the administrative record.[130]

The appellant must submit a completed Request for Appeal in order to appeal an AJD, and the Request for Appeal must be received by the division engineer within 60 days of the date of the Notification of Appeal.[131] The reason(s) for requesting an appeal of an AJD must be specifically stated in the Request for Appeal and must be "more than a simple request for appeal because the affected party did not like the approved JD." The Corps regulations provide examples of legitimate reasons for appeal: "[a] procedural error; an incorrect application of law, regulation or officially promulgated policy; omis-sion of material fact; incorrect application of the current regulatory criteria and associ-ated guidance for identifying and delineating wetlands; incorrect application of the Section 404(b)(1) Guidelines; or use of incorrect data."[132]

An AJD will be reconsidered by the district engineer if the affected party submits new information or data to the district engineer within 60 days of the date of the Notification of Appeal Process. A Request for Appeal that contains new information will either be returned to the district engineer for reconsideration or the appeal will be pro-cessed if the applicant withdraws the new information. The district engineer has 60 days from the receipt of such new information or data to review the new information or data, consider whether or not that information changes the previously approved JD, and, reis-sue the approved JD or issue a new approved JD. The reconsideration of an approved JD by the district engineer does not commence the administrative appeal process. The affected party may appeal the district engineer's reissued or new approved JD.[133]

If work is authorized by either general or individual permit, and the affected party wishes to request an appeal of the AJD associated with the general permit authorization or individual permit or the special conditions of the proffered individual permit, the appeal must be received by the Corps and the appeal process concluded prior to the commencement of any work in waters of the United States and prior to any work that could alter the hydrology of waters of the United States.[134]

Upon receipt of a Request for Appeal (RFA), the review officer must determine whether the RFA is acceptable (i.e., complete and meets the criteria for appeal). If the Request for Appeal is acceptable, the review officer must notify the appellant in writing within 30 days of receiving the acceptable Request for Appeal. If the review officer determines that the Request for Appeal is not complete, the review officer will notify the

129 *Id.* § 331.2.
130 *Id.* § 331.4.
131 *Id.* § 331.5(a)(1).
132 *Id.* § 331.5(a)(2).
133 *Id.* § 331.6(c).
134 *Id.* § 331.6(e).

appellant in writing within 30 days of receiving the Request for Appeal detailing the reasons why the Request for Appeal is not complete. No further administrative appeal is available, unless the appellant revises the Request for Appeal to correct the deficiencies notified in the letter from the Corps.

The revised Request for Appeal must be received by the division engineer within 30 days of the date of the Corps letter indicating that the initial Request for Appeal is not acceptable. If the review officer determines that the revised Request for Appeal is still not complete, the review officer will again so notify the appellant in writing within 30 days of the receipt of the Request for Appeal detailing the reasons why the Request for Appeal is not complete. If the division engineer determines that the revised Request for Appeal is still not acceptable, the division engineer will notify the appellant of this determination by certified letter within 30 days of the date of the receipt of the revised Request for Appeal, and will advise the appellant that the matter is not eligible for appeal. No further Requests for Appeal will be accepted after this point.[135]

The Corps regulations specifically allow for an informal meeting or conference call between the Corps and the appellant to review and discuss issues directly related to the appeal of an AJD for purpose of clarifying the administrative record. The regulations state that the AJD appeal meeting should be held at a location of reasonable convenience to the appellant and near the site where the approved JD was conducted.[136]

The appeal of an AJD is limited to the information contained in the administrative record by the date of the Notification of Appeal Process for the AJD, the proceedings of the appeal conference, and any relevant information gathered by the review office. Neither the appellant nor the Corps may present new information not already contained in the administrative record, but both parties may interpret, clarify or explain issues and information contained in the record.[137]

According to the regulations, because a decision to determine geographic jurisdiction depends on the facts, circumstances, and physical conditions particular to the specific project and/or site being evaluated, appeal decisions are of little or no precedential utility. Therefore, an appeal decision of the division engineer is applicable only to the instant appeal and has no other precedential effect. Such a decision may not be cited in any other administrative appeal, and may not be used as precedent for the evaluation of any other JD. While administrative appeal decisions lack precedential value and may not be cited by an appellant or a district engineer in any other appeal proceeding, the Corps' goal is to have the Corps regulatory program operate as consistently as possible, particularly with respect to interpretations of law, regulation, an Executive Order, and officially-promulgated policy. Therefore, a copy of each appeal decision will be forwarded to

135 *Id.* § 331.7(b). The Corps regulations also include provisions related to site visits by the Corps, if the review officer determines a site investigation is needed to clarify the administrative record. *Id.*

136 *Id.* § 331.7(e).

137 *Id.* § 331.7(f).

Corps Headquarters; those decisions are periodically reviewed at the headquarters level for consistency with law, Executive Orders, and policy.[138]

The division engineer will make a final decision on the merits of the appeal at the earliest practicable time. According to the regulations, the division engineer will normally make a final decision on the merits of the appeal within 90 days of the receipt of an acceptable Request for Appeal, unless any site visit is delayed. In such case, the review officer will complete the appeal review and the division engineer will make a final appeal decision within 30 days of the site visit. In no case will a site visit delay extend the total appeal process beyond 12 months from the date of receipt of an acceptable Request for Appeal.[139]

The division engineer will disapprove the entirety of or any part of the district engineer's decision only if he or she determines that the decision on some relevant matter was arbitrary, capricious, an abuse of discretion, not supported by substantial evidence in the administrative record, or plainly contrary to a requirement of law, regulation, an Executive Order, or officially promulgated Corps policy guidance. The division engineer will not attempt to substitute his or her judgment for that of the district engineer regarding a matter of fact, so long as the district engineer's determination was supported by substantial evidence in the administrative record, or regarding any other matter if the district engineer's determination was reasonable and within the zone of discretion delegated to the district engineer by Corps regulations. The division engineer may instruct the district engineer on how to correct any procedural error that was prejudicial to the appellant (i.e., that was not a "harmless" procedural error), or to reconsider the decision where any essential part of the district engineer's decision was not supported by accurate or sufficient information, or analysis, in the administrative record. The division engineer will document his or her decision on the merits of the appeal in writing, and provide a copy of this decision to the applicant (using certified mail) and the district engineer.[140]

The final decision of the division engineer on the merits of the appeal will conclude the administrative appeal process, and this decision will be filed in the administrative record for the project.[141] The Corps regulations include a flow chart illustrating the appeal process for an AJD (see Figure 7-1).

---

138 *Id.* § 331.7(g). The South Pacific Division posts the status of appeals and appeal decisions on its website. They can be accessed at http://www.spd.usace.army.mil/Missions/Regulatory/Regulatory-Appeals/Administrative-Appeals-Decisions/.

139 33 C.F.R. § 331.8.

140 *Id.* § 331.9(b).

141 *Id.* § 331.9(c).

FIGURE 7-1. ADMINISTRATIVE APPEAL PROCESS FOR APPROVED
JURISDICTIONAL DETERMINATIONS

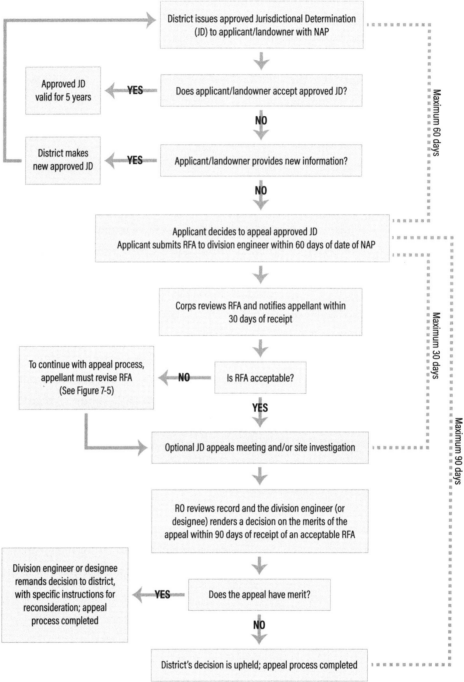

A JD can have significant implications for a landowner. In *United States Army Corps of Engineers v. Hawkes Co.*,[142] the U.S. Supreme Court held that AJDs are subject to judicial review because they are "final agency actions" reviewable under the Administrative Procedure Act in light of the test for "final agency actions" the Court articulated in

142 136 S. Ct. 1807 (2016).

Bennett v. Spear.[143] Based on that test, the Court first found that an AJD clearly "mark[s] the consummation" of the Corps' decisionmaking on the question of whether "there may be waters of the United States on a parcel of property."[144] The Court explained: "It is issued after extensive factfinding by the Corps regarding the physical and hydrological characteristics of the property, and is typically not revisited if the permitting process moves forward."[145] The Court also noted that the Corps itself describes AJDs as "final agency action."[146] Thus, the Court determined that the first prong of the *Bennett* test had been satisfied.

As to the second prong of the *Bennett* test, which evaluates whether the action is "one by which rights or obligations have been determined, or from which legal consequences will flow," the Court found that the "the definitive nature of approved JDs . . . gives rise to 'direct and appreciable legal consequences.'"[147] The Court reached this conclusion after considering the effect of an approved JD stating that a landowner's property does not contain jurisdictional waters—"a 'negative' JD, in Corps parlance."[148] A negative JD essentially creates a five-year safe harbor from civil enforcement proceedings for property owners under the Clean Water Act. According to the Court, "It follows that affirmative JDs have legal consequences as well: They represent the denial of the safe harbor that negative JDs afford." Thus, because "legal consequences flow" from approved JDs, they constitute final agency.[149]

Perhaps most notable about this decision is the Court's treatment of the Corps' argument that the landowner had two alternative approaches to challenging the approved JD—either discharge fill material without a permit, risking an EPA enforcement action during which they can argue that no permit was required, or apply for a permit and seek judicial review if dissatisfied with the results.[150]

As to the first alternative, the Court explained that "parties need not await enforcement proceedings before challenging final agency action where such proceedings carry the risk of 'serious criminal and civil penalties.'" Landowners "need not assume such risks while waiting for EPA to 'drop the hammer' in order to have their day in court."[151] As to the second alternative, the Court noted that the Section 404 "permitting process can be arduous, expensive, and long," generating information in support of a permit that will not "alter the finality of the approved JD, or affect its suitability for judicial review."[152]

---

143 520 U.S. 154 (1997).

144 136 S. Ct. at 1813.

145 *Id.* at 1813–14.

146 *Id.* at 1814 (citing 33 C.F.R. § 320.1(a)(6)).

147 *Id.* (citing *Bennett*, 520 U.S. at 178).

148 *Id.*

149 *Id.*

150 *Id.* at 1815.

151 *Id.*

152 *Id.* at 1816.

The Corps reacted quickly to the *Hawkes* decision. In October 2016, the Corps issued Regulatory Guidance Letter (RGL) No. 16-01 regarding the subject of "Jurisdictional Determinations" that provides guidance on which type of Jurisdictional Determination, either an AJD or a PJD, is appropriate for an activity. This RGL explains in detail the difference between an AJD and a PJD, essentially supplementing the definitions of these terms set forth in the Corps regulations. An important aspect of RGL No. 16-01 is that it expressly contemplates that for some activities, "no [Jurisdictional Determination] whatsoever" is necessary. For example, a Jurisdictional Determination may not be required when "jurisdictional questions [do] not arise," even when processing a standard permit. The RGL explains: "some jurisdictional inquiries may be resolved without a [Jurisdictional Determination] .... [A] letter confirming that no Corps permit is required for activities on a site may be sufficient for responding to requests in a particular case." Because of timing requirements and the costs involved, this flexibility can be vitally important for those projects where the Corps' jurisdiction is not

In light of the *Hawkes* decision, it is now clear that a landowner can seek judicial relief as to an AJD after exhausting the administrative appeal process.[153] See discussion below regarding judicial review of Army Corps decisions under Section 404 of the Clean Water Act.

REGULATED ACTIVITIES

Section 404 does not regulate all impacts to wetlands and other waters. It only regulates the discharge of dredged or fill material to those waters. Section 404 expressly states that permits are required only "for the discharge of dredged or fill material into the navigable waters at specified disposal sites."[154]

Discharge of Dredged or Fill Material

The Clean Water Act defines "discharge" to mean "a discharge of pollutant, and a discharge of pollutants."[155] The Act further defines "discharge of pollutant" to mean "any addition of any pollutant to navigable waters from any point source" and "any addition of any pollutant to the waters of the contiguous zone or the ocean from a point source other than a vessel or other floating craft."[156] The term "pollutant" is defined as "dredged spoil, solid waste, incinerator residue, sewage, garbage, sewage sludge, munitions, chemical wastes, biological materials, radioactive materials, heat, wrecked or discarded equipment, rock, sand, cellar dirt and industrial, municipal, and agricultural waste discharged into water."[157] While the word "discharge" is not defined in either the Corps or EPA's regulations, the phrases "discharge of dredged material" and "discharge of fill material" are defined in EPA's Section 404 Regulations.

The regulations define "discharge of dredged material" as "any addition of dredged material into, including redeposit of dredged material other than incidental fallback within, the waters of the United States."[158] The regulations indicate this term includes, but is not limited to, the following:

> the addition of dredged material to a specified discharge site located in waters of the United States

> the runoff or overflow, associated with a dredging operation, from a contained land or water disposal area

153 The Court did not directly address whether a plaintiff would be required to exhaust the administrative appeal process before seeking judicial relief against an AJD. The Court suggests that the plaintiffs did exhaust their administrative remedies by complying with the administrative appeal process. Presumably, the Court's conclusion rested on the implied fact that the plaintiff sought an administrative remedy before seeking judicial relief, and as such, the AJD constituted "final agency action."

154 33 U.S.C. § 1344(a).

155 *Id.* § 1362(16).

156 *Id.* § 1362(12). See *Rybachek v. U.S. Environmental Protection Agency*, 904 F.2d 1276, 1285 (9th Cir. 1990) (case involving placer mining, in which court concluded that because "material discharged is coming not from the streambed itself, but from outside, this clearly constitutes an 'addition.'").

157 *Id.* § 1362(6).

158 40 C.F.R. § 232.2(1).

> any addition, including redeposit other than incidental fallback, of dredged material, including excavated material, into waters of the United States which is incidental to any activity, including mechanized land-clearing, ditching, channelization, or other excavation[159]

The regulations specify that the term discharge of dredged material does not include the following:

> discharges of pollutants into waters of the United States resulting from the onshore subsequent processing of dredged material that is extracted for any commercial use (other than fill); these discharges are subject to section 402 of the Clean Water Act even though the extraction and deposit of such material may require a permit from the Corps or applicable state

> activities that involve only the cutting or removing of vegetation above the ground (e.g., mowing, rotary cutting, and chainsawing) where the activity neither substantially disturbs the root system nor involves mechanized pushing, dragging, or other similar activities that redeposit excavated soil material

> incidental fallback[160]

The regulations define "discharge of fill material" as "the addition of fill material into waters of the United States." The regulations elaborate:

The term generally includes, without limitation, the following activities: Placement of fill that is necessary for the construction of any structure or infrastructure in a water of the United States; the building of any structure, infrastructure, or impoundment requiring rock, sand, dirt, or other material for its construction; site-development fills for recreational, industrial, commercial, residential, or other uses; causeways or road fills; dams and dikes; artificial islands; property protection and/or reclamation devices such as riprap, groins, seawalls, breakwaters, and revetments; beach nourishment; levees; fill for structures such as sewage treatment facilities, intake and outfall pipes associated with power plants and subaqueous utility lines; placement of fill material for construction or maintenance of any liner, berm, or other infrastructure associated with solid waste landfills; placement of overburden, slurry, or tailings or similar mining-related materials . . . .

The regulations also govern the placement of pilings of waters of the United States:

[P]lacement of pilings in waters of the United States constitutes a discharge of fill material and requires a Section 404 permit when such placement has or would have the effect of a discharge of fill material. Examples of such activities that have the effect of a discharge of fill material include, but are not limited to, the following: Projects where the pilings are so closely spaced that sedimentation rates would be increased; projects in

159 *Id.* § 232.2(1)(i)–(iii).

160 *Id.*

which the pilings themselves effectively would replace the bottom of a waterbody; projects involving the placement of pilings that would reduce the reach or impair the flow or circulation of waters of the United States; and projects involving the placement of pilings which would result in the adverse alteration or elimination of aquatic functions.[161]

The "incidental fallback" exclusion is discussed in more detail below.

The Incidental Fallback Exclusion

A significant issue regarding the definition of "discharge of dredged material" is the phrase "incidental fallback." The issue is fairly straightforward: in some instances, work activities may not directly result in a discharge into a water of the United States, but a discharge may nonetheless occur as a result of fill incidentally "falling back" into the water of the United States. An example of this are the small amounts of soil that fall from a dredge bucket during excavation activities. The question then becomes, can the Corps regulate that incidental fallback under Section 404 and does it require a Section 404 permit?

This issue has been at the center of a storm of controversy since the early 1990s. In August 1993, the Corps and EPA issued a regulation defining the term "discharge of dredged material" as "any addition, including any redeposit, of dredged material, including excavated material, into waters of the United States which is incidental to any activity, including mechanized land-clearing, ditching, channelization, or other excavation." This regulation became known as the Tulloch Rule.[162] The American Mining Congress and several other trade associations challenged this regulation. In 1997, the U.S. District Court for the District of Columbia ruled that the regulation exceeded the agencies' authority under the Clean Water Act because it impermissibly regulated "incidental fallback" of dredged material.[163]

The court concluded that incidental fallback is not subject to the Clean Water Act as an "addition of pollutants" and declared the rule "invalid." The court also enjoined the agencies from applying or enforcing the regulation. The government appealed the court's ruling, and in June 1998, the U.S. Court of Appeals for the District of Columbia Circuit affirmed the district court's decision.[164]

Incidental fallback. Photo: Lindsay Teunis.

---

161 *Id.* § 232.2(1). The regulations provide even more detail regarding pilings:

Placement of pilings in waters of the United States that does not have or would not have the effect of a discharge of fill material shall not require a Section 404 permit. Placement of pilings for linear projects, such as bridges, elevated walkways, and powerline structures, generally does not have the effect of a discharge of fill material. Furthermore, placement of pilings in waters of the United States for piers, wharves, and an individual house on stilts generally does not have the effect of a discharge of fill material. All pilings, however, placed in the *navigable waters of the United States,* as that term is defined in 33 C.F.R. part 329, require authorization under section 10 of the Rivers and Harbors Act of 1899 (see 33 C.F.R. part 322). *Id.*

162 The Rule was issued after the Corps entered into a settlement agreement over an enforcement action related to the draining of wetlands without a permit. Tulloch was the name of the Corps District Engineer that was named in the complaint.

163 *American Mining Congress v. United States Army Corps of Engineers,* 951 F. Supp. 267, 272-76 (D.D.C. 1997).

164 *National Mining Association v. United States Army Corps of Engineers,* 145 F.3d 1339 (D.C. Cir. 1998).

The court of appeal described incidental fallback as "redeposit" of dredged material that "takes place in substantially the same spot as the initial removal."[165] The court further portrayed such fallback as "the situation in which material is removed from the waters of the United States and a small portion of it happens to fall back," and concluded that because such fallback represents a net withdrawal, it cannot constitute a regulable "addition" of a pollutant.[166] The court of appeal did not, however, conclude that all forms of redeposit were outside the government's regulatory authority. The court explained that its holding was limited to the question of whether the assertion of jurisdiction over "*any* redeposit, including incidental fallback, under the *Tulloch* rule outruns the Corps' statutory authority."[167] The court noted, for example, that "redeposits at some distance from the point of removal" could still be regulated.[168]

In May 1999, the agencies issued a final rule modifying the definition of "discharge of dredged material" in response to the court of appeals' decision.[169] This rule deleted the word "any" as a modifier of the term "redeposit," and it excluded "incidental fallback" from the definition of "discharge of dredged material." As explained in the preamble to that rulemaking, the determination whether a particular redeposit requires a Section 404 permit would be done on a case-by-case basis, consistent with the Clean Water Act authorities and governing case law.

After the agencies published the 1999 Rule, the National Association of Home Builders and others filed a motion with the district court that issued the original injunction seeking to compel compliance with that injunction. The Home Builders' motion asserted that the 1999 Rule violated the court's injunction by asserting unqualified authority to regulated mechanized land-clearing. In September 2000, the district court denied the Home Builders' motion. EPA and the Corps proposed further revisions to the definition of "discharge of dredged material" in August 2000[170] based on the agencies' understanding of language in the court decisions addressing "incidental fallback." The final rule was promulgated in January 2001 and became known as the Tulloch II Rule. This Rule retained the language from the 1999 Rule excluding "incidental fallback" from regulation, and adding in language defining "incidental fallback" as "the redeposit of small volumes of dredged material that is incidental to excavation activity in waters of the United States when such material falls back to substantially the same place as the initial removal."[171]

In February 2001, the National Association of Home Builders filed a facial challenge to the Tulloch II rule, asserting that the regulations created an impermissible rebuttable presumption that all unpermitted dredging results in unlawful discharge, and

165 *Id.* at 1401.

166 *Id.* at 1404.

167 *Id.* at 1405 (emphasis in original).

168 *Id.* at 1407, 1410 (Silberman, J., concurring).

169 64 Fed. Reg. 25,120, 25,123 (May 10, 1999).

170 65 Fed. Reg. 50,108.

171 66 Fed. Reg. 4575.

alleging that the rule exceeds the Corps' Section 404 authority by defining "incidental fallback" in terms of volume. In January 2007, the district court held that the Tulloch II rule violates the Clean Water Act because of the way the rule used volume to determine "incidental fallback." The district court declared the Tulloch II rule invalid.

In response to this court ruling, the agencies issued a rule that returned the definition of "discharge of dredged material" to that which was promulgated in the 1999 rule. As with the 1999 Rule, deciding when a particular redeposit of dredged materials is subject to Section 404 jurisdiction will essentially require a case-by-case evaluation. In addition to excluding "incidental fallback" from the scope of "discharge of dredged materials," the regulations now specify that Section 404 authorization is not required for the following:[172]

> Any incidental addition, including redeposit, of dredged material associated with any activity that does not have or would not have the effect of destroying or degrading an area of waters of the United States; however, this exception does not apply to any person preparing to undertake mechanized land-clearing, ditching, channelization and other excavation activity in a water of the United States, which would result in a redeposit of dredged material, unless the person demonstrates to the satisfaction of the Corps, or EPA as appropriate, prior to commencing the activity involving the discharge, that the activity would not have the effect of destroying or degrading any area of waters of the United States. The person proposing to undertake mechanized land-clearing, ditching, channelization or other excavation activity bears the burden of demonstrating that such activity would not destroy or degrade any area of waters of the United States.

> Incidental movement of dredged material occurring during normal dredging operations, defined as dredging for navigation in navigable waters of the United States with proper authorization from the Congress and/or the Corps; however, this exception is not applicable to dredging activities in wetlands.

> Certain discharges, such as those associated with normal farming, silviculture, and ranching activities, are not prohibited by or otherwise subject to regulation under section 404.

The Meanings of Fill Material and Dredged Material

"Fill material" is defined to mean material placed in waters of the United States where the material has the effect of: (1) replacing any portion of a water of the United States with dry land; or (2) changing the bottom elevation of any portion of a water of the

---

172 33 C.F.R. § 323.4(d)(3).

United States.[173] Examples of fill material include rock, sand, soil, clay, plastics, construction debris, wood chips, overburden from mining or other excavation activities, and materials used to create any structure or infrastructure in the waters of the United States.[174] The term "fill material" does not include trash or garbage.[175] "Dredged material" in only briefly defined in the regulations as "material that is excavated or dredged from waters of the United States."[176]

In *Resource Investments, Inc. v. U.S. Army Corps of Engineers*,[177] the Ninth Circuit considered whether Section 404 authorized the Corps to require a landowner to obtain a permit before constructing a municipal solid waste landfill on a wetlands site. The court held that the construction of a municipal solid waste landfill on a wetlands site is regulated by EPA or states with solid waste permit programs approved by EPA under the Resource Conservation and Recovery Act (RCRA),[178] not by the Corps under Section 404 of the Clean Water Act.[179] The court explained, "[T]he municipal solid waste that would be disposed of in the proposed landfill does not fall within the definition of either 'dredged material' or 'fill material.'"[180]

STATUTORILY EXEMPT ACTIVITIES

Section 404 of the Clean Water Act includes statutory exclusions that carve out application of the permitting requirements to certain activities. These are often referred to as Section 404(f) exemptions. They include the discharge of dredged or fill material:

RCRA = Resource Conservation and Recovery Act

173 33 C.F.R. § 323.2(e)(1)(i)–(ii); 40 C.F.R. § 232.2. See *Southeast Alaska Conservation Council v. U.S. Army Corps of Engineers*, 486 F.3d 638 (9th Cir. 2007) (discussing the history of the regulatory definition of "fill material"); *Resource Inv., Inc. v. U.S. Army Corps of Engineers*, 151 F.3d 1162 (9th Cir. 1998) (discussing the meaning "fill material" in the context of permitting a solid waste disposal site).

   As to that portion of the definition pertaining to changes to the bottom elevation of any portion of a water of the United States, see *Southeast Alaska Conservation Council v. U.S. Army Corps of Engineers*, 486 F.3d 638 (9th Cir. 2007). In *Southeast Alaska Conservation Council*, the Ninth Circuit concluded that even though the discharge of process wastewater containing tailings from a gold mine into a lake would raise the bottom elevation of the lake, the Corps' issuance of a Section 404 permit for that activity was improper because the discharge was instead subject to the effluent restrictions of Sections 301 and 306 of the Clean Water Act. Under those provisions, the discharge of the process wastewater was prohibited. According to the court, the Corps and EPA "clearly intended to exclude discharges subject to effluent limitations or performance standards from the . . . definition of 'fill material.'" *Id.* at 652.

174 33 C.F.R. § 323.2(e)(2); 40 C.F.R. § 232.2.

175 33 C.F.R. § 323.2(e)(3); 40 C.F.R. § 232.2.

176 33 C.F.R. § 323.2(c); 40 C.F.R. § 232.2. See *Resource Inv., Inc. v. U.S. Army Corps of Engineers*, 151 F.3d 1162 (9th Cir. 1998) (discussing the legislative history of this regulation and the definition of "dredged material").

177 151 F.3d 1162 (9th Cir. 1998).

178 The Resource Conservation and Recovery Act of 1976 (RCRA), as amended by the Hazardous and Solid Waste Amendments of 1984, 42 U.S.C. §§ 6941–6949a, establishes a comprehensive regime for the regulation of solid waste and hazardous waste disposal on land. RCRA gives EPA authority to issue permits for the disposal of solid waste. The EPA promulgated regulations providing minimum federal criteria with which all solid waste landfills must comply. Under these regulations, wetlands are given strong protection against degradation by solid waste landfills. A new municipal solid waste landfill cannot be constructed on a wetlands area unless the owner can make several demonstrations to the director of an "approved state." See *Resource Inv., Inc. v. U.S. Army Corps of Engineers*, 151 F.3d 1162, 1167–68 (9th Cir. 1998).

179 *Id.* at 1164.

180 *Id.* at 1168.

(1) from normal farming, silviculture, and ranching activities such as plowing, seeding, cultivating, minor drainage, harvesting for the production of food, fiber, and forest products, or upland soil and water conservation practices

(2) for the purpose of maintenance, including emergency reconstruction of recently damaged parts, of currently serviceable structures such as dikes, dams, levees, groins, riprap, breakwaters, causeways, and bridge abutments or approaches, and transportation structures

(3) for the purpose of construction or maintenance of farm or stock ponds or irrigation ditches, or the maintenance of drainage ditches

(4) for the purpose of construction of temporary sedimentation basins on a construction site which does not include placement of fill material into the navigable water

(5) for the purpose of construction or maintenance of farm roads or forest roads, or temporary roads for moving mining equipment, where such roads are constructed and maintained, in accordance with best management practices, to assure that flow and circulation patterns and chemical and biological characteristics of the navigable waters are not impaired, that the reach of the navigable waters is not reduced, and that any adverse effect on the aquatic environment will be otherwise minimized

(6) resulting from any activity with respect to which a state has an approved program under section 1288(b)(4) of this title which meets the requirements of subparagraphs (B) and (C) of such section[181]

These exemptions are not absolute. A further provision in Section 404 creates an exception to the application of these exemptions. This exception is sometimes referred to as the "recapture" provision. As described by the Ninth Circuit Court of Appeals, "To be exempt from the permit requirements, one must demonstrate that proposed activities both *satisfy* the requirements of § (f)(1) and *avoid* the exception to the exemptions (referred to as the 'recapture' provision) of § (f)(2)."[182] The recapture provision states:

> Any discharge of dredged or fill material into the navigable waters incidental to any activity having as its purpose bringing an area of the navigable waters into a use to which it was not previously subject, where the flow or circulation of navigable waters may be impaired or the reach of such waters be reduced, shall be required to have a permit under this section.[183]

SCOPE OF 404 AND AGRICULTURAL ACTIVITIES

The reach of the Clean Water Act over agricultural activities has been the subject of significant debate. At issue are questions of (1) the extent to which the Corps has jurisdiction over waters that have been converted to agricultural use (commonly referred to as

181 33 U.S.C. § 1344(f)(1).

182 *United States v. Akers*, 785 F.2d 814, 819 (9th Cir. 1986).

183 33 U.S.C. § 1344(f)(2).

"Prior Converted Croplands"); and (2) the extent to which the Clean Water Act covers routine agricultural activities.

PCC = prior converted cropland

NRCS = Natural Resources Conservation Service

Prior Converted Croplands

An issue that often arises in California agricultural production areas is the extent to which the Corps has jurisdiction over irrigated lands that would persist as wetlands in the absence of irrigation and meet the definition of wetlands under the 1987 Corps of Engineers Wetland Delineation Manual. This issue turns on the interpretation of "normal circumstances" in the Corps' definition of wetlands.

As described above, the Corps regulations define wetlands as "areas that are inundated or saturated by surface or groundwater at a frequency and duration sufficient to support, and that under *normal circumstances* do support, a prevalence of vegetation typically adapted for life in saturated soil conditions."[184] According to Regulatory Guidance Letter No. 90-07, the primary consideration in determining whether a disturbed area qualifies as a Section 404 wetland under "normal circumstances" involves an evaluation of the extent and relative permanence of the physical alteration of wetlands hydrology and hydrophytic vegetation.

To make that determination, the Corps provides guidance regarding how the concept of "normal circumstances" applies to areas that are in agricultural production:

> "Prior converted cropland" (PCC) is defined by the Soil Conservation Service (now known as the Natural Resources Conservation Service (NRCS)) as wetlands which were both manipulated (drained or otherwise physically altered to remove excess water from the land) and cropped before December 23, 1985, to the extent that they are no longer exhibit important wetland values.

> "Farmed wetlands" are wetlands which were both manipulated and cropped before December 23, 1985, but which continue to exhibit important wetland values.

> The definition of "normal circumstances" found in the Federal Manual for Identifying and Delineating Jurisdictional Wetlands, adopted by the Corps on January 10, 1989, is based on the premise that for certain altered wetlands, even though the vegetation has been removed by cropping, the basic soil and hydrological characteristics remain to the extent that hydrophytic vegetation would return if the cropping cease. This assumption is valid for "farmed wetlands" and as such these areas are subject to regulation under Section 404.

> "Prior converted croplands" generally have been subject to such extensive and relatively permanent physical hydrological modifications and alteration of hydrophytic vegetation that the resultant cropland constitutes the "normal circumstances" for purposes of Section 404 jurisdiction.

> If prior converted cropland is abandoned and wetland conditions return, then the area will be subject to regulation under Section 404. An area will be

184 33 C.F.R. § 328.3(b) (emphasis added).

considered abandoned if for five consecutive years there has been no cropping, management or maintenance activities related to agricultural production.

> For those cropped areas that have not been designated "prior converted cropland" or "farmed wetland" by the Soil Conservation Service, the Corps will consult with SCS staff and make appropriate use of SCS data in making a determination of "normal circumstances" for Section 404 purposes.

In a development context, one question that arises is whether land identified as prior converted cropland retains that status after the cessation of farming and the initiating of development activities. That is, is a PCC designation valuable only to a farmer, or does it also inure to the benefit of a developer who has purchased agricultural land for development purposes?

As noted above, RGL 90-7 states that, if prior converted cropland is abandoned and wetland conditions return, then the area will be subject to regulation under Section 404. An area will be considered abandoned if for five consecutive years there has been no cropping, management or maintenance activities related to agricultural production.

The preamble to the Corps' 1993 regulations specifically endorsed the provisions of RGL 90-07. "While the 1987 Manual does not address application of the 'normal circumstances' phrase as it relates to areas in agricultural production, both agencies continue to follow the guidance provided by RGL 90-7, which interprets our regulatory definition of wetlands to exclude PC cropland".[185] The preamble, however, expresses the concept of abandonment in a slightly different way, stating:

> PC cropland which now meets wetland criteria is considered to be abandoned unless: For once in every five years, the area has been used for the production of an agricultural commodity, or the area has been used or will continue to be used for the production of an agricultural commodity in a commonly used rotation with aquaculture, grasses, legumes or pasture production.[186]

There has been some debate as to whether a change in use from agriculture to a non-agricultural use changes the PCC status of the property. The clear answer in the 1993 preamble is "no." The preamble specifically states, "[t]his determination of [Clean Water Act] jurisdiction is made regardless of the types or impacts of the activities that may occur in those areas." Although joint guidance issued by the Corps and NRCS in 2005 discussed the concept of change of use, it does not relate to whether a PCC designation actually expires. Rather, the meaning of a "change in use" in the 2005 joint guidance is simply that the jurisdictional responsibility for wetland delineations shifts from the NRCS to the Corps at that time.

185 58 Fed. Reg. 45,032.
186 *Id.* at 45,034.

As described in *New Hope Power Co. v. Army Corps of Engineers*,[187] in 2009 the Corps began to implement a policy that suggested that PCC did not apply in the event of a change of use. When challenged, the district court held that this policy (known as the "Stockton Rules") was not valid because it had not been subject to a rulemaking procedure. In its opinion the court specifically noted that, prior to the Stockton Rules, "prior converted cropland that was shifted to non-agricultural use was treated as exempt."[188] Given the court's rejection of the Stockton Rules, that situation appears to remain the case today.

Normal Farming Activities

The "normal farming" exemption has been the source of much litigation, and the Corps has often used the recapture provision to determine that a proposal to change a current agricultural use in jurisdiction waters to a different use, such as a residential or retail use, is not exempt from the Section 404 permitting requirements.

In *Borden Ranch Partnership v. U.S. Army Corps of Engineers*,[189] a developer proposed to convert an approximately 8,400-acre ranch into vineyards and orchards, and to subdivide it into smaller parcels for sale. In order to prepare the ground for vineyards and orchards, the developer "deep ripped" the property, which is an agricultural process used to break through restrictive soil layers in order to accommodate deeper root systems. This process disgorges soil that is then dragged behind the "ripper." The developer conducted these activities without a Section 404 permit.

The Corps and EPA argued that these activities required a permit because deep ripping effectively redeposits material and therefore constitutes a discharge of a pollutant, which can be subject to the Clean Water Act. The developer disagreed with this analysis, and further argued that in any event deep ripping is exempt from the "farming exceptions" in Section 404(f)(1). The court concluded that deep ripping can constitute a discharge of pollutant under the Clean Water Act, and thus subject to Section 404 permitting requirements. The court further concluded that the developer's deep ripping activity was governed by the "recapture provision," because converting ranch land to orchards and vineyards is bringing the land "into a use to which it was not previously subject." The court also observed that activities that require "substantial hydrological alterations" require a permit. The court explained, "Although the Corps cannot regulate a farmer who desires 'merely to change from one wetland crop to another,' activities that require 'substantial hydrological alterations' require a permit."[190]

---

187 746 F. Supp. 2d 1272 (2010).

188 *Id.* at 1282.

189 261 F.3d 810 (9th Cir. 2001), aff'd, 537 U.S. 99 (2002).

190 *Id.* at 815–16. See also *Southeast Alaska Conservation v. U.S. Army Corps of Engineers*, 486 F.3d 638 (9th Cir. 2007) (finding that process wastewater from mining operation does not fall within any of the Section 404(f) exemptions).

SUBSTANTIVE STANDARDS FOR ISSUANCE OF A SECTION 404 PERMIT

Section 404 and the regulations identify several standards that must be met before the Corps can issue a Section 404 permit. As discussed in more detail below, these include, for example, a public interest review, where the Corps takes into account the public interest when evaluating whether to issue a permit, and the Section 404(b)(1) Guidelines, which creates certain presumptions that must be overcome in certain circumstances before a Section 404 permit can be issued.

General Policies for Evaluating Corps Permits

The Corps regulations include general policies that apply to applications for Corps Section 404 permits, including both standard permits (i.e., individual permits and letters of permission) and general permits (i.e., Regional General Permits, Programmatic General Permits, and Nationwide Permits). These general policies are set forth in Section 320.4 of the Corps regulations and are described below.

Public Interest Review

The Corps regulations require the Corps to take into account the public interest when evaluating a permit application.[191] More specifically, the Corps' decision whether to issue a permit is based on an evaluation of the probable impacts, including cumulative impacts, of the proposed activity and its intended use on the public interest. This involves a weighing of benefits and detriments associated with issuing the permit: "The benefits which reasonably may be expected to accrue from the proposal must be balanced against its reasonably foreseeable detriments."[192] Factors that are weighed in this balance include conservation, economics, aesthetics, general environmental concerns, wetlands, historic properties, fish and wildlife values, flood hazards, floodplain values, land use, navigation, shore erosion and accretion, recreation, water supply and conservation, water quality, energy needs, safety, food and fiber production, mineral needs, considerations of property ownership and, in general, the needs and welfare of the people.[193]

The Corps applies the following criteria when evaluating applications in the context of the public interest review:

> the relative extent of the public and private need for the proposed structure or work

> where there are unresolved conflicts as to resource use, the practicability of using reasonable alternative locations and methods to accomplish the objective of the proposed structure or work

---

191 33 C.F.R. § 320.4(a).

192 *Id.* § 320.4(a)(1).

193 *Id.*

> the extent and permanence of the beneficial and/or detrimental effects which the proposed structure or work is likely to have on the public and private uses to which the area is suited[194]

LEDPA = Least Environmentally Damaging Practicable Alternative

Although the public interest review infrequently serves as the basis for a permit denial, it can come into play where a project may have satisfied other regulatory tests (e.g., the project is the LEDPA and has offered adequate mitigation) but is unusually controversial for one reason or another. For example, tribal concerns or environmental justice problems can often trigger a negative public interest review where a project is otherwise consistent with the Corps regulations.

Effects on Wetlands in General

Related to the Corps' public interest review, another set of policies the Corps applies to permit applications is the effect on wetlands, and in particular with respect to wetlands that are "considered to perform functions important to the public interest." The Corps regulations suggest that the alteration or destruction of such wetlands should be discouraged as contrary to the public interest. Wetlands considered to perform functions important to the public interest include those that:

> serve significant natural biological functions

> have been set aside for study of the aquatic environment or as sanctuaries or refuges

> would affect detrimentally natural drainage characteristics, sedimentation patterns, salinity distribution, flushing characteristics, current patterns, or other environmental characteristics if the wetlands are destroyed or altered

> are significant in shielding other areas from wave action, erosion, or storm drainage

> serve as valuable storage areas for storm and flood waters

> are ground water discharge areas that maintain minimum baseflows important to aquatic resources and those which are prime natural recharge areas

> serve significant water purification functions

> are unique in nature or scarce in quantity to the region or local area[195]

No permit will be granted which involves the alteration of wetlands that are identified as "important" unless the Corps concludes, based on its public interest review, that the benefits of the proposed alteration outweigh the damage to the wetlands resource.[196]

Although important, these requirements are only one component of the overall impact analyses required to be conducted by the Corps. Additional, more specific standards are discussed below.

194 *Id.* § 320.4(a)(2)(i)–(iii).

195 *Id.* § 320.4(b)(2)(i)–(viii).

196 *Id.* § 320.4(b)(4).

Effects on Other Resources

The Corps regulations include a number of policies related to other natural resources issues, including fish and wildlife consultation requirements under the Fish and Wildlife Coordination Act;[197] certification of compliance with state water quality standards;[198] historic, cultural, scenic, and recreational values;[199] effects on limits of the territorial seas;[200] coastal zones;[201] marine sanctuaries;[202] floodplain management;[203] water supply and conservation;[204] and energy conservation and development.[205] The applicant should consult these policies when preparing a permit application to ensure that all relevant resource policies have been addressed.

Considerations of Property Ownership

Several policies pertain to property ownership and whether the issuance of a permit is itself some kind of property right. Many of these policies are repeated verbatim in a typical individual permit. They include, for example, policies stating that a Corps permit does not convey any property rights, either in real estate or material, or any exclusive privileges; a Corps permit does not authorize any injury to property or invasion of rights or any infringement of federal, state, or local laws or regulations; and an applicant's signature on a permit application is an affirmation that the applicant possesses or will possess the requisite property interest to undertake the activity proposed in the application.[206]

Other Federal, State, or Local Requirements

Because most projects requiring a Corps permit also involve permits from other agencies, including other federal, state, or local governments, the Corps has established policies relevant to those situations. Processing of an application for a Corps permit normally will proceed concurrently with the processing of other required federal, state, and/or local authorizations or certifications. Final action on the Corps permit will normally not be delayed pending action by another federal, state, or local agency. If these other agencies have denied an approval for a project before the Corps has issued its permit, the Corps will take this into account and either immediately deny the Corps permit without prejudice or continue processing the application to a conclusion, in which case the Corps may conclude by either denying the permit as contrary to the

197 *Id.* § 320.4(c).
198 *Id.* § 320.4(d).
199 *Id.* § 320.4(e).
200 *Id.* § 320.4(f).
201 *Id.* § 320.4(h).
202 *Id.* § 320.4(i).
203 *Id.* § 320.4(l).
204 *Id.* § 320.4(m).
205 *Id.* § 320.4(n).
206 *Id.* § 320.4(g)(6).

public interest, or denying it without prejudice indicating that except for the other agency's denial, the Corps permit could under appropriate conditions be approved.[207]

Another policy that may be important for projects involving complicated multi-agency approvals, including approvals from a local government, is the Corps' policy that the primary responsibility for determining zoning and land use matters rests with state, local, and tribal governments. Case law in the Ninth Circuit indicates that in some circumstances the Corps must take into account local land use controls. For example, in *Friends of Santa Clara River v. U.S. Army Corps of Engineers*, the Ninth Circuit explained that the Corps was required to take into consideration the objectives of a local government's Specific Plan for a proposed development.[208] Although this determination was in the context of a "least environmentally damaging practicable alternative" analysis, this rationale should apply to other aspects of the Corps' Section 404 permitting program. This is supported by the Corps regulations, which further indicate that the Corps will normally accept decisions by such governments on those matters unless there are significant issues of overriding national importance. These issues may include, for example, national security, navigation, national economic development, water quality, preservation of special aquatic areas, including wetlands, with significant interstate importance, and national energy needs.[209]

Economics

Economic policies are also identified in the Corps regulations. When the Corps receives an application for a permit from a private party, it is generally assumed that "appropriate economic evaluations have been completed, the proposal is economically viable, and is needed in the market place."[210] The regulations further explain, however, that the Corps "may make an independent review of the need for the project from the perspective of the overall public interest," noting that the "economic benefits of many projects are important to the local community and contribute to needed improvements in the local economic base, affecting such factors as employment, tax revenues, community cohesion, community services, and property values."[211]

THE LEAST ENVIRONMENTALLY DAMAGING PRACTICABLE ALTERNATIVE

One of the most rigorous aspects of the Section 404 permitting program is compliance with the *Section 404(b)(1) Guidelines for Specification of Disposal Sites for Dredged or Fill*

207 *Id.* § 320.4(j)(1). The Corps regulations define "denial without prejudice" in this context to mean that "there is no prejudice to the right of the applicant to reinstate processing of the [Corps permit] application if subsequent approval is received from the appropriate Federal, state and/or local agency on a previously denied authorization and/or certification." *Id.*

208 *Friends of Santa Clara River v. U.S. Army Corps of Engineers*, 887 F.3d 906 (9th Cir. 2018).

209 33 C.F.R. § 320.4(j)(2).

210 *Id.* § 320.4(q).

211 *Id.*

Material. Section 404(b)(1) of the Clean Water Act provides that disposal sites subject to a permit must be specified through the application of guidelines developed by EPA in conjunction with the Corps.[212] These guidelines have been provided as regulations promulgated by EPA and are commonly referred to simply as the "Section 404(b)(1) Guidelines."[213] As discussed in more detail below, the Section 404(b)(1) Guidelines create certain rebuttable presumptions that must be overcome before a Section 404 permit for the fill of wetlands can be issued. The documentation required to rebut those presumptions is often the most time-consuming and costly aspect of the overall processing effort for a Section 404 permit.

The purpose of the Guidelines is to restore and maintain the chemical, physical, and biological integrity of waters of the United States through the control of discharges of dredged or fill material.[214] Fundamental to the Guidelines is the principle that dredged or fill material should not be discharged into the aquatic ecosystem, unless it can be demonstrated that such a discharge will not have an unacceptable adverse impact either individually or in combination with known and/or probable impacts of other activities affecting the ecosystems of concern.[215]

Although the Section 404(b)(1) Guidelines have a number of components discussed further below, the Guidelines' requirement for an evaluation of alternatives to a proposed project are the most significant. This requirement is articulated as follows:

> [N]o discharge of dredged or fill material shall be permitted if there is a practicable alternative to the proposed discharge which would have less adverse impact on the aquatic ecosystem, so long as the alternative does not have other significant adverse environmental consequences.[216]

This requirement is categorical and admits of no exception, and effectively means the applicant must focus its efforts on establishing that there are no "practicable alternatives" as described. Put another way, if such a "practicable alternative" exists to the discharge of fill, then the Section 404 permit application must be denied. As described in the Guidelines, typical alternatives that are considered include (1) activities which do not involve a discharge of dredged or fill material into the waters of the United States; or (2) discharges of dredged or fill material at other locations in waters of the United States.

As a practical matter, a typical Section 404(b)(1) "Alternative Analysis," as they are usually called, consists of both off-site and on-site alternatives that are screened for purposes of this test. Off-site alternatives are typically off-site alternative project sites, meaning project sites other than the proposed project site where the project involving

212 33 U.S.C. § 1344(b)(1).

213 The *Section 404(b)(1) Guidelines for Specification of Disposal Sites for Dredged or Fill Material* can be found in Part 230 of Title 40 of the Code of Federal Regulations.

214 40 C.F.R. § 230.1(a).

215 *Id.* § 230.1(c).

216 *Id.* § 230.10(a).

the discharge of fill or dredged material can be located. For example, these off-site alternatives may include off-site project alternatives elsewhere in the city or county where the proposed project is located. The number of off-site alternatives evaluated in an Alternatives Analysis can vary. Projects that are more amenable to different locations within a geographic region may have 10 to 20 off-site alternatives, for example.

RGL = Regulatory Guidance Letter

On-site alternatives include alternative configurations of the proposed project that reduce impacts to waters of the United States or result in fewer environmental impacts. These alternatives usually include project designs that avoid or minimize the waters of the United States located on the project site, and those designs may require reconfiguration or elimination of project features. Like off-site alternatives, the number of on-site alternatives can vary. Four to six on-site alternatives is typical depending on the proposed project's size and relatively complexity.[217]

Another critical aspect of this requirement is the analytical sequencing it suggests. Based on the sequence of elements, the sequence is:

First, evaluate whether the alternative is practicable, which is a concept described in further detail below, but essentially requires its own sequencing:

(1) Is the alternative available?

(2) Is the alternative capable of being done after taking into consideration cost, existing technology, and logistics in light of overall project purposes?

Second, evaluate whether the alternative would have less adverse impact on the aquatic ecosystem, which is defined in the Section 404(b)(1) Guidelines as "waters of the United States, including wetlands, that serve as habitat for interrelated and interacting communities and populations of plants and animals."

Third, consider whether the alternative has other significant adverse environmental consequences, which may include an analysis of impacts to biological resources, water quality, historic and cultural resources, air quality, and other topics typically considered in a more general environmental analysis. Arguably, indirect effects to the aquatic ecosystem should be evaluated at this stage in the analysis because this analytical process is intended to evaluate a proposal to discharge fill or dredged material into delineated waters of the United States, which typically is viewed as a direct impact.

---

217 Regulatory Guidance Letter ("RGL") No. 93-02 regarding "Guidance on Flexibility of the 404(b)(1) Guidelines and Mitigation Banking" explains that although the Guidelines are binding regulations, they are inherently flexible, as described in the preamble to the Guidelines. This RGL states: "The Guidelines do not contemplate the same intensity of analysis will be required for all types of projects but instead envision a correlation between the scope of the evaluation and the potential extent of adverse impacts on the aquatic environment." (RGL No. 93-02 (Aug. 2, 1993).) For projects with minor impacts in particular, the RGL notes:

> Although sufficient information must be developed to determine whether the proposed activity is in the [sic] fact the least damaging practicable alternative, the Guidelines do not require an elaborate search for practicable alternatives if it is reasonably anticipated that there are only minor differences between the environmental impacts of the proposed activity and potentially practicable alternatives.

Id.

This sequencing can be important because it allows for alternatives to be "screened" out of further analysis at an earlier point in the process, making an Alternatives Analysis more efficient.

With respect to practicability, an alternative is practicable if it is available and capable of being done after taking into consideration cost, existing technology, and logistics in light of overall project purposes. If it is otherwise a practicable alternative, an area not presently owned by the applicant which could reasonably be obtained, utilized, expanded or managed in order to fulfill the basic purpose of the proposed activity may be considered.[218]

Critically important for this overall assessment are the following requirements, which create the two rebuttable presumptions that must be addressed in the Alternatives Analysis, evaluating whether the proposed activity is the least environmentally damaging practicable alternative (LEDPA) under the Section 404(b)(1) Guidelines.

> Where the activity associated with a discharge which is proposed for a special aquatic site . . . does not require access or proximity to or siting within the special aquatic site in question to fulfill its basic purpose (i.e., is not "water dependent"), practicable alternatives that do not involve special aquatic sites are presumed to be available, unless clearly demonstrated otherwise.[219]

> In addition, where a discharge is proposed for a special aquatic site, all practicable alternatives to the proposed discharge which do not involve a discharge into a special aquatic site are presumed to have less adverse impact on the aquatic ecosystem, unless clearly demonstrated otherwise.[220]

As to the first presumption, the Ninth Circuit has put the issue succinctly: "When the Corps recognizes that a project is not water dependent, considers a range of alternative sites for the project, and concludes that there are no practicable alternative sites available, the presumption is rebutted. [The court] then defer[s] to the Corps's approval of an alternative."[221]

The other element of the Guidelines critical for this analysis is the definition of "practicable."

> [P]racticable alternatives include, but are not limited to: (i) Activities which do not involve a discharge of dredged or fill material into the waters of the United States or ocean waters; (ii) Discharges of dredged or fill

---

218 40 C.F.R. § 230.10(a)(2).

219 *Id.* § 230.10(a)(3).

220 *Id.*

221 *Friends of Santa Clara River*, 887 F.3d at 912 (citing *Bering Strait Citizens for Responsible Res. Dev. v. U.S. Army Corps of Eng'rs*, 524 F.3d 938, 947 (9th Cir. 2008); see also *Butte Envtl. Council v. U.S. Army Corps of Eng'rs*, 620 F.3d 936, 945 (9th Cir. 2010) (stating that "the Corps applied the proper presumption and found that it had been rebutted" because "the Corps acknowledged that the proposed project was not water dependent").

material at other locations in waters of the United States or ocean waters.[222] [¶] An alternative is practicable if it is available and capable of being done after taking into consideration cost, existing technology, and logistics in light of overall project purposes.[223]

Another key element of the analysis is the determination of whether the discharge will result in the significant degradation of the waters of the United States:

> [N]o discharge of dredged or fill material shall be permitted which will cause or contribute to significant degradation of the waters of the United States. Findings of significant degradation related to the proposed discharge shall be based upon appropriate factual determinations, evaluations, and tests . . . , with special emphasis on the persistence and permanence of the effects . . . .

Factors the Corps considers when evaluating whether a discharge will result in a significant degradation of waters of the United States include significant adverse effects of the discharge of pollutants on human health or welfare, life stages of aquatic life and other wildlife dependent on aquatic ecosystems, aquatic ecosystem diversity, productivity, and stability, and recreational, aesthetic, and economic values.[224] The Guidelines require that the analysis of whether a discharge will result in a significant degradation of waters of the United States must occur after the Corps considers the potential impacts on physical and chemical characteristics of the aquatic ecosystem, potential impacts on biological characteristics of the aquatic ecosystem, potential impacts on special aquatic sites, and potential effects on human use characteristics. As part of that consideration, the Corps must place "special emphasis on the persistence and permanence" of these effects.[225]

Discussed in more detail below, a substantial body of case law has developed over the years interpreting many of the elements that comprise a Section 404(b)(1) Alternatives Analysis.

Basic Project Purpose

A project's basic purpose is typically associated with the question of whether the project is water-dependent, that is, whether the project requires "access or proximity to or siting within the special aquatic site in question to fulfill its basic purpose."[226] "Classification of an activity as 'non-water-dependent' does not serve as an automatic bar to issuance of a permit . . . . [It] simply necessitates a more persuasive showing than otherwise

---

222 40 C.F.R. § 230.10(a)(1).

223 *Id.* § 230.10(a)(2).

224 *Id.* § 230.10(c).

225 *Id.*

226 *Id.* § 230.10(a)(3). Note that "special aquatic sites" includes sanctuaries and refuges, wetlands, mud flats, vegetated shallows, coral reefs, and riffle and pool complexes, as those terms are defined in Subpart E of 40 C.F.R. Pt. 230.

concerning the lack of alternatives."[227] If a project is not a water-dependent activity, the Corps regulations presume that practicable alternatives are available "unless clearly demonstrated otherwise."[228] An alternative site does not have to accommodate components of a project that are merely incidental to the applicant's basic purpose.[229] In *Friends of the Earth v. Hintz*,[230] the Ninth Circuit Court of Appeal interpreted water dependency in the context of a project that involved a log storage facility on mudflats adjacent to a harbor. Because the log storage facility was tied to an exporting facility and formed an integrated complex, the court upheld the Corps' conclusion that the log storage facility was a water-dependent activity.

The Ninth Circuit has described the ways in which a basic project purpose differs from the overall project purpose. In *Friends of Santa Clara River v. U.S. Army Corps of Engineers*, the court explained that a project's "basic purpose (for determining water dependency) is distinct from the overall purpose (for determining practicable alternatives)."[231] The court further explained: "When a project's basic purpose is not water-dependent, practicable alternatives that do not involve special aquatic sites are presumed to be available, unless clearly demonstrated otherwise."[232]

The Corps issued an important "elevation decision" regarding this issue for a project proposed by Plantation Landing Resort, Inc.[233] In this decision, Corps Headquarters concluded that the alternatives analysis for Plantation Landing Resort, Inc.'s proposal incorrectly applied the "basic purpose" concept. This proposal included a "fully-integrated, waterfront, contiguous water-oriented recreational complex," in effect suggesting that the entire recreational resort complex was "water-dependent."[234] Corps Headquarters rejected this approach, finding that the "basic purpose of

---

227 *Louisiana Wildlife Fed'n, Inc. v. York*, 603 F. Supp. 518, 527 (W.D. La 1984), aff'd in part and vacated in part, 761 F.2d 1044 (5th Cir. 1985).

228 *Sylvester v. U.S. Army Corps of Engineers*, 882 F.2d 407 (9th Cir. 1989) (citing 40 C.F.R. § 230.10(a)(3)); see also *Friends of Santa Clara River v. U.S. Army Corps of Eng'rs*, 887 F.3d 906 (9th Cir. 2018) ("[C]lassification of an activity as 'non-water-dependent' does not serve as an automatic bar to issuance of a permit ... [it] simply necessitates a more persuasive showing than otherwise concerning the lack of alternatives.") (citing *Sylvester*, 882 F.3d at 409); *Utahns for Better Transp. v. U.S. Dep't of Transp.*, 305 F.3d 1152, 1163 (10th Cir. 2002) ("The presumption for a non-water-dependent project that a practicable alternative exists is not an automatic bar on issuance of a permit, but it does require that an applicant make a persuasive showing concerning the lack of alternatives."); *Northwest Envtl. Defense Ctr. v. Wood*, 947 F. Supp. 1371, 1376 (D. Or. 1996) ("When the proposed project is not water-dependent, the guidelines place the burden on the applicant to 'clearly demonstrate[]' that there are no practicable, less damaging sites.").

229 *Id.* at 409. The Ninth Circuit in *Sylvester* cites *Shoreline Assocs. v. Marsh*, 555 F. Supp. 169 (D.Md 1983), aff'd, 725 F.2d 677 (4th Cir. 1984), a case in which the Corps refused to issue a permit to a developer for building a number of waterfront town houses together with a boat storage and launching facility. The developer argued that the Corps' proposed alternative site for the town houses could not accommodate the boat storage and launch area. The court upheld the Corps' denial of the permit, observing that the boat facilities were merely "incidental" to the town house development.

230 800 F.2d 822 (9th Cir. 1986).

231 887 F.3d at 912 (quoting *Del. Riverkeeper Network v. U.S. Army Corps of Eng'rs*, 869 F.3d 148, 157 (3d Cir. 2017)).

232 *Id.* (citing 40 C.F.R. § 230.10(a)(3)).

233 U.S. Army Corps of Engineers, Director of Civil Works, Memorandum Regarding Permit Elevation, Plantation Landing Resort, Inc. (Apr. 21, 1989)).

234 *Id.* at 10.

each component element of the [proposal] must be analyzed in terms of its actual, non-water-dependent function. The basic purpose of the condominium housing [for the proposal] is housing (i.e., shelter); the basic purpose of the restaurant [for the proposal] is to feed people; etc." Activities such as these "do not gain the status of water-dependent activities merely because the applicant proposes to 'integrate' them with a marina, or proposes to build them on a piece of land contiguous to a marina, or proposes that any of these non-water-dependent facilities should be 'waterfront' or built on waterfront land." Corps Headquarters concluded that, "The concepts of 'integration', 'contiguity', and 'waterfront' must not be used to defeat the purpose of the 'water dependency' and 'practicable alternatives' provisions of the Guidelines, nor to preclude the existence of practicable alternatives."[235]

Based on this analysis, the Corps established an informal process for evaluating these kinds of proposals:

> First, determine whether each component part of the project is water-dependent or not in light of that component's *basic* purpose . . . . Second, for component parts of the project which are not water-dependent, a presumption arises that an alternative, upland site is available. The applicant may be able to rebut that presumption with clear and convincing evidence. Closely related to this inquiry is the question whether the non-water-dependent components of the project actually must be integrated with or contiguous to the water-dependent part(s) in such a manner as to necessitate their location in a special aquatic site. Once again, a presumption exists that the non-water-dependent components of the project do not have to be contiguous to or integrated with water-dependent parts . . . to be practicable (e.g., economically viable). As stated before, the applicant may be able to rebut the presumption with clear and convincing evidence. Only if the applicant rebuts these presumptions can the Corps conclude that some (or all) of the non-water-dependent components of the overall project pass the tests of 40 C.F.R. 230.10(a)(3).[236]

Overall Project Purpose

The Corps defines a practicable alternative as an alternative that "is available and capable of being done after taking into consideration cost, existing technology, and logistics in light of *overall project purposes*."[237] As such, the overall project purpose is critical because it essentially frames up the alternatives evaluated in an Alternatives Analysis.

235 *Id.* at 10–11.

236 *Id.* at 12.

237 40 C.F.R. § 230.10(a)(2) (emphasis added).

The Corps has a duty to consider the applicant's purpose where that purpose is "genuine and legitimate."[238] However, an applicant cannot define a project in order to preclude the existence of any alternative sites and thus make what is practicable appear impracticable.[239] In *Sylvester v. U.S. Army Corps of Engineers*, a case involving the fill of wetlands for a golf course that was to be part of a larger resort, opponents challenged the project on the basis that the project's overall purpose of constructing a golf course was too narrow and impermissibly skewed the alternatives analysis in favor of the project proponent. The Ninth Circuit held that while a project's purpose must be legitimate, the Corps properly considered alternatives to the golf course instead of the entire resort.[240]

In *Friends of Santa Clara River v. U.S. Army Corps of Engineers*, the Ninth Circuit acknowledged provisions in the Corps regulations regarding local land use controls and their application to an applicant's overall project purpose. The court explained that in determining the overall project purposes, the Corps will "normally accept decisions" by state, local, and tribal governments with respect to "zoning and land use matters," unless "there are significant issues of overriding national importance."[241] The court also acknowledged other provisions specifying that when the Corps approves or undertakes projects requiring the discharge of material into the waters of the United States, it must consider "officially adopted state, regional, or local land use classifications, determinations, or policies."[242] Based on these provisions and principles, the court rejected a plaintiff's argument that the Corps may not incorporate an applicant's project objectives or local use land objectives. The court found that "the Corps not only may, but must, consider [the applicant's] project objectives, provided that those project objectives are not so narrowly defined as to preclude alternatives, and must also consider the [local jurisdictions] Specific Plan objectives."[243]

Availability

Availability of an alternative is one of the elements of practicability under the Section 404(b)(1) Guidelines. An important case interpreting availability of alternatives is *Bersani v. Robichaud.*[244] In *Bersani*, a developer proposed a shopping mall project on wetlands in Massachusetts. EPA vetoed the approval (see discussion below regarding EPA's Section 404(c) veto authority) by the Corps of a permit to build the mall because

---

238 *Friends of Santa Clara Rivers*, 887 F.3d at 912; *Butte Envtl. Council v. U.S. Army Corps of Eng'rs*, 620 F.3d 936, 946 (9th Cir. 2010); *Sylvester v. U.S. Army Corps of Eng's*, 882 F.2d 407 (9th Cir. 1989) (quoting *Louisiana Wildlife Fed'n, Inc. v. York*, 761 F.2d 1044, 1048 (5th Cir. 1985) ("[I]t would be bizarre if the Corps were to ignore the purpose for which the applicant seeks a permit and to substitute a purpose it deems more suitable.")).

239 *Sylvester v. U.S. Army Corps of Eng'rs*, 882 F.2d 407 (9th Cir. 1989). See also *Northwest Envtl. Defense Ctr. v. Wood*, 947 F. Supp. 1371 (D. Or. 1996) (upholding an "overall project purpose" based on an applicant's "legitimate economic reasons" for constructing a project in certain a location).

240 *Sylvester*, 882 F.2d at 409.

241 *Friends of Santa Clara River*, 887 F.3d at 912 (citing 33 C.F.R. § 320.4(j)(2)).

242 *Id.* (citing 33 C.F.R. § 336.1(c)(11)(ii)).

243 *Id.* at 921 (citation omitted).

244 850 F.2d 36 (2nd Cir. 1988).

EPA found that an alternative site had been available to the developer at the time it entered the market to search for a site for the mall. The alternative site was purchased later by another developer and therefore arguably became unavailable by the time the original developer applied for a permit to build the mall. The developer argued that an alternative site's availability should be evaluated at the time of permit application, rather than at the time it enters the market. The Second Circuit Court of Appeals agreed with EPA and its "market entry theory," and held that availability must be evaluated at the time the applicant enters the market.

RGL = Regulatory Guidance Letter

The Second Circuit's analysis and conclusions related to the "market entry" approach to availability did not require as a matter of law that applicants use this approach to determining an alternative's availability. The court in *Bersani* was simply upholding EPA's use of this approach in that particular context. In the authors' view, the agencies often seek to use the approach taken in *Bersani*, and in most instances, that approach is overbroad and unnecessary. The better and more reasoned approach is to examine only those practicable alternatives that were available at the time of the permit review. A significant amount of time may pass between the time an applicant enters the market and the time the applicant applies for a permit. Developers and project proponents often "enter" the market early on to preliminarily gauge the economic climate for a particular project. In some instances, they may explore options, but based on economic conditions, such as those that occurred during the economic recession of 2008, they may hold out before committing themselves to the permit processes.

Consideration of Cost

The Corps must take into account an applicant's costs when evaluating an alternative's practicability. The Guidelines do not further elaborate on how the cost consideration is to be applied, but they do specify that an area not presently owned by the applicant which could reasonably be obtained, utilized, expanded or managed in order to fulfill the basic purpose of the proposed activity may be considered.[245] In addition, the Corps issued a Regulatory Guidance Letter (RGL) in 1993 explaining that the preamble to the Guidelines provides clarification on how costs are to be considered in determining practicability: "The term economic [for which the term 'cost' was substituted in the final rule] might be construed to include consideration of the applicant's financial standing, or investment, or market share, a cumbersome inquiry which is not necessarily material to the objectives of the Guidelines."[246] The RGL further explains,

> The determination of what constitutes an unreasonable expense should generally consider whether the projected cost is substantially greater than the costs normally associated with the particular type of project .... To the extent the Corps obtains information on the costs associated with the

245 40 C.F.R. § 230.10(a)(2).

246 Regulatory Guidance Letter No. 93-2 (Aug. 23, 1993), "Guidance on Flexibility of the 404(b)(1) Guidelines and Mitigation Banking".

project, such information may be considered when making a determination of what constitutes an unreasonable expense . . . . It is important to emphasize, however, that it is not a particular applicant's financial standing that is the primary consideration for determining practicability, but rather characteristics of the project and what constitutes a reasonable expense for these projects that are most relevant to practicability determinations.[247]

Some courts have interpreted the role costs play in a Section 404(b)(1) Alternatives Analysis. In *Friends of the Earth v. Hintz*, the court upheld the Corps' consideration of additional costs burdening a facility based on service fees, storage, overhead and inefficiency.[248] In *Sierra Club v. Van Antwerp*, the D.C. Circuit Court of Appeals upheld an applicant's cost analysis on a number of bases.[249] First, the court ruled that an applicant may use a site's fair market value as its cost instead of a lower out-of-pocket cost because opportunity costs (the value the owner could realize by a current sale) is a form of cost that can be used to test practicability.[250] Second, the court noted under the Corps regulations that the cost of an alternative project site would presumably be that site's market value.[251] Third, the court determined that the Guidelines can sensibly mean the cost of proceeding with the project as planned, and for this, the relevant measure of the developer's land cost is what it foregoes by proceeding (rather than selling the land and realizing its market value).[252] Fourth, whereas use of opportunity cost minimizes subjective, applicant-specific factors, reliance on the developer's acquisition cost would create the odd possibility that an alternative practicable for one applicant would be impracticable for another.[253] Finally, the use of out-of-pocket costs would create an anomaly: "an applicant with a low acquisition cost could resell the site at market value and thereby enable a successor developer to refute practicability claims that had been fatal for the seller."[254] Accordingly, the court deferred to the Corps' decision "to use the land's market value, rather than the developer's acquisition cost."[255]

In *Friends of Santa Clara River v. U.S. Army Corps of Eng'rs*, the court upheld the Corps' determination involving a large-scale specific plan project that it would be impracticably expensive for the project to adopt an alternative involving further

---

247 *Id.* § 3(b).

248 800 F.2d 822, 833 (9th Cir. 1986). In *Friends of the Earth*, the court upheld the Corps' determination that two alternatives for a proposed log storage facility were not practicable based on costs, noting that the applicant would have incurred additional costs of $1,785,700 per year for one alternative and $1,000,000 per year for another alternative.

249 661 F.3d 1147 (D.C. Cir. 2011).

250 *Id.* at 1151.

251 *Id.*

252 *Id.*

253 *Id.*

254 *Id.*

255 *Id.* The court also evaluated arguments raised by project opponents that the Corps impermissibly accepted the applicant's contentions that an eight percent rate of return was necessary to secure financing and that the planned project configuration was the only way to achieve that return. The court upheld the Corps' use of this rate of return in light of the fact that the record contained several reports justifying this rate. *Id.* at 1152.

avoidance and minimization of impacts to waters of the United States than the selected alternative. The court explained:

> The Corps's determination was reasonably based on its findings that [the alternative] would be more expensive than any previous comparable development project in southern California, and would also exceed the average and median costs for such projects by at least 56 percent. The alternative was 5.7 percent more costly than [the applicant's] preferred alternative, and significantly shrank the Project's footprint. The Corps's decision that [the alternative] was at the outer limit of cost practicability was thus based on a 'rational connection between facts found and the conclusion' made and [the court] defer[red] to its determination . . . .[256]

Other aspects of the court's decision in *Friends of Santa Clara River* regarding the consideration of costs in the Section 404(b)(1) Alternatives Analysis for the project at issue in this case are instructive. Many of the cost issues raised in this case are issues of first impression, and for that reason the court's discussion is quoted at length below.

> [Plaintiff] further criticizes three different aspects of the Corps's cost methodology. It claims that: (1) the Corps should have considered costs on a per-residential unit or per-commercial floor space basis rather than a per-acre basis; (2) the Corps was required to consider the Project's revenues; and (3) the Corps should have excluded land acquisition costs because those costs are sunk costs. We disagree. The Section 404(b) Guidelines do not require the Corps to use any particular metric for analyzing costs; rather, they merely instruct the Corps to assess alternatives in light of their "cost, existing technology, and logistics." Therefore, so long as the Corps's evaluation of costs is reasonable, we must defer to it. Here, the Corps adopted a reasonable methodology for calculating and evaluating costs, and therefore it is entitled to deference.
>
> The Corps's evaluation of costs on a per-acre basis was reasonable. As the Corps explained, [the applicant] intended to sell developable land by the acre, rather than developing the land itself and selling units or floor space. Accordingly, the Corps could reasonably conclude that determining [the applicant's] costs per acre made more sense than speculating about the type and density of units that might ultimately be built on that land. The Corps also noted that the per-acre cost metric was "more widely used in the industry."
>
> The Corps also reasonably declined to consider revenues as part of an alternative's costs. The regulations direct the Corps to assess practicability based on "cost, existing technology, and logistics." "Cost" means an

---

256 *Friends of Santa Clara River*, 887 F.3d at 922.

"expenditure or outlay," and does not include "revenues," which are items of income. Although revenues are not part of "costs," the Corps nevertheless stated that it took revenues into account "by looking at how each alternative affects developable acreage, which is the source of revenue for the project." Given the close relationship between the developable acreage resulting from the Project and revenues to [the applicant], the Corps did not fail to consider an important aspect of the problem.

Finally, the Corps did not err by including the acquisition costs of the property proposed for the Project site. The Section 404(b) Guidelines do not require a specified treatment of land acquisition costs, so we defer to the Corps's judgment unless its decision was arbitrary or capricious. Here, the Corps reasonably included the acquisition costs as part of its determination of whether an alternative is practicable. Because [the applicant] is investing (or contributing) its valuable site to the Project, the costs of the Project include the value of the property. Accordingly, the exclusion of the value of the property would have led to inaccurate comparisons between the costs for the [applicant's] project and the costs for comparable projects, which would require property acquisition. Indeed, the Corps would have arguably "entirely failed to consider an important aspect of the problem" had the Corps excluded land costs in its practicability analysis rather than included it.[257]

In practice, economic analyses used for cost considerations in an Alternatives Analysis often begin with a definition of the market area based on the nature and characteristics of a particular project. The next step is to identify financial or economic measures to evaluate the project and its alternatives. These measures can include, for example, a project's cost burden (comparing a project's basic infrastructure costs to its overall market value or revenue), residual land value (evaluating whether the project generates value that would be equal to or greater than the current price of land for a comparable project in a particular market after taking into account all the project's costs, impact fees, and infrastructure requirements), market absorption (whether there is enough market demand for a project to sell within an acceptable time frame that is sufficient enough to generate an acceptable financial return to carry the developer's investment in infrastructure and other project costs that typically occur up front), and fiscal impact (whether the project will generate annual revenues such as sales tax, property tax, etc.) to the local government to pay for the required annual (on-going) public services (such as police and fire) and other public benefits.

257 *Id.* at 922–23.

Consideration of Existing Technology

The Corps must take into account an alternative's technological constraints. Very little case law currently exists regarding this consideration. One court has found that an alternative to a water supply project involving desalinization was not a viable alternative because it was still experimental.[258]

Consideration of Existing Logistics

The Corps must also take into account an alternative's logistical constraints. As with existing technology, very little case law currently exists regarding consideration of existing logistics. One court has suggested that impracticable distances between an alternative site and a facility served by a proposed activity is a legitimate logistic consideration.[259] With respect to projects involving Section 408 requests, the Corp will not consider an alternative to be practible if Section 408 permission cannot be granted. "However, the need to seek a Section 408 permission does not make an alternative impracticable."[260]

SIGNIFICANT DEGRADATION DETERMINATION

The Section 404(b)(1) Guidelines specify that "no discharge of dredged or fill material shall be permitted which will cause or contribute to significant degradation of the waters of the United States."[261] The Guidelines require that a finding of significant degradation must be based on certain factual determinations, evaluations, and tests required under the Guidelines, with special emphasis on the persistence and permanence of the effects outlined in those portions of the Guidelines. According to the Guidelines, effects contributing to significant degradation considered individually or collectively include significantly adverse effects of the discharge on human health or welfare; life stages of aquatic life and other wildlife dependent on aquatic ecosystems; aquatic ecosystem diversity, productivity, and stability; and recreational, aesthetic, and economic values.[262]

In *Bering Strait Citizens v. U.S. Army Corps of Engineers*,[263] the Ninth Circuit Court of Appeal considered a challenge against a project raising claims related to the Corps' significant degradation determination. The project involved two open-pit gold mines, resulting in over 15,000,000 cubic yards of fill placed in 346.5 acres of wetlands. Project opponents argued that the Corps did not properly consider whether the project would "cause or contribute to significant degradation of the waters of the United States." The court held that the Corps acted properly, noting that the Corps correctly considered a

258 *James City County v. United States Environmental Protection Agency*, 955 F.2d 254, 260 (4th Cir. 1992).

259 *Friends of the Earth*, 800 F.2d at 833.

260 Army Corps of Engineering Circular (EC) 1165-2-220 (Sept. 10, 2018) at p. D-6.

261 40 C.F.R. § 230.10(c).

262 *Id.* §§ (c)(1), (c)(2), (c)(3).

263 524 F.3d 938 (9th Cir. 2008).

variety of impacts from the project and determined that the impacts would be localized or limited in time. The court also found persuasive the Corps' determination that the wetland that would be filled during the project are not unique to the site, and thus likely would have no impact on the greater ecosystem beyond the project site.

FACTUAL DETERMINATIONS UNDER THE GUIDELINES

The Section 404(b)(1) Guidelines include an entire section regarding factual determinations that the Corps must make related to the potential short-term and long-term effects of a proposed discharge of dredged or fill material on the physical, chemical, and biological components of the aquatic environment. Notably, these determinations should focus on the effects of the discharge of dredged or fill material, rather than the project that may occur as a result of that discharge. These factual determinations are used in making findings of compliance or non-compliance with the restrictions on discharge. Although the Corps is responsible for making these determinations at the conclusion of the permitting process, applicants should be prepared to provide any needed information required by the Corps to make these determinations. The determinations of effects of each proposed discharge must include the following analyses:

Physical Substrate Determinations

The Corps must determine the nature and degree of effect that the proposed discharge will have, individually and cumulatively, on the characteristics of the substrate at the proposed disposal site. The Corps must consider the similarity in particle size, shape, and degree of compaction of the material proposed for discharge and the material constituting the substrate at the disposal site, and any potential changes in substrate elevation and bottom contours, including changes outside of the disposal site which may occur as a result of erosion, slumpage, or other movement of the discharged material. The duration and physical extent of substrate changes must also be considered. The possible loss of environmental values and actions to minimize impact must also be considered in making these determinations. Potential changes in substrate elevation and bottom contours must be predicted on the basis of the proposed method, volume, location, and rate of discharge, as well as on the individual and combined effects of current patterns, water circulation, wind and wave action, and other physical factors that may affect the movement of the discharged material.[264]

Water Circulation, Fluctuation, and Salinity Determinations

The Corps must determine the nature and degree of effect that the proposed discharge will have individually and cumulatively on water, current patterns, circulation including downstream flows, and normal water fluctuation. The Corps must consider water chemistry, salinity, clarity, color, odor, taste, dissolved gas levels, temperature, nutrients, and eutrophication plus other appropriate characteristics. The Corps also must consider the

---

264 40 C.F.R. § 230.11(a).

potential diversion or obstruction of flow, alterations of bottom contours, or other sig-nificant changes in the hydrologic regime. Additional consideration of the possible loss of environmental values and actions to minimize impacts must be used in making these determinations. Potential significant effects on the current patterns, water circulation, normal water fluctuation and salinity must be evaluated on the basis of the proposed method, volume, location, and rate of discharge.[265]

Suspended Particulate/Turbidity Determinations

The Corps must determine the nature and degree of effect that the proposed discharge will have, individually and cumulatively, in terms of potential changes in the kinds and concentrations of suspended particulate/turbidity in the vicinity of the disposal site. The Corps must consider the grain size of the material proposed for discharge, the shape and size of the plume of suspended particulates, the duration of the discharge and result-ing plume and whether or not the potential changes will cause violations of applicable water quality standards. The Corps also must consider the possible loss of environmen-tal values and to actions for minimizing impacts. Consideration must include the pro-posed method, volume, location, and rate of discharge, as well as the individual and combined effects of current patterns, water circulation and fluctuations, wind and wave action, and other physical factors on the movement of suspended particulates.[266]

Contaminant Determinations

The Corps must determine the degree to which the material proposed for discharge will introduce, relocate, or increase contaminants. This determination must consider the material to be discharged, the aquatic environment at the proposed disposal site, and the availability of contaminants.[267]

Aquatic Ecosystem and Organism Determinations

The Corps must determine the nature and degree of effect that the proposed discharge will have, both individually and cumulatively, on the structure and function of the aquatic ecosystem and organisms. The Corps must consider the effect at the proposed disposal site of potential changes in substrate characteristics and elevation, water or sub-strate chemistry, nutrients, currents, circulation, fluctuation, and salinity, on the recolo-nization and existence of indigenous aquatic organisms or communities. Possible loss of environmental values and actions to minimize impacts must be examined. Tests may be required to provide information on the effect of the discharge material on communities or populations of organisms expected to be exposed to it.[268]

265 *Id.* § 230.11(b).
266 *Id.* § 230.11(c).
267 *Id.* § 230.11(d).
268 *Id.* § 230.11(e).

Proposed Disposal Site Determinations

Each disposal site must be specified through the application of the Section 404(b)(1) Guidelines. The mixing zone must be confined to the smallest practicable zone within each specified disposal site that is consistent with the type of dispersion determined to be appropriate by the application of the Section 404(b)(1) Guidelines. In a few special cases under unique environmental conditions, where there is adequate justification to show that widespread dispersion by natural means will result in no significantly adverse environmental effects, the discharged material may be intended to be spread naturally in a very thin layer over a large area of the substrate rather than be contained within the disposal site.[269]

Determination of Cumulative Effects on the Aquatic Ecosystem

As described in the Section 404(b)(1) Guidelines, cumulative impacts are the changes in an aquatic ecosystem that are attributable to the collective effect of a number of individual discharges of dredged or fill material. Although the impact of a particular discharge may constitute a minor change in itself, the cumulative effect of numerous such piecemeal changes can result in a major impairment of the water resources and interfere with the productivity and water quality of existing aquatic ecosystems.[270]

The Section 404(b)(1) Guidelines require that the cumulative effects attributable to the discharge of dredged or fill material in waters of the United States should be predicted to the extent reasonable and practical. The Corps must collect information and solicit information from other sources about the cumulative impacts on the aquatic ecosystem. This information must be documented and considered during the decision-making process concerning the evaluation of individual permit applications, the issuance of a general permit, and monitoring and enforcement of existing permits.[271]

Determination of Secondary Effects on the Aquatic Ecosystem

The Section 404(b)(1) Guidelines describe secondary effects as effects on an aquatic ecosystem that are associated with a discharge of dredged or fill materials, but do not result from the actual placement of the dredged or fill material. Information about secondary effects on aquatic ecosystems must be considered prior to the time final Section 404 action is taken by the Corps. Some examples of secondary effects on an aquatic ecosystem are fluctuating water levels in an impoundment and downstream associated with the operation of a dam, septic tank leaching and surface runoff from residential or commercial developments on fill, and leachate and runoff from a sanitary landfill located in waters of the United States. Activities to be conducted on fast land created by the discharge of dredged or fill material in waters of the United States may have secondary

269 *Id.* § 230.11(f).
270 *Id.* § 230.11(g)(1).
271 *Id.* § 230.11(g)(2).

impacts within those waters which should be considered in evaluating the impact of creating those fast lands.[272]

Mitigation Rule = Compensatory Mitigation for Losses of Aquatic Resources Rule

MITIGATION UNDER SECTION 404

One of the most important national policies driving mitigation requirements under Section 404 is the "no net loss" policy established during the George H.W. Bush Administration. In 1990, President George H.W. Bush signed an executive order that amended Executive Order 11990 signed by President Carter. The "no net loss" policy is intended to ensure that impacts to wetlands are mitigated such that no net loss of wetlands result.

A critical aspect of the Section 404 permitting process is the mitigation necessary to offset impacts associated with the fill of jurisdictional waters and to satisfy the Corps' "no net loss" policy. In the authors' experience, it is important to manage and understand the mitigation obligations imposed on a project because implementation of those obligations may make a project subject to onerous and potentially crippling economic costs.

The Section 404 Regulations include a comprehensive set of provisions and requirements that govern compensatory mitigation for losses of aquatic resources. The Corps and EPA established these provisions in 2008 after a significant rulemaking effort that culminated in the Compensatory Mitigation for Losses of Aquatic Resources Rule ("Mitigation Rule").[273] The Mitigation Rule applies to permits issued pursuant to Section 404 of the Clean Water Act and Sections 9 and 10 of the Rivers and Harbors Act of 1899.

Background and Sequence

Compensatory mitigation involves actions taken to offset unavoidable adverse impacts to wetlands, streams and other aquatic resources authorized by a Clean Water Act permit. As described in the preamble to the Mitigation Rule, the agencies view compensatory mitigation as a "critical tool" in helping the federal government meet the "no net loss" goal for wetland acreage and function.[274]

The agencies have long taken the position that mitigation for a project's impacts pursuant to Section 404 must follow a sequence: first, impacts must be avoided; second, to the extent those impacts cannot be avoided, they must be minimized; and third, any impacts that remain after avoidance and minimization must be compensated. The preamble to the Mitigation Rule explains this sequencing approach to mitigation. "For impacts authorized under [S]ection 404, compensatory mitigation is not considered

---

272 *Id.* § 230.11(h).

273 73 Fed. Reg. 19,594 (Apr. 10, 2008); 33 C.F.R. Pt. 332; 40 C.F.R. Pt. 230, Subpt. J. In January 2015, the Corps' South Pacific Division (whose jurisdiction includes California and other western states) issued its *Regional Compensatory Mitigation and Monitoring Guidelines* to supplement the Mitigation Rule for projects within the South Pacific Division.

274 73 Fed. Reg. 19,594.

until after all appropriate and practicable steps have been taken to first avoid and then minimize adverse impacts to the aquatic ecosystem . . . ."[275] As required in the Mitigation Rule, the Corps will issue a Section 404 permit "only upon a determination that . . . the permit applicant [will] take all appropriate and practicable steps to avoid and minimize adverse impacts to waters of the United States . . . . Compensatory mitigation for unavoidable impacts may be required to ensure that an activity requiring a section 404 permit complies with the Section 404(b)(1) Guidelines."[276]

In general, the required compensatory mitigation should be located within the same watershed as the impact site, and should be located where it is most likely to successfully replace lost functions and services, taking into account such watershed scale features as aquatic habitat diversity, habitat connectivity, relationships to hydrologic sources (including the availability of water rights), trends in land use, ecological benefits, and compatibility with adjacent land uses.

The preamble to the Mitigation Rule provides background that is essential to understanding the agencies' requirements for compensatory mitigation. As the preamble explains, compensatory mitigation can be carried out through four methods: (1) the *restoration* of a previously existing wetland or other aquatic site; (2) the *enhancement* of an existing aquatic site's functions; (3) the *establishment* (i.e., creation) of a new aquatic site; or (4) the *preservation* of an existing aquatic site.

There are three mechanisms for providing compensatory mitigation: (1) permittee-responsible compensatory mitigation; (2) mitigation banks; and (3) in-lieu fee mitigation. The preamble to the Mitigation Rule summarizes the characteristics of each of these mechanisms. According to the preamble, permittee-responsible is the most traditional form of compensation and represents the majority of compensation acreage provided. As its name implies, the permittee retains responsibility for ensuring that required compensation activities are completed and successful. Permittee-responsible mitigation can be located at or adjacent to the impact site (i.e., on-site compensatory mitigation) or at another location generally within the same watershed as the impact site (i.e., off-site compensatory mitigation).

Mitigation banks and in-lieu fee mitigation both involve off-site compensation activities generally conducted by a third-party, a mitigation bank sponsor or in-lieu fee program sponsor. When a permittee's compensatory mitigation requirements are satisfied by a mitigation bank or in-lieu fee program, responsibility for ensuring that required compensation is completed and successful shifts from the permittee to the bank or in-lieu fee sponsor. Mitigation banks and in-lieu fee programs both conduct consolidated aquatic resources restoration, enhancement, establishment and preservation projects.

---

275 *Id.*
276 33 C.F.R. § 332.1(c)(2).

The regulations establish a hierarchy of preference for compensatory mitigation projects.[277] In order of preference, this hierarchy is (1) mitigation bank credits; (2) in-lieu fee program credits; (3) permittee-responsible mitigation under a watershed approach; (4) permittee-responsible mitigation through on-site and in-kind mitigation; (5) permittee-responsible mitigation through off-site and/or out-of-kind mitigation.

Because of the important role permittee-responsible mitigation plays in the Section 404 permit process, this chapter focuses on this form of compensatory mitigation. For more information regarding mitigation banks and in-lieu fee programs, see Chapter 11.

Definition and Use of Permittee-Responsible Mitigation

The regulations define "permittee-responsible mitigation" as "an aquatic resource restoration, establishment, enhancement, and/or preservation activity undertaken by the permittee (or an authorized agent or contractor) to provide compensatory mitigation for which the permittee retains full responsibility."[278]

The regulations require that in general, compensatory mitigation requirements must be commensurate with the amount and type of impact that is associated with a particular Corps permit. Permit applicants are responsible for proposing an appropriate compensatory mitigation option to offset unavoidable impacts.[279] Compensatory mitigation may be performed using the methods of restoration, enhancement, establishment, and in certain circumstances preservation. According to the regulations, restoration should generally be the first option considered because the likelihood of success is greater and the impacts to potentially ecologically important uplands are reduced compared to establishment, and the potential gains in terms of aquatic resource functions are greater, compared to enhancement and preservation.[280]

As described above, the Corps has established a hierarchical preference for types of compensatory mitigation. Permittee-responsible mitigation approaches are last in the order of preference, and the regulations establish three different scenarios in which permit-responsible mitigation can be used. In order of preference, those scenarios are as follows:

Permittee-Responsible Mitigation under a Watershed Approach

Where permitted impacts are not in the service area of an approved mitigation bank or in-lieu fee program that has the appropriate number and resource type of credits available, permittee-responsible mitigation is the only option. Where practicable and likely to be successful and sustainable, the resource type and location for the required

---

277 *Id.* § 332.3(b)(1) ("When considering options for successfully providing the required compensatory mitigation, the [Corps] shall consider the type and location options in the order presented in paragraphs (b)(2) through (b)(6) of this section.").

278 *Id.* § 332.2.

279 *Id.* § 332.3(a)(1).

280 *Id.* § 332.3(a)(2).

Creek before mitigation. Photo: Lindsay Teunis.

Creek three years after mitigation. Photo: Photo: Lindsay Teunis.

Creek five years after mitigation. Photo: Photo: Lindsay Teunis.

permittee-responsible compensatory mitigation should be determined using the principles of a watershed approach.[281]

Permittee-Responsible Mitigation through On-site and In-Kind Mitigation

In cases where a watershed approach is not practicable, the Corps should consider opportunities to offset anticipated aquatic resource impacts by requiring on-site and in-kind compensatory mitigation. The Corps must also consider the practicability of on-site compensatory mitigation and its compatibility with the proposed project.[282]

Permittee-Responsible Mitigation through Off-site and/or Out-of-Kind Mitigation

If, after considering opportunities for on-site, in-kind compensatory mitigation, the Corps determines that these compensatory mitigation opportunities are not practicable, are unlikely to compensate for permitted impacts, or will be incompatible with the proposed project, and an alternative, practicable off-site and/or out-of-kind mitigation opportunity is identified that has a greater likelihood of offsetting the permitting impacts or is environmentally preferable to on-site or in-kind mitigation, the Corps should require that this alternative compensatory mitigation be provided.[283]

Other Important Considerations for Compensatory Mitigation

An important element of the Corps' compensatory mitigation requirement is its watershed approach. The Corps must use a watershed approach to establish compensatory mitigation requirements in Corps permits to the extent appropriate and practicable. The ultimate goal of a watershed approach is to maintain and improve the quality and quantity of aquatic resources within watersheds through strategic selection of compensatory mitigation sites.[284]

As described in the regulations, a watershed approach to compensatory mitigation considers the importance of landscape position and resource type of compensatory mitigation projects for the sustainability of aquatic resource functions within the watershed. Such an approach considers how the types and locations of compensatory mitigation projects will provide the desired aquatic resource functions, and will continue to function over time in a changing landscape. It also considers the habitat requirements of important species, habitat loss or conversion trends, sources of watershed impairment, and current development trends, as well as the requirements of other regulatory and non-regulatory programs that affect the watershed, such as storm water management or habitat conservation programs. It includes the protection and maintenance of terrestrial resources, such as non-wetland riparian areas and uplands,

281 *Id.* § 332.3(b)(4).
282 *Id.* § 332.3(b)(5).
283 *Id.* § 332.3(b)(6).
284 *Id.* § 332.3(c)(1).

when those resources contribute to or improve the overall ecological functioning of aquatic resources in the watershed.[285]

Locational factors (e.g., hydrology, surrounding land use) are important to the success of compensatory mitigation for impacted habitat functions and may lead to siting of such mitigation away from the project area. However, the regulations require that consideration should also be given to functions and services (e.g., water quality, flood control, shoreline protection) that will likely need to be addressed at or near the areas impacted by the permitted impacts.[286] A watershed approach should also include, to the extent practicable, inventories of historic and existing aquatic resources, including identification of degraded aquatic resources, and identification of immediate and long-term aquatic resource needs within watersheds that can be met through permittee-responsible mitigation projects, mitigation banks, or in-lieu fee programs. The regulations also specify that planning efforts should identify and prioritize aquatic resource restoration, establishment, and enhancement activities, and preservation of existing aquatic resources that are important for maintaining or improving ecological functions of the watershed.[287]

Site selection is an important aspect of the compensatory mitigation requirements. According to the regulations, the compensatory mitigation project site must be ecologically suitable for providing the desired aquatic resource functions. In determining the ecological suitability of the compensatory mitigation project site, the Corps must consider, to the extent practicable, the following factors:

> hydrological conditions, soil characteristics, and other physical and chemical characteristics

> watershed-scale features, such as aquatic habitat diversity, habitat connectivity, and other landscape scale functions

> the size and location of the compensatory mitigation site relative to hydrologic sources (including the availability of water rights) and other ecological features

> compatibility with adjacent land uses and watershed management plans

> reasonably foreseeable effects the compensatory mitigation project will have on ecologically important aquatic or terrestrial resources (e.g., shallow sub-tidal habitat, mature forests), cultural sites, or habitat for federally or state-listed threatened and endangered species

> other relevant factors including, but not limited to, development trends, anticipated land use changes, habitat status and trends, the relative locations of the impact and mitigation sites in the stream network, local or regional goals for the restoration or protection of particular habitat types or functions (e.g., re-establishment of habitat corridors or habitat for species of concern), water quality

---

285 *Id.* § 332.3(c)(2)(i).

286 *Id.* § 332.3(c)(2)(ii).

287 *Id.* § 332.3(c)(2)(iv).

goals, floodplain management goals, and the relative potential for chemical contamination of the aquatic resources[288]

The Corps may require on-site, off-site, or a combination of on-site and off-site compensatory mitigation to replace permitted losses of aquatic resource functions and services.[289]Applicants should propose compensation sites adjacent to existing aquatic resources or where aquatic resources previously existed.[290]

The regulations also discuss mitigation types and the Corps' preference as to which type of compensatory mitigation should be used. In general, in-kind mitigation is preferable to out-of-kind mitigation because it is most likely to compensate for the functions and services lost at the impact site. For example, tidal wetland compensatory mitigation projects are most likely to compensate for unavoidable impacts to tidal wetlands, while perennial stream compensatory mitigation projects are most likely to compensate for unavoidable impacts to perennial streams. Thus, typically the required compensatory mitigation must be of a similar type to the affected aquatic resource.[291]

If the Corps determines using a watershed approach that out-of-kind compensatory mitigation will serve the aquatic resource needs of the watershed, the district engineer may authorize the use of such out-of-kind compensatory mitigation. The basis for authorization of out-of-kind compensatory mitigation must be documented in the administrative record for the permit action.[292]

If further avoidance and minimization is not practicable for difficult-to-replace resources (e.g., bogs, fens, springs, streams), the required compensation should be provided, if practicable, through in-kind rehabilitation, enhancement, or preservation since there is greater certainty that these methods of compensation will successfully offset permitted impacts.[293]

The regulations also specify considerations related to the amount of compensatory mitigation. If the Corps determines that compensatory mitigation is necessary to offset unavoidable impacts to aquatic resources, the amount of required compensatory mitigation must be, to the extent practicable, sufficient to replace lost aquatic resource functions. In cases where appropriate functional or condition assessment methods or other suitable metrics are available, these methods should be used where practicable to determine how much compensatory mitigation is required. If a functional or condition assessment or other suitable metric is not used, a minimum one-to-one acreage or linear foot compensation ratio must be used.[294]

---

288 *Id.* § 332.3(d)(1)(i)–(vi).

289 *Id.* § 332.3(d)(2).

290 *Id.* § 332.3(d)(3).

291 *Id.* § 332.3(e)(1).

292 *Id.* § 332.3(e)(2).

293 *Id.* § 332.3(e)(3).

294 *Id.* § 332.3(f)(1).

The Corps must require a mitigation ratio greater than one-to-one where necessary to account for the method of compensatory mitigation (e.g., preservation), the likelihood of success, differences between the functions lost at the impact site and the functions expected to be produced by the compensatory mitigation project, temporal losses of aquatic resource functions, the difficulty of restoring or establishing the desired aquatic resource type and functions, and/or the distance between the affected aquatic resource and the compensation site. The rationale for the required replacement ratio must be documented in the administrative record for the permit action.[295]

Use of Preservation to Provide Compensatory Mitigation

An important aspect of the Corps compensatory mitigation requirements is the use of preservation. As discussed above, preservation is the least preferred of the compensatory mitigation methods typically accepted by the Corps. Often, however, preservation can be an essential component of an applicant's overall mitigation proposal.

According to the regulations, preservation may be used to provide compensatory mitigation for activities authorized by Corps permits when all the following criteria are met:

> the resources to be preserved provide important physical, chemical, or biological functions for the watershed

> the resources to be preserved contribute significantly to the ecological sustainability of the watershed. In determining the contribution of those resources to the ecological sustainability of the watershed, the Corps must use appropriate quantitative assessment tools, where available.

> preservation is determined by the Corps to be appropriate and practicable

> the resources are under threat of destruction or adverse modifications

> the preserved site will be permanently protected through an appropriate real estate or other legal instrument (e.g., easement, title transfer to state resource agency or land trust)[296]

Where preservation is used to provide compensatory mitigation, to the extent appropriate and practicable the preservation must be done in conjunction with aquatic resource restoration, establishment, and/or enhancement activities. This requirement may be waived by the Corps where preservation has been identified as a high priority using a watershed approach, but compensation ratios must be higher.[297] In addition, the Corps may require the restoration, establishment, enhancement, and preservation, as well as the maintenance, of riparian areas and/or buffers around aquatic resources where necessary to ensure the long-term viability of those resources. Buffers may also provide

---

295 *Id.* § 332.3(f)(2). If an in-lieu fee program will be used to provide the required compensatory mitigation, and the appropriate number and resource type of released credits are not available, the district engineer must require sufficient compensation to account for the risk and uncertainty associated with in-lieu fee projects that have not been implemented before the permitted impacts have occurred. *Id.* § 332.3(f)(3).

296 *Id.* § 332.3(h)(1)(i)–(v).

297 *Id.* § 332.3(h)(2).

habitat or corridors necessary for the ecological functioning of aquatic resources. If buffers are required by the Corps as part of the compensatory mitigation project, compensatory mitigation credit will be provided for those buffers.[298]

Compensatory Mitigation Specified in Permit Conditions

The regulations specify certain requirements related to conditions that must be included in a permit if compensatory mitigation is used. According to the regulations, the compensatory mitigation requirements for a permit, including the amount and type of compensatory mitigation, must be clearly stated in the special conditions of the individual permit or general permit verification. The special conditions must be enforceable.[299]

For an individual permit that requires permittee-responsible mitigation, the special conditions must:

> identify the party responsible for providing the compensatory mitigation

> incorporate, by reference, the final mitigation plan approved by the district engineer

> state the objectives, performance standards, and monitoring required for the compensatory mitigation project, unless they are provided in the approved final mitigation plan

> describe any required financial assurances or long-term management provisions for the compensatory mitigation project, unless they are specified in the approved final mitigation plan[300]

For a general permit activity that requires permittee-responsible compensatory mitigation, the special conditions must describe the compensatory mitigation proposal, which may be either conceptual or detailed. The general permit verification must also include a special condition that states that the permittee cannot commence work in waters of the United States until the district engineer approves the final mitigation plan, unless the district engineer determines that such a special condition is not practicable and not necessary to ensure timely completion of the required compensatory mitigation. To the extent appropriate and practicable, special conditions of the general permit verification should also address the requirements discussed above.[301]

---

298 *Id.* § 332.3(h)(2)(i).

299 *Id.* § 332.3(k)(1).

300 *Id.* § 332.3(k)(2)(i)–(iv).

301 *Id.* § 332.3(k)(3). If a mitigation bank or in-lieu fee program is used to provide the required compensatory mitigation, the special conditions must indicate whether a mitigation bank or in-lieu fee program will be used, and specify the number and resource type of credits the permittee is required to secure. In the case of an individual permit, the special condition must also identify the specific mitigation bank or in-lieu fee program that will be used. For general permit verifications, the special conditions may either identify the specific mitigation bank or in-lieu fee program, or state that the specific mitigation bank or in-lieu fee program used to provide the required compensatory mitigation must be approved by the district engineer before the credits are secured. *Id.* § 332.3(k)(4).

Other Administrative Considerations

The regulations provide a handful of other administrative items that should be taken into consideration when proposing compensatory mitigation. Below is a discussion of those administrative items, particularly as they pertain to permittee-responsible mitigation.

Party Responsible for Compensatory Mitigation

For permittee-responsible mitigation, the special conditions of the permit must clearly indicate the party or parties responsible for the implementation, performance, and long-term management of the compensatory mitigation project.[302]

Timing

Implementation of the compensatory mitigation project must be, to the maximum extent practicable, in advance of or concurrent with the activity causing the authorized impacts. The Corps must require, to the extent appropriate and practicable, additional compensatory mitigation to offset temporal losses of aquatic functions that will result from the permitted activity.[303]

Financial Assurances

The Corps must require sufficient financial assurances to ensure a high level of confidence that the compensatory mitigation project will be successfully completed, in accordance with applicable performance standards. In cases where an alternate mechanism is available to ensure a high level of confidence that the compensatory mitigation will be provided and maintained (e.g., a formal, documented commitment from a government agency or public authority) the Corps may determine that financial assurances are not necessary for that compensatory mitigation project.[304]

The amount of the required financial assurances must be determined by the Corps, in consultation with the project sponsor, and must be based on the size and complexity of the compensatory mitigation project, the degree of completion of the project at the time of project approval, the likelihood of success, the past performance of the project sponsor, and any other factors the Corps deems appropriate. Financial assurances may be in the form of performance bonds, escrow accounts, casualty insurance, letters of credit, legislative appropriations for government sponsored projects, or other appropriate instruments, subject to the approval of the Corps. The rationale for determining the amount of the required financial assurances must be documented in the administrative record for either the permit or the instrument. In determining the assurance amount, the Corps must consider the cost of providing replacement mitigation, including costs for land acquisition, planning and engineering, legal fees, mobilization, construction, and

---

302 *Id.* § 332.3(l)(1).

303 *Id.* § 332.3(l)(2).

304 *Id.* § 332.3(n)(1).

monitoring.[305] If financial assurances are required, the permit must include a special condition requiring the financial assurances to be in place prior to commencing the permitted activity.[306]

Financial assurances must be phased out once the compensatory mitigation project has been determined by the Corps to be successful in accordance with its performance standards. The permit or instrument must clearly specify the conditions under which the financial assurances are to be released to the permittee, sponsor, and/or other financial assurance provider, including, as appropriate, linkage to achievement of performance standards, adaptive management, or compliance with special conditions.[307]

A financial assurance must be in a form that ensures that the Corps will receive notification at least 120 days in advance of any termination or revocation. For third-party assurance providers, this may take the form of a contractual requirement for the assurance provider to notify the Corps at least 120 days before the assurance is revoked or terminated.[308] Financial assurances must be payable at the direction of the Corps or to a standby trust agreement. When a standby trust is used (e.g., with performance bonds or letters of credit) all amounts paid by the financial assurance provider must be deposited directly into the standby trust fund for distribution by the trustee in accordance with the Corps' instructions.[309]

Compliance with Applicable Law

The compensatory mitigation project must comply with all applicable federal, state, and local laws. The Corps permit must not require participation by the Corps or any other federal agency in project management, including receipt or management of financial assurances or long-term financing mechanisms, except as determined by the Corps or other agency to be consistent with its statutory authority, mission, and priorities.[310]

Compensatory Mitigation Planning and Documentation[311]

The regulations provide detailed instructions on the planning and documentation for compensatory mitigation. The summary below focuses on the use of permittee-responsible mitigation.

---

305 *Id.* § 332.3(n)(2).

306 *Id.* § 332.3(n)(3).

307 *Id.* § 332.3(n)(4).

308 *Id.* § 332.3(n)(5).

309 *Id.* § 332.3(n)(6).

310 *Id.* § 332.3(o).

311 For additional information regarding compensatory mitigation planning and documentation, the Corps' Regulatory Program's website provides several helpful documents and guidance materials. See https://www.usace.army.mil/Missions/Civil-Works/Regulatory-Program-and-Permits/mitig_info/.

As an initial matter, potential applicants for standard permits are encouraged to participate in pre-application meetings with the Corps and appropriate agencies to discuss potential mitigation requirements and information needs.[312]

The regulations require the preparation of a mitigation plan. For individual permits, the permittee must prepare a draft mitigation plan and submit it to the Corps for review. After addressing any comments provided by the Corps, the permittee must prepare a final mitigation plan, which must be approved by the Corps prior to issuing the individual permit. The approved final mitigation plan must be incorporated into the individual permit by reference.[313] For general permits, if compensatory mitigation is required, the district engineer may approve a conceptual or detailed compensatory mitigation plan to meet required time frames for general permit verifications, but a final mitigation plan, at a level of detail commensurate with the scale and scope of the impacts, must be approved by the Corps before the permittee commences work in waters of the United States.[314]

The mitigation plan typically includes the following elements:[315]

Objectives. A description of the resource type(s) and amount(s) that will be provided, the method of compensation (i.e., restoration, establishment, enhancement, and/or preservation), and the manner in which the resource functions of the compensatory mitigation project will address the needs of the watershed, ecoregion, physiographic province, or other geographic area of interest.

Site selection. A description of the factors considered during the site selection process. This should include consideration of watershed needs, on-site alternatives where applicable, and the practicability of accomplishing ecologically self-sustaining aquatic resource restoration, establishment, enhancement, and/or preservation at the compensatory mitigation project site.

Site protection instrument. A description of the legal arrangements and instrument, including site ownership, that will be used to ensure the long-term protection of the compensatory mitigation project site.

Baseline information. A description of the ecological characteristics of the proposed compensatory mitigation project site and, in the case of an application for a permit, the impact site. This may include descriptions of historic and existing plant communities, historic and existing hydrology, soil conditions, a map showing the locations of the impact and mitigation site(s) or the geographic coordinates for those site(s), and other site characteristics appropriate to the type of resource proposed as compensation. The baseline information should also include a delineation of waters of the United States on the proposed compensatory mitigation project site. A prospective permittee planning to secure credits from an approved mitigation bank or in-lieu fee program only

312 33 C.F.R. § 332.4(a).
313 33 C.F.R. § 332.4(c)(1)(i).
314 *Id.* § 332.4(c)(1)(ii).
315 *Id.* § 332.4(c)(2)–(14).

needs to provide baseline information about the impact site, not the mitigation bank or in-lieu fee project site.

Determination of credits. A description of the number of credits to be provided, including a brief explanation of the rationale for this determination. For permittee-responsible mitigation, this should include an explanation of how the compensatory mitigation project will provide the required compensation for unavoidable impacts to aquatic resources resulting from the permitted activity. For permittees intending to secure credits from an approved mitigation bank or in-lieu fee program, it should include the number and resource type of credits to be secured and how these were determined.

Mitigation work plan. Detailed written specifications and work descriptions for the compensatory mitigation project, including, but not limited to, the geographic boundaries of the project; construction methods, timing, and sequence; source(s) of water, including connections to existing waters and uplands; methods for establishing the desired plant community; plans to control invasive plant species; the proposed grading plan, including elevations and slopes of the substrate; soil management; and erosion control measures. For stream compensatory mitigation projects, the mitigation work plan may also include other relevant information, such as planform geometry, channel form (e.g., typical channel cross-sections), watershed size, design discharge, and riparian area plantings.

Maintenance plan. A description and schedule of maintenance requirements to ensure the continued viability of the resource once initial construction is completed.

Performance standards. Ecologically based standards that will be used to determine whether the compensatory mitigation project is achieving its objectives. Performance standards should relate to the objectives of the compensatory mitigation project, so that the project can be objectively evaluated to determine if it is developing into the desired resource type, providing the expected functions, and attaining any other applicable metrics (e.g., acres).[316] In addition, performance standards must be based on attributes that are objective and verifiable. Ecological performance standards must be based on the best available science that can be measured or assessed in a practicable manner. Performance standards may be based on variables or measures of functional capacity described in functional assessment methodologies, measurements of hydrology or other aquatic resource characteristics, and/or comparisons to reference aquatic resources of similar type and landscape position.[317]

Monitoring requirements. A description of parameters to be monitored in order to determine if the compensatory mitigation project is on track to meet performance standards and if adaptive management is needed. A schedule for monitoring and reporting on monitoring results to the district engineer must be included.[318]

---

316 *Id.* § 332.5(a).

317 *Id.* § 332.5(b).

318 For other requirements related to monitoring, see *id.* § 332.6.

Long-term management plan. A description of how the compensatory mitigation project will be managed after performance standards have been achieved to ensure the long-term sustainability of the resource, including long-term financing mechanisms and the party responsible for long-term management.[319]

Adaptive management plan. A management strategy to address unforeseen changes in site conditions or other components of the compensatory mitigation project, including the party or parties responsible for implementing adaptive management measures. The adaptive management plan will guide decisions for revising compensatory mitigation plans and implementing measures to address both foreseeable and unforeseen circumstances that adversely affect compensatory mitigation success.[320]

Financial assurances. A description of financial assurances that will be provided and how they are sufficient to ensure a high level of confidence that the compensatory mitigation project will be successfully completed, in accordance with its performance standards.

Other information. The Corps may require additional information as necessary to determine the appropriateness, feasibility, and practicability of the compensatory mitigation project.

TYPES OF PERMITS AND AUTHORIZATIONS

The Corps regulations provide for a variety of permit types. Most common among these is the "Individual Permit," which is a permit for a specific proposed activity. The Corps may also issue a type of "non-permit" for a specific activity or group of activities, which authorization is referred to as a "Letter of Permission." In addition, the Corps is authorized to issue various types of general permits applicable to broader classes of activities, either on a nationwide or regional basis.

These permits and the way they operate are described in this section. Because the procedural requirements for individual permits are more complicated, however, they are discussed in a separate section further below.

Letters of Permission

A letter of permission is a type of permit issued through an abbreviated process which includes coordination with federal and state fish and wildlife agencies, as required by the Fish and Wildlife Coordination Act, and a public interest evaluation, but without the publishing of an individual public notice.[321] A letter of permission identifies the permittee, the authorized work and location of the work, the statutory authority, any limitations on the work, a construction time limit and a requirement for a report of completed

---

319 For other requirements related to management, see *id.* §§ 332.6(a) and 332.6(d).

320 For other requirements related to adaptive management, see *id.* § 332.6(c).

321 *Id.* § 325.2(e)(1).

work. A copy of the relevant general conditions from ENG Form 1721 must be attached and incorporated by reference into the letter of permission.[322]

A letter of permission may be used in those cases subject to Section 10 of the Rivers and Harbors Act of 1899 when, in the opinion of the district engineer, the proposed work would be minor, would not have significant individual or cumulative impacts on environmental values, and should encounter no appreciable opposition. A letter of permission may be used in those cases subject to Section 404 of the Clean Water Act after all of the following have occurred:

> the district engineer, through consultation with federal and state fish and wildlife agencies, the regional administrator, Environmental Protection Agency, the state water quality certifying agency, and, if appropriate, the state Coastal Zone Management Agency, develops a list of categories of activities proposed for authorization under letter of permission procedures

> the district engineer issues a public notice advertising the proposed list and the letter of permission procedures, requesting comments and offering an opportunity for public hearing

> a Section 401 water quality certification has been issued or waived and, if appropriate, coastal zone management consistency concurrence obtained or presumed either on a generic or individual basis[323]

Letters of permission may not be used to authorize the transportation of dredged material for the purpose of dumping it in ocean waters.

The Corps Districts in California have established letter of permission procedures. For example, as revised on September 16, 2013, the Sacramento District implements a letter of permission procedure intended to more efficiently authorize activities with minor impacts on the aquatic environment which involve discharges of dredged or fill materials into waters of the United States under Section 404 of the Clean Water Act and/or work or structures in navigable waters under Section 10 of the Rivers and Harbors Act. This "Minor Impact" letter of permission is an optional abbreviated permit process available to all applicants for permits for activities meeting certain criteria and conditions. Specifically, to qualify for a letter of permission under this procedure activities must meet the following criteria: (1) the loss of waters of the United States does not exceed one acre or 500 linear feet of streambed or bank, and; (2) the loss of waters of the United States is compensated for at a minimum ratio of 2:1 for permittee-responsible mitigation or through an in-lieu fee program and/or the loss of waters of the United States is compensated for at a minimum ratio of 1:1 at a Corps-approved mitigation bank. For projects meeting these criteria, the project must satisfy a number of conditions related to, for example, navigation, aquatic life movements, spawning areas,

322 *Id.* § 325.5(b)(2).
323 *Id.* § 325.2(e)(1)(ii)(A)–(C).

migratory bird breeding areas, fills within 100-year floodplains, soil erosion and sediment controls, endangered species, and mitigation.[324]

RGP = regional general permit

General Permits

The Corps regulations provide for three kinds of general permits: Regional General Permits, Programmatic General Permits, and Nationwide Permits.[325]

Regional General Permits

Regional general permits are a type of general permit. They may be issued by a division or district engineer after compliance with the other procedures of the Corps regulations. After a regional permit has been issued, individual activities falling within those categories that are authorized by such regional permits do not have to be further authorized by the procedures of the Corps regulations. The issuing authority will determine appropriate conditions to protect the public interest. When the issuing authority determines on a case-by-case basis that the concerns for the aquatic environment so indicate, he or she may exercise discretionary authority to override the regional permit and require an individual application and review. A regional permit may be revoked by the issuing authority if it is determined that it is contrary to the public interest provided that the Corps regulations governing the modification, suspension, or revocation of permits are followed. Following revocation, applications for future activities in areas covered by the regional permit must be processed as applications for individual permits. The Corps regulations specify that no regional permit may be issued for a period of more than five years.[326]

Regional general permits typically cover routine or maintenance-type activities. For example, the Corps' Los Angeles District has issued Regional General Permit (RGP) 63, which provides a rapid response to requests for emergency work in waters of the United States. This RGP is restricted to situations of imminent threat to life or property. Los Angeles District RGP 54 authorizes small-scale maintenance dredging, structural repairs and in-kind structural replacement activities throughout portions of Newport Bay, located in the City of Newport Beach.[327]

Similarly, the Corps' San Francisco District has issued several RGPs, primarily for infrastructure construction and maintenance. For example, San Francisco District RGP 5 authorizes discharges of dredged or fill material into waters of the United States for necessary repair and protection measures associated with an emergency situation. San Francisco District RGP 4 is specific to public vector control agencies and authorizes the maintenance (but not construction) of currently serviceable water

---

324 For more information regarding the Sacramento District's Letter of Permission Procedure, see the District's Public Notice issued March 1, 2010 (revised September 16, 2013) regarding Minor Impact Letter of Permission Procedure (Action ID: 200901291).

325 See also 33 C.F.R. § 323.2(h).

326 *Id.* § 325.2(e)(2); *id.* § 325.5(c)(1).

327 For a current list of Los Angeles District RGPs, visit the District's website at http://www.spl.usace.army.mil/Missions/Regulatory/Regional-General-Permits/.

DWR = California Department
of Water Resources

PGP = Programmatic General
Permit

NWP = Nationwide Permit

NEPA = National Environmental
Policy Act

EA = Environmental
Assessment

PCN = pre-construction
notification

circulation ditches, sidecasting of fill incidental to the removal of debris, weeds, and emergent vegetation in natural channels where normal water circulation is impeded such that mosquito breeding can occur, and filling of existing, nonfunctional water circulation ditches to the extent necessary to achieve the required water circulation dynamics and restore ditched wetlands.[328]

The Corps' Sacramento District also has issued a number of similar types of RGPs. For example, Sacramento District RGP 5 streamlines the authorization for the repair of small erosion sites along levees maintained by the California Department of Water Resources (DWR) within the Sacramento River Flood Control Project and allows DWR to conduct work in waters of the United States associated with activities necessary to repair erosion damages to levees in a timely fashion to prevent further damages and avoid associated public safety risks and environmental impacts. Sacramento District RGP 14 provides a simple and expeditious means of providing Section 404 authorization for the construction of certain backbone infrastructure within the Placer Vineyards Specific Plan, which is comprised of improvements to existing roadways and intersections, new major roadways, and other infrastructure. This RGP is specifically designed to ensure that (1) construction occurs in a coordinated manner; (2) impacts to aquatic resources will be avoided, minimized, and compensated to the Corps' standards; and (3) no more than minimal individual or cumulative impacts will occur as a result of such activities.[329]

Programmatic General Permits

Programmatic general permits (PGPs) are a type of general permit based on an existing state, local or other federal agency program and designed to avoid duplication with that program.[330] Programmatic general permits are similar to regional permits and are typically administered by the Corps in much the same fashion. For example, Sacramento District PGP 10 authorizes minimal impact activities permitted in conjunction with the State of Utah's stream alteration program.[331]

Nationwide Permits

Nationwide permits (NWPs) are a type of general permit issued by the Corps. They represent Corps authorizations that have been issued for certain specified activities nationwide. If certain conditions are met, the specified activities can take place without the need for an individual or regional permit.[332] They are designed to regulate with little, if any, delay or paperwork certain activities having minimal impacts. The NWPs are

---

328 For a current list of San Francisco District RGPs, visit the District's website at http://www.spn.usace.army.mil/Missions/Regulatory/Regulatory-Overview/Regional-General-Permits/.

329 For a current list of Sacramento District RGPs, visit the District's website at http://www.spk.usace.army.mil/Missions/Regulatory/Permitting/Regional-and-Programmatic-General-Permits/.

330 33 C.F.R. § 325.5(c)(3).

331 PGPs can be found on the District websites provided above.

332 33 C.F.R. § 325.5(c)(2).

proposed, issued, modified, reissued (extended), and revoked from time to time after an opportunity for public notice and comment. Proposed NWPs or modifications to or reissuance of existing NWPs may be adopted only after the Corps gives notice and allows the public an opportunity to comment on and request a public hearing regarding the proposals. The Corps is required to give full consideration to all comments received prior to reaching a final decision.[333]

As part of the NWP proposal, issuance, modification, or reissuance process, the Corps complies with the National Environmental Policy Act (NEPA) by preparing a decision document for each NWP. Each decision document contains an Environmental Assessment (EA), to fulfill the requirements of NEPA. The EAs include the public interest review described in the Corps regulations at 33 C.F.R. Section 320.4(b), and they generally discuss the anticipated impacts the NWP will have on the human environment and the Corps' public interest review factors. If a proposed NWP authorizes discharges of dredged or fill material into waters of the United States, the decision document also includes an analysis conducted pursuant to Section 404(b)(1) of the Clean Water Act. Generally, before the NWPs go into effect, division engineers will issue supplemental decision documents to evaluate environmental effects on a regional basis (e.g., a state or Corps district) and to determine whether regional conditions are necessary to ensure that the NWPs will result in no more than minimal individual and cumulative adverse environmental effects on a regional basis.[334] In this way, the Corps has complied with NEPA as part of the NWP process, and therefore no further NEPA clearance is necessary when an applicant seeks coverage under an NWP.

An activity is authorized under an NWP only if that activity and the permittee satisfy all of the NWP's terms and conditions. Activities that do not qualify for authorization under an NWP still may be authorized by an individual or regional general permit. The Corps will consider unauthorized any activity requiring Corps authorization if that activity is under construction or completed and does not comply with all of the terms and conditions of an NWP, regional general permit, or an individual permit.[335]

As of the 2017 reauthorization of the Nationwide Permit Program, the Corps has authorized the NWPs shown in the table on the following page.[336]

The process for obtaining an NWP depends on the NWP being used. In most cases, permittees may proceed with activities authorized by NWPs without notifying the Corps. However, the prospective permittee should carefully review the language of the NWP to ascertain whether he or she must notify the Corps prior to commencing the authorized activity. For NWPs requiring advance notification, such notification must be

As compared to processing an individual permit, using a Nationwide Permit can be far less time-consuming and costly for a project proponent. Typical Nationwide Permits used by developers include NWP 18 for Minor Discharges, which authorizes fill of no more than 1/10-acre of waters of the United States; NWP 29 for Residential Developments, which authorizes discharges into waters of the United States for the construction or expansion of a single residence, a multiple unit residential development, or a residential subdivision, so long as the discharge does not result in the loss of greater than ½-acre of waters of the United States; and NWP 39 for Commercial and Institutional Developments, which authorizes discharges into waters of the United States for the construction or expansion of commercial and institutional building foundations and building pads and attendant features that are necessary for the use and maintenance of the structures, so long as the discharge does not result in the loss of greater than ½-acre of non-tidal waters of the United States.

333 *Id.* § 330.1(b).

334 For more discussion regarding the Corps' compliance with NEPA during the NWP process, see, for example, the Federal Register notice regarding the 2017 reissuance of the NWPS. (82 Fed. Reg. 1860, 1866 (Jan. 6, 2017)).

335 33 C.F.R. § 330.1(c).

336 Available at http://saw-reg.usace.army.mil/NWP2017/Summary_Final_2017NWPs_1-2017.pdf.

NATIONWIDE PERMITS

#	ACTIVITY	#	ACTIVITY
1	Aids to Navigation	28	Modifications of Existing Marinas
2	Structures in Artificial Canals	29	Residential Developments
3	Maintenance	30	Moist Soil Management for Wildlife
4	Fish and Wildlife Harvesting, Enhancement, and Attraction Devices and Activities	31	Maintenance of Existing Flood Control Facilities
5	Scientific Measurement Devices	32	Completed Enforcement Actions
6	Survey Activities	33	Temporary Construction, Access, and Dewatering
7	Outfall Structures and Associated Intake Structures	34	Cranberry Production Activities
8	Oil and Gas Structures on the Outer Continental Shelf	35	Maintenance Dredging of Existing Basins
9	Structures in Fleeting and Anchorage Areas	36	Boat Ramps
10	Mooring Buoys	37	Emergency Watershed Protection and Rehabilitation
11	Temporary Recreational Structures	38	Cleanup of Hazardous and Toxic Waste
12	Utility Line Activities	39	Commercial and Institutional Developments
13	Bank Stabilization	40	Agricultural Activities
14	Linear Transportation Projects	41	Reshaping Existing Drainage Ditches
15	U.S. Coast Guard Approved Bridges	42	Recreational Facilities
16	Return Water From Upland Contained Disposal Areas	43	Storm Water Management Facilities
17	Hydropower Projects	44	Mining Activities
18	Minor Discharges	45	Repair of Uplands Damaged by Discrete Events
19	Minor Dredging	46	Discharges in Ditches
20	Response Operations for Oil or Hazardous Substances	47	[reserved]
21	Surface Coal Mining Activities	48	Existing Commercial Shellfish Aquaculture Activities
22	Removal of Vessels	49	Coal Remining Activities
23	Approved Categorical Exclusions	50	Underground Coal Mining Activities
24	Indian Tribe or State Administered Section 404 Program	51	Land-Based Renewable Energy Generation Facilities
25	Structural Discharges	52	Water-Based Renewable Energy Generation Pilot Projects
26	[reserved]	53	Removal of Low-Head Dams
27	Aquatic Habitat Restoration, Enhancement, and Establishment Activities	54	Living Shorelines

made in writing as early as possible prior to commencing the proposed activity.[337] This notification is referred to as a "pre-construction notification," or "PCN."

WQC = Water Quality Certification

The permittee may presume that his or her project qualifies for the NWP unless he is otherwise notified by the Corps within 45 days. The 45-day period starts on the date of receipt of the notification in the Corps district office and ends 45 calendar days later regardless of weekends or holidays. If the Corps notifies the prospective permittee that the notification is incomplete, a new 45-day period will commence upon receipt of the revised notification. The prospective permittee may not proceed with the proposed activity before expiration of the 45-day period unless otherwise notified by the Corps. If the Corps fails to act within the 45-day period, the prospective permitee must initiate the process of modifying, suspending, or revoking the NWP authorization.[338]

The Corps will review the notification and may add activity-specific conditions to ensure that the activity complies with the terms and conditions of the NWP and that the adverse impacts on the aquatic environment and other aspects of the public interest are individually and cumulatively minimal.[339]

For some NWPs involving discharges into wetlands, the notification must include a wetland delineation. The Corps will review the notification and determine if the individual and cumulative adverse environmental effects are more than minimal. If the adverse effects are more than minimal the Corps will notify the prospective permittee that an individual permit is required or that the prospective permittee may propose measures to mitigate the loss of special aquatic sites, including wetlands, to reduce the adverse impacts to minimal. The prospective permittee may elect to propose mitigation with the original notification. The Corps will consider that proposed mitigation when deciding if the impacts are minimal. The Corps must add activity-specific conditions to ensure that the mitigation will be accomplished. If sufficient mitigation cannot be developed to reduce the adverse environmental effects to the minimal level, the Corps will not allow authorization under the NWP and will instruct the prospective permittee on procedures to seek authorization under an individual permit.[340]

To qualify for an NWP, the prospective permittee must comply with the general conditions established by the Corps during each reauthorization of the Nationwide Permit Program. These general conditions are included in the Federal Register notice that accompanies the reauthorization of the Program. As of the 2017 reauthorization of the Program, the Corps has established general conditions related to, for example, endangered species, migratory birds and bald and golden eagles, historic properties, and mitigation.

The prospective permittee also must comply with any regional conditions imposed by the Corps. As described above, the State of California is regulated by three Corps

337 33 C.F.R. § 330.1(e)(1).

338 *Id.* § 330.1(e)(1).

339 *Id.* § 330.1(e)(2).

340 *Id.* § 330.1(e)(3).

SAMP = Special Area
Management Plan

CZMA = Coastal Zone
Management Act

RGL = Regulatory Guidance
Letter

districts: Sacramento, San Francisco, and Los Angeles. Each district has its own unique regional conditions that may apply to an NWP, and the lists of these regional conditions should be consulted in addition to the general conditions that may apply to a project.[341]

As discussed below regarding the Section 401 Water Quality Certification (WQC) process, the State Water Resources Control Board has issued pre-certifications for only a few of the NWPs. As to those NWPs, no further Section 401 WQC process is required because the state of California has deemed the activities subject to those NWPs already certified.[342] As to the remaining NWPs, an applicant must obtain a Section 401 WQC from the State Board or Regional Board before the Corps will confirm that an NWP applies to the project.

Special Area Management Plans

One approach to Section 404 authorization that takes into consideration a regional approach to permitting is the Special Area Management Plan (SAMP). SAMPs were originally conceived under 1980 amendments to the Coastal Zone Management Act (CZMA) as a tool for use within the coastal zone. A SAMP is defined within the CZMA as "a comprehensive plan providing for natural resource protection and reasonable coastal-dependent economic growth containing a detailed and comprehensive statement of policies, standards and criteria to guide public and private uses of lands and waters; and mechanisms for timely implementation in specific geographic areas within the coastal zone."[343]

In 1986, the Corps issued Regulatory Guidance Letter (RGL) 86-10 that specifically addressed SAMPs. RGL 86-10 applies the SAMP concept to non-coastal wetland resources, stating that "[t]his process of collaborative interagency planning within a geographic area of special sensitivity is just as applicable in non-coastal areas." RGL 86-10 explains that because SAMPs are very labor-intensive, the following "ingredients" should usually exist before the Corps will become involved in a SAMP:

> The area should be environmentally sensitive and under strong developmental pressure.

341 For a list of the Sacramento District Regional Conditions, see http://www.spk.usace.army.mil/Portals/12/documents/regulatory/nwp/2017_nwps/Final_SPK_Regional_Conditions_for_Nevada_3_31_17.pdf?ver=2017-04-04-095504-693. For a list of the San Francisco District Regional Conditions, see https://www.spn.usace.army.mil/Missions/Regulatory/Regulatory-Overview/Nationwide/Regional-Conditions/. For a list of the Los Angeles District Regional Conditions, see https://www.spl.usace.army.mil/Portals/17/docs/regulatory/Permit_Process/FINAL%202017%20SPL%20regional%20conditions.pdf?ver=2017-03-15-140838-737.

342 The following 2017 NWPs have been certified: NWP 1 (Aids to Navigation); NWP 4 (Fish and Wildlife Harvesting, Enhancement, and Attraction Devices and Activities); NWP 5 (Scientific Measurement Devices); NWP 6 (Survey Activities); NWP 9 (Structures in Fleeting and Anchorage Areas); NWP 10 (Mooring Buoys); NWP 11 (Temporary Recreational Structures); NWP 12 (Utility Line Activities); NWP 20 (Response Operations for Oil and Hazardous Substances); NWP 22 (Removal of Vessels); NWP 28 (Modifications of Existing Marinas); NWP 32 (Completed Enforcement Actions); NWP 36 (Boat Ramps); and NWP 54 (Living Shoreline). State Water Resources Control Board, Clean Water Act Section 401 General Water Quality Certification and Order, Reg. Meas. ID: 411836.

343 16 U.S.C. § 1453(17).

> There should be a sponsoring local agency to ensure that the plan fully reflects local needs and interests.

> Ideally there should be full public involvement in the planning and development process.

> All parties must express a willingness at the outset to conclude the SAMP process with a definitive "regulatory product."

The RGL further elaborates on the concept of a "regulatory product." According to RGL 86-10, an "ideal SAMP" would culminate in two products: (1) "appropriate local/state approvals and a Corps general permit or abbreviated processing procedure for activities in specifically defined situations"; and (2) "a local/state restriction and/or an Environmental Protection Agency (EPA) 404(c) restriction (preferably both) for undesirable activities." The RGL explains, however, that an "individual permit review may be conducted for activities that do not fall into either category above. However, it should represent a small number of the total cases addressed by the SAMP." Notably, the RGL concludes that the Corps "recognize[s] that an ideal SAMP is difficult to achieve, and, therefore, it is intended to represent an upper limit rather than an absolute requirement."

The website for the Corps' Los Angeles District is an excellent resource for more information regarding the purpose of SAMPs and how, as a practical matter, they are developed.[344] As to their development, the Los Angeles District's website explains that the Corps devised a multi-step process that involves coordination and collaboration with multiple interested stakeholders over many years. Though each SAMP will follow its own trajectory, the foundational process is the same. This process is:

(1) The first step of a SAMP is to identify and assess the riparian ecosystem within a given study area. The assessment of ecosystem condition in a watershed context is used to score the riparian ecosystem's degree of modification in terms of hydrology, habitat, and water quality.

(2) Establishing aquatic resource management objectives is done collaboratively and concurrently with identifying the potential permitting needs and objectives of the regulated public.

(3) The next step is to identify sensitive aquatic resource areas whose conservation would help to maintain the overall integrity of the watershed.

(4) Building on all the data and analyses, the Corps is able to develop a watershed-specific permitting strategy and a complementary aquatic resource conservation strategy.

(5) Moving towards a plan for implementation entails the development and assessment of alternative strategies.

(6) Memorializing a SAMP for implementation occurs after the preparation of an Environmental Assessment and a decision document.

The flow chart in Figure 7-2 helps illustrate this process.

---

344 U.S. Army Corps of Engineers, SAMP Background, available at https://www.spl.usace.army.mil/Missions/Regulatory/SAMP-Permitting-and-Research/SAMP-Background/.

FIGURE 7-2. FLOWCHART FOR ESTABLISHING A SAMP

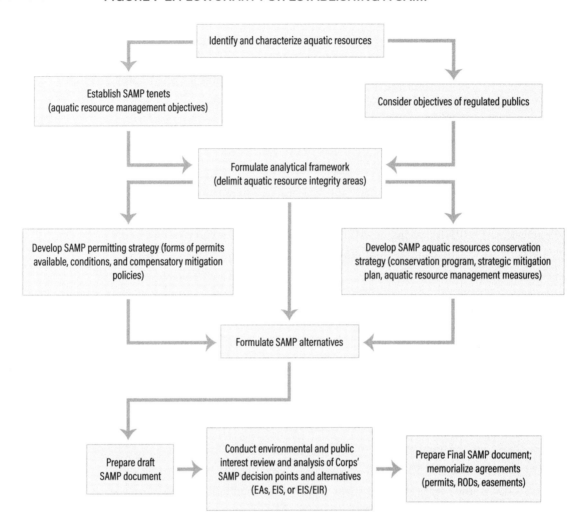

Existing SAMPs in California include SAMPs for the San Diego Creek Watershed, and the San Juan Creek and western San Mateo Creek Watersheds in Orange County; portions of the San Jacinto and upper Santa Margarita Watersheds in western Riverside County; and the Otay River Watershed in San Diego County.

INDIVIDUAL PERMIT PROCESSING

As discussed above, an individual permit is a form of Corps standard permit that is issued for a particular activity in a particular location. The process to obtain an individual permit can be time-consuming and costly for the applicant. An applicant should carefully evaluate whether a Nationwide Permit may cover the regulated activity and if not, whether the activity can be modified to avoid impacts to waters of the United States to obviate the need for a Section 404 permit, or to reduce impacts to waters of the United States to fit within one or more of the Nationwide Permit categories.

If an applicant Jurisdictional Determination indicates that an individual permit is required, then there are several procedural requirements that must be satisfied before the Corps will issue the Section 404 permit.

Pre-Application Meeting

The Corps regulations specify that the Corps must make staff available to advise potential applicants of studies or other information foreseeably required for later federal action on the project. Upon receipt by the applicant for a pre-application meeting, the Corps must assure the conduct of an orderly process which may involve other staff and affected agencies (federal, state, or local) and the public. This early process should be brief but thorough so that the potential applicant may begin to assess the viability of some of the more obvious potential alternatives in the application. At this stage, the Corps will endeavor to provide the potential applicant with all helpful information necessary in pursuing the application, including factors which the Corps must consider in its permit decisionmaking process.[345]

As to the environmental review that may be required for the permit under NEPA, the Corps regulations require that the staff coordinator for the project must maintain an open relationship with each potential applicant or the applicant's consultants so as to assure that the potential applicant is fully aware of the substance (both quantitative and qualitative) of the data required by the Corps for use in preparing an Environmental Assessment or an Environmental Impact Statement.[346]

Application Form

Applicants for all individual permits must use the standard application form. At this time, that form is designated ENG Form 4345 and is available for download on the Corps districts with jurisdiction in California. An appendix to the Corps regulations also includes a permit form along with typical permit conditions.[347] The Corps is authorized to use local variations of the application form for purposes of facilitating coordination with federal, state, and local agencies.[348]

Contents of Application

In addition to the application form, the applicants must submit other materials for a complete application. The application must include a complete description of the proposed activity including necessary drawings, sketches, or plans sufficient for public notice (detailed engineering plans and specifications are not required); the location, purpose and need for the proposed activity; schedule of the activity; the names and addresses of adjoining property owners; the location and dimensions of adjacent structures; and a list of authorizations required by other federal, interstate, state, or local agencies for the work, including all approvals received or denials already made.[349]

---

345 33 C.F.R. § 325.1(b).

346 *Id.* § 325.1(b).

347 *Id.* Pt. 325, App. A.

348 *Id.* § 325.1(c).

349 *Id.* § 325.1(d)(1).

NEPA = National Environmental
Policy Act

All activities which the applicant plans to undertake which are reasonably related to the same project and for which a Department of the Army permit would be required should be included in the same permit application. The Corps regulations specify that the Corps should reject as incomplete any permit application that fails to comply with this requirement. For example, a permit application for a marina will include dredging required for access as well as any fill associated with construction of the marina.[350]

For activities involving discharges of dredged or fill material into waters of the United States, the application must include a statement describing how impacts to waters of the United States are to be avoided and minimized. The application must also include either a statement describing how impacts to waters of the United States are to be compensated for or a statement explaining why compensatory mitigation should not be required for the proposed impacts.[351]

An application will be determined to be complete when sufficient information is received to issue a public notice. The issuance of a public notice will not be delayed to obtain information necessary to evaluate an application.[352] It is common for the Corps to determine an application is complete in order to issue a public notice, while other information required for the application, including a Section 7 Biological Assessment, Section 404(b)(1) Alternatives Analysis, or National Historic Preservation Act Section 106 determination, are still in process or preparation.

Public Notice

The public notice is the primary method of advising all interested parties of the proposed activity for which a permit is sought and of soliciting comments and information necessary to evaluate the probable impact on the public interest. The notice must, therefore, include sufficient information to give a clear understanding of the nature and magnitude of the activity to generate meaningful comment.

The notice should include the following items of information:

> applicable statutory authority or authorities
> the name and address of the applicant
> the name or title, address and telephone number of the Corps employee from whom additional information concerning the application may be obtained
> the location of the proposed activity
> a brief description of the proposed activity, its purpose and intended use, so as to provide sufficient information concerning the nature of the activity to generate meaningful comments, including a description of the type of structures, if any, to be erected on fills or pile or float-supported platforms, and a description of the type, composition, and quantity of materials to be discharged or disposed of in the ocean

350 *Id.* § 325.1(d)(2).
351 *Id.* § 325.1(d)(7).
352 *Id.* § 325.1(d)(10).

> a plan and elevation drawing showing the general and specific site location and character of all proposed activities, including the size relationship of the proposed structures to the site of the impacted waterway and depth of water in the area

> if the proposed activity would occur in the territorial seas or ocean waters, a description of the activity's relationship to the baseline from which the territorial sea is measured

> a list of other government authorizations obtained or requested by the applicant, including required certifications relative to water quality, coastal zone management, or marine sanctuaries

> if appropriate, a statement that the activity is a categorical exclusion for purposes of NEPA

> a statement of the Corps' current knowledge on historic properties

> a statement of the Corps' current knowledge on endangered species

> a statement on evaluation factors on which permit decisions are based

> any other available information which may assist interested parties in evaluating the likely impact of the proposed activity, if any, on factors affecting the public interest

> the comment period for the public notice, as determined by the Corps based on factors such as whether the proposal is routine or noncontroversial

> a statement that any person may request, in writing, within the comment period specified in the notice, that a public hearing be held to consider the application, and these requests for public hearings must state, with particularity, the reasons for holding a public hearing

> for non-federal applications in states with an approved Coastal Zone Management Plan, such as California, a statement on compliance with the approved Plan

> certain information for ocean dumping activities

Public notices will be distributed for posting in post offices or other appropriate public places in the vicinity of the site of the proposed work and will be sent to the applicant and to other interested parties identified in the Corps regulations. The Corps presumes that all interested parties and agencies will wish to respond to public notices, and therefore a lack of response will be interpreted as meaning that there is no objection to the proposed project.

The Corps regulations require that the Corps will consider all comments received in response to the public notice in its subsequent actions on the permit application. The Corps regulations mandate that the applicant be given an opportunity to review these comments. The regulations specifically provide that the Corps will provide the comments to the applicant for any views the applicant may wish to offer in response to such comments.[353]

---

353 *Id.* § 325.2(a)(3).

The comment period on the public notice should be for a "reasonable period of time within which interested parties may express their views concerning the permit."[354] The comment period must not be less than 15 days or more than 30 days from the date of the notice.[355]

Public Hearings

As discussed above, any person may request, in writing and within the comment period for the public notice, that a public hearing be held to consider the application. The Corps regulations provide additional guidance as to when a public hearing should be held and the process for such a hearing.

Upon receipt of any request for a public hearing, which must state with particularity the reasons for holding a public hearing, the Corps may expeditiously attempt to resolve the issues informally. Otherwise, the Corps must promptly set a time and place for the public hearing, and give due notice thereof as required in the regulations.[356]

Requests for a public hearing must be granted, unless the Corps determines that the issues raised are insubstantial or there is otherwise no valid interest to be served by a hearing.[357] In case of doubt, a public hearing must be held.[358]

Appropriate and Practicable Mitigation Measures

The Section 404(b)(1) Guidelines also require the Corps to include "appropriate and practicable" mitigation measures in permits.[359] Practitioners should be aware that this discussion in the Guidelines regarding mitigation is only a portion of the mitigation requirements and obligations specified in other portions of the Corps and EPA's Section 404 program. For example, the regulations discuss at length mitigation mechanisms that are available to a project applicant and the various requirements that apply to each of those mechanisms.

The Ninth Circuit Court of Appeals discussed this requirement in *Bering Strait Citizens v. U.S. Army Corps of Engineers*.[360] Project opponents argued that the Corps did not implement all of the mitigation measures suggested by EPA for the project. The court concluded, however, that the record demonstrated the Corps properly considered EPA's concerns, addressed them, and explained why it found them unpersuasive.[361] Project opponents also argued that the mitigation measures provided in the permit were insufficient because some of them had not yet been fully developed. Drawing upon

354 *Id.* § 325.2(d)(2).

355 *Id.*

356 33 C.F.R. § 327.4(b).

357 *Id.* See *Friends of Payette v. Horseshoe Bend Hydroelectric Co.*, 988 F.2d 989 (9th Cir. 1993) (upholding Corps' decision not to hold a public hearing because not warranted "to gather more technical data," and because "a hearing would be useful only as a forum to enable project proponents and opponents to air their views").

358 *Id.* § 327.4(c).

359 40 C.F.R. § 230.10(d).

360 524 F.3d 938 (9th Cir. 2008).

361 *Id.* at 950.

NEPA's mitigation requirements by analogy, the court held that these mitigation measures satisfied Clean Water Act requirements because:

> The mitigation measures that are to be developed after permit issuance are only one part of the overall mitigation requirements included in the permit. Where the Corps has undertaken a genuine effort to develop a detailed mitigation plan, the mere fact that one aspect of the plan is not yet finalized will not necessarily lead to the conclusion that the Corps' decision was arbitrary and capricious . . . . Finally, the Corps may be perfectly reasonable in its belief that additional on-site mitigation opportunities will present themselves once the project is underway. That the Corps intends to pursue additional mitigation opportunities at a later time does not conflict with the requirements of the [Clean Water Act] unless the mitigation measures that have been fully developed are inadequate.[362]

Compliance with Public Interest Review Requirements

In addition to evaluating permit applications relative to the Section 404(b)(1) Guidelines, the Corps is also required to evaluate permit applications pursuant to its "public interest review" requirements. These requirements are discussed above.

Issuance of Permit

The regulations require the Corps to make a decision on all applications not later than 60 days after receipt of a complete application.[363] This timing requirement is seldom met. The regulations provide certain exceptions to this time frame, which include (1) preclusion of a decision as a matter of law, (2) referral of the case to a higher authority, (3) extension of the comment period, (4) failure to receive from the applicant a timely submittal of information or comments, (5) request by the applicant to suspend processing of the application, (6) information needed by the Corps for a decision on the application cannot reasonably be obtained within the 60-day period.[364]

The Corps must prepare a statement of findings or, where an Environmental Impact Statement has been prepared pursuant to NEPA, a record of decision, on all permit decisions. The statement of findings or record of decision must include the Corps' views on the probable effect of the proposed work on the public interest, including conformity with the Section 404(b)(1) Guidelines.

The Corps' decision on a permit can be contrary to state or local decision related to that permit, which presumably could include a decision by the state or local government to deny a project approval. The regulations specify that if the Corps makes a decision on a permit application which is contrary to state or local decision, the Corps will include

---

362 *Id.* at 950–51.
363 33 C.F.R. § 325.4(d)(3).
364 *Id.* § 325.4(d)(3)(i)–(vi).

NAP = Notification of Appeal Process

RFA = Request for Appeal

JD = Jurisdictional Determination

in the decision document the significant national issues and explain how they are overriding in importance.[365]

ADMINISTRATIVE PERMIT APPEALS

A Corps' decision on a permit denial or a declined individual permit is subject to an administrative appeal by the affected party. The regulations do not allow for an administrative appeal of any issued individual permit that an applicant has accepted, unless the authorized work has not started in waters of the United States, and the issued permit is subsequently modified by the Corps. An applicant must exhaust any administrative appeal available pursuant to the Corps regulations and receive a final Corps decision on the permit application prior to filing a lawsuit in the federal courts based on a permit denial, or the terms and conditions of a declined permit.[366]

The process starts when an applicant receives notification of a Corps decision on those activities that are eligible for an appeal. As discussed earlier in this chapter, for Approved Jurisdictional Determinations, the notification includes a Notification of Appeal Process (NAP), which is a fact sheet explaining the criteria and procedures of the administrative appeal process, a Request for Appeal (RFA) form, which is used to initiate the appeal process, and a basis of Jurisdictional Determination. Other forms are provided depending on whether a permit has been denied, an initial proffered permit has been issued, or a permit has been declined.[367]

To initiate the appeal, the appellant must submit a completed RFA, and the reasons for requesting the appeal must be specifically stated. Examples of reasons for appeals include a procedural error; an incorrect application of law, regulation, or officially promulgated policy; omission of material fact; incorrect application of the current regulatory criteria and associated guidance for identifying and delineating wetlands; incorrect application of the Section 404(b)(1) Guidelines; or use of incorrect data.[368]

Certain actions are not subject to administrative appeal. These include: an individual permit decision (including a letter of permission or a standard permit with special conditions), where the permit has been accepted and signed by the permittee; any site-specific matter that has been the subject of a final decision of the federal courts; a final Corps decision that has resulted from additional analysis and evaluation, as directed by a final appeal decision; a permit denial without prejudice or a declined permit, where the controlling factor cannot be changed by the Corps decision maker; a permit denial case where the applicant has subsequently modified the proposed project; any request for the appeal of an Approved Jurisdictional Determination, a denied permit, or a declined permit where the RFA has not been received by the Corps within 60 days of the date of the NAP; a previously Approved Jurisdictional Determination (JD) that has

365 *Id.* § 325.2(a)(6).
366 *Id.* Pt. 331.
367 *Id.* § 331.4.
368 *Id.* § 331.5(a)(2).

been superseded by another Approved Jurisdictional Determination based on new information or data submitted by the applicant; an approved JD associated with an individual permit where the permit has been accepted and signed by the permittee; a preliminary JD or a JD associated with unauthorized activities, except as provided.[369]

RO = Reviewing Officer

An affected party appealing a permit denial or declined permit must submit an RFA that is received by the Corps within 60 days of the date of the NAP.

To initiate the appeal process regarding the terms and special conditions of an initial proffered individual permit, the applicant must write a letter to the Corps explaining its objections to the permit. The Corps may modify the permit in whole or in part, or refuse to modify the permit, and essentially re-proffer the permit, as modified or not, to the applicant. If the applicant still has objections, after receiving the second proffered permit (modified or unmodified), the applicant may decline the proffered permit, which may then be appealed to the Corps upon submittal of a complete RFA form.

After receiving an RFA, the Corps' division engineer determines whether the RFA is acceptable within 30 days. If the Corps determines that the RFA is acceptable, the Reviewing Officer (RO) will request the administrative record from the district engineer. The division engineer will normally make a final decision on the merits of the appeal within 90 days of the receipt of an acceptable RFA. In such case, the RO will complete the appeal review and the division engineer will make a final appeal decision within 30 days of the site visit.[370]

The division engineer will disapprove the entirety of or any part of the district engineer's decision only if he or she determines that the decision on some relevant matter was arbitrary, capricious, an abuse of discretion, not supported by substantial evidence in the administrative record, or plainly contrary to a requirement of law, regulations, an Executive Order, or officially promulgated Corps policy guidance.[371] The division engineer will document his or her decision on the merits of the appeal in writing, and provide a copy of this decision to the applicant and the district engineer. The final decision of the division engineer on the merits of the appeal concludes the administrative appeal process.[372]

The Corps regulations specify that appeal decisions are not to be treated as precedent and should not be relied upon by an applicant during an appeal process.[373] According to the Corps regulations, because the Corps' decision "to determine geographic jurisdiction, deny a permit, or condition a permit depends on the facts, circumstances, and physical conditions particular to the specific project and/or site being evaluated, appeal decisions would be of little or no precedential utility." Thus, an appeal decision is "applicable only to the instant appeal, and has no other precedential effect. Such a decision may not be cited in any other administrative appeal, and

369 *Id.* § 331.5(b).
370 *Id.* § 331.8.
371 *Id.* § 331.9(b).
372 *Id.* § 331.9(c).
373 *Id.* § 331.7(g).

Although the Corps' administrative appeal decisions are not binding as to other Corps permit or Jurisdictional Determination decisions, practitioners should be aware that they can be accessed online and can inform approaches to permitting or delineation issues. One notable example of an appeal decision issued by the South Pacific Division is the Administrative Appeal Decision re: Approved Jurisdictional Determination for Baccarat Fremont Developers, San Francisco District, File No. 23205S (Oct. 25, 2001). In this decision, the Corps' Review Officer remanded an Approved Jurisdictional Determination to the District to reconsider its conclusions regarding which wetlands on the project site were adjacent to jurisdictional waters of the United States. This decision ultimately found its way to the Ninth Circuit Court of Appeals, where the court held the Corps properly determined it had jurisdiction over the wetlands at issue in the case, finding that adjacency alone is sufficient for the Corps to assert jurisdiction over wetlands. (See *Baccarat Fremont Developers LLC v. United States Army Corps of Engineers*, 425 F.3d 1150 (9th Cir. 2005).)

FIGURE 7-3. ADMINISTRATIVE APPEAL PROCESS FOR PERMIT DENIALS AND PROFFERED PERMITS

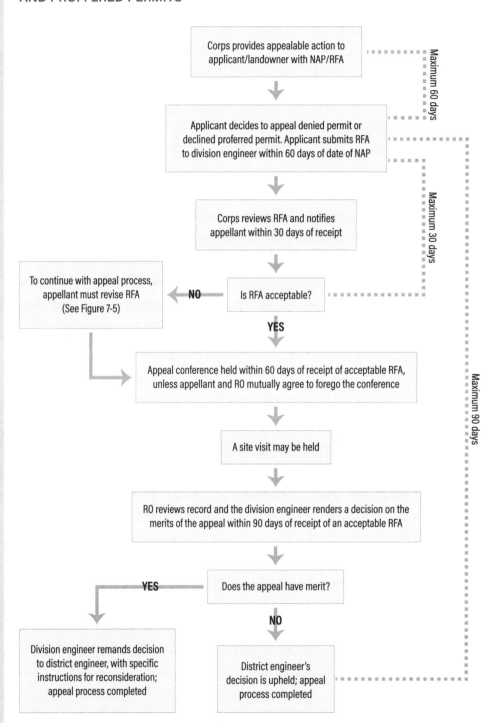

NOTE: If new information is provided to the Corps, the applicant will be asked if the applicant wishes to revise the project or record. If so, the appeal will be withdrawn and the case returned to the District for appropriate action. If not, then the Division Engineer will rule on the merits of the appeal based on the administrative record without consideration of the new information. however, the new information may cause the District Engineer to take action under 33 C.F.R. Section 325.7, independent of the appeal process.

FIGURE 7-4. APPLICANT OPTIONS WITH INITIAL PROFFERED PERMIT

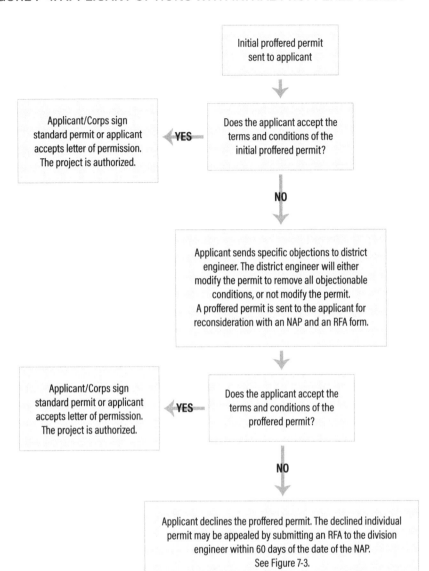

may not be used as precedent for the evaluation of any other Jurisdictional Determination or permit application." Nonetheless, the Corps regulations suggest that because the Corps seeks "to have the Corps regulatory program operate as consistently as possible, particularly with respect to interpretations of law, regulation, an Executive Order, and officially promulgated policy," copies of each appeal decision are forwarded to Corps Headquarters and are periodically reviewed at the headquarters level for consistency with law, Executive Orders, and policy. As such, although the practitioner may not rely on other appeal decisions for precedential value, appeal decisions may provide insight into how certain procedures, requirements, or other permitting concerns may be viewed by the Corps.[374]

374 The Corps' South Pacific Division archives appeal decisions on its website at https://www.spd.usace.army.mil/Missions/Regulatory/Regulatory-Appeals/Administrative-Appeals-Decisions/.

FIGURE 7-5. PROCESS FOR UNACCEPTABLE REQUEST FOR APPEAL

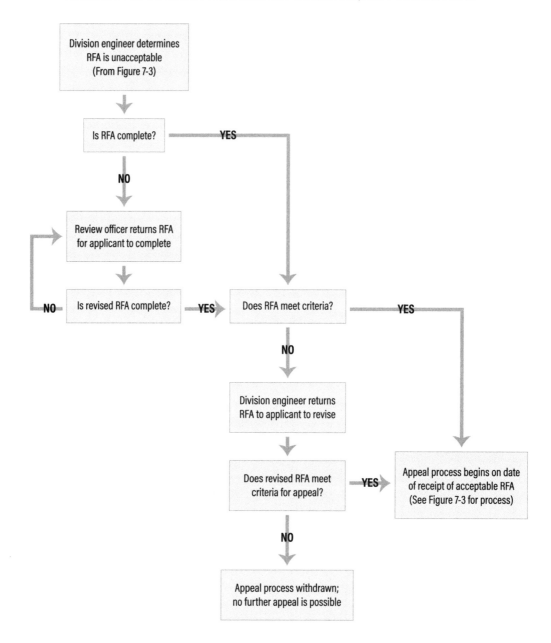

Conditioning of Permits

The Corps is authorized to add special conditions to permits when those conditions are necessary to satisfy legal requirements or to otherwise satisfy the public interest requirement. The regulations require that these conditions be directly related to the impacts of the proposal, appropriate to the scope and degree of those impacts, and reasonably enforceable.[375]

---

375 *Id.* § 325.4(a).

The Corps is authorized to deny a permit if the Corps determines that special conditions are necessary to insure the proposal will not be contrary to the public interest, but that those conditions would not be reasonably implementable or enforceable.[376]

If the Corps has reason to believe that the permittee might be prevented from completing work which is necessary to protect the public interest, the Corps may require the permittee to post a bond of sufficient amount to indemnify the government against any loss as a result of corrective action it might take.[377]

Duration of Permits

Corps permits may authorize both the work and the resulting use of that work, and that continue in effect until they automatically expire or are modified, suspended, or revoked.[378]

Permits for the existence of a structure or other activity of a permanent nature typically are for an indefinite duration with no expiration date. However, where a temporary structure is authorized, or where restoration of a waterway is contemplated, the permit will be of limited duration with a definite expiration date.[379] Permits for construction work, discharge of dredged or fill material, or other activity and any construction period for a structure with a permit of indefinite duration, as described above, will specify time limits for completing the work or activity. The permit may also specify a date by which the work must be started, normally within one year from the date of issuance.[380]

Authorization and construction periods automatically expire if the permittee fails to request and receive an extension of time. The Corps may grant an extension of time unless the Corps determines that an extension would be contrary to the public interest.[381]

Modification, Suspension, or Revocation of Permits

The Corps regulations govern modifications, suspensions, and revocations of permits. The Corps may reevaluate the circumstance and conditions of any permit on its own, at the request of the permittee, or a third party, and may initiate action to modify, suspend, or revoke a permit as may be made necessary by considerations of the public interest. The Corps must take into account the following factors when making this decision:

> the extent of the permittee's compliance with the terms and conditions of the permit

> whether or not circumstances relating to the authorized activity have changed since the permit was issued or extended, and the continuing adequacy of or need for the permit conditions

376 *Id.* § 325.4(c).
377 *Id.* § 325.4(d).
378 *Id.* § 325.6(a).
379 *Id.* § 325.6(b).
380 *Id.* § 325.6(c).
381 *Id.* § 325.6(d).

MOA = Memorandum of Agreement

> any significant objections to the authorized activity which were not earlier considered

> revisions to applicable statutory and/or regulatory authorities

> the extent to which modification, suspension, or other action would adversely affect plans, investments and actions the permittee has reasonably made or taken in reliance on the permit

If the Corps determines that the public interest requires a modification of the terms or conditions of a permit, the Corps will hold informal consultations with the permittee to ascertain whether the terms and conditions can be modified by mutual agreement. If mutual agreement can be reached, then the Corps will give the permittee written notice of the modification. If agreement cannot be reached, then the Corps will begin the process of suspending the permit if immediate suspension is warranted. If immediate suspension is not warranted but the Corps determines that the permit should be modified, the Corps will notify the permittee of the proposed modifications and the reasons for modifying the permit, which will then become effective on a date set by the Corps.[382]

The Corps may suspend a permit after preparing a written determination and finding that immediate suspension would be in the public interest. In which case, the Corps will notify the permittee and order the permittee to stop those activities previously authorized by the suspended permit.[383] The Corps must also advise the permittee that following the suspension a decision will be made to either reinstate, modify, or revoke the permit, and that the permittee may within 10 days of receiving the notice of suspension request a meeting with the Corps, after which the Corps will take action to reinstate, modify, or revoke the permit.[384] If revocation is found to be in the public interest, the Corps authority who made the decision on the original permit may revoke it.[385] The permittee is then advised in writing of the final decision.[386]

EPA's ROLE IN THE PERMIT PROCESS

Although the Corps is authorized to issue Section 404 permits, EPA has the ability to intervene in the process. Two of the most important mechanisms for EPA's involvement are the Section 404(q) elevation process and authority under Section 404(c) to "veto" permits.

Section 404(q) Elevation

Section 404(q) of the Clean Water Act establishes a requirement that the Secretary of the Army and the Administrator of EPA enter into an agreement assuring that delays in the issuance of permits under Section 404 are minimized. In August 1992, the Corps

---

382 *Id.* § 325.7(b).

383 *Id.* § 325.7(c).

384 *Id.*

385 *Id.* § 325.7(d).

386 *Id.*

and EPA released a Section 404(q) Memorandum of Agreement (MOA) that outlines the process and time frames for resolving disputes. This MOA essentially creates an elevation process, whereby EPA is authorized to elevate concerns regarding the Corps' issuance of permits.

The MOA requires the Corps to provide EPA with public notices of pending permits. EPA must submit any comments to the Corps within the basic comment period specified in the public notice. Within the basic or extended comment period, EPA has the authority to notify the Corps' district engineer by letter that in the opinion of EPA the project may result in substantial and unacceptable impacts to Aquatic Resources of National Importance, sometimes referred to as "ARNIs".

Although the Section 404(q) MOA does not specify what constitutes an ARNI, EPA has at least informally explained that the factors it uses in identifying ARNIs include: economic importance of the aquatic resource, rarity or uniqueness, and/or importance of the aquatic resource to the protection, maintenance, or enhancement of the quality of the nation's waters.[387]

Within 25 calendar days after the end of the comment period, the EPA regional administrator must notify the district engineer by letter that in EPA's opinion the discharge will have a substantial and unacceptable impact to aquatic resources of national important, stating in detail (1) why there will be substantial and unacceptable impacts to ARNIs; and (2) why the specific permit must be modified, conditioned, or denied to protect the ARNIs.

If the district engineer's decision is contrary to EPA's ARNI determination, or if the district engineer believes his decision resolves EPA's concerns, then the district engineer must forward the proposed decision to the Wetlands Division Director. Alternatively, if the district engineer, prior to reaching a decision on the permit, determines that the project has been modified or conditioned sufficiently so that there are no longer substantial adverse impacts on ARNIs, the district engineer will notify the Wetlands Division Director by letter of the project modifications or conditions that resolve EPA's concerns.

Within 15 calendar days from receipt of the draft permit, the EPA regional administrator will notify the district engineer that either (1) the regional administrator will not request higher level review; or (2) the regional administrator has forwarded the issue to the Corps' Assistant Administrator, Office of Water (AAOW) with a recommendation to request review by the Assistant Secretary of the Army for Civil Works (ASA(CW)). When the regional administrator requests elevation, the district engineer will hold in abeyance the issuance of a permit pending completion of the headquarters-level review.

If agency headquarters review is necessary, within 20 calendar days from the regional administrator's letter notifying the district engineer of the intent to request higher level review, the AAOW will either (1) notify the ASA(CW) that the AAOW

ARNIs = Aquatic Resources of National Importance

AAOW = U.S. Army Corps of Engineers Assistant Administrator, Office of Water

ASA(CW) = Assistant Secretary of the Army for Civil Works

---

387 U.S. Environmental Protection Agency, Clean Water Act Section 404(q) Dispute Resolution Process, available at https://www.epa.gov/sites/production/files/2015-05/documents/404q.pdf.

will not request further review; or (2) request the ASA(CW) to review the permit decision document.

Within 30 calendar days from the AAOW's request for review, the ASA(CW), through the Director of Civil Works, will review the permit decision document, and either (1) inform the district engineer to proceed with final action on the permit decision; or (2) inform the district engineer to proceed with final action in accordance with case specific policy guidance; or (3) make the final permit decision in accordance with the Corps regulations.

After ASA(CW) has reached its decision, the ASA(CW) will immediately notify the AAOW in writing of its decision. Under the MOA, EPA reserves the right to proceed with the Section 404(c) veto. The permit shall not be issued during a period of 10 calendar days after such notice unless it contains a condition that no activity may take place pursuant to the permit until the tenth day, or if EPA has initiated a Section 404(c) proceeding during the 10-day period, until the Section 404(c) proceedings are concluded and subject to final determination in such proceeding.

Section 404(c) Veto Authority

The Clean Water Act authorizes EPA to restrict, prohibit, deny, or withdraw the use of an area as a disposal site for dredged or fill material if the discharge will have unacceptable adverse effects on municipal water supplies, shellfish beds and fishery areas, wildlife, or recreational areas.[388]

EPA may exercise its Section 404(c) authority before a permit is applied for, while an application is pending, or after a permit has been issued.[389] An EPA regional administrator initiates a Section 404(c) action if he or she determines that the impact of a proposed permit activity is likely to result in:

> significant degradation of municipal water supplies (including surface or ground water)

> significant loss of or damage to fisheries, shellfishing, wildlife habitat, or recreation areas

The Section 404(c) veto process starts with EPA notifying the Corps and the project proponent of his or her intention to issue a public notice of a Proposed Determination to withdraw, prohibit, deny, or restrict the specification of a defined area for discharge of dredged or fill material. If EPA is not satisfied that no unacceptable adverse effects will occur, a notice of the Proposed Determination is published in the Federal Register.

This triggers a 30- to 60-day public comment period, during which a public hearing is usually held. Within 30 days of the public hearing or, if no public hearing is held, within 15 days of the end of the comment period, EPA prepares a Recommended

---

388 33 U.S.C. § 1344(c).

389 See *Mingo Logan Coal Co. v. U.S. Environmental Protection Agency*, 714 F.3d 608, 613 (D.C. Cir. 2013) (holding that EPA may exercise its veto power after issuance of the Section 404 permit).

Determination to withdraw, prohibit, deny, or restrict the specification of the defined area for disposing of dredged or fill material and forwards it along with the administrative record to the EPA Assistant Administrator for Water. Alternatively, EPA can withdraw the Proposed Determination at this time.

Within 30 days of receipt of the Recommended Determination, EPA contacts the Corps and project proponent and provides them 15 days to take corrective action to prevent unacceptable adverse effects. Within 60 days of the receipt of the Recommended Determination, EPA affirms, modifies, or rescinds the Recommended Determination and publishes notice of the Final Determination in the Federal Register.[390]

As a practical matter, EPA has used its Section 404(c) veto authority very sparingly, issuing only 13 final determinations since 1972 as of 2018.[391] When it has been used, the courts typically afford EPA broad discretion. For example, in *James City County v. Environmental Protection Agency*, EPA vetoed a Corps decision to allow a county in Virginia to build a dam and reservoir, finding that the county had practicable alternative water sources. On review by the Fourth Circuit Court of Appeals, the court held that EPA's determination was not supported by substantial evidence. However, the court also held that EPA's veto of this decision could be based solely on environmental harms without considering the community's need for water.[392]

Similarly, in *Alameda Water & Sanitation Dist. v. Reilly*, the U.S. District Court for the District of Colorado held that EPA did not exceed its veto authority regarding a Corps permit for a water storage project, despite the claim that the veto was improperly based upon recreational and fishing conditions not related to water quality changes, and the assertion that the Clean Water Act was concerned only with water quality, not quantity, impact.[393] Further, in *Mingo Logan Coal Company, Inc. v. United States Environmental Protection Agency*, the U.S. District Court for the District of Columbia held that EPA was not required to rely on substantial new information in vetoing specification of two streams as disposal sites after a coal mine operator had previously been issued a Section 404 permit. The court further noted that EPA was not constrained by a temporal limit in exercising its veto authority.[394]

The U.S. District Court for the District of Columbia has also held that EPA acted arbitrarily and capriciously by considering factors outside the scope of its statutory authority when it decided not to veto the Corps' issuance of a permit for a city's proposed reservoir project, where the EPA regional administrator based his decision on the determination that engaging in required notice and comment proceedings would divert resources; that given extensive public process provided by the Corps, another such process would be unlikely to add any new information; that there was a water supply

---

390 40 C.F.R. § 231.6.

391 See EPA's Clean Water Act Section 404(c) "Veto Authority" summary, available at https://www.epa.gov/sites/production/files/2016-03/documents/404c.pdf.

392 12 F.3d 1330 (4th Cir. 1993), *cert. denied,* 513 U.S. 823 (1993).

393 930 F. Supp. 486 (D. Colo. 1996).

394 70 F. Supp. 3d 151 (D.D.C. 2014).

shortfall that needed to be addressed; and that the permit would likely be subject to litigation in any event, rather than upon finding that the issuance of the permit would result in unacceptable adverse effects.[395]

Advance Specification of Disposal Areas

The Section 404(b)(1) Guidelines include a set of regulations that establish a planning process to identify wetlands and other waters that are generally suitable or unsuitable for the discharge of dredged and fill material. This process is referred to as the Advance Identification of Disposal Areas. According to EPA, the process is intended to add predictability to the wetlands permitting process as well as better account for the impacts of losses from multiple projects within a geographic area.[396]

Under these regulations, EPA and the Corps, on their own initiative or at the request of any other party and after consultation with any affected State that is not the permitting authority, may identify sites which will be considered as either possible future disposal sites, including existing disposal sites and non-sensitive areas, or areas generally unsuitable for disposal site specification.[397]

The regulations specify that the identification of any area as a possible future disposal site should not be deemed to constitute a permit for the discharge of dredged or fill material within such area or a specification of a disposal site. In addition, the identification of areas that generally will not be available for disposal site specification should not be deemed as prohibiting applications for permits to discharge dredged or fill material in such areas. Either type of identification constitutes information to facilitate individual or general permit application and processing.[398] However, the classification is strictly advisory.

Before establishment of an advanced identification of a disposal area, the regulations require that public notice of the proposed identification of such areas must be issued.[399] To provide the basis for advanced identification of disposal areas, and areas unsuitable for disposal, EPA and the Corps must consider the likelihood that use of the area in question for dredged or fill material disposal will comply with the Section 404(b)(1) Guidelines.[400] The permitting authority should maintain a public record of the identified areas and a written statement of the basis for identification.

OTHER RELEVANT FEDERAL STATUTES

Several other federal statutes are relevant to the Section 404 permitting process, and the practitioner should be mindful of the fact that a Section 404 permit is often accompanied by a constellation of other federal (and sometimes state) regulatory requirements.

---

395 *Alliance to Save the Mattaponi v. U.S. Army Corps of Engineers*, 606 F. Supp. 2d 121 (D.D.C. 2009).

396 EPA, ADID Fact Sheet, available at https://www.epa.gov/cwa-404/advance-identification-adid.

397 40 C.F.R. § 230.80(a).

398 *Id.* § 230.80(b).

399 *Id.* § 230.80(c).

400 *Id.* § 230.80(d).

Described below are the more significant federal statutes that often play a role in the Section 404 permitting process.

EA/FONSI = Environmental Assessment/Finding of No Significant Impact

EIS = Environmental Impact Statement

Section 401 Water Quality Certification

Section 401 of the Clean Water Act requires that any person applying for a federal permit or license, including a Section 404 permit, which may result in a discharge of pollutants into waters of the United States, must obtain a state water quality certification that the activity complies with all applicable water quality standards, limitations, and restrictions.[401] The Corps may not issue a Section 404 permit until certification required by Section 401 has been granted, and the Corps may not issue a Section 404 permit if certification has been denied. See Chapter 8 for further information regarding Section 401 and the role of the State Water Resources Control Board and the nine Regional Water Quality Control Boards in the Section 404 permit process.

National Environmental Policy Act

The issuance of a Section 404 permit constitutes a federal action subject to the National Environmental Policy Act (NEPA).[402] Environmental clearance under NEPA may take the form of a categorical exclusion, Environmental Assessment/Finding of No Significant Impact (EA/FONSI), or an Environmental Impact Statement (EIS), depending on the level of environmental impacts associated with the permit.

One of the most important issues relative to NEPA and Section 404 is the Corps' scope of its NEPA analysis for the Section 404 permit. As required by NEPA, the Corps has adopted its own NEPA implementing regulations.[403] Those regulations set forth a variety of administrative processes regarding the Corps' NEPA analysis, and specifically addresses the scope of the Corps' NEPA document in those situations where the application for a Section 404 permit covers only a part of a larger project that may include both federal and non-federal aspects.

This scenario is commonly referred to as the "small federal handle" problem, because it arises when the issue is the point at which a federal agency's involvement in a project proposed by a non-federal entity "federalizes" the entirety of the project, making the entire project subject to NEPA analysis and review. With respect to the Corps' Section 404 jurisdiction, the issue is whether the Corps' issuance of the permit causes the entirety of the project—i.e., both the federal portion and the non-federal portion—to be included within the scope of the Corps' NEPA analysis for the permit.

The resolution of this issue can be critical for a project, because an expanded scope of review often means that a much more robust, costly, and time-consuming EIS, rather than an EA/FONSI, may be required for a "federalized" project.

401 33 U.S.C. § 1341(a)(1).

402 42 U.S.C. §§ 4321–4347.

403 33 C.F.R. Pt. 325, App. B.

The first significant court decisions on this issue emerged in the early 1980s. Those decisions essentially established that the Corps could adopt a limited scope of NEPA review. In *Winnebago Tribe of Nebraska v. Ray*,[404] the applicant sought a Section 404 permit for a 1.25-mile river crossing for a 67-mile, non-federal power line. The Corps prepared an EA that covered only the river crossing, concluding that the issuance of the permit would result in no significant environmental impacts. Plaintiffs challenged the EA, arguing that, because the power line could not be built "but for" the Corps' Section 404 permit, the Corps had sufficient control over the entire project to require an environmental analysis of the entire 67-mile power line.

The Eighth Circuit determined that the Corps lacked sufficient control over the project based on a three-part test: (1) the degree of discretion exercised by the agency over the federal portion of the project; (2) whether the federal government has given any direct financial aid to the project; and (3) whether the overall federal involvement with the project is sufficient to turn an essentially private action into a federal action.[405]

In *Save the Bay v. U.S. Army Corps of Engineers*,[406] the applicant sought a Section 404 permit to construct a 2,200-foot wastewater discharge pipeline associated with a non-federal titanium dioxide manufacturing facility. The Corps analyzed in its EA the effects of building the pipeline, not the associated non-federal facility. Plaintiffs challenged the Corps' scope of NEPA analysis, arguing it should have included the entire facility. The Fifth Circuit upheld the Corps' analysis and found that there was an insufficient nexus between the Section 404 permit required for the pipeline and the construction of the non-federal plant. The court noted that the pipeline was not necessary to operate the plant because another method of discharge, not requiring a Corps permit, was available. Thus, the court held the Corps lacked factual control over the construction as well.

In response to these judicial decisions and to create guidance on when a federal permit "federalizes" otherwise non-federal aspects of a project, the Corps addressed these issues in Appendix B of their regulations. These regulations state:

> In some situations, a permit applicant may propose to conduct a specific
> activity requiring a [Corps] permit . . . which is merely one component of a
> larger project . . . . The district engineer should address the scope of the
> NEPA document (e.g., the EA or EIS) to address the impacts of the spe-
> cific activity requiring a [Corps] permit and those portions of the entire
> project over which the district engineer has sufficient control and respon-
> sibility to warrant Federal review . . . . The district engineer is considered to
> have control and responsibility for portions of the project beyond the lim-
> its of Corps jurisdiction where the Federal involvement is sufficient to turn
> an essentially private action into a Federal action. These are cases where

404 621 F.2d 269 (8th Cir. 1980).

405 621 F.2d at 272.

406 610 F.2d 322 (5th Cir. 1980).

the environmental consequences of the larger project are essentially products of the Corps permit action.[407]

CEQA = California Environmental Quality Act

The Appendix B regulations further elaborate on the "typical factors to be considered in determining whether sufficient 'control and responsibility' exists." Those factors include: "the extent to which the entire project will be within Corps jurisdiction" and "the extent of cumulative Federal control and responsibility."[408] The regulations explain:

> Federal control and responsibility will include the portions of the project beyond the limits of Corps jurisdiction where the cumulative Federal involvement of the Corps and other Federal agencies is sufficient to grant legal control over such additional portions of the project. These are cases where the environmental consequences of the additional portions of the projects are essentially products of Federal financing, assistance, direction, regulation, or approval . . . .[409]

A growing body of case law evaluates the Corps' implementation and interpretation of these regulations. One of the most important cases on the small federal handle problem was decided by the Ninth Circuit Court of Appeals in 1989. In *Sylvester v. U.S. Army Corps of Engineers*,[410] the court considered the Corps' NEPA review of a proposed resort that included a golf course located on wetlands and a ski resort located on adjacent uplands. The court held that the Corps could limit its NEPA review to the construction of the golf course on the wetlands, even though the golf course was part of a larger development. The court found that the golf course and the rest of the resort were not "two links of a single chain," because "each could exist without the other, although each would benefit from the other's presence."[411]

Since *Sylvester*, the Ninth Circuit has evaluated a number of cases involving the "small federal handle." For example, *Wetlands Action Network v. U.S. Army Corps of Engineers* involved a challenge to the Corps' decision to grant a permit to fill 16 acres of wetlands and to mitigate the fill by creating a 51-acre wetlands system for a large scale mixed-use development.[412] The Corps agreed to a division of the overall project into three phases for permitting purposes. The Corps also limited its analysis to the impacts resulting from the filling of the 16.1 acres of wetlands for the first phase of development. The court upheld the Corps' decision to limit its analysis, finding that the first phase encompassed development of approximately 600 acres, only 16 of which are subject to direct control by the Corps through the permitting process, and noting that the project could proceed without the permit. The court also noted that the project was not financed by federal money and state and local, not federal, regulations control the

---

407 33 C.F.R. Pt. 325, App. B, § 7(b).

408 *Id.* at Pt. 325, App. B, § 7(b)(2).

409 33 C.F.R. Pt. 325, App. B, § 7(b)(2)(A).

410 884 F.2d 394 (9th Cir. 1989).

411 *Id.* at 400–01.

412 222 F.3d 1105 (9th Cir. 2000).

overall design. Particularly noteworthy for projects in California, which are subject to environmental review under the California Environmental Quality Act (CEQA), the court was persuaded by the fact that the project had been "subjected to extensive state environmental review."[413]

Save Our Sonoran, Inc. v. Flowers involved a challenge to the Corps' decision to issue a permit for a gated community located on a 608-acre parcel of land in the desert near Phoenix.[414] The Corps based its permitting jurisdiction on the fact that water flowed through the washes and arroyos of the otherwise arid development site during periods of heavy rain, and those desert washes were considered navigable waters subject to Clean Water Act jurisdiction. The washes constituted approximately 31.3 acres, or about five percent of the site. The Corps issued an EA/FONSI for the project, examining only the washes rather than the entire project. The court held that the Corps improperly constrained its NEPA analysis to the washes, rather than considering the development's effect on the environment as a whole. The court pointed to the fact that the desert washes subject to Corps permits were "scattered throughout the entire property," appearing to "run through the property like lines run through graph paper." The court used another, even more colorful analogy: "Because the jurisdictional waters run throughout the property like capillaries through tissue, any development the Corps permits would have an effect on the whole property." Accordingly, the court held that "the NEPA analysis should have included the entire property."[415]

White Tanks Concerned Citizens, Inc. v. Strock involved a proposed master-planned community in an undeveloped desert area to house an estimated 60,000 people.[416] The site occupied 10,105 acres, with 144 acres of desert washes dispersed throughout the development site. The Corps issued the developer a permit to fill 26.8 acres of the desert washes, which were considered to be within the Corps' jurisdiction pursuant to the Clean Water Act. The Corps issued an EA/FONSI for the project, restricting its scope of NEPA analysis to the washes themselves and certain upland areas directly affected by the project's fill activities. The court described the *Wetlands Action Network* and *Save Our Sonoran* decisions as two opposite ends of a spectrum:

> At one end, the jurisdictional waters are concentrated in certain areas, making it easy to build around them, so that substantial development can go forward without a Section 404 permit. In these cases, the Corps' analysis may be limited to the effect on the waters. [*Wetlands Action Network*] is closer to this end of the spectrum. At the other end of the spectrum, the waters are dispersed throughout the site, so that any construction on the site would be impossible without affecting the waters, and a Section 404

---

413 *Id.* at 1117; see also *Sylvester*, 884 F.2d at 401 ("We, finally, draw comfort from the fact that ordinary notions of efficiency suggest a federal environmental review should not duplicate competently performed state environmental analyses.").

414 408 F.3d 1113 (9th Cir. 2004).

415 *Id.* at 1122.

416 563 F.3d 1033 (9th Cir. 2009).

permit would be required for any building. In these cases, the Corps' analysis must include the effects of the entire development. This is the end of the spectrum that [*Save Our Sonoran*] illustrates.

Based on this analytical construct, the court held that this case was closer to the *Save Our Sonoran* end of the spectrum. The court pointed out that the Section 404 permit application admitted that a "no-action alternative" was not feasible, because the project would have resulted in disconnected isolated clusters of development, given that the washes that would have required filling were not all confined to particular portions of the development site. In other words, the developers themselves admitted that without the permit, the project as they conceived it could not have proceeded. The court therefore concluded: "Because this project's viability is founded on the Corps' issuance of a Section 404 permit, the entire project is within the Corps' purview."[417]

Recently, the D.C. Circuit Court of Appeals has offered a much more limited view on the scope of Corps' responsibility under both NEPA and the ESA. This case, *Sierra Club v. United States Army Corps of Engineers*, is discussed in the following section.

The Endangered Species Act

Issuance of a Section 404 permit constitutes an agency action subject to Section 7 of the Endangered Species Act. As discussed in Chapter 1, the Section 7 process is administered by the U.S. Fish and Wildlife Service and the National Marine Fisheries Service. The Section 404 permitting process often involves Section 7 consultation because wetlands typically constitute habitat for special-status species.

With respect to the Corps' wetland permitting process, Section 7 requires the Corps to consult with the Service when any action the Corps carries out, funds, or authorizes (such as through a Section 404 permit) *may affect* a listed endangered or threatened species. This process usually begins as informal consultation, and starts when the Corps, typically in the early stages of project planning, requests the Service to initiate informal consultation. Discussions between the two agencies may include what types of listed species may occur in the proposed action area, and what effect the proposed action may have on those species.

If the Corps determines that the proposed action is not likely to affect any listed species in the project area, and if the Service concurs, the informal consultation is complete and the proposed project moves ahead. If it appears that the Corps' action may affect a listed species, the Corps may then prepare a Biological Assessment to assist in its determination of the project's effect on a species. In practice, the Biological Assessment is usually prepared by the applicant with significant input from the Corps before submittal to the Service.

If the Corps determines the proposed permitting action is *likely to adversely affect* a listed species, the Corps submits to the Service a request for formal consultation. During formal consultation, the Service and the Corps share information about the proposed

417 *Id.* at 1040–42.

project and the species likely to be affected. Formal consultation may last up to 90 days, after which the Service will prepare a Biological Opinion on whether the proposed activity will *jeopardize* the continued existence of a listed species. The Service has 45 days after completion of formal consultation to write the opinion. A Biological Opinion includes an incidental take statement, which authorizes the incidental take of listed species resulting from the permitted project.

Unlike the Endangered Species Act Section 10 incidental take permit/habitat conservation plan process, the Section 7 process includes definite timing parameters and is a more streamlined approach to incidental take authorization by comparison. As such, obtaining Section 7 incidental take authorization by virtue of a federal permitting nexus, such as that provided by a Section 404 permit, often is strategically advantageous to a project applicant. In fact, some developers essentially look to create a federal permitting nexus—including a Section 404 permit—in order to use Section 7, rather than Section 10, of the Endangered Species Act to authorize incidental take.

One of the issues that arises in this context is the extent to which the Service's Section 7 incidental take authorization covers construction and operation within non-jurisdictional portions of the project site. The Court of Appeals for the District of Columbia considered this issue in *Sierra Club v. United States Army Corps of Engineers*,[418] often referred to as the "Enbridge Decision," named after the corporate entity constructing a pipeline at issue in the case. The 600-mile long pipeline was designed to ship roughly 600,000 barrels of oil a day across Illinois, Missouri, Kansas, and Oklahoma. Enbridge applied to the Corps for permits associated with fill activities spanning in total approximately 10 miles of wetlands.

The Corps issued to Enbridge verifications for the use of Nationwide Permit 12 to authorize the fill activities in jurisdictional waters along the pipeline. Before it began construction, Enbridge considered applying to the Service for a Section 10 permit. Once the Service estimated that the Section 10 process could "take years to complete," Enbridge decided against the Section 10 route and instead opted only to participate in the speedier Section 7 process. Therefore, as part of that permitting effort, the Corps consulted with the Service pursuant to Section 7 regarding the project's potential impact on listed species. The Service issued a Biological Opinion that examined the entire length of the pipeline. No separate NEPA review was prepared in connection with this decision, given that the Corps verified the use of a Nationwide Permit for the fill activities.

The Sierra Club challenged the Corps decision, arguing that the agencies should have conducted NEPA review of the pipeline as a whole. The court held that the Service's issuance of the incidental take statement was not, standing alone, federal action triggering NEPA review. In so holding, however, the court also found that the Corps' implementation of the incidental take statement as a condition of its Clean Water Act verifications was a federal action, but with geographic scope far more limited than the

418 803 F.3d 31 (D.C. Cir. 2015).

NEPA review Sierra Club sought, i.e., a review that would have included the entire length of the pipeline. The court referred to the fact that the incidental take statement did not cover the entire length of the pipeline, only those portions of the pipeline involving fill activities subject to Corps jurisdiction.

The Enbridge Decision suggests that a Section 7 incidental take statement for a Section 404 permit required for only a portion of a project site does not extend take authorization to the remainder of the project. The policy rationale behind this view seems to be that there would be no NEPA analysis to provide the necessary environmental clearance for an expanded scope of take authorization. This position may lead to projects where Section 7 incidental take authorization attaches to those portions of the project requiring Section 404 permitting, while a Section 10 incidental take permit/habitat conservation plan may be required for the balance of the project.

CZMA = Coastal Zone Management Act

NMFS = National Marine Fisheries Service, administered by the National Oceanic and Atmospheric Administration

Fish and Wildlife Coordination Act

The Fish and Wildlife Coordination Act,[419] requires that fish and other wildlife receive equal consideration and be coordinated with other aspects of water resource development. This is accomplished by requiring consultation with the U.S. Fish and Wildlife Service, National Marine Fisheries Service (NMFS), and appropriate state agencies whenever any body of water is proposed to be modified in any way and a federal permit or license is required. In connection with this process, NMFS submits comments to federal licensing and permitting agencies on the potential harm to living marine resources caused by the proposed water development project and recommendations to prevent harm. Generally, comments submitted under the authority of the Fish and Wildlife Coordination Act may be integrated with the essential fish habitat consultation process.

Because water resource development projects covered by the Fish and Wildlife Coordination Act include those constructed by a non-federal entity under a federal permit or license, a proposed water resource development project that requires a Section 404 or Section 10 permit implicates this Act. As described in the Corps regulations, under the Fish and Wildlife Coordination Act, any federal agency that proposes to control or modify any body of water must first consult with the U.S. Fish and Wildlife Service or NMFS, as appropriate, and with the head of the appropriate state agency exercising administration over the wildlife resources of the affected state.[420]

National Historic Preservation Act

The Corps must comply with Section 106 of the National Historic Preservation Act[421] before issuing a Section 404 permit. Before undertaking or permitting an activity that may affect properties listed or eligible for listing on the National Register of Historic

419 16 U.S.C. §§ 661–667e.

420 33 C.F.R. § 320.3(e).

421 16 U.S.C. § 470.

Places, federal agencies must take into account the effect of the project on the historic properties and provide the Advisory Council on Historic Preservation an opportunity to comment on the activity. Compliance with Section 106 can be surprisingly time-consuming, and applicants should be aware that several steps may be involved to ensure full compliance with the statute.

Coastal Zone Management Act

The Coastal Zone Management Act[422] (CZMA) established a national program for the management, beneficial use, protection, and development of land and water resources of the United States' coastal zones. It requires that any applicant for a federal permit to conduct an activity affecting land or water uses in the coastal zone of that state must provide a certification that the proposed activity complies with the state's approved program and that such activity will be conducted in a manner consistent with the program. The federal agency may not grant the permit until the state or its designated agency has concurred with the applicant's certification.[423]

California's program is administered by three state agencies: California Coastal Commission, San Francisco Bay Conservation, and the California Coastal Conservancy. Depending on the location of the project, either the California Coastal Commission or the San Francisco Bay Conservation and Development Commission (BCDC) will be the agency that issues the CZMA consistency determination.

For those projects located within the California coastal zone but not within the San Francisco Bay, the Federal Consistency Unit of the California Coastal Commission implements the CZMA and administers the consistency determination process for federal agency activities and development projects, and consistency certification for federal permits and licenses. All consistency documents are reviewed for consistency with the policies identified in Chapter 3 of the California Coastal Act of 1976.[424] These policies pertain to issues such as public access, recreation, marine environment, land resources, development, and industrial development.

For those projects located within the Bay itself, a shoreline band of land extending inland for 100 feet from the shoreline of the Bay, or other features identified in the McAteer-Petris Act, BCDC uses its federally approved Management Program for the San Francisco Bay Segment of the California Coastal Zone to exercise its federal consistency authority under the CZMA. The Management Program provides that BCDC will generally follow its procedures for processing a permit application when it reviews a consistency determination for a federal project or activity, or a consistency certification for a non-federal project subject to consistency review. The Management Program specifically identifies Clean Water Act Section 404 and Rivers and Harbors Act of 1899

---

422 *Id.* § 1451–1465.

423 *Id.* § 1456.

424 Pub. Res. Code §§ 30200–30265.5.

Section 10 permits as being subject to the certification process for consistency with the Management Program.[425]

MOA = Memorandum of Agreement

ENFORCEMENT UNDER THE CLEAN WATER ACT

The Corps regulations discuss methods which can be used either singly or in combination to bring enforcement actions to ensure waters of the United States are not misused and to maintain the integrity of the permitting program. In furtherance of this policy, the regulations specify that the Corps should normally coordinate with EPA because it has independent enforcement authority under the Clean Water Act for unauthorized discharges.[426]

In January 1989, EPA and the Corps entered into a Memorandum of Agreement (MOA) regarding "Federal Enforcement for the Section 404 Program of the Clean Water Act." This MOA allocates enforcement responsibilities between EPA and the Corps and establishes a framework for Section 404 enforcement with very little overlap.[427] Under the MOA, the Corps generally acts as the lead enforcement agency for all violations of Corps-issued permits and for unpermitted discharge violations which do not meet the criteria for forwarding enforcement actions to EPA.

EPA acts as the lead enforcement agency when an unpermitted activity involves the following: (a) repeat violators; (b) flagrant violations; (c) where EPA requests a class of cases or a particular case; or (d) the Corps recommends that an EPA administrative penalty action may be warranted.[428] The Corps will act as the lead enforcement agency in all other unpermitted cases that do not involve these situations.[429] The Corps also will act as the lead enforcement agency for Corps-issued permit condition violations.[430] Where EPA requests the Corps to take action on a permit condition violation, the MOA establishes a "right of first refusal" for the Corps. Where the Corps notifies EPA that, because of limited staff resources or other reasons, it will not take an action on a permit condition violation case, EPA may take action commensurate with resource availability.[431] According to the MOA, an "appropriate enforcement response" may consist of an administrative order, administrative penalty complaint, a civil or criminal judicial referral or other appropriate formal enforcement response.[432]

---

425 See the Management Program for further information, available on the BCDC website at http://www.bcdc. ca.gov/publications/MgmtPrgrmSFBay.pdf.

426 33 C.F.R. § 326.2.

427 MOA ¶¶ I and II.A.

428 *Id.* ¶ III.D.1.

429 *Id.* ¶ III.D.2.

430 *Id.* ¶ III.D.3.

431 *Id.* ¶ III.D.4.

432 *Id.* ¶ III.E.

Wetlands and Other Waters of the State

This chapter discusses the protection of wetlands and other waters of the State under the Porter-Cologne Water Quality Control Act, which is California's analog to the federal Clean Water Act. The chapter begins with an overview of the programs administered by the State Water Resources Control Board and California's nine Regional Water Quality Control Boards under Porter-Cologne, including basin plans and beneficial uses, implementation of the federal National Pollutant Discharge Elimination System program for point and non-point source discharges (including storm water), and the process for issuance of Waste Discharge Requirements and Section 401 certifications. The chapter then turns to a detailed discussion of the State Water Resources Control Board's 2019 policy establishing a state-wide wetlands definition and procedures for the disposal of dredged and fill material into wetlands and other waters of the State.

HISTORY AND BACKGROUND

In its early years, water quality regulation in California was performed through a patchwork of state and local agencies. The State Department of Public Health's Division of Environmental Sanitation and Bureau of Sanitary Engineering issued permits for all sewage and waste disposal devices in the State of California, and it had the power to revoke those permits if discharges or a facility's disposal process became a menace to public health or a nuisance. The Department of Fish and Game (now the Department of Fish and Wildlife) and the Fish and Game Commission enforced provisions of the Fish and Game Code that prohibited depositing substances or materials deleterious to fish, plant, or bird life into water. The Department of Public Works was vested with the power to determine water rights, and its Division of Water Resources had broad investigative powers in all matters relating to water. Its Division of Architecture designed and regulated the operation of sewage treatment plants, which were not themselves subject to any state law. The Department of Industrial Relations governed sanitary conditions in industrial plants and sewage disposal by certain facilities. The Harbor and Navigation Code established regulations governing the disposal of wastes from vessels and dockside establishments. Local agencies regulated waste disposal as well.

This hodgepodge of regulation was not sufficient to meet modern challenges. The 1940s saw outbreaks of water-borne diseases and severe degradation of recreational and fishing waters during a time of significant population and industrial growth in California. A once-lauded sewage treatment plant in Los Angeles County was shuttered in 1945, having significantly polluted the waters of the Los Angeles basin. Industrial waste loads at plants in northern California caused septic conditions in the streams to which they discharged. The Department of Public Health's permitting system was strained due to lack of enforcement and an absence of coordination between the many interested state agencies. In the late 1940s, the California Assembly Committee on Water Pollution concluded that continuing to implement the existing laws and procedures was untenable.

In response to these shortcomings, the state legislature passed the Dickey Water Act in 1949 (the "Dickey Act"), which first established regional water boards and a state water board to coordinate state regulation of water pollution caused by industrial waste and sewage. Though somewhat limited in scope, the Dickey Act introduced concepts of water quality regulation that have since been expanded upon at the state level, and now make up key components of water quality regulation in California.

Under the Dickey Act's framework, the state and regional boards dealt exclusively with pollution and nuisance caused by sewage and industrial waste. "Pollution" and "contamination" were treated as distinct concepts. Pollution was defined as an impairment of water quality that did not result in adverse health effects, the purview of the water boards. Contamination was defined as an impairment of water quality that created actual adverse health effects. Critically, though, the Dickey Act protected the "beneficial use" of waters of the State, allowing the water boards to regulate discharges that could unreasonably interfere with a water body's beneficial use or uses, even though such discharges might not create any public health effect.

The nine regional boards established by the Dickey Act were responsible for issuing requirements to entities that caused or threatened to cause pollution or nuisance conditions. While the state board was given the responsibility of formulating a statewide policy for control of water pollution, the regional boards had significant discretion to consider how to regulate existing and proposed discharges of sewage and industrial waste. As California's population and industrial footprint continued to grow through the 1950s and 1960s, members of the state legislature became increasingly concerned with the limitations of the framework established by the Dickey Act. Of particular focus were the Dickey Act's restrictive scope, which did not extend beyond sewage and industrial waste and was not focused on environmental considerations, and the lack of coordination between regulation of water quality and regulation of water rights.

These concerns led to the establishment of the State Water Resources Control Board (SWRCB, or the "State Water Board") in 1967, merging regulation of both water quality and water rights under the authority of a single entity. Shortly following the creation of the State Water Board, Assembly Member Carley Porter of Compton requested the new entity to undertake a high-level study designed to update the Dickey Act. The State Water Board undertook this effort, which resulted in the passage in 1969 of the Porter-Cologne Water Quality Control Act ("Porter-Cologne)—legislation which remains the cornerstone of water quality regulation in California today, and which also served as a blueprint for key amendments to water quality legislation on the federal level.

Porter-Cologne retains the Dickey Act's basic structure of a State Water Board and nine Regional Water Quality Control Boards (the RWQCBs or "Regional Water Boards") responsible for administering a statewide program of water quality control. The State Water Board has jurisdiction throughout California, and holds authority to set statewide policy, coordinate Regional Water Board regulatory efforts, allocate funds, and review petitions challenging decisions administered by the Regional Water Boards.

The Regional Water Boards are organized around the major water basins in the state, and exercise regulatory and rulemaking authority within their particular jurisdictions. Because the Regional Water Boards' jurisdictions track hydro-geologic boundaries rather than county lines, different portions of the same county may be subject to the regulatory authority of different Regional Water Boards.

As a practical matter, it is generally the Regional Water Boards that issue the permits associated with specific development projects within their jurisdictions, including National Pollutant Discharge Elimination System (NPDES) permits and Waste Discharge Requirements (WDRs) for individual projects. In certain circumstances, the State Water Board may adopt a general permit applicable to a limited class of development projects, but projects that choose to opt in to general permit coverage must still register that status with the appropriate Regional Water Board. While the State Water

SWRCB = State Water Resources Control Board, or "State Water Board"

RWQCB = Regional Water Quality Control Board, or "Regional Water Board"

NPDES = National Pollutant Discharge Elimination System

WDRs = Waste Discharge Requirements

Board may set statewide policy that impacts a particular project or may review a challenged Regional Water Board decision, in the first instance, project developers are most likely to encounter and interact with the Regional Water Boards to secure necessary approvals and manage regulatory requirements for a project.

That being said, the State Water Board does hold a wide scope of authority. Critically, it is the state agency designated as the water pollution control agency for purposes of the federal Clean Water Act. It also conducts investigations and research pertaining to water quality issues; prepares the budgets for itself and the Regional Water Boards; adopts administrative regulations to implement legislative mandates to the State Water Board and Regional Water Boards; operates a grant and loan program for the construction of sewage treatment facilities; and licenses operators of sewage treatment facilities.

Porter-Cologne provides for any aggrieved party to petition the State Water Board to review Regional Water Board decisions, actions, or failures to act. A party must appeal a Regional Water Board action to the State Water Board within 30 days, or a Regional Water Board failure to act within 60 days after the petitioner requested that the Regional Water Board act.[1] However, the State Water Board reserves the power to review any Regional Water Board action on its own motion, and it is not constrained by the 30- and 60-day timeframes that apply to petitioners.[2] Once the State Water Board accepts an appeal, it reviews record evidence of the Regional Water Board's action and, if that record evidence is sufficient to render a decision, issues a draft order in response to the petition.[3] While the State Water Board more often than not upholds Regional Water Board determinations, where the State Water Board finds that a Regional Water Board action is inappropriate in whole or in part, it will direct the Regional Water Board to take the appropriate action.[4] A State Water Board decision on review of Regional Water Board action or inaction may be appealed in state court.

Building on the structure established by the Dickey Act, Porter-Cologne significantly expanded the enforcement authority of the water boards, as well as their mandate to engage in proactive planning to regulate California's water resources.

BASIN PLANNING AND BENEFICIAL USE

A key component of Porter-Cologne is the Water Code Section 13240 requirement that "[e]ach regional board shall formulate and adopt water quality control plans for all areas within the region." These plans are periodically reviewed and updated, as required by both California and federal law, and serve as general planning documents for water quality control within individual water basins.

California's definition of "waters of the State" is distinct from—and more expansive than—the federal definition of "waters of the United States." Under Section 13050(e) of Porter-Cologne, the term is defined as "any surface water or groundwater, including saline waters, within the boundaries of the state." As discussed in detail below, the water boards have relied on this definition to regulate not only traditional surface waters, but also seasonal wetlands and other areas that, some have asserted, would not be considered to constitute surface waters under traditional California water law.

1   Water Code § 13320(a).
2   *Id.*
3   *Id.* § 13320(b).
4   *Id.* § 13320(c).

A cornerstone of basin planning documents is their designation and protection of certain "beneficial uses" from degradation. Under Porter-Cologne, "beneficial uses" that may be protected against degradation in water quality include:

> domestic, municipal, agricultural, and industrial supply

> power generation

> recreation

> aesthetic enjoyment

> navigation

> preservation and enhancement of fish, wildlife, and other aquatic resources or preserves

The Regional Water Boards are mandated to establish water quality objectives within their basin plans that will ensure the reasonable protection of beneficial uses and the prevention of nuisance. Basin plan documents set forth an inventory of beneficial uses within the water basin, designating the beneficial uses, if any, of individual aquifers and waterways. Even if a basin plan establishes a particular beneficial use category or definition for planning purposes, specific water bodies are not considered designated for that beneficial use until a water quality standards action occurs to make the designation, meaning that if a water body was not designated for a particular beneficial use in the original approved basin plan, an amendment to the basin plan is typically required to add a designation for a particular water body. These designations are considered as the Regional Water Board sets water quality objectives, which are not merely water quality goals, but are standards that must be implemented and enforced by the Regional Water Boards.

When formulating or updating water quality objectives for a basin, Regional Water Boards are required to take into account a variety of factors, including:

> past, present, and probable future beneficial uses of water

> environmental characteristics of the hydrographic unit under consideration, including the quality of water available

> water quality conditions that could reasonably be achieved through the coordinated control of all factors which affect water quality in the area

> economic considerations

> the need for developing housing within the region

> the need to develop and use recycled water[5]

While Porter-Cologne contemplates that some change in water quality may be acceptable, any such change cannot "unreasonably" impact beneficial uses of water within a basin. To that end, in 1987, the State Water Board adopted Resolution 68-18, "Statement of Policy with Respect to Maintaining High Quality of Waters in California." This policy, commonly referred to as the "Antidegradation Policy," applies to "high quality waters"— waters of higher quality than the water quality standards applied to them—and requires that the quality of such waters be maintained unless it can be demonstrated that any

---

5   *Id.* § 13241.

EPA = Environmental Protection
Agency

WDRs = Waste Discharge
Requirements

change in quality (1) will not unreasonably affect either present or anticipated beneficial uses of the water and (2) will not result in water quality less than the prescribed standard for the water body in question.

The Antidegradation Policy also requires dischargers to high quality waters to secure WDRs to ensure that pollution or nuisance will not occur and that "the highest water quality consistent with the maximum benefit to the people of the State will be maintained." The Antidegradation Policy applies outside the basin planning context as well (to permitting, WDRs, Section 401 certifications, and cleanups of surface waters), and serves as an important consideration for Regional Water Boards as they adopt and update water quality objectives.

Beyond water quality objectives themselves, basin plans must also establish a program for implementation of the objectives. This includes not only a description of actions necessary to achieve water quality objectives (which recommends particular actions to be taken by private and public entities), but also a time schedule for undertaking these actions, and a description of the monitoring and oversight necessary to determine that the objectives have been met. Basin plans may also enumerate particular areas or conditions under which specific types of discharges will not be permitted. For example, water bodies of particular biological significance may be protected by special discharge prohibitions set forth in a basin plan.

Basin plans or amendments to them—including those designating or removing designations of beneficial uses for particular water bodies within the basin—are subject to notice and comment requirements, including a required public hearing and approval by the State Water Board. The State Water Board is required to act upon a basin plan or plan amendment within 60 days of a Regional Water Board's submission of the plan. If changes are required and the Regional Water Board resubmits the plan or amended plan, the State Water Board must act within 90 days. If a Regional Water Board does not make changes required by the State Water Board, the State Water Board has authority to hold a hearing in the area covered by the basin plan and make changes to the plan or plan amendment itself.

Where a basin plan covers waters regulated pursuant to the federal Clean Water Act, the Environmental Protection Agency (EPA) must also approve the basin plan or portion of the plan that applies to federally regulated waters. Once approved by EPA, the water quality objectives and beneficial use designations established by the basin plan or plan amendment become water quality standards under the Clean Water Act.

WASTE DISCHARGE REQUIREMENTS

Porter-Cologne requires that any person "discharging waste, or proposing to discharge waste, within any region that could affect the quality of the waters of the State, other than into a community sewer system" submit a report of waste discharge to the appropriate Regional Water Board.[6]

6   *Id.* § 13260(a)(1).

What Is "Waste"?

The precise nature of what constitutes "waste" has been explored in case law, as well as in opinions issued by the California Attorney General.[7] Generally, Porter-Cologne's definition of "waste" is considered to be expansive, and to capture a wide range of discharges associated both with human habitation and industrial operations. Under Porter-Cologne, the term "waste" can include "sewage and any and all other waste substances, liquid, solid, gaseous, or radioactive, associated with human habitation, or of human or animal origin, or from any producing, manufacturing, or processing operation, including waste placed within containers of whatever nature prior to, and for purposes of, disposal."[8] Discharges of fill material into waters of the State associated with development activity are treated by the Water Boards as discharges of waste under Porter-Cologne. Whether the Water Boards can exercise this authority has not been decided by the courts and, as recently as 2016, the U.S. Army Corps of Engineers (South Pacific Division) advised the State Water Board that clean fill does not constitute waste under California law.

When Has Waste Been "Discharged"?

Similarly, courts have considered the question of when waste has been "discharged" under Porter-Cologne. While the federal Clean Water Act regulates "point source" discharges (i.e., discharges that are attributable to a single specific source), courts have determined that Porter-Cologne places no such limitation on the discharges regulated under Porter-Cologne:

> [E]ven upon the assumption that a discharge . . . is [from] a nonpoint source
> of pollution, it remains subject to regulation by the laws of this state . . . .
> [There is] no suggestion the Legislature intended discharges of waste to be
> limited to point source discharges, particularly in light of the Legislature's
> express confinement of the "point source" definition to chapter 5.5 [of Porter-
> Cologne, dealing with compliance with the federal Clean Water Act].[9]

Accordingly, facilities or projects that plan to discharge to waters of the State— whether from a point source or otherwise—must notify the Regional Water Board of that fact prior to commencement of the discharge. A report of waste discharge is also required if there is any material change or proposed change in the character, location, or volume of discharge.[10] As discussed in greater detail below, a discharger that fails to file a report of waste discharge with the Regional Water Board is subject to a variety of

---

The Water Boards' authority to regulate discharges of fill material as "waste" under Porter-Cologne is presently the subject of legal challenge. Most recently, the San Joaquin Tributaries Authority filed litigation against the State Water Board's adoption of a permit program (discussed below) for the discharge of dredged or fill material into waters of the State. Similarly, the Santa Clara Valley Water District has challenged the San Francisco Regional Water Board's issuance of Waste Discharge Requirements for the construction and maintenance of certain channel modifications on Upper Berryessa Creek.

---

7   See, e.g., *Lake Madrone Water Dist. v. State Water Resources Control Bd.*, 209 Cal. App. 3d 16 (1989)
    (tailings from a dam were considered to be waste as defined by Porter-Cologne); 63 Ops.Cal.Atty.Gen.
    51 (1980) (silt-bearing drainage from Malakoff Diggins State Historical Park was considered waste under
    Porter-Cologne).

8   Water Code § 13050(d).

9   *Lake Madrone*, 209 Cal. App. 3d at 173–74.

10   Water Code § 13260(c).

enforcement actions by the Regional Water Board, which can range from administrative fines to a court action.

WDR Issuance Process

The report of waste discharge serves as an application for issuance of WDRs.[11] In the case of a development project, the application will typically be submitted by the project proponent. If the waters in question are also regulated by the federal Clean Water Act, the report of waste discharge may additionally serve as an application for a federal point-source discharge permit, typically referred to as an "NPDES" permit. Also as discussed below, an application for WDRs may also serve as an application for water quality certification of federal actions under Section 401 of the Clean Water Act. Following receipt of a report of waste discharge, the Regional Water Board will review the report for completeness and, within 30 days, request any additional information necessary to complete the application.

A Regional Water Board will review the complete report of waste discharge once submitted and, following discussions (i.e., negotiations) with the applicant, will then prepare draft WDRs. WDRs must implement any relevant water quality control plan, such as a basin plan, and must take into account:

> beneficial uses to be protected
> water quality objectives reasonably required to protect beneficial uses
> other waste discharges
> the need to prevent nuisance
> the factors relevant to establishment of the water quality objectives set forth in the basin plan, as outlined in Water Code Section 13241[12]

In prescribing WDRs, a Regional Water Board may set a time schedule for implementation in the WDR permit.

Importantly, the Regional Water Board is not required to authorize a discharger to utilize the full waste assimilation capacity of the receiving waters in question.[13] In other words, the Regional Water Board may authorize only a limited amount of discharge, even if the water receiving the waste still has capacity to accept waste. This concept fits with Porter-Cologne's mandate that the Regional Water Board consider other waste discharges to the water in question when approving WDRs.

Once draft WDRs have been prepared, the draft is sent to the discharger and to any other interested parties, such as other public agencies that may use the water in question.[14] The Regional Water Board may also hold a hearing on the draft WDRs if necessary; that hearing need include only three members of the Regional Water Board.[15]

11 *Id.* § 13260(a).
12 *Id.* § 13263.
13 *Id.* § 13263(b).
14 *Id.* § 13223.
15 *Id.* §§ 13228.14, 13263.

Once reviewed and after incorporating any additional modifications at the draft stage, the WDRs are placed on the Regional Water Board's agenda for public hearing and final approval.[16] At final approval stage, the full Regional Water Board must be present for the hearing. While the State Water Board retains jurisdiction to impose WDRs, it is typically the Regional Water Boards that are responsible for preparing and approving WDRs for individual facilities and/or projects.

A Regional Water Board may also act on its own to impose WDRs even when no report of waste discharge has been filed.[17] Where WDRs are imposed by independent action of the Regional Water Board, the appropriate procedures for preparation and approval of the WDR permit must still be followed. The Regional Water Board may also review and revise WDRs on its own motion, or upon application by any affected party. WDRs are required to be periodically reviewed.

While WDRs permit discharges to waters of the State if the conditions set forth in the WDRs are met, it is important to note that the issuance of a WDR does not create a vested right to continue the discharge.[18] Nor is there any vested right under Porter-Cologne to continue a discharge that has been ongoing without adherence to WDRs. Accordingly, it is within the Regional Water Board's authority to order termination or modification of a previously-permitted discharge.

General WDRs for Storm Water and Other Categories of Discharge

Under certain circumstances, the State Water Board or Regional Water Board may elect to create a general WDR order that is applicable to a particular category of discharges. To be covered by a general order, the category of discharges must:

> be produced by the same or similar operations

> involve the same or similar types of waste

> require the same or similar treatment standards

> be more appropriately regulated under general discharge requirements than individual discharge requirements[19]

For example, a commonly used general order in the development context is the state's General Permit for Storm Water Discharges Associated with Construction and Land Disturbance Activities, SWRCB Order No. 2009-009-DWQ ("Construction General Permit"). This permit covers construction activities that result in a land distur-bance of an acre or more, or less than an acre but part of a larger common plan of devel-opment or sale, and also serves as a permit under the State Water Board's authority to regulate non-point-source storm water discharges under the Clean Water Act.

The process for enrollment in the Construction General Permit is typical of the process to gain coverage under other general orders. Before commencing construction

16   *Id.* § 13228.14.

17   *Id.* § 13263(c).

18   *Id.* § 13263(g).

19   *Id.* § 13263(i).

FEDERAL NPDES PROGRAM

As discussed above, Porter-Cologne existed prior to, and in some senses, served as the inspiration for, the 1972 amendments to the federal Water Pollution Control Act, resulting in the Clean Water Act framework we know today. The Clean Water Act recognizes the interplay between state water quality control programs and federal requirements, and, in many instances, provides for state implementation of federal programs or state programs that comply with (or are more stringent than) the Clean Water Act's requirements. As a result, the State Water Board and Regional Water Boards implement both Porter-Cologne and portions of the federal Clean Water Act, including its permitting and planning provisions. The practical effects of this confluence include:

> when a project discharges to federally regulated waters, the State Water Board or a Regional Water Board will issue one discharge permit to an applicant for purposes of both state and federal law

> basin plan water quality objectives applicable to federally regulated waters are also incorporated into federal law as water quality standards once reviewed and approved by EPA

> when a project discharges fill and dredged material to wetlands, the State Water Board or a Regional Water Board must issue a certification consistent with Section 401 of the Clean Water Act before discharge can occur

The Clean Water Act established a permitting system to regulate point source discharges—discharges that are attributable to a single specific source, such as a pipe or ditch—to "navigable waters of the United States." This mandated permitting system is known as the National Pollutant Discharge Elimination System (NPDES). This system differs from Porter-Cologne's WDR permitting system in that it applies only to point source discharges and only to those discharges that occur to federally regulated waters. With respect to development activities, NPDES permits are often required for point source discharges of storm water or recycled wastewater into waters of the State.

EPA is the central permitting authority under the NPDES program. However, built into the statutory framework of the Clean Water Act is the ability for states to develop and administer their own NPDES program, subject to EPA approval and provided that the state's program is at least as strict as EPA's federal program. Accordingly, in late 1972, the California legislature amended Porter-Cologne, allowing the state to operate its own NDPES permitting program. The amended provisions of Porter-Cologne, found in Chapter 5.5 of Division 7 of the California Water Code, provide the State Water Board and Regional Water Boards with authority to issue fixed-term NPDES permits for periods not to exceed five years, inspect and monitor discharges, establish and enforce a pretreatment program, and enforce permit terms.

NPDES permits issued by the State Water Board and Regional Water Boards remain subject to the other provisions of Porter-Cologne, resulting in the dual-purpose permitting scheme administered by the Boards, whereby one permit is issued to satisfy the requirements of both Porter-Cologne and the Clean Water Act. State Water Board regulations enacted pursuant to Porter-Cologne provide that a facility's report of waste discharge—the permit application for WDRs—serves as the equivalent of an NPDES permit application.

While the State Water Board issues some NPDES permits, the Regional Water Boards issue the overwhelming majority of NPDES permits in California. The typical NPDES permitting process begins when a facility or project developer submits a report of waste discharge related to discharges of pollutants from point sources to the local Regional Water Board with jurisdiction over the facility or project area. The Regional Water Board then reviews the report and may exercise its authority to issue WDRs and/or an NPDES permit for the facility or project.

In issuing the joint WDR/NPDES permit, it is the Regional Water Board's responsibility to ensure that the permit is consistent not only with the requirements of Porter-Cologne, but with federal Clean Water Act regulations as well. This means that all WDRs applicable to point source discharges to federally regulated waters must comply with the Clean Water Act. Federal requirements that must be met include:

> adherence to pretreatment standards established for discharge to publicly owned treatment works; these include general and specific discharge prohibitions, as well as categorical pretreatment standards and local limits

> compliance with total maximum daily load (TMDL) standards for regulated waters; TMDLs establish the maximum amount of pollutant a water body can safely receive while still meeting water quality standards, and are consistent with basin plan water quality objectives

> required implementation of water quality control technology standards. The Clean Water Act requires that different levels of control technology—such as best available control technology economically achievable (BAT) or best conventional pollutant control technology (BCT) be implemented depending on the type of facility and nature of the discharge in question; water quality standards for a particular water body may necessitate the implementation of BAT or BCT

TDML = total maximum daily load

BAT = best available control technology economically achievable

BCT = best conventional pollutant control technology

SMARTS = Storm Water Multi-Application Report Tracking System

SWPPP = Storm Water Pollution Prevention Plan

NOI = notice of intent

activities, the legally responsible person for the project—most often the project propo-nent—will apply to the appropriate Regional Water Board by submitting the appropri-ate permit registration documents electronically through the Storm Water Multi-Application Report Tracking System (SMARTS), an online system set up by the Boards to track permit coverage and compliance. Those documents include a notice of intent (sometimes referred to by its acronym, NOI) to be covered by the Construction General Permit, a risk assessment, post-construction calculations, a site map, a Storm Water Pollution Prevention Plan (SWPPP, pronounced "*swip*"), a signed certification statement, and the first annual fee. Upon submitting this documentation, the Regional Water Board will issue an identification number to the applicant signifying its coverage under the permit.

Once a project is covered by the Construction General Permit, it is required to adhere to all of the permit's terms, including regularly updating its SWPPP, monitoring the discharge of pollutants identified in its SWPPP during storm events and reporting that data regularly through SMARTS, implementing best management practices identi-fied in the SWPPP, and undertaking appropriate reporting and improvements to on-site practices if discharges exceed mandated levels. Just as with individualized project-spe-cific WDRs, failure to adhere to the terms of a general permit exposes the permit appli-cant to penalties and potential court action.

Compliance with WDRs

Both general orders and individual WDRs contain monitoring and reporting require-ments that must be met by the discharger at the discharger's own expense. Dischargers must implement a monitoring and reporting program and must periodically submit self-monitoring reports to the Regional Water Boards through SMARTS.[20] WDRs also require regulated parties to report discharges that are out of compliance with a party's WDR permit.[21]

The required reporting frequency is dependent upon the nature and impact of the discharge in question. Larger dischargers may keep an individual on staff to ensure mon-itoring and reporting obligations are met, and to oversee implementation of any best management practices required; smaller dischargers sometimes contract this work out to a consultant.

The Regional Water Boards periodically inspect dischargers, with larger dischargers typically inspected on a more frequent basis than smaller dischargers.[22] Regional Water Board staff may inspect a discharge with the consent of the owner or, if the owner does not consent to the inspection, may obtain an inspection warrant to enter the property and observe the discharge. Typically, inspections occur with the voluntary consent of the owner.

20 See Water Code §§ 13267, 13383.

21 *Id.* § 13271.

22 See *id.* §§ 13267, 13383.

Enforcement Against Violations of WDR Terms

The State Water Board and Regional Water Board consider a number of WDR compliance violations to be priorities for enforcement actions:

> violations of discharge prohibitions contained in WDRs when the violation results in an adverse impact to beneficial uses or a condition of nuisance or pollution

> violation of the numeric effluent toxicity limits that are contained in WDRs

> failure to submit the reports required by WDRs within 30 days from their due dates

> submission of deficient or incomplete reports

> failure to comply with Porter-Cologne's discharge notice requirements

> failure to undertake required monitoring

The State Water Board or Regional Water Boards may exercise their enforcement authority with respect to such violations, including imposition of monetary penalties and, in some cases, referring the case for filing of civil or criminal suit against the discharger.

Penalties for WDR Reporting Violations

Failure to provide a report of waste discharge when requested by a Regional Water Board is a misdemeanor which carries monetary penalties. If those penalties are administratively imposed by the Regional Water Board, they can range up to $1,000 per day of violation; if the penalties are imposed by a court, they may range up to $5,000 per day of violation.[23]

An entity that discharges or proposes to discharge waste and willfully withholds information from a report of waste discharge, willfully fails to submit a report of waste discharge, or knowingly submits a false report is guilty of a misdemeanor and may be liable for administrative fines of up to $5,000 per day of violation or court-imposed fines of up to $25,000 per day of violation.[24]

Similarly, an entity that initiates a new discharge of waste or makes a material change to a discharge without filing a report of waste discharge, or before receiving WDRs, is guilty of a misdemeanor and may be liable for administrative fines of up to $1,000 per day of violation or court-imposed fines of up to $5,000 per day of violation.[25]

A failure to provide technical or monitoring reports to a Regional Water Board is a misdemeanor which carries administrative penalties of up to $1,000 per day of violation or court-imposed penalties of up to $5,000 per day of violation. A knowing violation of this obligation may also expose the violator to criminal liability.[26]

23 *Id.* § 13261.
24 *Id.*
25 *Id.* § 13264.
26 *Id.* § 13268.

NOV = notice of violation

Discharging hazardous waste without providing the required technical or monitoring reports is a misdemeanor that carries penalties of administrative fines of up to $5,000 per day of violation or court-imposed fines of up to $25,000 per day of violation, and a knowing failure to report the discharge may also result in criminal charges.[27]

These penalties apply only to the WDR provisions of Porter-Cologne; waste discharges for which an NPDES permit is required carry separate and distinct penalties, discussed later in this chapter.

ENFORCEMENT

The State Water Board and Regional Water Boards engage in both informal and formal enforcement actions pursuant to their authority under Porter-Cologne.

Informal Enforcement Actions

An informal enforcement action involves a communication from State Water Board or Regional Water Board staff regarding the violation or potential violation, typically to put the discharger on notice and provide an opportunity, if needed, to return to compliance. The first step of an informal enforcement action is often verbal communication from Regional Water Board staff, after which a follow-up enforcement letter may be sent.

The highest level of informal enforcement action is a notice of violation (NOV) letter to the discharger. NOV letters are signed by the Regional Water Board Executive Officer, and contain a description of the violations, a summary of potential enforcement options available to the Regional Water Board, and a request for written response, if appropriate.

While these informal actions may sometimes be petitioned to a Regional Water Board or Regional Water Board Executive Officer, they cannot be directly petitioned to the State Water Board.

Formal Enforcement Actions

Formal enforcement actions are actions provided for by statute to address a violation or threat of violation of Porter-Cologne. Formal enforcement orders issued by the State Water Board or Regional Water Boards contain a recitation of facts that establish enforcement authority under a particular statute. There are several types of formal enforcement actions that may be undertaken by the State Water Board or Regional Water Boards.

Notices to Comply

Notices to comply are issued by the State Water Board or Regional Water Boards to correct minor violations, such as inadvertent recordkeeping omissions or inadvertent violations of administrative provisions that do not involve a discharge or threat of discharge of waste. Typically, these violations can be corrected within a short period of time.

---

27 *Id.*

Notices of Storm Water Noncompliance

CAO = Cleanup and Abatement Order

The Regional Water Boards are required to notify storm water dischargers who fail to file a notice of intent to obtain permit coverage, a notice of non-applicability, a construction certification, or annual reports as required by Porter-Cologne.[28] If a discharger fails to file the applicable documentation after two notifications have been issued by the Regional Water Board, a mandatory civil penalty is assessed against the discharger. Failure to submit a required notice of intent to obtain coverage carries a penalty of no less than $5,000, while other violations carry penalties of no less than $1,000.[29]

Cleanup and Abatement Orders

The State Water Board and Regional Water Boards retain the authority to require any entity that has caused or permitted the discharge of waste that "creates, or threatens to create, a condition of pollution or nuisance . . . [to] clean up the waste or abate the effects of the waste, or, in the case of threatened pollution or nuisance, take other necessary remedial action, including, but not limited to, overseeing cleanup or abatement efforts . . . ."[30]

Under Porter-Cologne, "pollution" is "an alteration of the quality of waters of the State by waste to a degree which unreasonably affects . . . [t]he waters for beneficial uses [or] [f]acilities which serve these beneficial uses."[31] Pollution may include contamination. A "nuisance" is anything which is (1) injurious to health, indecent or offensive to the senses, or an obstruction to the free use of property; (2) affects at the same time an entire community or neighborhood, or any considerable number of persons; and (3) occurs during or as a result of the treatment or disposal of wastes.[32]

The State Water Board or Regional Water Board may accordingly adopt a Cleanup and Abatement Order (CAO) requiring the discharger to take any remedial action necessary. CAOs typically require dischargers to clean up the pollution to background levels or to the best water quality which is reasonable if background levels cannot be achieved. Cleanup levels are required to be sufficiently stringent to fully support the beneficial uses of the water body in question. If restoration cannot be achieved, the discharger may be required to provide alternate water supplies. Some CAOs require the submission of technical and monitoring reports, and may also require the discharger to pay Regional Water Board staff oversight costs.

Cease and Desist Orders

The State Water Board or Regional Water Boards may issue a Cease and Desist Order (CDO) to a discharger that is threatening to violate or is in violation of WDRs or other

28 *Id.* § 13399.25 *et seq.*

29 See *id.* § 13261.

30 *Id.* § 13304(a).

31 *Id.* § 13050(l).

32 *Id.* § 13050(m).

prohibitions imposed by the Boards. CDOs are typically employed in situations where a discharger has chronic noncompliance issues and compliance will involve extensive investment, such as large-scale capital improvements or operational changes. A CDO usually includes a compliance schedule, interim effluent limits (if appropriate), and a final compliance date.[33]

Modification or Rescission of WDRs

As discussed earlier in this chapter, the State Water Board or Regional Water Boards may modify or rescind WDRs in response to violations by a discharger. This enforcement action is typically considered appropriate where the discharger has the ability to prevent the discharge, and may occur in response to a failure to pay fees or penalties, or in response to a discharge that adversely affects beneficial uses of the water body in question. The discharger may challenge the modification or rescission of WDRs.

Administrative Civil Liability Complaints

Various provisions of the California Water Code assign administrative penalty amounts for particular statutory violations. For example, administrative penalty amounts associated with statutory violations of WDR requirements were discussed earlier in this chapter. An Administrative Civil Liability (ACL) complaint is the mechanism by which the state and regional water boards impose these penalties.[34]

An ACL complaint explains the violation and statutory provision authorizing imposition of civil liability, proposes a specific civil liability amount, and informs the discharger that a public hearing will be held within 90 days of service of the ACL complaint.[35] The discharger may waive the public hearing or agree to an extension of the hearing date. The hearing, if not waived, is held before a panel of the Regional Water Board, or before the Regional Water Board or State Water Board, depending on the circumstances and the body that issued the ACL complaint in question. After the hearing, the State Water Board or Regional Water Board will consider whether to affirm, modify, or reject the liability; in any case, liability cannot exceed the statutory maximum. If an ACL complaint is settled, a public comment period is required prior to approval of the settlement. ACL orders are final upon adoption, and can only be modified by the State Water Board or through a petition for writ of mandamus in state court.[36]

WATER QUALITY CERTIFICATIONS

Introduction

Section 401 of the Clean Water Act requires applicants for federal permits affecting waters of the United States to obtain certification from the state in which the discharge

33 *Id.* § 13301.
34 *Id.* § 13323 *et seq.*
35 *Id.* § 13323(b).
36 See *id.* § 13323(d).

will occur that the discharge will not violate state water quality standards. In 1990, the State Water Board formally instituted a Water Quality Certification (WQC) Program to implement the requirements of Section 401. Over time, the WQC Program has evolved and now stretches beyond administration of the Section 401 certification process.

WQC = Water Quality Certification

FERC = Federal Energy Regulatory Commission

While many WQCs are issued for activities involving discharges of dredged or fill material to wetlands and other waters of the United States pursuant to Section 404 of the federal Clean Water Act, those are not the only activities requiring a WQC. In addition to Section 404 permits, the following permits and licenses are subject to the WQC Program:

> permits issued under Sections 9 and 10 of the Rivers and Harbors Act (for example, to construct a dam, dike, or levee)

> licenses issued by the Nuclear Regulatory Commission

> licenses for hydroelectric power plants issued by the Federal Energy Regulatory Commission (FERC) under the Federal Power Act

To provide a WQC, the Regional Water Board must determine that the activity in question complies with all applicable water quality standards, limitations, and restrictions. Water quality standards (as defined by 40 CFR Part 131) considered by the Regional Water Board when issuing a WQC include:

> **Beneficial Uses.** The uses of water necessary for the survival or well-being of humans, plants, and wildlife. As discussed above, Porter-Cologne recognizes several categories of beneficial uses, and waters within a particular region are designated for certain beneficial uses in the regional basin plan.

> **Water Quality Objectives.** The constituent concentrations, levels, or narrative water quality standards or criteria representing the water quality that supports a particular beneficial use.

> **Antidegradation Policy.** As discussed above, this policy requires that the quality of "high quality" waters be maintained unless it can be demonstrated that any change in quality (1) will not unreasonably affect either present or anticipated beneficial uses of the water and (2) will not result in water quality less than the prescribed standard for the water body in question.

Application for Water Quality Certification

To receive a WQC, an applicant must provide:

> a complete application form, including the name, address, and telephone number of the applicant and the applicant's agent, and complete processing fee[37]

> a complete, technically accurate description of the entire activity, including its purpose and the final goal of the activity[38]

> a complete identification of all federal permits or licenses being sought for or applying to the proposed activity, including listing the federal agency granting

---

37   23 Cal. Code Regs. §§ 3833, 3856(a), 3856(g).

38   *Id.* § 3856(b).

the permit or license, the type of permit or license being granted, permit or license numbers (if applicable), and any available file numbers assigned by the federal agency or agencies in question[39]

> complete copies of either the federal permit or license applications, any notifications from federal agencies regarding the proposed activity if a permit or license is not required, or any correspondence between the applicant and any applicable federal agency if no notifications have been issued[40]

> a copy of any draft or final CEQA documents prepared for the activity[41]

> a complete description of the project, which in turn must include:

  • the names of any bodies of water that may receive a discharge

  • the types of water bodies that may receive a discharge (e.g., wetland type, riparian area)

  • the location of the activity area in latitude and longitude, township/range, or clearly indicated on a published map that allows for easy identification of the area and the receiving waters

  • for each water body type, the total estimated quantity of waters of the United States that may be temporarily or adversely impacted (in acres, or, for linear habitat such as shoreline, in linear feet)

  • for each water body type, the total estimated quantity (in acres or linear feet, as appropriate) of waters of the United States proposed to be created, restored, enhanced, set aside for protection, purchased from a mitigation bank, or otherwise identified as compensatory mitigation for any potential adverse impacts of the activity

  • a description of any other steps that have been or will be taken to mitigate the impacts to beneficial uses of waters of the State

  • the total size (in acres or linear feet, as appropriate), type, and description of the entire project area, including areas that are not waters of the United States

  • a brief list or description, including estimated adverse impacts, of any projects implemented by the applicant within the last five years or planned within the next five years that are in any way related to the proposed activity or may impact the same receiving waters as the proposed activity[42]

The application does not need to contain duplicative information, so if a federal application attached to the application contains information required for the WQC application, it need not be repeated again.[43] An applicant must submit two copies of its application.[44]

---

39 *Id.* § 3856(c).

40 *Id.* § 3856(d).

41 *Id.* § 3856(f); Gov't Code § 65941(b).

42 23 Cal. Code Regs. § 3856(h).

43 *Id.* § 3856.

44 *Id.* § 3832.

If an application may involve a FERC-licensed facility, a diversion of water, or an appropriation of water, the applicant must also notify the State Water Board Executive Director.[45]

EIR = Environmental Impact Report

Timeline for Review and Permit Streamlining

Once an application is submitted, the Regional Water Board must review the application and provide a written determination of the application's completeness to the applicant within 30 days pursuant to the State Water Board regulations and the California Permit Streamlining Act.[46] If the Regional Water Board deems the application incomplete, the applicant may resubmit a revised application, and the Regional Water Board will have another 30 days to determine whether the resubmitted materials are complete.

If the application is deemed complete, the Regional Water Board will notify the applicant, the federal agency issuing the permit or license in question, and EPA.[47] Once an application has been deemed complete by the Regional Water Board, the Regional Water Board may ask for additional materials to clarify the activity's impacts, mitigation for the proposed activity, evidence of compliance with the appropriate requirements of a water quality control plan, or other information regarding the application.[48]

Permit Streamlining Act deadlines apply to the Regional Water Board's ultimate decision on a WQC application as well, and are tied to CEQA compliance. Specifically, if the Regional Water Board is the lead agency, a decision on a WQC must follow within 180 days of an EIR certification, 60 days of adoption of a Negative Declaration or Mitigated Negative Declaration, or 60 days of a determination that the project is exempt from CEQA.[49] If the Regional Water Board is a responsible agency, a decision on a WQC must occur within the longer of 180 days from the lead agency's approval of the project or 180 days from the date that the WQC application was deemed complete.[50] If the Regional Water Board fails to act within the Permit Streamlining Act's mandated timeframes, the WQC will be deemed approved by operation of law.[51]

As discussed below, the application requirements for discharges of dredged or fill material are supplemental to those described in this section.

Certain federal agencies apply their own timelines to WQCs that are unaffected by the Permit Streamlining Act's requirements. For example, the Corps regulations for issuing Section 404 permits typically assume that a WQC will be made within 60 days of the request for certification, which deadline may be extended to the one-year maximum allowed under the Clean Water Act.[52] If the Regional Water Board fails to process a WQC within that timeframe, without an agreement to extend the deadline, the Corps may deem the WQC waived and proceed to grant the permit without it. To that end, the

---

45   *Id.* § 3855.

46   *Id.* § 3835(a); Gov't Code § 65943.

47   23 Cal. Code Regs. § 3835(d).

48   *Id.* § 3836(a).

49   Gov't Code § 65950.

50   *Id.* § 65950.1.

51   *Id.* § 65954.

52   33 C.F.R. § 325.2(b)(ii).

WQC regulations direct Regional Water Boards to issue WQCs or deny them before the federal period for certification of an activity expires.[53]

Approval or Denial of WQC Application

Approval or denial of a WQC application may be taken with or without a public hearing, but notice of the application must be given at least 21 days prior to the decision on the application.[54]

If the application is approved, the WQC can include conditions to ensure compliance with water quality standards or other requirements.[55] The WQC must include the names of the receiving waters, the certification action being taken and any required conditions, and a summary of the activity description information provided by the applicant. The WQC must be sent to the federal agency issuing the permit or license, EPA, and any other known interested persons or agencies within three days after the denial is issued. All WQCs must include conditions stating that the WQC is subject to revocation or modification upon administrative or judicial review and that certification does not apply to any activity involving a hydroelectric facility that requires a FERC license unless the application specifically identified that a FERC license was being sought.[56]

The Regional Water Board may deny a WQC application if:

> the activity requiring a federal license or permit will result in a discharge to waters of the United States that will not comply with applicable water quality standards or other appropriate requirements; or

> the Regional Water Board has not determined compliance with water quality standards or other appropriate requirements, but the application is procedurally inadequate (for example, a complete fee was not provided or it does not meet CEQA requirements)[57]

If the Regional Water Board denies the WQC application, it must notify the applicant in writing of the denial and the reasons for it. That written denial must also be sent to the federal agency issuing the permit or license, EPA, and any other known interested persons or agencies within three days after the denial is issued.[58]

Appeal from WQC Determinations

An applicant may petition the State Water Board to reconsider a WQC approval or denial.[59] Reconsideration should be initiated within 30 days from the decision on the

---

53   23 Cal. Code Regs. § 3859(1).

54   *Id.* § 3858.

55   *Id.* § 3859.

56   *Id.* § 3860.

57   *Id.* § 3837(b).

58   *Id.* § 3837(a).

59   *Id.* § 3867.

WQC application. Otherwise, any rescission or amendment of the certification action that results from reconsideration will not apply to a federal license or permit that was issued in reliance on the WQC determination before the federal agency was notified that reconsideration was being sought.

A reconsideration petition must contain:

> the name, address, and telephone number of the petitioner

> the specific action or failure to act that the State Water Board is being requested to reconsider and a copy of the WQC determination

> the date on which the WQC determination occurred

> a full and complete statement of why the WQC determination was improper

> the manner in which the petitioner is aggrieved

> the specific action by the State Water Board requested by the petitioner

> a list of persons known to have an interest in the subject matter of the petition

> a statement that the petition has been sent to the appropriate Regional Water Board

> a copy of any request for the administrative record

> a summary of the petitioner's participation in the administrative process leading up to the WQC determination

Once a petition for reconsideration is received by the State Water Board, the State Water Board will notify any other interested parties that they have 20 days to submit a response to the State Water Board.[60] After examining the petition and the administrative record, as necessary, the State Water Board may refuse reconsideration, deny the petition for reconsideration by finding the original WQC determination proper, set aside or modify the prior WQC determination, or direct the Regional Water Board to take action.[61] A decision by the State Water Board is appealable to state court.

General WQCs for Classes of Activities

The State Water Board or a Regional Water Board may, on its own action, take a "general" certification action on discharges within its jurisdictional area that result from a class or classes of activities without any application.[62] General WQCs only apply for five years after they are granted and require 45 days of public notice prior to issuance.[63] Proponents of projects falling under a general WQC must give the State Water Board and Regional Water Boards 21 days of notice before commencing a covered discharge.

---

60 *Id.* § 3867.1.

61 *Id.* § 3869.

62 *Id.* § 3861(a).

63 *Id.* § 3861(c).

STATE WETLANDS DEFINITION AND DREDGE AND FILL PROCEDURES

Background and Overview

At the federal level, the concept of "no net loss" of wetlands as a goal for national wetlands policy was first recommended at the National Wetlands Policy Forum in 1987, and was adopted by President George H.W. Bush in 1989 by executive order. Subsequent administrations have also reaffirmed the goal of "no overall net loss" of the United States' remaining wetlands, as well as the long-term goal of "increasing the quality and quantity of the Nation's wetland resource base," while stressing the need for efficient, fair, and flexible wetlands regulations that minimize and streamline regulatory impacts.[64] These goals have informed the nationwide Section 404 permitting program administered by the U.S. Army Corps of Engineers.

California began its first foray into wetlands regulation when Governor Pete Wilson in 1993 issued Executive Order W-59-93, which established a "no net loss" policy for California. Much like the federal policy, this order acknowledged the importance of wetlands, the historical conversion of wetlands to other uses, and the necessity of streamlining regulatory permitting processes. The comprehensive goal of the policy is to ensure "no overall net loss and long-term net gain in the quantity, quality, and permanence of wetlands acreage and values in California."

To achieve this goal, the executive order directed, among other things, the creation of a statewide wetlands inventory and accounting system, the development of a statewide policy concerning Corps-issued nationwide Section 404 dredge and fill permits, a pilot delegation of Section 404 permitting authority from the Corps to the San Francisco Regional Water Board, the development of a consistent regulatory definition of "wetlands," and the development of consistent standards and guidelines for mitigation and monitoring of impacts to wetlands.

Although the state never developed a pilot program for assumption of Section 404 permitting, following Governor Wilson's executive order the Regional Water Boards began to exercise closer scrutiny over federal dredge and fill permits. As more fully described below, when the U.S. Supreme Court limited the scope of the Section 404 program in 2001, the state fully entered the fray.

Following the U.S. Supreme Court's decision in *SWANCC*,[65] the State Water Board began to take steps it considered necessary to "fill the gap" left by that decision. The board's initial step was to issue a legal memorandum, dated January 25, 2001, asserting the authority of the Water Boards to regulate discharges to isolated waters. In 2003, in response to an advance notice of proposed rulemaking by EPA and the Corps to respond to *SWANCC*, the State Water Board submitted a letter (March

---

64 See White House Office of Environmental Policy, *Protecting America's Wetlands: A Fair, Flexible, and Effective Approach* (Aug. 24, 1993).

65 See Chapter 1 for a complete discussion of the *Solid Waste Agency of Northern Cook County v. U.S. Army Corps of Engineers*, or *"SWANCC"* decision.

2003) warning against any reduction in federal jurisdiction over non-navigable waters. In April 2003, the State Water Board submitted to the Legislature a report (*Regulatory Steps Needed to Protect and Conserve Wetlands Not Subject to the Clean Water Act*) identifying the need for regulatory mechanisms to "fill the gap," including a state wetland definition and state analog to the Section 404(b)(1) Guidelines. In May 2004, the State Water Board adopted (and continues to implement) general Waste Discharge Requirements for small discharges of dredged or fill material.

The State Water Board's program evolved further in 2008, when the Board adopted its Resolution No. 2008-0026, which directed staff to begin development of what finally evolved into the *State Wetland Definition and Procedures for Discharges of Dredged or Fill Material to Waters of the State*, adopted on April 2, 2019 (the "Procedures"). But the resolution envisioned the Procedures as really the first step in a larger program. Under the resolution, the Board's "Phase 1" directive was to establish a policy to protect wetlands from dredge and fill activities (i.e., the Procedures). "Phase 2" would expand the scope of the dredge and fill policies to protect wetlands from "all other activities impacting water quality." Finally, "Phase 3" of the work plan would be to extend the protection of the policies to riparian areas.

The Procedures began to take their current shape by June 2016, when the State Board issued its "Final Draft v1." Following a deluge of public comments, the State Water Board published an updated draft in July 2017. Again, the State Water Board received voluminous public comments and conducted a fall workshop that generated considerable attention from the building industry, the environmental community, and agricultural interests. Even the Corps weighed in, submitting a letter recommending against the State's incursion into this area of regulation.

Recognizing the need to address and reconcile these many comments, the State Water Board's staff thereafter spent a year and a half consulting with various stakeholders, holding Board and staff workshops, and ultimately promulgating a number of additional drafts during the winter of 2019. The Procedures were ultimately adopted by the State Water Board on April 2, 2019. The adopting resolution authorized and directed the Board's executive director to submit the Procedures and administrative record to the state's Office of Administrative Law (OAL) and, upon approval by that agency, to file a final notice of decision. The Procedures are set to become effective nine months following the completion of OAL review.

The Procedures establish a formal state-level definition of wetlands, but the permitting requirements included in the Procedures apply to all waters of the State. In particular, the Procedures regulate (1) the addition of *fill* material where the material has the effect of replacing any portion of a water of the State with dry land or changing the bottom elevation of any portion of a water of the State; and (2) the addition to waters of the State of *dredged* material, material that is excavated from waters of the State, including redeposit of dredged material other than incidental fallback. The Procedures are intended for inclusion in the regions' "Water Quality Control Plans for Inland Surface

OAL = Office of Administrative Law

Mr. Morrison represented the building and agriculture industries in these final negotiations.

In its August 2016 comment letter on the proposal, the Corps of Engineers asserted that the State lacks legal authority to regulate discharges of dredged or fill material into waters, arguing that such action is preempted by Section 404 of the Clean Water Act. The Corps cited as support Section 404(g) of the Clean Water Act, which "creates a specific mechanism for a State desiring to administer its own . . . permit program for the discharge of dredged or fill materials into waters of the United States that are within a State's jurisdiction." The Corps further stated that, "[b]ecause Congress created a specific process for States to obtain authority to regulate dredge and fill operations" through "assumption" of that authority under Section 404(g), Congress "intended to prohibit States from *otherwise* asserting such authority" (emphasis added).

Waters and Enclosed Bays and Estuaries and Ocean Waters in California," and will be used for both WQCs and WDRs. The Procedures use the term "Order" to include WDRs, waivers of WDRs, and WQCs.

The Procedures include essentially three major components. The first is a definition of wetlands. The second part consists of procedures for the review and consideration of permits, including standards for permit issuance. Thirdly, the Procedures include an "Appendix A," a multi-part document referred to as the "State Supplemental Dredge or Fill Guidelines," which incorporate certain federal wetlands regulations, but with modifications to fit the state's program. In particular, Subparts A through H of the Supplemental Guidelines are an adaptation of the federal Section 404(b)(1) Guidelines, 40 Code of Federal Regulations Section 230 *et seq.* Subpart J is an adaptation of the mitigation rule promulgated by the Corps in 2008, 33 C.F.R. Part 330 (commonly referred to as the "Mitigation Rule").

WETLAND DEFINITION AND EXCLUSIONS

Definition of Wetland

The wetlands definition contained in the Procedures does not (nor can it) affect the statutory definition of "waters of the State" (WOTS).[66] It does, however, identify wetlands as a type of WOTS, defining a wetland as follows:

> An area is a wetland if, under normal circumstances, (1) the area has continuous or recurrent saturation of the upper substrate caused by groundwater, or shallow surface water, or both; (2) the duration of such saturation is sufficient to cause anaerobic conditions in the upper substrate; and (3) the area's vegetation is dominated by hydrophytes or the area lacks vegetation.

This definition is modeled on the federal wetland definition found in the Corps' regulations at 33 Code of Federal Regulations Section 328.3(a)(8), but is different in several respects, the most important of which is its inclusion of areas that lack vegetation, but it also includes certain differences in the description of hydric soils.

Under the Clean Water Act, a wetland is a wetland only if it satisfies three established parameters: wetland hydrology, hydric soils, and the presence of certain concentrations of wetland plants.[67] The Procedures modify this long-standing federal "three parameter test" and designate an area as a wetland in certain circumstances even if it exhibits *no* wetland vegetation.[68] Under the Procedures, an area is considered to "lack" vegetation if it has "less than 5 percent areal [sic] coverage of plants at the peak of the growing season" (as described in certain federal wetland delineation manuals discussed below). Under this new "modified two parameter" test, any saturated, un-vegetated area

---

66 For the reader's ease of reference, the discussion in this section will use the acronyms WOTS and WOTUS to distinguish "waters of the State" and "waters of the United States."

67 40 C.F.R. § 232.2 (2011); see also U.S. Environmental Protection Agency, Section 404 of the Clean Water Act: How Wetlands are Defined and Identified, available at https://perma.cc/AH67-9A2Z.

68 2017 Dredge and Fill Procedures Final Draft, at 1-2.

will be treated as if it were a vernal pool or other wetland.[69] The State's definition does not, however, entirely dispense with a plant-based parameter. Where a saturated area does contain vegetation (i.e., at least five percent coverage at the peak of the growing season), that vegetation must be "dominated" by hydrophytic plants as described in certain federal delineation manuals discussed below.

Notably, the Procedures modify the function of the "normal circumstances" element of the federal definition. Under the Corps regulations, an area is jurisdictional if it has hydrophytic vegetation or would have such vegetation "under normal circumstances." This term has been included in the Corps regulations for years, and is intended to allow for situations in which wetland vegetation may not be present due to, among other things, farming or other human activity.

The State's definition appears to significantly expand this concept by applying the "normal circumstances" clause not just to vegetation, but also to a site's hydrology and soils. The Procedures defined the term "normal circumstances" to mean:

> The soil and hydrologic conditions that are normally present, without regard to whether the vegetation has been removed. The determination of normal circumstances exist in a disturbed area involves an evaluation of the extent and relative permanence of the physical alteration of wetland hydrology and hydrophytic vegetation and consideration of the purpose and cause of the physical alterations to hydrology and vegetation.

Notwithstanding such problems, the wetland delineation provisions found in Section III of the Procedures attempt to minimize conflicts between those definitions in a couple of small ways.

First, with respect to state wetland WOTS that are also federal wetland WOTUS, the Regional Water Boards, and the State Water Board when acting in a permitting capacity, are directed to by the Procedures to "rely on any final aquatic resources report verified by the Corps to determine boundaries of [WOTUS]."

Second, for state wetlands WOTS that do not constitute WOTUS, the State Water Board and the Regional Water Boards are directed to rely on three technical manuals used by consultants and the Corps (including the so-called "1987 Manual," the "Arid West" regional supplement to the 1987 Manual, and the "Western Mountains, Valleys, and Coast" regional supplement to the 1987 Manual). However, the methods described in these manuals must be adapted "to allow for the fact that the lack of vegetation does not preclude the determination that an area is a wetland under the State's definition."

Third, the Procedures treat the avoidance requirements for "2-parameter" wetlands differently, in an important respect, from federal "3-parameter" wetlands. Under the Section 404(b)(1) Guidelines, wetlands are treated as a "special aquatic site," which results in a rebuttable regulatory presumption that there are practicable alternatives to a project with less impact on aquatic resources. That is, for non-water-dependent projects,

WOTS = waters of the State

WOTUS = waters of the United States

---

69 *Id.*

CALIFORNIA'S RESPONSE TO THE TRUMPIAN ROLLBACK OF WETLAND PROTECTIONS UNDER THE CLEAN WATER ACT

Clark Morrison

The following discussion is a history of the Procedures, which was published in original form in the Hastings Environmental Law Journal, Vol. 24, No. 1, Fall 2017, and is reprinted with permission below in edited (i.e., updated) form. Because the procedures were adopted in modified form following publication of this article, discussion of the then-current draft of the procedures has been redacted.

Introduction

On February 28 of 2017, President Trump signed one of his first executive orders rolling back federal environmental protections for clean air and water.[1] This order, Presidential Executive Order on Restoring the Rule of Law, Federalism and Growth by Reviewing the "Waters of the United States Rule" ("Trump Executive Order"), directed the U.S. Army Corps of Engineers (Corps) and Environmental Protection Agency (EPA) to initiate the withdrawal of an Obama-era regulation that defined the scope of federal jurisdiction over wetlands and other "waters of the United States" (collectively, "WOTUS").[2]

That the President signed this executive order was not surprising. His newly-appointed EPA Administrator, Scott Pruitt, had made it his job as Oklahoma Attorney General to use litigation to rein in what he perceived as regulatory excesses of EPA. In fact, in that capacity, Mr. Pruitt had already initiated litigation against the very rule that the Trump Executive Order now seeks to withdraw.[3]

But the executive order did not stop there. Trump further directed the Corps and EPA to initiate a rulemaking to pare back the pre-Obama definition of WOTUS, updated and adopted by the Reagan Administration some 30

years ago.[4] The Executive Order explicitly endorsed a very narrow WOTUS definition promoted by the late Justice Scalia in his non-controlling plurality opinion in *Rapanos v. United States*.[5] On July 27, the Administration published a proposed rule "to initiate the first step in a comprehensive, two-step process intended to review and revise the definition of [WOTUS]" consistent with the President's executive order.[6] The rule is, quite literally, a proposal to "repeal and replace" President Obama's WOTUS Rule.

The State of California reacted swiftly. In 2019, the State Water Resources Control Board ("State Water Board") is adopted its own comprehensive program for the protection of wetlands and other "waters of the State."[7] This new program—the State Wetland Definition and Procedures for Discharges of Dredged or Fill Materials to Waters of the State (the "Dredge and Fill Procedures" or the "Procedures")—had been in the works for many years. But the Trump Administration's actions gave a renewed sense of urgency to this effort and parried long-standing arguments that the State's program would be duplicative of and in conflict with the federal program.

Originally intended to address the limited regulatory gap left by the Supreme Court's decision in *Solid Waste Agency of Northern Cook County v. U.S. Army Corps of Engineers*[8] *(SWANCC)*, as described below, the Procedures were ultimately crafted to fill the considerable regulatory void to be created by the President's pending retreat. In fact, the State's program went further than

4   "Sec. 3. *Definition of 'Navigable Waters' in Future Rulemaking.* In connection with the proposed rule described in section 2(a) of this order, the Administrator and the assistant secretary shall consider interpreting the term 'navigable waters,' as defined in 33 U.S.C. 1362(7), in a manner consistent with the opinion of Justice Antonin Scalia in *Rapanos v. United States*, 547 U.S. 715 (2006)." Waters of the United States Rule, *supra* note 1.

5   *Rapanos v. U.S.*, 547 U.S. 715 (2006).

6   82 Fed. Reg. 34,889 (2017) (Definition of "Waters of the United States" Proposed Rule).

7   State Water Res. Control Bd., Clean Water Act Section 401 – Certification and Wetlands (2017), https://perma.cc/HLS8-EAM6.

8   *Solid Waste Agency of N. Cook Cty. v. U.S. Army Corps of Eng'rs*, 531 U.S. 159 (2001).

1   82 Fed. Reg. 12,497–98 (2017) (Waters of the United States Rule).

2   33 U.S.C. § 1251 *et seq.* (1971) (which itself originated in the Federal Water Quality Control Act Amendments of 1972, 86 Stat. 816).

3   See *Murray Energy Corp., et al. v. U.S. Envtl. Prot. Agency, et al.*, 817 F.3d 261 (6th Cir. 2016).

existing federal regulations and, arguably, even further than the expansive Obama-era WOTUS definition.

These developments follow a long series of decisions in which the U.S. Supreme Court struggled to address the appropriate scope of federal jurisdiction under the Clean Water Act. This article will describe that judicial history, the evolution of the federal wetlands regulatory program in response to the Court's decisions (including the Trump Administration's current effort to pare back federal jurisdiction), and the State of California's ambitious program to fill the "Trump Gap" with its own protections for wetlands and other waters of the State.

Early History of the 404 Program

Since the passage of the Clean Water Act, the courts have been called on many times to determine the appropriate scope of federal jurisdiction over waters covered by that statute. Most of these cases have arisen in the context of Section 404 of the Clean Water Act, which prohibits the unpermitted discharge of dredged or fill material into covered wetlands and other types of waters.[9] The recurring issue in these cases is the extent to which a water must be "navigable" to be governed by Section 404.

This question about navigability is present in the very language of the statute. Although the statute prohibits discharges into "navigable waters," it defines this term without any reference to navigability whatsoever. That is, the Clean Water Act defines the term "navigable waters" to mean "the waters of the United States, including the territorial seas."[10] So, at its most basic level, the vexing question is whether a "navigable water" must be "navigable" at all.

Although the Corps initially viewed its jurisdiction as extending only to waters that were navigable-in-fact, in 1975 the Corps issued regulations redefining WOTUS to include not just navigable waters, but also tributaries, interstate waters and their tributaries, and non-navigable intrastate waters whose use or misuse could affect interstate commerce.[11] These regulations also covered

"freshwater wetlands" that were "adjacent" to other waters (without any specific requirement that those wetlands be navigable or have some connection to interstate commerce).[12]

Under the federal regulations that had been in effect since the 1980's (i.e., before Presidents Obama and Trump entered the fray), the Corps' jurisdiction under Section 404 covered (with certain exceptions) the following bodies of water:

All waters which are currently used, or were used in the past, or may be susceptible to use in interstate or foreign commerce, including all waters which are subject to the ebb and flow of the tide;

All interstate waters including interstate wetlands;

> all other waters such as intrastate lakes, rivers, streams (including intermittent streams), mudflats, sandflats, wetlands, sloughs, prairie potholes, wet meadows, playa lakes, or natural ponds, the use, degradation or destruction of which could affect interstate or foreign commerce including any such waters:
  - which are or could be used by interstate or foreign travelers for recreational or other purposes or
  - from which fish or shellfish are or could be taken and sold in interstate or foreign commerce or
  - which are used or could be used for industrial purpose by industries in interstate commerce
> all impoundments of waters otherwise defined as waters of the United States under the definition
> tributaries of waters identified in paragraphs (a) (1)–(4) of this section:
  - the territorial seas
  - wetlands adjacent to waters (other than waters that are themselves wetlands) identified in paragraphs (a) (1)–(6) of this section[13]

The first major case to test these regulations was *United States v. Riverside Bayview Homes, Inc.*,[14] in which the Supreme Court considered whether the Corps' assertion

9   33 U.S.C. § 1344 (1971).

10 33 U.S.C. § 1352(7) (1971); 33 C.F.R. § 328.3(a) (1986) (Army Corps Regulation Defining Waters of the U.S.).

11 40 Fed. Reg. 31,320 (1975) (Army Corps Regulation Defining Waters of the U.S.).

12 *Id.*

13 33 C.F.R. § 328.3 (1986) (Army Corps Regulation Defining Waters of the U.S.).

14 *U.S. v. Riverside Bayview Homes*, 474 U.S. 121 (1985).

of jurisdiction over "adjacent wetlands"[15] was valid under the Clean Water Act. In this case, the Sixth Circuit[16] held that the wetlands in question were not "adjacent" because they were not subject to actual flooding by nearby navigable waters. That is, the court was looking for some hydrologic connection sufficient to support jurisdiction. The Supreme Court reversed, holding that it was not unreasonable for the Corps to find that, as a general matter, adjacent wetlands are sufficiently "bound up" with nearby navigable waters to justify the assertion of jurisdiction without any fact-specific showing of that connection.[17]

In its analysis, the Court specifically considered the extent to which a water must actually be navigable to be subject to the Clean Water Act.[18] Citing a Senate report, the Court stated that "[a]lthough the Act prohibits discharges into 'navigable waters,' . . . the Act's definition of 'navigable waters' as 'waters of the United States makes it clear that the term 'navigable' as used in the Act is of limited import.'"[19]

Riverside Bayview Homes was followed several years later by the Supreme Court's decision in SWANCC.[20] SWANCC involved a non-navigable water-filled mining pit that was isolated from (and not adjacent to) any other body of water.[21] In asserting jurisdiction, the Corps relied on 33 C.F.R. § 328.3(a)(3), which covers "[a]ll other waters such as intrastate lakes, rivers, streams . . ., mudflats, sandflats, wetlands, sloughs, prairie potholes, wet meadows, playa lakes, or natural ponds, the use, degradation, or destruction of which could affect interstate commerce." The Corps had asserted a Commerce Clause connection over the SWANCC mining based upon its "Migratory Bird Rule,"

which posited that a Commerce Clause connection exists for any non-navigable isolated water "which are or would be used by . . . migratory birds that cross state lines."[22]

Given the attenuated Commerce Clause connection asserted by the Migratory Bird Rule, it was an easy target. In striking down the rule, the Court—in an opinion authored by Justice Rehnquist—struggled again with the import of the term "navigability" in the Clean Water Act. Distinguishing Riverside Bayview Homes, the Court reasoned:

> We cannot agree that Congress's separate definitional use of the phrase "waters of the United States" constitutes a basis for reading the term "navigable waters" out of the statute. We said in Riverside Bayview Homes that the word 'navigable' in the statute was of "limited import" . . . . But it is one thing to give a word limited effect and quite another to give it no effect whatever."[23]

California's Response to *SWANCC*

SWANCC generated regulatory tremors in California. Prior to *SWANCC*, the Water Board and its nine regional water quality control boards (the "Regional Water Boards") generally followed the federal definition of WOTUS when exercising their authority to "certify" proposed Corps permits under Section 401 of the Clean Water Act. When the Corps backed away from asserting jurisdiction over non-navigable isolated waters as a result of *SWANCC*, the Water Boards lost their ability to exercise their oversight (at least under Section 401) with respect to those waters.

To fill this gap, the Water Board's Office of Chief Counsel issued guidance advising the regional water boards to assert jurisdiction over isolated non-navigable waters through the Porter-Cologne Water Quality Control Act.[24] As stated in this guidance, "[g]iven the State [of California] and federal 'no net loss' of wetlands policy, the [Regional Water Boards] should consider regulating any

---

15   The term "wetlands" is defined in the Corps' regulations to mean "those areas that are inundated or saturated by surface or ground water at a frequency and duration sufficient to support, and that under normal circumstances do support, a prevalence of vegetation typically adapted for life in saturated soil conditions. Wetlands generally include swamps, marshes, bogs and similar areas." Army Corps Regulation Defining Waters of the U.S., 33 C.F.R. § 323.2(c) (1986).

16   *U.S. v. Riverside Bayview Homes*, 729 F.2d 391 (6th Cir. 1984).

17   *Riverside Bayview*, 474 U.S. at 134.

18   *Id.* at 133.

19   *Id.* (internal citations omitted, emphasis added).

20   *Solid Waste Agency of N. Cook Cty v. U.S. Army Corps of Eng'rs*, 531 U.S. 159 (2001).

21   *Id.* at 163.

22   51 Fed. Reg. 41,206, 41,217 (Preamble) (1986) (Proposed Rule Increasing Clarity on the Waters of the U.S.).

23   *Solid Waste Agency of N. Cook Cty*, 531 U.S. at 172.

24   Water Board Office of Chief Counsel, Effect of *SWANCC v. United States* on the 401 Certification Program, p. 5 (January 25, 2001); California Porter-Cologne Act of 1969, Cal. Water Code § 13000 *et seq.* (2017).

discharges of waste to waters that may no longer subject to [Corps] jurisdiction . . . ."[25] Ever since, the Regional Water Boards have asserted their own jurisdiction in these instances by requiring the issuance of "Waste Discharge Requirements" (i.e., permits under Porter-Cologne) for isolated non-navigable waters disclaimed by the Corps under *SWANCC*.

Despite its exclusive reliance on Clean Water Act section 401 to regulate wetland fills prior to *SWANCC*, the State of California had already initiated its own wetlands initiative in 1993.[26] In Executive Order W-59-93, Governor Wilson declared it to be the state's policy "[t]o ensure no overall net loss and long-term net gain in the quantity, quality, and permanence of wetlands acreage and values in California in a manner that fosters creativity, stewardship, and respect for private property."[27]

Governor Wilson's executive order included a number of subordinate policies and programs, including a proposal for a "pilot" delegation of Clean Water Act permitting authority in the San Francisco Bay Area to the San Francisco Regional Water Board and the Bay Conservation and Development Commission.[28] The executive order stated that this pilot project would be "part of a longer term effort to explore feasibility of Statewide delegation, with adequate funding, of the program."[29]

The delegation program never happened (and one wonders why it is not being considered today). Nonetheless, since Governor Wilson established the foundation for a California-based wetlands program, some of the regional water boards began to develop their own practices for the protection of wetlands. They did this partly through policies added to their basin plans, but mostly through certification conditions imposed on development projects on an ad hoc basis.[30] When *SWANCC* signaled a limited

federal retreat from the Clean Water Act, however, the Water Board initiated the establishment of a comprehensive state regulatory program for wetlands and other "waters of the State."[31]

Over the last several years, and with much interaction with environmental, business and other stakeholders, the State Water Board began to issue public drafts of such a policy. This policy was ultimately adopted by the State Water Board on April 2, 2019.[32] The originally-stated objective of what has become policy (often referred to as the "Procedures") was to "fill the gap" left by the Supreme Court's decision in *SWANCC*.[33] As noted above, however, the Water Board went much further than that in light of the Trump Administration's recent actions.

Rapanos and the Obama WOTUS Rule

The Water Board's effort was catalyzed by regulatory developments following the Supreme Court's 2006 decision in *Rapanos*. In this case, the Supreme Court again struggled with the question of how much connection a non-navigable water must have to a navigable water to establish jurisdiction under the Clean Water Act.[34] The case involved separate questions of jurisdiction over *non-navigable wetlands* (such as the adjacent wetlands considered in *Riverside Bayview Homes*) and *non-navigable tributaries* of traditional navigable waters (i.e. the extent to which federal jurisdiction creeps up to the headwaters of a navigable river), respectively.[35]

The Court found it difficult to reach agreement on these issues; the justices issued five separate opinions. To make things overly simple, although no single opinion won a majority of the Court, Justice Kennedy's opinion (which offered a generous theory of jurisdiction) generally is recognized as controlling.[36] Justice Scalia, in his own plurality opinion, offered a significant counter-weight (and

---

25   *Id.* at 5.

26   California Wetlands Policy, Executive Order W-59-93 (August 23, 1993).

27   *Id.* at Section II(1).

28   *Id.*

29   Executive Order W-59-93 (August 23, 1993) https://perma. cc/472A-Z28X.

30   See Los Angeles Regional Water Quality Control Board, Basin Plan for the Coastal Watersheds of Los Angeles and Ventura Counties, Chapter 5—Plans and Policies (Sept. 11, 2014).

31   See Clean Water Act § 401, 33 U.S.C. 1341, *supra* note 7.

32   Water Board, State Wetland Definition and Procedures for Discharges of Dredged or Fill Materials to Waters of the State (July 21, 2017) ("2017 Dredge and Fill Procedures Final Draft").

33   Effect of *SWANCC v. United States* on the 401 Certification Program, *supra* note 24.

34   *Rapanos, supra* note 5.

35   *Id.*

36   *Id.* at 759 (Kennedy, J. concurrence).

a far more restricted theory of jurisdiction) to the views of Justice Kennedy.[37]

From a lawyer's perspective, the interaction of the justices in this case is fascinating. Characteristically, Justice Kennedy offered a somewhat malleable view of navigability. Citing language from earlier decisions that focused on the nexus between navigable and non-navigable waters as the basis for limited extensions of jurisdiction (e.g., *Riverside Bayview Homes*), Kennedy expressed the general view that non-navigable waters may be subject to jurisdiction whenever they bear a "significant nexus" to other, navigable waters:

> When the Corps seeks to regulate wetlands adjacent to navigable-in-fact waters, it may rely on adjacency to establish its jurisdiction. Absent more specific regulations, however, the Corps must establish a significant nexus on a case-by-case basis when it seeks to regulate wetlands based on adjacency to non-navigable tributaries . . . . [I]n most cases regulation of wetlands that are adjacent to tributaries and possess a significant nexus with navigable waters will raise no serious constitutional or federalism difficulty. . . and as exemplified by *SWANCC*, the significant-nexus test itself prevents some problematic applications of the statute.[38]

Kennedy offered no clear rule, however, for determining when such a nexus might exist.

Not surprisingly, Scalia offered a more restrictive view of federal jurisdiction. Rather than the vague "significant nexus" theory offered by Kennedy, Scalia focused on the relative permanence of water in a given location.

> In sum, in its only plausible interpretation, the phrase 'waters of the United States' includes only those relatively permanent, standing or continuously flowing bodies of water 'forming geographic features' that are described in ordinary parlance as 'streams, . . . oceans, rivers and lakes (citation omitted). The phrase does not include channels through which waters flows

intermittently or ephemerally, or channels that periodically provide drainage for rainfall . . . . Therefore, only those wetlands with a continuous surface connection to bodies that are 'waters of the United States' in their own right, so that there is no clear demarcation between 'waters' and wetlands, are 'adjacent to' such waters and covered by the Act.[39]

Thus, for linear features, Scalia insisted on a "relatively permanent" flow to establish jurisdiction.[40] For non-linear features such as wetlands, Scalia insisted on a continuous surface water connection between the feature and some traditionally navigable water.[41] In short, Scalia rejected the flexible notions of navigability expressed by Justice Kennedy, as well the Court's decision in Riverside Bayview Homes and even, to some extent, *SWANCC*. It would require a fairly dramatic re-write if one were to incorporate Scalia's views into the list of WOTUS now contained in 33 Code of Federal Regulations Section 328.3.

On December 2, 2008—following the Presidential election but prior to the inauguration of President Obama—the Corps and EPA issued joint guidance entitled "Clean Water Act Jurisdiction Following the U.S. Supreme Court's Decision in *Rapanos v. United States & Carabell v. United States*" ("*Rapanos* Guidance").[42] The *Rapanos* Guidance, somewhat heroically, endeavored to formulate a policy that would reconcile the almost impossibly conflicting jurisdictional theories of Kennedy and Scalia.

As set forth below, the result was a marvelous regulatory pretzel:

> The agencies will assert jurisdiction over the following waters:
>
> • traditional navigable waters
>
> • wetlands adjacent to traditional navigable waters
>
> • non-navigable tributaries of traditional navigable waters that are relatively permanent where the

---

37   *Rapanos, supra* note 5, at 739–742 (Scalia, J. op.).

38   *Id.* at 782–783 (Kennedy, J. concurrence).

39   *Id.* at 739, 742 (emphasis in original).

40   *Id.* at 739.

41   *Rapanos, supra* note 5, at 742.

42   U.S. Army Corps of Engineers and U.S. Environmental Protection Agency, Clean Water Act Jurisdiction following the U.S. Supreme Court's Decision in *Rapanos v. United States & Carabell v. United States*, at 1 (Dec. 2, 2008).

tributaries typically flow year-round or have continuous flow at least seasonally (e.g., typically three months)

- wetlands that directly abut such tributaries

The agencies will decide jurisdiction over the following waters based on a fact-specific analysis to determine whether they have a significant nexus with a traditional navigable water:

- non-navigable tributaries that are not relatively permanent
- wetlands adjacent to non-navigable tributaries that are not relatively permanent
- wetlands adjacent to but that do not directly abut a relatively permanent non-navigable tributary
- the agencies generally will not assert jurisdiction over the following features:
- swales or erosional features (e.g., gullies, small washes characterized by low volume, infrequent, or short duration flow
- ditches (including roadside ditches) excavated whole in and draining only uplands and that do not carry a relatively permanent flow of water

The agencies will apply the significant nexus standard as follows:

- a significant nexus analysis will assess the flow characteristics and functions of the tributary itself and the functions performed by all wetlands adjacent to the tributary to determine if they significantly affect the chemical, physical and biological integrity of downstream traditional navigable waters
- significant nexus includes consideration of hydrologic and ecologic factors[43]

It is important to keep in mind that in formulating its own wetlands regulatory program, the State of California need not engage in these intellectual acrobatics. This is because state environmental structures for clean water are not tied to concepts of navigability.

Not surprisingly, the Obama Administration engaged in its own post-*Rapanos* rulemaking to define the scope of federal jurisdiction along the lines expressed by Justice Kennedy. The resulting rule, commonly known as the "WOTUS Rule," was adopted in June 2015.[44] The WOTUS Rule was promptly litigated by a number of states (one of which was, as noted above, represented by Scott Pruitt), farming interests, environmental groups and others, and the litigation continues.

Given the Trump Administration's proposal to "repeal and replace" Obama's WOTUS Rule, it may not survive. The rule is nonetheless important because it stretched Kennedy's "significant nexus" theory almost beyond recognition, generating the political reaction that led to its pending demise. In fact, the standards contained in the WOTUS Rule might better be characterized as based upon a theoretical rather than a significant nexus theory. It is hard to imagine a wetland or other water—other than those specifically exempted—that would not be subject to jurisdiction. It is not a stretch to say the Obama Administration had essentially brought us back, however briefly, to the days of the Migratory Bird Rule.

The Dredge and Fill Procedures originally were intended simply to fill the *SWANCC* gap. Their final purpose, however, is now to fill the much more considerable pending Trump gap. As finally adopted, they appear to do just that. At this point, the Procedures have only just been adopted, and it remains unclear whether litigation will ensue.

[The remainder of the article has been omitted.]

---

43   Clean Water Act Jurisdiction following the U.S. Supreme Court's Decision in *Rapanos v. United States & Carabell v. United States, supra* note 42, at 1.

44   Clean Water Rule: Definition of "Waters of the United States", 80 Fed. Reg. 37,054 (June 29, 2015) (to be codified at 40 C.F.R pts. 110, 112, 116, et al.).

the Section 404(b)(1) Guidelines *presume* that any project affecting a wetland is *not* the least environmentally damaging practicable alternative unless "clearly demonstrated otherwise." In response to suggestions made by the authors on behalf of industry, the January 3 draft of the Procedures was modified to clarify that "2-parameter wetlands" will *not* be considered a special aquatic site subject to this regulatory presumption.

It is important to keep in mind that fill of either a wetland *or* a non-wetland WOTS requires a permit under the Procedures. In fact, for the most part the procedures treat wetlands and non-wetland WOTS identically except in a couple of significant respects. That is, the State's broad wetland definition does not make jurisdictional any feature that is not already jurisdictional as a WOTS. If this is the case, then one might ask why the state needs a definition in the first place. As discussed below, the answer may be found in the limited exclusion over certain types of wetlands from the overall definition of waters of the State.

Section II of the Procedures lists those types of wetlands that are considered waters of the State. Any wetland that is not on this list is not a water of the State and is thus exempt from the permitting requirements established by the Procedures. If an aquatic feature meets the basic wetland definition discussed above, however, "the burden is on the applicant to demonstrate" that the wetland is not a WOTS.

Under the Procedures, the following wetlands are waters of the State:

> natural wetlands

> wetlands created by modification of a surface water of the state[70]

and

> artificial wetlands that meet any of the following criteria:

- artificial wetlands "approved by an agency as compensatory mitigation for impacts to other [WOTS]," except where the approving agency explicitly identifies the mitigation as being of a limited duration
- artificial wetlands specifically identified in a water quality control plan as a wetland or other WOTS
- artificial wetlands resulting from human activity, are not subject to ongoing operation and maintenance, and have "become a relatively permanent part of the natural landscape"
- artificial wetlands greater than one acre in size that were constructed, and currently used and maintained, for certain purposes (identified below) unless they were created by modification of a surface water of the state or were approved as compensatory mitigation, or are specifically identified in a water quality control plan

> Some of the features in this list, particularly those characterized as artificial wetlands, may not be wetlands at all under the definition.

---

70 Footnote 3 of the Procedures was added and clarified (at the authors' suggestion) to state that "modification of a water of the State" means that the wetland that is being created "was created by modifying an area that was a water of the State at the time of such modification. It does not include a wetland that is created in a location where a water of the State had existed historically, but had already been completely eliminated at some time prior to the creation of the wetland. The wetland being evaluated does not become a water of the State due solely to a diversion of water from a different water of the State."

According to Water Board staff, artificial wetlands that are less than an acre in size are not waters of the State, *regardless of the use to which they are put*, unless they were created by modification of a surface water of the State; approved as compensatory mitigation; or resulted from human activity, are not subject to ongoing operation and maintenance, and become a relatively permanent part of the natural landscape.

An artificial wetland described above equal to or greater than one acre in size is not jurisdictional only if it was constructed, and currently used and maintained, for one or more of the purposes set forth below. This limitation does not apply to artificial wetlands less than one acre in size.

> industrial or municipal wastewater treatment or disposal
> settling of sediment
> detention, retention, infiltration or treatment of storm water runoff and other pollutants or runoff subject to regulation under a municipal, construction, or industrial storm water permitting program
> treatment of surface waters
> agricultural crop irrigation or stock watering
> fire suppression
> industrial process or cooling
> active surface mining (even if the site is managed for interim wetlands functions and values)
> log storage
> treatment, storage or distribution of recycled water
> maximizing groundwater recharge (not including wetlands that have incidental groundwater recharge benefits)
> fields flooded for rice growing[71]

As noted above, this exemption is quite limited because it is not available if the artificial wetland (1) was created by modification of a WOTS; or (2) was "approved by an agency as mitigation for impacts to other [WOTS]," except where the approving agency explicitly identifies the mitigation as being of a limited duration; or (3) is specifically identified in a water quality control plan as being a wetland or other WOTS. These limitations render the exceptions to artificial wetlands to be quite narrow.

PROCEDURAL EXCLUSIONS

If a proposed activity may result in the discharge of dredged or fill material to a WOTS, an order may not be required because the Procedures identify a certain limited class of activities that are excluded from the permitting requirements. To some extent, albeit

As written, if one of the listed "artificial wetlands" does not meet the definition, then it is not a water of the State.

---

71 Footnote 5 of the Procedures further states that fields used for the cultivation of rice (that have not been abandoned due to five consecutive years of non-use for rice cultivation) that are determined to be a WOTS will not have beneficial uses applied to them except as required by federal law for WOTUS. The footnote further states that agricultural inputs legally applied to rice fields shall not constitute a discharge of waste into a WOTS, except to the extent they migrate to surface water or groundwater.

PCC = Prior Converted Cropland

imperfectly, these exclusions are intended to mirror some of the exclusions from Corps jurisdiction found in the Clean Water Act.

Section 404(f) Exclusions

The Procedures exclude from its permit procedures any activity that is exempt from federal regulation under Section 404(f) of the Clean Water Act (as further defined under 33 C.F.R. § 323.4 and 40 C.F.R. § 232.8. Section 404(f) excludes the discharge of dredged or fill material from certain activities, which are summarized as follows:

> from normal farming, silviculture, and ranching activities such as plowing, seeding, cultivating, minor drainage, harvesting for the production of food, fiber, and forest products, or upland soil and water conservation practices

> for the purpose of maintenance, including emergency reconstruction of recently damaged parts, or currently serviceable structures such as dikes, dams, levees, groins, riprap, breakwaters, causeways, and bridge abutments or approaches, and transportation structures

> for the purpose of construction or maintenance of farm or stock ponds or irrigation ditches, or the maintenance of drainage ditches

> for the purpose of construction of temporary sedimentation basins on a construction site which does not include the placement of fill material into the navigable waters

> for the purpose of construction or maintenance of farm roads or forest roads, or temporary roads for moving mining equipment, where such roads are constructed and maintained, in accordance with best management practices, to assure that flow and circulation patterns and chemical and biological characteristics of the navigable waters are not impaired, that the reach of the navigable waters is not reduced, and that any adverse effect on the aquatic environment will be otherwise minimized

Under the Clean Water Act, the exclusion for these activities may depend upon the *purpose* of the activity. More specifically, "[a]ny discharge of dredged or fill material into the navigable waters incidental to any activity having as its purpose bringing an area of the navigable waters into a use to which it was not previously subject, where the flow or circulation of navigable waters may be impaired or the reach of such waters be reduced, shall be required to have a permit under this section."[72] That is, these activities are not excluded if their purpose is to change jurisdictional conditions to non-jurisdictional conditions.

Prior Converted Cropland

Under federal law, wetlands that were converted to agricultural use prior to 1985 (referred to as "Prior Converted Cropland," or "PCC") are not treated as WOTUS unless their agricultural use is abandoned for five years and wetland conditions return.

---

72 33 U.S.C. § 1344(f)(2).

Under the Procedures, PCC *are* treated as WOTS under the definition to the extent they include surface or ground water. However, the Procedures exclude qualified PCC from permitting requirements except to the extent a discharge "converts wetlands areas to a non-agricultural use."

In particular, the Procedures exclude discharges into wetland areas:

> That qualify as [PCC] within the meaning of 33 CFR 328.3(b)(2). The applicant may establish that the area is PCC by providing relevant documentary evidence that the area qualifies as PCC and has not been abandoned due to five consecutive years of non-use for agricultural purposes, or by providing a current PCC certification by the Natural Resources Conservation Service, the Corps or the U.S. EPA. This exclusion does not apply to discharges of dredged or fill material that convert the wetland areas to a non-agricultural use.

Although not specifically stated in this definition, State Water Board staff has clarified that the term "qualified" incorporates the federal notion of five-year abandonment, which allows growers to maintain their PCC exclusion so long as they engage in certain agricultural activities at least one year out of any five-year period. It should be noted that, under federal law, PCC status is not affected by conversion to a non-agricultural use.

Rice

The specific exclusion for rice is contained in the Procedures' provisions regarding artificial wetlands, described above.

Exclusions for Certain Agricultural Facilities

The Procedures exclude certain specific features (regardless of whether they qualify as a regulable artificial wetland). These exclusions are analogous to those found in the Federal Register preamble to the Corps' 1986 regulations, and later modified by the Obama rule. As adopted for use in California, these exclusions include those set forth below, provided that these exclusions do not apply to discharges that convert these areas to a non-agricultural use:

> - ditches with ephemeral flow that are not a relocated WOTS or excavated in a WOTS
> - ditches with intermittent flow that are not a relocated WOTS or excavated in a WOTS, or that do not drain wetlands other than any wetlands described in the fourth or fifth bullets below
> - ditches that do not flow, either directly or through another water, into another WOTS
> - artificially irrigated areas that would revert to dry land should application of waters to that area cease

> artificial, constructed lakes and ponds created in dry land such as farm and stock watering ponds, irrigation ponds, and settling basins[73]

Suction Dredge Mining

The Procedures exempt suction dredge mining activities for mineral recovery as described under Section 402 of the Clean Water Act.

Public Emergency, Operation and Maintenance

Significantly, the Procedures exclude routine and emergency operation and maintenance activities conducted by public agencies, water utilities or special districts that result in discharge of dredged or fill material to artificial existing WOTS provided they are:

> currently used and maintained primarily for one or more of certain of the purposes that would qualify a wetland for exclusion as described above; or

> preserving the line, grade, volumetric or flow capacity within the existing footprint of a flood control or storm water conveyance facility

The Procedures state that the exclusion described above does not relieve public agencies, utilities and special districts of their obligation to seek an application for certification or WDRs for these activities so the water boards can determine whether the exclusion actually applies. The exclusion also does not relieve these agencies of their obligation to avoid and minimize adverse impacts to aquatic resources and associated beneficial uses.

In addition to the foregoing, the final version of the Procedures added an exclusion for routine operation and maintenance activities that result in discharges to certain artificial waters used for certain purposes that would exclude them as WOTS. This exclusion does not apply to discharges to (1) a WOTUS; (2) a water specifically identified in a water quality control plan; (3) a water created by modification of a WOTS; or (4) a water approved by an agency as compensatory mitigation.

Water Appropriations and Diversions

For activities associated with (1) an appropriation of water, (2) a hydroelectric facility where the proposed activity requires FERC license or an amendment thereto, or (3) any other diversion of water for beneficial use, the State Water Board's Division of Water Rights will inform an applicant as to whether the Procedures' application requirements are applicable.

APPLICATIONS AND PROCESSING

Except for excluded activities identified in Section IV.D of the Procedures, an application must be filed for any activity that "could" result in the discharge of dredged or fill

---

73   State Water Board staff has acknowledged that this category includes dairy ponds.

material to WOTS. That is, the Procedures apply to both water quality certifications *and* the issuance of WDRs for discharges to non-federal WOTS, both of which are referred to in the Procedures as "Orders." Note that the Procedures state that discharges of dredged or fill material (or other waste material) to areas that are not WOTS, but that could "affect the quality" of a WOTS, "may be addressed under other Water Board regulatory programs."

The Procedures will apply to all applications "submitted" after the effective date of the Procedures, which is scheduled to occur nine months following the completion of review by the Office of Administrative Law. Although the Procedures are not clear as to whether an application must be complete prior to the effective date in order to be grandfathered, the staff report for the final board action stated the following:

> [The provision stating that [t]he Procedures] do not apply to applications that are submitted prior to the [effective date] was added to the Procedures in an attempt to make it clear that, so long as a dredge or fill discharge application is submitted prior to the [effective date] they do not apply to that application. Instead, project application and Water Board review and approval will follow the policies and procedures in place at the permitting authority prior to the [effective date].
>
> This is true whether or not the application is ultimately deemed to be a 'complete' application by the Water Board. If the application is so obviously deficient that it is clear that it was submitted prematurely to avoid having to comply with the Procedures, however, then the Water Boards' recourse would be to deny the application without prejudice. The applicant can then finish the application and re-submit it. That resubmission of the application would have to be in accordance with the Procedures if the Procedures have taken effect by the time that the application is re-submitted.

The application requirements in the Procedures apply to "new discharges, proposed material changes in the character, location, or volume of existing discharges, and upon renewal of existing Orders for existing discharges. The permitting authority may amend an existing Order for the purpose of extending the expiration date without requiring a new application."

Section IV.A of the Procedures identifies certain materials that *must* be included in an application for an individual order. Applicants are specifically encouraged to consult with the appropriate Regional Water Board to determine the appropriate level of detail required for items to be included in an application. Required items include:

(1) **Materials required for Certification Procedures.** All materials identified in the State Water Board's requirements for a complete application for water quality certification as listed in California Code of Regulations, Title 23, Section 3856 ("Contents of a Complete Application").

(2) **Jurisdictional Analyses.** If the Corps requires an aquatic resources delineation report, a copy of the report verified by the Corps, and a delineation of any waters not reflected in a Corps-verified delineation, including wetlands.

(3) **Proposed Schedule.** When the projected commencement and completion dates of the "overall project activity" will take place and, if known, the dates upon which the permitted discharge is scheduled to occur.

CESA = California Endangered
Species Act

ESA = Endangered Species Act

LEDPA = least environmentally
damaging practicable
alternative

> The staff report states that, if the Corps does not require an aquatic resource delineation report, an applicant must submit a delineation of all waters, but the delineation need not be verified by the Corps. This language was added following insistence by the agricultural community that the Procedures specifically authorize the use of NRCS delineations, and that the Water Board defer to those delineations. Unfortunately, the language is less than explicit. However, Water Board staff added a "whereas" to the adopting resolution stating that "Water Board staff and agricultural landowners are encouraged to consult with [NRCS] regarding delineation of wetlands on agricultural lands and any other information that is relevant to the application of the Procedures to Agricultural Lands."

(4) **Project Maps.** Maps at a scale of at least 1:24,000 (1 inch = 2,000 feet) and of sufficient detail to accurately show:

> the boundaries of the property "owned or to be utilized" by the applicant (including grading limits, proposed land uses, and the location, dimensions and type of any structures erected or proposed to be erected); and

> all aquatic resources that "may" qualify as WOTS within the project boundaries and any such features outside the project boundaries that "could be impacted" by the project

(5) **Description of Potential Impacts and Mitigation.** This includes a description of the following:

> WOTS proposed to be impacted and the beneficial uses of those WOTS (as described in the applicable water quality control plan)

> a description of the discharge at each individual impact location; quantity of impact at each such location to the nearest 0.01 acre, lineal foot or (in the case of dredging) cubic yard

> an assessment of potential direct and indirect impacts and the mitigation proposed for such impacts

> an identification of existing water quality impairments and, if known, the source of those impairments

> the presence of species listed as rare, threatened or endangered under CESA, the federal ESA or the California Native Plant Protection Act

(6) **Alternatives Analysis.** An analysis of whether the proposed discharge represents the least environmentally damaging practicable alternative (LEDPA) in a manner consistent with the Corps' and EPA's Section 404(b)(1) Guidelines, unless the project is exempt from this requirement as more fully described below. Note that the limited exemption described below does not preclude a regional water board from requiring an applicant to demonstrate compliance with the Procedures' sequencing requirements.

In addition to these mandatory application requirements, the Procedures identify other types of information that might be required on a case-by-case basis:

(1) **Supplemental Field Data.** If any submitted delineation was conducted in the dry season, the Regional Water Board may require supplemental field data from the wet season to substantiate that delineation as required by the 1987 wetlands delineation manual and applicable supplements.

(2) **Mitigation Plans.** A mitigation plan, using a watershed approach as described below, for projects other than ecological restoration and enhancement projects.

(4) **Monitoring Plans.** If project activities include in-water work or diversions, a proposed water quality plan to monitor compliance with water quality objectives of the applicable water quality control plan. The plan must, at a minimum, include the type and frequency of sampling for each applicable parameter.

(5) **Restoration Plans.** Where temporary impacts are proposed, a draft restoration plan that "outlines design, implementation, assessment and maintenance" measures for restoring disturbed areas to pre-project conditions. The required components of the restoration plan are more fully described below.

(6) **Ecological Restoration and Enhancement Projects (EREPs).** For EREPs, a draft assessment plan that includes project objectives, description of performance standards, protocols for condition assessment, the timeframe and responsible party for performing condition assessments, and an assessment schedule. The assessment plan must include at least one overall assessment prior to restoration and two years following completion of the activity to determine success.

EREPs = Ecological Restoration and Enhancement Projects

The Procedures state that, within 30 days of an applicant submitting the mandatory application materials, the Regional Water Board may require the applicant to submit more of the "case-by-case" supplemental materials described above. Once the applicant has submitted the additional items, the Regional Water Board has 30 days to determine whether the application is complete. The Procedures allow an applicant to submit, as part of the permit application, materials that were also provided as a part of the applicant's Section 404 permit application, provided the applicant identify where in the federal application materials the state-required materials can be found.

The Procedures do not identify any particular timeline by which the Regional Water Board must act. However, Section 401 of the Clean Water Act provides that the certification requirement is waived if the state fails or refuses to act on a certification request within one year. The Corps regulations go further, allowing the Corps to find a waiver of certification if the state fails to act within a 60-day period. Moreover, the provisions of the Permit Streamlining Act apply to permit issuance under the Procedures.

It is important to note that the Procedures are intended to *supplement*, and do not replace, the state's procedures for water quality certification and WDRs. Thus, for orders issued under the Procedures as individual WDRs, the Water Board must provide public notice in accordance with Section 13167.5 of the California Water Code. For water quality certifications, the Water Board must provide public notice of an application in accordance with the State Water Board's regulations at Title 23, Section 3858 of the California Code of Regulations. If the Water Board receives comments on an application or there is substantial public interest in the project, the Water Board must also provide public notice of the draft order, or draft amendment of an order, unless circumstances warrant a shorter notice period.

OVERARCHING STANDARDS

Like the Clean Water Act and regulations issued thereunder, the Procedures include several fundamental requirements that underlie the consideration and issuance of Water Board orders. These fundamental standards are, in fact, analogous to those imposed under the Corps' permitting program under Section 404.

LEDPA = least environmentally damaging practicable alternative

These requirements include the following, and are more fully fleshed out in other parts of the Procedures:

(1) **Sequencing.** As is true under the Clean Water Act, the Procedures impose a "sequencing" requirement, which is essentially a system of priorities for the avoidance, minimization and mitigation of impacts to the aquatic environment. In particular, when considering an order, the Water Board is required to implement a sequence of actions to "first avoid; then to minimize; and lastly compensate for adverse impacts that cannot practicably be avoided or minimized to [WOTS]." At the federal level, and now presumably at the state level, some agency officials take the position that they cannot—from a temporal perspective—even discuss with the applicant any minimization or compensatory mitigation measures until all avoidance measures have been explored. In the authors' opinion, this position is legally tenuous. The point is that minimization and compensatory mitigation measures must be considered in light of practicability considerations relative to avoidance. There is no reason these cannot all be considered as part of a single and integrated administrative process. That is, the sequencing is analytical, not temporal, in nature.

(2) **No Net Loss.** The Procedures require that the potential impacts of a project will not contribute to a net loss of "the overall abundance, diversity, and condition of aquatic resources in a watershed," or multiple watersheds when compensatory mitigation is permitted in another watershed. This requirement is tied to the mitigation requirements set forth in the Procedures and reflects federal requirements set forth in the Corps' 2008 Mitigation Rule, which address the issues described above (abundance, diversity, condition and watershed).

(3) **State Water Quality Standards.** The discharge must not violate water standards and must be consistent with applicable water quality control plans and policies for water quality control.

(4) **Significant Degradation.** Finally, the discharge must not cause or contribute to significant degradation of WOTS.

ALTERNATIVES ANALYSES

In General

Under the Section 404(b)(1) Guidelines found in federal regulations, a discharge of dredged or fill material into a WOTUS may not be permitted if there is a practicable alternative to the proposed project that would be less environmentally damaging to the aquatic environment. That is, in order to be permitted, a proposed project must be the "LEDPA" (the "least environmentally damaging practicable alternative").

Under the Procedures, an applicant is required to submit an alternatives analysis that is more rigorous for smaller projects, and more specific in nature, than LEDPA analyses required by the Corps under Section 404. The structure of the analysis must be in accordance with *Appendix A* to the Procedures, which are essentially an adaptation of the federal Section 404(b)(1) Guidelines, and also include a state-level adaptation of the Corps' Mitigation Rule. Under the Procedures, a LEDPA analysis evaluates whether a project is the LEDPA "in light of all potential, direct, secondary (indirect), and cumulative impacts on the physical, chemical and biological elements of the aquatic ecosystem." Impacts to be considered must include both temporary and permanent impacts.

Second, the level of rigor required for small projects is higher than that required by the Corps. For small to medium projects, the Corps typically requires less rigor in LEDPA analyses, and typically does not require them at all for fills proposed under the Nationwide Permit program. By contrast, and as described below, the Procedures provide some relief from LEDPA requirements only for extremely small projects, all in accordance with a "tiering" system, as follows.

Tiering System for Alternatives Analyses

For discharges that directly impact (1) less than or equal to 0.10 acres of WOTS or (2) 100 or fewer lineal feet of WOTS ("Tier 1" projects), and unless the discharge meets the criteria for a "Tier 3" project as described below, the applicant need only provide a "description of any steps that have been or will be taken to avoid and minimize loss of, or significant adverse impacts to, beneficial waters of the State." Note that this discussion focuses not specifically on physical, chemical and biological elements of the aquatic ecosystem per se, but rather beneficial uses of the impacted WOTS.

For discharges impacting (1) more than 0.10 but less than 0.20 acres of WOTS or (2) more than 100 lineal feet but no more than 300 lineal feet for WOTS (unless the discharge meets the criteria for a "Tier 3" project as described below), and non-Tier-1 projects that inherently cannot be located at an alternative site ("Tier 2" projects), the applicant need only provide an on-site alternatives analysis.

For projects that exceed the permitted impact level for Tier 2 projects, or that directly impact (1) rare, threatened or endangered species habitat in WOTS; (2) wetlands or eelgrass beds, or (3) "Outstanding Natural Resource Waters" or "Areas of Special Biological Significance," and such project "inherently cannot be located at an alternative location ("Tier 3" projects), the applicant must provide both an on-site and an off-site alternatives analysis.

Prior to issuance of the January 3, 2019 draft, the Procedures provided discretion to the Regional Water Boards to require levels of analysis lower than would be required under the tiering system described above. That discretion was eliminated in the January 3 draft, but the January 3 version included language—retained in the finally adopted version—specifying that "[t]he level of effort required for an alternatives analysis within each of the three tiers" (including discharges exceeding Tier 3 thresholds) shall be "commensurate with the significance of the project's potential threats to water quality and beneficial uses." This is analogous to similar flexibility

CEQA = California
Environmental Quality Act

NEPA = National Environmental
Policy Act

built into the federal LEDPA requirements, although it remains to be seen how this flexibility will be applied in practice.

Exemptions from Alternatives Analysis Requirements

The Procedures contain very limited exemptions from the LEDPA requirement. The exemptions cover the following types of projects:

(1) **Corps Nationwide and other General Permits.** A project that involves non-federal WOTS but (when taken as a whole, i.e., the "entire project") would satisfy the terms of a Water Board pre-certified nationwide or other general permit, including any Corps-issued regional terms and conditions, if the impacted WOTS were also federal WOTUS. The exemption also covers projects qualifying for coverage under a *non-certified* nationwide or other general permit, *unless* the discharge would directly impact (1) more than 0.2 acres or 300 lineal feet of WOTS; (2) rare, threatened or endangered species habitat in WOTS; (3) a wetland or eel grass bed (i.e., the exemption is only applicable to "other waters"); or (4) an "Outstanding Natural Resource Water" or "Area of Special Biological Significance." Note that this exemption applies to projects that include *only* discharges to WOTUS.

(2) **Watershed Plans.** A project carried out in accordance with a "Watershed Plan" that has been approved for use by the Water Board and analyzed in an environmental document (i.e., a CEQA or NEPA document) that includes an alternatives analysis, monitoring provisions, and guidance on compensatory mitigation opportunities.

(3) **Ecological Restoration and Enhancement Projects.** EREPs are those projects that are "voluntarily undertaken for the purpose of assisting or controlling the recovery of an aquatic ecosystem that has been degraded, damaged or destroyed to restore some measure of its natural condition and to enhance the beneficial uses, including potential beneficial uses of water." These projects must be undertaken pursuant to an enhancement or restoration agreement entered into by the applicant and one of many natural resource agencies or a non-governmental conservation organization. Certain types of restoration and enhancement projects, defined more fully in the Definitions section of the Procedures, are not eligible for this exemption.

(4) **Temporary Impacts.** A project that has (1) no permanent impacts to aquatic resources and (2) no impacts to habitat for rare, threatened or endangered species, wetlands or eel grass beds, or "Outstanding Natural Resource Waters" or "Areas of Special Biological Significance"; and all implementation actions in the restoration plan can reasonably be concluded within one year.

Reliance on Federal Alternatives Analyses

An applicant is permitted to submit an alternatives analysis that has been prepared for the Corps. The Procedures appear to require, though, that any such draft submitted to the Corps must also be submitted to the Water Board in draft form. Any such alternatives analysis "may satisfy some or all of" the requirements of the Procedures.

With respect to discharges to WOTS that are also WOTUS, the Water Board is required to defer to the Corps' determinations on the adequacy of the alternatives analysis, or to rely on a draft federal alternatives analysis if no final federal determination has been made. This required deference, however, is conditional. The Water Board may choose not to rely upon or defer to such a federal analysis if the Water Board's Executive Director of Executive Officer determines that (1) the Water Board was not provided an adequate opportunity to "collaborate" in the development of the analysis; (2) the analysis does not adequately address aquatic resource issues identified in writing to the Corps by the Executive Director or Executive Officer during the development of the analysis; or (3) the proposed project and *all* of the identified alternatives would not comply with water quality standards.

If the proposed project would include discharges to non-federal WOTS, the Water Board must require the applicant to supplement any federal analysis to include those non-federal WOTS, unless the applicant has consulted with the permitting authority and the alternatives analysis addresses all issues identified by the permitting authority during the consultation process. If the Corps has not required a federal LEDPA analysis for WOTUS associated with the project, the Water Board must (unless the project is exempt) require an alternatives analysis for the entire project.

COMPENSATORY MITIGATION

Subpart J of the Procedures includes a comprehensive set of policies regarding compensatory mitigation for aquatic impacts. These policies are essentially an adaptation of the Corps' Mitigation Rule, which is described more fully in Chapters 7 and 10. Summarized below are those specific mitigation requirements found in the body of the Procedures, which supplement the requirements of Subpart J.

The Policies state that compensatory mitigation may be required by a water board in connection with permit issuance. In determining the required mitigation, a water board is required, where feasible, to consult and coordinate with other public agencies that have "concurrent" mitigation requirements. The stated purpose of this coordination is to achieve "multiple environmental benefits" with a single mitigation project, thereby reducing the cost of compliance.

Amount of Mitigation

The amount of compensatory mitigation is to be decided on a case-by-case basis in accordance with Subpart J.

In the final negotiations over the Procedures, the definition of "Watershed Plan" was clarified to ensure that most HCPs and NCCPs can qualify for the alternatives analysis exemption, as well as the Procedures' mitigation standards for watershed plans. The Procedures define a watershed plan as "a document, or a set of documents, developed in consultation with relevant stakeholders, a specific goal of which is aquatic resource [conservation] . . . The permitting authority may approve the use of . . . Habitat Conservation Plans (HCPs) [or] Natural Community Conservation Plans (NCCPs) if they substantially meet the [criteria stated above]. Any NCCP approved by [CDFW] before December 31, 2020, and any regional HCP approved by [USFWS] before [the same date], which includes biological goals for aquatic resources, shall be used by the permitting authority as a watershed plan for aquatic resources, unless the permitting authority determines in writing that the HCP or NCCP does not substantially meet the definition of a watershed plan for such aquatic resources."

As noted below, the amount of mitigation will depend upon which of two watershed-based planning approaches are built into the mitigation. In either case, however, a minimum of one-to-one mitigation ratio, measured as area of length, must be satisfied for wetland or stream losses. The Procedures clarify that this mitigation ratio may be met "using methods of restoration, enhancement, establishment, and in certain cases preservation," consistent with the Procedures' overall specifications for mitigation type, provided that restoration is "generally" the first option considered. The Procedures further clarify that, with respect to the one-to-one minimum, "a higher overall mitigation ratio shall be used where necessary to ensure replacement of lost aquatic functions .... Where temporary impacts will be restored to pre-project conditions, the permitting authority may require compensatory mitigation for temporal impacts."

The Procedures specifically provide that, in determining the amount of mitigation, a Water Board may take into account "recent anthropogenic degradation" to the aquatic resource and existing functions and conditions of the resource. They also note that the amount of mitigation may be reduced "if buffer areas adjacent to the compensatory mitigation" are also required to be maintained as part of the compensatory mitigation management plan.

Mitigation Based on Watershed Planning Concepts

As noted above, compensatory mitigation may take the form of restoration, enhancement, establishment and, in certain circumstances, preservation. The Procedures clarify, however, that restoration should generally be "the first option considered" because "the likelihood of success is greater and the impacts to potentially ecologically important uplands are reduced compared to establishment, and the potential gains in terms of aquatic resource functions are greater compared to enhancement and preservation."

The amount of compensatory mitigation may vary depending on the use of one of two identified strategies to locate the mitigation site within a watershed, as follows:

> Strategy 1: Applicant locates compensatory mitigation using a watershed approach based on a watershed profile developed from a watershed plan that (1) has been approved for use by the [Water Board] and analyzed in [a CEQA or NEPA document], (2) includes monitoring provisions, and (3) includes guidance on compensatory mitigation strategies.

> Strategy 2. Applicant locates compensatory mitigation using a watershed approach based on a watershed profile developed for a project evaluation area and demonstrates that the mitigation project will contribute to the sustainability of watershed functions and the overall health of the watershed area's aquatic resources.

The Procedures indicate that the amount of mitigation required under Strategy 1 will be less than that required under Strategy 2. This is due to an increased confidence in the success of mitigation where an approved watershed plan is in place.

Similarly, a water board will evaluate the *type* and *location* of proposed mitigation based upon the use of a watershed approach that is itself based on a watershed profile. In particular, the appropriate type and location of compensatory mitigation will be based on watershed conditions, impact size, location and spacing, aquatic resource values, relevant watershed plans, and other considerations.

The required compensatory mitigation generally should be located within the same watershed as the impact site, but the Water Board *may* approve out-of-watershed mitigation in some circumstances. For example, if a proposed development project straddles more than one watershed, it may be appropriate to locate all of the mitigation in one watershed if that is ecologically preferable.

In furtherance of this watershed approach, the Procedures use the term "Project Evaluation Area" to describe the area of impacts of, and mitigation for, a particular project. This term is defined to mean an area that (1) includes the project impact site, and/or the compensatory mitigation site, and (2) is sufficiently large to evaluate the effects of the project or compensatory mitigation on "the abundance, diversity, and condition of the aquatic resources in an ecologically meaningful unit of the watershed." The size and location of the "ecologically meaningful unit" must be based upon a "reasonable rationale." As used in this definition, the term "abundance" represents an "estimate of the amount of aquatic resources by type in a watershed area, and what types of aquatic resources are most and least prevalent." The term "diversity" is defined to mean "the relative proportion of aquatic resource types, classification, connectivity, and spatial distribution within a watershed area."

Mitigation Plans

The applicant's mitigation plan will be reviewed to ensure that it comports with the provisions of Subpart J, the Water Code, applicable water quality standards, and state law. The level of detail in the mitigation plan must be sufficient to allow an evaluation of whether the mitigation offsets impacts considering the overall size and scope of impact. The mitigation plan must also provide a reasonable assurance that replacement of the full range of lost aquatic resources and functions will be provided in perpetuity.

The Procedures contain fairly detailed requirements for the contents of mitigation plans to be included in an application, although projects relying on mitigation banks or in-lieu fee programs are relieved of some of these specific items. Generally speaking, however, a proposed mitigation plan must include:

> a watershed profile for the "Project Evaluation Area" for both the fill and the
> mitigation activities

> an assessment of the overall condition of aquatic resources proposed to be
> impacted and their likely stressors

> a description of how the impacts and mitigation would not cause a "net loss of
> the overall abundance, diversity, and condition of aquatic resources, based on
> the watershed profile." If the mitigation is located in the same watershed as the

project, no net loss will be determined on a watershed basis. If located in multiple watersheds, no net loss will be determined considering all affected watersheds collectively.

> preliminary information about ecological performance standards, monitoring, and long-term protection and management
> a timetable for implementation
> design criteria and monitoring requirements for any proposed buffers
> if required by the Regional Water Board, an assessment of reasonably foreseeable impacts to the mitigation associated with climate change, and any measures to minimize or avoid those impacts
> to the extent the mitigation involves creation (i.e., establishment) or restoration, notification to identified local governments (e.g., flood control districts, airport land use commissions, vector control districts) *prior to initial site selection*
> for activities including in-water work or diversions, a water quality monitoring plan that includes, at a minimum, type and frequency of sampling for each applicable parameter
> for projects involving temporary impacts, a draft restoration plan that meets certain detailed requirements, including provisions outlining design, implementation, assessment, and maintenance for restoring impacted areas to pre-project conditions
> for EREPs, a draft assessment plan satisfying certain detailed requirements

The Procedures provide some additional requirements, as follows:

> The Procedures state that a permitting authority will approve a final compensatory mitigation plan when it issues an order. Where compliant with CEQA, however, the permitting authority may approve a final compensatory mitigation plan after it issues the order. In such cases the permitting authority must include as a condition that the applicant receive final approval prior to the discharge, and must specify a process for approving the final mitigation plan.
> Where necessary, a Water Board may require that financial security (e.g., letter of credit or performance bond) be provided as assurance that the mitigation plan will be implemented. The financial security must be in a form consistent with California law (which is described more fully in Chapter 10).
> A Water Board may also establish mitigation performance standards and long-term management funding requirements that must be met before an applicant will be released from his or her mitigation obligations under the order.
> The Water Board may specify in the order the conditions that must be met in order for the permittee to be released from the mitigation obligation, including performance standards and long-term management funding obligations.

POST-ADOPTION IMPLEMENTATION OF THE PROCEDURES

Although many clarifications were made to the Procedures in the run-up to final action by the Water Board, the policy remains quite complicated and, in some places, difficult to understand. Moreover, the economic impact of the Procedures on housing, agriculture and other regulated industries remains unclear. Accordingly, the industry coalition led by the California Building Industry Association sought and secured inclusion of several provisions in the board's adopting resolution.

In that resolution, the Water Board:

> authorized the Executive Director to make minor, non-substantive modifications to the language of the Procedures if the State Water Board or the California Office of Administrative Law determines that such changes are needed for clarity or consistency, of which changes the board must be informed

> directed staff to work with stakeholders, relevant state agencies, and scientific organizations to develop best practices for conducting a climate change analysis as required by the Procedures

> directed staff to develop implementation guidance for potential applicants and conduct staff training prior to the effective date of the Procedures, and to solicit informal input from stakeholders prior to finalizing the guidance

> directed staff to provide periodic progress reports to the State Water Board regarding implementation issues, including updates regarding application processing timelines and environmental performance measures

On May 1, 2019, the San Joaquin Tributaries Authority filed a legal action against the Procedures. The Authority's petition and complaint alleges that (1) the Procedures illegally regulate waters outside of the Water Board's delegated authority under the Clean Water Act; (2) dredged and fill material do not constitute "waste" within the meaning of Porter-Cologne; (3) the State Water Board's action violated statutory notice requirements; and (4) the Procedures do not satisfy the legal requirements for amendments to the state's water quality control plans.

CHAPTER 9

Rivers, Streams, and Lakes

This chapter covers the California Department of Fish and Wildlife's regulatory program under Section 1600 of the California Fish and Game Code, which requires certain types of impacts to rivers, streams, and lakes in California to be permitted through the issuance of "lake and streambed alteration agreements."

HISTORY AND BACKGROUND

Section 1600 *et seq.* of the Fish and Game Code ("Section 1600") is descended from the earliest of the state's system of protections for rivers, streams and lakes. Administered by the Department of Fish and Wildlife ("Department"), the statute arises out of the Legislature's belated recognition that mining activities—particularly during the Gold Rush—had vastly diminished the amount and quality of salmon and steelhead spawning habitat.

Early hydraulic mining operation. Photo: Oakland Museum of California, h92.0.1432. Licensed under CC 2.0.

As described by one court in 1983:

> Over 100 years, gold drew throngs of adventurers to early mining communities in the Sierra Nevada. When the halcyon years were over, a few earnest argonauts decamped and went to the river bottoms, and pointed great water cannons, called monitors, at the hillsides hoping to dislodge sparkles of gold from the sandy detritus . . . .

> Although considerable quantities of gold washed down and were separated from the gravel, the hydraulic mines annually discharged 600,000 cubic yards of debris, which soon choked the American and Sacramento Rivers with tailings, raised the beds of these rivers, impairing navigability, fouling the waters, and angering farmers.[1]

Following an early California Supreme Court injunction of hydraulic mining based upon theories of public trust and nuisance,[2] the Legislature passed a series of laws—directed at mining, timber and other industries—that served as statutory precursors to Section 1600, including one law requiring county approval of alterations or diversions of nonnavigable streams during mining operations.[3]

By the early 1960s, concerns over aggregate mining had drawn the attention of the Legislature due to silt that had affected salmon and steelhead by preventing spawning and suffocating eggs and fry. In 1961, the Senate "Permanent Fact Finding Report on Natural Resources" received a progress report describing these impacts in some detail.[4]

Soon thereafter, Sections 1600–02 were added to the Fish and Game Code. In this early form, the statute required all governmental agencies to submit general plans for any project "which will divert, obstruct or change the natural flow or bed of any river, stream or lake designated by the department." The Department was then to propose non-binding modifications to the acting agency's proposal to protect fish and game. In addition, Section 1602 required any person to notify the Department of proposed changes in any river, stream, or lake and to await the Department's recommendations before proceeding. These recommendations were non-binding in nature.[5]

> Although the scope of Section 1600 is limited to rivers, streams, and lakes, the Department has broader jurisdiction under Section 5650 of the Fish and Game Code, which makes it unlawful to "deposit in, permit to pass into, or place where it can pass into the waters of the State" a variety of pollutants, including "[a]ny substance deleterious to fish, plant life, mammals, or bird life." In some circumstances, this may include clean fill material. However, Section 5650 exempts any discharge or release that is expressly authorized by the state or regional water boards pursuant to waste discharge requirements or a Section 401 certification.

1   *People v. Weaver*, 147 Cal. App. 3d Supp. 23, 30 (1983).

2   *People v. Gold Run D. & M. Co.*, 66 Cal. 3d 138 (1884).

3   *People v. Weaver*, 147 Cal. App. 3d Supp. at 30–31.

4   *Report of Senate Permanent Fact Finding Committee on Natural Resources, Aggregate Removal from Streambeds*, section 1, pages 13, 17, 18, 2 *Appendix to Journal of the Senate* (1961 Reg. Sess.).

5   See *Willadsen v. Justice Court*, 139 Cal. App. 3d 171 (1983), for a discussion of this legislative history.

The statute was strengthened in 1970, when the Legislature added provisions *pro-hibiting* either an agency or an individual from proceeding with a project until an agreement was reached with the Department. Thus, the Department's recommendations were no longer advisory, and the statute's provisions made the prohibitions against public and private action roughly parallel. The bill added provisions making a violation of Section 1602 a misdemeanor, and created an arbitration feature that, in a different form, continues to be a part of the statute today.[6]

LSAA = Lake and Streambed Alteration Agreement

Although these early versions of the statute limited the act's application to waterways "designated by the Department," the Department thereafter adopted a regulation protecting *all* rivers, streams, lakes, and streambeds in the State of California, "including all rivers, streams and streambeds which may have intermittent flows of water . . . ."[7] This action was unsuccessfully challenged in the *Willadsen* case, discussed below, which held that the Legislature implicitly recognized this broad scope of coverage when it adopted subsequent amendments to the statute in 1976.

In 1976, the Legislature reorganized the statute, moving the governmental restrictions to Section 1602 and the provisions relating to other parties to Section 1603. In 2003, the Legislature collapsed the distinction between private and public entities, consolidating the basic prohibitions into a new Section 1602, applying its provisions to all "entities," a category that includes any person, state or local governmental agency, or public utility. Subsequent amendments to the statute occurred in 2014 and 2016.

BASIC PROHIBITIONS

The basic prohibition in the statute is found in Section 1602, which states that "[a]n entity shall not substantially divert or obstruct the natural flow of, or substantially change or use any material from the bed, channel, or bank of, any river, stream, or lake, or deposit or dispose of debris, waste, or other material containing crumbled, flaked, or ground pavement where it may pass into any river, stream, or lake" unless the entity submits a notice to the Department and secures a Lake and Streambed Alteration Agreement (LSAA) or otherwise follows the requirements of the statute.

There is a common misperception that the Department's mission under Section 1600 is to protect the river, stream, or lake *itself* from all types of environmental impacts. This is not exactly the case. Although the statute regulates various types of alterations or discharges to these features, the Department's job is to recommending measures to protect *fish and wildlife resources*. If there are no impacts to fish and wildlife resources, then no agreement is required to engage in that activity and, in fact, the Department is required to so notify the notifying party.

As stated in the legislative findings and declarations found in Section 1600:

> The Legislature finds and declares that the protection and conservation of
> the fish and wildlife resources of this state are of utmost public interest. Fish

6   See 57 Ops.Cal.Atty.Gen. 475, 476 (1974).

7   14 Former Cal. Admin. Code § 720.

and wildlife are the property of the people and provide a major contribution to the economy of the state, as well as providing a significant part of the people's food supply; therefore their conservation is a proper responsibility of the state. This chapter is enacted to provide conservation for these resources.

In particular, the Department's responsibility when presented with a notification of a proposed activity is to identify "reasonable measures" necessary to protect any "fish or wildlife resource" that may be substantially and adversely affected by the proposed activity. In practice, however, the Department tends to assert jurisdiction over, and require mitigation for any impacts to, a lake, river, or stream regardless of whether there will be any impacts at all (let alone substantial adverse effects) to a fish or wildlife resource.

That said, those activities requiring advance notification to the Department fall into three categories: (1) substantial diversions and obstructions of the natural flow of a river, stream or lake; (2) substantial changes to, or use of materials from, a river, stream or lake; and (3) deposit or disposal of certain debris, waste or other material where it "may pass into" any river, stream or lake.

Substantiality as a Threshold Question

Regulated diversions and obstructions of flow, and regulated changes in or use of material from beds and banks, must be "substantial" in order to require notice to the Department. There is little judicial guidance on when a potentially regulated activity moves from "less than substantial" to "substantial" under Section 1600. Not surprisingly, the courts have simply concluded that it depends on the circumstances.

For example, the term "substantial" was defined in *Rutherford v. State of California*[8] commonly to mean "something as ample or of considerable amount, quantity or size; while within the legal context, [it is defined to mean] important or material and of considerable amount or value rather than inconsequential or small."

In *People v. Weaver*,[9] the court found that the term "substantial" is a relative term and must be gauged by the circumstances. It went on to state that "we feel confident that the Legislature was not concerned with children skipping rocks across a stream, or building sandcastles, or hikers dislodging a few stones as they climbed on the banks of a river. On the contrary, by using the word substantially, the Legislature certainly intended to prohibit an owner from bulldozing material in a streambed which would cause the stream to change its course materially, or a like change which might interfere with the spawning grounds of anadromous fish . . . ."

Skipping stones as insubstantial alteration. Photo: Lindsay Teunis, ICF. Licensed under CC 2.0.

Finally, in *Siskiyou County Farm Bureau v. Department of Fish and Wildlife*,[10] the court considered the substantiality question in the context of water diversions that did not result in physical alterations to a bed or bank. Citing a 1973 Attorney General opinion issued two years before *Weaver*, the court concluded that whether a diversion is

---

8   188 Cal. App. 3d 1267 (1987).

9   147 Cal. App. 3d Supp. 23 (1983).

10   237 Cal. App. 4th 411 (2015).

substantial depends on the facts of the case. Quoting the Attorney General, the court stated that, "All pump diversions are capable of diverting small fish, fry and eggs out of a stream, river or lake, but a general rule cannot be laid down for what would constitute a substantial diversion, because of the innumerable factual variations."

LSAA = Lake and Streambed Alteration Agreement

The court further reasoned:

> Some of these considerations are the amount of water taken relative to the supply, the use to which such water is applied, the historical usage by the diverter and its predecessors, and the needs of the fish, given the palpable fact that—due to yet another in a series of drought conditions in California—there simply is not enough water to satisfy all legitimate needs.[11]

So how does an entity proposing activity in a stream determine whether an activity is substantial and requires authorization? The Department's answer, and it is reinforced by the *Rutherford* decision, is that the entity should submit a notification and the Department will make that determination. As stated in both *Rutherford* (and later quoted in *Siskiyou*), "[I]t is the role of the Department to determine whether the individual's proposed activity will affect the existing fish or wildlife resources. Consequently, because notice is required under the statute before an individual acts . . . , this determination rests on the Department and not the individual."[12]

Thus, the statute requires an entity to notify the Department of a proposed activity, following which the Department is required to determine whether the activity will affect fish and wildlife resources and, only in that event, to recommend measures to protect the identified resources. If the entity objects to the measures proposed, the Department is actually required to meet with the entity to resolve any disagreements. If they agree, the parties then enter into an agreement (referred to as a "Lake and Streambed Alteration Agreement or "LSAA") that incorporates the mutually acceptable measures. If they cannot agree, the matter actually goes to arbitration, resulting in a final "agreement" that is binding on both parties.

Substantial Diversion or Obstruction of Natural Flow

Notification to the Department is required whenever an entity proposes to substantially divert or obstruct the natural flow of any river, stream, or lake. Although the meaning of this provision appears to be clear on its face, for many decades the Department did not prioritize the regulation of water diversions, per se, under Section 1600. When the Department began to require notifications under Section 1600 for water diversions that did not otherwise result in actual physical alterations of the bed or banks of a stream, the reaction was unsurprising.

---

11 *Id.* at 429. See also *People v. Murrison*, 101 Cal. App. 4th 349 (2002) (in which the court failed to disturb a trial court finding that a rancher's construction of a rock and gravel dam across a creek for diversion purposes was substantial within the meaning of Section 1600).

12 *Rutherford*, 188 Cal. App. 3d at 1280, fn. 4.

In *Siskiyou County*, the Court of Appeal put this question to rest, setting aside the Farm Bureau's arguments that the statutory meaning of "diversion" is ambiguous and that diversions as traditionally understood are not regulated under Section 1600. Citing dictionary definitions, common law, judicial definitions, related statutory usages, legislative history, and the Department's own administrative interpretations, the court made clear that a diversion is nothing more than "the *taking* of water from a stream or river, and not the mere blocking or altering the course of the stream or river itself.[13] A diversion is a diversion, and it requires notification to the Department.

The courts have rejected claims that Section 1600 improperly interferes with the exercise of duly established water rights. In *People v. Murrison*,[14] a rancher appealed a criminal judgment against him under Section 1600, arguing that his exercise of pre-1914 appropriative rights could not be limited by the application of Section 1600, and further argued that any effort by the state to do so would create an unconstitutional taking.

Not surprisingly, the court concluded that the appellant's water rights were subject to reasonable regulation by the State of California. The court cited Article X Section 2 of the California Constitution, which proscribes the waste or unreasonable use or diversion of water, rejecting Murrison's argument that this provision was the *only* permissible restriction on the use of his water rights.

The court also rejected Murrison's argument under Water Code Section 1201 that, because his water rights were pre-1914, any otherwise permissible regulatory structure would not apply to his activities. As for Murrison's takings claim, the court held that it was not ripe because Murrison had never submitted a notification under Section 1600, and so no restrictive action had been taken by the Department in the first place.

Substantial Change or Use of Material from a Bed, Channel, or Bank

There is little judicial gloss on what it means to "change or use any material" from the bed, channel, or bank of any river or stream. Because the plain meaning of this phrase is broad, however, it has historically been the most common hook for state jurisdiction under Section 1600. Certainly grading, culverting and similar development activities fall within the ambit of this provision, and the usual question is whether the change or use is substantial.

Occasionally, there are disagreements with the Department as to whether certain types of crossings are regulated under Section 1600 where they do not physically alter the bed or banks. Examples of these disputes include free-span bridges that do not have abutments below the top of bank but may nonetheless have "shadowing" or other riparian impacts; and jack-and-bore operations that take place entirely beneath the bed of a creek or river. In the former case, the Department will typically take the position that, to the extent the improvements touch ground within the riparian zone, they are regulated under Section 1600. With respect to jack-and-bore operations, CDFW staff may assert

Bridge crossing over American River Canyon. Photo: Nick Ares. Licensed under CC 2.0.

13 *Siskiyou County*, 237 Cal. App. 4th at 436.

14 101 Cal. App. 4th 349 (2002).

that the potential for "fracking" of the creek bed requires the submission of a notification under Section 1600.

CDFW or the "Department" = California Department of Fish and Wildlife

Disposal of Debris, Waste, or Other Materials

Although the third notification trigger under Section 1602 is ostensibly the broadest, historically it has been the least used basis for CDFW jurisdiction. This trigger requires notification for the "deposit or [disposal of] debris, waste or other material containing crumbled, flaked, or ground pavement where it may pass into any river, stream, or lake . . . ." Although it has not been used much in the past, the Department is becoming increasingly muscular about using this trigger to regulate activities that occur well beyond the bed and banks of streams. It is important to note that the "pass into" notification trigger does not have any substantiality threshold like the other two notification triggers.

Given the focus of this provision on debris and waste, there is doubt as to whether this trigger covers the deposit of clean fill in upland areas. The Department insists that it does, in some cases relying on the broad definition of "waste" under the Porter-Cologne Water Quality Control Act. Under Porter-Cologne, the term "waste" can include "sewage and any and all other waste substances, liquid, solid, gaseous, or radioactive, associated with human habitation, or of human or animal origin, or from any producing, manufacturing, or processing operation, including waste placed within containers of whatever nature prior to, and for purposes of, disposal."[15] It is not clear that this definition is applicable to clean fill.

There is also a question as to whether the "debris, waste other material" triggering the permit requirement under this prong of the statute must contain "crumbled, flaked, or ground pavement." Not surprisingly, the Department's view is that it is only the "other material" that must include pavement to trigger review, and that *any* debris or waste may act as a trigger, regardless of whether it contains crumbled, flaked or ground pavement.

EXEMPTIONS

Section 1600 contains some exemptions from the requirement to obtain an LSAA, although in each of these instances some form of notification is still required.

The Department has begun to assert jurisdiction over any activity occurring within the watershed of, or in an area that is somehow hydrologically connected to, a river, stream or lake. In many cases the Department will decline to state whether such an assertion is based on a broad definition of stream or, instead, a broad reading of the "pass into" trigger. In either case, the Department's assertions of jurisdiction often are overly broad, leaving potential applicants in the position of deciding whether to notify or not and, in the latter case, risking potential enforcement.

"No Substantial Adverse Effect" Determination

If an entity has paid the necessary fees and the Department has determined the entity's application is "complete" under the Permit Streamlining Act, Government Code Section 65920, an LSAA is not required if the Department "informs the entity, in writing, that the activity will not substantially adversely affect an existing fish or wildlife resource, and that the entity may commence the activity without an agreement."[16]

---

15 Water Code § 13050(d).

16 Fish & Game Code § 1602(a)(4)(A)(i).

Failure of the Department to Respond to Notification

If an entity has paid the necessary fees and the Department has determined its application is complete under the Permit Streamlining Act, an LSAA is not required if the Department fails to provide a draft LSAA within 60 days following the Department's determination that the application is complete.[17] As described more fully below, this exemption applies only if the entity conducts the activity as described in the notification, including any mitigation measures contained in the notification, and the authorization may not be assigned.

If an entity is uncertain as to whether the criteria for this exemption have been satisfied, or needs some written confirmation to satisfy a lender, local agency or other interested party, the entity may request the Department for that confirmation. In these instances, the Department may issue a letter commonly referred to as an "Op-Law" letter, meaning the activity has been approved by operation of law.

Emergency Work

Section 1600 contains an exemption for certain emergency work, provided the entity performing the emergency work notifies the Department in writing within 14 days of beginning the work.[18] This exemption covers:

> immediate emergency work necessary to protect life or property

> immediate emergency repairs to public service facilities necessary to maintain service as a result of a disaster in an area in which the governor has declared a state of emergency under Government Code Section 8550

> emergency projects undertaken, carried out, or approved by a state or local agency to maintain, repair, or restore an existing highway (as defined in Vehicle Code Section 360), within the existing right-of-way, that has been damaged as a result of fire, flood, storm, earthquake, land subsidence, gradual earth movement, or landslide, within one year of the damage. Corrective grading work outside of the right-of-way is also permitted if ongoing mudslides, landslides or erosion pose an immediate threat to the highway, as is work to restore damaged roadways "to their pre-damage condition and functioning." This exemption does not cover any project undertaken, carried out or approved to expand or widen a damaged highway. It also does not apply to work on an official state scenic highway under Section 262 of the Streets and Highways Code.

The term "emergency" is defined under Section 1601, as it is defined under the California Environmental Quality Act (CEQA), to mean "a sudden, unexpected occurrence, involving a clear and imminent danger, demanding immediate action to prevent or mitigate loss of, or damage to, life, health, property, or essential public services," and includes "such occurrences as fire, flood, earthquake, or other soil or geologic movements, as well as such occurrences as riot, accident, or sabotage."[19]

17 Fish & Game Code § 1602(a)(4)(D).

18 *Id.* § 1610.

19 *Id.* § 1601, Cal. Pub. Res. Code § 21060.3.

In *Rutherford v. State of California*,[20] the Court of Appeal rejected a defendant's claim that his work was "emergency work" because it consisted of grading operations occurring over the course of a year. Similarly, in *Martin v. Riverside County Department of Code Enforcement*,[21] the Court of Appeal sustained the trial court's finding that an emergency did not exist when access to a secondary residence was wiped out by flood waters and the property owner did not repair the damage for seven months. The court further found that, even if the work qualified as emergency work under Section 1600, that exemption did not preempt the County's ability to require a grading permit under local codes.

Any work described in a 14-day post-work notification must meet the criteria set forth above and, if it does not, it will be considered a violation of Section 1600.

Routine Maintenance

Under Section 1602(b)(1), projects involving the routine maintenance and operation of water supply, drainage, flood control, or waste treatment and disposal facilities do not require notification if (1) the entity secured an agreement with the Department *prior to 1977* (and provides proof of that agreement to the Department), and (2) the work described in the agreement, and conditions affecting fish and wildlife resources adversely affected by the project, have not changed.

Cannabis Cultivation

Under Section 1602(d), an entity is not required to secure an LSAA for any activity under a cannabis cultivation license issued by the Department of Food and Agriculture, if:

> the entity submits to the Department a copy of the license or renewed license issued by the Department of Food and Agriculture that includes requirements specified in Section 26060.1 of the Business and Professions Code (application requirements for license for cultivation); the Department's application fees; and a written notification to the Department comporting with the usual requirements for a notification under the statute

> the Department determines in its sole discretion that the requirements included in the license, in accordance with Section 26060.1 of the Business and Professions Code, will adequately protect existing fish and wildlife resources without the need for additional measures that would be included in an LSAA

> the Department affirmatively notifies the entity that the exemption applies to the proposed activity

The Department has 60 days from the date an application is complete, and the fee has been paid, to notify the entity that the exemption applies.

In addition, Fish and Game Code Section 1617 authorizes the Department to adopt regulations providing for the issuance of a "general agreement" for a category or categories of activities related to cannabis cultivation. Compliance with such an agreement

20   188 Cal. App. 3d 1267 (1987).

21   *Martin v. Riverside County Department of Code Enforcement*, 166 Cal. App. 4th 1406 (2008).

Cannabis sativa. Photo: Manuel MV.
Licensed under CC 2.0.

alleviates the need to secure a more standard LSAA or follow the procedures to confirm an exemption for a licensed cannabis cultivation activity under Section 1602(d), although the Department is authorized to collect a fee for a general agreement.

In December 2017, pursuant to Section 1617, the Department noticed an emergency rulemaking action under the Administrative Procedure Act to adopt such a statewide general agreement for activities related to cannabis cultivation. After a brief notice period, the regulations became effective on January 2, 2018.[22] The general agreement is restricted to specific activities related to cannabis cultivation that meet the eligibility criteria identified in the regulations. Specifically, the activities covered are restricted to the construction, reconstruction, maintenance, or repair of stream crossings in the form of bridges, culverts, rock fords, and water diversions on any non-finfish bearing river, stream, or lake in the state. As a result, the Department does not expect all cultivators to be eligible for the general agreement.

To seek coverage under the general agreement, an entity must apply through the Department's website by providing information to confirm whether the entity's proposed activity or activities meet the eligibility criteria in the regulations for coverage under the general agreement, certifying some of this information, and by paying a fee. The fee will be the same fee the entity would pay to obtain a regular standard agreement. The term of coverage under the general agreement is five years. The regulations also provide a sunset date: the regulations will expire on January 1, 2023, unless the Department repeals the regulations or extends the date before the regulations expire. The reader should note that, under California Water Code Section 13149(a)(1)(A)–(a) (2), the Department is required to coordinate with the State Water Board on principles and guidelines for the diversion and use of water for cannabis cultivation. As state policy is rapidly unfolding on cannabis cultivation, this book does not intend to provide comprehensive coverage of that subject.

PROTECTED FEATURES

It is common parlance to refer to areas under 1602 jurisdiction as "waters of the State." This is a misnomer.

CDFW's Section 1602 jurisdiction is not over waters per se. CDFW's jurisdiction is over certain physical features in the landscape, not the water itself, except as articulated in *Siskiyou County Farm Bureau v. Department of Fish and Wildlife*.[23] In addition, Fish and Game Code Section 89.1 contains a precise definition of "waters of the State," adopting the definition found in the Porter-Cologne Water Quality Control Act. Under Section 13050(e) of Porter-Cologne, the term is defined as "any surface water or groundwater, including saline waters, within the boundaries of the state." That is, the term "waters of the State" defines the jurisdictional scope of the State Water Resources Control Board (SWRCB) under Porter-Cologne, *not* the jurisdictional scope of CDFW over

22   See 14 Cal. Code Regs. § 722.

23   237 Cal. App. 4th 411 (2015).

streambeds and banks. In fact, the term "waters of the State" does not appear within Section 1600 *et seq.*, but it is found in other provisions of the Fish and Game Code which are not relevant here.

Lakes

Section 1.56 of Title 14 contains the regulatory definition of "Lake," which "[i]ncludes natural or man-made reservoirs."[24]

Rivers and Streams

When Section 1603 (the predecessor to Section 1602) was added to the Fish and Game Code in 1976, the statute prohibited substantial alterations, etc., to rivers, streams, and lakes designated by the Department. In 1977, CDFW adopted regulations to implement this provision, designating "all rivers, streams, lakes, and streambeds in the State of California, including all rivers, streams and streambeds which may have intermittent flows of waters" for protection under the statute.[25]

The breadth of this designation was challenged by a defendant facing a misdemeanor violation of the statute. In *Willadsen v. Justice Court*,[26] the defendant asserted that, by delegating to CDFW the power to designate which features are subject to protection, the Legislature must have intended that some—but not all—of those features should be protected. The court rejected this argument, noting that, prior to 1976, the statute did not contain the limitation to those features designated by the Department. Accordingly, the statutory amendments that added this restriction merely codified what had already been the Department's practice.

Historically, the Department limited its jurisdictional reach over streams to those physical features containing bed and banks, typically defining the banks as extending to the edge of riparian vegetation along the stream. In recent years, however, CDFW has begun to expand its assertions of jurisdiction, claiming that a stream may extend to the edge of the associated floodplain or, in the alternative, any area that has seen some discernable flow over the last two hundred years.

These broad assertions of jurisdiction, both in the permitting process and the enforcement context, took the regulated community by surprise because the new definitional construct was not circulated for public review and comment, let alone a rulemaking under California's Administrative Procedure Act. Instead, these assertions of jurisdiction are based upon two *technical* reports prepared by CDFW staff.

These technical reports—*Appendix G: The MESA Field Guide, Mapping Episodic Stream Activity* (February 2014) and *A Review of Stream Processes and Forms in Dryland Watersheds* (December 2010)—were intended to articulate the environmental processes surrounding streams and their watersheds. Naturally, these reports illustrate how activities

---

24 14 Cal. Code Regs. § 1.56.

25 *Id.* § 720. Note that the regulation distinguishes between *streams* and *streambeds,* a distinction not made in the statute itself.

26 *Willadsen v. Justice Court,* 139 Cal. App. 3d 171 (1983).

MESA = Mapping Episodic
Stream Activity

OHWM = ordinary high water
mark

CEQA = California
Environmental Quality Act

For simplicity, this chapter
focuses primarily on
the MESA Field Guide,
although the Dryland
Watersheds Report is
based largely upon the
same principles.

Desert wash. Photo: Lindsay Teunis,
ICF. Licensed under CC 2.0.

outside the statutory definition of "stream" (but relevant to stream ecology and processes) might impact areas within the statutory definition of "stream." But these reports take it a step further by explicitly rejecting the statutory definition of stream.

MESA defines a stream as:

> a body of water that flows perennially or episodically and that is defined by the area in which water currently flows, or has flowed, over a given course during the historic hydrologic regime, and where the width of its course can reasonably be identified by physical or biological indicators. The historic hydrologic regime is defined as circa 1800 to the present.

This definition is now commonly used, and expanded upon, by CDFW staff in CEQA comment letters on lead agency environmental documents. The following quote from one such letter is included below to illustrate the "flexibility" inherent in a MESA-based stream definition:

> The Department's jurisdiction includes the bed, bank and channel and any associated habitat including areas where water has flowed and where the width of its course can be identified by physical or biological indicators. This may include the floodplain or associated contributing drainage areas. The Ordinary High Water Mark (OHWM) usually only takes into account the low-flow channel or thalweg. Riparian vegetation is not the end of our jurisdiction either. In some cases there may be no vegetation. When determining jurisdiction, the Department must consider the fluvial geomorphology of the system including the following: (1) where water currently flows, has flowed, over a given course during the historic hydrologic regime (can be subsurface flows), (2) the maximal extent of the expression of a stream on the landscape, (3) the connectivity between the groundwater table and surrounding landscape (may include springs, swales, surface runoff source areas that are a source of water to the stream), and (4) the nexus between the stream and all life associated with the streams. Riparian can include areas adjacent to the perennial, intermittent, and ephemeral streams, lakes and estuarine marine shorelines that are transitional between terrestrial and aquatic ecosystems and are distinguished by gradients in biophysical conditions, ecological process, and biota. They are areas through which surface and subsurface hydrology connect waterbodies with their adjacent uplands. Riparian areas connect upland and aquatic environments through both surface and subsurface hydrologic flow paths.

To understand the legal significance of this regulatory shift, one must understand how the courts, as well as the Department's regulations, historically have defined the terms "stream" and "bed and banks."

MESA DEFINITIONS

These MESA-based definitions of the Department's jurisdiction are contained in typical LSAAs:

Bank: The land, including its vegetation, that bounds the channel (defined herein) of a stream (defined herein), and that defines the lateral extent of that feature's waters. Banks are the land that confines or otherwise defines the boundary of a stream when its water rises to the highest point of confinement in a definite watercourse. In some cases, the banks can be slight or nearly imperceptible. The landward extent of a stream bank for concrete-lined or modified earthen channels is defined by the horizontal distance necessary to protect the stability of the bank; the horizontal boundary of the bank is commonly defined by the distance twice that of the bank height.

Bed: The land beneath a stream and its outermost banks; the portion of a stream directly beneath the water as defined by the highest stream flow at which these waters are confined to a definite watercourse. The bed may extend laterally beneath the banks where subsurface hydrologic connectivity exists between the stream and the surrounding land.

CDFW jurisdictional area: The stream bed, bank, channel, and associated riparian vegetation (all defined herein) within and adjacent to the [project construction footprint].

Channel: The course of a stream through which water flows perennially, intermittently, or ephemerally. The channel is defined by the area in which water currently flows, or has flowed over a given course during the historic hydrologic regime, and where the width of the course can reasonably be defined by geomorphic or vegetative indicators. The historic hydrologic regime is that which existed prior to the anthropogenic changes to the Californian landscape and waterbodies that increased with the accelerated settlement of the state after 1800. The channel is not defined by a particular flow event, but rather by the topography or elevations of land that confine the water to a definite course when the water rises to its highest point.

The 1983 decision *People v. Weaver*[27] evaluated the physical scope of CDFW's jurisdiction. The court in this case reasoned that a stream need not be perennial in order to invoke CDFW jurisdiction, stating that a continuous flow of water "is not necessary to constitute a stream and its waters [sic] stream waters." The court did, however, define the term "stream" by reference to the physical structure of the land containing the feature:

---

27   147 Cal. App. 3d Supp. 23 (1983).

> A stream is a watercourse having a source and terminus, banks and channel, through which waters flow, at least periodically. Streams usually empty into other streams, lakes, or the ocean, but a stream does not lose its character as a watercourse even though it may break up and disappear. Streams are usually formed by surface waters gathering together in one channel and flowing therein. The waters then lose their character as surface waters and become stream waters.[28]

In other words, according to the court in *Weaver*, a stream is not a stream until it is constrained by some form of channel. If waters are not so constrained, then they constitute surface flows and not a stream.

In 1987, this reasoning was reasserted in *Rutherford v. State of California*.[29] *Rutherford* involved the prosecution of a rancher who had engaged in activities to reclaim his land following a severe flooding event. Rutherford's property was a meadow that served as a water storage area, although the property had not previously seen flooding during the period of Rutherford's ownership. When Rutherford began to build roadways across his still-saturated meadow, he used material from the "high sides of [a] streambed" that apparently crossed his property. It is unclear from the opinion whether Rutherford's conviction resulted from his substantial alteration of the streambed or whether CDFW also claimed that his activities in the meadow were illegal.

Rutherford challenged his conviction on the basis that the statute (including the meaning of the terms "stream" and "streambed") was unconstitutionally vague. The Court of Appeal disagreed with Rutherford, citing the "commonly understood" definition of a stream as "a watercourse having a source and terminus, banks and channel, through which water flows, at least periodically." Relying on *Black's Law Dictionary*, the court further defined the term "streambed" as:

> the hollow or channel of a water course; the depression between the banks worn by the regular and usual flow of the water. The land that is covered by the water in its ordinary low stage. Area extending between the opposing banks measured from the foot of the banks from the top of the water at its ordinary stage, including sand bars which may exist between the foot of said banks as thus defined. It includes the lands below ordinary high water mark.[30]

More recently, in 2004, the Court of Appeal considered whether a suction dredging operation violated the statute by dredging "into the bank" of a stream without an LSAA. In *People v. Osborn*,[31] the court engaged in a fairly exhaustive discussion of where the bed and banks of a stream begin and end. Here, and with reference to

---

28 *Id.* at 30 (citations and internal quotation marks omitted).

29 188 Cal. App. 3d 1267 (1987).

30 *Id.* at 1279–80.

31 116 Cal. App. 4th 764 (2004).

California's law governing suction dredging,[32] and the regulations promulgated under that statute,[33] the court defined the term "bank" as including "the slope or elevation of land that bounds the bed of the stream in a permanent or long standing way, and that confines the stream water up to its highest level."[34] The court stated that this definition "aligns with common knowledge," citing the *American Heritage Dictionary* and *Black's Law Dictionary*, as well as the *Rutherford* decision and one other early case involving the interpretation of a deed.[35]

It is notable that, in MESA, the Department both (1) abandons written regulatory guidance that had been employed by the Department since at least 1994 and (2) disavows the applicability of Title 14 of the California Code of Regulations, Section 1.72, which the Department had traditionally used to determine the scope of its jurisdiction under the Lake and Streambed Statute.

In its 1994 *Field Guide to Lake and Streambed Alteration Agreements*, which is no longer in use as described in MESA, the Department stated:

> The outer edge of riparian vegetation is generally used as the line of demarcation between riparian and upland habitats and is therefore a reasonable and identifiable boundary for the lateral extent of a stream. In most cases, the use of this criterion should result in protecting the fish and wildlife resources at risk . . . . Most streams have a natural bank which confines flows to the bed or channel except during flooding. In some instances, particularly on smaller streams or dry washes with little or no riparian habitat, the bank should be used to mark the lateral extent of a stream.

Similarly, Section 1.72 of Title 14 of the California Code of Regulations defines the term "stream," which includes both "rivers and creeks," as "a body of water that flows at least periodically or intermittently through a bed or channel having banks and supports fish or other aquatic life. This includes watercourses having a surface or subsurface flow that supports or has supported riparian vegetation."

Beginning in 2015, the regulated community began to object to the Department's new definition. The Department's Office of General Counsel (OGC) responded in writing that Section 1.72 is not applicable to the Department's decisions under Section 1600, taking the position that, in adopting the regulation, the California Fish and Game Commission intended primarily to regulate sport-fishing. This position differs, however, from a legal opinion issued by OGC in 1990, which explicitly relied upon Section 1.72 as a source of authority relating to the scope of the Department's jurisdiction under Section 1600.

In response to industry pressure and assertions that the Department had promulgated and was applying an underground regulation, the Department's Deputy Director

---

32 Fish & Game Code § 5653.

33 14 Cal. Code Regs. § 228.

34 *Osborn*, 116 Cal. App. 4th at 765.

35 *Id.* at 770 (citing *Mammoth Gold Dredging Co. v. Forbes*, 39 Cal. App. 2d 739 (1940)).

issued guidance to CDFW staff indicating that they "may, but are not required to, use" MESA to implement Section 1600. It appears this guidance was intended to undercut any argument that the Department had promulgated an underground regulation by establishing that MESA is voluntary in nature. It did not change staff practice, however, and as of today, MESA is still being implemented throughout the state.

The judicial decisions discussed above generally resulted from challenges to the constitutional vagueness of Section 1600. The courts set aside these challenges based upon the common or dictionary meaning of the term "stream." By redefining the term in MESA, the Department raises anew these questions of vagueness. As stated by the court in *People v. Weaver*:

> [T]he void for vagueness doctrine requires that a penal statute define the criminal offense with sufficient definiteness that ordinary people can understand what conduct is prohibited and in a manner that does not encourage discriminatory enforcement. When the Legislature fails to establish minimal guidelines to govern law enforcement, a criminal statute may permit 'a standardless sweep [that] allows policemen, prosecutors and juries, to pursue their own personal predilections.'[36]

To illustrate the "pernicious aspects" of vague penal legislation, the court recalled a scene from Lewis Carroll's *Alice's Adventures in Wonderland*:

> At this moment the King, who had been for some time busily writing in his notebook, called out "Silence!" and read out from his book, "Rule Forty-two. All persons more than a mile high to leave the court."
>
> Everybody looked at Alice.
>
> "I'm not a mile high," said Alice . . . .
>
> "You are," said the King.
>
> "Well, I shan't go, at any rate," said Alice; "besides, that's not a regular rule. You invented it just now."[37]

In August 2017, the Department informally announced that it intended to initiate a rulemaking process under Section 1600. As of the publication of this book, this process had not formally been initiated.

The Department's "Questions and Answers," included on the CDFW website, state that Section 1602 applies to "all perennial, intermittent, and ephemeral rivers, streams, and lakes in the state." Unfortunately, the Department does not have a process by which an applicant may secure a pre-permit Jurisdictional Determination of whether a particular feature qualifies for protection under Section 1602. Given the considerable uncertainty surrounding the scope of CDFW jurisdiction, it would be helpful to have such a process, including a right to administrative appeal (such as that provided by the U.S.

---

36   147 Cal. App. 3d Supp. at 34–35.

37   *Id.* at 35 fn.8.

Army Corps of Engineers for waters of the United States). A link to more information on CDFW's program under Section 1600 can be found at https://www.wildlife.ca.gov/conservation/lsa.

In the meantime, the Department takes the position that it will not evaluate the scope of geographic jurisdiction without an entity first providing notification to the Department under Section 1602. That is, the Department "recommends" that a person initiate a full permit process (and pay the established fees) before knowing whether a proposed activity is regulated in the first place.[38] Even in this instance, the Department offers no means of appealing its determination of geographic scope other than completing the permit process and then (1) requesting a meeting with CDFW; and (2) pursuing arbitration of the protective measures recommended for inclusion in the LSAA.

This situation leaves members of the regulated community with a difficult choice when presented with a feature that may not be jurisdictional in the first place: either pay fees, submit a notification (i.e., actually apply for a permit), complete a permit process, and provide compensatory mitigation for the activity in question; or proceed with the project *without* notification to the Department and risk an enforcement action.

The latter course can be tricky because, in an enforcement context, the Department has no difficulty determining the scope of jurisdiction in advance of any permit application. Moreover, the Department takes the view that, once it issues a notice of violation to a person, the right of arbitration is immediately eliminated under Section 1614 of the Fish and Game Code. That is, there is no administrative due process available for an alleged violator of the Section 1600. Thus, the consequences of guessing wrong about the scope of the Department's jurisdiction may be considerable.

PENALTIES AND ENFORCEMENT

Violations of Section 1600 create both potential criminal and civil liability. With respect to criminal penalties, a violation of Fish and Game Code Section 1600 is a misdemeanor and subject to a fine of not more than $1,000, imprisonment in a county jail for not more than six months, or both the fine and imprisonment.[39] Further, for the second and each subsequent violation on the same project or streambed alteration agreement, the punishment increases to a fine of not more than $5,000 or imprisonment in the county jail for a period not to exceed one year, or both the fine and imprisonment.[40]

Section 1615 also establishes civil penalties of not more than $25,000 per violation. In determining the amount of a civil penalty, a court must consider all relevant circumstances, including but not limited to the nature, circumstance, extent and gravity of the violation. The court may also consider:

> the degree of toxicity of the discharge

> the volume of the discharge

---

38 See *LSA Questions and Answers (When must I notify CDFW?)*, California Department of Fish and Wildlife.

39 Fish & Game Code § 12002(a).

40 *Id.* § 12007.

> the extent of harm caused by the violation

> whether the effects of the violation may be reversed or mitigated

With respect to the defendant, the court may also consider:

> the defendant's ability to pay

> the effect of any civil penalty on the defendant's ability to continue in business

> any voluntary clean-up efforts undertaken

> any prior history of violations

> the gravity of the behavior

> the economic benefit, if any, resulting from the violation

> any other matters the court determines that justice may require[41]

The Department itself is not authorized to initiate a civil action. Such an action may only be brought by the Attorney General upon complaint by the Department or by a district attorney or city attorney brought in the name of the people of the State of California.[42]

In addition to civil penalties, the attorney general, district attorney or city attorney may seek injunctive relief in the form of a temporary restraining order, preliminary injunction or permanent injunction. The standards for injunctive relief are low. In such a proceeding the attorney general, district attorney or city attorney is not required to allege or prove, at any stage of the proceeding, that either (1) irreparable damage will occur if the order is not issued; or (2) the remedy at law is inadequate.[43] Moreover, the law specifies that the court *shall* issue injunctive relief without these allegations or proof.[44]

As noted below, the Department has a right under Section 1612 to revoke an LSAA if the entity is not in compliance with the terms and conditions of that LSAA. It should also be noted that, following receipt of a notification but prior to issuance of an LSAA, the Department may suspend processing of the notification if the Director of CDFW notifies the entity that the proposed activity, "or any activity or conduct by the entity directly related thereto," violates Section 1600 or any regulation that implements the statute.[45] In this case, the 60-day permit processing times established under Section 1602 do not apply, nor do the timelines established under Section 1603. These provisions cease to be applicable, however, if (1) the Department determines that the violation has been remedied; (2) legal action to prosecute the action is not filed within the applicable statute of limitations; or (3) legal action to prosecute the violation has been terminated.[46]

---

41 *Id.* § 1615(c).

42 *Id.* § 1615(d).

43 *Id.* § 1516(e)(1).

44 *Id.* § 1516(e)(2).

45 *Id.* § 1613.

46 See *id.* § 1603(a)–(c).

The Department takes the position that, if an entity has submitted a notification in response to a notice of violation from the Department, none of the procedures established under Sections 1603 are available. That is, the entity has no right to object to protective measures included in a draft LSAA, no right to meet with the Department to discuss the acceptability of such measures, and no right to arbitration under Section 1603(b). The stated basis for the Department's position is Section 1614, which states that if an entity is required to "perform work subject to" Section 1600 "pursuant to a court or administrative order or notice," *the entity shall include in the agreement* the measures proposed by the Department to protect fish and wildlife resources, and those measures are not subject to arbitration.

The Department's position is questionable in a couple of respects:

First, this Section explicitly applies *only* to arbitration under Section 1603(b), and it has no application to the notice and conferral requirements established under Section 1603(a).

Second, Section 1614 only applies to those situations in which an entity is under a judicial or administrative order to undertake some sort of work within a stream. The point of Section 1614 is that, in this instance, an entity may not arbitrate protective measures imposed to address the impacts of activity under the judicial or administrative order.

PERMITTING

Section 1600 is unusual in that it does not require a permit to engage in the activities covered by the statute. Rather, except in certain instances described below, it requires the entity to provide the Department with written notification of the proposed activity and enter into a written agreement with the Department (i.e., an LSAA) that authorizes the proposed activity. Courts have recognized this distinction in the context of whether Section 1600 is preempted by the Federal Power Act, and it may also be relevant to the question of whether Section 1600 is applicable to activities occurring on federal lands.[47]

Notification Requirements

Notification to the Department is required to include:

> a detailed description and map of the location of the project
> the name (if any) of the river, stream, or lake affected
> a detailed project description including, but not limited to, construction plans and drawings
> a copy of any CEQA document
> copies of other local, state or federal permits or agreements that have already been issued
> any other information required by the Department[48]

Like incidental take permits, LSAAs may be challenged by third parties. However, administrative mandamus is not an appropriate vehicle for such a challenge because a LSAA is not an adjudicatory decision that requires a hearing or factual findings. Instead, as the name denotes, an LSAA is a contract entered by an entity with CDFW. Accordingly, review is governed by traditional mandamus. *Environmental Protection Information Center v. California Department of Forestry and Fire Protection*, 44 Cal. 4th 459 (2008) (*EPIC*).

47 See, e.g., *Mega Renewables v. County of Shasta*, 644 F. Supp. 491 (E.D. Cal. 1986); see also *California Coastal Commission v. Granite Rock Company*, 480 U.S. 572 (1987).
48 Fish & Game Code § 1602(a)(1).

PSA = Permit Streamlining Act

The Department has not promulgated regulations for the administration of Section 1600. It has, however, published informal guidance for use in the application process. This guidance, which can be found on the Department's website, includes questions and answers, notification forms and other helpful materials.

It should be noted that, although the statute requires the submission of a detailed project description, the resulting LSAA may be somewhat protected against third-party challenge if such detail is not initially provided. In *Environmental Protection Information Center v. California Department of Forestry & Fire Protection* (*"EPIC"*),[49] for example, the court held that a notification need not identify the exact dates and locations of proposed diversions or obstructions. According to the court, the notification required by the statute is simply a notice of the proposed activity. That is, the court appeared satisfied with some level of generality in the initial notice based upon the fact that the terms and conditions of the LSAA itself would contain the necessary detail.[50]

Under Section 1608, the Department must provide any entity that submits a notification with all of the following information:

> the time period for review of the notification

> an explanation of the entity's right to object to any measures proposed by the Department

> the time period within which objections may be made in writing to the Department

> the time period within which the Department is required to respond, in writing, to the entity's objections

> an explanation of the right of the entity to arbitrate any measures in a draft LSAA

> the procedures and statutory timelines for arbitration, including, but not limited to, information about the payment requirements for arbitrator fees

> the current schedule of fees to obtain an LSAA

> departmental Response to Notifications

Section 1602(a)(2) requires the Department to determine whether a notification is complete, within the meaning of the Permit Streamlining Act (PSA),[51] "irrespective of whether the activity constitutes a development project for the purposes of that chapter." Under the PSA, the Department has 30 days to determine whether a notification is complete and, if it fails to do so, the application (i.e., the notification) will be deemed complete as a matter of law. The Department is not required to determine whether a notification is complete, or otherwise process the notification, until the Department has received the applicable fees.[52]

---

49 44 Cal. 4th 459 (2008).

50 *Id.* at 518–20.

51 Gov't Code § 65920.

52 Fish & Game Code § 1602(c).

Under Section 1602, an entity is not authorized to proceed with a non-exempt activity until (1) application fees have been paid; (2) the application (i.e., the notification) is determined by the Department—or deemed as a matter of law—to be complete; and (3) one of the following events has occurred:

> the Department informs the entity that the proposed activity will not substantially adversely affect an existing fish or wildlife resource (in which case the entity may carry out the activity without an LSAA provided the activity is as described in the notification, including any protective measures described in the notification)

> the Department determines that the activity may substantially adversely affect an existing fish and wildlife resource and issues an LSAA that includes "reasonable" measures necessary to protect the resource (in which case the entity may carry out the activity in accordance with the LSAA)

> a panel of arbitrators has issued a final LSAA to the entity in accordance with Section 1603(b) (provided the entity carries out the activity in accordance with that LSAA)

> the Department does not provide a draft LSAA within 60 days (in which case the entity may carry out the activity without an LSAA provided the activity is carried out as described in the notification, including any protective measures described in the notification that are intended to protect fish and wildlife resources)

Issuance of Draft LSAA

If the Department determines that a proposed activity *may substantially affect* an existing fish and wildlife resource, the Department must provide a draft LSAA to the entity within 60 days after the notification is complete.[53] That draft agreement must describe the fish and wildlife resources that may be substantially affected by the proposed activity. This description must be specific and detailed, and the Department must make available, upon request, the information upon which its determination of substantial adverse effect is based.[54]

The purpose of these requirements is to generally enable the affected person to enter into informed and intelligent negotiations with the Department.[55] Because the purpose of these requirements is for the benefit of the applicant, in the *EPIC* decision, the court demonstrated little patience with a third-party petitioner's assertion that the information was not sufficiently detailed.

In addition to its "effects determination," the Department's draft agreement must contain "measures to protect" the potentially affected fish and wildlife resources. Although the statute does not provide explicit authority for the Department to require

---

53   *Id.* § 1603(a); see also *id.* § 1602(a)(4)(D).

54   *Id.* § 1603(a).

55   See *EPIC*, 44 Cal. 4th at 518–20.

off-site compensation mitigation, the Department routinely includes such requirements in its "measures to protect." That is, it is the Department's view that protective measures are not limited to minimization measures intended to protect the resources affected by the activity, and that compensatory mitigation is an appropriate form of "protection." The statute does not define what types of "measures to protect" are permissible.

Negotiation and Arbitration Process

Within 30 days following receipt by the entity of a draft LSAA, the entity must notify the Department whether the measures to protect fish and wildlife resources are acceptable.[56] Although the statute does not explicitly authorize the applicant to question whether the resource-related effects by the Department are properly characterized, the need for those measures, in light of whether the effects as characterized may actually occur, are probably fair game. Accordingly, the entity may properly question (1) whether the Department has appropriately restricted its review to fish and wildlife resources associated with a "stream" or "lake" as properly characterized under Section 1600; (2) whether the potential effects as characterized by the Department satisfy the statutory standard; and (3) whether the protection measures proposed by the Department are within its statutory authority.

If the measures proposed by the Department are not "acceptable," then the entity must specify the measures that are not acceptable.[57] The statute does not specify any particular standard for determining whether the measures are acceptable. It simply allows the entity to identify the problematic measures, which are then subject to the negotiation and arbitration procedures specified in the statute. If the entity does not respond to the Department within 90 days, however, the Department may "withdraw" the agreement and require the entity to resubmit a notification to the Department prior to undertaking the activity.

Upon written request, which is typically associated with an entity's statement of objections, the Department must meet with the entity within 14 days following receipt of the entity's objection. The stated purpose of the meeting is to "resolve any disagreement" regarding the proposed protective measures. If the parties are unable to reach agreement at this meeting, the entity may request, in writing, a request for the appointment of a panel to conduct binding arbitration to resolve the disagreement.

If the entity makes this request, a panel of arbitrators must be appointed within 14 days. The panel is evenly balanced between the entity and the Department, being comprised of three panelists: one "representative" selected by the Department; one selected by the entity; and a third mutually agreed upon by the Department and the entity. This third panelist serves as the chair of the panel. If the parties cannot agree on a panel chair, the third person is appointed in the manner provided under Section 1281.6 of the Code of Civil Procedure, which specifies the manner in which a court

---

56 Fish & Game Code § 1603(a).

57 *Id.*

may appoint an arbitrator. In any event, the panel chair must have "scientific expertise" relevant to (1) the fish and wildlife resources that may be substantially adversely affected by the proposed activity, and (2) the measures proposed by the Department to protect those resources.

The Department tends to insist that, because the statute limits the arbitrators' jurisdiction to questions relating to the reasonableness of protective measures imposed by the Department, questions regarding the scope of the Department's jurisdiction may not be arbitrated. In a 1999 arbitration involving a golf course in Los Angeles, however, the Department lost on this question. This is probably the correct result, because questions regarding the reasonableness of mitigation necessarily depend on the acreage or lineal footage of the feature being affected.

The decision of the arbitration panel must be issued within 14 days after the panel was established, which is a tall order. The panel's decision is *binding* on both the entity *and the Department*, but it must be made based upon "the best scientific information reasonably available at the time of the arbitration." Except for a decision to extend an agreement without modification, the decision must be made in the form of a final agreement that includes, without modification, all measures from the original agreement that were not made subject to arbitration. Each party must pay the expenses of their selected representative and pay one-half the expenses of the third person. Decisions by an arbitration panel are in turn appealable to a court of competent jurisdiction for confirmation, correction, or vacation of the decision.[58]

Deemed Approval and "Op-Law" Letters

As noted above, if the Department does not issue a draft LSAA within 60 from the date notification is complete, the entity may proceed with its proposed activity provided it conducts that activity "as described in the notification," including any measures in the notification that were intended to protect fish and wildlife resources.[59] This circumstance occurs more often that one would suspect, and the delay is often intentional on the part of the Department.

For those entities who require assurance from the Department that the LSAA requirement has been waived, either for financing or sale purposes, the Department historically has been willing to provide those assurances. Upon request, the Department will often issue a letter (commonly referred to as an "Op-Law" letter) confirming that the Department has waived its permit requirement and that the entity may proceed, provided its actions are consistent with those described in the notification.

From an applicant's perspective, there are limitations on the value of Op-Law letters. The first is that they cannot be assigned, because the Department's view of the statute is that the "entity" that submitted the notification is the only person who is relieved of any permit requirement. The Department is also of the view that Op-Law

58   Fish & Game Code § 1604.
59   *Id.* § 1602(a)(4)(D).

authorizations may not be amended, because there is actually no agreement to amend. These limitations can be tricky when a land developer secures an Op-Law letter and then wants to sell the property to, say, a retail homebuilder. In these situations, the retail homebuilder may undertake the authorized activity as a contractor to the "entity" that originally submitted the notification. But this solution may become more attenuated if the property has already been transferred to the buyer at the time the activity occurs. To avoid these complicated contractual scenarios, it is often better to insist that the Department issue a written LSAA rather than rely upon the statute's op-law deadline.

Extensions of LSAAs

Generally speaking, LSAAs are required to be issued with terms not exceeding five years.[60] Even after expiration, however, an entity is responsible for complying with any "mitigation or other [protective] measures" specified in the agreement.[61]

Prior to expiration of an LSAA, an entity may request one extension of a previously approved agreement. Where an extension is requested, the original agreement will remain in effect until the Department grants the request or new measures are imposed through the negotiation and/or arbitration processes, but not for more than one year following the expiration of the original LSAA.[62] If the entity fails to submit an extension request prior to expiration of the original LSAA, the entity must submit a new notification before proceeding with the proposed activity.[63]

The Department is *required* to grant the extension unless it determines that the agreement requires modification "because the [protective] measures in the agreement no longer protect" the potentially affected fish and wildlife resources.[64] In the event the Department makes that determination, it must propose measures intended to protect those resources. As noted above, however, if the entity disagrees with these measures (or the Department's determination that the LSAA must be modified), then the entity may invoke the arbitration procedures established under Section 1603(b).

Long-Term Agreements

Notwithstanding the provisions of Section 1605(a)(1), the Department may issue an LSAA that otherwise satisfies the requirements of the statute for more than five years if the following conditions are satisfied:

> the entity submits a complete notification
> the entity agrees to submit a status report every four years, which status report must include: a copy of the original agreement; the status of the activity covered by the agreement; an evaluation of the success or failure of the protective

60 *Id.* § 1605(a)(1).
61 *Id.* § 1605(a)(2).
62 *Id.* §§ 1605(b)–(e).
63 *Id.* § 1605(f).
64 *Id.* § 1605(b).

measures; and a discussion of any factors that could increase the predicted adverse effects on fish and wildlife resources; and a description of the resources that may be adversely affected[65]

If the Department approves a long-term LSAA, it must review the four-year status report when submitted and conduct an on-site inspection to confirm that (1) the entity is in compliance with the LSAA; and (2) the protective measures continue to protect the identified fish and wildlife resources. If the entity fails to provide a status report in a timely manner, the Department may suspend or revoke the agreement.[66] The statute gives the Department express authority to conduct on-site inspections, on reasonable notice, that are relevant to the agreement.[67]

If the Department determines that the measures in the LSAA "no longer protect" the adversely affected fish and wildlife resources, the Department, "in consultation with the entity" and within 45 days of receipt of the report, shall impose "one or more new measures" to protect the adversely affected fish and wildlife resources.[68] If requested to do so by the entity, the Department must make available the information upon which it determined that the original agreement "no longer protects" the identified fish and wild-life resources.

In this instance, an entity has only seven days to notify the Department that it disagrees with the new measures, and the entity and the Department have only seven days to consult regarding the disagreement. If they fail to reach agreement, then the entity may request, in writing, the appointment of a panel of arbitrators to resolve the disagreement. The panel of arbitrators must be appointed within 14 days of the completed consultation, and a decision must be issued within 14 days thereafter. All of the other arbitration provisions in Fish and Game Code Section 1603(b) otherwise apply.

The Department is of the view that the "Op-Law" provisions of Section 1602(a) do not apply to long-term agreements.[69] Although there is a minor ambiguity in the statute, the Department is probably correct on this point. This does not, however, relieve the Department of the timelines—including the timeline for deemed approval—that exist under California's Permit Streamlining Act.

For complex or long-term projects, or actions involving multiple but similar projects, the Department will enter into a "Master Streambed Alteration Agreement." These agreements are available for projects for which "specific detailed plans" have not been prepared at the time of the original notification, and they describe a procedure (usually through "sub-notifications") that the entity must follow for construction, maintenance or other projects. Master streambed alteration agreements are essentially one form of long-term LSAA.

---

65   Fish & Game Code § 1605(g).

66   *Id.* § 1605(g)(3).

67   *Id.* § 1605(g)(4).

68   *Id.* § 1605(g)(3).

69   See *id.* § 1605(g)(5).

CEQA = California
Environmental Quality Act

Enforcement of LSAA Terms and Conditions

Under Fish and Game Code section 1612, the Department may suspend or revoke an LSAA at any time if it determines that the entity is not in compliance with the terms of the agreement or, in the case of a long-term agreement, fails to provide timely status reports under Section 1605(g). The statute requires the Department to establish regulations establishing the procedure for suspension or revocation of an agreement. These regulations are required to, among other things, require the Department to provide (1) written notice explaining the basis for a suspension or revocation; and (2) an opportunity for the entity to correct any deficiency before the Department revokes or suspends an agreement.[70] To date, the Department has not proposed these regulations.

CEQA Compliance

LSAAs are subject to CEQA. For most development projects, the Department will serve as a responsible agency and rely on the CEQA document that has already been prepared. In many cases, however, CEQA documents are prepared for most projects well before much design detail has been developed for that component of the project that will affect a river, lake, or stream. In those cases where an EIR or Mitigated Negative Declaration mention the need for a lake or streambed alteration, or where there have been changes to the design or location of the alteration, the Department is comfortable relying on an addendum provided the thresholds set forth in Public Resources Code Section 21166 (providing for subsequent environmental review) have not been met. The Department will rely upon an addendum prepared by the lead agency or, in some instances, an addendum prepared for the Department to act upon as responsible agency.

Application Fees under Section 1600

Not surprisingly, the statute requires the payment of fees established by the Department under Section 1609 of the Fish and Game Code.[71] Section 1609 states that these fees shall be established in an amount "necessary to pay the total costs incurred by the department in administering and enforcing [the statute], including, but not limited to, preparing and submitting agreements and conducting inspections."

The Department's application fees must be annually adjusted pursuant to Section 713 of the Fish and Game Code and must not include a fee that exceeds $5,000 for "any single project." The meaning of the term "any single project" is significant because, historically, the Department has treated every lake or streambed alteration as a separate project even though multiple alterations are part of a larger development project. By way of example, a development project that requires the installation of three bridges across a drainage would be charged three separate fees, even if all crossings are covered by a single LSAA.

70   *Id.* § 1612.

71   *Id.* § 1602(a)(3).

On January 1, 2016, the Department adopted a new set of rules for the calculation and payment of fees under the FWPC Act.[72] These rules specify the fees applicable to various types of LSAAs, including among other things "standard" agreements, "routine maintenance" agreements, "master agreements," and extensions. In addition, the rules specify methods for payment and include provisions for refunds to be issued in certain limited instances.[73] The Department's fees are updated annually and can be found on the Department's website. The 2019 schedule of fees can be found at https://nrm.dfg.ca.gov/FileHandler.ashx?DocumentID=162284&inline.

FWPC Act = Federal Water Pollution Control Act

---

72   14 Cal. Code Regs. § 699.5.

73   *Id.* § 699.5.

PART III

OTHER RESOURCES
AND PROCESSES

CHAPTER 10

Conservation Transactions

Much of the discussion in Parts I and II of this book is devoted to the compensatory mitigation requirements of the resource agencies. That is, Parts I and II address what types and amounts of mitigation may be required to offset, in whole or in part, the environmental effects of permitted actions. This chapter is devoted to the means by which mitigation projects are carried out, including the financial, contractual, and structural vehicles used to deliver mitigation projects. It covers conservation easements and associated financial assurances; mitigation and conservation banks; and in-lieu fee programs under the Corps of Engineers' 2008 mitigation rule.

PRM = permittee-responsible mitigation

HCP = Habitat Conservation Plan

NCCP = Natural Community Conservation Plan

BACKGROUND

Generally speaking, compensatory mitigation may involve the preservation of existing natural resources; the enhancement of existing natural resources whose functions can be improved through physical modification; the restoration of resources where they once existed but may have been eliminated from the landscape or greatly impaired (sometimes called "re-establishment"); or the creation of new resources where they did not previously exist (sometimes called "establishment"). Moreover, compensatory mitigation may take the form of preservation of natural resources even without enhancement, restoration or similar activities. In each of the foregoing cases the agencies typically require the preservation of the mitigation lands through a "site-protection instrument" such as a conservation easement.

The various agencies use different terms to describe the foregoing activities and, in some cases, different language to describe mitigation activities in general. This may result in confusion to an applicant, particularly where the different agencies insist on the use of different language to describe single mitigation projects addressing the requirements of multiple agencies. In the interest of brevity, in this chapter we have employed interchangeably the agencies' different usages relative to different types of compensatory mitigation. Also for brevity, we have used the term "mitigation" in this chapter to refer to "compensatory mitigation." There are actually many forms of mitigation that are not necessarily compensatory in nature because they are not intended to provide replacement habitat (e.g., minimization measures).

Despite these difficulties in translation, the agencies have over the years devoted considerable effort (although not always successful) to create some consistency in policies governing the *means* by which mitigation is delivered. For example, the agencies all tend to recognize that mitigation projects may be provided in accordance with three different models: (1) through a mitigation or conservation bank or an in-lieu fee program; (2) by a permittee's completion of a project to mitigate the impacts of that permittee's particular activity (which mitigation projects are generally referred to as "permittee-responsible mitigation" or PRM projects); or (3) through some other mechanism such as a Habitat Conservation Plan (HCP) or Natural Community Conservation Plan (NCCP) that may, for practical purposes, operate like an in-lieu fee program.

In each of these cases, there is one common denominator: the area identified as mitigation must be protected in perpetuity through a conservation easement or similar instrument. During the 1980s and 1990s this process was fairly simple and, in many cases, the agencies would rely on a deed restriction or declaration of covenants to protect a property. Those tools are used less frequently today, because deed restrictions lack the third-party oversight associated with a conservation easement. Over the last two decades, the use of conservation easements has itself become quite complicated. This is due largely to the perception that mitigation projects were at risk of failure for a variety of reasons, including questions regarding the solvency of nonprofits accepting grants of conservation easements.

In California, these perceptions led to the development of laws and policies intended to shore up what had been a fairly informal set of expectations relative to the protection of mitigation properties. These include, among other things, laws and policies (1) requiring financial security for the completion of the physical activity through which mitigation is provided (e.g., restoration, enhancement) and the long-term management of the land; and (2) establishing criteria and approval processes for entities desiring to hold a conservation easement or the associated short- or long-term financial assurances.

This chapter provides an overview of the principal mechanisms by which land mitigation transactions are conducted in California, including conservation easements and related contractual arrangements; PRM projects; mitigation and conservation banks; and in-lieu fee programs. Although mitigation transactions come in many different forms, and it is difficult to give this subject its due in the context of a single chapter, we have endeavored here to outline the basic rules and considerations that should be taken into account when structuring and implementing such projects. In any case, there are four fundamental questions that must be answered in planning a mitigation project:

> Who will own the land?
> Who will manage the land?
> Who will hold the conservation easement?
> Who will hold the endowment?

Approaches to these and related questions are described below.

SUMMARY OF AGENCY POLICIES

In California, the three *primary* drivers of mitigation projects are the California Department of Fish and Wildlife (Department), the U.S. Fish and Wildlife Service (Service or USFWS), and the U.S. Army Corps of Engineers (Corps). Among these, the Department tends to have the most exacting procedures for the establishment of a mitigation project, and the other agencies tend to defer to the Department's standards. It is likely that, as the State Water Resources Control Board's dredge and fill procedures mature over the next several years, we will see more formalized mitigation guidance from the Water Boards. In the meantime, however, the *structuring* of mitigation projects tends to follow the policies and guidance of these other agencies.

U.S. Fish and Wildlife Service

Until fairly recently, the Service had not given a great deal of attention to mitigation policy. In 1981, USFWS published its first overall policy on mitigation,[1] which established rudimentary mitigation thresholds (e.g., no net loss, minimization of loss) for different categories of resources and replaced even more primitive policies promulgated in the 1970s. But this policy had shortcomings, including its failure to give proper importance to the concept of *compensatory* mitigation. In 1983, the Service supplemented this policy with its *Guidance for the Establishment, Use, and Operation of*

Department = California Department of Fish and Wildlife

USFWS or the "Service" = U.S. Fish and Wildlife Service

Corps = U.S. Army Corps of Engineers

Water Boards = State Water Resources Control Board and Regional Water Quality Control Boards

1   46 Fed. Reg. 7656 (Jan. 23, 1981).

Conservation Banks[2] and, in 2008, promulgated guidance on the evaluation of recovery crediting efforts.[3] Although these policies were relatively general, they remained in place until near the end of the Obama Administration, when the Service began to modernize its mitigation policies to reflect practices that had developed since the 1980s.

In 2016, the Service published an updated and comprehensive ESA Compensatory Mitigation Policy,[4] which provided specific guidance regarding the role of compensatory mitigation under the federal ESA. The 2016 Mitigation Policy—which was not long-lived—reflected a conscious shift from project-by-project mitigation to a landscape-scale approach to planning and implementing compensatory mitigation. The 2016 Mitigation Policy applied to all compensatory mitigation requirements under the ESA,[5] including permittee-responsible mitigation, conservation banking, in-lieu fee programs, and other third-party mitigation mechanisms.[6]

On July 30, 2018, the Trump Administration withdrew the 2016 Mitigation Policy based primarily on constitutional concerns with respect to the policy's "net gain" goal, citing the U.S. Supreme Court's decision in *Koontz v. St. Johns River Water Management District*, 570 U.S. 595 (2013), and its predecessors, the *Nollan* and *Dolan* decisions. Although the "net conservation gain" goal was only a part of the Mitigation Policy, the adminstration took the position that, "[b]ecause the net conservation gain standard is so prevalent throughout the Mitigation Policy, the Service is . . . withdrawing the Mitigation Policy."[7] In fact, the net conservation gain was technically severable from the rest of the policy. In any event, it provided an easy target for the Trump Administration, which threw the baby out with the bathwater.

Despite its withdrawal, the 2016 Mitigation Policy is important because it represented a significant modernization of the Service's approach to mitigation, and it is possible that the principles expressed in the Mitigation Policy (and the Obama Administration's subsequent "Interim Guidance" discussed below) may still find their way into the Service's decision-making processes.

The 2016 Mitigation Policy encouraged strategic planning at the landscape level and established standards that mitigation programs and projects must meet to achieve conservation that is both effective and sustainable. The 2016 Mitigation Policy emphasized that the goal of mitigation is not necessarily based on total habitat area conserved, but rather on numbers of individuals, size and distribution of populations, the quality and carrying capacity of habitat, or the capacity of the landscape to support stable or increasing populations of the affected species after the project (including all proposed conservation measures) is implemented. In adopting the 2016 Mitigation Policy, the Service concluded that this approach would achieve the best conservation outcomes for

---

2   68 Fed. Reg. 24,753 (May 8, 2003).

3   73 Fed. Reg. 44,761 (July 31, 2008).

4   81 Fed. Reg. 95,316, 95,316–49.

5   *Id.* at 95,334.

6   *Id.* at 95,335.

7   83 Fed. Reg. 36,472 *et seq.*

listed, proposed, and at-risk species through management of the risks associated with compensatory mitigation. As noted above, under the 2016 Mitigation Policy, the Service sought to achieve a "net gain" or, at a minimum, a "no net loss" mitigation goal (the latter of which was intended to minimize the constitutional concerns).

ILF = in-lieu fee

The 2016 Mitigation Policy encouraged a landscape-level approach to conservation banking, in-lieu fee programs, and other third-party mitigation mechanisms such as "habitat credit exchanges" (a concept that has yet to be put into practice). The 2016 Mitigation Policy also encouraged the use of programmatic approaches to compensatory mitigation, such as through the use of HCP and NCCP devices, which have the advantages of advance planning and economies of scale to: (1) achieve a net gain in species' conservation; (2) reduce the unit cost of compensatory mitigation; and (3) improve regulatory procedural efficiency.

Just weeks after adoption of the 2016 Mitigation Policy, and during the final days of the Obama Administration, the Service published supplemental interim guidance to assist in the implementation of the 2016 Mitigation Policy ("Interim Guidance").[8] The Interim Guidance was intended to replace both the Service's 2003 guidance on conservation banks and its 2008 guidance on recovery crediting. The Interim Guidance is far more specific than, and implements, the broad goals and policies of the 2016 Mitigation Policy. Despite the withdrawal of the 2016 Mitigation Policy, it is possible that USFWS personnel will look informally to its provisions in reviewing mitigation projects. For this reason and for ease of use, this chapter refers to the Interim Guidance as if it is presently in use.

Section 5 of the Interim Guidance provides operational detail on the review, establishment, use, and operation of compensatory mitigation projects and programs as tools for offsetting adverse impacts to species, including conservation banks and in-lieu fee (ILF) programs.[9] Generally speaking, Section 5 is drafted to roughly mirror the procedures set forth in the Corps' 2008 Mitigation Rule.

Under Section 5 of the Interim Guidance, to secure approval of a mitigation project, an applicant begins by submitting a draft mitigation proposal, which is analogous to a "draft prospectus" under the Corps' Mitigation Rule. Following initial agency comments on the draft, the applicant then submits for approval a variety of additional documents that must satisfy some fairly detailed requirements set forth in the Interim Guidance.

These additional documents include a formal mitigation proposal; a draft "mitigation instrument" (which may take the form of a Bank-Enabling Instrument or in-lieu fee program instrument); a "mitigation work plan" (i.e., a plan for the enhancement, restoration or establishment of habitat if proposed); service area maps; credit tables and release schedules (for conservation banks and ILFs); interim and long-term management plans; proposed conservation easement or other "site protection instrument"; short-term, interim and long-term financial assurances (discussed further below);

---

8   Interim Guidance on Implementing the Final Endangered Species Act Compensatory Mitigation Policy, USFWS (Jan. 17, 2017) ("Interim Guidance").

9   *Id.* at p. 1.

BLM = Bureau of Land
Management

certain corporate information; and a closure plan. Section 5 also includes a set of criteria for the identification of the holders of conservation easements and financial assurances, respectively. If acceptable to the Service, these documents serve as the basis for a mitigation project intended to offset the impacts associated with some federal action reviewed by the Service.

The balance of the *Interim Mitigation Policy* is devoted to a number of specific subjects, including: requirements for the "durability" of compensatory mitigation on public lands; criteria for the use of third-party mitigation vehicles such as banks; management of risk and uncertainty through adaptive management; and compliance monitoring and tracking of compensatory mitigation projects. A brief discussion of the *Interim Mitigation Policy*'s guidance on these topics is provided below.

The Service has recognized that ensuring the durability of compensatory mitigation on public lands (e.g., lands held by BLM, National Forest Service, certain state agencies) presents particular challenges, especially regarding site protection assurances, long-term management, and funding assurances for long-term stewardship, as well as concerns about developers taking advantage of public land resources for private mitigation purposes. This lack of predictability, in part, is due to the fact that mechanisms available for ensuring durability of land protection for compensatory mitigation on public lands vary from agency to agency, are subject to site-specific limitations, and are likely to be politically and administratively challenging to secure.

To that end, the *Interim Mitigation Policy* establishes a number of required strategies for ensuring adequate long-term management of public lands, including assurance that: incompatible uses are removed or precluded to ensure that uses of the public lands do not conflict with or compromise the conservation of the species for which the compensatory mitigation project was established; the project authorization, permit, or license include in whole or by reference a final mitigation plan as a formal condition of the authorization; if the compensatory mitigation obligation will be satisfied through use of a conservation bank or other third-party mitigation provider, that the authorization, permit, or license identify the party responsible for providing the compensatory mitigation and the type(s) and amount(s) of credits that must be secure; and agreements enabling mitigation on public lands include provisions for equivalent alternative mitigation if subsequent changes in public land management directives result in actions on public land that are incompatible with the conservation needs of the species.

The *Interim Mitigation Policy* also establishes criteria for the use of third-party mitigation vehicles such as banks, including means of assuring transfer of liability for mitigation and addressing the permitted "stacking" of mitigation, particularly in multi-agency contexts. When a project sponsor engages a third-party mitigation sponsor, such as a bank operator, under the *Interim Mitigation Policy* the sponsor assumes liability for the success of the mitigation through the transfer of credits (or other quantified allocation of mitigation) via a mitigation instrument. The *Interim Mitigation Policy* requires that credit sales be recorded in a fully executed sales contract between the permittee and the mitigation sponsor that specifically stated the transfer of liability to be legally binding.

The *Interim Mitigation Policy* also allows for "stacking" of mitigation within a mitigation site, which allows for more than one credit type on spatially overlapping areas. However, the *Interim Mitigation Policy* provides that the stacked credits cannot be used to provide mitigation for more than one permitted impact action even if all the resources included in the stacked credit are not needed for that action. This policy was intended to avoid a double counting of mitigation credits. Additionally, the *Interim Mitigation Policy* allows for a compensatory mitigation project used under one Service program (e.g., Ecological Services) to be used to satisfy the requirements of another Service program (e.g., Migratory Birds), or other federal, state, or local agency programs; however, the same credits cannot be used for more than one authorized or permitted action (i.e., no double counting of mitigation credits) and all credits must be tracked using a credit ledger.

The *Interim Mitigation Policy* includes guidance regarding the management of risk and uncertainty through adaptive management, the use of buffers, the timing and approval of credit releases, the evaluation of mitigation ratios, and reserve credit accounts. Adaptive management allows for an iterative approach to decisionmaking, and provides the opportunity to adjust initial and subsequent decisions in light of learning with an overarching goal of reducing uncertainty over time. In developing and implementing long-term management plans for individual compensatory mitigation projects, the *Interim Mitigation Policy* requires that frameworks such as the Service's strategy habitat conservation model (USFWS and USGS 2006) and the Department's technical guidance (Williams et al. 2009) be used to inform metrics for compensatory mitigation programs. The *Interim Mitigation Policy* notes that certain compensatory mitigation programs should consider the use of buffers, used to protect compensatory mitigation sites from undesirable edge effects (e.g., introduction of invasive species, garbage dumping, erosion, etc.), particularly for small mitigation sites or sites with a high edge-to-area ratio.

Under the *Interim Mitigation Policy,* certain transactional provisions for managing uncertainty include credit release schedules, mitigation ratios, and reserve credit accounts. Credit release schedules permit credit releases only when specific performance criteria are met, which allows for mitigation project remediation rather than failure in situations in which default or other unintended events occur.

The *Interim Mitigation Policy* states that mitigation ratios are permitted to address the uncertainty of any mitigation program or for policy-based incentives, but cannot be used to compensate for limited understanding of species' conservation needs. The policy also provides that mitigation ration may be adjusted over time to achieve conservation goals. For example, mitigation ratios can be adjusted upward to create an incentive for avoidance of impacts in areas of high conservation concern, or adjusted downward to provide an incentive for project applicants to use conservation banks or in-lieu fee programs that conserve habitat in high priority conservation areas rather than PRM, which is likely to be of lower quality due to smaller parcel size.

ECOS = Environmental
Conservation and Online
System

RIBITS = Regulatory In-Lieu Fee
and Bank Information Tracking
System

HCE = Habitat Credit Exchange

NMFS = National Marine
Fisheries Service

EPA = Environmental Protection
Agency

The *Interim Mitigation Policy* provides that reserve credit accounts may be used to manage risk associated with mitigation projects or programs by spreading the risk among mitigation providers and providing assurance that the mitigation program is achieved. The uses of reserve credits may include offsetting catastrophic natural events such as wildfire or flooding or an adjacent land use that negatively affects a mitigation site. In those circumstances, the use of reserve credits allow the mitigation program to continue uninterrupted (i.e., prevent the need for temporary suspension of credit transfers while the landscape recovers or the situation is resolved).

Finally, the *Interim Mitigation Policy* sets forth minimum requirements for compliance monitoring and tracking of compensatory mitigation projects. Credit withdrawals from Service-authorized mitigation programs or projects that are unrelated to ESA compliance and are not approved by the Service also must be tracked in the same tracking system. Monitoring reports and other documents used to evaluate compensatory mitigation projects compliance are to be uploaded into the Service's Environmental Conservation and Online System (ECOS) or the Regulatory In-Lieu Fee and Bank Information Tracking System (RIBITS), as appropriate. Permittee-responsible mitigation is required to be tracked in ECOS. The *Interim Mitigation Policy* also anticipates that ILF programs and HCEs would be tracked in RIBITS when sufficient modifications to RIBITS have been made to accommodate these mitigation mechanisms. Until that time, the *Interim Mitigation Policy* provides that ILF programs and HCEs must be accessible to the Service and the public, as appropriate.

Corps of Engineers

As discussed earlier in this book, the Corps has long been guided by a "no net loss" policy in formulating wetland mitigation requirements under the Clean Water Act. For many years, however, the implementation of this principle was conducted on an ad hoc basis, with mitigation ratios varying widely and no formal policy established relative to the requirements of delivering wetland mitigation (e.g., legal instruments, financial assurances, long-term management, and similar questions).

Although the Corps formally stepped into the banking world in 1995, when the Corps, EPA, the Service, National Marine Fisheries Service (NMFS) issued joint *Federal Guidance for the Establishment, Use and Operation of Mitigation Banks*,[10] it was not until 2008 that the Corps (along with EPA) provided comprehensive guidance on the delivery of permittee-responsible mitigation projects, mitigation banks and ILF programs.[11]

10   60 Fed. Reg. 58, 605–58, 614 (Nov. 28, 1995).

11   Section 314 of the National Defense Authorization Act for the federal government's Fiscal Year 2004 required the Secretary of the Army, acting through the Chief of Engineers, to issue regulations establishing performance standards and criteria for the use, consistent with Section 404 of the Federal Water Pollution Control Act (33 U.S.C. §1344) ("Clean Water Act"), of on-site, off-site, and in-lieu fee mitigation and mitigation banking as compensation for lost wetlands functions in permits issued by the Secretary of the Army under such section. In response to this directive, the Corps and EPA published a proposed rule in Part II of the March 28, 2006 issue of the Federal Register (71 Fed. Reg. 15,520). In the preamble to the March 2006 proposal, the Corps and EPA noted their decision, in light of their respective statutory roles in the Section 404 program, to pursue the proposed rulemaking as a joint effort between the two agencies.

Significantly, the 2008 Mitigation Rule established a regulatory preference for mitigation banking over both in-lieu fee programs and PRM, and a regulatory preference for ILF programs over PRM projects.[12]

Like the Service's *Interim Mitigation Policy* (which was fashioned in large measure based upon the Corps' rule), the 2008 Mitigation Rule includes a list of detailed requirements for the review and approval of mitigation projects, whether in the PRM, bank or ILF context. In particular, Section 332.4 ("Planning and Documentation") reads much like Section 5 of the *Interim Mitigation Policy,* perhaps the most significant difference being that the Corps' policy specifically includes a requirement for public review and comment on mitigation proposals through the Corps' usual public notice requirement.

The reader is referred to Section 332.4 for more information than can be provided here. Generally speaking, however, like the *Interim Mitigation Policy,* the 2008 Mitigation Rule includes a requirement for review and approval of draft and final mitigation plans (at least for permittee-responsible projects).[13] Mitigation plans must include, but are not limited to, the following contents:

> a statement of objectives (including form of mitigation) describing the resource type(s) and amount(s) that will be provided, the method of compensation (i.e., restoration, establishment, enhancement, and/or preservation), and the manner in which the resource functions of the compensatory mitigation project will address the needs of the watershed ecoregion, physiographic province, or other geographic area of interest

> description of site selection factors to be considered during the site selection process, including consideration of watershed needs, onsite alternatives where applicable, and the practicability of accomplishing ecologically self-sustaining aquatic resource restoration, establishment, enhancement, and/or preservation at the compensatory mitigation project site

> description of the proposed site protection legal arrangements and instrument, including site ownership, that will be used to ensure the long-term protection of the compensatory mitigation project site

> baseline information and credit information (or, in the case of PRM, a justification of the adequacy of the proposed mitigation) that describes the ecological characteristics of the proposed compensatory mitigation project site and, in the case of an application for a DA permit, the impact site

> a mitigation work plan providing a detailed description regarding specifications and work descriptions for the compensatory mitigation project, including, but not limited to, the geographic boundaries of the project; construction methods timing, and sequence; source(s) of water, including connections to existing waters and uplands; methods for establishing the desired plant community; plans to control invasive plant species; the proposed grading plan, including

DA = Department of the Army

As of the date of publication, the Corps was seeking stakeholder input on a potential update to the Migitation Rule. A formal rule-making procedure is expected to commence in late 2019.

12 33 C.F.R. § 332.3(b)(2), (3).
13 *Id.* § 332.4(c).

RCIS = Regional Conservation Investment Strategy

CEQA = California Environmental Quality Act

CESA = California Endangered Species Act

CDFW or the "Department" = California Department of Fish and Wildlife

In 2016, the Corps and EPA published a helpful guide describing the different form of site protection instrument that might be used under the 2008 Mitigation Rule. This guide, entitled *Compensatory Mitigation Site Protection Instrument Handbook for the Corps Regulatory Program*, was updated in 2017 and can be found at https://www.epa.gov/cwa-404/compensatory-mitigation-site-protection-instrument-handbook-and-fact-sheet.

elevations and slopes of the substrate; soil management; and erosion control measures

> ecological performance standards that will be used to determine whether the compensatory mitigation project is achieving its objectives

> monitoring requirements providing a description of parameters to be monitored in order to determine if the compensatory mitigation project is on track to meet performance standards and if adaptive management is needed, and a schedule for monitoring and reporting

> long-term and adaptive management plans providing a description of how the compensatory mitigation project will be managed after performance standards have been achieved to ensure the long-term sustainability of the resource, including long-term financing mechanisms and the party responsible for long-term management

> description of financial assurances that will be provided and how they are sufficient to ensure a high level of confidence that the compensatory mitigation project will be successfully completed, in accordance with its performance standards[14]

Much of this information must be very specific and detailed, and much of it applies to the review and approval of projects to be included in mitigation banks and ILF programs.

California Department of Fish and Wildlife

The California Department of Fish and Wildlife (CDFW) has not promulgated a single, comprehensive policy on the structuring of mitigation transactions. CDFW is governed by the "full mitigation" requirement of CESA, as well as the requirements of CEQA, the NCCP Act, the 1602 program and the Regional Conservation Investment Strategy (RCIS) program, but there is little formal guidance describing how to satisfy these substantive requirements, except as provided under CEQA itself.

Despite the lack of a formal comprehensive mitigation, however, CDFW has developed a number of specific processes relating to conservation easements, financial assurances, banks and related matters that, in most cases, have made CDFW the agency leader in the structuring of mitigation deals, particularly permittee-responsible mitigation transactions. These various policies are discussed below where relevant.

In 2014, following the state legislature's adoption of Senate Bill 1148, which established a formal process for CDFW review and approval of mitigation and conservation bank applications, CDFW promulgated its *Conservation and Mitigation Banking Guidelines*. The 2014 Guidelines were intended to clarify the mitigation and conservation bank review and approval process as defined in the Fish and Game Code in order to assist bank sponsors, partner agencies, the public, and CDFW staff.

Under the 2014 Guidelines, applicants seeking CDFW approval to establish a bank must submit a series of application documents during the bank review process. The required documents typically include a prospectus and a bank agreement package,

14   *Id.* §§ 332.4(c), 332.5, 332.6, 332.7.

which is comprised of a conservation bank enabling instrument, a conservation easement, property assessment and warranty, and long-term management plan. The 2014 Guidelines state that this phased approach allows CDFW to consider bank concepts and initial proposals *before* the bank sponsor invests the time and resources to prepare a full bank agreement package. Establishment of banks subject to other state or federal agency review requires joint review by the Interagency Review Team (IRT), as discussed further below. Under the 2014 Guidelines, a bank sponsor may, but is not required to, submit a draft prospectus providing a brief, concept-level proposal prior to filing a formal prospectus with CDFW. The draft prospectus is recommended when a bank sponsor is scoping the concept for a bank or contemplating a specific mitigation or conservation bank idea, or for those new to the banking process. The formal agency review process begins upon submission of a prospectus, as discussed in detail under Section 1797.5(h) of the Fish and Game Code, which establishes a statutory procedure for bank consideration and approval.

IRT = Interagency Review Team

The Department of Fish and Wildlife maintains its own forms of easement for use in different situations. Although these forms are similar to the multi-agency template discussed below, they are not identical. Moreover, modifications to the Department's form may be required to accommodate permitting situations involving the U.S. Fish and Wildlife Service, the Water Boards or the Corps.

CONSERVATION EASEMENTS AND OTHER SITE PROTECTION INSTRUMENTS

Each of the permitting agencies requires mitigation projects to be protected by a "site protection instrument." In almost all cases this term refers to a conservation easement, although the Corps retains some flexibility in its regulations to allow for other types of protective instruments (e.g., a deed restriction, which does not offer the same third-party oversight provided by an easement). Like all real property interests, conservation easements are creatures of state law, and the federal agencies tend to defer to California real property law when it comes to questions involving site protection.[15] As more fully discussed below, California's requirements for conservation easements are found in Section 815 *et seq.* of the California Civil Code (the "Conservation Easement Statute").

Nature of Conservation Easements

A conservation easement is an interest in real property that is established by agreement between a landowner (grantor) and a land conservation organization, government entity or other qualified entity (grantee) for the purpose of (1) limiting the landowner's use of the underlying property to certain permitted uses that are compatible with conservation, (2) identifying and assigning responsibility for the restoration or enhancement measures required under the permit or permits that generated the need for the easement, and (3) providing for compliance monitoring and enforcement.

In California, a conservation easement is defined to mean:

> Any limitation in a deed, will, or other instrument in the form of an easement, restriction, covenant or condition, which is or has been executed by or on behalf of the owner of the land subject to the easement and is binding upon successive owners of such land, and the purpose of which is to

15   Interim Guidance, § 5.2.3.5.

retain land predominantly in its natural, scenic, historical, agricultural, forested, or open-space condition.[16]

The Conservation Easement Statute further specifies that a conservation easement is an interest in real property that is "freely transferable in whole or in part . . . by any lawful method for the transfer of interests in real property" in California.[17] Even though a conservation easement may be negative in character, it is still considered an interest in real property and is not personal in nature.[18] Moreover, even if a conservation easement is created by an instrument that does not normally create an interest in real property (e.g., a declaration of restrictions, covenants or conditions), it retains its character as real property. No conservation easement is considered unenforceable in California even if (1) there is a lack of privity of contract; (2) there is a lack of benefit to particular land (i.e., there is no "benefited property") or (3) the instrument does not state that it runs with the land.[19]

Significantly, California law provides considerable flexibility with respect to the types of instruments that can be used to create conservation easements. That is, a conservation easement need not be in the form of an actual *easement*. A conservation easement may be in the form of a declaration of restrictions or restrictive covenants, even though under California law such instruments may not otherwise create an interest in real property. As real property instruments, conservation easements must be recorded in the office of the applicable county recorder, and are subject in all respects to the state's recording laws.[20]

Rights and Obligations of Grantors

Under a conservation easement, a grantor or his or her successor in interest retains fee title to the underlying property and may continue to use the land subject to the restrictions contained in the easement. By statute, all interests *not* transferred and conveyed by the instrument "shall remain in the grantor of the easement, including the right to engage in all uses of the land not affected by the easement nor prohibited by the easement or by law."[21] The particular characteristics of a conservation easement are those "granted or specified in the instrument creating or transferring the easement."[22]

Given the statutory default allowing a grantor to engage in all uses not prohibited, much attention is typically given in the negotiation of a conservation easement to identifying a list of both "permitted" *and* "prohibited" uses to govern the landowners' long-term use of the property. Where a particular use is not identified in one of these lists,

---

16   Civ. Code § 815.1.

17   *Id.* § 815.2(a).

18   *Id.* § 815.2(c).

19   *Id.* § 815.7(a).

20   *Id.* § 815.5.

21   *Id.* § 815.4.

22   *Id.* § 815.2(d).

under statute that use is considered a permitted use. However, most conservation easements include a broad statement of conservation "purposes" or "values" to be protected under the easement, usually prohibiting any activity that would run afoul of these conservation purposes or values even if not specifically prohibited by the easement.

Permitted Grantees

Under the Conservation Easement Statute, only the following types of entities are authorized to hold conservation easements:

> > a tax-exempt nonprofit organization qualified under section 501(c)(3) of the Internal Revenue Code and qualified to do business in California, provided the organization has as its *primary purpose* the preservation, protection, or enhancement of land in its natural, scenic, historical, agricultural, forested, or open-space condition or use

> > the state or any state or local government entity, including any city, county, or district, provided that the government entity is otherwise authorized to acquire and hold title to real property

> > a federally recognized California Native American tribe or non-federally recognized California Native American tribe that is on the contact list maintained by the American Heritage Commission to protect a California Native American prehistoric, archaeological, cultural, spiritual or ceremonial place[23]

Although any of these entities is authorized by law to hold a conservation easement, for mitigation properties, the agencies tend to advise against the grant of mitigation easements on tribal land due to challenges associated with tribal sovereignty; similarly, the recordation of easements on land held by the United States or the State of California (particularly the Department of Fish and Wildlife) can be problematic.[24]

In recent years the agencies have become increasingly rigorous in their approval of proposed easement holders. Under the Service's *Interim Mitigation Policy*, for example, a proposed easement holder must be accredited by the Land Trust Accreditation Commission if such an accredited entity is available.[25] If one is not available, then the proposed easement holder will be scrutinized closely by the Service to confirm it satisfies various criteria set forth in the *Interim Mitigation Policy*.[26]

The Department of Fish and Wildlife tends to be the strictest of the agencies, and requires entities seeking to hold conservation easements or manage mitigation lands to complete and submit to CDFW for approval an "Application to Hold and Manage Mitigation Land" that allows the Department to conduct a fairly rigorous due diligence process. Each CDFW region maintains its own list of approved easement holders.

---

23 *Id.* § 815.3.

24 *Interim Mitigation Policy,* § 5.2.3.5.

25 *Id.* § 5.4.

26 *Id.*

Rights and Remedies of Grantees

The grantee of a conservation easement assumes the responsibility to monitor the use of the covered property to ensure compliance with the terms of the easement and to enforce the terms if a violation occurs. In addition to the right to enforce the negative covenants created by a conservation easement, a grantee may be given responsibility to undertake the various physical land improvements that may be needed for restoration or enhancement purposes.

Under California law, any actual or threatened injury to or impairment of a conservation easement, or actual or threatened violation of the terms of a conservation easement, may be prohibited or restrained by a court of law.[27] Any such action may be initiated by either the easement holder *or* the grantor of the easement. In addition to injunctive relief, an easement holder may recover money damages for any injury to the easement or violation of the terms thereof.[28] Recoverable damages may include, among other things, the cost or restoration; the loss of scenic, aesthetic, or environmental values protected by the easement; and reasonable attorneys' fees incurred by the prevailing party.[29]

In addition to the foregoing, California Government Code Section 65967(e) provides that, where a permitting agency determines that mitigation property is not being held, monitored, or stewarded for conservation purposes in the manner specified in the easement, the property shall revert to the agency, or to another public agency, governmental entity, special district, or nonprofit organization approved by the agency.

Scope of Protections

A conservation easement is not required to restrict land *entirely* to conservation purposes. That is, land covered by a conservation easement need only be used "predominantly" for conservation purposes. Moreover, the conservation purposes protected by an easement are not necessary related to natural resources. That is, the purpose of a conservation easement may be to protect scenic resources, agricultural or forest resources, or simply open space or natural conditions, regardless of whether those activities promote or protect values related to wetlands or endangered species.[30]

This flexibility is sufficient to allow a broad variety of non-conservation activities, at least as a matter of statute, and is most often used to facilitate the ongoing use of a pre-existing homestead, ranch facilities or similar features. But it may be used more broadly to allow activities such as power generation or transmission, water storage and conveyance facilities, oil and gas, roadways, and other intensive activities. For mitigation purposes, however, the permitting agencies are loathe to allow any but the least intensive activities, and unusual situations (or deviations from the agency template) typically require review by the agency's legal counsel.

27   Civ. Code § 815.7(b).

28   *Id.* § 815.7(c).

29   *Id.*

30   *Id.* § 815.1

Perpetual Nature of Conservation Easements

Although not necessarily required by the resource agencies in all permitting situations, the Conservation Easement Statute requires easements to be perpetual in nature.[31] This requirement is repeated in the Government Code, which applies the perpetuity requirement to both conservation easements and "open-space easements" (discussed below).[32] This perpetuity requirement raises questions as to whether a conservation easement can be amended or replaced after it has been granted. The Internal Revenue Service tends to frown on such transactions, and thus nonprofit easement holders are reluctant to consider them. Some nonprofits, however, have established processes for amendment where an amendment or exchange can be shown to produce a net conservation benefit, but such transactions are fairly rare.

Voluntary Nature of Conservation Easements

In enacting the Conservation Easement Statute, the Legislature found and declared it to be the public policy and in the public interest of the state to encourage the voluntary conveyance of conservation easements to qualified organizations. Section 815.2 of the Civil Code specifically defines a conservation easement as an interest in real property that is "voluntarily created." In fact, under Section 815.3, state and local governmental organizations and tribes are authorized to hold conservation easements only if the easement is "voluntarily conveyed," and that section explicitly prohibits local governmental agencies from conditioning the issuance of a land use entitlement on the grant of a conservation easement. Moreover, although the prohibition is expressly limited to local government, the statute provides that *any* conservation easement must be voluntarily conveyed, regardless of whether the conveyance requirement is imposed by a local, state, or federal governmental agency.

The prohibition against requiring conservation easements, however, is not absolute. In *Building Industry Assn. of Cent. California v. County of Stanislaus*,[33] the court held that a county general plan provision conditioning conversions from agricultural to residential use on obtaining conservation easements on an equal number of acres of other farmland within the county limits *did not violate* Section 815.3 because the general plan provision allowed the applicant to arrange for a third party to grant a conservation easement as an alternative to the applicant itself granting such an easement. The court emphasized that Section 815.3 only prevents a government entity from requiring an involuntary conveyance of a conservation easement. The court noted that under the general plan policy, the developer was required to arrange for the granting of a conservation easement in order to obtain a development approval, most likely by a purchase, but that no particular landowner would be required to grant the conservation easement. Rather, the actual grant of the conservation easement would be

---

31 *Id.* § 815.2(b).

32 Gov't Code § 65966(a).

33 190 Cal. App. 4th 582 (2010).

voluntary. In arriving at its holding, the court noted that this narrow interpretation of Section 815.3 is consistent with the legislative mandate to liberally construe the provisions of the conservation easement chapter in order to preserve "one of California's most important environmental assets."[34]

Notwithstanding the foregoing, when the Legislature enacted SB 1094 in 2012, it implicitly recognized that state and local agencies may require a project proponent to "transfer property" to mitigate adverse natural resource impacts caused by permitting the development of a project or facility,[35] and there is authority under CEQA to utilize land replacement for "mitigation" to offset project impacts.[36] There is therefore some ambiguity under the California law as to the extent to which property owners may be required by the government to convey permanent easements in a permitting situation. Moreover, the U.S. Supreme Court has weighed in on requirements for the transfer of real property in permitting situations, in one case holding that government may be liable if it requires an easement where the underlying property may already be protected by local zoning controls.[37]

Note that creation of a conservation easement for compensatory mitigation purposes does not trigger certain state laws governing division and transfer of land. A 2007 Attorney General Opinion[38] concluded that the granting of an easement to a qualified nonprofit organization for the purpose of protecting a listed species under the federal Endangered Species Act does not constitute a "subdivision" of land for purposes of the Subdivision Map Act.[39] The question addressed by the Opinion was whether the creation of an easement resulted in a "subdivision" as defined under Government Code Section 66424 of the act:

> the division, by any subdivider, of any unit or units of improved or unimproved land, or any portion thereof, shown on the latest equalized assessment roll as a unit or as contiguous units, for the purpose of sale, lease or financing, whether immediate or future.

The opinion concluded that the grant of a conservation easement does not effect a "sale, lease or financing, whether immediate or future," because the purpose of granting a conservation easement "is to retain land predominantly in its natural, scenic, historical, agricultural, forested, or open-space condition." Otherwise stated, the grant of an

---

34   *Id.* at 593–94.

35   Gov't Code § 65967(a).

36   CEQA provides that "public agencies should not approve projects as proposed if there are . . . feasible mitigation measures available which would substantially lessen the significant environmental effects of such projects." (Pub. Res. Code § 21002.) To that end, CEQA agencies must mitigate significant effects of projects they approve "whenever it is feasible to do so." (Pub. Res. Code § 21002.1(b).) The CEQA Guidelines note that some mitigation measures do not avoid or reduce an impact directly, but rather compensate for it by providing a substitute resource. Such mitigation may include acquisition and enhancement of wetlands or species habitat through establishment of a conservation easement. (See 14 Cal. Code Regs. §15370(e).)

37   *Nollan v. California Coastal Commission*, 483 U.S. 825 (1987); *Dolan v. City of Tigard*, 512 U.S. 374 (1994).

38   06 Ops.Cal.Atty.Gen. 801 (2007).

39   Gov't Code §§ 66410–66499.37.

easement is not a "sale" because ownership does not change hands. The Attorney General rejected the suggestion that a corporation's receipt of mitigation credits in exchange for granting the conservation easement, or the subsequent sale and use of such credits, would constitute a "subdivision" under the Act given that such credit does not grant an interest in any specific property.

Form and Contents of Conservation Easements

While the contents of a conservation easement may vary considerably, generally, instruments creating conservation easements will contain the following components: a preamble discussing the purposes of the conservation; the reserved uses and rights of the affected property; the extinguished or prohibited uses and rights of the affected property; the affirmative rights and obligations of the easement holder; and various administrative provisions regarding the relationship between the landowner and easement holder.

Although the Service's *Interim Mitigation Policy* is not specific as to the form of a conservation easement or other site protection instrument, any such instrument must designate the Service as a third-party beneficiary with a right of enforcement. It must also, among other things, (1) incorporate the interim and long-term management plans, (2) prohibit incompatible uses "to the extent appropriate and practicable," and (3) contain a provision requiring 60-day advance notice before any action is taken to void or modify the instrument, including any transfer of title to or establishment of any legal claims over the mitigation site (which may not be binding on superior land interests). The Service's "approval of" a specific site protection instrument must be obtained in advance of, or concurrently with, the permitted impacts.[40]

Many of these same requirements can be found in the 2008 Mitigation Rule,[41] although the Corps tends to be more forgiving than the wildlife agencies in allowing the use of real estate instruments other than conservation easements, explicitly allowing the use of restrictive covenants to the extent they can provide adequate site protection.[42]

MITIGATION SITE DUE DILIGENCE

In General

In addition to reviewing the ecological rationale for mitigation at a particular site, each of the resource agencies requires some form of real estate due diligence relative to a site proposed for mitigation. In particular, the agencies want to assure that a proposed mitigation property has clean title, and that severed mineral or water rights have been extinguished or that the potential for their use is negligible. Typical due diligence also includes the production of Phase 1 reports to assure that a mitigation property is not compromised by contamination.

CNRA = California Natural Resources Agency

NMFS = National Marine Fisheries Service

EPA = Environmental Protection Agency

NRCS = Natural Resources Conservation Service

State Water Board = State Water Resources Control Board

The following agencies have developed a common template conservation easement for mitigation and conservation banks in California: the Corps South Pacific Division's Sacramento, San Francisco, and Los Angeles Districts, along with USFWS, CDFW, the California Natural Resources Agency (CNRA), the National Marine Fisheries Service (NMFS), the federal Environmental Protection Agency (EPA), the State Water Resources Control Board (State Water Board), and the Natural Resources Conservation Service (NRCS). The template can be found at http://www.spd.usace.army.mil/Portals/13/docs/regulatory/banking/CE2017F.pdf

40   *Interim Mitigation Policy,* § 5.2.3.5.

41   33 C.F.R. § 332.7(a).

42   *Id.*

The *Interim Mitigation Policy* includes helpful due diligence checklists (Appendices B-1 and B-2) to assist in the evaluation of these questions. With respect to title, the Service requires a title report and legal description, as well as a "plat map" (although an A.L.T.A. survey would be more helpful), and it directs Service employees to look for existing easements and leases; mortgages and other liens; severed mineral or water rights; and title exceptions contained in the legal description itself.

Similarly, the Department supplies to applicants a "Habitat Management Land Acquisition Package Checklist" that outlines the submittal requirements for approval of a site to serve as a mitigation property. The Department's checklist requires a form of conservation easement; Phase 1 site assessment report; preliminary title report with copies of exceptions; various maps; a final management plan; a biological resources report; and a draft summary of the proposed transaction.

During the due diligence process, there are two sets of problems that often arise in a manner that frustrates the objectives of a proposed mitigation project. The first is when mitigation is proposed on lands that have already been preserved in one form or another. The second is when mineral or other subsurface rights have the potential to undermine the conservation values sought to be achieved through the easements. The Department has issued guidance on both of these issues.

CDFW Policies on Publicly Owned and Already Preserved Lands

The Department is often presented with conservation easement proposals that seek to mitigate impacts on wildlife resources through the protection of lands that are publicly owned or already protected for conservation or other purposes, including: state- or federally owned lands and lands already protected by easements.[43] CDFW has published the following policy statement to address these situations:

> Mitigation for impacts to fish and wildlife resources may occur on publicly owned, Department own[ed], and conserved lands if it has been determined by the Department that: (1) the mitigation is consistent with requirements of the law under which the mitigation is being sought; (2) its relative value as mitigation is equal to or greater than it would be if the same mitigation were situated on non-public or non-conserved lands; (3) it results in a clear and quantifiable improvement or positive change above that currently present or reasonably expected to exist under current conditions on the site; (4) the future uses of the land, including encumbrances or easements, will not preclude or diminish the mitigation; (5) the mitigation will not preclude, diminish or interfere with the funding or purpose of acquisition, encumbrances, or management plan for the property; and (6) it will not result in a net loss of existing conservation values.[44]

43 CDFW, Departmental Bulletin No. 2012-2, *Policy for Mitigation on Publicly Owned, Department Owned, and Conserved Lands* (Mar. 1, 2012).

44 *Id.*

For publicly owned or already protected lands that will be used for mitigation in connection with a CESA permit, a long-term conservation assurance mechanism must be in place to protect the land in perpetuity and ensure the biological value of the land remains intact.

For mitigation to occur on publicly owned or already protected land, the following requirements must be met:

> mitigation must be consistent with the current and future uses of the land including any encumbrances, easement or public use values

> mitigation must be consistent with the purpose for which the land was acquired and the funding source used for the acquisition

> mitigation must not preclude, diminish or interfere with encumbrances, or the management plan for the property

> mitigation must maintain or enhance the current ecological and public use values of the land

> full cost of the mitigation must be accounted for, including but not limited to, all capital improvements, restoration, enhancement, monitoring, long-term management and maintenance, and reimbursement for any CDFW staff time, including enforcement

> a memorandum of understanding must be in place prior to the project sponsor undertaking the project, which must be developed in cooperation with the land manager, reviewed for statewide consistency by CDFW's Lands Program and signed by the District Assistant Chief and CDFW Regional Manager, the land management agency or nonprofit, and the project sponsor; the memorandum must define the mitigation purpose, permit requirements, agreement term, scope of work, schedule, management and/or maintenance requirements, monitoring, and responsibilities of the parties to the agreement[45]

Compliance with the California Environmental Quality Act and all other state, federal, and local permits is the responsibility of the project sponsor and must be complete prior to implementation of the mitigation project.[46] Note that the 2008 Mitigation Rule, discussed above, establishes requirements for compensatory mitigation projects that are conducted on agricultural lands and National Forest System lands. While such mitigation is permitted, the 2008 Mitigation Rule does not permit a Section 404 or other Corps permittee to take credit for resources that have been or will be restored, established, enhanced or preserved to satisfy the requirements of other federal programs. However, Corps district engineers may evaluate and approve on a case-by-case basis situations where a consolidated project is used to satisfy more than one set of requirements, provided the same resource is not "double-counted."

45   *Id.*

46   *Id.*

Mineral Rights on Conserved Lands

The Department also requires an assessment of the risk of mineral exploration and development that may impact the conservation value of that property—referred to as a "Minerals Assessment Report."[47] Where there is a moderate or high risk that mining would occur from the property's surface in the foreseeable future, CDFW will then evaluate feasibility of actions to avoid, minimize or mitigate the risks.[48] The assessment informs CDFW's final determination as to whether to accept the proposed conservation for conservation purposes.

CDFW's requirement to assess the risk of use of conservation property for mining purposes results from the fact that fee title ownership of real property may be divided between the owner of the surface estate and one or more owners of the subsurface mineral estate.[49] However, even in instances in which the surface estate ownership has not been severed from mineral rights, CDFW requires completion of a Minerals Assessment Report to determine whether conservation purposes can be achieved and maintained.

CDFW has established a procedure for evaluating lands already held by CDFW or subject to a conservation easement (referred to as "Category 1" property) and lands newly proposed for acquisition, conservation easement recordation or other form of conservation (referred to as "Category 2" property). The procedures for addressing potential mineral development include the following four phases:

> risk assessment through preparation of a Minerals Assessment Report
> evaluation of context for mining risk and methods to avoid, minimize or mitigate impacts
> determination by CDFW's Regional Manager regarding what, if any, action should be taken with respect to the property
> documentation of CDFW's determination[50]

Minerals Assessment Reports generally require the following information:

> overview of report purpose, location maps, and legal description of the property
> title report review, including preliminary title report and final title report (if available)
> description of the surface and mineral estate ownerships, including all changes in ownership over the 15 preceding years and rights to access the surface by the owners of the mineral estate
> specific mineral resources included and excluded in the mineral estate
> review of locatable, useable and salable mineral resources on the property
> maps and aerial photographs of property with delineated mineral estates
> assessment of mineral resource potential, including a map showing locations

---

47 Department of Fish and Wildlife, Departmental Bulletin No. 2015-1, *Policy and Procedural Guidance for Managing Risks of Mining on Conservation Lands* (Feb. 3, 2015).

48 *Id.*

49 *Id.*

50 *Id.*

> discussion of environmental constraints which may constrain mining
> opinion as to the likelihood of surface mining or other forms of mining, including a determination of whether the "probability of surface mining is so remote as to be negligible"
> references cited
> report preparer's qualifications[51]

The *Interim Mitigation Policy* also includes provisions addressing split mineral estates, including mechanisms to address unresolved situations, which may include: (1) using a crediting methodology that accounts for future uncertainty, (2) establishing a reserve credit account, (3) entering into a subsurface use agreement with the mineral rights owner, or (4) entering into a mineral subordination agreement with the mineral rights owner.[52]

FINANCIAL ASSURANCES FOR MITIGATION PROJECTS

The resource agencies require various forms of financial "assurances" (i.e., security) relative to the development and long-term management of a mitigation project. The Corps' requirements for financial assurances can be found at 33 Code of Federal Regulations Sections 332.3(n), 332.4(c) and (n), and 332.7(d). Section 5.2.3.6 of the *Interim Mitigation Policy* also contains the Service's specific guidance for "short-term," "interim" and "long-term" financial assurances.

Generally speaking, "short-term" financial assurances are those required to guarantee the performance of physical measures undertaken in connection with a mitigation project (e.g., fencing or wetland restoration), and are phased out once certain performance criteria have been satisfied, usually in accordance with a schedule that has been negotiated with the regulatory agencies. Short-term assurances typically cover the cost of performing the mitigation, but in some cases the agencies will require additional security to guarantee the remediation of a mitigation project that does not meet performance standards.

"Interim" financial assurances are those required to assure the general management of a mitigation project (typically for a three-year period) until the long-term financial assurances can begin to supply funding for management into perpetuity. Like short-term assurances, interim assurances are phased out over time.

Short-term and interim financial assurances are typically provided through a cash deposit or letter of credit, but in many cases the agencies will accept a bond, which is a far more efficient form of security. The Department maintains template letter of credit and bond forms that must be used for these purposes, and the Department's counsel disfavors any deviation from these forms. Usually, the Service, the Corps and the Regional Water Boards will defer to the Department relative to the form and amounts of short-term and interim security, but this deference may change in the

51   *Id.*
52   *Interim Mitigation Policy* § 4.1.3.

CFD = Community Facilities
District

GHAD = Geological Hazard
Abatement District

future as the Regional Water Boards gain experience under the state's pending wet-lands definition and dredge and fill procedures. (See Chapter 8 for more details regarding these procedures.)

From an applicant's perspective, the cost of short-term and interim assurances can be very high, but at least they are temporary in nature. Long-term assurances, how-ever, must fund the stewardship of the mitigation property in perpetuity and take the form of an endowment, although the Corps' regulations are more flexible and appear to allow for mechanisms other than an endowment.[53] These long-term assurances are described below.

Endowments

The Service's specifications for long-term assurances are described in Section 5.2.3.62 of the *Interim Mitigation Policy,* and include requirements that, among other things, (1) the endowment holder be held to a "prudent investor" standard (e.g., consistent with the Uniform Prudent Management of Institutional Funds Act of 2006); (2) accounting standards are consistent with those promulgated by the Financial Accounting Standards Board or, if a governmental entity, the Governmental Accounting Standards Board; and (3) funds be disbursed to the easement holder on a timely basis and annual fiscal reports provided to the Service.

Under California law, the requirements for long-term assurances are statutory. In particular, California Government Code Section 65966(b) provides that any state or local agency requiring the transfer of a real property interest (including fee title or any partial interest such as a conservation easement)[54] for mitigation purposes may identify how the funding needs of the long-term stewardship of the property will be met. In almost all cases, the permitting agencies require the establishment of an up-front endow-ment—in the form of a charitable trust—to generate the cash flow that will be used over time to fund the easement holder's long-term activities.

Although special districts such as community facilities districts (CFDs) and geolog-ical hazard abatement districts (GHADs) can provide secure funding for long-term management, the agencies are reluctant to rely on these mechanisms, generally on the theory that taxes imposed under these vehicles can be voted out by the public (despite the improbability of such events). Although California law explicitly authorizes the use of mechanisms other than endowments,[55] the agencies tend to employ a "cash is king" approach, which is a highly inefficient way of funding land management but which the agencies view as relatively foolproof.

In 2012, the Legislature adopted Senate Bill 1094 (amending Government Code Sections 65965 through 65968), which included, among other things, new requirements relative to the ownership and control of mitigation lands and the establishment and

53   33 C.F.R. § 332.7(d).

54   Gov't Code § 65966(b).

55   *Id.*

management of endowments. Under this statute, the term "endowment" is defined to mean "funds that are conveyed solely for the *long-term stewardship* of a mitigation property."[56] The term "stewardship" is defined to encompass "the range of activities involved in controlling, monitoring, and managing for conservation purposes a property, or a conservation or open-space easement . . . and its attendant resources."[57]

PAR = Property Analysis Record

Endowment funds are held as charitable trusts that are permanently restricted to paying the costs of long-term management and stewardship of the mitigation property for which the funds were set aside.[58] Notably, the statutory definition states that endowments do *not* include funds conveyed for meeting the short-term performance objectives of a mitigation project.

The amount of an endowment is determined using a present value algorithm approved by the permitting agency or agencies (the most common of which is called a "Property Analysis Record" or "PAR"). As discussed below, because endowments must be managed conservatively, the interest rate assumed for purposes of calculating present value is fairly low, which significantly inflates the amount of funds required for the endowment. Permittees are often surprised by the millions of dollars that may be required to endow the stewardship of even a small piece of mitigation property.

Endowment Holders

The Department is not permitted to designate a particular endowment holder as a condition of approval of an incidental take permit or other permit, clearance, agreement, or mitigation approval.[59] The Government Code does, however, limit the types of entities or organizations permitted to hold endowment funds. With certain exceptions, under state law endowment funds must be held by one of the following:

> the agency or agencies that required the mitigation

> the governmental entity, special district, or nonprofit organization that either holds the property, or holds an interest in the property, for conservation purposes

> the governmental entity or special district that retains the property after conveying an interest in the property for conservation purposes if that governmental entity or special district is protecting, restoring, or enhancing the property that was retained[60]

For purposes of mitigation endowment management, a "government entity" means any state agency, office, officer, department, division, bureau, board, commission, public postsecondary educational institution, city, county, or city and county, or a joint powers authority formed pursuant to the Joint Exercise of Powers Act. A joint powers authority

---

56 Gov't Code § 65965(a).

57 *Id.* § 65965(*l*).

58 *Id.* § 65965(a).

59 *Id.* § 65968(k).

60 *Id.* § 65968(b)(1).

NCCP = Natural Community
Conservation Plan

seeking to hold and manage a mitigation endowment must either have been created for the purpose of (1) the direct protection or stewardship of land, water, or natural resources, including, but not limited to, agricultural lands, wildlife habitat, wetlands, endangered species habitat, open-space areas, and outdoor recreational areas; or (2) constructing, maintaining, managing, controlling, and operating transportation infrastructure, such as major thoroughfares and bridges.[61]

Notably, SB 1094 explicitly authorized endowments to be held by the same governmental entity, special district or nonprofit that holds the underlying conservation easement, a practice that previously had been frowned upon by the regulatory agencies.[62]

The Government Code establishes certain exceptions regarding the entity that may hold a mitigation endowment. If any of the following exceptions apply, the endowment may be held by another qualified entity not listed above:

> an endowment held by an entity other than the state or holder of the mitigation property as of January 1, 2012

> an endowment that is held by another entity, qualified under the Code and pursuant to the terms of an NCCP or a state safe harbor agreement; in order for this exception to apply, the implementation agreement that is a part of an approved NCCP, the planning agreement for any NCCP that has not yet been approved, or a safe harbor agreement must address qualifications of the endowment holder, capitalization rate, return objectives, and the spending rule and disbursement policies

> if existing law prohibits the holder of the mitigation property to hold the endowment, including for-profit entities

> if the project proponent and the holder of the mitigation property or conservation easement agree that a community foundation or a congressionally chartered foundation shall hold the endowment

> if the mitigation property is held or managed by a federal agency

> if any of the same mitigation property is required to be conveyed pursuant to both a federal and state governmental approval, and the federal agency does not approve one of the entities[63]

Some projects rely on the National Fish and Wildlife Foundation (NFWF) to hold endowments for conservation easements. NFWF is a federally chartered corporation and operates widely in California, and has even established its own large-scale in-lieu fee program in the Central Valley. More information on NFWF can be found at https://www.nfwf.org/Pages/default.aspx.

These are not the only statutory requirements relative to endowment holders. In particular, an entity wishing to hold an endowment must certify to the project proponent (landowner) or the holder of the mitigation property or a conservation easement (easement holder), and to CDFW, that it meets all of the requirements outlined in Government Code Section 65968, subdivision (e), including that the entity:

> has the capacity to effectively manage the mitigation funds

> has the capacity to achieve reasonable rates of return on the investment of those funds similar to those of other prudent investors for endowment funds

61 *Id.* §§ 65965(e)(1)–(2).

62 *Id.* § 65968(a).

63 *Id.* § 65968(b)(2).

> manage and invest the endowment consistent with the Uniform Prudent Management of Institutional Funds Act

> utilize generally accepted accounting practices

> will be able to ensure that funds are accounted for, and tied to, a specific property

> if the holder is a nonprofit organization, a community foundation, or a congressionally chartered foundation, it has an investment policy that is consistent with the Uniform Prudent Management of Institutional Funds Act

From the Service's perspective, an endowment holder must be accredited by the Land Trust Accreditation Commission (Commission) or otherwise meet certain specific requirement set forth in Section 5.4 of the *Interim Mitigation Policy*. Land trusts and other entities that are accredited by the Commission and are in good standing will automatically meet the minimum requirements for holding real estate and financial assurance instruments and be approved by the Service.[64] In those areas where an entity accredited by the Commission is not available to act as endowment holder, the *Interim Mitigation Policy* establishes a number of requirements that must be satisfied. Broadly, a non-accredited endowment holder must be either a nonprofit organization or a government entity with a purpose of direct protection or stewardship of land, water, or natural resources, and must demonstrate a successful track record of holding and managing funds for conservation purposes.

Management of Endowments

California Government Code Section 65966(b) requires that, if an endowment if conveyed or secured at the time a mitigation property is protected, the following requirements apply:

> the endowment must be held, managed, invested and disbursed soley for, and permanently restricted to, the long-term stewardship of the specific property for which the endowment was created

> the endowment must be calculated to include a principal amount that, when managed and invested, is reasonably anticipated to cover annual stewardship costs in perpetuity

> the endowment must be held, managed, invested, disbursed, and governed in accordance with the Uniform Prudent Management of Institutional Funds Act

If an endowment is held by a local agency, the agency must comply with the foregoing requirements to the extent allowed by law; disburse funds on a timely basis to meet the stewardship expenses of the easement holder; and utilize accounting standards consistent with those promulgated by the Governmental Accounting Standards Board or successor entity.[65]

---

64   *Interim Mitigation Policy,* § 5.4 .

65   Gov't Code § 65966(d).

HCP = Habitat Conservation
Plan

NCCP = Natural Community
Conservation Plan

Unless a different process is established under a mitigation agreement, an endowment holder must submit annual fiscal reports to CDFW to ensure the endowment is managed in accordance with California law.[66] These reports must contain at least the following eight elements:

> the balance of each individual endowment at the beginning of the reporting period

> the amount of any contribution to the endowment during the reporting period including, but not limited to, gifts, grants, and contributions received

> the net amounts of investment earnings, gains, and losses during the reporting period, including both realized and unrealized amounts

> the amounts distributed during the reporting period that accomplish the purpose for which the endowment was established

> the administrative expenses charged to the endowment from internal or third-party sources during the reporting period

> the balance of the endowment or other fund at the end of the reporting period

> the specific asset allocation percentages including, but not limited to, cash, fixed income, equities, and alternative investments

> the most recent financial statements for the organization audited by an independent auditor who is, at a minimum, a certified public accountant[67]

Section 65966 includes a number of other miscellaneous provisions, including (1) authorization for governmental agencies to impose fees for the review of conservation transactions; (2) authorization for the imposition of a one-time fee to provide for the first three years of stewardship while the long-term endowment funds begin to accumulate investment earnings; (3) a requirement that funds paid in connection with the condemnation of mitigation property be used to replace the lost mitigation property to the extent reasonably feasible; (4) an exemption for funds used for the management of property under an HCP or NCCP; and (5) a variety of other provisions governing endowments and easement in certain specific situations.

California Government Code Section 65965(f) also establishes the concept of a "mitigation agreement," which is an agreement between a project proponent (i.e., permittee) and the easement holder or endowment holder to govern the long-term stewardship of a mitigation property and the associated endowment. Except for mitigation agreements prepared by a state agency, any mitigation agreement authorizing endowment funds to be conveyed to a governmental entity, community foundation, special district, congressionally chartered foundation or nonprofit organization must include a requirement causing the endowment to revert to the permitting agency if the entity holding the endowment ceases to exist, is dissolved, or becomes bankrupt or insolvent.[68]

---

66 *Id.* § 65966(e).

67 *Id.* §§ 65966(e)(1)(A)–(H).

68 *Id.* § 65968(g).

Under the 2008 Mitigation Rule, the Corps requires that any provisions necessary for long-term financing must be addressed in the Bank-Enabling Instrument. The Corps district engineer may also require provisions be incorporated in the Bank-Enabling Instrument to address inflationary adjustments and other contingencies, as appropriate.

Other Types of Financial Assurances

Endowments are an inefficient way to assure an adequate source of long-term funds for property management. This is particularly true in light of the fact that endowment holders will assume that the corpus builds at low interest rates, thus requiring a higher corpus to begin with. In some circumstances, the agencies have allowed the use of special taxes and assessments to fund long-term management of easement areas, usually through either a Community Facilities District (Mello-Roos) or Geological Hazard Abatement District (GHAD), but the agencies are often reluctant to allow even these mechanisms given the theoretical chance that the affected residents may vote to eliminate the taxes, unless the sponsoring public agency provides some other form of credit enhancement. Although some applicants propose the use of homeowners' association or property owner association fees to fund long-term maintenance, such proposals are usually dead upon arrival.

It is important to note that, because an endowment may be used to fund long-term stewardship but not the short-term objectives of a particular mitigation project (e.g., the construction and monitoring of a particular restoration project), in many cases the endowment is only one part of the overall financial security package for a project.

As described above, CDFW or the other permitting agencies may require additional cash security, bonds or letters of credit for the initial construction project; short-term or "interim" management (often a three-year period) by the easement holder (as authorized under California Government Code Section 65966); additional costs associated with the failure of a project to meet identified conservation objectives (including easement enforcement costs); and other items. Moreover, if a permittee desires to proceed with construction prior to recording the required conservation easement, the permittee will be required to post security for the cost of acquisition of the easement itself.

MITIGATION AND CONSERVATION BANKS

As described above, the development and implementation of a permittee-responsible mitigation project based upon an individually negotiated conservation easement can be complex. Moreover, applicants for agency permits are typically private developers or public agencies who are not in the business of, or have little expertise in, PRM projects. Thus, in many cases it may be easier for a permittee to pay a third party to provide the mitigation required by an agency permit. This is often done through what is referred to as a "turnkey" mitigation deal, in which a third party (typically a company in the mitigation business) acquires the conservation easement, assembles the management plan, posts all of the security and acts as the easement holder or land manager for the mitigation site.

Another alternative is for the permittee to purchase mitigation credits from an agency-approved mitigation bank or conservation bank. A conservation or mitigation bank is essentially a financial vehicle through which a "bank sponsor" builds a large-scale mitigation project and then, by way of analogy, sells undivided interests (in the form of "mitigation credits") in the enhanced environmental values created by the mitigation project. The credits are not actually an interest in real property, but rather a fictional currency authorized for sale by the agencies to compensate the bank sponsor for its establishment of the mitigation project. Nonetheless, the credits themselves are typically tied to the acreage of the banked property (e.g., a credit may be equal to one net acre of property after accounting for buffers, setbacks, and exclusions of areas covered by utility or other easements).

The term "mitigation bank" is defined by the Corps to mean "a site, or suite of sites, where resources (e.g., wetlands, streams, riparian areas) are restored, established, enhanced, and/or preserved for the purpose of providing compensatory mitigation for impacts authorized by [Corps] permits. In general, a mitigation bank sells compensatory mitigation credits to permittees whose obligation to provide compensatory mitigation is then transferred to the mitigation bank sponsor."[69] Similarly, the *Interim Mitigation Policy* defines the term "conservation bank" to mean "a site, or suite of sites, that is conserved and managed in perpetuity and provides ecological functions and services expressed as credits for specified species that are later used to compensate for impacts occurring elsewhere to the same species."[70]

By way of very crude example, suppose a bank sponsor purchases a conservation easement on a piece of land and then restores 100 acres of vernal pools on the site. The Corps, as the agency approving the mitigation bank, would then authorize the bank sponsor to sell 100 "wetlands restoration credits" to third-party developers or public agency permittees. Let's then suppose a water district applies to the Corps for a Section 404 permit to fill five acres of wetlands. If the Corps were to require the water district to mitigate at a 2:1 ratio, then the water district would approach the mitigation banker (i.e., the bank sponsor) to purchase 10 of the wetland restoration credits from the bank. The banker would then have 90 credits remaining to sell to other permittees.

> To accomplish 100 acres of vernal pool restoration, a bank sponsor may actually have to purchase a much larger site to account for the relatively low density of the restorable wetlands. For example, if a property exhibits 10 percent wetland coverage (which is itself a very high figure), the overall property preserved would be roughly 1,000 acres.

Overview of State and Federal Mitigation Banking Policies

As discussed above, over the last ten years the state and federal resource agencies have promulgated a number of policies relating to compensatory mitigation strategies, including mitigation and conservation banking and ILF programs. These include the Corps' 2008 Mitigation Rule, the Service's *Interim Mitigation Policy,* and the Department's Conservation and Mitigation Banking Guidelines.

69   33 C.F.R. § 332.2.

70   *Interim Mitigation Policy,* Appendix A.

TABLE 10.1. STATE AND FEDERAL MITIGATION BANK APPROVAL TIME COMPARISON

Event	Corps/EPA 2008 Mitigation Rule (225 days max)	Federal Running Total	CDFW Guidance	Comparison
Draft Prospectus Submitted				
agency comments on draft	30 days	30 days	30 days	state/federal timelines in alignment
Final Prospectus Submitted				
agency completeness review	30 days	30 days	30 days	
Corps public notice published	30 days from completeness determination	60 days		
public review period	30 days	90 days		
comments distributed to IRT and bank sponsor	within 15 days of close of Public Notice comment period	105 days		
initial evaluation letter to bank sponsor	within 30 days of close of public comment period	120 days (90 days from completeness date)	CDFW approval 90 days from completeness (i.e., same as mitigation rule)	state/federal timelines in alignment
Draft Instrument				
completeness review	30 days	30 days	30 days	
Corps distributes to complete draft BEI to IRT				
start of IRT review period	5 days after Corps distributes draft BEI	35 days		
IRT review period	30 days	65 days		
internal IRT discussions/issue resolution	60 days (variable)	125 days (variable)		
notice to sponsor re: status of IRT review	90 days from distribution to IRT	best case 125 days (90 days from start of IRT review)	CDFW informational request (90 days from completeness) (120 days total)	state timeline 5 days faster than federal (assuming no state-level unsolicited changes)
Final Instrument				
Corps notifies IRT of intent to approve/ not approve final instrument	within 30 days from Corps' receipt of BEI	30 days	CDFW completeness review 30 days	
bank approval or initiation of IRT dispute resolution process	within 45 days following Corps' receipt of final BEI (i.e., within 15 days of receipt of Corps' notice of intent to approve)	45 days	CDFW approval 90 days (total 120 days) unless unsolicited changes (each an additional 90 days)	federal timeline at least 75 days faster than state timeline assuming no IRT dispute resolution

ILF = in-lieu fee

PRM = permittee-responsible mitigation

MOU = Memorandum of Understanding

CNRA = California Natural Resources Agency

EPA = Environmental Protection Agency

Corps = U.S. Army Corps of Engineers

NMFS = National Marine Fisheries Service

IRT = Interagency Review Team

BEI = Bank-Enabling Instrument

ESA = Endangered Species Act

To better coordinate their efforts, in 2011 a number of agencies entered into a multi-agency memorandum of understanding to streamline the state and federal agencies processes and standardize conservation and mitigation bank document templates.[71] The signatory agencies to the Memorandum of Understanding (the "Bank MOU") included: the CNRA, CDWF, the U.S. Army Corps of Engineers (the Corps), USFWS, federal EPA, U.S. Department of Agriculture/Natural Resources Conservation Service, National Oceanic and Atmospheric Association/National Marine Fisheries Service, and State Water Resources Control Board.

Following the model established in the Corps' 2008 Mitigation Rule, the Bank MOU adopts a multi-agency bank approval process that may involve any of the following five agencies: the Corps, EPA Region IX, NMFS, and CDFW. As described in the Bank MOU, these agencies comprise and are referred to jointly as the Interagency Review Team (IRT). An IRT has the responsibility of reviewing proposed mitigation and conservation banks and ILF programs. IRTs are assigned such review authority generally based on the regulatory boundaries of the Corps districts in California (e.g., Los Angeles, San Francisco, and Sacramento). Typically, IRTs are composed of a representative from a Corps district and a representative from each responsible agency, as appropriate.

Under the Bank MOU, the agencies also committed to the preparation of a number of templates, guidance documents, and other process-related documents to help assure consistency during the bank approval process. To date, the agencies have prepared a template "Bank-Enabling Instrument" (BEI) and bank conservation easement, as well as a template long-term management plan and various other materials.

BANKS UNDER THE 2008 MITIGATION RULE

Because the Corps tends to serve as the lead agency for any IRT, a more detailed discussion of the 2008 Mitigation Rule's banking provisions is in order.

The Interagency Review Team

Generally speaking, where a bank sponsor seeks to sell bank credits under multiple authorities (e.g., wetland credits under Section 404, species credits under the federal ESA), the process for bank formation and operation is overseen by a group of representatives from the various agencies acting as a mitigation review team or IRT.[72] Both the 2008 Mitigation Rule and the 2011 Memorandum of Understanding describe the role of the IRT in some detail. Generally speaking, however, the IRT is responsible for reviewing bank proposals and decisionmaking over various operational questions (e.g., review and approval of credit releases, monitoring compliance, etc.) arising during the life of the bank. The IRT also takes the lead on providing opportunities for public review and comment as may be required by agency policy.

---

71 Memorandum of Understanding, Mitigation and Conservation Banking and In-Lieu Fee Programs in California (Sept. 22, 2011) ("Memorandum of Understanding").

72 Interim Guidance, p. 8.

The Prospectus

To initiate the process to establish a mitigation bank, a prospective bank sponsor must prepare and submit a draft bank proposal (known as the "prospectus") to the IRT for approval. Generally speaking, a prospectus must include a broad spectrum of information including, among other things, (1) information on the location and current condition of the property; (2) a description of how the mitigation bank will be established and operated, including the proposed ownership arrangements and long-term management strategy, and any phases planned; (3) the qualifications of the proposed "Bank Sponsor" to successfully complete the types of mitigation projects proposed; (4) delineations and biological resource surveys; (5) a statement of need and proposed service area; (6) bank objectives and conceptual plan; (7) an explanation of how the proposed bank would contribute to connectivity and ecosystem function and a discussion of potential conflicts and compatibility with any conservation plans, conceptual area plans, or other land use plans, policies, or regulations; and (8) various materials regarding title, water rights, mineral rights, and other issues. Once the IRT has approved a final prospectus, the bank sponsor begins preparation (and negotiation with the agencies regarding the terms) of the various documents that make up the mitigation or conservation bank.

The Bank-Enabling Instrument

The most fundamental document in a bank transaction is the "Mitigation Banking Instrument" (MBI) or "Bank-Enabling Instrument" (BEI), which is a contract between the bank sponsor and the agencies approving the bank, and it is the core legal document pursuant to which a bank is formed and operated. As noted above, in 2017 the Sacramento, San Francisco, and Los Angeles Districts of the Corps along with the other state and federal signatory agencies to the 2011 Memorandum of Understanding, updated the template for banks established in California.

The current template requires the BEI to include information regarding the following topics:

> objectives of the bank
> evaluation of baseline conditions of the mitigation site, including biological resources; geographic location and features; topography; hydrology; vegetation; past, present, and adjacent land uses; species and habitats occurring on the site
> phase 1 environmental site assessment results
> project approvals and phasing
> property assessment and warranty
> accounting system that will be used to track credits, funding and other reporting requirements
> financial assurances
> bank location maps
> service area maps and descriptions

MBI = Mitigation Banking Instrument

> development plan associated with the project
> bank management and operation documents, including interim and long-term management and monitoring
> real estate records and assurances
> potential additional requirements for business entities
> bank closure plan[73]

The BEI itself is a complex instrument and, in many respects, does not favor the banker. The BEI includes specific schedules for credit releases, but the agencies retain broad rights to withhold or delay credit releases if they have concerns about the performance of the bank, and to impose requirements for remedial action plans on the bank sponsor. Although the template BEI provides some protection for the banker against extraordinary circumstances that might affect bank performance, the agencies' remedies under the BEI are fairly broad and may afford limited opportunities to cure.

Conservation Easement and Long-Term Management Plan

The management plan is the roadmap for the bank manager to operate and maintain the bank. The plan outlines the necessary measures the bank manager will take in order to maintain the conservation purposes of the bank. It should list the responsibilities of the manager and outline the estimated costs of maintaining the bank. The management plan should also be incorporated by reference into the conservation easement.[74] In May 2008, the Sacramento, San Francisco, and Los Angeles Districts of the Corps along with the other state and federal signatory agencies to the 2011 Memorandum of Understanding, updated the long-term management plan template for use with mitigation banks that are established within California.

The current template requires the long-term management plan to include the following information:

> property description, including geographical setting, adjacent land uses, open-space plans, geology and cultural or historic features on-site
> description of baseline biological resources, setting, location, history and types of land use activities, geology, soils, climate, hydrology, habitats present on-site
> overall management, maintenance, and monitoring goals; specific tasks and timing of implementation; and a discussion of any constraints which may affect goals
> biological monitoring scheme including a schedule, appropriate to the species and site; biological monitoring over the long term is not required annually, but must be completed periodically to inform any adaptive management actions that may become necessary over time
> reporting schedule for ecological performance and administrative compliance
> cost-analysis of all long-term management activities

73 *Id.* at pp. 11–12.
74 *Id.* at p. 15.

> discussion of adaptive management principles and actions for reasonably fore-seeable events, possible thresholds for evaluating and implementing adaptive management, a process for undertaking remedial actions, including monitoring to determine success of the changed/remedial actions, and reporting

> rights of access to the mitigation area and prohibited uses of the mitigation area, as provided in the real estate protection instrument

> procedures for amendments and notices

> reporting schedule for annual reports to the Service

Certain Corps Districts post management plans that can be used as templates. For example, the San Francisco District of the Corps provides a template management plan that incorporates the above suggestions.[75]

Financial Assurances

Approval of a mitigation bank requires "sufficient financial assurances to ensure a high level of confidence that the compensatory mitigation project will be successfully completed, in accordance with applicable performance standards."[76] As discussed above, financial assurances may be in the form of performance bonds, escrow accounts, casualty insurance, letters of credit, legislative appropriations for government sponsored projects, or other appropriate instruments, subject to the approval of the district engineer.[77] In determining the financial assurance amount, a number of factors may be considered, including the cost of providing replacement mitigation, including costs for land acquisition, planning and engineering, legal fees, mobilization, construction, and monitoring.

The amount of required financial assurances must be determined by the Corps, in consultation with the mitigation project sponsor (defined as any public or private entity responsible for establishing, and in most circumstances, operating a mitigation bank or in-lieu fee program), and must be based on the size and complexity of the compensatory mitigation project approval, the likelihood of success, the past performance of the mitigation project sponsor, and any other factors deemed appropriate by the Corps.[78]

The rationale for determining the amount of the required financial assurances must be documented in the administrative record for either the issued permit or the bank enabling instrument.[79] Financial assurances may be phased out once the mitigation project has been determined by the Corps to be successful in accordance with its performance standards.[80] The permit or mitigation banking or in-lieu fee program instrument must clearly specify the conditions under which the financial assurances are to be released to the permittee, sponsor, or other financial assurance provider, including the

---

75 Bank Management Plan Template, revised May 2008.

76 33 C.F.R. § 332.3(n)(1).

77 *Id.*

78 *Id.*

79 *Id.*

80 *Id.* § 332.3(n)(4).

linkage to achievement of performance standards, adaptive management, or compliance with special conditions.[81]

Service Area

A "service area" is the land outside of the conservation or mitigation bank where development creates the environmental impacts that may be offset by credits from the bank.[82] With limited exceptions, permittees may only purchase credits from conservation and mitigation banks if their project is within the bank's service area.[83] With respect to conservation banks, the bank owner and the Service determine the service area based on the habitat and species to be preserved by the bank.[84]

For mitigation banks, the service area is the area a bank can reasonably be expected to provide appropriate compensation for impacts to wetlands and other aquatic resources. The mitigation bank service area should be designated in the banking instrument, and should be guided by a watershed-based rationale for the delineation of each service area that includes an analysis of historic aquatic resource loss in the service area and a statement of aquatic resource goals and objectives the service area.[85]

Credits

The credits made available through mitigation and conservation banks are a unit of measure representing the accrual or attainment of habitat or aquatic functions at a compensatory mitigation site. For mitigation banks, the measure of aquatic functions is based on the resources restored, established, enhanced, or preserved.[86] The bank sponsor[87] receives a monetary benefit by selling credits in addition to the benefit of preserving species and wetlands habitat. Generally, the bank sponsor will calculate the full bank development costs, and then determine a cost per unit of credit and establish a per credit fee amount that is equal to or greater than such cost per unit. Credits are then sold by the sponsor to developers who need to mitigate a project's impacts. The standards and rationale for the determination of credit value must be clearly articulated in the relevant banking agreement or instrument. In regard to mitigation banks, it is the bank sponsor who determines the actual monetary price of the credit.[88] To make banks an affordable option to mitigation buyers (relative to the cost of a permittee-responsible mitigation project), the price of credits is driven in large part by the cost of land. Nonetheless, a

---

81 *Id.*

82 *Id.* § 332.2; Interim Guidance, p. 25.

83 Interim Guidance, p. 25.

84 Interim Guidance, p. 13.

85 33 C.F.R. § 332.8 (c)(2).

86 *Id.* § 332.2.

87 A bank sponsor is "any public or private entity responsible for establishing and, in most circumstances, operating a mitigation [or conservation] bank." 33 C.F.R. § 332.2; Interim Guidance, p. 3.

88 33 C.F.R. § 332.8(o)(5).

developer may prefer a somewhat higher cost of bank credits due to the ease of purchasing them as opposed to pursuing an independent permittee-responsible project.

Mitigation bank credits are based on the accrual or attainment of aquatic functions at the bank.[89] In general, bank credit systems should be expressed in the same units as the impacts of the development projects that will utilize the bank. Examples of conservation bank credit units include: (1) an acre of habitat for a particular species; (2) the amount of habitat required to support a breeding pair; (3) a wetland unit along with its supporting uplands; or (4) some other measure of habitat or its value to the listed species.

A credit tracking system is essential to ensuring compliance with the mitigation instruments used to implement compensatory mitigation programs. It is the bank sponsor's responsibility to account for the credit sales,[90] although the USFWS typically requires its own signature on credit sales agreements to avoid unapproved sales transactions. The money used to buy the credits will then help to maintain a bank's lands.

For conservation banks, USFWS will review each proposed use of credits to determine if the mitigation program is in good standing (i.e., is in compliance with the instrument and site protection mechanism) and has the appropriate available credits.[91] If upon review, USFWS determines that the mitigation program is in good standing and has the appropriate available credits, USFWS will provide authorization in writing approving the pending credit transfer.[92] All conservation bank credit transfers must be tracked using the so called "RIBITS" system.[93]

For mitigation banks, the banking enabling instrument must contain a provision requiring the sponsor to establish and maintain a ledger to account for all credit transactions. Each time an approved credit transaction occurs, the sponsor must notify the appropriate Corps district engineer.[94] The credit release schedule is tied to achievement of specific milestones.[95] Credit releases for mitigation banks must be approved by the district engineer. In order for credits to be released, the sponsor must submit documentation to the appropriate Corps district engineer demonstrating that the appropriate milestones for credit release have been achieved and requesting the release.[96]

Management and Monitoring

A critical component of the operation of the bank is the management and monitoring performed by the bank sponsor. As discussed above, the long-term management plan is a specific, long-term plan that ensures the mitigation or conservation bank is managed

RIBITS = Regulatory In-Lieu Fee and Bank Information Tracking System

Regulatory Guidance Letter (RGL) 19-01 establishes additional guidance with respect to credit release schedules for mitigation banks. Prior to RGL 19-01, it had been common for a bank to include an initial release, several interim releases tied to achievement of performance standards, and a final release upon achievement of all performance standards. RGL 19-01 facilitates the expedited release of credits by authorizing a *single* interim credit release upon construction of the bank. To the extent performance standards relevant to those interim credits have not been achieved, financial security may be provided to support the larger interim release.

---

89   *Id.* § 332.2.

90   33 C.F.R. § 332.8(p); Interim Guidance, p. 31.

91   Interim Guidance, p. 31.

92   *Id.*

93   *Id.*

94   33 C.F.R. § 332.8(p)(1).

95   *Id.* § 332.3(b)(2).

96   33 C.F.R. § 332.8(o)(8).

and maintained in perpetuity. As part of the management plan, monitoring requirements must also be outlined in the bank agreement or instrument. Each monitoring program is specific to the particular needs of that bank and must be approved by the approving agencies. For mitigation banks, specific monitoring requirements are set forth under Section 332.6 of the 2008 Mitigation Rule.

Reporting

For conservation banks, reports are required at least annually to document the compensatory mitigation program's or project's performance. Reports generally include a description of the mitigation site conditions, attainment of performance criteria, status of the endowment fund or other financial assurance mechanism, expenditures, and management actions taken and expected to be taken in the future.[97] Reports must be submitted at least annually. For mitigation banks, reports are required as determined by the appropriate Corps district engineer.[98] Generally, the content and level of detail for those monitoring reports must be commensurate with the scale and scope of the compensatory mitigation project, as well as the compensatory mitigation project type.[99]

End of Bank Operation

A mitigation bank ends its operational life once all credits have been exhausted or banking activity is voluntarily terminated with written notice to the Corps. The end of bank operations cannot affect the long-term management and protection of bank lands or wetlands, which is ensured by the long-term management plan and conservation easements.

Conservation banks may obtain additional credits after the initial allotment through a phased establishment of the bank.[100] A bank sponsor may decide to only obtain credits for a portion of the bank property to gauge demand before committing the entire property. USFWS may also want a phased establishment of the bank whereby credits for high quality habitat are allotted first, and if there is a need, credits for lower quality habitat given at a later time. Another way to receive additional credits is through an incentive program. This mechanism would allot an initial number of credits based on the best available information available on species average population sizes. Additional credits may be awarded based on subsequent performance; when specified mitigation outcomes or conservation milestones are reached, the USFWS may allot additional credits. There is no explicit mechanism to obtain additional credits for a mitigation bank, but presumably, the bank sponsor and agencies could negotiate an additional allotment of credits if the bank sponsor can demonstrate the ability to preserve or create additional

97   Interim Guidance, p. 30.

98   33 C.F.R. § 332.6(b)(3).

99   *Id.* § 332.6(a)(1).

100 Interim Guidance, p. 27.

aquatic resources than stated in the enabling instrument. In any case, the number of credits created will never exceed the raw acreage of the mitigation property.

ILF = in-lieu fee

USFWS or the "Service" = U.S. Fish and Wildlife Service

IN-LIEU FEE PROGRAMS

ILF programs involve the restoration, establishment, enhancement, and/or preservation of habitat through funds paid to a governmental or nonprofit natural resources management entity (i.e., ILF program sponsor) to satisfy compensatory mitigation requirements for impacts to particular species or habitat.[101] For compensatory mitigation required by USFWS, ILF programs may be used to collect fees from permittees that have been approved by the Service to use ILF programs instead of providing permittee-responsible mitigation.[102] ILF program sponsors, which may be nonprofit organizations or government agencies, collect and deposit fees into an ILF account, and funds are disbursed from that account to purchase land or perform an activity, as specified in the ILF instrument.[103]

From a regulatory context, mitigation banks and ILF programs are structurally similar. Both mitigation banks and ILF programs involve off-site compensation activities generally conducted by a third party, a mitigation bank sponsor, or ILF program sponsor. Ultimately, when compensatory mitigation requirements are satisfied by the purchase of credits from a mitigation bank or payment into an ILF program, any further mitigation compliance responsibility shifts from the permittee to the bank or ILF sponsor.

The most substantial difference between mitigation banks and ILF programs relate to timing of mitigation and financing. Very roughly speaking, a bank is implemented prior to impacts occurring, whereas ILFs are typically executed following the impacts being mitigated. ILF programs typically are not able to capitalize compensatory mitigation projects prior to project impacts occurring, but rather collect funds from permittees before they can secure a suitable site and develop and implement a compensatory mitigation project. To ameliorate this temporal lag and ensure funds are spent on mitigation, the Compensatory Mitigation Rule establishes rules limiting the use of ILF program funds for the selection, design, acquisition, implementation, and management of ILF projects, with a small percentage allowed for administrative costs.

As is the case for banks, the 2008 Mitigation Rule sets forth requirements governing the establishment, use, operation, and maintenance of ILF programs as a means of providing compensatory mitigation for unavoidable adverse impacts to wetlands, streams, and other aquatic resources authorized by Clean Water Act Section 404. Also as discussed above, the 2011 multi-agency Memorandum of Understanding, contemplates the use of ILF programs to offset unavoidable adverse impacts to resources under the jurisdictions of the California Natural Resources Agency, California Department of Fish and Wildlife, State Water Resources Control Board, the Corps, USFWS, NMFS, the federal EPA, and

---

101 33 C.F.R. § 332.2.

102 Interim Guidance, p. 3.

103 *Id.*

COMPARISON OF BANKS AND ILFs

Regulatory Guidance Letter (RGL) 19-01 (Appendix) contains the following helpful discussion describing the differences between banks, ILF programs and permittee-responsible mitigation projects, as follows:

> First, mitigation banks are usually (though not always) operated for profit by private entities whereas in-lieu fee programs are administered by governments or non-profit natural resources management agencies.
>
> Second, mitigation banks usually rely on private investment for initial financing to initiate compensatory mitigation projects while in-lieu fee programs rely on fees collected from permittees.
>
> Third, and most importantly, mitigation banks must achieve certain milestones, such as selecting a site, approving a plan, and securing financial assurances, before they can sell credits to permittees, and generally sell a majority of their credits only after the physical development of compensatory mitigation project sites has begun. In-lieu fee programs generally initiate compensatory mitigation projects only after collecting a sufficient amount of fees to secure an in-lieu fee project site and implement an approved mitigation plan. When advance credits from an in-lieu fee program are used to fulfill the compensatory mitigation requirements of a [Corps] permit, there can be a substantial time lag between the occurrence of the permitted impacts and the production of released credits by an in-lieu fee project that fulfills the obligation incurred by the sponsor through the sale of those advance credits.
>
> Permittee-responsible mitigation differs from mitigation banks and in-lieu fee programs, in that it is conducted by the permittee or his or her contractor, and the permittee retains responsibility for ensuring that the compensatory mitigation project is successfully implemented and achieves its objectives. Permittee-responsible mitigation can be located at or adjacent to the impact site . . . or at another location generally within the same watershed as the impact site . . . .

Natural Resources Conservation Service. Under the 2011 MOU, the signatory agencies are authorized to draft an ILF Enabling Instrument that documents the objectives and administration of an ILF program, and the legal characteristics of the ILF program and physical characteristics of mitigation project sites. It is also worth noting that, under the current regime, an ILF generally must expend dollars within three years of receiving them.

This section provides an overview of the regulatory features unique to establishment and operation of an ILF program (as compared with a mitigation or conservation bank) as satisfaction of compensatory mitigation requirements.

Establishment of an ILF

While the rules governing the operation and use of ILF programs differ in some ways from the rules governing operation and use of conservation and mitigation banks, the operation and use of an ILF program are similarly governed by a programmatic enabling instrument—an ILF program-enabling instrument.[104] To initiate establishment of an ILF program, a prospective sponsor must prepare and submit a draft mitigation proposal to the permitting agencies, referred to as a Prospectus.[105] As with the establishment of mitigation and conservation banks, applicants for an ILF program are encouraged to contact the applicable agencies early in their site selection and project planning processes. Like a mitigation bank, review and approval of ILF programs in California is accomplished through an interagency review teams, or IRT. For wetland and stream mitigation banks and in-lieu fee programs authorized by the Corps and the federal EPA, in which the mitigation sponsor also seeks mitigation credits for species under Service authority (e.g., a joint bank), the Service will serve on the IRT as a co-chair.[106] The Service may also serve on the IRT in an advisory capacity as a member, rather than as a co-chair, when there are no proposed credits that would fall under USFWS jurisdiction. The ILF program sponsor must submit a final enabling instrument to the appropriate agency for approval, with supporting documentation that explains how the final instrument addresses any comments previously provided by the agency.[107]

Program Account

The in-lieu fee program sponsor must establish a program account after the enabling instrument is approved by the Corps district engineer, prior to accepting any fees from permittees.[108] All interests and earnings accruing to the program account must remain in that account for use by the in-lieu fee program for the purposes of providing compensatory mitigation.[109] Generally, the program account may only be used for the selection, design, acquisition, implementation, and management of in-lieu fee compensatory mitigation projects, except for a small percentage (as determined by the Corps district engineer in consultation with the IRT and specified in the instrument) that can be used for administrative costs.[110] To release funds from the program account, the sponsor must submit proposed ILF projects to the appropriate Corps district engineer for funding approval.[111] The ILF program sponsor must provide

---

104 33 C.F.R. § 332.8.

105 *Id.* § 332.8(d)(2).

106 *Id.* § 332.8(b)(1).

107 *Id.* § 332.8(d)(8).

108 *Id.* § 332.8(i)(3).

109 *Id.*

110 *Id.*

111 *Id.*

annual reports to the Corps district engineer and the IRT as specified under Section 332.8 of the 2008 Mitigation Rule. The program account is subject to audit.[112]

ILF Mitigation Plan Approval

As in-lieu fee project sites are identified and secured, the sponsor must submit mitigation plans to the Corps district engineer that include all applicable items listed in Section 332.4(c)(2) through (14).[113] The mitigation plan must also include a credit release schedule consistent with Section 332.4(o)(8) that is tied to achievement of specific performance standards.[114]

Allocation of Advance Credits

ILF programs allow for a limited number of credits that the sponsor can sell before securing a compensatory mitigation project site and conducting aquatic resource restoration, establishment, enhancement, and/or preservation at that site, referred to as "advance credits."

These advance credits are to be made available to permittees when the ILF program enabling instrument is approved.[115] The number of advance credits will be determined by the Corps district engineer, in consultation with the IRT, and will be specified for each service area in the instrument. The number of advance credits must be based on certain considerations, including:

> the compensation planning framework

> the sponsor's past performance for implementing aquatic resource restoration, establishment, enhancement, and/or preservation activities in the proposed service area or other areas

> the projected financing necessary to begin planning and implementation of in-lieu fee projects

As credits are produced by ILF projects, they must be used to "fulfill" any advance credits that have already been provided within the project service area before any remaining released credits can be sold or transferred to permittees.[116] Once previously provided advance credits have been fulfilled, an equal number of advance credits is re-allocated to the sponsor for sale or transfer to fulfill new mitigation requirements, consistent with the terms of the instrument. The number of advance credits available to the sponsor at any given time to sell or transfer to permittees in a given service area is equal to the number of advance credits specified in the instrument, minus any that have already been provided but not yet fulfilled.[117]

---

112 *Id.* § 332.8(i)(4).
113 *Id.* § 332.8(j).
114 *Id.*
115 *Id.* § 332.8(n).
116 *Id.*
117 *Id.*

Timeframe for Completion of ILF Project

As a means of ensuring accountability and success of an ILF program sponsored project, the land acquisition and initial physical and biological improvements established under the ILF program enabling instrument must be completed by the third full growing season after the first advance credit in that service area is secured by a permittee, unless the Corps district engineer determines that more or less time is needed to plan and implement an in-lieu fee project.[118] The sponsor is responsible for complying with the terms of the ILF program enabling instrument. Permittees that secured credits from the in-lieu fee program are not responsible for in-lieu fee program compliance.

Credit Valuation

The cost per unit of ILF program credits must include the expected costs associated with the restoration, establishment, enhancement, and/or preservation of aquatic resources in that service area.[119] These costs must be based on full cost accounting, and include, as appropriate, expenses such as land acquisition, project planning and design, construction, plant materials, labor, legal fees, monitoring, and remediation or adaptive management activities, as well as administration of the ILF program.[120] The cost-per-unit credit must also take into account contingency costs appropriate to the stage of project planning, including uncertainties in construction and real estate expenses, and the resources necessary for the long-term management and protection of the ILF project.[121] In addition, the cost-per-unit credit must include financial assurances that are necessary to ensure successful completion of ILF projects.[122]

---

118 *Id.* § 332.8(n)(4).

119 *Id.* § 332.8(o)(5)(ii).

120 *Id.*

121 *Id.*

122 *Id.*

CHAPTER 11

Conservation Planning

Chapters 1 and 2 of this book describe the standard processes for securing incidental take authority under Section 7 of the federal Endangered Species Act and Section 2081 of the California Endangered Species Act. This chapter describes an alternative vehicle for federal ESA and CESA permitting: the habitat conservation plan. HCPs and their state counterpart, the Natural Community Conservation Plan, are discussed separately in this chapter because they provide a common vehicle by which an applicant can secure both state and federal permitting through a single vehicle. HCPs and NCCPs serve as a planning tool by which incidental take authorization can be issued on a regional basis. They can also be used to establish a framework for wetland permitting on a regional basis. In addition to HCPs and NCCPs, this chapter covers the recently-adopted state program establishing Regional Conservation Investment Strategies.

ESA = Endangered Species Act

CESA = California Endangered Species Act

HCP = Habitat Conservation Plan

NCCP = Natural Community Conservation Plan

ITP = incidental take permit

INTRODUCTION

Although Section 2080.1 of the Fish and Game Code provides a vehicle for the Department of Fish and Wildlife to pursue coordinated issuance of state and federal incidental take authorizations through consistency determinations, in most cases an applicant will undertake separate permit processes under the ESA and CESA. One exception to this general rule, however, is conservation planning. Both Section 10 of the ESA and Section 2035 of the Fish and Game Code (the "Natural Community Conservation Planning Act" or "NCCP Act") allow the preparation of a single, joint conservation plan (i.e., a joint HCP/NCCP) that provides the basis for issuance of state and federal incidental take authority for species covered by that plan.

HCPs and NCCPs may be undertaken separately, however, and HCPs are commonly secured separately in cases where a project or plan will affect only federally listed species. Where a project will take both state and federal species, an HCP may be undertaken in coordination with an NCCP or, alternatively, a simple incidental take permit (ITP) process under Section 2081 of the Fish and Game Code. NCCPs, however, are generally not prepared except in coordination with a federal HCP.

One benefit of both HCPs and NCCPs is that they can provide take coverage not just for individual projects, but also for broad classes of activities (e.g., housing, energy, mining) that may occur throughout an entire county or even many counties. In fact, although HCPs are often prepared for single projects, NCCPs are only prepared to provide permit issuance for many projects or activities on a regional basis.

One other common element of HCPs and NCCPs is that they provide a certain level of regulatory "assurances" that are not available under either Section 7 of the ESA or Section 2081 of CESA. That is, when an applicant has secured incidental take authority under an HCP or NCCP, the government is not permitted (with some exceptions) to change the terms of the deal (e.g., require additional mitigation) if circumstances change in unforeseen ways over the life of the permit. These assurances, described below, are commonly referred to as "no surprises" assurances.

From a conservation perspective, HCPs and NCCPs are generally considered superior to ordinary permit processes because they can accommodate regional strategies for both avoidance and mitigation that are not easily available under Sections 7 or 2081, which tend to provide for avoidance and mitigation on more of a project-by-project basis.

According to the Service's HCP Handbook, only 10 HCPs were produced during the first decade of the regulatory program. From 1992 to 1997, 225 HCPs were completed and, by 2009, more than 500 HCPs covered approximately 46 million acres of non-federal lands. As of 2016, this number had grown to over 1,000 HCPs.

Set forth below is a discussion of HCPs and NCCPs, including applicable legal requirements and how these plans are actually created and implemented in practice. The reader is advised that the subject of HCPs and NCCPs is deserving of its own book, as the complexities of the conservation plan process cannot be illustrated in a single chapter. Accordingly, this chapter provides only a very broad overview of the HCP process and should not be relied upon for specific guidance. In fact, the best reference guide to HCPs is the Services' 2016 HCP Handbook, discussed below. No such guide yet exists for NCCPs.

HABITAT CONSERVATION PLANS

Background

As discussed in Chapter 1, Section 9 of the ESA prohibits the take of listed species.[1] "Take" is defined as "to harass, harm, pursue, hunt, shoot, wound, kill, trap, capture, or collect, or to attempt to engage in any such conduct."[2] Because of the terms "harass" and "harm," the meaning of "take" is quite broad under the ESA. The Service's ESA regulations further define "harass" to mean "an intentional or negligent act or omission which creates the likelihood of injury to wildlife by annoying it to such an extent as to significantly disrupt normal behavioral patterns which include, but are not limited to, breeding, feeding or sheltering."[3] "Harm" is further defined to include "an act which actually kills or injures wildlife [including] significant habitat modification or degradation where it actually kills or injures wildlife by significantly impairing essential behavioral patterns, including breeding, feeding, or sheltering."[4]

The U.S. Supreme Court upheld this broad view of "take" by finding that the definition of "harm" as including "significant habitat modification or degradation that kills or injures wildlife" was reasonable, and that the Department of the Interior's interpretation was supported by the ordinary understanding of the word "harm" and legislative history establishing Congress' intent that "take" applies broadly to cover indirect as well as purposeful actions.[5]

For a project to be exempt from these strict and broad take prohibitions under the ESA, the project proponent must obtain authorization for take that is incidental to the otherwise lawful activity being proposed.

For projects with a federal "nexus" (e.g., a Corps of Engineers permit), incidental take authorization can come through an incidental take statement in a biological opinion issued by the Service under Section 7. For those projects or activities where there is

---

1   16 U.S.C. § 1538(a)(1).

2   *Id.* § 1532(20).

3   50 C.F.R. § 17.3.

4   *Id.*

5   *Babbitt v. Sweet Home Chapter of Communities for a Great Oregon*, 515 U.S. 687 (1995). See also *Marbled Murrelet v. Babbitt*, 83 F.3d 1060 (9th Cir. 1996), amended on denial of rehearing, cert. denied, 519 U.S. 1108 (1996) (a habitat modification which significantly impairs the breeding and sheltering of a protected species amounts to "harm" under the ESA, and "harm" therefore includes the threat of future harm); *Forest Conservation Council v. Rosboro Lumber Co.*, 50 F.3d 781, 784 (9th Cir. 1995) (harm is "defined in the broadest possible manner to include every conceivable way in which a person can 'take' or attempt to 'take' any fish or wildlife."); *National Wildlife Fed'n v. Burlington N.R.R., Inc.*, 23 F.3d 1508, 1513 (9th Cir. 1994) (includes habitat degradation that prevents or possibly retards recovery of species); *Building Industry Ass'n of California v. Babbitt*, 979 F. Supp. 893 (D.D.C. 1997) (term "harm" as used in the ESA's definition of "take" includes significant habitat modification or degradation where it actually kills or injures wildlife).

no federal nexus—in other words, projects on non-federal land and subject to no federal permitting, funding, or other involvement triggering Section 7—the only other mechanism for incidental take is an incidental take permit supported by an HCP pursuant to Section 10 of the ESA.[6]

In effect, a Section 10(a)(1)(B) incidental take permit (ITP) allows a permit holder to proceed with an activity that is legal is all other respects, but that results in the incidental taking of a listed species.[7] Applying to receive this form of take authorization is voluntary. An important purpose of including this process in the ESA was to give non-federal landowners seeking to develop or use their property incentives to establish conservation measures for protected species.

This is reflected in the legislative history for the 1982 ESA amendment that established HCPs:

> The proposed amendment should lead to resolution of potential conflicts between endangered species and the actions of private developers, while at the same time encouraging these developers to become more actively involved in the conservation of these species.[8]

An HCP is different from a biological opinion in that, in many respects, an HCP can actually *look like* a land use plan approved by a local agency. Although the Service does not really approve the land uses per se, it does approve any incidental take resulting from the project (often the project footprint), the manner in which it is carried out, and the lands to be conserved in exchange for the permitted development.

As described more fully below, an HCP can be prepared for a specific project or group of projects in one location, or it can be prepared for a broad range of projects in an entire region. A number of regional HCPs have been created in California (often in conjunction with the Department of Fish and Wildlife's NCCP program) and, as of the date of publication of this book, a number more were in process. Whereas a project-specific HCP may *look like* a land use permit, a regional HCP can look more like a city or county general plan. These are rough analogies, of course, but they serve to illustrate the broad variety of scopes and scales than an HCP can take.

At its most fundamental, the Section 10 ITP and HCP are intended to give non-federal landowners with listed species on their property some measure of incentive to negotiate with the Service for the establishment of a conservation plan for those species and their habitat, while receiving an exemption from the Section 9 take prohibitions in the form of an incidental take permit. Moreover, and very importantly, they offer long-term protection (sometimes up to 50 years) against the possibility that new listings or unforeseen events will result in changes to the permit terms. This so-called "No Surprises Policy" is more fully described below.

More information on HCPs and NCCPs in California, including a list of approved plans, can be found at the "ECOS" website maintained by USFWS at https://ecos.fws.gov. The Department also maintains its own NCCP website, which can be found at https://www.wildlife.ca.gov/Conservation/Planning/NCCP.

6   16 U.S.C. § 1539(a)(1)(B).

7   *Id.* § 1539(a)(1)(B) (allowing the take of listed species under certain conditions when the "taking is incidental to, and not the purpose of, the carrying out of an otherwise lawful activity").

8   Senate Rep. No. 97-418, 97th Cong., 2d Sess. 10 (1982).

History of Habitat Conservation Planning

Before Section 10 was added to the ESA, Section 7 Biological Opinions were the only vehicle available for landowners to secure incidental take authorization for their projects or activities. As more and more species were listed—particularly in California—it became apparent that the Section 7 process was insufficient, particularly for projects that had no federal nexus. These problems came to a head in connection with a controversial development proposal for San Bruno Mountain on San Francisco Bay. The USFWS intended to designate a large portion of the mountain as critical habitat for the listed mission blue butterfly and another species proposed for listing. Given the lack of a federal nexus, there would have been no way for the landowners or the affected cities to secure federal authorization for the development.

After much struggle, the problem found its way to Congress, which amended the federal ESA in 1982 to provide authority for the issuance of ITPs for non-federal projects under the auspices of an HCP. At its very simplest, under Section 10, an applicant (or group of applicants) prepares and submits a draft habitat conservation plan for review by the Service and, if it satisfies the statutory criteria established under Section 10, the Service will issue an incidental take permit (or group of permits) with a requirement that the applicant complies with the terms of the HCP. In practice the process is much more complex than this, but this represents the basic legal structure.

During the Clinton Administration, the Service began to make regulatory adjustments to the HCP process to make it more effective and to provide greater incentives for landowner participation. In 1996, the Services published a *Habitat Conservation Planning Handbook* that provided informal guidance to agency officials, consultants and landowners as to how an HCP is prepared and processed and incidental take authority ultimately issued.

Also during this period, the Service began heavily to promote the use of regional HCPs, particularly in Southern California. As an incentive for landowner participation, the Clinton Administration promulgated the federal "No Surprises" policy, which ultimately found its way into formal regulation in 1998 and is more fully described below.[9] These regulatory assurances are available to all HCPs, regardless of whether they are regional or project-specific in nature.

In 2000, the Services published a "Five-Point Policy" as an addendum to the 1996 Handbook. The Policy focused on the expanded use and integration of five particular components of the HCP program: (1) biological goals and objectives, (2) adaptive management, (3) monitoring, (4) permit duration, and (5) public participation.

In 2016 these principles, discussed more fully below, were integrated into a revised and updated *Habitat Conservation Planning and Incidental Take Permit Processing Handbook* (the "HCP Handbook"). The updated HCP Handbook is essentially a modernization of the HCP process based upon years of successes and failures in the HCP program. It also integrates a variety of other guidance documents issued by the Services

An HCP does not itself authorize take. In fact, an HCP is technically the *applicant's* document and is submitted as a part of its application for an ITP under Section 10(a). It is only the ITP issued by the Service that actually authorizes take. Nonetheless, with apologies to our readers at the Service, for simplicity this chapter may refer occasionally to an HCP "permitting" the covered activities covered by the plan.

9   63 Fed. Reg. 8859.

NEPA = National Environmental
Policy Act

over the prior two decades, including the 5-Point Policy,[10] the "No Suprises" policy, the Service's 2007 permit revocation rule, the Service's 2007 policy for "General Conservation Plans,"[11] the Service's 2011 policy relative to incidental take of eagles under the Bald and Golden Eagle Protection Act, and the Service's very helpful 2015 guidance on the issuance of ITPs in multiple-application situations.

The HCP Handbook is an invaluable tool for anyone involved in the HCP process. It includes many practical tips for practitioners and agency officials, and the electronic version includes a link to an online "HCP Toolbox" with many helpful forms and other materials. The HCP Handbook can be found online at https://www.fws.gov/endangered/what-we-do/hcp_handbook-chapters.html. Note that the HCP Handbook is written as guidance to agency staff who will review and approve HCPs. However, it remains a valuable guide to HCP applicants and stakeholders as well.

Overview of the Process

It is impossible the capture the complexities of the HCP process in a single chapter. At a very rudimentary level, however, the HCP Handbook identifies four phases in the preparation and approval of an HCP: (1) the pre-application process; (2) development of the HCP and NEPA (National Environmental Policy Act) documents; (3) permitting decision and ITP issuance; and (4) implementation and compliance monitoring. As noted in the Handbook, this process is "not linear, it is iterative and some steps should occur concurrently."

Phase 1: Pre-Application (HCP Handbook Chapters 3 and 4)

Phase 1 largely consists of informal communications between the applicant and the Service regarding the applicant's project and possible coverage under Section 10(a)(1)(B) of the ESA to authorize incidental take. During Phase 1, the Service provides the applicant with guidance as to whether an ITP is appropriate, and if so, the type and scale of the HCP. The Service also begins to assess the appropriate level of NEPA analysis for the ITP.

Phase 2: Developing the HCP and Environmental Compliance Documents (HCP Handbook Chapters 5 through 13)

During Phase 2, the applicant (in coordination with the Service) prepares the HCP and submits to the Service a complete application package, which includes the permit application, the draft HCP, and the application fee. The Service conducts a NEPA review for the ITP and HCP, and also initiates an "intra-service" Section 7 consultation during this phase, in which the Service consults with itself under Section 7 to ensure that the plan will not result in jeopardy to listed species or adverse modification of critical habitat.

10   65 Fed. Reg. 35,242.

11   50 C.F.R. 22.11.

Phase 3: Processing, Making a Permitting Decision, and Issuing the Incidental Take Permit (HCP Handbook Chapters 14 through 16)

During Phase 3, the Service publishes in the Federal Register an announcement of the availability of the HCP, providing an opportunity for the public to provide comments on the HCP and the NEPA documentation for the HCP, the length of which period depends on the required level of required NEPA compliance (i.e., a NEPA categorical exclusion, Environmental Assessment, or Environmental Impact Statement). After public comments are received and addressed, the HCP and its accompanying NEPA documentation are revised and finalized, and the Service concludes its intra-Service Section 7 process. At the conclusion of this phase, the Service makes its decision whether to issue the ITP to the applicant.

Phase 4: Implementing the HCP and Compliance Monitoring (HCP Handbook Chapter 17)

During Phase 4, the permittee begins its "covered activities" (i.e., the activities permitted under the HCP) and implements the HCP's conservation strategy, including mitigation for the take permitted under the HCP. This phase also includes implementing the avoidance, minimization, monitoring, and reporting activities set forth in the HCP.

The HCP process can be relatively straightforward or complicated, largely determined by the scope of the HCP (i.e., number of applicants, number of covered species, complexity of covered activities). Like any state or federal permit process, the HCP process involves considerable coordination between the applicant and the Service, and often involves other stakeholders such as local government and conservation organizations. And, of course, there is also the possibility of third-party litigation against the HCP or NEPA document once adopted.

Eligible Applicants

As described in Section 3.3 of the HCP Handbook, any individual, non-federal agency, business, or other entity that has the authority to conduct activities on non-federal property, or any state, municipal, or tribal government agency that has the authority to regulate land use can apply for an ITP under Section 10. But to do so the applicant must have enough legal control over the covered lands to implement the HCP, usually through fee simple ownership or a long-term lease, but also through other contractual arrangements. It is also a requirement that the applicant have direct control over any other parties who will implement the terms of the HCP. This includes employees and contractors and, in the case of a regional HCP in which incidental take authority is issued to a land use agency, it may mean those under the regulatory authority of that agency (e.g., developers).

Applicants must also cover at least one federally listed wildlife species to pursue an HCP. Because take of listed plants on non-federal lands is not prohibited by the federal ESA, listed plants by themselves are insufficient to prepare an HCP. However, listed and non-listed plants can be covered by an HCP that includes at least one listed animal.

CEQA = California Environmental Quality Act

Types of Habitat Conservation Plans

There are many different types, or permutations, of HCPs, ranging from fairly simple single-applicant HCPs to HCPs involving many or even an indefinite number of applicants. A brief summary can be found in Table 3-4 of the HCP Handbook.

Single-Applicant HCPs

A single-applicant HCP is used for one applicant requesting a single permit. Typical projects suitable for a single-applicant HCP include projects involving individual lot owners on a fraction of an area, subdivisions, timber or utility operations, or a set of recurring activities across a large, multi-tract, set of properties.

Low-Effect HCPs

Low-effect HCPs, usually in the form of a single-applicant HCP, can be used for projects involving minor or negligible direct, indirect, or cumulative effects on species and their habitat, and all other environmental resources. Projects subject to these plans can include development of a single-family residence or small housing development; small-scale forestry or a site-specific oil and gas operation; farm or ranch operations, or any other activities that would result in smaller-scale take of listed species. For an HCP to qualify as low-effect, it must also qualify as a categorical exclusion under NEPA. The Service can consider mitigation proposed by the applicant when determining the level of effects under NEPA.

An HCP that might otherwise have significant effects on the environment (and would not qualify for a categorical exclusion) can be "mitigated into" low-effect status. Very roughly, one might think of this as analogous to a Mitigated Negative Declaration under CEQA. The benefits of a low-effect HCP include, among other things, a shortened public review period and the fact that such HCPs need not be initially noticed in the Federal Register.

Programmatic or Regional HCPs

As shown in Table 3-4 of the HCP Handbook, a programmatic—or regional HCP—is used for regional scale planning and to expedite the processing of future projects anticipating incidental take authorization. For these HCPs, a *master permit holder* administers its normal regulatory authority to convey incidental take coverage to eligible landowners via local regulatory instruments or certificates of inclusion. In California, there are many HCPs in which a city or county becomes the administrator of a regional HCP and holder of a regional ITP and then passes down incidental take authority to developers and others operating in its jurisdiction. That is, a developer under a regional HCP essentially secures his or her own ITP through the city or county grading or building permit process. In some cases, this extension of take authorization is done through the issuance by the city or county of a "certificate of inclusion" to the developer.

As observed by the court in one case:

This litigation concerns the issuance of an ITP on a regional scale. An important purpose of this regional approach was to streamline the permit process so that the City would issue ESA take permits directly to developers (known as "Third Party Beneficiaries"). The City obtained an "umbrella" permit from the FWS to kill species with mitigation, and developers seeking approval of specific projects obtain authorization from the City rather than going through their own cumbersome application and review process with the FWS.[12]

FWS = U.S. Fish and Wildlife Service

Classic examples of this type of structure can be found in many urbanizing areas of the state including Orange County, Riverside County, San Diego County, East Contra Costa County and Santa Clara County. As of the date of publication of this book, additional programmatic HCPs were in the development and approval stages in other areas of the state, including Butte County, Placer County, Yolo County, Solano County, and South Sacramento County.

In Regional or Programmatic HCPs, incidental take authority is issued to one or more land use agencies, but that authority may pass through to many parties. The basic requirement is that the permittee must, under 50 Code of Federal Regulations 13.25(d), have "direct control" over the other parties intended to receive incidental take authority. This control exists when the master permittee extends direct control over (1) those under the jurisdiction of the master permittee and the master permit provides that those people may carry out the proposed activity; or (2) those who receive a permit from, or have executed a written agreement with, a master permittee who is a government entity.

Multiple Project/Applicant or Umbrella Plans

Another way of authorizing take for multiple applicants through a single regional HCP is an "Umbrella," or "Multiple Applicant," HCP. In this case, there is no master permittee, but the HCP covers a number of applicants conducting activity within a given region.

A good example of a multiple-applicant HCP is the Upper Santa Ana River HCP currently under development. This HCP would cover the activities of a dozen water-related utilities operating on the Santa Ana River. Each of the agencies will be conducting different activities (e.g., flood control, water supply, wastewater treatment, groundwater recharge), but all of them cumulatively will have adverse effects on the listed Santa Ana sucker and a few other aquatic species. Because none of these agencies has direct control over the others, a programmatic HCP is not feasible. Although each of the agencies legally could secure its own permit under the HCP, in this case the applicants have chosen to pursue a single ITP for the joint benefit of all of the agencies.

Santa Ana sucker. Photo: Riverside County Resource Conservation District.

These multiple-applicant HCPs can be far more complicated to put together than a programmatic HCP due to the number of parties working directly with the Service, sometimes represented by a trade organization. A good example of this complexity can be found in the proposed Desert Renewable Energy Conservation Plan (DRECP),

12 *Southwest Center for Biological Diversity v. Bartel*, 470 F. Supp. 2d 1118, 1128 (2006) (citations omitted).

DRECP = Desert Renewable
Energy Conservation Plan

GCP = General Conservation
Plan

which was intended to cover tens of millions of acres of land in the California desert, and provide incidental take coverage to wind, solar, and other renewable energy developers and operators.

General Conservation Plans

A General Conservation Plan (GCP) is prepared by the Service itself—rather than an applicant or group of applicants—to fit the needs of potential applicants for projects with similar species effects in a specific area. Eligible applicants can incorporate the plan into their ITP application as if it were their own HCP. If the Service determines that an applicant satisfies criteria defined under the GCP, the Service may issue an individual ITP to the applicant. In a sense, GCPs are roughly analogous to a regional general permit issued by the Army Corps of Engineers. Applicants proceeding under a GCP can benefit from considerable streamlining, both under NEPA and under the HCP issuance criteria themselves. More specific guidance on GCPs can be found in the Service's October 5, 2007 *Final General Conservation Plan Policy*, which can be found in the Service's HCP Toolbox. General Conservation Plans work best when they provide incidental take for many small projects with landowners who might not otherwise be able to afford to prepare their own HCP or where preparing their own HCP would be very inefficient. There are no approved GCPs in California, but one is under development in Santa Barbara County for the oil and gas industry and its potential effects on California tiger salamander. Examples of operating GCPs can be found in Oklahoma (for American burying beetle), Alabama (for Alabama beach mouse), and Florida (for Florida scrub jay).

Other Permutations

HCPs can be used as a vehicle to address other state and federal permitting requirements. Most importantly, as mentioned above, they are often combined with NCCPs adopted under the NCCP Act. An HCP can also be used as a vehicle for incidental take authorization under the federal Bald and Golden Eagle Protection Act. In addition, it is theoretically possible to combine an HCP with a programmatic safe harbor agreement or candidate conservation agreement (discussed in Chapter 1) replete with regulatory assurances.

In California, HCP applicants, the Service, and the Corps of Engineers are pioneering methods by which an HCP can be used to support the issuance of Clean Water Act Section 404 permits. In recent years the Corps has issued or is planning to issue regional general permits for very small fill projects carried out under and implemented by HCPs (e.g., Butte County, East Contra Costa County, Santa Clara County, Placer County, and South Sacramento County). The Corps has also experimented with the idea that an HCP can serve as a "regional alternatives analysis" that might reduce the need for individual permit applicants to conduct exhaustive off-site analyses under the Section 404(b)(1) Guidelines.

There are many significant challenges to the potential for full integration of Section 404 permitting and HCPs due to, among other things, the different standards and regulatory priorities of the Corps and the Service, as well as the different lexicons used by the two agencies in their regulatory processes. The agencies continue to work to address this problem, and are beginning to identify effective solutions. The Placer County Conservation Plan is perhaps the most advanced example of how this might occur. In that situation, the agencies are using a Corps-approved in-lieu fee program (as well as a tool referred to as an "aquatic resources plan") to bridge the gap between Sections 7 and 10 of the ESA, on one hand, and Section 404, on the other. If this works as envisioned, the PCCP may serve as a model for future HCPs in California and elsewhere.

PCCP = Placer County Conservation Plan

A Note on Severability

In 2013, in recognition of the complexity and wide variety of permutations of programmatic and umbrella plans (as well as "General Conservation Plans" described below), the Service issued its *Final Guidance for Endangered Species Act Incidental Take Permits Covering Multiple Projects or Project Owners*, which clarifies questions like "direct control," the applicability of "no surprises" assurances, and the availability of co-permittee structures. This guidance can be found in the HCP Toolbox.

One significant issue that must be resolved in HCP situations involving multiple permittees is the extent to which permit obligations are severable. As described in the HCP Handbook:[13]

> In any permit structure, the Services and the applicants must consider roles and responsibilities so that any incidental take permit is enforceable, and that each permittee, or enrollee in a programmatic permit, can be held responsible for their respective implementation obligations. As the number of applicants and potential enrollees increases, these considerations become more vital to successful implementation of the plan.
>
> Permit severability refers to the ability to suspend or revoke any one permit without jeopardizing the take authorization of the other permittees. Permit severability essentially divides a plan into separate administrative processes/responsibilities, different covered species, different activities, or geographically by jurisdiction into multiple sub-plans with discrete roles for each applicant. The Services, before issuing a permit, must find that each piece of the plan is viable on its own without relying on other pieces of the plan . . . .

The HCP Handbook suggests that activities and responsibilities among the applicants be allocated to avoid the potential that problems with one applicant would put at risk the incidental take authority enjoyed by another. This may be straightforward in HCPs in which applicants implement their mitigation independently of one another. But this is more easily said than done in HCPs where applicants are very interdependent in their mitigation obligations. In some cases, as recognized by the HCP Handbook, it

---

13   HCP Handbook, p. 3-17.

may be appropriate to create legal instruments (possibly including indemnities, step-in cure rights, etc.) to allocate the rights and responsibilities of a group of co-permittees.

Regulatory Assurances and the "No Surprises" Rule

Background

In 1998, the Service adopted a final rule to provide regulatory assurances to permitted under Section 10(a)(1)(B) of the ESA.[14] According to the HCP Handbook, these are called "no surprises" assurances "and essentially mean that 'a deal is a deal.'"[15] The handbook further notes:

> As long as the permittee is properly implementing the HCP, the Service[] will not impose additional requirements or restrictions. If an unforeseen circumstance occurs, unless the permittee consents, the Service[] will not require him/her to commit additional land, water, or financial compensation or impose additional restrictions of the use of land, water, or other natural resources beyond the level agreed to in the HCP. The Service will honor these assurances as long as the permittee is implementing the requirements of the HCP, permit, and other associated documents in good faith, and their permitted activities will not jeopardize the species.[16]

Changed Circumstances

In practice, the terms of an HCP will spell out what types of changed circumstances fall within and outside the "no surprises" protections. The Service uses the term "changed circumstances" to identify those "affecting a species or geographic area covered by [an HCP] that can reasonably be anticipated by [plan] developers and the Service[] and that can be planned for (e.g., the listing of new species, or a fire or other natural catastrophic event in areas prone to such events)."[17] That is, an HCP does not provide protection against modifications to applicant commitments based upon changed circumstances. However, the HCP should articulate what circumstances may trigger modifications, and must include remedial measures to address the changed circumstances and funding for those measures.

If additional conservation and mitigation measures are deemed necessary to respond to changed circumstances, and such measures were provided for in the HCP, the permittee will be required to implement such measures.[18] By contrast, if additional conservation and mitigation measures are deemed necessary to respond to changed circumstances, and such measures were *not* provided for in the HCP, the Service will not

14   63 Fed. Reg. 8859.

15   HCP Handbook, p. 103.

16   *Id.*

17   50 C.F.R. § 17.3.

18   *Id.* §§ 17.22(b)(5)(i), 17.32(b)(5)(i); *id.* § 222.307(g)(1).

require any additional measures beyond those provided for in the HCP, without the consent of the permittee, provided the HCP is being properly implemented.[19] That is, even in the event of changed circumstances, an applicant is provided regulatory assurances against measures that were not anticipated by the plan itself.

Unforeseen Circumstances

"Unforeseen circumstances" are defined as changes in circumstances affecting a species or geographic area covered by a conservation plan that could *not* reasonably have been anticipated by plan developers and the Service at the time of the negotiation and development of the HCP, and that result in a substantial and adverse change in the status of the covered species.[20] The Service bears the burden of demonstrating that unforeseen circumstances exist using the best available scientific and commercial data available while considering certain factors.[21]

The Service will not require the commitment of additional land, water or financial compensation or additional restrictions on the use of land, water or other natural resources beyond the level otherwise agreed upon for the species covered by the HCP without the consent of the permittee.[22] That is, if additional conservation and mitigation measures are deemed necessary to respond to unforeseen circumstances, the Service may require additional measures of the permittee where the HCP is being properly implemented only if such measures are limited to modifications within conserved habitat areas, if any, or to the HCP's operating conservation program for the affected species, and maintain the original terms of the plan to the maximum extent possible.[23]

According to the HCP Handbook, if unforeseen circumstances are found, the permittee is not required to provide additional resources or funds to remedy unforeseen circumstances, but the Service and the permittee should work together to determine an appropriate response within the original resource commitments in the HCP.[24]

Contents of HCPs
Section 10(a)(2)(A) of the ESA states:

> No permit may be issued by the [Service] authorizing any taking referred to in paragraph (1)(B) [i.e., taking that "is incidental to, and not the purpose of, the carrying out of an otherwise lawful activity"] unless the applicant therefor submits to the [Service] a conservation plan that specifies:

19 *Id.* §§ 17.22(b)(5)(ii), 17.32(b)(5)(ii); *id.* § 222.307(g)(2).

20 *Id.* § 17.3.

21 *Id.* §§ 17.22(b)(5)(iii)(C) and 17.32(b)(5)(iii)(C); *id.* § 222.307(g)(3)(iii).

22 *Id.* § 17.22(b)(5)(iii)(A); *id.* § 222.307(g)(3)(i).

23 *Id.* §§ 17.22(b)(5)(iii) and 17.32(b)(5)(iii)(B); *id.* § 222.307(g)(3)(ii).

24 See *Spirit of Sage Council v. Kempthorne*, 511 F. Supp. 2d 31 (D.D.C. 2007) (finding that "no surprises" rule, providing for regulatory assurances to holders of ITPs that they would not be required to commit additional resources to mitigate effects of unforeseen circumstances on protected species and their habitats, was not inconsistent with the requirements under the ESA that before issuing permit, agencies must find that doing so was not likely to jeopardize the continued existence of any listed species).

(i)   the impact which will likely result from such taking;

(ii) what steps the applicant will take to minimize and mitigate such impacts, and the funding that will be available to implement such steps;

(iii) what alternative actions to such taking the applicant considered and the reasons why such alternatives are not being utilized; and

(iv) such other measures that the [Service] may require as being necessary or appropriate for purposes of the plan.

The Service's ESA regulations essentially mirror these requirements:

A person wishing to get a permit for an activity prohibited by [the ESA regulations] submits an application for activities under this paragraph. The Services provides Form 3-200 for the application to which all of the following must be attached: . . . (iii) A conservation plan that specifies:

(A) The impact that will likely result from such taking;

(B) What steps the applicant will take to monitor, minimize, and mitigate such impacts, the funding that will be available to implement such steps, and the procedures to be used to deal with unforeseen circumstances;

(C) What alternative actions to such taking the applicant considered and the reasons why such alternatives are not proposed to be utilized; and

(D) Such other measures that the [Service] may require as being necessary or appropriate for purposes of the plan.[25]

The HCP Handbook provides much more complete guidance on the contents of an HCP, and it recommends an outline for any HCP that is intended to assure that the required statutory and regulatory elements are adequately covered. Generally speaking, an HCP should include, in addition to a title page and executive summary, the following chapters:

> introduction, including the applicant's goals, plan and permit areas, permit duration, coordination with federal and state agencies and, as appropriate, a description of the permit structure

> a description of the covered activities

> a list of covered species (including non-listed species) and species accounts that describe, among other things, their habitats and status in the plan area

> a discussion of environmental setting and biological resources

> potential effects on the covered species and take assessment

> the conservation strategy, which includes avoidance, minimization, and mitigation measures; alternatives to the taking; and monitoring and adaptive management

> changed and unforeseen circumstances

> implementation costs and funding

> permit/HCP Administration (Optional)

> references, tables and appendices

25   50 C.F.R. § 17.22(b)(1).

The more important components of an HCP are summarized below.

S-M-A-R-T = specific, measurable, achievable, result-oriented, and time-fixed

The Conservation Strategy

According to the HCP Handbook, a fundamental element of the HCP is the conservation strategy. It is the foundation upon which the HCP is built. The conservation strategy defines the HCP's biological goals, defines the required mitigation, explains how the applicant will track progress through the HCP's monitoring program, and describes how the applicant will adjust implementation of the HCP through adaptive management and changed circumstances. The goal of every HCP should be to fully offset the impacts of take, and every HCP must minimize and mitigate the impacts of take to the maximum extent practicable. An HCP's conservation strategy typically includes the following elements:

Biological Goals and Objectives. The biological goals describe the desired future conditions of an HCP. Each goal steps down to one or more biological objectives that define how these future conditions will be achieved. Objectives should be specific, measurable, achievable, result-oriented, and time-fixed (S-M-A-R-T). The applicant should develop the HCPs goals and objectives in coordination with the Service.

Conservation Measures. Conservation measures describe the specific actions that the permittee will implement to achieve the objectives in support of the HCPs goals. They usually take one of the following forms: avoiding the impact through project design, minimizing the impact through best management practices, minimizing the impacts of the taking by reducing or eliminating other threats, or mitigating impacts by restoring degraded habitat, enhancing functional habitat, preserving habitat, creating new habitat, or translocating or repatriating species.

Minimization and Mitigation. The HCP Handbook identifies three general approaches to mitigation. Permittee-implemented mitigation or permittee-responsible mitigation, conservation banks, or in-lieu fee mitigation. Permittee-responsible mitigation occurs when applicants use their own contractors, funding, and long-term management to provide mitigation to offset incidental take. Permittee-responsible mitigation can occur on or off the project site. Conservation banks are sites established under a conservation bank instrument, approved by the Service, that are conserved and managed to provide ecological functions and expressed as credits for species. In-lieu-fee mitigation occurs when a permittee provides funds to an in-lieu-fee sponsor, acting on behalf of the permittee, instead of completing project-specific mitigation themselves or purchasing credits from a mitigation bank. In all three cases, mitigation land is typically protected in perpetuity by legally binding conservation easements or similar mechanisms, and endowments or other long-term funding sources for long-term management.

Under the ESA, the impacts of the incidental take must be minimized and mitigated "to the maximum extent practicable."[26] According to the HCP Handbook, this statutory standard will always be met if the HCP applicant demonstrates that the impacts of the

---

26   16 U.S.C. § 1539(a)(2)(B)(ii).

taking will be fully offset by the measures incorporated into the plan. However, the statutory standard will also be met where the applicant demonstrates that while the HCP will not completely offset the impacts of the taking, the minimization and mitigation measures provided in the plan represent the most the applicant can practically accomplish. When the applicant cannot "fully offset" impacts, the Service will determine if the proposed conservation measures minimize and mitigate the effects of the actions to the maximum extent practicable by evaluating whether there are rigid restrictions on how a project can be development and there are insufficient options for implementing additional mitigation, or whether there are financial constraints that limit the ability of the applicant to practically do more.

Changed and Unforeseen Circumstances. As described above, the No Surprises Rule provides that, as long as a permittee is properly implementing the HCP and ITP, no additional commitment of land, water, or financial compensation will be required with respect to covered species, and no restrictions on the use of land, water, or other natural resources will be imposed beyond those specified in the HCP without the consent of the permittee. As described above, these assurances are not unlimited. In any particular HCP, the limits on regulatory assurances are defined by its descriptions of "changed circumstances" and "unforeseen circumstances."

Findings Required for ITP Issuance

Section 10 includes specific findings that must be made before the Service can issue an ITP, as follows:

> If the [Service] finds, after opportunity for public comment, with respect
> to a permit application and the related conservation plan that:
> (i)   the taking will be incidental;
> (ii) the applicant will, to the maximum extent practicable, minimize and mitigate
>   the impacts of such taking;
> (iii) the applicant will ensure that adequate funding for the plan will be provided;
> (iv) the taking will not appreciably reduce the likelihood of the survival and
>   recovery of the species in the wild; and
> (v)   the measures, if any, [that the Service may require as being necessary or
>   appropriate for purposes of the HCP] will be met;
>
> and [the Service] has received such other assurances as [it] may require
> that the [HCP] will be implemented, the [Service] shall issue the permit.
> The permit shall contain such terms and conditions as the [Service] deems
> necessary or appropriate to carry out the purposes of this paragraph,
> including, but not limited to, such reporting requirements as the [Service]
> deems necessary for determining whether such terms and conditions are
> being complied with.[27]

---

27   16 U.S.C. § 1539(a)(2)(B)(ii).

Mirroring the statute, the Service's regulations include essentially the same finding requirements:

> Upon receiving an application [for an ITP], the [Service] will decide whether or not a permit should be issued. The [Service] . . . shall issue the permit if [it] finds that:
>
> (A) The taking will be incidental;
>
> (B) The applicant will, to the maximum extent practicable, minimize and mitigate the impacts of such takings;
>
> (C) The applicant will ensure that adequate funding for the conservation plan and procedures to deal with unforeseen circumstances will be provided;
>
> (D) The taking will not appreciably reduce the likelihood of the survival and recovery of the species in the wild;
>
> (E) The measures, if any, [that the Service may require as being necessary or appropriate for purposes of the HCP] will be met; and
>
> (F) [It] has received such other assurances as [it] may require that the plan will be implemented.[28]

As described below, case law provides the practitioner with helpful guidance on the interpretation and application of these findings.

Minimization and Mitigation to the Maximum Extent Practicable

The Section 10 mitigation requirement has been the source of some confusion. The court in *National Wildlife Federation v. Norton* described well the inherent ambiguity in this phrase. According to the court, "the term 'maximum extent practicable' is not defined in the statute, nor in any formal agency regulations. It joins together two somewhat opposing concepts, 'maximum' and 'practicable,' without providing the key to their reconciliation."[29]

Generally, the courts have deferred to the Service's informal approach to "maximum extent practicable" by looking at whether the mitigation is "rationally related to the level of take under the plan." In *National Wildlife Federation v. Norton*, the court stated:

> The words "maximum extent practicable" signify that the applicant may do something less than fully minimize and mitigate the impacts of the take where to do more would not be practicable. Moreover, the statutory language does not suggest that an applicant must ever do more than mitigate the effect of its take of species. Thus, if a permit authorized the destruction of one acre of habitat that normally supports one individual member of a protected species, it would not be necessary for the applicant to create 100 acres of new habitat that would support some 100 individuals of the species, even if the particular developer could afford to do so . . . . Because the

---

28   50 C.F.R. § 17.22(b)(2).

29   306 F. Supp. 2d 920, 927 (E.D. Cal. 2004).

phrase "maximum extent practicable" is at best ambiguous, the court will defer to the construction of the agency, so long as it is reasonable. The Service's view of the statutory language as requiring that the level of mitigation must be "rationally related to the level of take under the plan" is entirely reasonable and avoids absurd results. It also avoids unduly enmeshing the Service in developers' economic affairs and projections.[30]

Giant garter snake. Photo: CDFW. Licensed under CC 2.0.

In *Norton*, the court evaluated an HCP for a development project of approximately 2,000 acres located next to the Sacramento International Airport. The development would have included commercial, light industrial, and office space, hotels, a golf course, and necessary roads and infrastructure. The site was composed almost entirely of agricultural lands, mostly rice fields. When in active rice cultivation, the land provides valuable habitat for the giant garter snake; in its current fallow state, however, the habitat value of the land is minimal to both the snake and the Swainson's hawk, the two species of greatest concern. The ITP for the project covered 14 species, but the litigation in this case focused on the snake and the hawk. The snake is a threatened species under both the federal and the state Endangered Species Acts, and the hawk is threatened under the California Endangered Species Act.[31]

The HCP for the project (which was based upon the conservation strategy for the Natomas Basin HCP evaluated in *National Wildlife Federation v. Babbit* as described below) required that, for every acre of land developed, half an acre of habitat must be permanently protected and managed to maximize its conservation plan. Because the HCP contemplated development of the entire site, the conservation land would be purchased off-site. Seventy-five percent of the mitigation lands were to be maintained as rice fields or managed marsh, primarily to benefit the snake. The remaining 25 percent were to be maintained as upland habitat, primarily benefiting the hawk. At full development, the HCP required the purchase and maintenance of 1,208 acres of mitigation land. The Service made a finding that "the level of mitigation provided for in the [HCP] more than compensates for the impacts of take that will occur under the plan."[32] According to the court, based on this finding, the Service was under no obligation to inquire whether additional mitigation was financially possible because all that was reasonably required to mitigate had been included in the HCP. That is, once an impact has been fully mitigated, nothing more is required. As stated by the court, the ESA does not require "mitigation up to the financial breaking point."[33]

Swainson's hawk. Photo: Great Sand Dunes National Park. Licensed under CC 1.0.

The foregoing case followed the court's decision in *National Wildlife Federation v. Babbitt*,[34] an earlier case in which the court considered the legality of the Natomas Basin HCP, which includes approximately 53,000 acres in the Sacramento Valley north of the

30   *Id.* at 927–28.

31   *Id.* at 921–22.

32   *Id.* at 928.

33   *Id.* at 928–29.

34   128 F. Supp. 2d 1274 (E.D. Cal. 2000).

City of Sacramento. In this earlier case, the National Wildlife Federation argued that the Service's finding that the plan would minimize and mitigate take to the maximum extent practicable was arbitrary and capricious because the Service failed to consider the practicability of any alternatives involving a higher level of mitigation.

The court agreed, reasoning that "the most reasonable reading of the statutory phrase 'maximum extent practicable ... requires the Service to consider an alternative involving greater mitigation.'"[35] In the context of the Natomas Basin HCP, the court found that "to consider an alternative providing greater mitigation, ... the record should provide some basis for concluding, not just that the chosen mitigation fee and land preservation ratio are practicable, but that a higher fee and ratio would be impracticable."[36] In addition, the court found that the "maximum extent practicable" standard is "not satisfied by a fee set ... at the minimum amount necessary to meet the minimum biological necessities of the covered species," and that the record in that case lacked "adequate evidence and analysis of whether a fee higher than that initially proposed by [the HCP's working group] would be economically practicable."[37]

By contrast, at least one court has held that a project is not required under the ESA to further mitigate impacts by reducing takings until further reduction was impracticable.[38] Moreover, another court has held that this finding does not impose a "sequencing" requirement in an HCP context. That is, ESA does not require an applicant *first* to demonstrate that it will minimize the number of individual members of the species taken to the maximum extent practicable, and *then* mitigate the taking to the maximum extent practicable. The words "mitigate" and "minimize" should be read jointly and together, rather than independently and sequentially.[39] If these combined minimization and mitigation measures fully offset take, then it does not matter if the applicant could do more. This alone will satisfy what is required under ESA. Moreover, the term "impacts" refers to the effect of the taking on the species as a whole, which necessarily includes populations and subpopulations, rather than the discrete number of individual members of the species.

In *Klamath-Siskiyou Wildlands v. National Oceanic and Atmospheric Administration*,[40] the court evaluated the significance of the word "applicant" in the provision requiring that "the applicant will, to the maximum extent practicable, minimize and mitigate the impacts of such taking." This case involved an HCP and ITP to take northern spotted owls on the applicant's lands in connection with timber harvest operations.

In evaluating the HCP, the Service found that the applicant would to the maximum extent practicable minimize and mitigate the impacts of such taking because of the applicant's proposed establishment of "conservation support areas" consisting of

35 *Id.* at 1292.

36 *Id.*

37 *Id.* at 1293.

38 *Union Neighbors United, Inc. v. Jewell*, 83 F. Supp. 3d 280 (D.D.C. 2015).

39 *Union Neighbors United, Inc. v. Jewell*, 831 F.3d 564, 577–84 (D.C. Cir. 2016).

40 99 F. Supp. 3d 1033 (N.D. Cal. 2015).

land on which the applicant committed to preserve or manage and maintain. These conservation support areas were located on lands owned by the applicant and that focused on owl activity centers with high conservation values, to provide demographic support to owl populations on adjacent federal lands, i.e., lands administered by the U.S. Forest Service.[41]

Plaintiffs had argued that the Service wrongly "credited" the applicant for the conservation value that the Forest Service—i.e., someone other than "the applicant"—would provide. According to the plaintiffs, the Service's "minimize and mitigate" finding was arbitrary and capricious because under Section 10(a)(2)(B)(ii), the Service may only consider minimization and mitigation efforts of "the applicant," and may not factor into its analysis the minimization and mitigation efforts by neighboring landowners.[42]

The court agreed, holding that the Service improperly factored in efforts by entities other than the applicant to make the "minimize and mitigate" finding. The court summed it up by saying: "Applicant landowners seeking to perform actions that would lead to a taking of an endangered or threatened species should not be permitted to obtain incidental take permits by piggybacking off of already-existing conservation efforts by their non-applicant neighbors."[43]

The court also considered whether the applicant's commitments to proposed mitigation measures were enforceable. According to the court, one of the key mitigation measures to offset impacts to the northern spotted owl in the HCP was unenforceable by the Service, and nothing in the Plan actually obligated the applicant to commit to those measures. The court concluded that the Service cannot make the Section 10(a)(2)(B)(ii) finding by relying on mitigation that the Services cannot enforce.[44]

Funding Assurances

Funding for an HCP must be dependable and not speculative. In *Southwest Center for Biological Diversity v. Bartel*,[45] the District Court for the Southern District of California evaluated a claim against an HCP prepared by the City of San Diego, in which it was alleged that the plan failed to identify adequate funding to implement and monitor its conservation program.

Under the HCP, the city had identified two main categories of expenses: (1) the money to acquire the land that it must contribute to the preserve to be established pursuant to the Plan, and (2) the funds required to administer it for the life of the Plan. For the land purchase, the city estimated it would need to acquire 2,400 acres from willing sellers at fair market costs, and the land acquisitions must be completed within 30 years. The city anticipated that it would acquire 1,000 acres for the preserve through

41 *Id.* at 1041–43.

42 *Id.* at 1049–50.

43 *Id.* at 1052.

44 *Id.* at 1053–54.

45 470 F. Supp. 2d 1118 (S.D. Cal. 2006).

mitigation from developers who impact land outside the preserve through open-space easements and land use regulations.[46]

The court determined that the Service arbitrarily concluded that the city ensured adequate funding for the plan because the city identified undependable and speculative sources for the necessary funds. "While an applicant need not acquire all the land nor set aside a trust account of ready cash before obtaining an ITP, the City's reluctance to confirm that it would fund the long-term conservation plan raises a red flag."[47] In particular, the court found that the city's reliance on future actions, such as a regional plan with other jurisdictions, a possible bond issue requiring voter approval, and raising sales tax, were too uncertain and unreliable.[48]

In *National Wildlife Federation v. Babbitt*, discussed above,[49] the court considered an allegation that the Service improperly found that the City of Sacramento would ensure that adequate funding would be provided for the HCP. Although the city expressly rejected the imposition of liability on the city to "ensure" the Plan, the Service issued the ITP "despite the possibility that, should funding under the City's [ITP] prove inadequate, no entity [would] be responsible for making up the funding shortfall, and there may not be any future permittee to whom increased costs may be shifted."[50]

The court determined that it was not "clear that a funding mechanism that is not backed by the applicant's guarantee could ever satisfy the requirement . . . that the applicant 'ensure' funding for the Plan. Assuming, however, that a cost shifting mechanism 'ensures' funding . . . in these circumstances, where the adequacy of funding depends on whether third parties decide to participate in the Plan, the statute requires the applicant's guarantee." The fact that the permit could be revoked does not satisfy the requirement that the applicant "ensure" funding. "The Service's discretion to revoke a permit for violation of a condition . . . does not seem to satisfy the statute's requirement that the *applicant* ensure the adequacy of funding."[51]

Provisions in covenants, conditions, and restrictions giving a homeowner's association the authority to impose any necessary supplemental fees on already-developed parcels such that the first developers may yet be liable for an additional assessment if future land costs soar, and provisions that require the association to impose supplemental fees if necessary to fully implement the plan, can be used to support a finding of adequate funding.[52] In those situations, it is important that the association must not be authorized to dissolve without prior consent of the Service.

Following the *National Wildlife Federation v. Babbitt* decision, the parties to that HCP revised the Plan to assure that no impacts would occur beyond the level of impacts

46   *Id.* at 1155–56.

47   *Id.* at 1156.

48   *Id.* at 1156–57.

49   128 F. Supp. 2d 1274 (E.D. Cal. 2000).

50   *Id.* at 1294.

51   *Id.* at 1295 (emphasis in original).

52   *National Wildlife Fed'n v. Norton*, 306 F. Supp. 2d 920, 926–27 (E.D. Cal. 2004).

HCP = Habitat Conservation Plan

ITP = Incidental Take Permit

that had already been mitigated through the payment of HCP fees and the acquisition of conservation easements on land in the Plan area, and the court found that this was an appropriate way to address the findings required under Section 10. This practice has become standard in HCPs in California, where the Service requires a master permittee to "get ahead" and "stay ahead" so that mitigation always stays in front of impacts and mitigation is both financed and accomplished with a reasonable degree of security.

No Appreciable Reduction in the Likelihood of the Survival and Recovery of the Species

The Service may rely on an applicant's acquisition of mitigation lands to determine whether the "taking will not appreciably reduce the likelihood of the survival and recovery of the species in the wild." The applicant need not identify *specific* mitigation lands for acquisition and management so long as the Service can rationally conclude that the HCP's acquisition criteria and management scheme ensure that the mitigation lands will provide habitat that is superior to the habitat that is lost as a result of development. Moreover, the mitigation lands generally need not be purchased prior to issuing a permit conditioned upon mitigation through habitat acquisition.[53] In fact, there is no general rule requiring purchase of mitigation lands prior to ground disturbance, although that has become fairly standard practice for programmatic HCPs in California.

In *National Wildlife Federation v. Babbitt*,[54] the Natomas Basin HCP was challenged on the grounds that the Service failed to adequately support this finding. Notably, the court framed the issue in the context of the "no jeopardy" standard of Section 7 of the Endangered Species Act, presumably because plaintiffs' ESA challenge was brought as a Section 10 challenge against the HCP and the ITP, and as a Section 7 challenge against the Biological Opinion prepared for the ITP. The court described the issue as whether the Service "failed adequately to explain how habitat loss authorized by the HCP would avoid jeopardizing the continued survival" of the species covered under the HCP.[55]

The court determined that as to the HCP, the Service's findings were adequate, largely because the Service's need to speculate about the likely success of the Plan's conservation measures and to make certain assumptions about the loss of potential habitat for the species were proper. The court concluded that "[a] certain degree of what plaintiffs label 'speculation' and 'uncertainty' is inevitable in any decision-making process, particularly one as complicated as that which led to the issuance of the ITP. The law does not require that the [Service] achieve certainty before acting."[56]

However, the court determined that the Service acted arbitrarily and capriciously with respect to this finding for the ITP. According to the court, the HCP assumed that other

---

53 *Id.*

54 128 F. Supp. 2d 1274.

55 *Id.* at 1289.

56 *Id.* at 1298.

agencies would seek permits under the Plan, which presumably would ensure adequate funding for the Plan by virtue of the mitigation fees associated with the agencies' project approvals. Moreover, the Service did not consider whether the monitoring and adaptive management provisions of the HCP could be effective if the City of Sacramento was the sole permittee.[57] This has led to a practice that, in evaluating an HCP involving multiple permittees, the Service must consider whether non-participation by one or more intended permittees would compromise the legal adequacy of the plan. This issue is relevant to, among other things, the severability requirement addressed above in this chapter.

ESA = Endangered Species Act

It is important to keep in mind that *enhancement* of the survival of the species or *recovery* of the species is not an element of the statutory finding.[58] An HCP need only mitigate its own impacts and, unlike an NCCP in California, need not affirmatively contribute to the recovery of a species. Nonetheless, some courts have found that an HCP's effect of enhancing the survival of a covered species can support the Service's finding that the taking not appreciably reduce the likelihood of the survival and recovery of the species.[59]

HCP Implementing Agreements

Implementing agreements are documents jointly prepared by the Service and the applicant that clarify provisions of an HCP and specify how the HCP will be carried out. They are not required under Section 10 of the ESA, but they can be useful for complex multi-party HCPs where it may be helpful to further explain and allocate obligations of the parties. Implementing agreements can also be helpful in clarifying the minimization and mitigation commitments in the HCP, the time frames for completing specific tasks set forth in the HCP, and the parties' roles in preparing, reviewing, and approving post-HCP documents, such as management plans.

According to the HCP Handbook, the Service does not consider implementing agreements as contracts, and they do not have any independent legal force and effect. Typically, they are incorporated by reference into the ITP as a term and condition, and a failure to comply with the implementing agreement may be grounds for suspending or revoking the ITP. If the Service and an applicant decide to use an implementing agreement, all parties must agree to its contents. If the applicant submits a draft implementing agreement as part of its application, it must be made available for public review when the Notice of Availability for the draft HCP and the draft NEPA document are published.

---

57 *Id.* at 1298–1300.

58 But see *National Wildlife Fed'n v. Norton*, 306 F. Supp. 2d 920, 925 (E.D. Cal. 2004) (stating that the use of mitigation lands to support this finding must include lands providing superior habitat and "enhance" the covered species' "prospects for survival"); *Sierra Club v. Babbitt*, 15 F. Supp. 2d 1274, 1278 n.3 (S.D. Ala. 1998) (an applicant for an ITP must submit an HCP "that will—as the name plainly connotes—help 'conserve' the entire species by facilitating its survival and recovery").

59 *Friends of Endangered Species v. Jantzen*, 760 F.2d 976, 982–84 (9th Cir. 1985) (an HCP's likely enhancement of the survival of a listed species can support the Service's finding that "the taking will not appreciably reduce the likelihood of the survival of the species").

NEPA = National Environmental
Policy Act

On August 31, 2017,
the Deputy Secretary
of the Interior issued
Secretary's Order 3355,
which imposed strict time
limits (365 days) and
page limits (i.e., 150–300
pages) for the preparation
of Environmental Impact
Statements. On April 27,
2018, he issued additional
direction for implementing
Order 3355. This order
has created significant
logistical problems in the
preparation of environmental documents for habitat
conservation plans, which
are highly technical and
complex documents.

NEPA Review of HCPs

The National Environmental Policy Act, or NEPA, requires federal agencies to analyze the impacts of their actions on aspects of the human environment, such as water quality, cultural resources, other biological resources, and socioeconomic values.[60] Because issuing an ITP is a federal action under NEPA, the Service must conduct an environmental analysis and document that analysis pursuant to NEPA.

As described in the HCP Handbook, the applicant must evaluate its project and alternatives from the perspective of its effects on listed species and other natural resources of concern to the Service. This information is provided in the HCP, and this serves as the essential core of the proposed federal action for analysis in the Service's NEPA document. This federal action is described by the Service in the HCP Handbook as the "issuance of an incidental take permit in response to that HCP and permit application." In its NEPA documentation, the Service evaluates issuing the permit from the perspective of its potential effects on the human environment.

When the Service concludes that a project will result in significant effects, it will prepare an Environmental Impact Statement. If the Service is uncertain of the effects or if the effects of the action will be less than significant, the Service will prepare an Environmental Assessment that results in either a Finding Of No Significant Impact or continue to prepare an Environmental Impact Statement. The Service also has the option of bypassing an Environmental Assessment and beginning with an Environmental Impact Statement if the Service knows it will be necessary at the outset. If the action has effects that are individually or cumulatively not significant, the action may be categorically excluded from further analysis. For an HCP to qualify for a categorical exclusion, none of the "extraordinary circumstances" listed in Section 46.215 of Title 43 of the Code of Federal Regulations can apply. These include, for example, significant impacts on public health or safety, highly controversial environmental effects, highly uncertain and potentially significant environmental effects, or establishment of a precedent for future action.

As the NEPA process begins, the Service must define its "purpose and need" for the proposed action, which is a statement that articulates the goals and objectives that the Service intends to fulfill by taking an action under the ESA. As described in the HCP Handbook, the applicant's project description defines the applicant's proposed activity that would result in incidental take, and the possible incidental take is the underlying "need" for the proposed federal action. The Service does not consider the need for a particular development or land use, but rather a narrow need to determine whether this non-federal activity complies with the ESA.

The scope of the Service's environmental analysis includes the impacts of the specific activity requiring the incidental take permit. The Service analyzes issues in an environmental document if they are related to potentially significant effects of the federal action, or if they help lead to a reasoned choice among the alternatives. For each aspect

60   42 U.S.C. § 4321.

of the federal action, the Service must evaluate (1) direct effects caused by the federal action at the immediate time and place; (2) indirect effects caused by the federal action later in time, or at a distance, but that are reasonably foreseeable; and (3) cumulative effects due to the incremental impact of the federal action when added to other past, present, and reasonably foreseeable future actions.

NEPA alternatives differ from HCP alternatives. NEPA alternatives analyzed in an Environmental Assessment (EA) or Environmental Impact Statement (EIS) are alternatives to the federal action of issuing the ITP based on the HCP proposed by the applicant and including terms and conditions to comply with the HCP. These alternatives are not necessarily the same as the HCP's alternatives to the taking. The Service is responsible for developing the NEPA alternatives, and those alternatives should meet the purpose and need of the action, which essentially is to fulfill the Service's conservation obligations under Section 10 of the ESA while responding to the applicant's request for authorization of incidental take. The range of alternatives typically includes (1) the proposed action (i.e., the applicant's proposed HCP), (2) a no action alternative, and (3) one or more variations of the proposed action, usually with more or less take, a shorter or longer permit, or different covered activities. The Service must also discuss alternatives it considered but rejected, and the reasons why it rejected those alternatives from further analysis.

NEPA requires the Service to provide notice and in most cases an opportunity for public review and comment related to its NEPA documentation. The HCP Handbook, together with a later April 2018 memorandum issued by management at the Service, establishes public comment periods for review of draft NEPA and HCP documents:

> low-effect and Environmental-Assessment-level HCPs need only the 30-day notice period as required by Section 10(c) of the ESA

> preparation of an EIS requires:

  • a notice of intent to prepare an EIS

  • scoping public notice, which can be combined with the notice of intent (30 days)

  • a Notice of Availability of the proposed HCP and the draft EIS (45 days)

  • a Notice of Availability for the HCP, final EIS, and Record of Decision (30 days)

At the end of the process, the NEPA decision documents should summarize the reasons for selecting a particular alternative. In making a decision on an Environmental Assessment, if the Service determines the proposed action would not constitute a major federal action significantly affecting the quality of the human environment, then the Service prepares a Finding Of No Significant Impact (FONSI). A FONSI serves two functions. It documents the Service's finding that no significant impacts would occur if the proposed HCP is implemented, and it explains the rationale used in selecting the alternative for implementation. It is not necessary to notify the public that the completed EA and FONSI are available before the Service issues the permit, unless certain

EA = Environmental Assessment

EIS = Environmental Impact Statement

FONSI = Finding Of No Significant Impact

ROD = Record Of Decision

circumstances described in the NEPA regulations apply, in which case the Service must make the draft FONSI available to the public for at least 30 days before it decides whether to implement the FONSI or prepare an EIS.

Following completion of a final EIS, the Service must prepare the Record Of Decision (ROD). The ROD documents the ultimate choice of an alternative, mitigation measures, and the decision rationale. Contents of the ROD are set forth in the Council on Environmental Quality Regulations. Public comments and the Service's responses may be attached to the ROD, or they may be included as an appendix to the final EIS.

HCP applicants should know that the Service expects the applicant to pay for preparation of the NEPA document on the Service's behalf. The applicant will typically contract with a consultant to prepare the NEPA document under the Service's sole direction and guidance. The same consultant preparing the HCP can prepare the NEPA document as long as different staff are assigned to each document. This separation, or "firewall," helps to ensure for the Service that the analysis conducted in the NEPA document is an independent assessment of the effects on the human environment of the issuance of the ITP and the implementation of the HCP.

Section 7 Consultation for an HCP

Section 7(a)(2) of the ESA requires that each federal agency consult with the USFWS or NMFS, whichever is appropriate, to ensure that any action that the agency authorizes, funds, or carries out is not likely to jeopardize the continued existence of a listed species or result in the destruction or adverse modification of designated critical habitat.[61] The federal agency taking the action is often referred to as the "action agency." In those circumstances where the USFWS or NMFS itself is taking an action, the USFWS or NMFS is the action agency, and it must essentially "consult with itself" through a process referred to as an intra-Service Section 7 consultation.[62] Because USFWS or NMFS issuance of an ITP is a federal action for purposes of Section 7 of the ESA, that action requires intra-Service Section 7 consultation. The Service identifies specific considerations and approaches for the Section 7 consultation process and formats for a Biological Opinion specific to HCPs.[63]

In *Environmental Protection Information Center v. Simpson Timber Co.*,[64] the Ninth Circuit Court of Appeals considered an HCP prepared for an ITP issued to a timber company for impacts to the northern spotted owl. Plaintiffs argued that the Service violated Section 7 by refusing to reinitiate consultation with itself about the effect that the ITP might have on two other species that were added to the threatened species list after

---

61   16 U.S.C. § 1507.

62   See, e.g., *National Wildlife Fed'n v. Babbitt*, 128 F. Supp. 2d 1274, 1286 (E.D. Cal. 2000) ("When the action agency is the Service itself, as when the Service is considering whether to issue an ITP, it must engage in internal consultation under § 7, and may issue the permit only upon a finding that it 'is not likely to jeopardize the continued existence of' a protected species, or result in the destruction or adverse modification of critical habitat").

63   See HCP Handbook, pp. 14-26 to 14-29.

64   255 F.3d 1073 (9th Cir. 2001).

the Service issued the ITP to the timber company. The plaintiff alleged that the Service's duty to reinitiate consultation had been triggered because the Service retained discretionary involvement or control over the action permitted by the ITP, and two species that inhabit the land covered by the HCP had been added to the threatened species list.[65]

The court explained that the Service did not retain discretionary control to make new requirements to protect species that subsequently might be listed as endangered or threatened. The court further explained that language in the biological opinion indicating that reinitiation of consultation would be required if "a new species is listed or critical habitat designated that may be affected by this action" did not give the Service this discretionary control. According to the court, this "is not a statement of any continuing discretionary power retained by the [Service] over [the timber company's ITP]. It simply restates the general regulatory requirement found [in the Service's regulations], a requirement which becomes applicable *only when* sufficient discretionary involvement or control has been retained to trigger reinitiation of consultation."[66] The court concluded that because the Service had not retained discretionary control over the timber company's ITP that would inure to the benefit of the two species added to the threatened species list, the Service was not required to reinitiate consultation to consider the permit's effects on those species.[67]

HCPs and the National Historic Preservation Act

The Service considers HCPs and their associated ITPs to constitute federal undertakings requiring compliance with Section 106 of the National Historic Preservation Act (NHPA). Guidance for NHPA compliance in the HCP context can be found in *Appendix A* to the HCP Handbook. The Service's compliance with the NHPA is typically addressed in the NEPA document.

Permit Administration

The Service's regulations govern administrative issues related to permits in general, including ITPs. Under these regulations, an ITP can be renewed subject to certain criteria (for example, the applicant has not been assessed a civil penalty or convicted of any criminal provision related to the permit subject to renewal, the applicant has not failed to disclose material information or made false statements as to any material fact, etc.), and any person holding a valid renewable permit may continue the activities authorized by the expired permit until the Service acts on the application for renewal if the permit is currently in force and has not been suspended or revoked and the person has otherwise complied with the regulations.[68]

NHPA = National Historic Preservation Act

---

65   *Id.* at 1075–76.

66   *Id.* at 1081 (emphasis in original).

67   *Id.* at 1083.

68   50 C.F.R. § 13.22.

A permit may also be amended, either at the permittee's own request or by the Service for just cause at any time during the term of the permit. If a permittee determines that circumstances have changed so that he or she desires to have any condition of the permit modified, then the permittee must submit a full written justification and supporting information to the Service for approval.[69] The Service's regulations also provide for the right of succession by certain persons,[70] the transfer of permits and scope of permit authorization,[71] the discontinuance of permit activity,[72] permit suspension,[73] and permit revocation.[74]

NATURAL COMMUNITY CONSERVATION PLANS

The Natural Community Conservation Planning Act authorizes the voluntary development of Natural Community Conservation Plans (NCCP) approved by the California Department of Fish and Wildlife for the conservation of the natural communities identified in the applicable NCCP. An NCCP identifies and provides for the regional or area-wide protection of plants, animals, and their habitats, while allowing compatible land use and economic activity.[75] An NCCP is intended to promote wildlife diversity through conservation of unfragmented habitat on an ecosystem level, and is a mechanism for developing early planning frameworks for proposed development projects within the planning area in order to avoid, minimize, and compensate for project impacts to wildlife.[76]

An approved NCCP will provide the basis for issuance of state take authorizations for those species specifically identified in the plan, whether or not a species is listed as threatened or endangered under CESA or the federal ESA. If combined with an HCP, the same plan can provide the basis for issuance of federal endangered species permits.

Background and History

Unlike the original ESA, which was later amended to include the HCP process and availability of an ITP, the Natural Community Conservation Planning Act[77] (the "NCCP Act") was enacted specifically to perform similar regional planning functions in the California state context. Like its federal analog, an NCCP takes a broad-based ecosystem approach to planning for the protection and perpetuation of biological diversity. The incentive for a project proponent to agree to an NCCP is the incidental take

---

69   *Id.* § 13.23(a), (b).

70   *Id.* § 13.24.

71   *Id.* § 13.25.

72   *Id.* § 13.26.

73   *Id.* § 13.27.

74   *Id.* § 13.28.

75   Fish & Game Code § 2801.

76   *Id.* § 2801(d).

77   Fish & Game Code §§ 2800–2835.

authorization that flows from the plan, similar to the incidental take authorization granted by virtue of a Section 10 ITP and HCP.

RCIS = Regional Conservation Investment Strategy

The statutory requirements for an NCCP are, however, far more exacting than those established for an HCP and the process for establishment more complex. Notably, and as described below, while an HCP requires mitigation to the maximum extent "practicable," the NCCP Act requires a plan to go much further. In particular, an NCCP must meet a "conservation" standard, which means that the plan must include the use of methods and procedures that are necessary to bring any covered species to the point at which listing measures identified in CESA are not necessary, and for covered species that are not listed pursuant to CESA, to maintain or enhance the condition of that species so that listing will not become necessary.[78] The plan area of NCCPs rarely encompasses the entire range of covered species, so the practical effect of this requirement is that an NCCP must contribute to the recovery (or prevention of listing if the species is not yet listed) of each covered species.

Accordingly, in some cases where an applicant seeks an HCP, the applicant may choose to forego an NCCP and instead simply apply for state take authorization under Section 2081 of CESA. In fact, the state has recognized that the complexity of NCCPs has become problematic, and the Legislature recently amended the Fish and Game Code to authorize another kind of conservation plan, called a "Regional Conservation Investment Strategy" (RCIS) (discussed below).

The NCCP program began when the California legislature enacted the state's Natural Community Conservation Planning Act of 1991, which was codified as Chapter 10 to Division 3 of the California Fish and Game Code, commencing with Section 2800. Amendments were added to the 1991 NCCP Act in 1996 and 2000. The Act was then superseded by the NCCP Act of 2003, which was subsequently amended on several occasions.

The NCCP Act originated in the early 1990s during the housing boom in southern California. The state recognized that a new solution was needed to address the growing challenges of project-by-project permitting and the poor mitigation it often produced. The coastal California gnatcatcher, a small songbird found only in coastal sage scrub, was rapidly being lost to urban development. The state, led by then Governor Pete Wilson, devised the NCCP program to incentivize regional conservation planning for the gnatcatcher and other species. The federal government recognized this innovative approach by listing the species as threatened instead of endangered, and providing exemptions from take prohibitions under a 4(d) rule for communities willing to prepare and implement an NCCP. Since its inception in 1991, the legislative findings in the NCCP Act have reflected a statutorily prescribed balance between protection and conservation of the state's natural resources on the one hand and development and growth on the other hand, although some in the development community argue that this balance is not particularly even.

---

78 *Id.* § 2805(d).

The NCCP Act of 2012 states: "There is a need for broad-based planning to provide for effective protection and conservation of the state's wildlife heritage while continuing to allow appropriate development and growth."[79] The Act also states: "Natural community conservation planning is an effective tool in protecting California's natural diversity while reducing conflicts between protection of the state's wildlife heritage and reasonable use of natural resources for economic development."[80] Focusing on the effects of conservation for federally listed species, the Ninth Circuit Court of Appeals has found that the purpose of the NCCP Act is to encourage planning among affected interests for habitat protection of species to avert their listing under the federal Endangered Species Act.[81]

Overview of the NCCP Process

In general, an NCCP is a plan for the conservation of natural communities that takes an ecosystem approach and encourages cooperation between private and government interests.[82] The Plan identifies and provides for the regional or area-wide protection and perpetuation of plants, animals, and their habitats, while allowing compatible land use and economic activity. An NCCP seeks to anticipate and prevent the controversies caused by species' listings by focusing on the long-term stability of natural communities.

Unlike an HCP, the scope of an NCCP is necessarily regional in nature (i.e., there are no project-specific NCCPs). Within the planning region, effective NCCP "subregional planning units" may be delineated to reflect both biological and administrative boundaries. An NCCP is based on a scientific and procedural framework that must effectively address cumulative impact concerns and integrate them with multi-jurisdictional or subregional planning efforts. The ecosystem conservation elements of a Plan promote wildlife diversity through conservation of habitat on an ecosystem level. The definition of "wildlife" used by the agency includes all wild animals, birds, plants, fish, amphibians, and related ecological communities, including the habitat upon which wildlife depend for their continued viability.[83] Nonetheless, a Plan allows compatible economic activity including resource utilization and development. Species that are included within an NCCP are referred to as "covered species," which are defined under the NCCP Act as species, both listed under CESA and unlisted, that are conserved and managed under an approved NCCP and that may be authorized for take.[84]

---

79   *Id.* § 2801(b).

80   *Id.* § 2801(c).

81   *Southwest Center for Biological Diversity v. Berg*, 268 F.3d 810 (9th Cir. 2001).

82   The California Department of Fish and Wildlife adopted guidelines in 1998 to implement the NCCP Act as it was originally enacted in 1991. Except as provided in Fish & Game Code Section 2830, these guidelines have been superseded by subsequent enactments of the NCCP Act. Nonetheless, they continue to provide practitioners with helpful guidance as to the characteristics and components of an NCCP. See Fish & Game Code § 2825 (authorizing CDFW to adopt regulations for the development and implementation of NCCPs consistent with the NCCP Act).

83   Fish & Game Code § 711.2.

84   *Id.* § 2805(e).

NCCP Planning Agreements

The NCCP Act requires the California Department of Fish and Wildlife (CDFW) to enter into agreements with any person or public entity for the purpose of preparing and implementing an NCCP, in cooperation with a local agency that has land use permit authority over the activities proposed to be addressed in the plan.[85] A planning agreement identifies the scope of the plan to be prepared and the participating parties. More specifically, the planning agreement:

> shall be entered into by, and binding upon,[86] all parties, including CDFW, other participating federal, state, or local agencies, and participating private landowners

> shall identify those natural communities, and the endangered, threatened, proposed, candidate, or other species known, or reasonably expected to be found in those communities, which will be the focus of the plan

> should establish a process for the identification of target species, which may include listed species, and which shall collectively serve as indicators of the natural communities which are the focus of the plan

> shall establish a process for the collection of data, information, and independent input necessary to meet scientifically sound principles for the conservation of species coverage in the plan

> shall establish a process for public participation throughout plan development and review

> should establish an interim process (during plan development) for project review by which projects that potentially conflict with goals of the plan are discussed with CDFW prior to formal processing by the jurisdiction

> shall provide that draft documents associated with an NCCP shall be available for public review and comment, and this review period may run concurrent with the review period provided for the CEQA document associated with the NCCP; however, this does not limit the discretion of a city or county to revise any draft documents at a public hearing

The approval of the planning agreement itself is not considered a project subject to review under CEQA.[87] Prior to CDFW approval of the planning agreement, the public shall have 21 calendar days to review and comment on the proposed planning agreement.[88]

---

85 *Id.* § 2810(a).

86 In practice, Planning Agreements are loose commitments to prepare an NCCP that looks something like the outlines in the Planning Agreement. NCCPs are allowed to deviate from the initial ideas in the Planning Agreement.

87 Fish & Game Code § 2810(c).

88 *Id.* § 2810(d).

Natural Community Conservation Plan Document

As noted above, an NCCP should be tailored to meet the resource needs of a particular region or subregion. The plan must specify a strategy for achieving the required objectives of natural community conservation and compatible land use and economic activity. The strategy might include such techniques as reserve assembly or watershed management. Planning considerations and key plan elements should include, but are not limited to, the following:

Preparation of an NCCP should take into account, and coordinate with, ongoing scientific research that will be helpful in future management adaptations. It should consider the impact of the plan on the use of existing agricultural lands and on conversion of agricultural land to non-agricultural purposes. The plan preparation should also consider methods by which CDFW's responsibilities under Fish and Game Code Section 1600 *et seq.* can be integrated with future NCCP planning processes and with the responsibilities of various federal agencies for regulation of waterways and wetlands.

The statute requires key plan elements of an NCCP to be addressed as follows:

> **Scope.** Describe the natural communities and geographic area of the plan. Also identify the conservation goals for the plan area.

> **Covered Species.** Identify those species to be conserved and managed within the plan area and may therefore be authorized for taking pursuant to Fish and Game Code Section 2835, and summarize how the ecological needs of those species are met by the plan.

> **Anticipated Activities.** Describe the activities or categories of activities anticipated to be authorized by plan participants, which will result in the taking of species pursuant to Fish and Game Code Section 2835 within the plan area. Activities shall be described in sufficient detail to allow CDFW to evaluate the impact of such activities on the ecosystems, natural communities, and species identified in the plan. The combined effect of these activities must not negate the conservation benefits of the plan for any covered species.

> **Principles of Conservation Biology.** Delineate the scientifically sound principles of conservation biology used in formulating those provisions of the plan to protect, restore, or enhance the ecosystems, natural communities and habitat types within the plan area. Demonstrate accepted principles of conservation biology for species covered have been used in formulating the plan.

> **Conservation Strategy.** Identify conservation measures, those actions to be undertaken to protect, restore, or enhance the natural communities within the plan area. Identify compatible uses, those appropriate activities, and any restrictions on activities, within the conserved areas. Set forth a schedule for the implementation of conservation measures. Set forth objective, measurable goals to ensure that the conservation measures identified in the plan are carried out in accordance with the schedule and goals set forth in the plan.

> **Monitoring**. Include a monitoring program that provides periodic evaluations of monitoring results and other new information to be used to evaluate compliance with plan implementation mechanisms; evaluate biological performance of the plan; and determine whether management objectives remain appropriate and whether new or different techniques could be utilized to better achieve management goals.

> **Adaptive Management**. Develop a management plan which will provide for adaptive management. The plan will provide for the implementation of an adaptive management program which establishes a flexible, iterative approach to long-term management of natural communities, habitat types, and species within the plan area. Management will be refined and improved over time based upon the results of ongoing monitoring activities and other relevant information. Elements of a management plan subject to adaptive management may include habitat management and enhancement, fire management, management of human impacts, and exotic species control.

> **Funding**. Set forth an adequate funding source or sources to ensure that the conservation actions identified in the plan are carried out in accordance with the schedule and goals set forth in the plan.

> **Assurances**. An NCCP may include, in both the plan and in a separate implementing agreement, assurances that provide for the long-term reconciliation of new land development in the planning area and the conservation and protection of endangered species. Departmental assurances will be determined for individual plans according to the level of conservation each plan affords. If warranted, CDFW will provide its assurance that the NCCP provides measures sufficient to conserve the species addressed in the plan and that no further land dedications, land use restrictions, water use commitments, or financial compensation will be required by CDFW, except in defined extraordinary circumstances.

NCCP Implementation Agreement

NCCP participants commit to implementing the NCCP by preparing and signing an Implementation Agreement, and an Implementation Agreement is a required element of an NCCP.[89] As with an HCP, the Implementation Agreement for an NCCP defines the obligations of the signatories and other parties; provides legally binding and enforceable assurances that the plan will be implemented and adequately funded; and provides a process for amendment of the Plan. The Implementation Agreement may provide that a separate management plan or plans will be adopted in the future or at periodic intervals provided that the management plan(s) meets criteria set forth in the NCCP. Where appropriate, CDFW may require additional memoranda of understanding that CDFW believes would assist in the implementation of the Plan. CDFW maintains a template Implementation Agreement that applicants should follow closely to minimize lengthy

---

89   Fish & Game Code § 2820(b).

reviews by CDFW. In addition, it is important that as much as possible of the Implementation Agreement be stated first in the NCCP and then repeated or copied into the Implementation Agreement. Past NCCPs encountered challenges when new concepts were introduced into the Implementation Agreement that inadvertently affected or changed elements of the NCCP. Applicants should strive to avoid situations in which the Implementation Agreement conflicts with the NCCP.

An Implementation Agreement must include the following:

> provisions defining species coverage, including any conditions of coverage
> provisions for establishing the long-term protection of any habitat reserve or other measures that provide equivalent conservation of covered species
> specific terms and conditions, which, if violated, would result in the suspension or revocation of the permit, in whole or in part. CDFW must include a provision requiring notification to the plan participant of a specified period of time to cure any default prior to suspension or revocation of the permit in whole or in part. These terms and conditions must address, but are not limited to, provisions specifying the actions CDFW must take under all of the following circumstances:
  • if the plan participant fails to provide adequate funding
  • if the plan participant fails to maintain the rough proportionality between impacts on habitat or covered species and conservation measures
  • if the plan participant adopts, amends, or approves any plan or project without the concurrence of the wildlife agencies that is inconsistent with the objectives and requirements of the approved plan
  • if the level of take exceeds that authorized by the permit
> provisions specifying procedures for amendment of the Plan and the Implementation Agreement
> provisions ensuring implementation of the monitoring program and adaptive management program
> provisions for oversight of plan implementation for purposes of assessing mitigation performance, funding, and habitat protection measures
> provisions for periodic reporting to the wildlife agencies and the public for purposes of information and evaluation of plan progress
> mechanisms to ensure adequate funding to carry out the conservation actions identified in the Plan
> provisions to ensure that implementation of mitigation and conservation measures on a plan basis is roughly proportional in time and extent to the impact on habitat or covered species authorized under the Plan. These provisions must identify the conservation measures, including assembly of reserves where appropriate and implementation of monitoring and management activities, that will be maintained or carried out in rough proportion to the impact

on habitat or covered species and the measurements that will be used to determine if this is occurring.[90]

Public Participation Process

CDFW must establish, in cooperation with the parties to the planning agreement, a
process for public participation throughout the development and review of the NCCP
to ensure that interested persons, including landowners, have an adequate opportunity
to provide input. The statutory minimum for this process includes a requirement that
draft documents associated with an NCCP must be available for public review and comment for at least 60 days prior to the adoption of that draft document. Preliminary public review documents must be made available by the NCCP lead agency at least 10
working days prior to any public hearing addressing these documents. These review
periods may run concurrently with the review period provided for any document
required by CEQA that is associated with the NCCP.

The Ninth Circuit Court of Appeals has found that the balance of equities and public interest require full and diverse participation in the NCCP process. In *Starkey v.
County of San Diego*, the court supported the issuance of injunctive relief where a cattle-
men's association had been removed from an NCCP steering committee.[91] In practice,
many NCCPs proponents have established local stakeholder committees to provide
input and advice throughout the process. These stakeholder committees are typically
composed of representatives of local interest groups such as developers, landowners,
farmers or ranchers, and environmental groups. When the members are chosen carefully
and the process managed well, these stakeholder groups can provide valuable local support at the final approval process.

Findings Required for Approval of NCCP

As set forth in Section 2820 of the California Fish and Game Code, CDFW must make
the following findings based upon substantial evidence in the record before approving
an NCCP:

> the Plan has been developed consistent with the process identified in the plan-
> ning agreement
> the Plan integrates adaptive management strategies that are periodically evalu-
> ated and modified based on the information from the monitoring program and
> other sources, which will assist in providing for the conservation of covered spe-
> cies and ecosystems within the Plan area
> the Plan provides for the protection of habitat, natural communities, and species
> diversity on a landscape or ecosystem level through the creation and long-term
> management of habitat reserves or other measures that provide equivalent

90   Fish & Game Code § 2820(b).
91   346 Fed. Appx. 146 (9th Cir. 2009).

conservation of covered species appropriate for land, aquatic, and marine habitats within the Plan area

> the development of reserve systems and conservation measures in the Plan area provides, as needed for the conservation of species, all of the following:

  • conserving, restoring, and managing representative natural and seminatural landscapes to maintain the ecological integrity of large habitat blocks, ecosystems function, and biological diversity

  • establishing one or more reserves or other measures that provide equivalent conservation of covered species within the Plan area and linkages between them and adjacent habitat areas outside of the Plan area

  • protecting and maintaining habitat areas that are large enough to support sustainable populations of covered species

  • incorporating an range of environmental gradients (such as slope, elevation, aspect, and coastal or inland characteristics) and high habitat diversity to provide for shifting species distributions due to changed circumstances

  • sustaining the effective movement and interchange of organisms between habitat areas in a manner that maintains the ecological integrity of the habitat areas within the Plan area

> the Plan identifies activities, and any restrictions on those activities, allowed within reserve areas that are compatible with the conservation of species, habitats, natural communities, and their associated ecological functions

> the Plan contains specific conservation measures that meet the biological needs of covered species and that are based upon the best available scientific information regarding the status of covered species and the impacts of permitted activities on those species

> the Plan contains a monitoring program

> the Plan contains an adaptive management program

> the Plan includes the estimated timeframe and process by which the reserves or other conservation measures are to be implemented, including obligations of landowners and Plan signatories and consequences of the failure to acquire lands in a timely manner

> the Plan contains provisions that ensure adequate funding to carry out the conservation actions identified in the Plan[92]

Regarding the finding to ensure adequate funding, many NCCPs are able to utilize public funding sources unavailable to regional HCPs. Because NCCPs must provide conservation that exceeds mitigation requirements (i.e., contribute to species recovery in the Plan area), NCCPs can qualify for funding sources such as federal grants, state grants, or state bond funds earmarked for conservation purposes (not mitigation). Some NCCPs have also received support from private foundations. This ability to pay for large

---

92   Fish & Game Code § 2820(a).

shares of NCCP costs with public funds is sometimes cited as one of the primary reasons the local agencies and some private companies have pursued an NCCP.

Concurrent with the approval of a final NCCP, CDFW must establish a list of species that are authorized for take pursuant to Section 2835 of the NCCP Act and make the findings identified above to support coverage. For purposes of determining whether a species should receive coverage under a Plan, CDFW must use, in addition to the standards required for the adoption of a Plan, one or more of the following criteria:

> coverage is warranted based upon regional or landscape level consideration, such as healthy population levels, widespread distribution throughout the Plan area, and life history characteristics that respond to habitat-scale conservation and management actions

> coverage is warranted based on regional or landscape level considerations with site-specific conservation and management requirements that are clearly identified in the Plan for species that are generally well distributed, but that have core habitats that must be conserved

> coverage is warranted based upon site-specific considerations and the identification of specific conservation and management conditions for species within a narrowly defined habitat or limited geographic area within the Plan area[93]

CDFW must also find that the mitigation measures specified in the Plan and imposed by the Plan participants are consistent with Section 2081(b) of the California Fish and Game Code. See discussion below.[94]

Take Authorization under an NCCP

Section 2835 of the California Fish and Game Code allows CDFW to authorize incidental take in an NCCP. Take may be authorized for any identified species whose conservation and management is provided for in the Plan, whether or not the species is listed as threatened or endangered. Identified species that are not listed are treated as if listed pursuant to the California Endangered Species Act either by addressing the species themselves or by addressing species whose habitat and survival needs are demonstrably similar to those of the identified species.

According to CDFW's 1998 guidelines, the NCCP should demonstrate that it contributes to the recovery of listed species authorized for take within the area subject to the NCCP. This position appears to be based on language in the NCCP Act defining the terms "conserve," "conserving," and "conservation" to mean using methods and procedures that are necessary to bring any covered species to the point at which listing measures identified in the California Endangered Species Act are not necessary, and for covered species that are not listed pursuant to the California Endangered Species Act, to maintain or enhance the condition of that species so that listing will not become

93 *Id.* § 2821(a).
94 *Id.* § 2821(b).

necessary.[95] This is one of the key differences in the NCCP Act, as compared to the Section 10 Habitat Conservation Plan permitting regime, in which there is no recovery standard or requirement.

To ensure compliance with the California Endangered Species Act, authorization for taking of species identified in the NCCP must also meet the following conditions required by Section 2081(b) of the California Fish and Game Code:

> the taking is incidental to an otherwise lawful activity
> the impacts of the authorized take must be minimized and fully mitigated. Impacts of taking include all impacts on the identified species that result from any act that would cause the proposed taking:
  • the measures required to meet this obligation must be roughly proportional in extent to the impact of the authorized taking on the species
  • where various measures are available to meet this obligation, the measures required must maintain the applicant's objectives to the greatest extent possible; and
  • all required measures must be capable of successful implementation
> the authorization is consistent with any regulations adopted pursuant to Sections 2112 and 2114 of the California Fish and Game Code (Recovery Strategies)
> the applicant shall ensure adequate funding to implement the measures required and for monitoring with, and effectiveness of, those measures

Under fairly recent amendments to the NCCP Act, CDFW was given authority to permit the incidental take of fully protected species subject to California Fish and Game Code Sections 3511, 4700, 5050, and 5515. The NCCP Act specifically refers to fully protected species in the definition of "covered species," stating that notwithstanding the code sections governing these species, fully protected species may be included as "covered species" in an NCCP and "taking of fully protected species may be authorized pursuant to Section 2835 for any fully protected species conserved and managed as a covered species under an approved [NCCP]."[96] This is expressly set forth in Section 2835, which provides:

> At the time of plan approval, [CDFW] may authorize by permit the taking of any covered species, including species designated as fully protected species pursuant to Sections 3511, 4700, 5050, and 5515, whose conservation and management is provided for in a natural community conservation plan approved by [CDFW].

Take authorization for fully protected species is not allowed by a California Fish and Game Code Section 2081(b) permit, so the only way to obtain take authorization for fully protected species is through an approved NCCP.

95   *Id.* § 2805(d).
96   *Id.* § 2805(e).

CDFW has the authority to suspend or revoke any permit, in whole or in part, issued for the take of a species subject to Section 2835 of the Fish and Game Code if the continued take of the species would result in jeopardizing the continued existence of the species.[97]

Regulatory Assurances

Like its federal analog, an NCCP can include assurances and provisions regarding unforeseen circumstances. Under the NCCP Act, CDFW may provide assurances for Plan participants commensurate with long-term conservation assurances and associated implementation measures pursuant to the approved NCCP.

When providing assurances, CDFW's determination of the level of assurances and the time limits specified in the Implementation Agreement for assurances may be based on localized conditions and must consider all of the following:

> the level of knowledge of the status of the covered species and natural communities

> the adequacy of analysis of the impact of take on covered species

> the use of the best available science to make assessments about the impacts of take, the reliability of mitigation strategies, and the appropriateness of monitoring techniques

> the appropriateness of the size and duration of the Plan with respect to quality and amount of data

> the sufficiency of mechanisms for long-term funding of all components of the Plan and contingencies

> the degree of coordination and accessibility of centralized data for analysis and evaluation of the effectiveness of the Plan

> the degree to which a thorough range of foreseeable circumstances are considered and provided for under the adaptive management program

> the size and duration of the Plan

The NCCP Act defines "unforeseen circumstances" as changes affecting one or more species, habitat, natural community, or the geographic area covered by a conservation plan that could not reasonably have been anticipated at the time of plan development, and that result in a substantial adverse change in the status of one or more covered species.[98] If there are unforeseen circumstances, additional land, water, or financial compensation or additional restrictions on the use of land, water, or other natural resources shall not be required without the consent of Plan participants for a period of time specified in the Implementation Agreement, unless CDFW determines that the Plan is not being implemented consistent with the substantive terms of the Implementation Agreement.[99]

97   *Id.* § 2823.

98   *Id.* § 2805(k).

99   *Id.* § 2820(f)(2).

RCIS = Regional Conservation
Investment Strategy

RCA = Regional Conservation
Assessment

The regulatory assurances available with an NCCP are not available through a California Fish and Game Code Section 2081(b) permit. This has important practical considerations. For example, applicants can only receive through an NCCP state regulatory assurances for species not yet listed. If the NCCP has adequately covered not-yet-listed species then no further conservation actions will be required if that species becomes listed during the term of NCCP permit.

Environmental Review Requirements

NCCPs must provide for compliance with CEQA as required by Section 2826 of the California Fish and Game Code. The NCCP Act does not exempt a project proposed in a natural community conservation planning area from CEQA or otherwise alter or affect the applicability of CEQA.[100] The CEQA document for the NCCP must include a specific mitigation and implementation monitoring program, consistent with the requirements of CEQA. Ordinarily, CDFW will act as a CEQA responsible agency for the purpose of approving an NCCP. In certain circumstances, CDFW may act as a CEQA lead agency. In either case, CEQA review of NCCPs must be coordinated with CDFW.

If the impacts on one or more covered species and its habitat are analyzed and mitigated pursuant to a program Environmental Impact Report for a plan adopted pursuant to the NCCP Act, a plan participant that is a lead agency or a responsible agency for CEQA purposes must incorporate in the review of any subsequent project in the plan area the feasible mitigation measures and alternatives related to the biological impacts on covered species and their habitat developed in the program Environmental Impact Report.[101]

REGIONAL CONSERVATION INVESTMENT STRATEGIES

Background and History

In 2016, the State of California passed legislation (AB 2087) to enable a certain form of resource conservation planning that authorized CDFW to establish a mitigation program based upon a regional conservation plan that is not as difficult to complete as an NCCP. These plans, called "Regional Conservation Investment Strategies" (RCIS) allow the creation of *advance* mitigation credits on a regional basis that can later be used by public agencies and private developers to mitigate the impacts of their projects. In essence, an RCIS and its attendant structures essentially combine the features of the conservation strategy of an HCP and a conservation bank, but without the burdensome procedural and substantive requirements of an HCP or NCCP. The RCIS program is technically not a regulatory program, and does not result in a permit, but local agencies and landowners have expressed ongoing concern that identification of potential mitigation opportunities may have a chilling effect on areas within their jurisdiction or ownership (analogous to justified concerns about federal recovery programs, which also have

100 *Id.* § 2826.
101 *Id.* § 2820(e).

no "regulatory effect" but which clearly guide federal permitting and conservation decisions).

RCA = Regional Conservation Assessment

One of the themes in AB 2087 is that an RCIS is intended to guide voluntary investments in conservation and mitigation, and that it is not intended to be regulatory in nature. In fact, they may have utility independent of the use of advance mitigation techniques or the use of "Mitigation Credit Agreements" (described below). This is because they are intended to develop a body of scientific and planning information that can be used to guide all types of decisionmaking relative to resource issues. The statute points out that RCISs (and their companion documents, "Regional Conservation Assessments" or "RCAs") are intended to have no effect on the land use authority of local governments. In fact, these instruments are supposed to acknowledge and consider local general plans, infrastructure projects and housing needs. Nonetheless, RCISs and RCAs will undoubtedly be used as a source of information in CEQA, NEPA, and other planning and environmental review processes.

Setting aside the broader informational purposes of RCISs and RCAs, a private party or public agency may—through the use of Mitigation Credit Agreements—secure mitigation credit in other permitting efforts through investment in conservation consistent efforts with an already-established RCIS.

Overview of the RCIS

An RCIS can be prepared only by a public agency, including CDFW. An RCIS must be developed in consultation with local agencies having land use jurisdiction in the plan area.[102]

The purpose of an RCIS is to inform science-based nonbinding and voluntary "conservation actions" and "habitat enhancement actions" that would advance the conservation of "focal species," including the ecological processes, natural communities and habitat connectivity upon which those species depend.[103] A more complete definition of the term RCIS is found in Fish and Game Code Section 1851(l). The RCIS is intended for:

> identification of wildlife and habitat conservation priorities (including actions to address climate change and other wildlife stressors)

> investments in resource conservation

> infrastructure

> identification of areas for compensatory mitigation for impacts to species and natural resources

An RCIS is required to contain 15 different components, which are expressed in detail in the statute and in Guidelines that CDFW has published on their web site, and can be summarized as follows:

> conservation purpose and need for the RCIS

102 *Id.* § 1852(a).
103 *Id.* § 1852(b).

> geographic area of the strategy and its relationship to surrounding areas
> description of the focal species to be addressed by the strategy
> important resource conservation elements within the strategy area
> a summary of historic, current, and projected future resource stressors in the planning area
> consideration of major infrastructure facilities, urban development areas, and local agency general plans that accounts for, among other things, the need for housing and renewable energy
> provisions to ensure that the strategy will be in compliance with all applicable state and local requirements and does not preempt the authority of local agencies to implement infrastructure and urban development in local general plans
> conservation goals and measurable objectives
> prioritized conservation actions that could achieve the stated conservation goals and objectives
> provisions assuring that the strategy is consistent with overlapping NCCPs and HCPs
> an explanation of consistency with any other RCIS, state or federal recovery plan, or other approved state or federal conservation strategy
> a summary of mitigation and conservation banks with overlapping service areas
> an adaptive management strategy responsive to climate change
> a discussion of the best available scientific information used to support the strategy
> consideration of (1) the conservation benefits of preserving lands for agricultural uses; (2) reasonably foreseeable development of infrastructure; (3) reasonably foreseeable housing and other projects; and (4) any draft NCCPs[104]

Regional Conservation Assessments

Although it is not required by the statute, the Department may also approve an RCA for areas covered by an RCIS. An RCA may be proposed by the Department or any other public agency and, if it covers the area of an already adopted RCIS, must describe the relationship of the RCA to that RCIS.[105]

It does not appear that an RCA has any specific legal utility. Rather, the purpose of an RCA is to provide context for the conservation strategies and actions set forth in an RCIS.[106] An RCA is intended to be "nonbinding [and] voluntary, and does not create, modify, or impose regulatory requirements or standards, regulate the use of land, establish land use designations, or affect the land use authority of, or the exercise of discretion by, any public agency." Nonetheless, it is not entirely irrelevant to local

---

104 Fish & Game Code § 1852(c), (e).
105 *Id.* § 1853(a), (b).
106 *Id.* § 1851(k).

governmental processes, because an RCA does generate information that could be used in a local CEQA process (whether by a lead agency or a project opponent).

OPR = Office of Planning and Research

Like an RCIS, an RCA must include certain statutorily required components, including (1) an identification and summary of relevant regional pressures and stressors, including climate change vulnerability, conservation areas, and habitat connectivity values; (2) an identification of the best available scientific information and analysis of the distribution of species and natural communities; (3) the use of spatial analyses of certain ecological information; (4) for standardization purposes, the use of standard or prevalent vegetation and ecoregional classifications; (5) a consistent format allowing upload and interaction on an internet web portal; (6) a demonstration of consistency with NCCPs, regional HCPs and approved recovery plans; (7) consideration of existing and reasonably foreseeable major infrastructure facilities, including renewable energy and housing; (8) provisions ensuring compliance with applicable state and local requirements and that the strategy does not preempt the authority of local agencies to implement infrastructure and urban development in their general plans; (9) explanations of consistency with overlapping NCCPs and HCPs and (10) explanations of consistency with other assessments, RCISs and recovery plans.[107]

Approval Processes

The Department may approve an RCIS, or certain amendments thereto, for an initial period of up to 10 years. An RCIS may be extended for an additional 10 years if the strategy is updated and complies with the requirements of Section 1852.

If a public agency desires to create an RCIS, it must publish a notice of intent with the Governor's Office of Planning and Research (OPR) and the county clerk of each affected county. Once a draft RCIS (or an amendment thereto) is submitted to the Department for review, the Department has 30 days to determine whether the strategy is "complete." Within 30 days of completeness, the Department must publish the strategy on its website for a 30-day public review period.[108]

In addition to the foregoing, the public agency proposing an RCIS must hold a public meeting on the strategy early in the process of preparing it.[109] The statute includes a number of requirements relative to the local public review and meeting process, including a requirement that notice be given to (1) local governments with territory within or adjacent to the RCIS planning area; (2) the implementing entity for any overlapping HCP or NCCP; and (3) any person or entity who has requested notice of any RCIS effort.[110]

At least 60 days prior to submitting an RCIS (or amendment thereto) to the Department, the public agency proposing the strategy must notify the board of supervisors and city council of each county or city, respectively, with territory in the RCIS

---

107 *Id.* § 1853(c).

108 *Id.* § 1854.

109 *Id.*

110 *Id.* § 1854(c).

planning area, and must provide those legislative bodies at least 30 days for review and comment.[111]

Although this requirement does not appear to be consistent with the 30-day completeness review described above, the Department has 30 days following submission of a "final" RCIS to either (1) approve the RCIS or (2) explain in writing to the submitting public agency what is needed to approve the strategy.

Limitations

During the negotiations over AB 2087, considerable concern was expressed by the building industry, and cities and counties, that the RCIS process might be used by the Department to usurp the land use planning authority of local agencies. Accordingly, as expressed above, the statute contains abundant language requiring RCISs and RCAs to take into consideration local general plans and anticipated infrastructure and housing needs. In this respect, the RCIS should be prepared in a manner that respects state housing law, including requirements that cities bear their fair shares of regional and statewide housing needs. An RCIS that fails to recognize these requirements is vulnerable to legal challenge.

In addition to the provisions described above, the statute includes specific "limitations" that also provide protection to local agencies, landowners and other parties. In particular, the law states that an RCIS shall not:

> affect the authority or jurisdiction of any public agency and shall not be binding upon public agencies other than a party to a mitigation credit agreement. Nothing in this chapter increases or decreases the authority of the Department regarding any land use, species, habitat area, resource, plan, process or corridor. Regional conservation investment strategies are intended to provide scientific information for the consideration of public agencies. Nothing in this chapter or any other provision of law requires any public agency . . . to adopt, implement, or otherwise adhere to [an RCIS or RCA].[112]

In addition to this general limitation, the statute contains a number of protections for existing governmental standards and processes. In particular, Section 1855(b) states that the approval or existence of an RCIS or mitigation credit agreement (described below) does not do any of the following:

> modify the standards for issuance of Section 2081 incidental take permits, Section 2080.1 consistency determinations, lake and streambed alteration agreements under Section 1600 of the Fish and Game Code, or NCCPs

> modify in any way the standards under CEQA or in any way limit a lead or responsible agency's discretion, in connection with any determination of whether a project may or may not have a significant effect "or in any way

111 *Id.*

112 Fish & Game Code § 1855(a).

establish a presumption" in connection with any such determination or whether the impacts of a project would be mitigated

MCA = Mitigation Credit Agreement

> prohibit or authorize any project or project impacts

> create a presumption that any proposed project will be approved or permitted, or that any proposed impact will be authorized, by any state or local agency

> create a presumption that any project will be disapproved or prohibited, or that any proposed impact will be prohibited, by any state or local agency

> alter or affect, or create additional requirements for, any local general plan

Moreover, the approval or existence of an RCIS or mitigation credit agreement does not constitute any of the following for the purposes of CEQA:

> a plan, policy, or regulation adopted for the purpose of avoiding or mitigating an environmental effect

> a local policy or ordinance protecting biological resources

> an adopted local, regional, or state habitat conservation plan

The RCIS statute includes language intended to make clear that an RCIS is not binding in nature. For example, under the statute, project proponents are not required to follow the guidance in an RCIS (i.e., adopt an RCIS conservation action or enhancement action) when they develop mitigation for their individual projects. Nor are they required to either develop a Mitigation Credit Agreement (MCA) or purchase mitigation credits under an MCA. In particular, nothing in the RCIS statute may require someone seeking to provide compensatory mitigation under a Lake and Streambed Alteration Agreement, Section 2081 ITP, NCCP or consistency determination under Section 2080.1 to (1) undertake "conservation actions" or "habitat enhancement actions" identified in an RCIS; (2) implement, continue to fund or otherwise comply with the actions identified in an RCIS; (3) require or otherwise compel a project proponent to enter into a mitigation credit agreement or use or purchase mitigation credits established thereunder.[113] Notwithstanding the foregoing, nothing in the statute prevents a project proponent from proposing mitigation consistent with an RCIS.[114] However, the Department is prohibited from rejecting "biologically appropriate and adequate" compensatory mitigation on the basis that the proposed mitigation is not a "conservation action" or "habitat enhancement" identified in an RCIS.

Conservation Actions and Habitat Enhancement Actions

As noted above, an RCIS must identify "conservation actions" and "habitat enhancement actions" intended to further the goals of the RCIS. These actions and enhancements may be used under the statute to create mitigation credits that can be used to compensate for impacts to focal and other species addressed in an RCIS, habitat, and other natural resources.[115]

---

113 *Id.* § 1855(c).

114 *Id.*

115 *Id.* § 1856.

Once created by an MCA, these mitigation credits can be used to fulfill, in whole or in part, compensatory mitigation requirements established under any state or federal law including, without limitation, NCCPs, Lake and Streambed Alteration Agreements (provided one satisfies a mitigation standard that is higher than the standard expressed under Section 1602 of the Fish and Game Code), and CEQA.[116]

The statute defines a "conservation action" as:

> an action to preserve or to restore ecological processes, and wildlife corridors, to protect those resources permanently, and to provide for their perpetual management, so as to help to achieve one or more biological goals and objectives for one or more focal species. Conservation actions may include, but are not limited to, actions to offset impacts to focal species.[117]

The statute defines a "habitat enhancement action" as:

> an action to improve the quality of wildlife, or address risks or stressors to wildlife, that has long-term durability but does not involve land acquisition or permanent protection of habitat, such as improving in-stream flows to benefit fish species, enhancing habitat connectivity, or invasive species control or eradication.[118]

Note that, under the statute, the "durability" of a habitat enhancement action must be ensured by the Department.[119] For a habitat enhancement action to be used for crediting purposes in an MCA, the action must "remain in effect" at least until the site of the environmental impact is returned to pre-impact ecological conditions. This is a notable innovation. Before the RCIS program, mitigation credits created through traditional mitigation banks or conservation banks in California were required to be permanent. Mitigation values in conservation banks, for example, are guaranteed through mechanisms such as a permanent conservation easement. For the first time, non-permanent habitat enhancement actions can generate mitigation credits that can be sold or used for non-permanent impacts (i.e., temporary or short-term impacts).

For either a conservation action or habitat enhancement action to be used to create mitigation credit, the RCIS identifying those measures must include certain additional information, including (1) an adaptive management and monitoring strategy; (2) a process for updating the scientific information contained in the RCIS and tracking progress in meeting biological goals and objectives and satisfying mitigation requirements at least once every 10 years; and (3) identification of a public or private entity responsible for the required monitoring and updates .[120]

---

116 *Id.* § 1856(c).
117 *Id.* § 1851(d).
118 *Id.* § 1851(g).
119 *Id.* § 1856(d).
120 *Id.* § 1856(b).

Requirements for a Mitigation Credit Agreement

A Mitigation Credit Agreement (MCA) must identify the type and number of mitigation credits proposed to be created and the terms and conditions under which they may be used.[121] Mitigation credits may *not* be created on a site that has already been permanently protected and has been or is currently being used to fulfill compensatory mitigation requirements for one or more projects. Once mitigation credits have been created, they may sold or transferred with the approval of the Department.

The process for agreement approval begins with the submission of a draft agreement to the Department. Within 5 days of deeming a draft agreement complete, the Department must publish notice of availability of the agreement (with OPR, the county clerks and anyone else who has requested notice) and provide a public comment period of 45 days.[122] Following completion of the public review period, the Department must respond to written comments and may approve the agreement, approve it with revisions, or disapprove it.

To approve an MCA, the Department must find that the agreement does all of the following 18 items, all of which are described more fully in Fish and Game Code Section 1856(f) and in Mitigation Credit Agreement Guidelines that CDFW intends to publish:

> identifies and establishes the qualifications of the party entering into the agreement with the Department, the person, or entity to manage the site of the Conservation Action or Habitat Enhancement Action, and any contractors or consultants

> fully describes the proposed Conservation Actions or Habitat Enhancement Actions, explaining how they will achieve RCIS conservation objectives that have not already been achieved

> identifies the location of the proposed Conservation Actions or Habitat Enhancement Actions, as specified

> includes aerial and ground-level photos of the proposed location and surrounding properties

> explains how the credits will be created, including ownership structures, long-term management and phasing

> identifies conservation and mitigation banks approved by the Department as an alternative mitigation alternative and explains how credits in those banks will be purchased or used in combination with credits created under the RCIS or, if they will not be used, the reasons why they will not be used

> includes an evaluation that documents baseline conditions and adjacent land uses

> identifies protected public lands in the vicinity

MCA = Mitigation Credit Agreement

---

121 *Id.* § 1856(e).

122 *Id.* § 1856(f).

LSAA = Lake and Streambed
Alteration Agreement

> fully describes the type and quantity of proposed credits and the supporting rationale, which credits must "directly correlate" to the focal species and other species and other resources addressed by the proposed actions

> identifies consistent metrics or indicators to evaluate the success of the proposed actions, including the net ecological gain from the proposed actions

> describes proposed land ownership structures

> includes a template conservation easement or other protective instruments (consistent with any NCCP in the area) and an explanation of how the long-term durability of the sites of any Habitat Enhancement Actions will be ensured

> ensures adequate funding of any Conservation Action or Habitat Enhancement Action, including the long-term protection and management of the site, in accordance with the requirements of the Department as set forth in Section 65965 of the California Government Code or, in the case of a public agency, another comparable funding method approved by the Department in accordance with an adopted statewide policy regarding funding for long-term management and operation of mitigation sites

> includes a template monitoring and long-term management plan

> explains the terms for sale or transfer of mitigation credits, including accounting, reporting, and record-keeping of credit creation, release and use, sale, or transfer

> includes enforcement provisions

> ensures that the information that is legally required for the establishment of a mitigation bank (under Sections 1798 and 1798.5 of the Fish and Game Code) will be provided with respect to the site on which the actions will be carried out even though the actions do not involve establishment of a mitigation bank

> includes a proposed credit ledger and release schedule satisfying the requirements of Section 1856(g)

Establishment and Release of Mitigation Credits

As more fully set forth in Section 1856(g), and as with a mitigation or conservation bank or in-lieu fee program, the release of credits under a Mitigation Credit Agreement must be tied to performance-based milestones and achievement of ecological performance standards.

These performance-based milestone must include, without limitation, (1) recordation of a conservation easement (for a conservation action) or the establishment of measures to establish durability of a habitat enhancement action, (2) completion of construction of a habitat enhancement action, (3) achievement of temporal ecological performance standards for habitat restoration (e.g., for periods one, three or five years following the initiation of construction), and (4) full achievement of identified performance standards.

For credits to be released, the implementing party must demonstrate to the Department that the applicable milestones and performance standards have been met. If the milestones and performance standards established under a Mitigation Credit Agreement are *not* achieved, the Department may suspend the release of credits, reduce the number of credits, or otherwise modify the credit release schedule accordingly.

Mitigation credits can be used in connection with mitigation projects provided under NCCPs or Lake and Streambed Alteration Agreements (LSAAs), but *only* to the extent that a project that improves wildlife habitat or addresses wildlife stressors in a manner that "quantifiably exceeds" the mitigation requirements established under those other programs. That is, to the extent that an applicant "over-mitigates" under an LSAA or an NCCP, credits may be assigned and released for that excess mitigation.[123] One example given in the statute is the construction of a setback levee that creates more floodplain or riparian habitat than is required to compensate for construction impacts.

Section 1856(h) includes provisions describing how an applicant may concurrently process a Mitigation Credit Agreement along with an LSAA or NCCP application. This process is not permitted, however, for incidental take permits under Section 2081 of the Fish and Game Code.

Other Provisions

The statute includes several other miscellaneous provisions, as follows:

> Section 1856(i) clarifies that the statute is not intended to limit or impose additional conditions on conservation or mitigation banks under Section 1797 of the Fish and Game Code

> Section 1856(j) is intended to clarify that mitigation credits created within the area of an NCCP are properly coordinated with the NCCP

> Section 1856(k) requires the Department to make mitigation credit and release information available on its website

> Section 1857 allows the Department to require payment of the Department's costs associated with an RCIS, RCA or Mitigation Credit Agreement (CDFW has established fees to review and process a draft RCIS or RCA; they will soon establish similar fees for Mitigation Credit Agreements)

> Section 1858 authorizes the Department to adopt guidelines and criteria to aid in the implementation of the RCIS program (CDFW has adopted guidelines to prepare RCAs and RCISs; they are expected to adopt guidelines for Mitigation Credit Agreements but as of the publication of this book, they have not yet done so)

Additional Guidance

The Department maintains a useful website describing the RCIS program, which can be found at https://www.wildlife.ca.gov/conservation/planning/regional-conservation.

---

123 Fish & Game Code § 2086(h).

The website includes links to the Department's RCIS Guidelines (2018), as well as a fee schedule, FAQs, and a "Guide to AB 2087." As of July 2018, local public agencies have produced two draft RCIS documents which cover Yolo County and Santa Clara County, respectively. Several more RCISs are in preparation including in the Antelope Valley of Los Angeles County, the Sacramento Valley of Colusa and Sutter Counties, and the eastern San Francisco Bay Area (Contra Costa and Alameda Counties).

CHAPTER 12

Cultural Resources

This chapter addresses state and federal requirements for agencies to consider the effects of their actions on cultural resources, particularly tribal cultural resources. After briefly discussing relevant state and federal executive orders, the chapter turns to the requirements of Section 106 of the National Historic Preservation Act, and then California's requirements for the consideration of cultural resource impacts. This chapter does not cover the broader requirements of NEPA or CEQA with respect to cultural resources, which are addressed in other books.

OMB = Office of Management and Budget

EXECUTIVE DIRECTIVES TO CONSULT TRIBES

Federal

Executive Order 13175, issued in November 2000, requires agencies to adhere to three criteria when formulating and implementing policies that have tribal implications:

> "Agencies shall respect Indian tribal self-government and sovereignty, honor tribal treaty and other rights, and strive to meet the responsibilities that arise from the unique legal relationship between the Federal Government and Indian tribal governments"

> "With respect to Federal statutes and regulations administered by Indian tribal governments, the Federal Government shall grant Indian tribal governments the maximum administrative discretion possible"

> "When undertaking to formulate and implement policies that have tribal implications, agencies shall: (1) encourage Indian tribes to develop their own policies to achieve program objectives; (2) where possible, defer to Indian tribes to establish standards; and (3) in determining whether to establish Federal standards, consult with tribal officials as to the need for Federal standards and any alternatives that would limit the scope of Federal standards or otherwise preserve the prerogatives and authority of Indian tribes."[1]

Additionally, agencies must consult tribes when developing regulatory policies that have tribal implications. Pursuant to this executive order, each agency has a consultation process that it has submitted to the Office of Management and Budget (OMB) and a designated official whose principal responsibility is implementation of this executive order. That official must submit a certification when an agency transmits a final draft regulation that has tribal implications to the OMB attesting to the agency's timely and meaningful compliance with its consultation and other requirements under the executive order.

State

In September 2011, the California governor issued Executive Order B-10-11 to strengthen the state's relationship with its tribes.[2] Among other things, this executive order established the position of Governor's Tribal Advisor ("Tribal Advisor") in the Office of the Governor.[3] The Tribal Advisor oversees government-to-government consultation between the governor's office and tribes on policies that affect California tribal communities. The Tribal Advisor's duties include serving as a direct link between tribes and the governor; facilitating communication and consultations between the tribes, the governor's office, state agencies, and agency tribal liaisons; and reviewing and making recommendations on state legislation and regulations affecting tribes.[4]

1 Exec. Order No. 13175, 65 Fed. Reg. 67,249 (2000).

2 Cal. Exec. Order No. B-10-11 (Sept. 19, 2011), https://www.gov.ca.gov/2011/09/19/news17223/.

3 *Id.*

4 *Id.*

This executive order also requires the Office of the Governor to meet regularly with the elected officials of California tribes to discuss state policies that may affect tribal communities.[5] In addition, every state agency and department subject to the governor's control must "encourage communication and consultation with California Indian Tribes" and "permit elected officials and other representatives of tribal governments to provide meaningful input into the development of legislation, regulations, rules, and policies on matters that may affect tribal communities."[6] Natural resource agencies subject to the governor's control include the California Department of Fish and Wildlife (CDFW), California Coastal Commission, and State Water Resources Control Board (SWRCB). Pursuant to Executive Order B-10-11, the California Department of Fish and Wildlife adopted a tribal consultation policy on June 10, 2015, which can be found at https://www.wildlife.ca.gov/General-Counsel/Tribal-Affairs; the California Coastal Commission adopted a tribal consultation policy on August 8, 2018, which can be found at https://www.coastal.ca.gov/env-justice/tribal-consultation; and, as of the date this book was published, the SWRCB had promulgated a draft tribal consultation policy, which can be found at https://calepa.ca.gov/wp-content/uploads/sites/6/2018/12/2018_SWRCB_Draft-Tribal-Policy_181015.pdf.[7] Broadly speaking, these policies require the applicable agency to communicate and consult with tribes early in the decisionmaking process.

THE NATIONAL HISTORIC PRESERVATION ACT

Background

Section 106 of the National Historic Preservation Act of 1966 (NHPA), as amended[8] requires federal agencies to take into account the effects of their "undertakings" on historic properties and, in various ways, to consult with both the Advisory Council on Historic Preservation ("Council") and the relevant state's historic preservation officer (SHPO) as to the Corps' findings.

In the arena of wetlands and endangered species regulation, the NHPA expresses itself most often in the Corps of Engineers' permitting processes. As described further below, the Corps' procedures under Section 106 can be confusing, because the Corps maintains its own regulations for the purposes of implementing the NHPA, and these regulations conflict with those promulgated by the Council and followed by the California Office of Historic Preservation, which reviews and comments on federal proposals in California. Complicating this even further are federal "government-to-government" processes

CDFW or the "Department" = California Department of Fish and Wildlife

SWRCB = State Water Resources Control Board

NHPA = National Historic Preservation Act

SHPO = State Historic Preservation Officer

5 *Id.*

6 *Id.*

7 In addition, the California Natural Resources Agency adopted a tribal consultation policy on November 20, 2012, available at http://resources.ca.gov/docs/tribal_policy/Final_Tribal_Policy.pdf.

8 54 U.S.C. § 306108. Preservationists and people who deal with preservationists are more likely to discuss Section 106 than 54 U.S.C. Section 306108, which is where the National Historic Preservation Act is codified.

ESA = Endangered Species Act

NEPA = National Environmental Policy Act

NAGPRA = Native American Graves Protection and Repatriation Act

CEQA = California Environmental Quality Act

conducted by the Corps, which require independent discussions with tribes that do not include the same type of applicant participation provided for under Section 106.[9]

Although the U.S. Fish and Wildlife Service complies with the Section 106 process for Habitat Conservation Plans, the Service takes the position that its consideration and issuance of Biological Opinions under Section 7 of ESA does not constitute an undertaking within the meaning of the NHPA.[10] When the Service must comply with Section 106, the Service generally relies on the Council regulations discussed below.[11] Specifically, the Service's Manual states that it will comply with the Section 106 regulations in the Federal Register.[12]

Where possible, it is generally beneficial for the agency that must comply with Section 106 to coordinate Section 106 compliance with reviews required under NEPA, the Native American Graves Protection and Repatriation Act (NAGPRA), the American Indian Religious Freedom Act, the Archeological Resources Protection Act, CEQA (AB 52), SB 18, and agency-specific legislation, such as Section 4(f) of the Department of Transportation Act, to increase efficiency and duplicative efforts.[13] Where consistent with the procedures in Section 106, the agency may be able to use information developed for other federal, state, and local reviews, or tribal law, to satisfy its Section 106 obligations.[14]

Making the Effects Determination

The First Step: Defining the Scope of Review under Section 106

The first analytical step under Section 106 process is to determine whether there is an "undertaking" and, if so, the scope of that undertaking. An "undertaking" is defined under the Council's regulation as "a project, activity, or program funded in whole or in part under the direct or indirect jurisdiction of a federal agency, including those carried out by or on behalf of a federal agency; those carried out with federal financial assistance; those requiring a federal permit, license or approval; and those subject to state or local regulation administered pursuant to a delegation or approval by a federal agency."[15]

The Council's regulations require that the federal agency take into account the direct *and indirect* effects that the undertaking may have on historic properties, which are defined as those that are either listed on, or eligible for inclusion in, the National

---

9   36 C.F.R. § 800.2(c)(5).

10   See U.S. Fish & Wildlife Service Manual, 614 FW 2 (August 2016), available at https://www.fws.gov/policy/614fw2.html#section27. Although the Service's Manual states that merely because an activity is not discussed in the section regarding compliance with the NHPA, in our experience, and based on the Service's Endangered Species Consultation Handbook (available at https://www.fws.gov/endangered/esa-library/pdf/esa_section7_handbook.pdf), the Service does not consider a Biological Opinion to be an undertaking requiring Section 106 consultation.

11   U.S. Fish & Wildlife Service Manual, 614 FW 3 (August 2016), available at https://www.fws.gov/policy/614fw3.html.

12   *Id.*

13   36 C.F.R. § 800.3(b).

14   *Id.*

15   *Id.* § 800.16.

Register of Historic Places. This concept of direct and indirect effects has been problem-atic for Corps undertakings at the outset when defining the undertaking when only a portion of a project requires a federal permit, such as the issuance of a Section 404 per-mit for authorized fill of waters of the United States within a larger development foot-print. Generally speaking, if a portion of a contiguous project is carried out with a federal permit, then the entire project is "federalized" for the purposes of Section 106.[16] The Corps' Appendix C regulations, however, reject this notion; the Corps routinely cites a lack of jurisdiction over uplands. This disagreement frequently manifests during Section 106 consultation.

APE = Area of Potential Effects

The California Office of Historic Preservation or the State Historic Preservation Officer (both of which we refer to in this chapter as the "SHPO") typically rejects the Corps' use of Appendix C and has offered its own specific guidance on this question, taking the position that non-federal portions of a project should be considered part of a federal undertaking where the two components serve a "unified end," and offering the following examples:

> A road that is being built from Point A to Point B with federal and state dollars cannot extract or exclude a section in the middle of the road from Section 106 review even if only state funds will be used to construct that middle section because that middle section would not be built absent the project between Points A and B.

> Suppose a community wants to build a conference center with local funds, but the site they have chosen would require that the Federal Highway Administration construct a highway off-ramp to access the project. The new conference center, regardless of the resources used to construct it, would be sub-ject to Section 106 review because its very existence depends on the highway off-ramp.

In other words, if not but for the federal undertaking, historic properties may be indirectly affected. For this reason (and much to the chagrin of SHPO and Council), the Corps has increasingly utilized an argument of independent utility to narrow its jurisdic-tion to that which is more consistent with its own Appendix C regulations.

But the inquiry does not end with a determination of the scope of the undertaking itself. The next step is to determine the "Area of Potential Effects" (APE) of the under-taking. The APE is defined broadly under Council's regulations to include the "geo-graphic area or areas within which an undertaking may directly or indirectly cause changes in the character or use of historic properties, if any such properties exist," and "is influenced by the scale and nature of an undertaking and may be different for differ-ent kinds of effects caused by the undertaking."[17]

16   *Colorado River Indian Tribes v. Marsh*, 605 F. Supp. 1425, 1438 (C.D. Cal. 1985) (holding that the Corps violated the NHPA by failing to examine potential adverse effects outside within the Corps' permit area, but within the area to be disturbed by the proposed development).

17   36 C.F.R. § 800.16.

THPO = Tribal Historic
Preservation Officer

The location of the APE—which is typically depicted as a line on a map—depends on the likely direct physical effects that the undertaking may have on historic properties, including visual, auditory, and sociocultural effects, as well as indirect or secondary effects. Indirect effects can include urban decay or increased development due to the project (for example, a roadway project that creates new access to an undeveloped area). Indirect effect may also include neglect of a historic structure, or damage caused by increased visitation to archaeological sites that would not have been possible without the project. The size of the APE may or may not match the physical footprint of the undertaking. For example, the APE for the construction of infrastructure for a proposed mixed-use community could exceed the property boundaries because that infrastructure could induce future development in the area, result in changes in traffic volumes, or changes in land use, all of which could have an adverse impact on historic properties.

The Second Step: Identifying Consulting Parties

As part of its initial planning, the acting federal agency must identify the appropriate SHPO and, where applicable, the appropriate "Tribal Historic Preservation Officer" (THPO) as designated under Section 106.[18] Typically, this can be done as soon as an undertaking is defined although, if the APE turns out to be larger than the permit area, then there may be more consulting parties than initially thought.

If an undertaking will occur on or affect historic properties located on tribal lands, and the relevant tribe has assumed SHPO's responsibilities for Section 106, the agency consults with that tribe as the THPO rather than the State's SHPO. Certain owners of property on tribal lands can, however, request SHPO involvement in addition to the THPO. If the relevant tribe has not assumed SHPO responsibilities for Section 106, the acting federal agency will consult with both the tribe and SHPO.[19] If more than one state is involved in an undertaking, the involved SHPOs may agree to designate a lead SHPO to act on their behalf.[20]

Once the right SHPO and/or THPO have been identified, the acting federal agency should work with those entities to identify any other person or entity entitled to be "consulting parties" and invite them to participate as such.[21] The usual consulting parties include local governments, project applicants, and Indian tribes or Native Hawaiian organizations that may attach religious and cultural significance to resources in the APE.[22] Indeed, because the project sponsor will be responsible for carrying out the project as may be modified as the result of Section 106, the project sponsor's input during consultation as to feasibility is also critical and is often inadvertently overlooked as a consulting party. The acting federal agency can invite others to participate as consulting

---

18   36 C.F.R. § 800.3(c).

19   *Id.*

20   *Id.* § 800.3(c)(2).

21   *Id.* § 800.3(f).

22   *Id.* §§ 800.2(c)(3), 800.2(c)(4), 800.2(c)(5), 800.3(f)(1), 800.3(f)(2).

parties as the Section 106 process moves forward, and consider written requests from individuals and organizations wishing to participate as consulting parties.[23] In addition to identifying the consulting parties, the agency should decide how and when to involve the public.[24]

The Third Step: Identifying Resources

Once the APE is established, in addition to identifying the consulting parties, the APE must be researched and surveyed to determine whether it contains any historic properties, which are defined to include "any prehistoric or historic district, site, building, structure, or object included in, or eligible for inclusion in, the National Register of Historic Places."[25] Federal agencies must make a reasonable and good faith effort to identify historic resources that retain integrity in the APE, which can include background research, consultation, oral history interviews, sample field investigation, and field surveys, as well as working with the consulting parties.[26]

A resource is considered "eligible for inclusion in" the National Register if it is not listed but nonetheless meets the criteria for listing. Districts, sites, buildings, structures, and objects that "possess integrity" of location, design, setting, materials, workmanship, feeling, or association *and* meet one of the four criteria are eligible for listing on the National Register. These criteria treat as eligible any resource that:

> is associated with events that have made a significant contribution to the broad patterns of American history

> is associated with the lives of persons significant in America's past

> embodies the distinctive characteristics of a type, period, or method of construction, or that represent the work of a master, or that possess high artistic values, or that represent a significant and distinguishable entity whose components may lack individual distinction; or

> has yielded or may be likely to yield, information important in prehistory or history[27]

The term "integrity" describes the ability of a property to convey its historic significance. Historic properties either retain integrity—the essential qualities that define both why a property is significant and when it was significant—or they do not. The evaluation of integrity requires an understanding of how a property's physical features relate to the reasons it is eligible for listing (or listed) on the National Register. A property that lacks some of its historic physical features or characteristics can still be eligible for listing in the National Register if it nevertheless retains sufficient integrity. In addition, depending upon why the property is significant, the condition of the property does not necessarily correlate

---

23   *Id.* § 800.3(f).

24   *Id.* § 800.3(e).

25   *Id.*

26   *Id.* § 800.4(b)(1).

27   *Id.* § 60.4.

to integrity. For example, regardless of the conditions of structures on the land that housed Washington's troops for two winters, the location itself may retain sufficient integrity to convey its significance in the Revolutionary War.[28]

The National Register contains a wide range of historic property *types*, including: (1) buildings, structures, and sites; (2) groups of buildings, structures or sites that form historic districts; (3) landscapes; and (4) individual objects. Together, these properties reflect many different kinds of significance, including in architecture, history, archeology, engineering, and culture. For purposes of the NHPA, "culture" is understood to mean the traditions, beliefs, practices, lifeways, arts, crafts, and social institutions of a community, be it an Indian tribe, a local ethnic group, or the people of the nation as a whole.[29]

One kind of cultural significance a property may possess is traditional cultural significance. "Traditional" refers "to those beliefs, customs, and practices of a living community of people that have been passed down through the generations, usually orally or through practice."[30] A traditional cultural property is a property "that is eligible for inclusion in the National Register because of its association with cultural practices or beliefs of a living community that (a) are rooted in that community's history, and (b) are important in maintaining the continuing cultural identity of the community."[31] The National Park Service provides the following examples of properties possessing traditional cultural significance that may make them eligible for listing on the National Register:

> a location associated with the traditional beliefs of a Native American group about its origins, its cultural history, or the nature of the world

> a rural community whose organization, buildings and structures, or patterns of land use reflect the cultural traditions valued by its long-term residents

> an urban neighborhood that is the traditional home of a particular cultural group, and that reflects its beliefs and practices

> a location where Native American religious practitioners have historically gone, and are known or thought to go today, to perform ceremonial activities in accordance with traditional cultural rules of practice

> a location where a community has traditionally carried out economic, artistic, or other cultural practices important in maintaining its historic identity.

As these examples illustrate, identifying resources eligible for listing on the National Register may require both research in archives as well as discussions with current community members. Although Native American traditional cultural properties are one of the most common types, these properties need not be associated with Native American culture.

---

28 Morristown National Historical Park, National Register Number 66000053; nomination packet available at https://npgallery.nps.gov/AssetDetail/NRIS/66000053.

29 National Register Bulletin 38, Appendix I, available at https://www.nps.gov/nr/publications/bulletins/nrb38/nrb38%20apendix%201.htm.

30 National Register Bulletin 38.

31 *Id.*

The Fourth Step: Effects Determination

Once the acting federal agency has determined that a cultural resource may be present with an APE, the agency must then assess the effects that a project may have on that property, making one of the following three findings: (1) no historic properties affected, (2) no adverse effect to historic properties, or (3) adverse effect to historic properties.[32] When making this determination, "consideration shall be given to all qualifying characteristics of a historic property, including those that may have been identified subsequent to the original evaluation of the property's eligibility for the National Register."[33]

The determination "no historic properties affected" means that either there are no historic properties in the APE or that there are historic properties, but the project will have no effect on them.[34]

"No adverse effect" means there are historic properties present in the APE and the project will have an effect on them, but this effect is not adverse.[35] Typically, this finding is reached when the project activities avoid the properties or mitigation adequately protects the properties.[36] A no adverse effect finding may also be concluded when effects are considered de minimus and that post-project integrity of the historic property will not differ from pre-project integrity. Because there will be no adverse effects on historic properties, no mitigation to resolve adverse effects is required; however, project sponsors may elect to incorporate project design changes that will result in a no adverse effect finding.

A finding of "adverse effect" means that there are historic properties present in the APE, the project will have an effect on them, and this effect is adverse.[37] An adverse effect is an action that may "alter, directly or indirectly, any of the characteristics that qualify the property for inclusion in the National Register in a manner that would diminish the integrity of the property's location, design, setting, materials, workmanship, feeling, or association."[38] Adverse effects can "include reasonably foreseeable effects caused by the undertaking that may occur later in time, be farther removed in distance or be cumulative."[39]

Adverse effects include, but are not limited to:

> demolition
> alteration that is inconsistent with the Secretary of the Interior's standards for the treatment of historic properties and applicable guidelines
> removal of a resource from its historic location
> change in use or of physical features within the property's setting that contribute to its historic significance

32   *Id.* § 800.5(a), (b).

33   *Id.* § 800.5(a)(1).

34   *Id.* § 800.4(d)(1).

35   *Id.* § 800.5(b).

36   *Id.*

37   *Id.* § 800.5(d)(2).

38   *Id.* § 800.5(a)(1).

39   *Id.*

MOA = Memorandum of Agreement

PA = Programmatic Agreement

> neglect or abandonment
> introduction of visual, atmospheric, or audible elements that diminish the integrity of the property's significant historic features
> transfer, lease, or sale of the property out of federal ownership without adequate and legally enforceable restrictions or conditions to ensure long-term preservation of the property's historic significance.[40]

Because an adverse effect will occur, the federal agency is required to take efforts to avoid, minimize, or resolve (mitigate) those adverse effects, in that order of preference. As discussed in the next section, mitigation often is determined through consultation, resulting in a Memorandum of Agreement (MOA) or Programmatic Agreement (PA), depending on the type of project and its effects on historic resources. Implementation of the undertaking in accordance with the finding as documented fulfills the agency official's Section 106 responsibilities.[41]

Once the federal agency has made its determination, it notifies SHPO and, where appropriate, the THPO and consulting tribes or Native Hawaiian Organization, sending them its determination and reasons supporting the determination. In practice, the federal agency affords these consulting parties 30 days to review the determination; however, the Council's regulations implementing Section 106 only require that the federal agency afford the Council (via SHPO) 30 days to comment. If SHPO does not respond within 30 days, the agency may move forward.[42] With respect to other consulting parties, the federal agency need only take into account the comments provided by those parties when making a determination. "Approval" from SHPO, THPO, tribes, or consulting parties is not required. The exception is when the Section 106 consultation process terminates in a MOA or PA, for which signatories and invited signatories (but not concurring or consulting parties) must agree in order to execute the agreement document.

The California SHPO may respond in several ways to the request for comment from a federal agency. Although SHPO concurrence is *not* required by the Council's regulations, the most favorable response for a project is a response from SHPO of "I concur." This response constitutes an agreement with the federal agency. The next best response is "I do not object," in which SHPO may not fully concur, but will not stand in the way of the federal agency. In some cases, a response of this type may be accompanied by conditions, such as that the federal agency incorporates certain permit conditions. The third best response is no response at all. As described above, a response from SHPO is not required, but as a practical matter, federal agencies (and typically the Corps) do not feel comfortable exercising their rights to proceed absent SHPO concurrence. The least favorable response from SHPO is "I object," which has a similar response from the Corps.

40 *Id.*

41 *Id.* § 800.5(d)(1).

42 A SHPO's failure to respond to an agency's determination proposal is not a "concurrence," but instead "no response." The regulations do not require SHPO to respond to the agency.

If there is a disagreement, the federal agency can either consult with the dissenting party to resolve the issue or follow dispute resolution procedures by requesting that the Council review the finding and determination (or the consulting party can request Council review). If it is requested to do so, the Council has 30 days to review the determination and reasons supporting it and can then either agree or disagree. If the Council disagrees, the Council must provide the agency a written opinion within 15 days of receiving the documented finding from the agency official. The Council, at its discretion, may extend that time period for another 15 days.

If the Council provides an opinion, the acting federal agency must take it into account when making a final decision on the finding. The person to whom the Council addresses its opinion (the agency official or the head of the agency) must prepare a summary of the decision that contains the rationale for the decision and evidence of consideration of the Council's opinion, and provide it to the Council, SHPO/THPO, and the consulting parties. If the agency official's initial finding will be revised, the agency official shall proceed in accordance with the revised finding. If the final decision of the agency is to affirm the initial finding of no adverse effect, once the summary of the decision has been sent to the Council, SHPO/THPO, and the consulting parties, the agency official's responsibilities under Section 106 are fulfilled.

TCP = traditional cultural property

TCR = tribal cultural resource

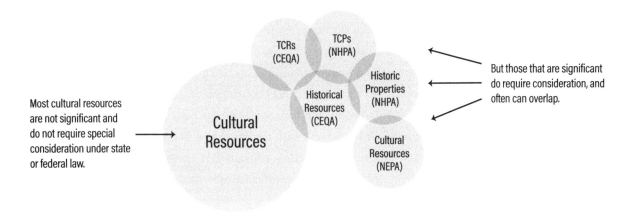

Diagram courtesy of Lisa Westwood.

The Consultation Process

If historic properties are identified within the APE and the undertaking would adversely affect them, the acting federal agency must consult with the consulting parties, which can include SHPO, THPO, Indian tribes and Native Hawaiian organizations, and the project applicant, to resolve the adverse effect.[43] The agency and consulting parties together develop and evaluate alternatives or modifications to the undertaking that could avoid, minimize, or mitigate adverse effects on historic properties.[44] The agency

43   *Id.* § 800.5(d)(2).

44   *Id.* § 800.6(a).

official also must notify the Council of the adverse effect and can invite the Council to participate in the consultation. The SHPO/THPO, an Indian tribe, a Native Hawaiian organization, or any other consulting party also may, at any time, independently request the Council participate in consultation. After receiving a request, the Council has 15 days to advise whether it will participate.

When an Indian tribe is a consulting party, the tribe may request discussions with the lead agency on a government-to-government basis, and ask that the applicant be excluded from those discussions. To the extent such discussions cover specifics about how to minimize the undertaking's adverse effects on resources important to the tribe, they ultimately may lengthen the consultation process and result in disappointing or frustrating both the tribe and the applicant. For example, an agency and tribe may agree that relocating a proposed pipeline would best protect historic properties. But when the agency presents this conclusion to the applicant, the applicant may explain that it already looked at that solution, but cannot relocate the pipeline as requested because that would place the pipeline directly on an active fault and require disturbance of bio-logically sensitive vegetation. When the agency returns to the tribe to explain that the agreed approach will not work, the tribe may lose confidence that the agency is address-ing its concerns and negotiating in good faith. If the consulting parties distrust each other, the Section 106 consultation typically lasts longer than when the parties have a good relationship and more likely leads to results that neither the tribe nor the applicant support. This hypothetical illustrates the importance of the applicant in the Section 106 process. The applicant, as the party that wants and will implement the undertaking, best understands the on-the-ground practicalities and constraints of construction and oper-ation, and thus provides a key voice during consultation.

Once consultation begins, the agency official has a duty to provide all consulting parties with relevant information, with the exception of confidential archeological, Native Hawaiian, and tribal information, relevant to resolving the adverse effects. The agency official also makes non-confidential information available to the public and provides an opportunity for the public to express their views on resolving the under-taking's adverse effects. These views are considered when resolving the adverse effects. Consultation should lead to a MOA or PA, but also can end with a failure to resolve adverse effects. Whereas PAs are used when the effects of an undertaking are not fully known, MOAs are used to resolve known and definable adverse effects on historic properties.

Programmatic Agreements

A programmatic agreement (PA) is a legally binding agreement between the consulting parties and any invited signatories and which establishes a process for consultation, review, and compliance with the NHPA and other federal laws concerning historic pres-ervation. It can be a tool for the implementation of approaches that do not follow the normal Section 106 process, particularly where an atypical approach will streamline and enhance historic preservation and project objectives.

NCSHPO = National Conference of State Historic Preservation Officers

PAs are particularly encouraged for large, complex projects or programs that have at least one of the following features:

> similar and repetitive effects of historic properties
> the effects cannot be fully determined prior to approval of the project
> nonfederal parties are delegated major decisionmaking responsibilities
> effects would result from routine maintenance
> circumstances warrant a departure from the normal Section 106 process[45]

The development of a PA involves lengthy consultation and public participation, and frequently takes more than a year to complete.[46] Once signed, compliance with the procedures established by the PA satisfies the federal agency's obligations under Section 106 for all undertakings covered by the agreement until it expires or is terminated by the federal agency, the president of the National Conference of State Historic Preservation Officers (NCSHPO) when a signatory, or the Council.[47] Termination by a SHPO or THPO only terminates the application of a regional programmatic agreement within the jurisdiction of SHPO or THPO.[48] Concurring or consulting parties that sign the PA (but not as signatories) have no power to terminate the PA. Failure of a concurring party to sign the PA does not invalidate the agreement. Once the PA is executed by all signatories, the federal agency's pre-project consultation under Section 106 is complete and the agency can proceed with permit issuance, authorization, or funding. The PA—either through a Cultural Resources Management Plan or similar document—will stipulate the phasing and completion of the agreed-upon measures, and the timing of such activities relative to the project.

The Council also may create a prototype PA that may be used for the same type of program or undertaking in more than one case or area.[49] One example in California is the PA between the California Department of Transportation ("Caltrans"), SHPO, and the Federal Highway Administration. When an agency official uses such a prototype PA, the agency official may develop and execute the agreement with the appropriate SHPO and THPO and the agreement becomes final without need for Council participation in consultation or Council signature.[50]

In March 2018, the Corps' Sacramento, San Francisco, and Los Angeles Districts (the "Districts") issued a notice that they would be developing a PA as a program alternative for compliance with Section 106 in California. The goal is to reduce the overall permit application review times for activities subject to the Districts' authorization by

45 *Id.* § 800.14(b)(1).
46 *Id.* § 800.14(b)(2).
47 *Id.* § 800.14(b)(2)(iii).
48 *Id.*
49 *Id.* § 800.14(b)(4).
50 *Id.*

accomplishing the objectives of Section 106 in a more flexible and expeditious manner. The regulated community hopes that another outcome of this process will be to make the Corps' existing, controversial process for cultural resource review set forth in Appendix C to the Corps' regulations (discussed below) more compatible with the Council's regulations. The proposed PA would cover activities now considered under Appendix C, but would exclude undertakings that occur on or affect tribal lands unless the affected tribe requests in writing to have the proposed project considered in accordance with the PA.

The proposed California PA would cover the following actions by the Districts:

> exclusion from consultation with the California SHPO regarding any finding of "no historic properties affected" when there are no identified cultural resources within or immediately adjacent to the permit area and APE and the following conditions are met:

  (1) completion of a defined minimum level of effort regarding cultural resource identification

  (2) consultation with appropriate interested and consulting parties, including but not limited to federally recognized tribes

  (3) no indirect effects to historic properties located outside the permit area are identified; and

  (4) internal review of "no historic properties affected" determination by a person meeting specified qualifications and appropriate documentation of such review

> exclusion from consultation with the California SHPO regarding any finding of "no historic properties affected" when there are historic properties within or immediately adjacent to the permit area and APE, but the historic properties will not be affected and the following are met:

  (1) completion of a defined minimum level of effort regarding cultural resource identification

  (2) consultation with appropriate interested and consulting parties, including but not limited to federally recognized tribes

  (3) appropriate avoidance measures are included in the project proposal to ensure avoidance of any identified historic properties

  (4) no indirect effects to historic properties located outside the permit area are identified; and

  (5) internal review of "no historic properties affected" determination by a person meeting specified qualifications and appropriate documentation of such review

> exemption from Section 106 review if the nature of a specific activity is unlikely to adversely affect historic properties, even if one were present; a list and description of activities would be defined during development of the proposed PA

In addition to the above, the Districts propose to include reporting procedures, including an annual report to the Council and the California SHPO summarizing all Districts' authorizations reviewed under the PA.[51]

Memoranda of Agreement

If the agency official and SHPO and (if applicable) THPO agree on how the adverse effects will be resolved, and if the criteria for use of a PA are not met, they will execute an MOA.[52] An MOA must include a provision that addresses termination and reconsideration of terms if the undertaking has not been implemented within a specified time and may include provisions to deal with the subsequent discovery or identification of additional historic properties affected by the undertaking.[53] The agency official must ensure that the undertaking is carried out in accordance with the MOA and, where appropriate, can include a provision for monitoring and reporting on the MOA's implementation.[54] The agency official submits a copy of the executed MOA, along with the required documentation, to the Council prior to approving the undertaking in order to meet the requirements of Section 106.[55]

Depending on whether the Council is a signatory, the MOA signatories will be the agency official, SHPO/THPO, and if it so chooses, Council.[56] The agency official also can invite additional parties to be signatories, including an Indian tribe or Native Hawaiian organization that attaches religious and cultural significance to historic properties located off tribal lands, and should invite the party that will be responsible for performing the undertaking.[57] All signatories have the same rights with regard to seeking amendment or termination of the MOA. The agency official can invite all consulting parties to concur in the MOA and the signatories may agree to invite others to concur.[58] The refusal of any invited or concurring party to concur in the MOA does not invalidate the MOA.[59] Failure of a concurring party to sign the MOA does not invalidate the agreement. If a MOA requires amendment, it must be executed in the same manner as the original MOA.[60]

Similar to a PA, once the MOA is executed by all signatories, the federal agency's pre-project consultation under Section 106 is complete and the agency can proceed with permit issuance, authorization, or funding. However, the MOA—either through a

---

51 Letter from Michael S. Jewell, Chief, Regulatory Division, Sacramento Division to Dr. John T. Eddins, Ph.D., Federal Permitting, Licensing, and Assistance Section Office of Federal Agency Programs, Advisory Council on Historic Preservation (April 27, 2017).

52 36 C.F.R. § 800.6(b)(1)(iv).

53 *Id.* § 800.6(c)(4)–(8).

54 *Id.* § 800.6(c)(4).

55 *Id.*

56 *Id.* § 800.6(c)(1).

57 *Id.* § 800.6(c)(2).

58 *Id.* § 800.6(c)(3).

59 *Id.* § 800.6(c)(2)(iv).

60 *Id.* § 800.6(c)(7).

Historic Properties Treatment Plan or similar document—will stipulate the requirements for the completion of the agreed-upon measures, and the timing of such activities relative to the project. In many cases, the standard treatments established by the Council provide an appropriate basis for an MOA.[61] Standard treatments are a program alternative that allows the Council to establish standardized practices for dealing with certain categories of undertakings, effects, historic properties, or treatment options and carry the Council's explicit endorsement. Federal agencies are not obligated to follow approved standard treatments, but may elect to do so when they feel standard treatments will be of benefit in meeting their Section 106 compliance requirements.

As a practical matter, most mitigation must be completed to the satisfaction of the federal agency before a project proponent may proceed with authorized activities. Depending upon the amount of mitigation required by the MOA, this may lead to delays between permit issuance and actual start of construction.

Failure to Resolve Adverse Effects

After consulting to resolve adverse effects, the agency official, SHPO/THPO, or the Council may determine that further consultation will be unproductive and terminate consultation.[62] Any party that terminates consultation must notify the other consulting parties and provide them the reasons for terminating in writing.[63] If the agency official terminates consultation, the head of the agency or an Assistant Secretary or other officer with major department-wide or agency-wide responsibilities requests that the Council comment on the proposed termination. If SHPO terminates consultation, the agency official and the Council can execute a MOA without SHPO's involvement, in which case SHPO will not be a signatory. If a THPO terminates consultation regarding an undertaking occurring on or affecting historic properties on its tribal lands, the THPO must notify the Council and ask for Council comment. The agency must consider the Council's comments when making the final termination determination. If the Council terminates consultation, the Council notifies the agency official, the agency's federal preservation officer and all consulting parties of the termination. The head of the agency must document the termination by (1) preparing a summary of the decision that contains the rationale for the decision and evidence of consideration of the Council's comments and providing it to the Council prior to approval of the undertaking, (2) providing a copy of the summary to all consulting parties; and (3) notifying the public and making the record available for public inspection.[64]

When a PA or an MOA is terminated by one of the signatories, the federal agency must default back to "straight Section 106 compliance," which means that any streamlining or phasing afforded by the PA or MOA are no longer in effect.

---

61 *Id.* § 800.6(b)(1)(ii).

62 *Id.* § 800.7(a).

63 *Id.*

64 *Id.* § 800.7(c)(4).

Post-Review Discoveries

It is not uncommon to encounter unknown resources during the undertaking. PAs and MOAs generally include procedures for how to handle finds that occur after the Section 106 process is completed.[65] If a resource is discovered after Section 106 review has occurred and the agency takes actions in conformance with the agreed PA or MOA process to resolve adverse effects on resources discovered after beginning the undertaking, the agency is deemed to satisfy its Section 106 obligations.[66]

If the agency did not establish a process to deal with discoveries and new historic properties are discovered or unanticipated effects on known historic properties are found after Section 106 is done, the agency must make reasonable efforts to avoid, minimize or mitigate adverse effects to such properties.[67] If the agency has not approved the undertaking or if construction on an approved undertaking has not commenced, then the agency can reopen the Section 106 consultation. Alternatively, the agency, SHPO/THPO, and any tribe or Native Hawaiian organization that might attach significance to the affected property can agree that such property is of value solely for its scientific, prehistoric, historic or archeological data. In such a case, the agency may comply with the Archeological and Historic Preservation Act instead of reopening the Section 106 process, and provide the Council, SHPO/THPO, and the Indian tribe or Native Hawaiian organization with a report on the actions within a reasonable time after they are completed.[68]

If the new resource or unanticipated adverse effect is discovered after the project applicant has begun construction and off tribal land, and there is no agreed process for dealing with unanticipated effects on historic properties, then the agency must determine how to resolve adverse effects and, within 48 hours of the find, notify SHPO/THPO, any Indian tribe or Native Hawaiian organization that might attach significance to the affected property, and the Council of the discovery. The notification needs to describe the agency's assessment of whether the discovered resource is eligible for the National Register and the proposed actions to resolve adverse effects.[69] The SHPO/THPO, Indian tribe or Native Hawaiian organization, and Council have 48 hours to respond to the notification, and the agency should consider their input when deciding the appropriate course of action.[70] The agency, in consultation with SHPO/THPO, also can choose to assume the discovery is Register-eligible for the purposes of Section 106 and determine the appropriate action to minimize adverse effects based on that assumption.[71] After the action is complete, the agency must provide SHPO/THPO, Indian

---

65   *Id.* § 800.13(a)(1), (2).

66   *Id.*

67   *Id.* § 800.13(b).

68   *Id.* § 800.13(b)(1), (2).

69   *Id.* § 800.13(b)(3).

70   *Id.*

71   *Id.* § 800.13(c).

MMS = Minerals Management
Service

EIS = Environmental Impact
Statement

tribe or Native Hawaiian organization, and Council a report describing the agency's action. If the new resources or unanticipated adverse effect is discovered after the project applicant has begun construction and is on tribal land, and there is no agreed process for dealing with unanticipated effects on historic properties, the agency must comply with applicable tribal regulations and procedures and obtain the concurrence of the Indian tribe on the proposed action to minimize adverse effects on the resource.[72]

Foreclosure

The Section 106 process should begin well before an agency approves a project. When a federal project is approved and started without Section 106 consultation, the Council's opportunity to comment on the undertaking is "foreclosed." The Council may review a case to determine whether a foreclosure has occurred.[73] When this occurs, the Council notifies the agency official and the agency's federal preservation officer that it believes the agency failed to comply with Section 106 and gives the agency 30 days to provide information regarding its compliance. After reviewing the agency response, if the Council determines foreclosure has occurred, the Council transmits the determination to the agency official and the head of the agency, and makes the determination available to the public and any parties known to be interested in the undertaking and its effects upon historic properties.[74] A foreclosure finding can prevent an agency from approving an environmental certification and also cause the Council to take a closer look at an agency's Section 106 practices.

Foreclosure can occur when tribal consultation is delayed, ultimately causing project delays. For example, the Corps and the Minerals Management Service (MMS) allegedly failed to undertake timely tribal consultation prior to the approval of the Cape Wind project in Nantucket Sound. After the MMS released the final Environmental Impact Statement (EIS), the Keeper of the National Register of Historic Places ("Keeper") determined the Nantucket Sound is National Register-eligible as a Traditional Cultural Property. The Council criticized the belated consultation in comments to the Secretary of the Interior, although the Secretary of the Interior approved the project, with the condition that the plans be modified to protect sacred and cultural sites and the promise to engage in additional consultation. Had consultation occurred at the beginning of the environmental review process rather than after the release of the EIS, the Section 106 consultation could have informed the EIS's alternative analysis and post-approval delays may have been lessened or avoided.

Foreclosure also can occur when a project applicant intentionally takes an action that causes an adverse effect to a historic property with the intent to avoid the Section 106

72 *Id.* § 800.13(d).

73 *Id.* § 800.9(b).

74 *Id.*

process.[75] In such a case, NHPA Section 110(k) is applicable. That section is discussed in Section III, below.

ACHP = Advisory Council on Historic Preservation

CORPS OF ENGINEERS PROCEDURES

The Corps has adopted a regulatory program (33 Code of Federal Regulations 325, Appendix C ("Appendix C") with implementing regulations for NHPA compliance, although the Council has not approved this program. Appendix C is organized to follow the Corps standard permit process and clarifies how the Corps will consider and address historic properties during the processing and evaluating of permit applications. Appendix C does not apply to the Corps' Section 408 authorizations for modifications of federal levees.

Due to controversy over Appendix C, particularly over its differences with the Council regulations related to the area examined for potential adverse impacts to historic properties, definition of adverse effects, triggers for tribal consultation, and treatment of confidential information, not all district engineers rely on Appendix C. Instead, some district engineers follow the Council regulations, particularly for projects that involve tribal land or cultural resources, or make their consultation co-compliant with both sets of regulations. As discussed below, Appendix C tends to narrow the area where the Corps considers impacts to historic properties and the scope of the actions that may cause adverse effects as compared to the Council regulations. Thus Section 106 compliance under Appendix C generally takes less time and results in fewer project modifications than Section 106 compliance under the Council regulations; however, the Corps' use of the Appendix C regulations is nearly always met with objection from SHPO and the Advisory Council on Historic Preservation (ACHP).

Initial Review

Under Appendix C, the district engineer is generally the "agency official" within the Corps responsible for ensuring that Corps permits comply with Section 106. The Corps' process under Appendix C begins with the agency's initial review of an application, including district files and records, the National Register, lists of properties determined eligible for the National Register, and other sources of information, to determine if there are any designated or undesignated historic properties that may be affected by the proposed undertaking. As part of the initial review, the Corps must determine the "permit area" (i.e., the Corps' interpretation of an APE) which consists of those areas comprising the waters of the United States that will be *directly affected* by the proposed work or structures and uplands *directly affected* as a result of authorizing the work or structures. Under Appendix C and in conflict with the Council's regulations, the Corps does not typically consider indirect effects that the issuance of its permit will have on historic properties that are in uplands, even if those properties fall within the project's overall footprint. Appendix C states that the following three factors all must be satisfied

75   *Id.* § 800.9(c).

NPS = National Park Service

for an activity undertaken outside the waters of the United States to be included in the permit area:

(1) the activity would not occur but for the authorization of the work or structures within the waters of the United States

(2) the activity must be integrally related to the work or structures to be authorized in waters of the United States or the work or structures in the water of the United States must be essential to the completeness of the overall project or program; and

(3) the activity must be directly associated with the work or structures to be authorized. Appendix C provides three examples of how to apply the three factors to determine if work occurring outside the waters of the United States should be included in the permit area. These examples are quoted on the facing page.

If the Corps determines that a historic property is unlikely to exist or be affected, then a statement to that effect will be included in its public notice. The Corps may reach this conclusion if the undertaking will occur in an area that has been extensively modified, was created relatively recently (such as a man-made island), or the undertaking is extremely limited in nature and scope. Conversely, if the Corps determines that the undertaking may affect a historic property, the Corps discusses as early as possible with the applicant measures or alternatives to avoid or minimize effects on historic properties.

The Corps must release a public notice when it receives an application for a permit under Section 404. This notice must include the district engineer's current knowledge of the presence or absence of historic properties and the anticipated effects of the undertaking on them. This notice is sent to SHPO, the regional office of the National Park Service (NPS), any relevant local governments certified to carry out responsibilities under the NHPA, Indian tribes, and interested citizens. If there are designated historic properties or properties that likely meet the criteria for inclusion in the NRHP that could be affected by the undertaking, the public notice also is sent to the Council. Interested parties have 30 days from the date of the public notice to submit comments to the Corps. If the district engineer discovers during its evaluation of the application that additional historic resources that were not identified at the time of permit application may be affected by the undertaking, the district engineer immediately informs the applicant, SHPO, the appropriate certified local government and the Council. Commencing from the date of the district engineer's letter, these entities have 30 days to submit additional comments.[76]

Further Investigations

If the undertaking, including any upland areas, would occur in a location with a potentially eligible property, the district engineer will determine if further investigation is

---

76 Both the Corps' Appendix C regulations and the Council regulations have emergency procedures that streamline the Section 106 process when action must occur quickly. The discussion in this chapter does not address the emergency procedures.

CORPS GUIDANCE ON PERMIT AREA (APPENDIX C)

[C]onsider an application for a permit to construct a pier and dredge an access channel so that an industry may be established and operated on an upland area.

(1) Assume that the industry requires the access channel and the pier and that without such channel and pier[,] the project would not be feasible. Clearly then, the industrial site, even though upland, would be within the "permit area." It would not be established "but for" the access channel and pier; it also is integrally related to the work and structure to be authorized; and finally it is directly associated with the work and structure to be authorized. Similarly, all three tests are satisfied for the dredged material disposal site and it too is in the "permit area" even if located on uplands.

(2) Consider further that the industry, if established, would cause local agencies to extend water and sewer lines to service the area of the industrial site. Assume that the extension would not itself involve the waters of the United States and is not solely the result of the industrial facility. The extensions would not be within the "permit area" because they would not be directly associated with the work or structure to be authorized.

(3) Now consider that the industry, if established, would require increased housing for its employees, but that a private developer would develop the housing. Again, even if the housing would not be developed but for the authorized work and structure, the housing would not be within the permit area because it would not be directly associated with or integrally related to the work or structure to be authorized.[1]

Consider a different example. This time an industry will be established that requires no access to the navigable waters for its operation. The plans for the facility, however, call for a recreational pier with an access channel. The pier and channel will be used for the company-owned yacht and employee recreation. In the example, the industrial site is not included within the permit area. Only areas of dredging, dredged material disposal, and pier construction would be within the permit area.

Lastly, consider a linear crossing of the waters of the United States; for example, by a transmission line, pipeline, or highway.

(1) Such projects almost always can be undertaken without Corps authorization, if they are designed to avoid affecting the waters of the United States. Corps authorization is sought because it is less expensive or more convenient for the applicant to do so than to avoid affecting the waters of the United States. Thus the "but for" test is not met by the entire project right-of-way. The "same undertaking" and "integral relationship" tests are met, but this is not sufficient to make the whole right-of-way part of the permit area. Typically, however, some portion of the right-of-way, approaching the crossing, would not occur in its given configuration "but for" the authorized activity. This portion of the right-of-way, whose location is determined by the location of the crossing, meets all three tests and hence is part of the permit area.

(2) Accordingly, in the case of the linear crossing, the permit area shall extend in either direction from the crossing to that point at which alternative alignments leading to reasonable alternative locations for the crossing can be considered and evaluated. Such a point may often coincide with the physical feature of the waterbody to be crossed, for example, a bluff, the limit of the flood plain, a vegetational change, etc., or with a jurisdictional feature associated with the waterbody, for example, a zoning change, easement limit, etc., although such features should not be controlling in selecting the limits of the permit area.

---

1 This portion of the example makes the most sense if the timing, extent, and impacts of housing could not be reasonably assessed by the project applicant, and the development of housing could proceed without the issuance of the Corps permit (authors' note).

required in light of the information already available. Investigations may consist of any of the following: further consultations with SHPO, the State Archeologist, local governments, Indian tribes, local historical and archeological societies, university archeologists, and others with knowledge and expertise in the identification of historical, archeological, cultural and scientific resources; field examinations; and archeological testing. The Corps generally requires that the applicant conduct the investigations at his or her expense.

Appendix C limits the Corps' responsibility to seek eligibility determinations for potentially eligible historic properties to resources located within waters of the United States and upland areas that are directly affected by the undertaking or related upland activities. Appendix C also states that the Corps is not responsible for identifying or assessing potentially eligible historic properties outside the permit area, although it will consider the effects of undertakings on any such known historic properties.

Eligibility Determination

For a historic property in the permit area that will be directly affected by the undertaking, the district engineer will: (1) treat the historic property as a "designated historic property" if both SHPO and the district engineer agree that it is eligible for inclusion in the National Register; or (2) treat the historic property as not eligible if both SHPO and the district engineer agree that it is not eligible for inclusion in the National Register.

If SHPO and the district engineer disagree or the Council or the Secretary of the Interior request, the district engineer will request a determination of eligibility from the Keeper.[77] If the Keeper determines that the resources are not eligible for listing in the National Register or fails to respond within 45 days of receipt of the request, the district engineer can conclude his or her action on the permit application. Alternatively, if the district engineer and SHPO do not agree and SHPO notifies the district engineer that he or she is nominating a potentially eligible historic property that may be affected by the undertaking for the National Register, the district engineer will wait 30 days for SHPO to nominate the historic property plus 45 days for the Keeper of the National Register to make such determination.

Assessing Effects

During the public notice comment period or within 30 days after the discovery of a history property, the district engineer coordinates with SHPO and determines if there is an effect and if so, assesses the effect. An undertaking has an effect on a designated historic property when the undertaking may alter characteristics of the property that qualified the property for inclusion in the National Register. For the purpose of determining effect, alteration to features of a property's location, setting, or use may be

---

77 The option to request a determination of the Keeper is not unique to Appendix C, but is available to any agency undertaking the Section 106 process.

relevant, and depending on a property's important characteristics, should be considered. An undertaking is considered to have an adverse effect when the effect on a designated historic property may diminish the integrity of the property's location, design, setting, materials, workmanship, feeling, or association. Adverse effects on designated historic properties include, but are not limited to: (1) physical destruction, damage, or alteration of all or part of the property; (2) isolation of the property from or alteration of the character of the property's setting when that character contributes to the property's qualification for the National Register; (3) introduction of visual, audible, or atmospheric elements that are out of character with the property or alter its setting; (4) neglect of a property resulting in its deterioration or destruction; and (5) transfer, lease, or sale of the property. The district engineer can find effects of an undertaking that would normally be adverse *not adverse* under Appendix C in the following instances: (1) when the designated historic property is of value only for its potential contribution to archeological, historical, or architectural research, and when such value can be substantially preserved through the conduct of appropriate research, and such research is conducted in accordance with applicable professional standards and guidelines; (2) when the undertaking is limited to the rehabilitation of buildings and structures and is conducted in a manner that preserves the historical and architectural value of affected designated historic properties through conformance with the Secretary's "Standards for Rehabilitation and Guidelines for Rehabilitating Historic Buildings"; or (3) when the undertaking is limited to the transfer, lease, or sale of a designated historic property, and adequate restrictions or conditions are included to ensure preservation of the property's important historic features.

If SHPO concurs with the district engineer's determination of no effect or fails to respond within 15 days of the district engineer's notice to SHPO of a no effect determination, then the district engineer may proceed with the final decision. If the district engineer, based on his coordination with SHPO determines that an effect is not adverse, he or she will notify the Council and request comments. The district engineer's notice will include a description of both the project and the designated historic property; both the district engineer's and SHPO's views, as well as any views of affected local governments, Indian tribes, federal agencies, and the public, on the no adverse effect determination; and a description of the efforts to identify historic properties and solicit the views of those above. The district engineer may conclude the permit decision if the Council does not object to the district engineer's determination or if the district engineer accepts any conditions requested by the Council for a no adverse effect determination, or the Council fails to respond within 30 days of receipt of the notice. If the Council objects or the district engineer does not accept the conditions proposed by the Council, then the effect shall be considered as adverse.

If the undertaking would cause an adverse effect on designated historic properties, the district engineer will notify the Council and coordinate with SHPO to seek ways to avoid or reduce those adverse effects. Either the district engineer or SHPO may request the Council to participate. The Council also may participate without such a request. At some point, the district engineer, SHPO, or the Council may find that further coordination will be unproductive. If the district engineer determines that coordination with SHPO is unproductive or the Council, within the appropriate comment period, requests additional information to provide its comments, or the Council objects to any agreed resolution of impacts on designated historic properties, then the district engineer, normally within 30 days, provides the Council with additional project information, including a project description, a listing and description of the designated historic properties that will be affected, a description of the anticipated adverse effects of the undertaking on the designated historic properties and of the proposed mitigation measures and alternatives considered, and the views of any commenting parties regarding designated historic properties. The district engineer also sends copies of this information to the applicant, SHPO, and any appropriate Indian tribe or certified local government.

The Council has 60 days from the date of the district engineer's letter to provide its comments. If the Council does not comment by that time, the district engineer can complete processing of the permit application. If the permit decision delayed for another reason, the district engineer will provide additional time for the Council to comment consistent with, but not extending beyond, that delay.

At any time during permit processing, the district engineer may consult with the involved parties to discuss and consider possible alternatives or measures to avoid or minimize the adverse effects on historic properties of a proposed activity. The district engineer terminates consultation when he or she determines that further consultation is not productive. If consultation results in a mutual agreement among SHPO, Council, applicant and the district engineer regarding the treatment of designated historic properties, then the district engineer may formalize that agreement either through permit conditioning or by signing a MOA with these parties, and proceed with the permit decision.

As illustrated by the above description, Appendix C has a less defined and robust role for tribal consultation that the Council's regulations. But the Corps also has to comply with its government-to-government consultation obligations, so the amount of tribal consultation typically is similar to what would occur if the Corps followed the Council's regulations rather than Appendix C.

Decision

In making a public interest determination on a permit application, the district engineer weighs a number of factors, including the effects of the undertaking on historic properties, comments of the Council and SHPO, and views of other interested parties. The district engineer must add permit conditions to avoid or reduce effects on historic properties where feasible, taking into account the Secretary of the Interior's Standards and

Guidelines for Archeology and Historic Preservation.[78] If the district engineer concludes that permitting the activity would result in the irrevocable loss of important scientific, prehistoric, historical, or archeological data, the district engineer, in accordance with the Archeological and Historic Preservation Act of 1974, advises the Secretary of the Interior (by notifying the National Park Service (NPS)) of the extent to which the data may be lost if the undertaking is permitted, any plans to mitigate such loss that will be implemented, and the permit conditions that will be included to ensure that any required mitigation occurs.

NPS = National Park Service

Discoveries During Permit Activities

After the permit has been issued, if the district engineer finds or is notified that the permit area contains a previously unknown, potentially eligible historic property which he or she reasonably expects will be affected by the undertaking, he or she must inform the Department of the Interior Departmental Consulting Archeologist and the regional office of the NPS. The district engineer will require voluntary avoidance of construction activities that could affect the historic property pending a recommendation from the NPS. Based on the circumstances of the discovery, equity to all parties, and considerations of the public interest, the district engineer can modify, suspend or revoke a permit.

Criticisms of Appendix C

The Council has, as have others, criticized Appendix C as not fully satisfying the requirements of Section 106. These criticisms generally fall into the following five categories:

> Inappropriately limits the APE. Appendix C limits the APE to the permit area rather than the geographic area within which a project may directly or indirectly cause alterations in the character or use of historic properties.

> Narrows the definition of adverse effects. Appendix C limits the Corps' responsibilities by narrowing the definition of adverse effects from the Council's regulations that consider the direct and indirect effect of projects.

> No requirement for tribal consultation. Appendix C states that tribes "may" be consulted unlike the Council's regulations, which require tribal consultation.

> Failure to protect confidentiality. Unlike the NHPA, the Corps only protects information from disclosure where there is a substantial risk of harm, theft, or destruction.

> No authority to promulgate Appendix C. Congress did not delegate regulation authority to the Corps to promulgate its own Section 106 regulations. The Council's regulations are the only approved procedures to implement Section 106. While federal agencies can enact alternate regulations, those must be approved for use by the Council. Because the Council has not approved (and does not intend to approve) Appendix C, the Corps' use of Appendix C is

78   48 Fed. Reg. 44,716.

A STREAMLINED CONSULTATION PROCESS GOES WRONG

Commenced in 2014, the Dakota Access Pipeline (DAPL) is a 1,172-mile, privately owned crude-oil pipeline that delivers crude oil produced in the Bakken region of North Dakota through South Dakota, Iowa, and Illinois to major refining and distribution centers. DAPL made national news in 2016, when thousands of protesters camped on and near the Standing Rock Sioux Reservation in North Dakota to protest the project, and additional protests occurred around the country.

No federal agency has jurisdiction over crude-oil pipelines, but because the pipeline would cross waters of the United States in four states, it required a Corps permit.[1] The Corps thus defined an APE, identified cultural resources, determined whether the project could adversely affect such resources, and undertook Section 106 consultation, with over 389 tribal meetings.[2]

But interested tribes, including the Standing Rock Sioux Tribe and Cheyenne River Sioux Tribe (the "Tribes") claimed that the Corps failed to meaningfully engage with the Tribes and listen to their concerns about the pipeline.[3] The Standing Rock Sioux Tribe had expressed concerns about the proposed pipeline alignment beginning in 2014.[4] In particular, the Tribe was concerned about the location of the pipeline's crossing of the Missouri River, approximately a half-mile upstream from the Tribe's reservation on treaty land that includes sacred sites and burial grounds.[5] That land was particularly sensitive to the Tribe; it already had been subject to litigation when the Tribe stopped the Corps' eminent domain proceedings to take the land in 1958, only to have the judicial outcome overturned by legislation, resulting in the creation of the Lake Oahe reservoir.[6]

In 2016, the Corps issued a Nationwide Permit (NWP), which is a streamlined Corps permitting program for lineal infrastructure projects such as pipelines, that authorized all water crossings except that over Lake Oahe, a reservoir on

1   Troy A. Eid, Beyond Dakota Access Pipeline: Why Embracing Tribal Consultation Makes Sense for the Energy Industry, Denver Law Review, Vol. 95:3 (August 2017), http://static1.1.sqspcdn.com/static/f/276323/27945279/1531287528983/Vol95_Issue3_Eid_FINAL.pdf?token=Qz4amYoeUz4v1em1fU3wkHMDrLI%3D.

2   Corps' Opposition to Plaintiff's Motion for Preliminary Injunction, U.S. District Court, District of Columbia, Case No. 1:16-cv-01534 (JEB) (Aug. 18, 2016).

3   *Standing Rock Sioux Tribe warns of "same mistakes" with new Dakota Access study*, Indianz.Com (March 7, 2018), https://www.indianz.com/News/2018/03/07/standing-rock-sioux-tribe-warns-of-same.asp.

4   Justin Worland, What to Know About the Dakota Access Pipeline Protests, TIME (Oct. 28. 2016), http://time.com/4548566/dakota-access-pipeline-standing-rock-sioux/.

5   Timothy Q. Purdon, Katerine S. Barrett Wiik, and Dr. Aryn Conrad, *DAPL: Storm Clouds on the Horizon in Indian Country*, The Federal Lawyer, pp. 63–68 (June 2017), https://www.robinskaplan.com/~/media/pdfs/dapl%20storm%20clouds%20on%20the%20horizon%20in%20indian%20country.pdf?la=en.

6   Eid, *supra*, note 76.

perceived as a violation of Section 106 (a comment with which the Corps vehemently disagrees).

Since first promulgated, the Corps has revised Appendix C and issued interim guidance on compliance. The interim guidance also clarifies that the Corps will not undertake Section 106 compliance if another federal agency has greater responsibility for the undertaking and that the Corps will generally accept the outcome of other agencies' Section 106 consultation. Further, the interim guidance clarifies that the Corps must consult the same parties as required by the Council regulations, including any Indian Tribe, Alaska Native village or regional corporation, or Native Hawaiian organization that places historic and cultural significance to historic properties, including traditional cultural properties, that may be affected by an undertaking, even if those historic properties are located on private lands. But despite criticism, the guidance clarifies that the

the Missouri River.[7] For that crossing, the Corps issued a separate Section 408 permit and easement.[8]

The Standing Rock Sioux Tribe, later joined by the Cheyenne River Sioux Tribe (the "Tribes") and environmental groups, sued the Corps in federal court, raising a number of environmental claims, including that the Corps failed to adequately consult with the Tribes, thereby violating the NHPA.[9] After a district court judge upheld the Corps' NWP determinations, the Tribes focused their claims on the Lake Oahe pipeline crossing.[10] While litigation was pending, the Tribes continued to request additional consultation with executive branch officials.[11]

On September 9, 2016, the Tribes received both a judicial order denying a motion for a preliminary injunction until the Corps engaged in additional Section 106 consultation and a joint statement from the Corps and the U.S. Departments of Justice and the Interior halting DAPL construction on federal land and asking the pipeline company to voluntarily halt all construction within 20 miles east or west of Lake Oahe.[12] On November 14, 2016, the

Corps reopened consultation regarding the easement on Corps-administered land at Lake Oahe and, a few weeks later, denied the easement.[13]

Just days after taking office in 2017, President Trump issued a memorandum declaring DAPL to be in the national interest and directing federal agencies to review and approve it "in an expedited manner, to the extent permitted by law and as warranted."[14] The Corps reversed course and granted the easement later that same year, and today DAPL is an operating pipeline.[15]

The DAPL saga serves as a cautionary tale. Even though the pipeline company was able to proceed with DAPL, by 2016, project delays were costing DAPL's private investors more than $83.3 million per month and had already totaled $450 million.[16] Thus, while the letter of the NHPA may be followed, unless the spirit is too, tribes likely will be dissatisfied. The subsequent litigation can result in more delays than continued consultation.

7 *Id.*
8 *Id.*
9 *Id.*
10 *Id.*
11 *Id.*
12 Rebecca Hersher, *Key Moments in the Dakota Access Pipeline Fight*, National Public Radio (Feb. 22, 2017), https://www.npr.org/sections/thetwo-way/2017/02/22/514988040/key-moments-in-the-dakota-access-pipeline-fight.

13 Amy Sisk, Timeline: *The Long Road To #NoDAPL*, Inside Energy (Jan. 23, 2017), http://insideenergy.org/2017/01/23/timeline-the-long-road-to-nodapl/.
14 White House Office of the Press Secretary, Memorandum for the Secretary of the Army, *Construction of the Dakota Access Pipeline* (Jan. 24, 2017), https://assets.documentcloud.org/documents/3410448/Construction-of-the-Dakota-Access-Pipeline.pdf.
15 Sisk, *supra*, note 88.
16 Eid, *supra*, note 76.

Corps does not believe that Council regulations change the scope of analysis for the consideration of historic properties in the Corps regulatory program and that the term "permit area" in Appendix C, including the three tests in that definition quoted above, should continue to be used.

The Council and various other groups have remained critical of the guidance, mainly for being inconsistent with Section 106. As discussed above, the Districts are seeking approval of a PA that would attempt to make Appendix C in California compatible with the Council's regulations and, because it would be adopted through proper procedures, resolve some of the controversy that surrounds Appendix C.

SECTION 110 OF THE NHPA

Section 110 of the NHPA requires federal agencies to consider historic preservation strategies in the management of properties under federal ownership or control.[79] Among other things, agencies must carry out their programs and projects in accordance with the purposes of the NHPA and requires agencies to minimize harm to landmarks and obtain Council review of an undertaking that may directly and adversely affect a national landmark.[80] The review required by Section 110(f) is similar to that required under Section 106, but involves a higher standard of care because the historic properties are under the ownership of the federal government, which must act as its steward. Generally, Section 110(f) review is accomplished under the Council's procedures implementing Section 106.

Most relevant to obtaining a Corps permit, Section 110 directs federal agencies to withhold approvals or other assistance to applicants who intentionally significantly and adversely affect historic properties.[81] This provision, known as the "anticipatory demolition" section, is designed to deter applicants from destroying historic properties prior to seeking federal assistance in an effort to avoid the Section 106 process. Section 110 also requires the head of a federal agency to document any decision under Section 106 where a MOA has not been executed.[82] It further clarifies that when an MOA is executed, that MOA governs implementation of the undertaking in a binding manner.[83]

TRIBAL CULTURAL RESOURCES CONSULTATION UNDER THE CALIFORNIA ENVIRONMENTAL QUALITY ACT

The California Environmental Quality Act (CEQA) requires lead agencies to examine impacts on cultural resources. Under CEQA, there are four types of cultural resources: historical[84], archeological, paleontological, and tribal cultural resources.[85] Of these, tribal consultation is required only for tribal cultural resources.[86] The requirement for tribal consultation on all projects requiring a Negative Declaration or Environmental Impact Report was enacted in 2014, through Assembly Bill 52 (AB 52), and took

---

79 16 U.S.C. § 470h-2.

80 *Id.* § 470h-2(d), (f).

81 *Id.* § 470h-2(k). This provision does allow assistance if, after consultation with the Council, the agency determines that circumstances justify granting the assistance.

82 *Id.* § 470h-2(l).

83 *Id.*

84 CEQA and the CEQA Guidelines refer to "historical resources" when referring to historic (i.e., historically significant) resources and although grammatically incorrect that convention is followed in this section.

85 A proposed update to Appendix G of the CEQA Guidelines would relocate questions related to a project's impact on paleontological resources from the cultural resources section to the geology and soils section. Governor's Office of Planning and Research, *Proposed Updates to the CEQA Guidelines* (Nov. 2017), available at http://opr.ca.gov/docs/20171127_Comprehensive_CEQA_Guidelines_Package_Nov_2017.pdf.

86 CEQA is premised on public disclosure, but tribes are the only group of the public that are entitled to additional consultation outside the general forums for public participation during the CEQA process. Pub. Res. Code § 21080.3.1.

effect on July 1, 2015. Prior to the adoption of AB 52, CEQA required tribal consulta- AB = Assembly Bill
tion only for projects that involved a General Plan or Specific Amendment or adop- SB = Senate Bill
tion or dedication of open space for the purpose of protecting cultural places,
sometimes referred to as "SB 18" consultation. The SB 18 consultation requirements
are discussed below.

CEQA defines "tribal cultural resources" as:

> > sites, features, places, cultural landscapes, sacred places, and objects with cul-
> tural value to a California Native American tribe that are either of the following
> included or determined to be eligible for inclusion in the California Register of
> Historical Resources or included in a local register of historical resources

> > a resource the lead agency determines, taking into account the significance of
> the resource to a California Native American tribe and substantial evidence, to
> be significant based on the criteria for listing on the National Register.[87]
> California Native American tribes traditionally and culturally affiliated with a
> project's geographic area may have expertise concerning their tribal cultural
> resources that provide substantial evidence.[88]

> > a cultural landscape that is geographically defined in terms of the size and scope
> of the landscape also can be tribal cultural resources if it fits the definition; in
> addition, to the extent it fits the definition, a historical resource (a resource that
> is listed in or eligible for the California Register of Historical Resources) and an
> archaeological resource can be a tribal cultural resource[89]

A project that would cause a substantial adverse change in the significance of a tribal
cultural resource is a project that would have a significant impact on the environment
under CEQA.[90] CEQA requires lead agencies to mitigate a project's significant impacts
to the extent feasible.[91] Nevertheless, a lead agency can approve a project that has a significant impact on the environment as long as consultation concluded (either with or
without agreement with the tribe(s)) or did not occur because it was either not
requested or after the request, the tribe failed to engage in the process, and the agency
adopts a statement of overriding considerations and all feasible mitigation to minimize
the impact.[92]

---

87 Pub. Res. Code § 21074.

88 *Id.* § 21080.3.1. Evidence that may support a lead agency's finding that something is a tribal cultural
resources includes elder testimony, oral history, tribal government archival information, testimony of
a qualified archaeologist certified by the relevant tribe, testimony of an expert certified by the Tribal
Government, official tribal government declarations or resolutions, formal statements from a THPO,
and historical notes, such as those found in the Harrington Papers and other anthropological records.
Governor's Office of Planning and Research, *Technical Advisory: AB 52 and Tribal Cultural Resources in
CEQA* (June 2017).

89 *Id.*

90 14 Cal. Code Regs., Appendix G.

91 Pub. Res. Code § 21002.

92 *Id.* § 21082.3(d), (e).

Consultation Procedures under AB 52

Under CEQA, consultation is between the lead agency and California Native American tribes.[93] If a tribe wishes to be notified of projects within its traditionally and culturally affiliated area, the tribe must submit a written request to the relevant lead agency.[94] The lead agency can include the project sponsor in the consultation, but is not required to do so.[95]

For discretionary projects that require CEQA review that may result in a Negative Declaration (ND), Mitigated Negative Declaration (MND), or Environmental Impact Report (EIR), a lead agency must provide formal advance notification, in writing, to the tribes that have requested notification of proposed projects within 14 days of determining that a project application is complete, or to undertake a public agency project. The 14-day notification must include a description of the project, its location, and must state that the tribe has 30 days to request consultation. If a tribe responds within that 30-day period, the lead agency must begin consultation with that tribe within 30 days and before the release of the ND, MND, or EIR.[96]

Consultation is required for lead agencies to obtain the information necessary to understand the significance of and impact of a project on a tribal cultural resource. This understanding is necessary for the agency to fulfill CEQA's directive to "avoid damaging effects to any tribal cultural resource" where feasible.[97] Consultation allows a lead agency to determine appropriate mitigation for a tribal cultural resource, which may differ from typical mitigation for archeological resources. Consultation can be ongoing throughout the CEQA process.

The lead agency is authorized to consult on a wide range of topics if requested by the consulting tribe, including the type of environmental review necessary, the significance of tribal cultural resources, the significance of the project's impacts on the tribal cultural resources, and, if necessary, project alternatives or the appropriate measures for preservation or mitigation that the tribe may recommend to the lead agency.[98] If the tribe requests consultation regarding alternatives to the project, recommended mitigation measures, or significant effects, the consultation must include those topics.[99] As a part of the consultation, the parties may propose mitigation measures capable of avoiding or substantially lessening potential significant impacts to a tribal cultural resource or alternatives that would avoid significant impacts to a tribal cultural resource.[100] A lead agency must recommend any mitigation measures agreed on in the consultation for inclusion in the environmental document and in the

93 *Id.* § 21080.3.1(b).
94 *Id.*
95 *Id.* § 21080.3.2(d).
96 *Id.* § 21080.3.1(b), (e).
97 *Id.* § 21084.3(a).
98 *Id.* § 21080.3.2(a).
99 *Id.*
100 *Id.*

mitigation monitoring and reporting program if those measures avoid or lessen the impact on tribal cultural resources.[101]

Typically, information exchanged during the CEQA process is part of the CEQA record, but there are exceptions for sensitive tribal information. For example, information about the location of an archeological site or sacred lands, Native American graves, cemeteries, and sacred places and records of Native American places, features, and objects are exempt from disclosure and kept confidential.[102] Confidential cultural resource inventories or reports generated for environmental documents should be maintained by the lead agency under separate cover and are not to be made available to the public.

In addition, information submitted by a California Native American tribe during the environmental review process cannot be included in the environmental document or disclosed to the public without the prior written consent of the tribe. This confidentiality protection extends to a tribe's comment letter on an environmental document, if that comment letter is specifically stamped as "confidential." The lead agency and the tribe may agree to share confidential information regarding tribal cultural resources with the project applicant and its agents. In that case, the project applicant is responsible for keeping the information confidential, unless the tribe consents to disclosure in writing, to prevent looting, vandalism, or damage to the cultural resource. The project applicant must use a reasonable degree of care to protect the information. When describing its analysis of cultural resources, the lead agency should use general terms in the environmental document, providing enough information to inform the public while maintaining confidentiality.[103]

The lead agency may not take action on the CEQA document (certify or adopt) until the tribal consultation, if initiated, has been concluded. Consultation ends when either (1) the parties agree to measures to mitigate or avoid a significant effect, if a significant effect exists, on a tribal cultural resource, or (2) a party, acting in good faith and after reasonable effort, concludes that mutual agreement cannot be reached.[104]

Examples of Mitigation Measures

If the lead agency determines that a project may cause a substantial adverse change to a tribal cultural resource, and measures are not identified in the consultation process, CEQA offers example mitigation measures that, if feasible, may avoid or minimize the significant adverse impacts.[105] These examples are:

---

101 *Id.* § 21082.3(a).

102 14 Cal. Code Regs. § 15120(d).

103 Pub. Res. Code § 21082.3(c)(4).

104 *Id.* § 21080.3.2(b)(1) & (2).

105 *Id.* § 21084.3(b).

> avoiding the resources or preserving the resources in place by, for example, protecting the cultural and natural context during construction and incorporating parks or other open space in the design with appropriate management criteria
> treating the resource with culturally appropriate dignity taking into account the tribal cultural values and meaning of the resource, including:
>   • protecting the cultural character and integrity of the resource
>   • protecting the traditional use of the resource, and
>   • protecting the confidentiality of the resource
> creating permanent conservation easements or other interests in real property, with culturally appropriate management criteria, to preserve or use the resources or places
> protecting the resource[106]

AB 52 did not expand an agency's authority under CEQA.[107] Therefore, mitigation must have a nexus and be roughly proportional to the impacts caused by the project.[108] In addition, CEQA requires mitigation only for physical impacts or social impacts that have physical manifestations and not for purely psychological or spiritual harms.[109]

Key Differences between Section 106 and AB 52

Just as there is overlap between NEPA and CEQA, there also is overlap between Section 106 and AB 52 consultations. To the extent practical, it is beneficial to coordinate these consultations so that the end result is one set of harmonized mitigation measures.

Nonetheless, the requirements of AB 52 are not completely coextensive with Section 106 consultation. The two primary differences are:

> Tribes to Consult. The list of tribes to contact initially under AB 52 is broader because it includes non-federally recognized tribes
> Timing of the Consultation. While Section 106 consultation can trail the release of the NEPA document, AB 52 assumes consultation is coordinated with the CEQA document. Thus, as discussed above, AB 52 imposes deadlines based on the CEQA process. In addition, because AB 52 encourages consultation regarding the type of CEQA document to prepare, and requires consultation regarding mitigation measures and alternatives, the consultation necessarily must be done near the beginning of the CEQA process.

Despite the above differences, the substance of the consultation is similar, with both Section 106 and AB 52 consultation aimed at identifying tribal cultural resources (among other resources) and determining the best way to protect those resources during and after project construction.

---

106 *Id.*

107 See 14 Cal. Code Regs. § 15040 (explaining an agency's CEQA authority).

108 *Id.* § 15041(a).

109 *Id.*; see *Preserve Poway v. City of Poway*, 245 Cal. App. 4th 560, 580–81 (2016); *Martin v. City & County of San Francisco*, 35 Cal. App. 4th 392, 404 (2005); *Cathay Mortuary, Inc. v. San Francisco Planning Commission*, 207 Cal. App. 3d 275, 279 (1989).

TABLE 12-1. SECTION 106 AND AB 52 COMPARISON

	Section 106	AB 52	Comparison
Purpose	Account for effects of undertaking on historic properties, and afford Council and federally recognized tribes opportunity to comment. 36 C.F.R. § 800.1(a).	Require consultation with California Native American tribes that are traditionally and culturally affiliated with the geographic area of a project. Pub. Res. Code § 21080.3.1. "Tribes" are all those on the contact list maintained by NAHC, which is broader than just federally recognized tribes. Pub. Res. Code § 21073.	Section 106 is designed to protect "historic properties" and operates independently from NEPA. Section 106 includes consultation with a SHPO unless tribe takes over as THPO. AB 52 is designed to give California Native American tribes a more active role in the CEQA process. It requires consultation with a broader array of tribes, as tribes need not be federally recognized.
What resources are covered?	"Historic properties": listed or eligible for listing in National Register. These may include prehistoric or historic districts, sites, buildings, structures, objects, or properties of traditional religious and cultural importance to an Indian tribe. 36 C.F.R. § 800.16(l)(1). Includes "traditional cultural property": eligible for listing in National Register because of its association with cultural practices or beliefs of a living community that (a) are rooted in that community's history, and (b) are important to maintaining the community's continuing cultural identity. NPS Bulletin 38.	"Tribal cultural resources": > either (1) sites, features, places, and objects with cultural value to descendent communities or cultural landscapes that are (a) included in the California Register, (b) included in local register, *or* (2) a resource determined by the lead agency, in its discretion, and supported by substantial evidence, to be significant pursuant to criteria used to determine if a resource is eligible for the California Register. In applying this criteria, the lead agency shall consider the significance of the resource to a California Native American tribe > a cultural landscape that meets the criteria listed above is a tribal cultural resource to the extent that the landscape is geographically defined in terms of the size and scope of the landscape > a historical resource, a unique archaeological resource, or a "nonunique archaeological resource" may also be a tribal cultural resource if it conforms with the criteria in the first bullet above Pub. Res. Code § 21074.	AB 52 and Section 106 are similar here, with the differences being: > on which Register the resource is listed or meets the criteria for listing; > definition of "tribe" to which the resource would be of value; and > whether the agency must consider the significance of the resource to the tribe when making a determination
What is an "adverse effect"?	"Adverse effect" is found when a project, activity, or program ("undertaking") may directly or indirectly alter a characteristic of a historic property that qualifies the property for inclusion in the National Register in a manner that would diminish the integrity of the property's location, design, setting, materials, workmanship, feeling, or association. 36 C.F.R. § 800.5(a)(1).	Significance thresholds for determining whether an impact to a tribal cultural resource is significant: Would the project cause a substantial adverse change in the significance of a tribal cultural resource that is: > listed or eligible for listing in the California Register of Historical Resources, or in a local register of historical resources, or > a resource determined by the lead agency, in its discretion and supported by substantial evidence, to be significant pursuant to California Register criteria and considering the significance of the resource to a California Native American tribe	Section 106 is concerned with resources eligible for the National Register and AB 52 is concerned with resources eligible for the California Register.

TABLE 12-1, CONTINUED. SECTION 106 AND AB 52 COMPARISON

	Section 106	AB 52	Comparison
Timing of consultation	Complete process prior to approval of the expenditure of federal funds on the undertaking or prior to the issuance of any license. 36 C.F.R. § 800.1(b).	Begin consultation prior to release of Negative Declaration or EIR prepared pursuant to CEQA. Pub. Res. Code § 21080.3.1(b). To ensure consultation is timely, AB 52 has noticing and response deadlines: > lead agency provides notice to tribes that have requested notice of projects in the lead agency's jurisdiction within 14 days of determining to undertake a project > tribe responds within 30 days of receipt of notification of project and, if desired, requests consultation	Although Section 106 consultation can conclude after NEPA document is released, consultation results may change the NEPA determination and so should coordinate Section 106 consultation and NEPA review. AB 52 assumes consultation results coordinated with CEQA.
Consulting parties	Required: > federal agency permitting the project > SHPO/THPO > federally recognized Indian tribes that may attach significance to an historic property at issue > project applicant > representatives of local governments with jurisdiction over areas that may be affected by the project The federal agency also needs to decide how to involve the public. Discretionary: Individuals and organizations with a demonstrated interest in the undertaking, which may include local historic preservation officials, historic preservation groups, community organizations, individual property owners, and other stakeholders. These invited consulting parties have the right to receive information and make their views known at various points in the process, but do not have the right to veto a project decision.	Required: > lead agency > California Native American Tribe: Native American tribe located in California and on the contact list maintained by the NAHC. Pub. Res. Code § 21074 Discretionary: > project proponent and/or its consultants. Pub. Res. Code § 21080.3.2(c)(2), (d)	In addition to the permitting agency and tribe, Section 106 consultation always includes the project applicant. AB 52 does not require the project applicant be included in consultation.
Consultation process	Consultation regarding eligibility determinations can be conducted in many different ways; there is no prescribed process. Consultation can include one or more public meetings or can be conducted by circulating a technical report for review and comment.	According to CEQA's Tribal Consultation Guidelines, effective consultation is an ongoing process, not a single event. The process should focus on identifying issues of concern to tribes pertinent to the cultural place(s) at issue, including cultural values, religious beliefs, traditional practices, and laws protecting California Native American cultural sites, and on defining the full range of acceptable ways in which a local government can accommodate tribal concerns.	Similar

TABLE 12-1, CONTINUED. SECTION 106 AND AB 52 COMPARISON

	Section 106	AB 52	Comparison
Content of consultation	> assess whether adverse effects > resolve adverse effects, if found 36 C.F.R. § 800.5	> assess project's impact to identified resources > if tribe requests consultation to include alternatives, mitigation measures, or significant effects, consultation must do so. Consultation may also include discussion of type of environmental review necessary Pub. Res. Code § 21080.3.2(a).	Section 106 and AB 52 are similar. Consultation should include a discussion of the resources that would be affected by the project and alternatives and mitigation to resolve/mitigate identified adverse effects.
Resolution of adverse effects/ potentially significant impacts, if found	Continue consultation to develop and evaluate alternatives or modifications to the undertaking that could avoid, minimize, or mitigate adverse effects on historic properties. 36 C.F.R. § 800.6(a), (b). Alternatives and measures developed during consultation must be described in the NEPA document. If agreement, enter into MOA with SHPO/THPO. If no agreement, request Council to join consultation.	Any mitigation measures agreed upon during consultation "shall be recommended for inclusion in the environmental document and in an adopted mitigation monitoring program" if determined to avoid or lessen a significant impact on a tribal cultural resource. If a project "may have a significant impact on a tribal cultural resource," the environmental document would be required to discuss both of the following: > whether the proposed project has a significant impact on an identified tribal cultural resource > whether feasible alternatives or mitigation measures, including those measures that may be agreed to [during consultation], avoid or substantially lessen the impact on the identified tribal cultural resource Pub. Res. Code § 21082.3(a), (b).	Both AB 52 and Section 106 require that alternatives and mitigation developed during consultation be analyzed in the CEQA/NEPA document. Both favor formal agreement with tribe on alternatives or measures to be implemented.
Termination of consultation	After consulting to resolve adverse effects, agency, SHPO/THPO, or Council may determine that further consultation will not be productive and terminate consultation by notifying other consulting parties and providing them the reasons for termination in writing. 36 C.F.R. § 800.7(a).	The parties agree to measures to mitigate or avoid a significant effect, if a significant effect exists, on a tribal cultural resource, or A party, acting in good faith and after reasonable effort, concludes that mutual agreement cannot be reached concerning appropriate measures to be taken that would mitigate or avoid a significant effect, if a significant effect exists, on a tribal cultural resource. Pub. Res. Code § 21080.3.2(b).	Similar; consultation concludes with agreement, or a good faith determination by the agency that agreement cannot be reached.
Coordination with environmental laws	NEPA: agency may use the process and documentation required for EA/FONSI or EIS/ROD to comply with Section 106 if the agency notifies in advance SHPO/THPO and Council. 36 C.F.R. § 800.8(c). Otherwise, processes should be coordinated.	CEQA: Where project would have a significant impact on a tribal cultural resource, the lead agency may only certify an EIR or adopt a Negative Declaration if: > consultation has occurred and concluded > the tribe has requested consultation and failed to comment or otherwise engage in the consultation process, or > the tribe failed to request consultation within 30 days of receiving notice as required If no agreement on mitigation occurs during consultation, lead agency must still evaluate and select feasible mitigation in the CEQA document to mitigate a potentially significant impact.	Section 106 anticipates coordination with the NEPA process, whereas AB 52 consultation is explicitly made a part of the CEQA process.

TRIBAL CONSULTATION UNDER SENATE BILL 18

Senate Bill 18 requires cities and counties to consult with California Native American Tribes that are on the contact list maintained by the California Native American Heritage Commission with traditional lands within the city or county's jurisdiction prior to the adoption of or any amendment to a General Plan or Specific Plan or the dedication of open space for the purpose of preserving a cultural place.[110] Similar to AB 52, "consultation" means the meaningful and timely process of seeking, discussing, and considering carefully the views of others, in a manner that is cognizant of all parties' cultural values and, where feasible, seeking agreement.[111] Consultation should occur about potential impacts from the project to a Native American sanctified cemetery, place of worship, religious or ceremonial site, or sacred shrine, as well as a Native American historic, cultural, or sacred site, that is listed or may be eligible for listing in the California Register of Historic Resources, including any historic or prehistoric ruins, any burial ground, and any archaeological or historic site. The consultation process is similar to that required under AB 52. While the city and county must undertake consultation in good faith, consultation can end even if the local jurisdiction and tribes fail to come to an agreement. Once a city or county asks tribes for consultation, tribes have 90 days to reply.[112] Consultation occurs if requested and the city or county must send notice to the tribes 45 days before taking action on the General Plan adoption or amendment.[113]

110 Gov't Code § 65352.3.

111 *Id.* § 65352.4.

112 *Id.* § 65352.3.

113 *Id.* § 65352.

TABLE 12-2. SUMMARY OF CULTURAL RESOURCE CONSULTATION MECHANISMS

Regulatory Context	Agency	Tribes	When Applies	Party Initiating Contact	Reaction	Timing	Schedule	Resource Considered
Section 106 NHPA	federal	federally recognized	prior to issuance of a permit, license, or funding	federal agency	proactive	tends to be later in the process, post-CEQA	no time frames	historic properties and traditional cultural properties
Senate Bill 18	local (cities/counties)	California Native American tribes	prior to general plan and specific plan adoptions or amendments	local agency	proactive	tends to be earlier in the process, in conjunction with CEQA	90-day window to initiate, followed by City Council or Board of Supervisors noticing (45 and 10 days)	Native American cultural resources
Public Comment: CEQA	state/local	any member of the public	CEQA	tribes	reactive	near the end of CEQA, after the draft environmental document has been released to the public	initial study: 30 calendar days; EIR: 45 calendar days	historical resources, unique archaeological resources, and tribal cultural resources
Public Comment: NEPA	federal	any member of the public	NEPA (note: this often occurs in conjunction with Section 106)	tribes	reactive	near the end of NEPA, after the draft environmental document has been released to the public	EA: 30 calendar days; EIS: 45 calendar days	historic properties and cultural resources
Assembly Bill 52	state/local	California Native American tribes	CEQA	tribes	proactive	earliest point in the process, at the start of CEQA	14 days from start; 30-day response window; 30-day initiation window; then no time frames	tribal cultural resources

Chart courtesy of Lisa Westwood.

CHAPTER 13

Bay and Coastal Resources

The Legislature has established separate statutory structures for certain regions in the state. The most notable of these are California's laws protecting San Francisco Bay and the California coastline. Regulatory jurisdiction over these resources is delegated to the Bay Conservation and Development Commission and the California Coastal Commission, respectively. This chapter provides a high-level overview of the programs administered by these two agencies.

BAY CONSERVATION AND DEVELOPMENT COMMISSION

History and Background

In 1965 the Legislature passed the McAteer-Petris Act, which created the San Francisco Bay Conservation and Development Commission (BCDC). The act was a legislative response to the piecemeal filling of the San Francisco Bay and the lack of a cohesive regime to regulate those activities.

As one contemporary commenter noted:

> San Francisco Bay has been disappearing at the rate of three and one-half square miles a year. Over the last hundred years, filling and diking have removed over 240 square miles from the Bay. At the present rate, it will take less than one hundred years to deprive the Bay of the 326 miles still susceptible of reclamation . . . .

> The Bay is in the hands of hundreds of private owners, twenty cities, three counties, one harbor district, the State of California, and the federal government. [Citation.] Each entity has its own proprietary interest; each contributes to the lack of uniform control which the Legislature intended to cure by creating BCDC.[1]

The findings of the McAteer-Petris Act declare:

> that uncoordinated, haphazard filling in San Francisco Bay threatens the bay itself and is therefore inimical to the welfare of both present and future residents of the area surrounding the bay; that while some individual fill projects may be necessary and desirable for the needs of the entire bay region, and while some cities and counties may have prepared detailed master plans for their own bay lands, a governmental mechanism must exist for evaluating individual projects as to their effect on the entire bay; and that further piecemeal filling of the bay may place serious restrictions on navigation in the bay, may destroy the irreplaceable feeding and breeding grounds of fish and wildlife in the bay, may adversely affect the quality of bay waters and even the quality of air in the bay area, and would therefore be harmful to the needs of the present and future population of the bay region.[2]

Indeed, according to the BCDC's website, when the agency was established only four miles of the Bay shoreline was publicly accessible.

---

1   *Leslie Salt Co. v. San Francisco Bay Conservation and Dev. Comm.*, 153 Cal. App. 3d 605, 616 n. 13. (1984); *Acme Fill Corp. v. San Francisco Bay Conservation and Dev. Comm.*, 232 Cal. App. 3d 1056, 1072 n. 9 (1986) (both quoting *San Francisco Bay: Regional Regulation for its Protection and Development*, 55 Cal.L.Rev. 728 (1967)).

2   Gov't Code § 66601.

BCDC Jurisdiction

BCDC has jurisdiction over the San Francisco Bay (including all sloughs, tidelands, and marshlands); salt ponds (consisting of all areas which have been diked off from the bay and historically used for solar evaporation); managed wetlands (areas that have been diked off from the bay and historically used as duck hunting preserves, game refuges or for agriculture); and a list[3] of certain waterways that are tributary to the San Francisco Bay.[4] BCDC also has jurisdiction over a "shoreline band" reaching 100 feet landward of, and parallel to, the shoreline of the San Francisco Bay.[5]

The "San Francisco Bay" generally includes all areas in the bay subject to tidal action, including areas connected to the bay through artificial means such as culverts.[6] Case law has clarified that the San Francisco Bay and the shoreline band should be measured to the mean high tide line.[7] BCDC's marshland jurisdiction extends landward over any marshlands, but not beyond a line five feet above the mean sea level.[8]

Fill activities undertaken prior to the establishment of BCDC affect the extent of BCDC's jurisdiction (i.e., if fill activities removed areas from tidal action, those areas would no longer be considered part of the bay).[9] BCDC jurisdiction will also change due to changes in the mean high tide line resulting from sea-level rise.[10] Similar to the Corps of Engineers Section 404 jurisdiction, as waters rise, the reach of BCDC's jurisdiction will expand.

The Bay Plan

Originally, BCDC was intended to be a temporary agency charged with developing a master plan for the conservation and development of the Bay—the San Francisco Bay Plan ("Bay Plan"). In 1969, the McAteer-Petris Act was amended to make BCDC a permanent agency charged with implementing the Bay Plan. The Bay Plan contains two overarching objectives: 1) protect the Bay as a great natural resource for the benefit of present and future generations; and 2) develop the Bay and its shoreline to their highest potential with a minimum of Bay filling.

---

3   This list includes: (1) Plummer Creek in Alameda County, to the eastern limit of the saltponds; (2) Coyote Creek (and branches) in Alameda and Santa Clara counties, to the easternmost point of Newby Island; (3) Redwood Creek in San Mateo County, to its confluence with Smith Slough; (4) Tolay Creek in Sonoma County, to the northerly line of Sears Point Road (State Highway 37); (5) Petaluma River in Marin and Sonoma counties to its confluence with Adobe Creek, and San Antonio Creek to the easterly line of the Northwestern Pacific Railroad right-of-way; (6) Napa River, to the northernmost point of Bull Island; (7) Sonoma Creek, to its confluence with Second Napa Slough; (8) Corte Madera Creek in Marin County to the downstream end of the concrete channel on Corte Madera Creek which is located at the U.S. Army Corps of Engineers Station No. 318+50 on the Corte Madera Creek Flood Control Project. Gov't Code § 66610(e).

4   Gov't Code § 66610.

5   *Id.* § 66610(b).

6   *Id.* § 66610(a); *Blumenfeld v. BCDC*, 43 Cal. App. 3d 50, 56–57 (1974).

7   *Littoral Dev. Co. v. BCDC*, 24 Cal. App. 4th 1050, 1064 (1994).

8   *Id.* at 1054.

9   *Id.* at 1057.

10   *Id.* at 1065 n. 5.

Policies Related to Fill

Generally speaking, the Bay Plan allows the minimum fill necessary to achieve its purpose, and only when it meets *one* of the following three conditions: 1) the fill is in accord with Bay Plan policies "as to the Bay-related purposes for which filling may be needed (i.e. ports, water-related industry, and water-related recreation) and is shown on the Bay Plan maps as likely to be needed; or 2) the filling is in accord with Bay Plan policies as to purposes for which some fill may be needed if there is no other alternative (i.e., airports, roads, and utility routes); or 3) the filling is in accord with the Bay Plan policies as to minor fills for improving shoreline appearance or public access. Housing is generally considered a non-water-oriented use and ordinarily would not justify the placement of fill in the Bay.[11]

Shoreline Band and Priority Use Areas

The Bay Plan and the "Plan Maps" designate "priority use areas" that are intended to be reserved for specific uses such as ports, wildlife refuges, and water-oriented recreation. Generally, BCDC may deny a project located in its shoreline band jurisdiction if it "fails to provide maximum feasible public access to the Bay and shoreline consistent with the proposed project." But if a project is located in a priority use area, the Commission may also deny it if it is would conflict with Bay Plan policies related to those priority uses.

Sea Level Rise

In 2011, BCDC adopted new Bay Plan findings and policies related to climate change and sea level rise. These are intended to apply only to projects, or portions of projects, located in BCDC's jurisdiction and not to projects reviewed solely under the Coastal Zone Management Act that are outside BCDC's jurisdiction. The policies require that large projects prepare a risk assessment for a 100-year flood elevation that takes into account the best estimates of future sea level rise for 2050 and 2100. To protect public safety and the environment, projects within areas that a risk assessment determines are vulnerable to future shoreline flooding that threatens public safety are required (with limited exceptions) to be resilient to 2050 sea level rise. Projects that have a lifespan lasting past 2050 should also be designed to accommodate adaptation strategies to address longer term sea-level rise impacts. If a project is located only in the shoreline band jurisdiction, BCDC will focus on the resiliency of the project's public access areas.

11   *Mein v. BCDC*, 218 Cal. App. 3d 727 (1990).

Activities Requiring a Permit

A project proponent is required to obtain a permit from BCDC for any fill, material extraction, or any substantial change in the use[12] of any water, land or structure within BCDC's jurisdiction.[13] BCDC's definition of "fill" is broader than that used by the Army Corps of Engineers. Under the McAteer-Petris Act, "fill" includes "earth or any other substance or material, including pilings or structures placed on pilings, and structures floating at some or all times and moored for extended periods, such as houseboats and floating docks."[14] This means that, unlike under the Section 404 permitting regime, a fill permit is required for structures *over* water even if no material is placed in jurisdictional waters.

Types of Permits

BCDC has separate application and processing requirements for administrative (or minor) permits, emergency permits, and major permits.

Administrative Permits

Administrative permits are generally limited to minor repairs and improvements which are defined to include certain defined activities. For work on San Francisco Bay, these include:

> the construction of a new single boat dock no larger than 1,000 square feet or a new multiple boat dock no larger than 5,000 square feet, or up to 20,000 square feet of expansion of boat docking facilities within an existing marina

> the installation of new protective works and repairs to existing protective works, such as bulkheads and riprap, that meet certain criteria

> the placement of outfall pipes approved by the California Regional Water Quality Control Board, San Francisco Bay Region

> the placement of utility cables on or under the bottom of the Bay

> routine repairs, reconstruction, replacement, removal, and maintenance that do not involve any substantial enlargement or change in use

> minor fills for shoreline appearance or public access that do not exceed 1,000 square feet

12   A "substantial change in use" includes any one of the following:
        (a) as to any "salt pond" or "managed wetland," any change in use including abandonment which, for the purposes of this section, shall include any draining of water except temporary draining for a short period of time in accordance with routine operating practice; or
        (b) . . . any construction, reconstruction, alteration, or other activity, whether or not involving a structure, if the activity either: (1) has an estimated cost of $250,000 or more; (2) involves a change in the general category of use of a structure or of land, i.e., agriculture, residential, commercial, office, industrial, recreational, vacant non-use, etc.; (3) involves a substantial change in the intensity of use; (4) adversely affects existing public access or future public access as shown on any Commission permit, the San Francisco Bay Plan, any Commission special area plan, or any other Commission planning document; or (5) is any subdivision of land pursuant to the Subdivision Map Act (Gov't Code § 66410 *et seq.*) or other division of land, including a lot split, where the subdivision or other division of land will substantially affect either present or future public access to or along the shoreline or substantially affect either the present or future suitability of a water-oriented priority land use site for that priority use, but not a subdivision or other division of land that is brought about in connection with the acquisition of an interest in such land by a public agency for wildlife habitat, marsh restoration, public recreation, or public access. 14 Cal. Code Regs. § 10125.

13   Gov't Code § 66632(a).

14   *Id.* § 66632.

The regulations include additional, different lists of activities that may be permitted within the 100-foot shoreline band, in salt ponds and managed wetlands, in Suisun Marsh, and in other areas under the Commissioner's jurisdiction.

An administrative permit may be acted on by the Executive Director unless either of the following occurs:

> when the Commission holds a meeting within 14 days of the mailing of the public notice of the pending application, one or more Commissioner has objected at the meeting to the issuance of the administrative permit and the Commission has determined at that meeting by a majority of those present and voting that the Commission should process the application as a major permit application

> when the Commission does not hold a meeting within 14 days of the mailing of the public notice of the pending application, one or more Commissioner has submitted to the Executive Director a written objection to the issuance of the administrative permit within 14 days of the mailing of the administrative listing and the Commission has determined at the first meeting following the objection by a majority of those present and voting that the Commission should process the application as a major application[15]

If the Executive Director denies an administrative permit, a project applicant may bring its application before the commission so long as it supplements its application with all the requirements for a major permit.[16]

Emergency Permits

Emergency permit application procedures are somewhat informal. An application can be made through a letter, or if the nature of the emergency does not allow for sufficient time for a letter, by telephone or in person.[17] The application must state the nature of the emergency, the location of the emergency, and the work proposed. The amount of information needed to describe these aspects of the emergency must be consistent with the time the emergency allows.[18]

Once an emergency application is submitted, the Executive Director will confirm the existence of the emergency, and if time permits, consult with the chair of the Commission, prior to issuing an emergency permit.[19] The Executive Director will issue the permit if the nature of the emergency prevents the use of normal procedures and if the proposed work is otherwise consistent with the McAteer Petris Act provisions, the Bay Plan, or if applicable, other BCDC regulations related to the Suisun Marsh.[20]

15   *Id.* § 10621.
16   *Id.* § 10624.
17   *Id.* § 10640.
18   *Id.* § 10641.
19   *Id.* §§ 10650–51.
20   *Id.* § 10652.

Major Permits

Any activity that does not qualify for an administrative or emergency permit will require a major permit. To secure a major permit, the project proponent must submit a detailed application containing among other things:

> a list of previous BCDC permits for the site

> a detailed description and purpose of the proposed fill, including photographs of current conditions

> a detailed narrative explanation of how the fill would comply with McAteer-Petris Act and Bay Plan policies; this includes why the fill is the minimum amount necessary and why there are no alternative upland locations for the project that would avoid the need for fill

> a vicinity map and project site plan

> a mitigation plan

> public access information

> evidence that the applicant has obtained all required local discretionary approvals

> evidence of environmental clearance, such as a certified EIR

> public notice information

> a list of campaign contributions to BCDC commissioners in the preceding 12 months

> a sliding scale application fee based on the total project cost (as of publication of this book, these fees are between $350 and $600,000)

BCDC and several other state and federal agencies have agreed to accept a standard application form to reduce the documentary burden on an applicant. According to BCDC staff, the Joint Aquatic Resource Permit Application (JARPA) does not dispense with the need to have early contact with staff from each relevant agency to determine the specific information required by each agency and to ensure that the project is designed in a manner satisfactory to each agency. Contact with the staff of each agency will clarify if using JARPA or agency-specific applications would be more efficient.

Advisory Bodies and Pre-Application Hearings

Design Review Board

Although not mandatory, BCDC staff encourages applicants to participate in a pre-application Design Review Board hearing to provide the applicant advice on adjusting proposed work to address significant issues the Board may identify at the front end of the application process. The Design Review Board serves as an advisory board to the Commission and its staff and is comprised of members with landscape architecture, architecture, and civil engineering expertise. The Design Review Board focuses on a project's effects on appearance, design and scenic views and public access. After an application is submitted, staff will encourage one or more subsequent hearings with the Design Review Board to continue to shape a project so that by the time a project reaches the Commission,

JARPA = Joint Aquatic Resource Permit Application

EIR = Environmental Impact Report

all major issues have been ironed out. While the Commission will consider the Design Review Board's recommendations, the Commission cannot deny a permit solely on the basis of the appearance or design of the project except to the extent it relates to the project providing the maximum public access feasible.

Engineering Criteria Review Board

Projects that involve significant in-water work that could pose seismic risks (such as the construction of a bridge or levee), or that involve significant coastal engineering, flooding, or sea level rise issues, may be requested to go before the Engineering Criteria Review Board which, like the Design Review Board, serves as an advisory body to staff and the Commission. The Engineering Criteria Review Board makes recommendations related to the safety of fills and structures placed on fill.

Major Permit Processing

Once BCDC receives an application, the Commission's staff has 30 days to determine whether the application is complete.[21] After the Commission's staff determines that an application is complete, the staff files and distributes the application to the Commission and certain state agencies.[22] BCDC staff also prepares a summary of the application that is distributed to the Commission, certain state agencies and the public.[23] At least 28 days after the application has been filed and at least 10 days after the summary has been distributed, the Commission will hold a public hearing on the application.[24] Unless the applicant agrees to provide the Commission with more time, the Commission must vote on a permit application within 90 days of the filing of the application.[25]

Advisory Hearings

As noted above, staff often strongly encourages projects to go before the Design Review Board for an advisory recommendation to the Commission. In addition to a potential pre-application hearing, a hearing is usually scheduled after the application has been submitted but usually after any draft environmental document on the project has been circulated. While the Commission can deny an application if it agrees with a Design Review Board finding that the project does not include sufficient public access, the Commission cannot deny a permit solely on the basis of the appearance or design of the project.

---

21 14 Cal. Code Regs. § 10350.

22 *Id.* § 10360.

23 *Id.* § 10380.

24 *Id.* §§ 10400–10401.

25 Gov't Code § 66632(f); 14 Cal. Code Regs. §§ 10400–10403, 10505.

Commission Hearing

BCDC regulations require a noticed public hearing on an application.[26] The Commission will often vote on a project application at a second meeting without reopening the public hearing. At the first meeting, the applicant or applicant's representative can describe the project and explain why the permit should be granted.[27] Ten minutes is usually allowed for the applicant's presentation. At the next meeting, the Commission's staff presents its recommendation,[28] and the Commission votes on the application.[29] The applicant has an opportunity to comment on the staff's recommendation before the Commission votes.[30] Thirteen members of the 27-member Commission must vote in favor of a project in order for a project to be approved.[31]

Design Review Board

As noted above, to assist the Commission in evaluating the appearance, design and provision of maximum feasible public access, many applications for major projects are evaluated by the Commission's Design Review Board, an advisory board made up of architects, landscape architects, engineers, and other design professionals.[32] Special drawings and exhibits are needed for this review.[33] The Board advises the Commission on appearance and design issues as well as on the adequacy of the public access in a proposed project. The Design Review Board's evaluation of a proposed project is normally scheduled to take place prior to the Commission's public hearing on the application, but usually after any draft environmental document on the project has been circulated. As noted above, while the Commission can deny an application if it agrees with a Design Review Board finding that the project does not include sufficient public access, the Commission cannot deny a permit solely on the basis of the appearance or design of the project.

Engineering Criteria Review Board

Buildings or other facilities constructed on Bay fill pose particular risks during earthquakes. To assist the Commission in evaluating the safety of such proposals, they may be evaluated by the Commission's Engineering Criteria Review Board, an advisory panel composed of civil engineers, geologists, soils engineers, structural engineers, and other

---

26   14 Cal. Code Regs. § 10420.

27   *Id.* § 10410.

28   To ensure full compliance with the Commission's laws and policies, permits granted by the Commission generally include several conditions that must be carried out as part of the authorized project. Gov't Code § 66632(f); 14 Cal. Code Regs. § 10503. Typical permit conditions include requirements to construct, guarantee and maintain public access to the Bay, specified construction methods to assure safety or to protect water quality, plan review requirements that must be met before construction can begin, and mitigation requirements to offset the adverse environmental impacts of the project.

29   14 Cal. Code Regs. §§ 10500, 10504.

30   *Id.* § 10505.

31   Gov't Code §66632(f); 14 Cal. Code Regs. § 10512.

32   14 Cal. Code Regs. § 10270.

33   *Id.* § 10315.

The CZMA procedural burden is minimal if the project applicant is also submitting an application for a BCDC permit. One wrinkle with a BCDC CZMA certification, however, is that BCDC may potentially look beyond its jurisdictional area under the McAteer-Petris Act and reach projects that would not otherwise require a BCDC permit. In *Acme Fill Corp. v. BCDC*, BCDC requested that a landfill expansion project receiving a Corps permit obtain a BCDC CZMA consistency review even though the project was located entirely landward of BCDC's 100-foot shoreline band jurisdiction. The project applicant challenged this requirement, arguing that the Bay Plan should not be applied to projects outside of BCDC's jurisdiction. The Court of Appeal disagreed. It upheld BCDC's position that a CZMA certification is required for projects located outside its jurisdiction but that "may have a substantial effect" on the resources within its jurisdiction. (*Acme Fill Corp. v. San Francisco Bay Conservation and Dev. Comm.*, 232 Cal. App. 3d 1056 (1986))

seismic experts. Special drawings and exhibits are needed for this review.[34] BCDC staff has indicated that that the Board is only used for projects with significant seismic concerns such as bridges or levees and that the review would take place around the same time as any review by the Design Review Board.

Coastal Zone Management Act Certification

The Coastal Zone Management Act[35] (CZMA) was enacted to encourage coastal states to develop comprehensive programs to manage and balance competing uses of, and impacts to, coastal resources. Section 307 of the CZMA requires that any applicant for a federal permit in or outside of the coastal zone that affects any coastal zone land, or water use or natural resource, must submit a "consistency certification" to the federal agency certifying that the activity complies with the state's Coastal Management Program. For projects within the San Francisco Bay coastal zone, the state agency that reviews this consistency certification is BCDC, which determines whether a project is consistent with the Bay Plan.

CALIFORNIA COASTAL COMMISSION

The California Coastal Act of 1976

Development located in California's "coastal zone" is subject to regulation under the California Coastal Act of 1976 (Coastal Act).[36] The Coastal Act establishes comprehensive goals for the protection of the "coastal resources" of California. Those "coastal resources" include wetlands and environmentally sensitive habitat areas (ESHA), as well as resources such as water quality, public access and recreation, agriculture, natural landforms, and scenic values. The following discussion highlights relevant provisions of the Coastal Act, regulations adopted by the California Coastal Commission (Coastal Commission) to implement the Coastal Act[37] (Commission Regulations), and policies of the Coastal Commission which bear upon the regulation of wetlands and ESHAs. This discussion is intended to provide general background and identify the types of issues that might be encountered by development proposals along California's coast. It is not intended to provide a comprehensive level of guidance, as is provided in other chapters of this book covering, e.g., wetlands and endangered species.

History and Background

In 1972, California voters passed Proposition 20, the Coastal Zone Conservation Act.[38] The product of growing environmental and public access concerns arising from development along California's coastline, Proposition 20 created the California

34 14 Cal. Code Regs. § 10316.

35 16 U.S.C. § 1451 *et seq.*

36 The Coastal Act is found in Pub. Res. Code § 3000 *et seq.*

37 The Commission Regulations are found at 14 Cal. Code Regs. § 13001 *et seq.*

38 COASTAL ZONE CONSERVATION ACT California Proposition 20 (1972). http://repository.uchastings.edu/ca_ballot_props/771.

Coastal Zone Conservation Commission (Conservation Commission). This body was tasked with preparing a "comprehensive, coordinated, enforceable plan for the orderly, long-range conservation and management of the natural resources"[39] of California's coast. That area, called the "permit area of the coastal zone," was defined to be "that portion of the coastal zone lying between the seaward limit of the jurisdiction of the state and 1,000 yards landward from the mean high tide line, subject to various exceptions," referred to as "Coastal Zone" for purposes of this discussion.

The Conservation Commission was given four years to do its work. For that interim period, Proposition 20 gave the Conservation Commission and six regional commissions permit authority within the permit area, which began the regulatory interplay between local government and the State along California's coast. The Conservation Commission delivered its California Coastal Zone Conservation Plan to the Legislature on December 1, 1975. Subsequently, the California Coastal Act of 1976 was enacted and the Coastal Commission replaced the Conservation Commission and the regional commissions.

The Coastal Act prioritizes preservation and enhancement of public access to the coast, coastal-dependent development, and coastal resources, including wetlands and ESHA. Through the Coastal Act and the Commission Regulations, various policies and permitting procedures are now applicable within the boundaries of the Coastal Zone. There are 61 cities and 15 counties whose boundaries include land within the Coastal Zone.

CZMA = Coastal Zone Management Act

ESHA = environmentally sensitive habitat area

The Commission—Members and Staff

The Coastal Commission is comprised of fifteen members,[40] twelve of whom are appointed voting members and three of whom are non-voting members.[41] Of the twelve voting Commissioners, four are appointed by the Governor, four by the Senate Rules Committee, and four by the Speaker of the Assembly.[42] Six of the twelve Commissioners are local elected officials from six coastal regions.[43] The other six voting members are public representatives "at large."

The day-to-day activities of the Coastal Commission are overseen by an Executive Director, with the support of administrative, planning, enforcement, and legal staff.

Coastal Commission Jurisdictional Boundaries

The Coastal Commission regulates land and water uses within the Coastal Zone, which includes roughly 1.5 million acres along the 1,100 miles of California's coastline. California's nine offshore islands also are within the jurisdiction of the Coastal

---

39   *Id.*

40   Pub. Res. Code § 30301.

41   *Id.* §§ 30301(a)–(c), 30301.5. The three non-voting members are the secretary of the Resources Agency, the secretary of the Business and Transportation Agency, and the chairperson of the State Lands Commission, or their designees.

42   *Id.* § 30301(d)–(e).

43   Pub. Res. Code §§ 30301(e), 30301.2(a).

LCP = Local Coastal Program

LUP = Land Use Plan

IAP = Implementing Actions Plan

Commission. As a general statement subject to many exceptions, the Coastal Zone extends inland "generally 1,000 yards from the mean high tide line of the sea."[44] Of particular relevance to natural resource issues is the definition of the "sea":

> "Sea" means the Pacific Ocean and all harbors, bays, channels, estuaries, salt marshes, sloughs, and other areas subject to tidal action through any connection with the Pacific Ocean, excluding nonestuarine rivers, streams, tributaries, creeks, and flood control and drainage channels. "Sea" does not include the area of jurisdiction of the San Francisco Bay Conservation and Development Commission . . . .[45]

Clearly, for Coastal Act purposes, the "sea" means much more than "the ocean." This distinction might become particularly important, for example, in delineating wetlands on land adjacent to a river which flows into the ocean more than 1,000 yards downstream. If that adjacent river is part of the "sea," the property likely is in the Coastal Zone. If so, what may not be "wetlands" outside of the Coastal Zone may now fall under the Coastal Commission's more expansive wetlands definition, discussed below.

Coastal Zone boundary maps are available on the Coastal Commission's website.[46] Notably, the Commission's jurisdiction does not extend to the San Francisco Bay, which is regulated by the San Francisco Bay Conservation and Development Commission as described above.[47]

Local Coastal Programs

The Coastal Act requires local agencies whose boundaries include property within the Coastal Zone to prepare Local Coastal Programs (LCPs). An LCP consists of both a Land Use Plan (LUP) and an Implementing Actions Plan (IAP). Functionally, the LUP will establish land uses and related policies, while the IAP will consist of zoning ordinances, zoning maps, and other implementing actions needed to carry out the provisions of the LUP.

After preparing and approving the LCP locally, the LCP is submitted to the Coastal Commission for certification. An LCP is certified only when both the LUP and the IAP have been certified. The local agency has options as to how it submits the LCP to the Coastal Commission.

The LUP may be submitted alone and may be certified by the Commission before the IAP is prepared and submitted. Or, the agency may submit and seek certification of the LUP and IAP together.[48] A third option is for the agency to process LUPs and IAPs, either separate or together, for different geographic units of its Coastal Zone.[49] This often occurs

By analogy, LUP provisions are similar to general plan land use provisions and IAP provisions are similar to zoning provisions. There is no standard format for an LCP. Some local agencies prepare standalone documents, some include a Local Coastal Element within their general plan, and others incorporate their general plan and zoning requirements by reference.

---

44   *Id.* § 30103(a).

45   *Id.* § 30115.

46   https://www.coastal.ca.gov/maps/czb/.

47   http://www.bcdc.ca.gov/.

48   Pub. Res. Code § 30511(a)–(b).

49   *Id.* § 30511(c).

when a specific geographical area requires more focused attention and is, therefore, "white holed" to allow the balance of the LCP to proceed toward certification.

As a general statement which does have exceptions, permitting authority within the Coastal Zone rests with the Coastal Commission before an LCP is certified and with the local agency after the LCP is certified. This is discussed in further detail below.

Development within the Coastal Zone

Scope of Regulated Development

The Coastal Act's definition of "development" is broad.[50] "Development" means:

> . . . on land, in or under water, the placement or erection of any solid material or structure; discharge or disposal of any dredged material or of any gaseous, liquid, solid, or thermal waste; grading, removing, dredging, mining, or extraction of any materials; change in the density or intensity of use of land, including, but not limited to, subdivision pursuant to the Subdivision Map Act (commencing with Section 66410 of the Government Code), and any other division of land, including lot splits, except where the land division is brought about in connection with the purchase of such land by a public agency for public recreational use; change in the intensity of use of water, or of access thereto; construction, reconstruction, demolition, or alteration of the size of any structure, including any facility of any private, public, or municipal utility; and the removal or harvesting of major vegetation other than for agricultural purposes, kelp harvesting, and timber operations which are in accordance with a timber harvesting plan . . . .

To further emphasize the breadth of "development" under the Coastal Act, a "structure" "includes, but is not limited to, any building, road, pipe, flume, conduit, siphon, aqueduct, telephone line, and electrical power transmission and distribution line."[51]

In addition, a "change in the density or intensity of use of land" has been interpreted by the courts to include both an increase and a *decrease* in the intensity of a use, "such as by limiting public access to the coastline or reducing the number of lots available for residential purposes."[52] For example, the closing of a gate to a beach has been found to be "development" under the Coastal Act definition.[53]

---

50 *Id.* § 30106.

51 *Id.*

52 *Pacific Palisades Bowl Mobile Estates, LLC v. City of Los Angeles,* 55 Cal. 4th 783, 795 (2012).

53 *Surfrider Foundation v. Martins Beach 1, LLC* (2017) 14 Cal. App. 5th 238, 253–54 (finding that closing public access constituted "development" requiring a Coastal Development Permit under Pub. Res. Code § 30106). Review denied by the California Supreme Court on October 25, 2017. Certiorari denied by the U.S. Supreme Court on October 1, 2018 (139 S.Ct. 54).

CDP = Coastal Development
Permit

Coastal Development Permits

With very limited exceptions, development within the Coastal Zone requires a Coastal Development Permit (CDP).[54] The CDP is in addition to all other permits required by other agencies.[55] Depending upon the circumstances, either the Coastal Commission or the local agency will have primary permitting authority. Where the local agency has primary permitting authority, appeal to the Coastal Commission is possible in limited circumstances.[56] Where the Coastal Commission has primary permitting authority, there is no appeal. A decision of the Coastal Commission may be challenged only through litigation.

Although the Coastal Act broadly defines "development," it also provides exemptions[57] and opportunities for exclusions[58] from its permitting requirements. In addition, Public Resources Code Section 30624.7 allows for a waiver of CDP requirements by the Executive Director for a proposed development considered to be *de minimis.*

For purposes of this chapter, it is not necessary to review the full range of those exemptions, exclusions, and waivers. It is important to note, however, the potential role that coastal resources—in particular, wetlands and ESHA—can play in disqualifying an exemption, exclusion, or waiver. In almost all cases, an exemption, exclusion, or waiver will not be available if the proposed development may have an adverse effect on coastal resources.[59] The issuance of administrative and emergency permits, though not addressed in this chapter, also is constrained by concerns related to impacts upon coastal resources.

Coastal Commission's Permitting Authority

The Coastal Act provides the Coastal Commission with *permanent* authority, often referred to as either "original permit jurisdiction" or "retained permit jurisdiction," over the approval of CDPs for certain categories of development. Those are "any development proposed or undertaken on any tidelands, submerged lands, or on public trust lands" in the Coastal Zone,[60] some port development, and development "within any state university or college within the Coastal Zone."[61] In these instances, the Coastal Commission's permitting authority does not shift to local government even after certification of the local agency's LCP.

---

54 Pub. Res. Code § 30600. Practitioners should note that the Commission's regulations specify that when development for which a CDP is required also requires a permit from one or more cities or counties or other state or local governmental agencies, the Commission will not accept an application for the CDP unless all such governmental agencies have granted at a minimum their preliminary approvals for such development. 14 Cal. Code Regs. § 13052. Certain exceptions may apply. *Id.* § 13053. As a result of this sequencing requirement, the need for a CDP may prolong the time it takes to fully entitle a project.

55 *Id.* § 30600(a).

56 *Id.* §§ 30603, 30625.

57 See *id.* § 30610(a)–(d) and (f)–(h).

58 For example, see *id.* § 30610(e) and (i).

59 For example, see *id.* § 30610(a), (b), (d), (e), (f), and (i); *id.* § 30624.7.

60 *Id.* § 30519(b).

61 *Id.*

With respect to other development within the Coastal Zone in local jurisdictions, the Coastal Commission generally holds permitting authority until the LCP for the local agency has been certified by the Coastal Commission.

Finally, the Coastal Act allows the Coastal Commission to act upon a "consolidated" CDP if (1) the development requires a CDP from both the Commission and a local agency with a certified LCP and (2) the applicant, the local agency, and the Commission all agree to consolidate the permit action for determination by the Commission.[62]

Transfer of Permitting Authority to the Local Agency

It is commonly stated that the Coastal Commission has primary authority for acting on CDPs within a local agency's jurisdiction if that agency does not yet have a certified LCP. As a practical matter, that is generally accurate. Nonetheless, the Coastal Act does provide an option for a local agency to assume, with some exceptions,[63] permit authority within its jurisdiction prior to certification of its LCP.[64] While it is rare for a local agency to take the steps necessary to exercise that option, it has happened. In 1978, the City of Los Angeles opted to approve or deny CDPs in its Coastal Zone prior to certification of its LCP and developed a permit program to do so.[65] Since then, the City has acted pursuant to that permit program while it has developed and obtained certification of LCPs for various geographical units of the City.

In general, once a local agency's LCP is certified, the primary authority to act upon CDPs shifts to the local agency.[66] Public Resources Code Section 30519(a) provides:

> Except for appeals to the commission, as provided in Section 30603, after a local coastal program, or any portion thereof, has been certified and all implementing actions within the area affected have become effective, the development review authority provided for in Chapter 7 (commencing with Section 30600) shall no longer be exercised by the commission over any new development proposed within the area to which the certified local coastal program, or any portion thereof, applies and shall at that time be delegated to the local government that is implementing the local coastal program or any portion thereof.

It is important, however, to note the use of the words "new development" in Section 30519(a). These words have been interpreted and applied by the Coastal Commission to mean that, after LCP certification, if a proposed development modifies either (1) the terms or conditions of a CDP approved by the Commission before LCP certification or (2) a development approved by the Coastal Commission before LCP certification, then it is not "new development" and the Commission retains primary permitting authority. On

---

62   *Id.* § 30601.3
63   *Id.* § 30600(b)(2).
64   *Id.* §§ 30600(b), 30620.5.
65   Sec. 12.20.2, Los Angeles Municipal Code.
66   Pub. Res. Code §§ 30600(d), 30519.

the other hand, if the development activity is "new development," the local government has primary permitting authority. There is not always a bright line between "new" and "modified" development.

Even where the Coastal Commission has primary CDP authority, the development typically will first need to be approved by the local agency as an "approval in concept" before it can be submitted to the Coastal Commission for the approval of a CDP.

Appeals of Locally Approved CDPs

Appeals from local agency CDP decisions generally must meet the following requirements in order to be heard by the Coastal Commission:

First, the appeal must comply with the procedural requirements set forth in Sections 30602 and 30603 of the Coastal Act,[67] as applicable, and Section 13318 of the Commission Regulations.[68] These provisions identify who may appeal and the timing for an appeal.

Second, after LCP certification, the development must fall within specific categories,[69] the most notable of which are developments:

> located between the sea and the first public road paralleling the sea or within 300 feet of the inland extent of any beach or of the mean high tideline of the sea where there is no beach, whichever is the greater distance;[70] or

> located on tidelands, submerged lands, public trust lands, within 100 feet of any wetland, estuary, or stream, or within 300 feet of the top of the seaward face of any coastal bluff;[71] or

> located in a sensitive coastal resource area;[72] or

> a major public works project or major energy facility[73]

Third, the Coastal Commission must find that "no substantial issue" exists as to the appeal.[74] The "substantial issue" hearing is held separate from the actual appeal hearing, solely to determine if there is a basis for the appeals process to move forward to a hearing.

De Novo Hearing

The Coastal Act provides that Coastal Commission hearings on CDP appeals shall be conducted on a de novo basis. This has potentially significant implications for natural resource issues relative to the California Environmental Quality Act (CEQA). In acting upon a CDP application, the local agency will prepare the appropriate environmental

---

67 Pub. Res. Code §§ 30602, 30603.

68 14 Cal. Code Regs. § 13318.

69 Pub. Res. Code § 30603(a).

70 *Id.* § 30603(a)(1).

71 *Id.* § 30603(a)(2).

72 *Id.* § 30603(a)(3).

73 *Id.* § 30603(a)(5).

74 *Id.* § 30625(b); 14 Cal. Code Regs. § 13115.

review documentation under CEQA. When the Coastal Commission considers approval of a CDP, whether originally or on appeal, it may rely for its environmental evaluation upon the regulatory program certified by the Secretary of the Resources Agency pursuant to Section 21080.5 of CEQA. Because the Coastal Commission is acting de novo on appeal, once the "no substantial issue" determination has been made and the appeal has been accepted, the decision of the local agency to approve the CDP has been ruled to be a nullity. In *Fudge v. City of Laguna Beach*,[75] the City of Laguna Beach had issued a CDP for the demolition of a home. Mark Fudge filed an action under CEQA challenging the approval by the City. But he also appealed the City's approval of the CDP to the Coastal Commission. The court held that once the appeal was accepted by the Commission, the CEQA action in state court was rendered moot because the Coastal Commission would be acting "de novo" on the CDP using the certified regulatory program for its environmental analysis—and not the EIR used by the City. Therefore, the court reasoned, the CEQA case was properly dismissed once the Commission accepted the appeal.[76]

CEQA = California Environmental Quality Act

The Standard of Review

Different standards of review can be applied to a CDP determination depending upon the context of the proposed development. Before LCP certification, the standard is that (1) the development is in conformity with Chapter 3 of the Coastal Act and (2) approval of the development will not prejudice the preparation of an LCP which is in conformity with Chapter 3.[77] After LCP certification, the standard of review shifts to conformity with the LCP.[78] If the property lies between "the nearest public road and the sea or the shoreline of any body of water located within the coastal zone," a finding also must be made that the development is in conformity with the public access and public recreation policies of Chapter 3 of the Coastal Act.[79]

With respect to wetlands and ESHA issues, the difference between the pre-certification standard and the post-certification standard can be significant. Whereas Chapter 3 of the Coastal Act primarily contains policy statements subject to varying interpretations and applications, certified LCPs generally contain provisions implementing those Chapter 3 policies with specific development standards and requirements. As a result, in the context of a CDP application in a jurisdiction without a certified LCP, the Coastal Commission has greater discretion in applying Chapter 3 policies to the specific coastal resource issues (including wetlands and ESHA issues) presented by the CDP application. On the other hand, if an LCP has been certified, the Coastal Commission, on appeal, must evaluate those resource issues only for conformity with the LCP which, in most cases, will specifically state how those issues must be addressed.

---

75   32 Cal. App. 5th 193 (2019).

76   *Id.* at 204–05.

77   Pub. Res. Code § 30604(a).

78   *Id.* § 30604(b).

79   *Id.* § 30604(c).

Coastal Wetlands and ESHA

Coastal Commission decisions related to wetlands and ESHA are principally guided by Coastal Act definitions and policies set forth in Chapter 3 of the Coastal Act (Chapter 3 Policies).[80] The Chapter 3 Policies provide the focal point for the evaluation and treatment of wetlands and ESHA issues. They set the broad general standards by which the adequacy of LCPs is evaluated and determine the conditions on which Coastal Commission-issued CDPs may be approved, if at all.[81]

Chapter 3 Policies are legislatively enacted policies found within the Coastal Act itself, and should be distinguished from the Coastal Commission's interpretation and application of the Coastal Act which is reflected in Commission Regulations, Coastal Commission "guidance" (Commission Guidance), and the Commission's internal policies and practices. Commission Regulations have been adopted by the Commission at the direction of the Coastal Act. Commission Guidance is reflected in documents published by the Coastal Commission which, although not legally binding, reflect the Commission's policies and suggested guidance for local agencies as they prepare or amend their LCPs and act upon CDPs.

Commission Regulations and Commission Guidance, of course, may not expand the authority granted to the Coastal Commission by the Coastal Act. However, in reviewing regulations adopted at the direction of a statute, the courts will consider the specialized knowledge and expertise of the agency charged with the implementation of the statute.[82] This is particularly true "where the statute at issue is a complex, technical one" and where the regulations were adopted pursuant to the Administrative Procedure Act.[83] In the case of the implementation of the Chapter 3 Policies related to wetlands and ESHA, the technical criteria applied to the determination of the presence of wetlands or ESHA, as will be discussed below, are found primarily in Commission Regulations, Commission Guidance, and the Commission's practice.

It is important to note that, while there may be overlap in some circumstances, wetlands are not necessarily ESHA and ESHA does not necessarily include wetlands.

Wetlands

The Coastal Act defines "wetland" as follows:

> "Wetland" means lands within the coastal zone which may be covered periodically or permanently with shallow water and include saltwater marshes, freshwater marshes, open or closed brackish water marshes, swamps, mudflats, and fens.[84]

---

80   Pub. Res. Code §§ 30210–30265.5.

81   *Id.* § 30200.

82   *California Building Industry Assn. v. Bay Area Air Quality Management District*, 62 Cal. 4th 369, 381 (2015).

83   *Id.*

84   Pub. Res. Code § 30121.

The Chapter 3 Policies most relevant to wetlands begin with Section 30231, which provides a broad directive with respect to the protection of natural resources in the Coastal Zone:

> The biological productivity and the quality of coastal waters, streams, wetlands, estuaries, and lakes appropriate to maintain optimum populations of marine organisms and for the protection of human health shall be maintained and, where feasible, restored through, among other means, minimizing adverse effects of waste water discharges and entrainment, controlling runoff, preventing depletion of ground water supplies and substantial interference with surface water flow, encouraging waste water reclamation, maintaining natural vegetation buffer areas that protect riparian habitats, and minimizing alteration of natural streams.

The definition of "wetland" requires interpretation supported by technical justification and criteria. During the course of its history, although the Coastal Act's definition of "wetland" has not changed, the Coastal Commission's classification of property as a "wetland" has evolved through practice and policy.[85] Through that evolution, the Coastal Commission's policies and practices have led to significant differences between the delineation and treatment of wetlands in the Coastal Zone and those outside of the Coastal Commission's jurisdiction, as will be discussed below. In the Coastal Zone, the jurisdictions of the Corps and of the Coastal Commission will overlap when the applicable criteria of both agencies indicate that wetlands are present. In those cases, the requirements of both agencies must be met. However, it is common for conditions which are not considered by the Corps to constitute wetlands to nonetheless be considered wetlands within the Coastal Zone.

The circumstances in which wetlands and other protected areas may be filled, dredged, or diked are itemized in Section 30233(a). By virtue of what it omits, this Section stands as a ban on the filling of wetlands under all circumstances not included within this list.

> The diking, filling, or dredging of open coastal waters, wetlands, estuaries, and lakes shall be permitted in accordance with other applicable provisions of this division where there is no feasible less environmentally damaging alternative, and where feasible mitigation measures have been provided to minimize adverse environmental effects, and shall be limited to the following:
>
> (1) New or expanded port, energy, and coastal-dependent industrial facilities, including commercial fishing facilities
>
> (2) Maintaining existing, or restoring previously dredged, depths in existing navigational channels, turning basins, vessel berthing and mooring areas, and boat launching ramps

85 Coastal Commission Wetlands Workshop, April 2016. https://www.coastal.ca.gov/meetings/workshops/.

(3) In open coastal waters, other than wetlands, including streams, estuaries, and lakes, new or expanded boating facilities and the placement of structural pilings for public recreational piers that provide public access and recreational opportunities

(4) Incidental public service purposes, including but not limited to, burying cables and pipes or inspection of piers and maintenance of existing intake and outfall lines

(5) Mineral extraction, including sand for restoring beaches, except in environmentally sensitive areas

(6) Restoration purposes

(7) Nature study, aquaculture, or similar resource dependent activities

In addition to limiting the types of development for which the fill of wetlands and other coastal waters may be allowed, Section 30233(a) stipulates that such development is permitted only where "no feasible less environmentally damaging alternative" exists and where "feasible mitigation measures have been provided to minimize adverse environmental effects." Further guidance on these mitigation measures is found in Section 30607.1 which reads as follows:

Where any dike and fill development is permitted in wetlands in conformity with Section 30233 or other applicable policies set forth in this division, mitigation measures shall include, at a minimum, either acquisition of equivalent areas of equal or greater biological productivity or opening up equivalent areas to tidal action; provided, however, that if no appropriate restoration site is available, an in-lieu fee sufficient to provide an area of equivalent productive value or surface areas shall be dedicated to an appropriate public agency, or the replacement site shall be purchased before the dike or fill development may proceed. The mitigation measures shall not be required for temporary or short-term fill or diking if a bond or other evidence of financial responsibility is provided to assure that restoration will be accomplished in the shortest feasible time.

The use of Section 30607.1 has not been widespread. It has been used for public works projects, for example, to offset both wetland impacts resulting from critical highway construction[86] and temporary impacts to eelgrass and soft bottom habitat necessary to keep public access to a local island open during bridge construction.[87]

Commission Regulations provide further criteria for permit and appeal jurisdiction boundary determinations. Section 13577(b) states that the "precise boundaries" of the jurisdictional area for wetlands is to be determined using these criteria:

(1) Measure 100 feet landward from the upland limit of the wetland. Wetland shall be defined as land where the water table is at, near, or above the land

86 LCP Amendment MCO-MAJ-1-08, August 7, 2008. https://documents.coastal.ca.gov/reports/2008/8/Th27b-8-2008.pdf.

87 Application No. 5-14-1668, June 11, 2015. https://documents.coastal.ca.gov/reports/2015/6/th6b-6-2015.pdf.

surface long enough to promote the formation of hydric soils or to support the growth of hydrophytes, and shall also include those types of wetlands where vegetation is lacking and soil is poorly developed or absent as a result of frequent and drastic fluctuations of surface water levels, wave action, water flow, turbidity or high concentrations of salts or other substances in the substrate. Such wetlands can be recognized by the presence of surface water or saturated substrate at some time during each year and their location within, or adjacent to, vegetated wetlands or deep-water habitats.

For purposes of this section, the upland limit of a wetland shall be defined as:

(A) the boundary between land with predominantly hydrophytic cover and land with predominantly mesophytic or xerophytic cover

(B) the boundary between soil that is predominantly hydric and soil that is predominantly nonhydric; or

(C) in the case of wetlands without vegetation or soils, the boundary between land that is flooded or saturated at some time during years of normal precipitation, and land that is not

(2) For the purposes of this section, the term "wetland" shall not include wetland habitat created by the presence of and associated with agricultural ponds and reservoirs where:

(A) the pond or reservoir was in fact constructed by a farmer or rancher for agricultural purposes; and

(B) there is no evidence (e.g., aerial photographs, historical survey, etc.) showing that wetland habitat pre-dated the existence of the pond or reservoir. Areas with drained hydric soils that are no longer capable of supporting hydrophytes shall not be considered wetlands.

It is the interpretation and application of this regulation that has come to be known as the Coastal Commission's "one parameter" method of wetlands delineation. This contrasts with the "three parameter" delineation policy employed by the Army Corps of Engineers and the "two parameter" (or "modified three parameter") test applied by the Water Boards. The three parameters typically applied by the Corps and the Water Boards are hydrology, soils, and vegetation, each of which requires identification in the field of substantial evidence of indicators.

By contrast, the Coastal Commission's "one parameter" approach requires the presence of only one of the three indicators to conclude that a wetland is present. The result is that in many instances the Coastal Commission's delineators find wetlands to be present on a site, while the Corps or the Water Boards do not. Because the Commission Regulations do not define the characteristics set forth in Section 13577(b) (such as

Water Boards = State Water Resources Control Board and Regional Water Quality Control Boards

OBL = obligate species (species that occur almost always in wetlands)

FAC = facultative species (those species that are equally to occur in wetland or non-wetlands)

FACW = facultative wetland species (species that usually occur in wetlands)

what constitutes "hydric soils" or hydrophytic vegetation), reference to sources such as the 1987 USACE (U.S. Army Corps of Engineers) Wetland Delineation Manual is generally required to complete a wetlands delineation performed by Coastal Commission biologists. On occasion, the Commission's "delineators" will exercise their independent professional judgment in the delineation process if they believe that conditions in the field make the application of scientific methods and observations of indicators (or the absence of indicators) subject to uncertainty or error.[88]

A "one parameter" wetlands determination, though typically stated as a hard and fast rule by Coastal Commissioners and Coastal Staff, may be subject to qualification under a seldom-invoked, but nonetheless legally reasonable, policy stated by Commission staff as follows:[89]

> The Coastal Commission has found that OBL, FACW, and FAC species in the U.S. Fish and Wildlife Service's "National list of plant species that occur in wetlands: California (Region 0)" are presumptively "hydro-phytic" and, in general, a preponderance of those species is presumptive evidence of a wetland. The strength of this test is greater where most dominant wetland indicator species are classed as FACW or OBL. In recognition of the fact that a proportion of wetland indicator plants occur in uplands, the wetland presumption may be falsified where there is strong, positive evidence of upland conditions (as opposed to a lack of evidence, for example, of hydrology).

In other words, using prior methodology, the "one parameter rule" provided a rebuttable presumption that a wetland exists, which allowed an applicant to provide evidence to establish "strong, positive evidence of upland conditions" to overcome the one-parameter determination. As noted in a footnote to the above statement, the justification for this "presumption" approach is that facultative (FAC) species "are not reliable wetland indicators" given that only 34–66 percent of their occurrences are in wetlands. It is not clear whether the rationale behind this rebuttable presumption would apply equally to the wetlands delineation methodology used today. However, to the extent that a one-parameter wetland determination based upon the presence of hydrophytic vegetation relies upon the presence of FAC species for its conclusion, there may continue to be a legal rationale for providing "strong, positive evidence of upland conditions" to challenge that "one-parameter" wetlands determination.

Beyond Section 13577(b), the Commission Regulations are most notable in how the presence of wetland can influence the course of a particular process. For example, Section 13253 of the Commission Regulations identifies the circumstances under which improvements to an existing structure, other than a single-family residence or public works facility, requires a CDP. Among those circumstances:

---

88 Coastal Commission *Wetlands Briefing Background Information Handout*, October 5, 2011.

89 Commission Staff Report, June 25, 2003, Application No. 5-03-091, Exhibit 19, pp. 3–4 (https://documents.coastal.ca.gov/reports/2003/7/W9h-7-2003.pdf).

Improvement to any structure if the structure or the improvement is located: on a beach; in a wetland, stream, or lake; seaward of the mean high tide line; in an area designated as highly scenic in a certified land use plan; or within 50 feet of the edge of a coastal bluff....[90]

These examples demonstrate how the presence of wetlands (a similar provision of Section 13253 applies to ESHA) can dictate the process that a development applicant must undertake. While, on the surface, this regulation simply answers the question of whether or not a CDP is required, it potentially triggers the substantive determination as to whether wetland conditions exist on the property. If a CDP is required, in addition to limitations and conditions potentially placed on the proposed improvement, the CDP process easily could delay construction by 9 to 24 months.

Environmentally Sensitive Habitat Areas (ESHA)

The Coastal Act defines ESHA as follows:

"Environmentally sensitive area" means any area in which plant or animal life or their habitats are either rare or especially valuable because of their special nature or role in an ecosystem and which could be easily disturbed or degraded by human activities and developments.[91]

The use in this definition of terms such as "rare," "especially valuable," "special nature," and "easily disturbed" leave room for interpretation requiring technical support and criteria. That interpretation is not clearly defined in the Coastal Act or the Commission Regulations. In practice, the Coastal Commission approaches the designation of a specific area as an ESHA by evaluating both the development site and adjacent areas for the presence of those rare or especially valuable species. The California Natural Diversity Database and the Vegetation and Classification Mapping Program are the primary tools in this exercise,[92] providing data on special status plant and animal species, assessing the rarity of species identified on site, and providing mapping to assist in setting the boundaries of the ESHA.

Once identified, the treatment of ESHA is controlled by Section 30240 of the Coastal Act, which reads as follows:

a) Environmentally sensitive habitat areas shall be protected against any significant disruption of habitat values, and only uses dependent on those resources shall be allowed within those areas.

b) Development in areas adjacent to environmentally sensitive habitat areas and parks and recreation areas shall be sited and designed to prevent impacts which would significantly degrade those areas, and shall be compatible with the continuance of those habitat and recreation areas.

90   14 Cal. Code Regs. § 13253(b)(1).

91   Pub. Res. Code § 30107.5.

92   Coastal Commission ESHA Workshop, April 2016. https://www.coastal.ca.gov/meetings/workshops/.

Notably, while the wetland policy set forth in Section 30233(a) specifically references "feasible mitigation measures ... to minimize adverse environmental effects," there is no similar reference with respect to ESHA. Section 30240(a) mandates that ESHA "shall be protected" and 30240(b) requires that development *adjacent* to ESHA must be "sited and designed to prevent impacts." The only uses within ESHA mentioned by the statute as permissible are those that are dependent upon the resources within the ESHA and that do not disrupt the ESHA's habitat values.

In *Bolsa Chica Land Trust v. Superior Court*,[93] the absence of any indication to the contrary in Section 30240 led the Court of Appeal to conclude that the replacement of a degraded eucalyptus grove in one location with a new raptor habitat consisting of nesting poles, native trees, and other native vegetation in another location violated the express terms of Section 30240:

> [T]he language of section 30240 does not permit a process by which the habitat values of an ESHA can be isolated and then recreated in another location. Rather, a literal reading of the statute protects the area of an ESHA from uses which threaten the habitat values which exist in the ESHA. Importantly, while the obvious goal of section 30240 is to protect habitat values, the express terms of the statute do not provide that protection by treating those values as intangibles which can be moved from place to place to suit the needs of development. Rather, the terms of the statute protect habitat values by placing strict limits on the uses which may occur in an ESHA and by carefully controlling the manner uses in the area around the ESHA are developed.[94]

Similarly, in *McAllister v. California Coastal Commission*,[95] the Coastal Commission granted a CDP to homeowners who proposed to build a home on the Big Sur coast in the middle of the Coastal Range for an endangered butterfly. The project, the Commission found, had the potential to impact plants that represented one of only two species of host plants for the butterflies. The Commission approved mitigation for that potential impact, requiring the applicant to enlarge the remaining habitat by replacing the removed host plants at a 3:1 ratio. The Commission also found that the project site was within a larger habitat area for coastal bluff scrub. Nonetheless, the Commission approved the CDP, claiming that it was "compelled to relax the resource-dependent-use restriction and approve the Project in order to avoid an unconstitutional taking" of the applicants' property.[96] Finding, among other factors, that the record was silent on the avoidance of a taking as justification for deviating from the strict application of Section 30240 and that the

---

93 71 Cal. App. 4th 493 (1999).

94 *Id.* at 507 (citation omitted).

95 169 Cal. App. 4th 912 (2009).

96 *Id.* at 937.

Commission failed to avail itself of the provisions of the Coastal Act allowing it to resolve policy conflicts,[97] the court reversed the Commission's approval of the CDP.

These court decisions reflect the stringent protections accorded ESHA by the Coastal Act. They clearly preclude the loss of ESHA habitat values even where what might otherwise be considered adequate mitigation is provided.

Climate Change and Sea Level Rise

In recent years, the Coastal Commission has turned its attention to the potential effects of climate change on coastal resources. Citing its charge to protect, maintain, and enhance coastal resources, the Commission is preparing to "take planning and regulatory steps aimed at slowing global warming."[98] Some of the Commission's more prominent concerns are sea level rise, increased storm frequency and intensity, coastal erosion, and coastal flooding. From a natural resources perspective, the Commission sees potentially devastating effects upon coastal and marine habitats, wetlands, and water quality.

While it is too early to anticipate the full scope of the Coastal Commission's regulatory response to the effects of global climate change, the Commission has adopted a "California Coastal Commission Sea Level Rise Policy Guidance" (SLR Guidance).[99] The SLR Guidance sets forth interpretive guidelines which may be used by both the Coastal Commission and local agencies in preparing LCPs and in evaluating CDP applications. The SLR Guidance is not a regulatory document, but rather an advisory document. The SLR Guidance does not bind the Commission or local agencies to any particular course of conduct. Nonetheless, it does serve as a starting point for understanding the direction the Commission is likely to take as it reviews and evaluates LCP and CDP applications.

For LCP preparation and amendment, the SLR Guidance proposes, first, a sea level rise vulnerability assessment. This assessment consists of applying appropriate sea level rise projections to the planning area, identifying potential SLR impacts, and assessing the risks to coastal resources, including wetlands and ESHA. Next, the SLR Guidance proposes that the local agency identify "adaptation measures" and policy options. Finally, the policies will be included within the LCP and, after certification by the Commission, implemented.

An example of the many categories of issues addressed by the SLR Guidance is the question of whether wetlands and other coastal habitats have room to migrate inland. The implications include the need, under certain circumstances, to develop land use policies to ensure that open space is available into which the wetland will be able to migrate in the future.

With respect to the review of CDP applications, the SLR Guidance notes that, in general, sea level rise is only likely to be a factor in "those projects that are on low-lying

---

97 On occasion, the context of proposed development will present a conflict between Chapter 3 policies, often with respect to wetlands and ESHA issues. Section 30200(b) of the Coastal Act designates Section 30007.5 as the mechanism to be used to resolve any such conflicts.

98 Coastal Commission website: https://www.coastal.ca.gov/climate/whyinvolved.html.

99 Coastal Commission website: https://www.coastal.ca.gov/climate/slrguidance.html.

land, on eroding coastal bluffs, are in close proximity to water, or rely upon a shallow aquifer for water supply."[100] For those CDPs that do require an evaluation of the potential effects of sea level rise, the SLR Guidance offers a five-step analytical process:[101]

> Establish the projected sea level rise for the proposed project. The factors to address include the expected life of the project and the potential sea level rise scenarios, based on best available science.

> Determine how sea level rise may constrain the project site. Considerations include potential erosion, flooding, inundation, and wave impacts.

> Determine how, as a result of sea level rise, the project may impact coastal resources over time. Potentially impacted resources to evaluate include wetlands and ESHA.

> Identify project alternatives to both avoid and minimize resource impacts. This principle suggests relocating the project to a site that avoids sea level rise impacts. It also proposes an adaptation strategy to address unavoidable impacts.

> Finalize project design and submit CDP application. The prior steps lead to a potentially redesigned project and a project application that has taken into consideration the issues that Commission staff and the Commission are likely to raise.

• With respect to wetlands and ESHA issues, the SLR Guidance promotes the evaluation of the potential impacts of sea level rise on wetlands, ESHA, biological productivity in coastal waters, the boundaries of coastal habitats, and water quality. Once potential impacts, such as saltwater intrusion into wetlands, are identified, the SLR Guidance indicates that planning for the project (i.e., special conditions applied to the CDP approval) "should anticipate the migration and natural adaptation of coastal resources (beaches, access, wetlands, etc.) . . . to avoid future impacts to those resources from the new development."

For greater detail and insight into the planning and permitting implications of sea level rise, the SLR Guidance may be reviewed on the Coastal Commission's website.[102]

---

100 Coastal Commission website: https://www.coastal.ca.gov/climate/slrguidance.html (p. 21).

101 Coastal Commission website: https://www.coastal.ca.gov/climate/slrguidance.html (pp. 21, 100, 115).

102 Coastal Commission website: https://www.coastal.ca.gov/climate/slr/planning-permitting/.

CHAPTER 14

The Public Trust Doctrine

This chapter discusses the public trust doctrine, which is an overarching common law and California constitutional principle requiring state natural resource agencies to administer their programs for the benefit of the people and their interest in, among other things, water and wildlife resources.

INTRODUCTION TO THE PUBLIC TRUST DOCTRINE

The protection of wetlands, special-status species and other natural resources in California is primarily driven by state and federal statutes, such as the state and federal Endangered Species Acts, Migratory Bird Treaty Act, Bald and Golden Eagle Protection Act, Clean Water Act, Porter-Cologne Water Quality Control Act, National Environmental Policy Act, California Environmental Quality Act, and various provisions in the California Fish and Game Code. Practitioners must be well-acquainted with these statutes and interpretive case law to navigate a project through the various permitting processes and agencies that manage wetlands and special-status species.

Operating as an overlay to these statutory structures in California is the public trust doctrine. In American jurisprudence this is the principle that certain natural resources are understood to be held in trust by the government for the people, and that the government is subject thereby to certain trust obligations. The California Supreme Court has embraced the public trust doctrine as a legal tool to protect environmental and other public trust values, originally with respect to tidelands and navigable waters (as a matter of title) and later broadened to include water, wildlife, and other such resources. Accordingly, natural resource practitioners in California should have at least a passing familiarity with the doctrine, its scope and application, and the mechanisms by which it is enforced.

ORIGINS OF THE PUBLIC TRUST DOCTRINE

Most scholars agree that the public trust doctrine is rooted in ancient Roman law.

> By the law of nature these things are common to mankind—the air, running water, the sea and consequently the shores of the sea.[1]

From these earliest references to resources held in common by the public, English common law derived what we know today as the public trust doctrine, under which the sovereign owns "all of its navigable waterways and the lands lying beneath them 'as trustee of a public trust for the benefit of the people.'"[2]

As described in the seminal law review article *The Public Trust Doctrine in Natural Resources Law: Effective Judicial Intervention* by Joseph Sax, the doctrine is founded on several key principles, including the view that:

> [I]t [is] "inconceivable" that any person should claim a private property interest in the navigable waters of the United States . . . . An allied principle holds that certain interests are so particularly the gifts of nature's bounty that they ought to be reserved for the whole of the populace . . . . Finally, there is often a recognition, albeit one that has been irregularly perceived in legal doctrine, that certain uses have a peculiarly public nature that makes their adaptation to private use inappropriate. The best known example is

---

1   *National Audubon Society v. Superior Court*, 33 Cal. 3d 419, 434–35 (1983) (citing Institutes of Justinian 2.1.1).

2   *Id.* at 435 (citing *Colberg, Inc. v. State of California ex rel. Dep't Pub. Works*, 67 Cal. 2d 408, 416 (1967)).

found in the rule of water law that one does not own a property right in water in the same way he owns his watch or his shoes, but that he owns only an usufruct—an interest that incorporates the needs of others. It is thus thought to be incumbent upon the government to regulate water uses for the general benefit of the community and to take account thereby of the public nature and the interdependency which the physical quality of the resource implies.[3]

These principles and concepts began to emerge by the late nineteenth century, particularly in connection with the U.S. Supreme Court's decision *Illinois Central Railroad v. Illinois*,[4] which essentially announced the existence of the public trust doctrine in the United States. This decision is still regarded as the primary authority setting forth the rationale and general parameters of the doctrine.

Illinois Central Railroad involved an 1869 grant by the Illinois Legislature to the Illinois Central Railroad Company of fee simple title to 1,000 acres of tidal and submerged lands, representing virtually the entire waterfront of Chicago:

> The only limitations upon the grant were that the railroad company could not authorize obstruction of the harbor or impair the public right of navigation, and that the Legislature retained the right to regulate wharfage fees when docks were built. Four years later, the Legislature thought better of its action and enacted a measure to revoke the grant, an action which was challenged by the railroad.[5]

As described in a later public trust case, the *Illinois Central Railroad* court determined that the title a state holds to land under navigable waters:

> is held in trust for the people of the state, in order that they may enjoy the navigation of the waters and carry on commerce over them, free from obstruction or interference by private parties; that this trust devolving upon the State in the public interest is one which cannot be relinquished by a transfer of the property; that a State can no more abdicate its trust over such property, in which the whole people are interested, so as to leave it under the control of private parties, than it can abdicate its police powers in the administration of government and the preservation of the peace; and that the trust under which such lands are held is governmental so that they cannot be alienated, except to be used for the improvement of the public use in them.[6]

3   Joseph Sax, The Public Trust Doctrine in Natural Resources Law: Effective Judicial Intervention, 68 Mich. L. Rev. 471, 484–85 (1970) (citations omitted).

4   146 U.S. 387 (1892).

5   *City of Berkeley v. Superior Court*, 26 Cal. 3d 515, 521 (1980).

6   *Long Sault Development Co. v. Call*, 242 U.S. 272, 278–79 (1916) (citing *Illinois Central Railroad v. Illinois*, 146 U.S. 387 (1892)).

A core principle that emerges from the *Illinois Central Railroad* decision is that "[w]hen a state holds a resource which is available for the free use of the general public, a court will look with considerable skepticism upon *any* governmental conduct which is calculated *either* to reallocate that resource to more restricted uses *or* to subject public uses to the self-interest of private parties."[7] Because of its unique history and geography, this principle is reflected in the public trust doctrine in California with more than a few nuances and embellishments.

OVERVIEW OF THE PUBLIC TRUST DOCTRINE IN CALIFORNIA

The California Supreme Court expressly recognized that there are two distinct public trust doctrines: public trust duties that are derived from statutes, and the common law doctrine involving the government's affirmative duty to take the public trust into account.[8] These two approaches to the public trust doctrine often overlap, and it can be helpful for the practitioner to understand the difference between the two.

Courts have interpreted Section 4 of Article 10 of the California Constitution as providing a foundation for the public trust doctrine in California. This section reads in full:

> No individual, partnership, or corporation, claiming or possessing the frontage or tidal lands of a harbor, bay, inlet, estuary, or other navigable water in this State, shall be permitted to exclude the right of way to such water whenever it is required for any public purpose, nor to destroy or obstruct the free navigation of such water; and the Legislature shall enact such laws as will give the most liberal construction to this provision, so that access to the navigable waters of this State shall be always attainable for the people thereof.[9]

This section is focused primarily on what might be considered public trust easements and access rights. Other statutory authority in the state has expanded upon this rather narrow articulation of the doctrine to include an obligation by certain state agencies to protect resources held in trust for the public regardless of actual title.

For example, the California Legislature has incorporated the public trust doctrine into the Public Resources Code. Section 6009 provides legislative findings that reference several public trust concepts:

(1) Upon admission to the United States, and as incident of its sovereignty, California received title to the tidelands, submerged lands, and beds of navigable lakes and rivers within its borders, to be held subject to the public trust for

---

7   Sax, 68 Mich. L. Rev. at 490 (emphasis in original).

8   *Environmental Protection Information Center v. California Dep't of Forestry and Fire Protection*, 44 Cal. 4th 459, 515 (2008).

9   Cal. Const. Art. 10, Sec. 4.

statewide public purposes, including commerce, navigation, fisheries, and other recognized uses, and for preservation in their natural state.

CDFW or the "Department" = California Department of Fish and Wildlife

(2) The state's power and right to control, regulate, and utilize its tidelands and submerged lands when acting within the terms of the public trust is absolute.

(3) Tidelands and submerged lands granted by the Legislature to local entities remain subject to the public trust, and remain subject to the oversight authority of the state by and through the State Lands Commission.

(4) Grantees are required to manage the state's tidelands and submerged lands consistent with the terms and obligations of their grants and the public trust, without subjugation of statewide interests, concerns, or benefits to the inclination of local or municipal affairs, initiatives, or excises.

(5) The purposes and uses of tidelands and submerged lands is a statewide concern.[10]

Several other California statutes either expressly or impliedly require natural resource agencies to take into account the "public trust" when evaluating permits or authorizations or taking other actions that bear on the use of public trust resources.

Examples of natural resource agencies in California that must take into account public trust concerns include the following.

State Lands Commission

The State Lands Commission is subject to public trust obligations in connection with its administration and control over public trust lands. For example, the Commission must take the public trust into account when authorizing oil, gas, and mineral leases on tidal and submerged lands and the beds of navigable waters.[11] The Commission also has the authority to acquire or condemn a right-of-way easement across privately owned land or other land that it deems necessary to provide access to public land subject to the "public trust for commerce, navigation, and fisheries."[12]

California Department of Fish and Wildlife

CDFW is subject to public trust obligations in connection with the management of fish and wildlife resources.[13] More recently, in 2017 the Legislature has specifically addressed the Department's responsibilities in light of declining state revenues for the Department, noting that CDFW's "responsibilities have increased in order to protect public trust resources in the face of increasing population and resource management demands."[14]

---

10 Pub. Res. Code § 6009.

11 *Id.* § 6879 ("Each such agreement shall provide that any impairment of the public trust for commerce, navigation or fisheries to which said granted lands are subject is prohibited and shall be submitted to the State Lands Commission for approval. If the State Lands Commission shall find that said agreement so provides and that the entering into and the performance of such agreement is in the public interest, then the State Lands Commission may approve such agreement on behalf of the State.").

12 *Id.* § 6210.9.

13 Fish & Game Code § 711.7(a).

14 *Id.* § 710.5(a).

Delta Stewardship Council

The Delta Stewardship Council, created by the Sacramento-San Joaquin Delta Reform Act of 2009, manages certain water supply and land use issues in the Sacramento-San Joaquin Delta. The Act confirms that "[t]he longstanding constitutional principle of reasonable use and the public trust doctrine shall be the foundation of state water management policy and are particularly important and applicable to the Delta."[15]

SCOPE OF THE DOCTRINE

Although references to the public trust doctrine, or at least references to the "public trust," can be found scattered throughout the California Code and regulations, the primary guidance on what constitutes the public trust, its scope, and means of its enforcement is found in California case law.[16]

Beginnings of the Doctrine in California

Originally, the focus of the public trust doctrine in California mirrored the U.S. Supreme Court announcement in *Illinois Central Railroad* that "the public trust is not limited by the reach of the tides, but encompasses all navigable lakes and streams."[17] Since 1854, a significant amount of case law has established the common law concept that the State of California holds all of its navigable waterways and the lands lying beneath them "as trustee of a public trust for the benefit of the people."[18] The state's power to control, regulate, and utilize these resources within the terms of the trust is absolute except as limited by the paramount supervisory power of the federal government over navigable waters.[19]

Coupled with these concepts is the general principle that the acts of the state with regard to these resources are within trust purposes when they are done "for purposes of commerce, navigation, and fisheries for the benefit of all the people of the state."[20] For example, public trust easements have been traditionally defined in terms of navigation,

---

15 Water Code § 85023.

16 The California Supreme Court has addressed the existence of statutory enactments codifying the obligations of certain state agencies to consider public trust uses of resources. The court explained:

> These enactments do not render the judicially fashioned public trust doctrine superfluous. Aside from the possibility that statutory protections can be repealed, the noncodified public trust doctrine remains important both to confirm the state's sovereign supervision and to require consideration of public trust uses in cases filed directly in the courts without prior proceedings before the board.

> *National Audubon Society*, 33 Cal. 3d at 446 fn.27.

17 *Id.* at 435 (noting that this principle is well settled in the United States generally and in California, and citing *Illinois Central Railroad Co. v. Illinois*, 146 U.S. 387 (1892); *State of California v. Superior Court (Lyon)*, 29 Cal. 3d 210 (1981); *State of California v. Superior Court (Fogerty)*, 29 Cal. 3d 240 (1981); *People v. Gold Run D & M. Co.*, 66 Cal. 138 (1884); *Hitchings v. Del Rio Woods Recreation & Parks Dist.*, 55 Cal. App. 3d 560 (1976)).

18 *Colberg, Inc. v. State of California ex rel. Dep't of Pub. Wks.*, 67 Cal. 2d 408, 416 (1967); see *Eldridge v. Cowell*, 4 Cal. 80, 87 (1854); *Ward v. Mulford*, 32 Cal. 365, 372 (1867); *People v. Gold Run Ditch & Min. Co.*, 66 Cal. 138, 151 (1884); *People v. California Fish Co.*, 166 Cal. 576, 584 (1913); *Henry Dalton & Sons v. Oakland*, 168 Cal. 463, 465, 467–68 (1914); *City of Long Beach v. Lisenby*, 175 Cal. 575, 579 (1917); *Katenkamp v. Union Realty Co.*, 6 Cal. 2d 765, 769 (1936); *Miramar Co. v. City of Santa Barbara*, 23 Cal. 2d 170, 174 (1943).

19 *Colberg, Inc.*, 67 Cal. 2d at 416–17; see *Gray v. Reclamation Dist. No. 1500*, 174 Cal. 622, 637 (1917). See also *Shively v. Bowlby*, 152 U.S. 1, 26–31 (1894); *United States v. Mission Rock Co.*, 189 U.S. 391, 404 (1903).

20 *Colberg, Inc.*, 67 Cal. 2d at 417 (quoting *Mallon v. City of Long Beach*, 44 Cal. 2d 199 (1955)).

commerce, and fisheries, and have been held to include the right to fish, hunt, bathe, swim, to use for boating and general recreation purposes the navigable waters of the state, and to use the bottom of the navigable waters for anchoring, standing, or other purposes.[21]

The *National Audubon Society* Decision and Environmental Values

The most important case in California concerning the public trust doctrine is *National Audubon Society v. Superior Court*.[22] A decade earlier, however, the California Supreme Court began to expand its views of the doctrine in its 1971 decision *Marks v. Whitney*. This case concerned a quiet title action to settle a boundary dispute caused by overlapping and defective surveys and to enjoin the defendant from asserting any claim or right in or to the plaintiff's property. The dispute was complicated by the fact that part of plaintiff's property was tidelands[23] acquired under an 1874 land patent, and a portion of those tidelands adjoined almost the entire shoreline of defendant's upland property. The tidelands were located on the westerly side of Tomales Bay in Marin County. Plaintiff was proposing to develop the tidelands with a marina.

Plaintiff argued it had complete ownership of the tideland and the right to fill and develop them. Defendant argued in response that this would cut off his rights as a littoral owner and as a member of the public in these tidelands and the navigable waters covering them; as such, defendant requested a declaration that plaintiff's title to the land was burdened with a public trust easement.

The California Supreme Court held that these tidelands were subject to the public trust. The court's analysis began by emphasizing important policy issues: "This matter is of great public importance, particularly in view of population pressures, demands for recreational property, and the increasing development of seashore and waterfront property." The court found that the public uses to which tidelands are subject "are sufficiently flexible to encompass changing public needs," essentially establishing the principle that public trust easements can be defined more broadly than navigation, commerce, and fisheries. As the court explained:

> There is a growing public recognition that one of the most important public uses of the tidelands—a use encompassed within the tidelands trust—is the preservation of those lands in their natural state, so that they may serve as ecological units for scientific study, as open space, and as environments which provide food and habitat for birds and marine life, and which favorably affect the scenery and climate of the area. It is not necessary to here define precisely all the public uses which encumber tidelands.[24]

---

21   *Marks v. Whitney*, 6 Cal. 3d 251, 259 (1971).

22   33 Cal. 3d 419 (1983).

23   The court defined "tidelands" as "those lands lying between the lines of mean high and low tide covered and uncovered successively by the ebb and flow thereof." *Id.* at 258 (citations omitted).

24   *Id.* at 259.

Accordingly, the "traditional triad of uses—navigation, commerce and fishing—did not limit the public interest in the trust res."[25] This case therefore makes "clear that protection of these values is among the purposes of the public trust."[26]

The court quickly pointed out however, that this is not to suggest that the state (through the Legislature) may not free such lands from the trust. "The state in its proper administration of the trust may find it necessary or advisable to cut off certain tidelands from water access and render them useless for trust purposes."[27] But, "[i]n the absence of state or federal action the court may not bar members of the public from lawfully asserting or exercising public trust rights on these privately owned tidelands."[28]

The California Supreme Court revisited this expansive understanding of the public trust doctrine in *National Audubon Society v. Superior Court*.[29] *National Audubon Society* involved permits granted by the state Division of Water Resources (the predecessor to the California Water Resources Board) to the Department of Water and Power (DWP) of the City of Los Angeles for the diversion of virtually the entire flow of four of the five streams that flow into Mono Lake. As a result of the diversions, the level of the lake dropped, causing "both the scenic beauty and the ecological values of Mono Lake [to be] imperiled."[30]

Environmental organizations filed suit to enjoin the DWP diversions on the theory that the shores, bed, and waters of Mono Lake are protected by the public trust. In this lawsuit, the California Supreme Court considered a case that brought together "for the first time two systems of legal thought: the appropriative water rights system . . . , and the public trust doctrine which, after evolving as a shield for the protection of tidelands, now extends its protective scope to navigable lakes." As the court described it, "Ever since [the court] first recognized that the public trust protects environmental and recreational values, the two systems of legal thought have been on a collision course."[31]

The key issue for the court was the fact that although Mono Lake itself is a navigable waterway, and the bed, shores, and waters of the lake are "without question protected by the public trust," the streams that were being diverted by DWP that once flowed into Mono Lake were not themselves navigable. Thus, the court framed the question as "whether the public trust limits conduct affecting nonnavigable tributaries to navigable waterways."[32]

Mono Lake. Photo: Bonnie Peterson.

25 *National Audubon Society*, 33 Cal. 3d at 434 (citing and quoting *Marks v. Whitney*, 6 Cal. 3d 251 (1971)).

26 *Id.*

27 *Marks v. Whitney*, 6 Cal. 3d 251, 259–60 (1971) (citing *City of Long Beach v. Mansell*, 3 Cal. 3d 462 (1970)); see also *id.* at 261 ("It is a political question, within the wisdom and power of the Legislature, acting within the scope of its duties as trustee, to determine whether public trust uses should be modified or extinguish[ed], and to take the necessary steps to free them from such burden.").

28 *Id.* at 251.

29 33 Cal. 3d 419 (1983).

30 *Id.* at 424.

31 *Id.* at 425 (citation omitted).

32 *Id.* at 435.

To answer this question, the court turned to two prior California decisions that at least obliquely considered this issue. The first, *People v. Gold Run D. & M. Co.*,[33] involved the use by mining operators of huge water cannons to wash gold-bearing gravel from hillsides. This practice resulted in a significant amount of sand and gravel debris, which raised the beds of the American and Sacramento Rivers, impairing navigation, polluting waters, and creating flood dangers. The California Supreme Court upheld an injunction against the practice, finding that the "right of the people in the navigable rivers of the State are paramount and controlling. The State holds the absolute right to all navigable waters and the soils under them . . . . The soil she holds as trustee of a public trust for the benefit of the people; and she may, by her legislature, grant it to an individual; but she cannot grant the rights of the people to the use of the navigable waters flowing over it."[34]

Historic "Monitor" water cannon exhibit at the Mariposa Museum and History Center, Mariposa, California. Photo: Scott Birkey and Davis Bryant.

The second decision, *People v. Russ*,[35] involved the erection of dams on sloughs which adjoined a navigable river. The California Supreme Court reversed a trial court decision that gave judgment for the defendants on the basis that the sloughs were nonnavigable. The Supreme Court directed the trial court to make a finding as to the effect of the dams on the navigability of the river, noting that "if the dams upon these sloughs result in the obstruction of Salt River as a navigable stream, they constitute a public nuisance."[36]

The Supreme Court in *National Audubon Society* found that the principles recognized in these prior decisions "apply fully to a case in which diversions from a nonnavigable tributary impair the public trust in a downstream river or lake." Accordingly, the court concluded that the public trust doctrine protects navigable waters from harm caused by diversion of nonnavigable tributaries.[37]

National Audubon Society is important because of its expansion of the scope of the public trust doctrine. Equally important, however, is the court's holdings as to the duties and powers of the state as trustee for the public trust. Relying on the U.S. Supreme Court's decision in *Illinois Central Railroad Company v. Illinois*, and the California Supreme Court's decisions in *People v. California Fish Co.* and *City of Berkeley v. Superior Court*, the court found a "continuing power of the state as administrator of the public trust, a power which extends to the revocation of previously granted rights or to the enforcement of the trust against lands long thought free of the trust." Based on that finding, the court held:

> [T]he public trust is more than an affirmation of state power to use public property for public purposes. It is an affirmation of the duty of the state to protect the people's common heritage of streams, lakes, marshlands and

---

33 66 Cal. 138 (1884).

34 *Id.* at 151–52.

35 132 Cal. 102 (1901).

36 *Id.* at 106.

37 *National Audubon Society*, 33 Cal. 3d at 437.

tidelands, surrendering that right of protection only in rare cases when the abandonment of that right is consistent with the purposes of the trust.[38]

As discussed above, *National Audubon Society* is notable because it addresses the relationship between the public trust doctrine and the California water rights system. The court reached three conclusions as to this relationship, which provide useful guidance for state agencies as to their roles and obligations related to the public trust doctrine.

> The state retains continuing supervisory control over its navigable waters and the lands beneath those waters, and this principle applies to rights in flowing waters as well as to rights in tidelands and lakeshores; it prevents any party from acquiring a vested right to appropriate water in a manner harmful to the interests protected by the public trust.

> The Legislature, acting directly or through an authorized agency such as the State Water Resources Control Board, has the power to grant usufructuary licenses that will permit an appropriator to take water from flowing streams and use that water in a distant part of the state, even though this taking does not promote, and may unavoidably harm, the trust uses at the source stream.

> The state has an affirmative duty to take the public trust into account in the planning and allocation of water resources, and to protect public trust uses whenever feasible.[39]

Because "no responsible body has ever determined the impact of diverting the entire flow of the Mono Lake tributaries" to the City of Los Angeles, the court explained that no legislative, administrative, or judicial body has ever determined whether "the needs of Los Angeles outweigh the needs of the Mono Basin," and whether "the benefit gained is worth the price." Because no such determination had taken place, the court concluded that "it is clear that some responsible body ought to reconsider the allocation of the waters of the Mono Basin."[40]

Post-*National Audubon Society* Views of the Public Trust Doctrine

The effect of the *National Audubon Society* decision on the evolution of the public trust doctrine in California cannot be overstated. Most decisions regarding the doctrine since then are effectively mere footnotes to this landmark case. But certain themes have evolved since its issuance in 1983.

Feasibility of Protection

The California Supreme Court in *National Audubon Society* was not absolutist in its description of the state's duty to take the public trust into account. The court explained: "The state has an affirmative duty to take the public trust into account in the planning and

---

38 *Id.* at 441.

39 *Id.* at 445–47.

40 *Id.* at 447–48.

allocation of water resources, and to protect public trust uses *whenever feasible*."[41] In *State Water Resources Control Board Cases*,[42] environmental organizations argued that the language "whenever feasible" requires that conflicts between public trust values and competing water uses must, whenever possible, be resolved in favor of public trust protection. They also argued that by failing to do more to implement salmon objectives, the State Water Resources Control Board failed to comply with its duties under the public trust doctrine to protect the Bay-Delta's fishery resources "whenever feasible." The court rejected these arguments, noting that the plaintiffs appeared to be taking the position that the Board was obligated under the public trust doctrine to implement more generous flow objectives because it would have been "feasible" to do so. The court stated that "what is 'feasible' . . . is a matter for the Board to determine." Pointing to other language in *National Audubon Society*, the court held that "in determining whether it is 'feasible' to protect public trust values like fish and wildlife in a particular instance, the Board must determine whether protection of those values, or what level of protection, is 'consistent with the public interest.'" The court noted: "It was for the Board in its discretion and judgment to balance all of these competing interests in adopting water quality objectives and formulating a program of implementation to achieve those objectives."[43]

CEQA = California Environmental Quality Act

Process for Public Trust Considerations

In *Citizens for East Shore Parks v. California State Lands Commission*,[44] plaintiffs brought a CEQA challenge against the State Lands Commission alleging that the Commission failed to comply with CEQA and violated the public trust doctrine when it approved a lease allowing a petroleum company to continue operating a marine terminal along the shores of the San Francisco Bay. The court found that the public trust doctrine does not create some kind of "procedural matrix" that resource agencies must use to evaluate a request for a public trust use. More specifically, the court explained that no case discussing the public trust doctrine requires an agency to identify other public trust uses, analyze the impact of maintaining the existing public use on those other uses, or determine and require measures to mitigate those impacts to the greatest extent possible. "Imposing such procedural constraints would be inconsistent with the recognition that the state is free to choose between public trust uses and that selecting one trust use 'in preference to . . . [an]other cannot reasonably be said to be an abuse of discretion.'"[45] The court determined that where no change is being made to a public trust use and there has been compliance with CEQA, the public trust doctrine does not independently impose an

---

41 *Id.* at 434 (emphasis added).

42 136 Cal. App. 4th 674 (2006). This case consisted of eight appeals and three cross-appeals in seven coordinated cases known collectively as the *State Water Resources Control Board Cases*, Judicial Council Coordinated Proceeding No. 4118.

43 *Id.* at 778. Notably, this discussion and the court's analysis assumes without argument that fish and wildlife resources can be considered public trust values.

44 202 Cal. App. 4th 549 (2011).

45 *Id.* at 576–77 (quoting *Higgins v. City of Santa Monica*, 62 Cal. 2d 24, 30 (1964)).

additional impact analysis requirement or require the consideration of additional project alternatives and mitigation measures in connection with other public trust uses.[46] By contrast, in *San Francisco Baykeeper, Inc. v. State Lands Commission*,[47] plaintiffs argued the State Lands Commission violated the public trust doctrine when it approved leases for sand mining operations in the San Francisco Bay. The Commission argued it fulfilled its public trust duties by conducting a CEQA review. The court disagreed, noting that the Commission's record of its CEQA proceedings did not affirmatively demonstrate that it complied with its public trust obligations. The court distinguished prior case law raising similar issues, explaining that that case law did not stand for the broader proposition that CEQA review of a project involving sovereign property necessarily satisfies the Commission's public trust obligations.[48] The court in *San Francisco Baykeeper* also rejected the Commission's view that *Citizens for East Shore Parks* is "unequivocal" authority that the state can satisfy its public trust doctrine obligations by complying with CEQA.[49]

Further Expansion of the Doctrine

Since *National Audubon Society*, courts continue to explore the contours of the public trust doctrine. Those contours were pushed even further in the case *Center for Biological Diversity v. FPL Group, Inc.*[50] In *FPL Group*, environmental plaintiffs filed suit against owners and operators of wind turbine electric generators, alleging that by operating their wind turbines, they were responsible for killing and injuring raptors and other birds in violation of the public trust doctrine. The court agreed with the plaintiffs that the public trust doctrine applies to wildlife, including raptors and other birds. In reaching this decision, the court explained that although *National Audubon Society* recognizes that an important purpose of the public trust over bodies of water is to protect habitat for wildlife, the case does not address whether a public trust protects the wildlife itself.[51] According to the court, "it has long been recognized that wildlife are protected by the public trust doctrine."[52] However, the court cited to a minimal amount of authority, primarily relying on the concept of state ownership of wildlife, to draw this conclusion. Nonetheless, the court unequivocally held that the doctrine can be expanded that far: "Thus, whatever its historical derivation, it is clear that the public trust doctrine encompasses the protection of undomesticated birds

---

46 *Id.* at 577–78.

47 242 Cal. App. 4th 202 (2015).

48 *Id.* at 240–41 (distinguishing *State Water Resources Control Bd. Cases v. California State Lands Commission*, 136 Cal. App. 4th 674 (2006)).

49 *Id.* at 241–42 (distinguishing *Citizens for East Shore Parks*, 202 Cal. App. 4th 540 (2011)).

50 166 Cal. App. 4th 1349 (2008).

51 *Id.* at 1361. The court also evaluated this issue relative to the case *City of Berkeley v. Superior Court*, 26 Cal. 3d 515 (1980), which, like *National Audubon Society*, reflects "the property rights rationale that historically underlies the doctrine, reiterating that the state holds tidelands and navigable waters 'not in its proprietary capacity but as trustee for the public.'" *Id.* at 1360.

52 *Id.* at 1361.

and wildlife. They are natural resources of inestimable value to the community as a whole. Their protection and preservation is a public interest that is now recognized in numerous state and federal statutory provisions."[53]

SGMA = Sustainable Groundwater Management Act

Although the courts thus far have found that the doctrine does not extend to groundwater resources,[54] in *Environmental Law Foundation v. State Water Resources Control Board*[55] the Third Appellate District Court of Appeal considered whether the public trust doctrine applies to the extraction of groundwater that adversely impacts a navigable waterway, and whether the California Legislature intended to occupy the entire field of groundwater management and thereby abolish all fiduciary duties to consider potential adverse impacts on a navigable waterway and public trust resource.

As to the first issue, the court found that "the dispositive issue is not the source of the activity, or whether the water that is diverted or extracted is itself subject to the public trust, but whether the challenged activity allegedly harms a navigable waterway."[56] Thus, the court held that the public trust doctrine does apply to the extraction of groundwater that adversely impacts a navigable waterway. As to the second issue, the court considered this question in the context of the Sustainable Groundwater Management Act (SGMA).[57] The court rejected the argument that in enacting SGMA the Legislature had precluded the State Water Resources Control Board from acting to protect the public trust from groundwater extraction except in limited circumstances, and thus, the board's public trust duties did not survive the enactment of SGMA.[58] The court held that SGMA does not supplant the common law public trust doctrine.

Agency Preference of Trust Uses

The court in *National Audubon Society* suggested in a footnote that resource agencies have the discretion to "promote" one trust purpose over another.[59] Subsequent cases have further established this principle. For example, in *Carstens v. California Coastal Commission*,[60] plaintiffs sought judicial review of a California Coastal Commission decision to approve an amendment to a Coastal Development Permit for construction of portions of the San Onofre Nuclear Generating Station. The amendment modified conditions relating to beach access in conflict with safety measures required by the Nuclear Regulatory Commission. Among other things, plaintiffs argued that the amendment violated the public trust doctrine because it failed to protect the right of free access to

---

53 *Id.* at 1363 (citing, among other authorities, Fish & Game Code §§ 711.7(a), 1600, 1801, 1802, 2000, 2052, 3503.5, 3511, 3513, 3800,12000; Pen. Code § 597; 14 Cal. Code Regs §§ 472, 509).

54 *Santa Teresa Citizen Action Group v. City of San Jose*, 114 Cal. App. 4th 689, 884 (2003) ("[T]he doctrine has no direct application to groundwater sources.").

55 Slip Op. Case No. C083239 (3rd App. Dist. Aug. 29, 2018).

56 *Id.* at Slip Op. p.14.

57 *Id.* at Slip Op. p.17.

58 *Id.* at Slip Op. p.22.

59 *National Audubon Society*, 33 Cal. 3d at 439 fn.21.

60 182 Cal. App. 3d 277 (1986).

the tidelands. The court viewed this argument as implying that the Commission must preserve recreational access to the tidelands at issue in this case "without consideration of other competing public trust purposes." The court disagreed, finding that the Commission was not precluded from considering commerce as well as recreational and environmental needs in carrying out the public trust doctrine.[61] By contrast, in *San Francisco Baykeeper Inc. v. State Lands Commission*,[62] plaintiffs alleged the State Lands Commission violated the public trust doctrine by failing to consider whether sand mining leases issued in the San Francisco Bay constituted a permissible use of public trust property. The Commission argued it was not required to consider whether the project violated the doctrine because sand mining is categorically a public trust use, and the agency had sole discretion to prefer one public trust use over any other. The court rejected the Commission's view that it had "unfettered discretion to prefer sand mining as a preauthorized public trust use of the lease parcels." The court explained: "[A] use does not qualify as a trust use simply because it might confer a public benefit. The scope of this public right is expansive and flexible in order to accommodate changing needs. But, by its very essence, a public trust use facilitates public access, public enjoyment, or public use of trust land. The private activity of removing valuable soil sediment for commercial profit from beneath the bay does not necessarily comport with that definition."[63] The court concluded that the concept of a public trust use as encompassing any private activities that benefit commerce is unsupported by the case law and the principles underlying the public trust doctrine.

Permanent Alienation of Trust Resources

The *National Audubon Society* decision concerned a government action that had the effect of alienating permanently a public trust resource. In *San Francisco Baykeeper, Inc. v. State Lands Commission*,[64] the State Lands Commission pointed to this fact, and argued that *National Audubon Society*'s holding that the public trust doctrine imposes affirmative duties on the state or its trustee applies only in cases that involve a permanent alienation of a trust resource. Thus, according to the Commission, since mineral extraction is not a permanent alienation of the trust res, a mining lease does not trigger the affirmative trust duties discussed in *National Aubudon Society*. The court rejected this line of argument finding that, first, the mining of bay sand depletes a trust resource; second, the legal authority does not support the Commission's legal theory that mining leases are exempt from public trust analysis; and, third, the Public Resources Code provisions conferring the Commission its public trust jurisdiction provides that the Commission "may lease or otherwise dispose of [trust] lands, as provided by law, and therefore the

---

61 *Id.* at 289; see also *Boone v. Kingsbury*, 206 Cal. 148 (1928); *Martin v. Smith*, 184 Cal. App. 2d 571 (1960); *Colberg, Inc. v. State of California ex rel. Dept. Pub. Wks.*, 67 Cal. 2d 408 (1967).

62 242 Cal. App. 4th 202 (2015).

63 *Id.* at 235–36 (distinguishing *Boone v. Kingsbury*, 206 Cal. 148 (1928), and rejecting the view that *Boone* establishes a rule that mineral extraction is per se a public trust use of sovereign lands).

64 242 Cal. App. 4th 202 (2015).

Commission "is not exempt from the law, but must comply with the requirements of the common law trust doctrine when administering trust lands."[65]

ENFORCEMENT OF THE PUBLIC TRUST DOCTRINE

Use of the public trust doctrine to challenge projects on environmental grounds has gained momentum since *National Audubon Society*, which in many ways confirms the view articulated by Professor Sax in 1970 that the public trust doctrine could be used in judicial enforcement of environmental regulations.

In the authors' experience, most public trust doctrine challenges are coupled with the typical suite of causes of action alleged by opponents of a project, such as Planning and Zoning Law claims under the California Government Code and claims raised under the California Environmental Quality Act. Factors to consider related to enforcing or defending against a public trust doctrine include:

Standing

The case of *Center for Biological Diversity v. FPL Group, Inc.*[66] clarified whether members of the public have standing to enforce the public trust doctrine. Discussed in more detail above, *FPL Group* involved challenges brought by environmental organizations against owners and operators of wind turbine electric generators, alleging that by operating their wind turbines, they were responsible for killing and injuring raptors and other birds in violation of the public trust doctrine. Defendants argued that although *National Audubon Society* recognized "any member of the general public . . . has standing to raise a claim of harm to the public trust," this only applied to actions to enforce "the traditional public trust interest in navigable and tidal waters and tidelands." The court disagreed and held that "the public retains the right to bring actions to enforce the trust when the public agencies fail to discharge their duties." This includes actions to enforce the trust when it applies to wildlife.[67]

Proper Defendants

FPL Group also provides guidance on who or what entities are proper defendants in a claim for breach of the public trust. Plaintiffs in *FPL Group* brought their lawsuit only against private parties, i.e., the owners and operators of the wind turbine generators, rather than against any permitting or other government agencies. The court held that plaintiffs brought their lawsuit against the wrong parties. They should have instead "proceeded against the County of Alameda, which has authorized the use of the wind turbine generators, or against any agency such as the California Department of Fish and Wildlife that has been given the statutory responsibility of protecting the affected natural resources."[68]

---

65   *Id.* at 239–40 (citing Pub. Res. Code § 6301).

66   166 Cal. App. 4th 1349 (2008).

67   *Id.* at 1365–67.

68   *Id.* at 1367–68.

Standard of Review

In *Citizens for East Shore Parks v. California State Lands Commission*,[69] plaintiffs alleged the State Lands Commission violated the public trust doctrine when it approved a lease allowing a petroleum company to continue operating a marine terminal along the shores of the San Francisco Bay. Plaintiffs argued the renewal of the lease was a quasi-adjudicatory decision, and therefore the Commission's determination to continue the existing public trust use of the Bay land and waters should be reviewed under the abuse of discretion standard set forth in California Code of Civil Procedure Section 1094.5, which applies when the underlying administrative proceeding is one "in which by law a hearing is required to be given, evidence is required to be taken, and discretion in the determination of facts is vested" in the agency.[70] The defendant focused on the fact that the Commission's decision continued an existing public trust use, namely the maintenance and use of a marine terminal. Defendant argued that the Commission's choice of this trust use, rather than another, is a quasi-legislative determination subject to judicial review under California Code of Civil Procedure Section 1085, which is the traditional mandamus statute for quasi-legislative actions and subject to a more deferential, arbitrary and capricious standard of review. The court ultimately determined it need not decide whether the Commission's decision to continue a long-standing public trust use is adjudicatory or legislative in character. Instead, the court determined that plaintiffs raised a legal issue subject to de novo review under both Section 1094.5 and 1085.[71]

---

69 202 Cal. App. 4th 549 (2011).

70 Code Civ. Proc. § 1094.5(a).

71 202 Cal. App. 4th at 573.

ACRONYMS

AAOW = U.S. Army Corps of Engineers Assistant Administrator, Office of Water

AB = Assembly Bill

ACHP = Advisory Council on Historic Preservation

ACL = Administrative Civil Liability

AJD = Approved Jurisdictional Determination

APE = Area of Potential Effects

ARNIs = Aquatic Resources of National Importance

ASA(CW) = Assistant Secretary of the Army for Civil Works

BAT = best available control technology

BCDC = San Francisco Bay Conservation and Development Commission

BCT = best conventional pollutant control technology

BEI = Bank-Enabling Instrument

BGEPA = Bald and Golden Eagle Protection Act

BLM = U.S. Bureau of Land Management

CAO = Cleanup and Abatement Order

CDFW or the "Department" = California Department of Fish and Wildlife

CDNPA = California Desert Native Plants Act

CDO = Cease and Desist Order

CDP = Coastal Development Permit

CEQA = California Environmental Quality Act

CESA = California Endangered Species Act

CFD = Community Facilities District

CNDDB = California Natural Diversity Database

CNPS = California Native Plant Society

CNRA = California Natural Resources Agency

Corps = U.S. Army Corps of Engineers

CSPA = California Species Preservation Act

CTS = California tiger salamander

CZMA = Coastal Zone Management Act

DA = Department of the Army

Department = California Department of Fish and Wildlife

DFW = Department of Fish and Wildlife

DOI = Department of the Interior

DPS = distinct population segment

DRECP = Desert Renewable Energy Conservation Plan

DWP = Department of Water and Power of the City of Los Angeles

DWR = California Department of Water Resources

EA = Environmental Assessment

EA/FONSI = Environmental Assessment/ Finding Of No Significant Impact

ECOS = Environmental Conservation and Online System

EFH = essential fish habitat

EIR = Environmental Impact Report

EIS = Environmental Impact Statement

EMU = Eagle Management Unit

EPA = Environmental Protection Agency

EREPs = Ecological Restoration and Enhancement Projects

ESA = Endangered Species Act

ESHA = environmentally sensitive habitat area

ESU = evolutionarily significant unit

FAC = facultative species

FACW = facultative wetland species

FERC = Federal Energy Regulatory Commission

FONSI = Finding Of No Significant Impact

FWPC Act = Federal Water Pollution Control Act

FWS = Fish and Wildlife Service

GCP = General Conservation Plan

GHAD = Geological Hazard Abatement District

HCE = Habitat Credit Exchange

HCP = Habitat Conservation Plan

IAP = Implementing Actions Plan

ILF = in-lieu fee

INRMP = Integrated Natural Resources Management Plan

IRT = Interagency Review Team

ITP = incidental take permit

JARPA = Joint Aquatic Resource Permit Application

JD = Jurisdictional Determination

LAP = Local Area Population

LCP = Local Coastal Program

LEDPA = least environmentally damaging practicable alternative

LSAA = Lake and Streambed Alteration Agreement

LUP = Land Use Plan

MBI = Mitigation Banking Instrument

MBTA = Migratory Bird Treaty Act

MCA = Mitigation Credit Agreement

MESA = Mapping Episodic Stream Activity

Mitigation Rule = Compensatory Mitigation for Losses of Aquatic Resources Rule

MMPA = Marine Mammal Protection Act

MMS = Minerals Management Service

MND = Mitigated Negative Declaration

MOA = Memorandum of Agreement

MOU = Memorandum of Understanding

NAGPRA = Native American Graves Protection and Repatriation Act

NAP = Notification of Appeal Process

NCCP = Natural Community Conservation Plan

NCCPA = Natural Community Conservation Planning Act

NCCP Act = Natural Community Conservation Planning Act

NCSHPO = National Conference of State Historic Preservation Officers

ND = Negative Declaration

NEPA = National Environmental Policy Act

NGO = non-governmental organization

NHPA = National Historic Preservation Act

NMFS or NOAA Fisheries = National Oceanic and Atmospheric Administration's National Marine Fisheries Service

NOAA = National Oceanic and Atmospheric Administration

NOI = notice of intent

NOV = notice of violation

NPDES = National Pollutant Discharge Elimination System

NPPA = Native Plant Protection Act

NPS = National Park Service

NRCS = Natural Resources Conservation Service

NRDC = Natural Resources Defense Council

NWP = Nationwide Permit

OAL = Office of Administrative Law

OBL = obligate species

OHWM = ordinary high water mark

OMB = Office of Management and Budget

OPR = Office of Planning and Research

PA = Programmatic Agreement

PAR = Property Analysis Record

PCC = prior converted cropland

PCCP = Placer County Conservation Plan

PCN = pre-construction notification

PGP = Programmatic General Permit

PJD = Preliminary Jurisdictional Determination

PRM = permittee-responsible mitigation

PSA = Permit Streamlining Act

RCA = Regional Conservation Assessment

RCIS = Regional Conservation Investment Strategy

RCRA = Resource Conservation and Recovery Act

RFA = Request for Appeal

RGL = Regulatory Guidance Letter

RGP = Regional General Permit

RIBITS = Regulatory In-Lieu Fee and Bank Information Tracking System

RO = Reviewing Officer

ROD = Record Of Decision

RWQCB = Regional Water Quality Control Board, or "Regional Water Board"

SAMP = Special Area Management Plan

SB = Senate Bill

Service = U.S. Fish and Wildlife Service

SGMA = Sustainable Groundwater Management Act

SHPO = State Historic Preservation Officer

SLR = sea level rise

S-M-A-R-T = specific, measurable, achievable, result-oriented, and time-fixed

SMARTS = Storm Water Multi-Application Report Tracking System

SPD = South Pacific Division

SSC = Species of Special Concern

State Water Board = State Water Resources Control Board

SWPPP = Storm Water Pollution Prevention Plan

SWRCB = State Water Resources Control Board, or "State Water Board"

TCP = traditional cultural property

TCR = tribal cultural resource

TDML = total maximum daily load

Commission = California Fish and Game Commission

THPO = Tribal Historic Preservation Officer

USACE or the "Corps" = U.S. Army Corps of Engineers

USFWS or the "Service" = U.S. Fish and Wildlife Service

Water Boards = State Water Resources Control Board and Regional Water Quality Control Boards

WDR = Waste Discharge Requirement

WOTS = waters of the State

WOTUS = waters of the United States

WQC = Water Quality Certification

INDEX

Note: Page numbers in *italics* indicate information in figures, maps and tables.

A

AB 52 (2014), 568–572, *573–575*, 576, 577

AB 454 (2019), 212

AB 2087 (2016), 531, 534

AB 2640 (2018), 213

accidental take, 180

Accord Citizens Interested in Bull Run, Inc. v. Edrington, 191

Acme Fill Corporation v. San Francisco Bay Conservation and Development Commission, 580, 588

action area, *104–105*

administrative appeal process
administrative permit appeals, 350–356
approved jurisdictional determinations, 286–292
permit denials and proffered permits, 350–352

Administrator, Environmental Protection Agency, Defenders of Wildlife v., 66

Advisory Council on Historic Preservation (ACHP), 543–544

Affirming California's Protections for Migratory Birds, 212

AFL-CIO v. Martin, 276

AJD (Approved Jurisdictional Determination), 286–294

Akers, United States v., 300

Alabama-Tombigbee Rivers Coalition v. Kempthorne, 17

Alameda Water & Sanitation District v. Reilly, 359

Alaska Oil and Gas Association v. Jewell, 68

Alliance to Save the Mattiponi v. U.S. Army Corps of Engineers, 360

Alsea Valley Alliance v. Evans, 31–33

American Forest and Paper Association v. Environmental Protection Agency, 66

American Mining Congress v. United States Army Corps of Engineers, 296

American Petroleum Institute, Industrial Union Department v., 69

Anderson-Cottonwood Irrigation District, Department of Fish and Game v., 161–162

Andrews, Riverside Irrigation District v., 109–110

Andrus, Conservation Law Foundation v., 66

Andrus, Pacific Legal Foundation v., 132, 150

APE (Area of Potential Effects), 545

Apollo Energies, Inc., United States v., 194, 195

Appendix C (Corps of Engineers), 559–567

Approved Jurisdictional Determination (AJD), 286–294

aquatic ecosystems, 311–321

Aquatic Resources of National Importance (ARNIs), 357

Area of Potential Effects (APE), 545

Arizona Cattle Growers' Association v. Salazar, 47

Army Corps of Engineers, Friends of Boundary v., 195, 201

Army Corps of Engineers, New Hope Power Company v., 303

ARNIs (Aquatic Resources of National Importance), 357

ASA(CW) (Assistant Secretary of the Army for Civil Works), 8–9, 357

Assistant Secretary of the Army for Civil Works ASA(CW), 8–9, 357

at-risk species, 256–257

avian protections
Bald and Golden Eagle Protection Act (BGEPA), 197–210
under California law, 210–214
Migratory Bird Treaty Act (MBTA), 186–197

B

Babbitt, Building Industry Association of California v., 493

Babbitt, Douglas County v., 132, 133

Babbitt, Gibbs v., 17

Babbitt, Marbled Murrelet v., 55, 63, 138, 493

Babbitt, Mausolf v., 96

Babbitt, National Wildlife Federation v., 508, 511

Babbitt, Sierra Club v., 63, 64, 513

Babbitt v. Sweet Home Chapter of Communities for a Great Oregon, 37, 54, 56, 99, 162, 191

Baccarat Fremont Developers, LLC v. United States Army Corps of Engineers, 270, 352

Bald and Golden Eagle Protection Act (BGEPA), 197–202, 210

Bank-Enabling Instrument (BEI), 479–480

Bartel, Southwest Center for Biological Diversity v., 53, 499, 510

bay and coastal protections, 580–604

Bay Area Air Quality Management, California Building Industry Association v., 596

Bay Plan (San Francisco Bay Plan), 581–582

BCDC (San Francisco Bay Conservation and Development Commission), 580–588

Beaudreau, Public Employees for Environmental Responsibility v., 195

bed of stream, defined, 431

BEI (Bank-Enabling Instrument), 479–480

Bennett v. Spear, 96, 136, 293

Berg, Biological Diversity v., 520

Bering Strait Citizens for Responsible Resource Development v. U.S. Army Corps of Engineers, 310, 319, 348

Bernal, Defenders of Wildlife v., 55

Bersani v. Robichaud, 314–315

Betchart v. Department of Fish and Game, 183

BGEPA (Bald and Golden Eagle Protection Act), 197–202, 210

Biodiversity Legal Foundation v. Norton, 53

Biological Diversity v. Berg, 520

Biological Diversity v. Jewell, 36

biological opinion
analysis, scope of, 106–107
beneficial effects, analysis of, 114
conservation recommendations, 124
content of, 94
cumulative effects, analysis of, 110–111
on destruction or adverse modification of critical habitat, 118–120
direct effects, analysis of, 108–109
environmental baseline, 102–106
vs. habitat conservation plan (HCP), 494
incidental take statements, 95–100
indirect effects, analysis of, 109–110
interrelated and interdependent actions, analysis of, 111–114
jeopardy analysis, 115–118
monitoring and reporting, 124–125
proposed action and scope of, 100–102
reasonable and prudent alternatives, 120–122
reasonable and prudent measures, 122–123
species and habitat, factors in analysis of effects upon, 107–108
terms and conditions, 123–124

birds, fully protected in California, 214, 252

Birds of Conservation Concern, 187

Black, Yaak Committee v., 138

Blackwood, Blue Mountains Biodiversity Project v., 135

Blanket 4(d) Rule, 37–38

BLM (U.S. Bureau of Land Management), 62, 114

Blue Mountains Biodiversity Project v. Blackwood, 135

Blumenfeld v. San Francisco Bay Conservation and Development Commission, 581

Bolsa Chica Land Trust v. Superior Court, 602

Boone v. Kingsbury, 618

Final Guidance for Endangered Species Act Incidental Take Permits Covering Multiple Projects or Project Owners, 501
findings required for approval of NCCP, 525–527
findings required for ITP issuance, 506–507
ITP reconsideration and appeal, process for, 176–177
mineral rights on conserved lands, 468–469
minimization and mitigation to the maximum extent practicable, 507–510
nesting birds, uniform standards and definitions for, 212
no appreciable reduction, 512–513
permit administration, 517–518
public participation process, 525
publicly owned and already preserved lands, policy on, 466–468
rare species, 257
as responsible agency, 174–175
special status species, at-risk species, and special animals, 256–257
species of special concern, 255–256
take of rare plants, authorization of, 227
CDNPA (California Desert Native Plants Act), 227–229
CDP (Coastal Development Permit), 592
Center for Biological Diversity v. Bureau of Land Management, 98, 116, 221
Center for Biological Diversity v. California Department of Fish and Wildlife, 163, 253
Center for Biological Diversity v. California Fish and Game Commission, 155
Center for Biological Diversity v. FPL Group, Inc., 616, 619
Center for Biological Diversity v. Pirie, 195
Center for Biological Diversity v. Salazar, 38
Center for Marine Conservation v. Brown, 96
Central Coast Forest Association v. California Fish and Game Commission, 156
CEQA (California Environmental Quality Act)
NCCP compliance with, 530
plant and oak woodlands protections, 230–231
tribal cultural resources consultation, 568–572, 573–575
CESA (California Endangered Species Act)
90-day review, 153
2081 permits and "no surprises" assurances, 170
agricultural activities, provisions governing, 180–182
candidate species, review of, 157–158
CEQA, listing decisions and, 149–150
components of, 147–148
conservation mandate, 145–146
consideration of petition and evaluation report, 153–154
consistency determinations under Section 2080.1, 179–180
emergency listings, 160
fish and game protections, 1909–1997, 142
history of, 144–145
incidental take permits (ITP) (Section 2081), 163–171

indirect harm, 162–163
initial listing petition steps, 150–151
listing decisions, reconsideration of, 156–157
listing process, 148–161
may be warranted finding, 155–156
minimization and full mitigation, 164–168
penalties and enforcement, 183
periodic review, 160–161
permit process, 171–180
petition for final consideration, 158–159
plant species, classifications of, 216–219
post-permit considerations, 177–179
rare and threatened species, pre-CESA protections, 143–144
scientific, educational and management authorizations, 180
state agencies, role of, 147–148
take in the form of pursue, catch and capture, 163
take prohibition, overview of, 161–162
channel, defined under Fish and Game Code, 431
Chevron USA, Inc. v. Natural Resources Defense Council, Inc., 26
Citgo Petroleum Corporation, United States v., 190, 192
Citizens for East Shore Parks v. California State Lands Commission, 615
City & County of San Francisco, Martin v., 572
City Council, Orsi v., 175
City of Berkeley v. Superior Court, 607, 613
City of Culver City, Ehrlich v., 165
City of Healdsburg, Northern California River Watch v., 270, 276
City of Laguna Beach, Fudge v., 595
City of Long Beach, Mallon v., 610
City of Long Beach v. Lisenby, 610
City of Long Beach v. Mansell, 612
City of Los Angeles, Pacific Palisades Bowl Mobile Estates, LLC v., 591
City of Moreno Valley, San Bernardino Valley Audubon Society v., 144
City of Ojai, Palmer v., 175
City of Poway, Preserve Poway v., 572
City of Sacramento (Natomas), Environmental Council of Sacramento v., 166, 211
City of San Jose, Santa Teresa Citizen Action Group v., 617
City of Santa Barbara, Miramar County v., 610
City of Santa Monica, Higgins v., 615
City of Sausalito v. O'Neill, 196, 201
City of Tigard, Dolan v., 164, 464
Clean Water Act
discharge of dredged or fill material, 294–296
exclusions, 404–406
history and background, 262
overview of federal statutes regulating wetlands and other waters, 262–264
statutory exclusions, 299–300
wetland, defined, 394–395
wetlands and other waters regulated by, 265–278
climate change and sea level rise, 603–604

CNDDB (California Natural Diversity Database), 256–257
CNPS (California Native Plant Society), 217–219
CNRA (California Natural Resources Agency), 465
Coastal Act *see* California Coastal Commission
Coastal Development Permit (CDP), 592
Coastal Zone Management Act (CZMA), 264, 368
Colberg, Inc. v. State of California, 606, 610
Coleman, National Wildlife Federation v., 106, 109
Colorado River Indian Tribes v. Marsh, 545
Commission *see* California Fish and Game Commission
Community Association for Restoration of the Environment v. Henry Bosma Dairy, 138, 139, 140
Community Facilities District (CFD), 470, 475
comparison of banks and ILFs, 486
compensatory mitigation
administrative considerations, 331–332
documentation, 332–335
financial assurances for projects, 469–475
means of delivery, 450
overview, 450–451
watershed approach, 325–329, 414–415
conference processes, 61
Conner v. Burford, 62, 66
conservation easements, defined, 459–460
Conservation Law Foundation v. Andrus, 66
Conservation Northwest v. Kempthorne, 53
conservation planning, 492–540
conservation transactions
agency policies, summary of, 451–459
background, 450–451
banks under 2008 mitigation rule, 478–485
conservation easements and site protection instruments, 459–465
in-lieu fee (ILF) programs, 485–489
mitigation and conservation banks, 475–478
mitigation projects, financial assurances for, 469–475
mitigation site due diligence, 465–469
conserved lands, mineral rights on, 468–469
Consultation Handbook: Procedures for Conducting Consultation and Conference Activities Under Section 7 of the Endangered Species Act, 57
Corbin Farm Service, United States v., 193, 195
Corps *see* U.S. Army Corps of Engineers
Corps guidance on permit area (Appendix C), 561
Corrow, United States v., 194
Cottonwood Environmental Law Center v. U.S. Forest Service, 93, 137
Council of Volusia County, Loggerhead Turtle v., 136
County of Mendocino, Masonite Corporation v., 168
County of San Diego, Starkey v., 525
County of Shasta, Mega Renewables v., 437
County of Sonoma, California River Watch v., 136
County of Stanislaus, Building Industry Association of Central California v., 463
Cowell, Eldridge v., 610
Coxe, Strahan v., 136